LOGICAL REASONING

Class 8

with **Chapter-wise Previous**
5 Year (2018 - 2022) Questions

DISHA Publication Inc.

45, 2nd Floor, Maharishi Dayanand Marg,
Corner Market, Malviya Nagar, new Delhi -110017
Tel: 49842349/ 49842350

Typeset By

DISHA DTP Team

Preface

We are pleased to launch the 2nd edition of **Olympiad Champs Logical Reasoning Class 8** which is the first of its kind book on Olympiad in many ways.

The Unique Selling Proposition of this new edition is the inclusion of past year questions till 2022 of different Olympiad exams held in schools.

The book is aimed at achieving not only success but deep rooted learning in children. It is prepared on content based on National Curriculum Framework prescribed by NCERT. All the text books, syllabi and teaching practices within the education programme in India must follow NCF. Hence, Olympiad Champs become an ideal book not only for the Olympiad Exams but also for strengthening the concepts for Class 8.

There is an exhaustive range of thought provoking questions in MCQ format to test the student's knowledge thoroughly. The questions are designed so as to test the knowledge, comprehension, evaluation, analytical and application skills. Solutions and explanations are provided for all questions. The questions are divided into two levels - Level 1 and Level 2. The first level, Level 1, is the beginner's level which comprises of questions like fillers, analogy and odd one out. When the child covers Level 1, it means his basic knowledge about the subject is clear and now it is ready for Level 2. The second level is the advanced level. Level 2 comprises of techniques like matching, chronological sequencing, picture, passage and feature based, statement correct/ incorrect, integer based, puzzle, grid based, crossword, venn diagram, table/ chart based and much more.

The first concern which each parent faces is how to make their children read a book especially when it is based on academics. Keeping this in mind interesting facts, real life examples, historical preview, short cut to problem solving, charts, diagrams, illustrations and poems are added. In addition to this, we have introduced comic strip which increases the readability quotient and make the reading experience for the children more exciting.

With the vision to remove all the misconception a child may have pertaining to the subject, to relate his knowledge to the real world and to develop a deeper understanding of the subject this book will cater all the requirements of the students who are going to appear in Olympiads.

While preparing this book, some errors might have crept in. We request our readers to identify those errors and send it across on **feedback_disha@aiets.co.in.**

We wish you all the best for your Olympiads and happy reading.......

Team Disha

For feedback : feedback_disha@aiets.co.in.

CONTENTS

10 Principles to CRACK ANY EXAM

1. Chase consistency, not intensity.

Doing intensive study makes your day. But it also exhausts you in the long run, leading to lesser output and added pressure. Toppers always focus on doing consistent work daily, for consistency is far more valuable than intensity. Remember consistent study of 4 hours every day is more important and powerful than studying 12 hours a day and then not studying at all for next 2 days.

UTILISATION
5h
4h
6h
DAYS
CONSISTENT EFFORTS

UTILISATION
12h
2h
1h
DAYS
INTENSIVE EFFORTS

2. Go beyond the surface.

Most students only see a few reasons (teacher, coaching, books, etc) behind Toppers' success, which is only the tip of the iceberg. What they donot see is Toppers Mindset, self belief, habits and discipline and that is where the real problem is.

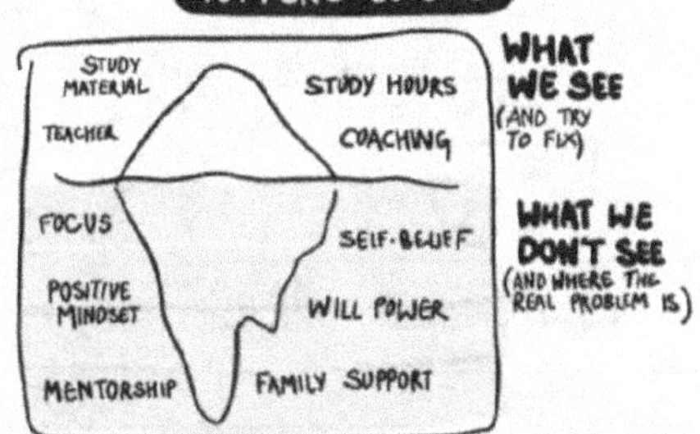

3. Focus on giving your best, not chasing the best.

We want the best coaching, the best teacher, best batch and the best books but we are not ready to give our BEST. Success comes only when we are ready to give our best. We must focus on giving our best than chasing excuses to cover up our failures.

4. Clarity of concept is the key

PROBLEM SOLVING

THEORY → SOLVE QUESTION → SOLVE MORE QUESTIONS → FACE PROBLEMS → THEORY

Concept clarity is critical. If you cannot solve a question, you must go back to the theory and thoroughly examine the concept instead of referring to the solutions. Remember question is one of the chehra(face) of the concept. When toppers get stuck in a problem, they go back and refer the theory(read the concept again and again on which the question is based)

5. Every failure should be a lesson learned.

Most students do not learn from their failures and repeat their mistakes. Toppers also face failures, but they learn from mistakes and elevate themselves. Making mistakes and learning from them is the key to success.

6 Choosing the quality of resources is more important than quantity.

More than 90% of the questions in most books are the same as their substitutes. Instead of practicing from four books and failing to complete them, it is best to prepare from two books and complete them with thorough revisions.

7 Difficult things become easy by taking it one day at a time.

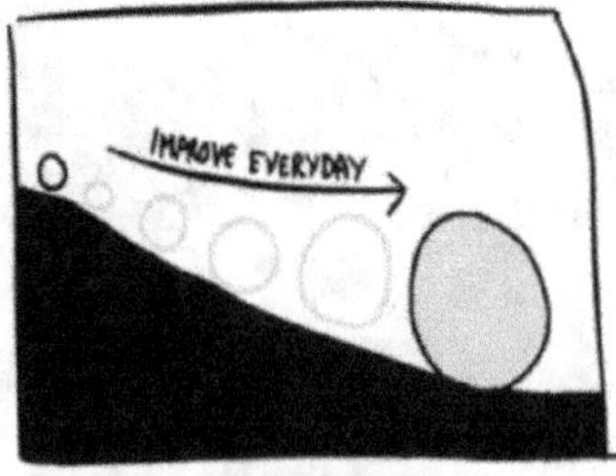

The best way to take any preparation forward is by taking it one day at a time. It makes the impossible possible by taking small steps every day.
Starting a difficult subject. No worries. Keep on working session by session, day by day and week by week and one day you will become unstoppable force.

8. Everything is easy

Before starting everything looks difficult. Once you take a first step, it slowly starts looking easy and over a period of time you become master in the activity. This is toppers secret to become master in any subject.

9. Nobody is gifted

We think toppers are god gifted. We think toppers have high IQ. We think toppers are special/lucky. But the truth is every topper was once an average student(no body is born topper). What makes them different is their consistent and focused efforts

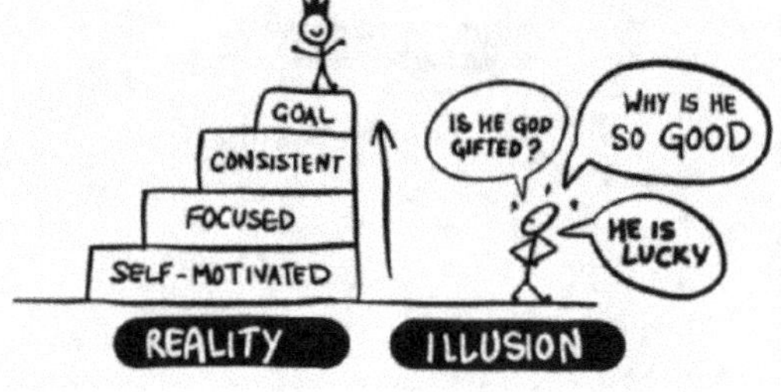

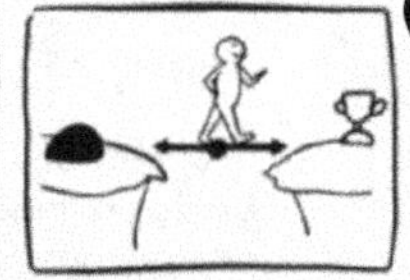

10. Believe in your journey and success will come to you.

There is never a straight path to success; hard work & patience is required for the results to show up. Keep on working hard without thinking too much about the results and success will come to you eventually.

CHAPTER

Analogy and Classification

CLASSIFICATION

Classification means 'to sort the items of a given group on the basis of a certain common quality they possess and then spot the stranger or odd one out'.

ODD ONE OUT WORDS CONCEPTS :

In this type of classification, four words are given, out of which three are almost same in matter or meaning and one word is different from the other three. One has to find out the word which is different from the rest.

DIRECTIONS (ILLUSTRATION 1-10) : Choose the option which is least like the others in the group.

ILLUSTRATION 1:

(a) Copper (b) Zinc

(c) Brass (d) Aluminium

Sol. Here, all except Brass are metals, while Brass is an alloy. Hence, the answer is (c).

ILLUSTRATION 2:

(a) Volume : Litre

(b) Time : Seconds

(c) Length : Metre

(d) Pressure : Barometer

Sol. In all other pairs, except (d), the second word is the unit to measure the first. On the other hand, barometer is an instrument.

ILLUSTRATION 3:

(a) Painter : Gallery (b) Actor : Stage

(c) Mason : Wall (d) Farmer : Field

Sol. Clearly, the answer is (c). In all other pairs, second is the working place of the first.

ILLUSTRATION 4:

(a) Lion : Roar (b) Snake : Hiss

(c) Frog : Bleat (d) Bees : Hum

Sol. Clearly, the answer is (c). In all other pairs, second is the noise produced by the first.

ODD ONE OUT LETTER COMPARISON:

In this classification of letters, four groups of letters or a series of letters are given as options. One has to select the option as answer which does not share the commonness of the others.

ILLUSTRATION 5:

(a) ABC : CBA (b) JKL : KLJ

(c) XYZ : ZYX (d) MNO : ONM

Sol. Clearly, the answer is (b). In all other pairs of groups, the letters in the second group are the letters of the first group written backwards.

GROUP OF NUMBERS :

The group of numbers can be consecutive numbers in natural or reverse series, multiplication, subtraction and mathematical rules can also be used to frame the groups.

ILLUSTRATION 6:

(a) 14, 28 (b) 40, 80

(c) 16, 32 (d) 15, 35

Sol. In each pair the second number is double the first number. In option (d), the number 35 should have been 30, the very reason as to why it is the odd one out.

ILLUSTRATION 7:

(a) 70 : 80 (b) 54 : 62

(c) 28 : 32 (d) 21 : 24

Sol. In each of the pairs except (b), the ratio of the two numbers is 7 : 8.

ILLUSTRATION 8:

(a) 16 : 64 (b) 9 : 36

(c) 36 : 216 (d) 49 : 343

Sol. Clearly, the answer is (b). In all other pairs contain square and cube of the same number e.g. $36 = 6^2$ and $216 = 6^3$.

CHOOSING THE ODD NUMERAL :

In this type of question, certain numbers are given, out of which all except one have some common property and hence are alike, while one is different and this number is to be chosen as the answer.

ILLUSTRATION 9:

(a) 8 (b) 64

(c) 125 (d) 28

Sol. **(d).** All except 28 are perfect cubes of some number.

ILLUSTRATION 10:

(a) 131 (b) 151

(c) 161 (d) 171

Sol. **(c)** The sum of the digits of each of the numbers except 161, is an odd number.

ANALOGY

In questions based on analogy, a particular relationship is given and another similar relationship has to be identified from the alternatives provided.

For example :

1. Action Object Relationship

ILLUSTRATION 1:

Shoot is to Gun as Eat is to ....

(a) Hunger (b) Thirst

(c) Dinner (d) Fruit

Sol. **(d)** The relationship between the given words is that 'shoot' is the action and 'Gun' is the specified object of action . Similarly 'eat' is the action and 'fruit' is the specified object.

2. Antonym Relationship

ILLUSTRATION 2:

INTROVERT :EXTROVERT

(a) ANGLE : TANGENT

(b) EXTREME : INTERIM

(c) AGAINST : FAVOUR

(d) ACTION : LAW

Sol. **(c)** The related words are opposite in meaning.

3. Grammatical Relationship

ILLUSTRATION 3:

Clever is to Beautiful as Sour is to.........

(a) Lemon (b) Cunning

(c) Loathing (d) Taste

***Sol.* (b)** The related words are Adjectives.

4. Part Whole Relationship

ILLUSTRATION 4:

MAN : MAMMAL

(a) HALL : SNOW

(b) NATIVE : INHABITANT

(c) OFFSPRING : FAMILY

(d) LIBERTY : URBANISM

***Sol.* (c)** Man is a part of the whole species of mammal, so is an offspring of the whole family.

5. Sequence Relationship

ILLUSTRATION 5:

.........is to Dusk as Summer is to Monsoon.

(a) Evening

(b) Dawn

(c) Night

(d) Noon

***Sol.* (a)** Summer season is immediately followed by monsoon (rainy season) and evening is immediately followed by dusk.

6. Volume Relationship

ILLUSTRATION 6:

GALLONS : SWIMMING POOL

(a) SPECTATORS : AUDITORIUM

(b) CURRENCY : SHARES

(c) DUST : MOUNTAIN

(d) BOOKS : CATALOGUE

***Sol.* (a)** Gallons of water is needed to fill a swimming pool and large number of spectators can be admitted into an auditorium .

COMMON RELATIONSHIPS

1. Country and currency :

India : Rupee

Argentina : Peso

China : Yaun,

Iraq : Dinar

Kuwait : Dinar

Thailand : Baht

Bangladesh : Taka

Greece : Drachma

Japan : Yen

UK : Pound

UAE : Dirham

Burma : Kyat

Iran : Rial,

Korea : Won

USA : Dollar

Turkey : Lira

2. Quantity and Unit :

Length: Metre

Metre is the unit of measuring length.

Mass : Kilogram

Time : Seconds

Energy: Joule

Resistance: Ohm

Angle : Radians

Power: Watt

Work: Joule

Current: Ampere

Area: Hectare

Temperature: Degrees

Luminosity: Candela

Magnetic field: Oersted

Force: Newton

Volume : Litre

Potential : Volt

Pressure : Pascal

Conductivity: Mho

3. **Animal and Young One :**

Cow: Calf

Calf is the young one of cow.

Bear : Cub

Hen: Chick

Horse : Colt/Filly/Foal Lion/tiger : Cub

Duck: Duckling

Sheep : Lamb

Butterfly : Caterpillar

Stag: Fawn

Dog: Puppy

Deer: Fawn

Cockroach: Nymph

Cat : Kitten

Man : Child

Insect: Larva

Frog: Tadpole

Swan: Cygnet

4. **Animal and Movement:**

Duck: Waddle

Waddling is the name given to the movement of the duck.

Bird: Fly

Cock: Strut

Owl : Flit

Bear: Lumber

Elephant: Amble

Horse : Gallop

Lion: Prowl

Mouse: Scamper

Eagle : Swoop

Donkey: Trot

Lamb : Frisk

Rabbit : Leap

5. **Animal/Thing and Sound:**

Lion: Roar

Roar is the sound produced by a lion.

Donkey: Bray

Frog: Croak

Horse: Neigh

Snake : Hiss

Mice : Squeak

Cat: Mew

Camel : Grunt

Elephant : Trumpet

Cock: Crow

Owl : Hoot .

Crow: Caw

Duck: Quack

Bells : Chime

Drum : Beat

Thunder: Roar

Leaves : Rustle

Goat : Bleat

Jackal: Howl

Cattle : Low

Monkey: Gibber

Sparrow: Chirp

Hen: Cackle

Coins : Jingle

Rain : Patter

6. Individual/Thing and Class :

Lizard: Reptile

Lizard belongs to the class of Reptiles.

Man: Mammal	Butterfly : Insect
Ostrich: Bird	Snake : Reptile
Frog: Amphibian	Pen: Stationery
Chair: Furniture	Cup: Crockery
Whale: Mammal	Rat : Rodent
Curtain: Drapery	Shirt: Garment

7. Animals/Things and Keeping Place:

Car : Garage

A car is kept in a garage.

Aeroplane : Hangar	Bees : Apiary
Animals : Zoo	Clothes : Wardrobe
Grains: Granary	Guns: Armory
Medicine: Dispensary	Patient: Hospital
Birds: Aviary	Fish: Aquarium
Curios : Museum	Wine : Cellar

8. Games and Place of Playing:

Badminton : Court

Badminton is played on a court

Boxing: Ring	Athletics : Stadium
Hockey: Ground	Skating: Rink
Race: Track	Tennis: Court
Exercise: Gymnasium	Cricket: Pitch
Wrestling: Arena	

9. Worker and Tool:

Blacksmith : Anvil

Anvil is the tool used by a blacksmith.

Carpenter : Saw	Chef: Knife
Author: Pen	Soldier: Gun
Doctor : Stethoscope	Farmer: Plough
Gardener: Harrow	Mason: Plumbline
Labourer: Spade	Tailor: Needle
Woodcutter: Axe	Warrior: Sword
Surgeon: Scalpel	Sculptor : Chisel

10. Worker and Working Place:

Chef: Kitchen .

A chef works in a kitchen.

Farmer: Field	Teacher: School
Sailor : Ship	Engineer: Site
Doctor: Hospital	Servant: House
Painter: Gallery	Waiter: Restaurant
Umpire: Pitch	Gambler: Casino
Artist: Theatre	Actor : Stage
Lawyer: Court	Scientist : Laboratory
Clerk: Office	Warrior : Battlefield
Grocer: Shop	Worker: Factory
Beautician : Parlour	Mechanic: Garage
Astronomer:Observatory	

11. Worker and Product:

Mason: Wall

A mason builds a wall.

Choreographer: Ballet Dramatist : Play

Editor: Newspaper

Producer: Film

Architect: Design

Tailor: Clothes

Farmer: Crop

Author: Book

Carpenter: Furniture

Butcher: Meat

Cobbler : Shoes

Chef: Food

Poet : Poem

Goldsmith: Ornaments

Teacher: Education

12. Word and Synonym :

Abode: Dwelling

Abode means almost the same as Dwelling. Thus, Dwelling is the synonym of Abode.

Blend: Mix	Solicit : Request
Presage: Predict	Assign : Allot
Flaw: Defect	Fierce: Violent
Substitute: Replace	Mend: Repair
Presume: Assume	Brim : Edge
Sedate : Calm	Dissipate : Squander
Abduct: Kidnap	Vacant: Empty

13. Study and Topic:

Ornithology: Birds

Ornithology is the study of birds.

Seismology : Earthquakes

Entomology: Insects

Anthropology: Man

Cardiology: Heart

Pathology : Diseases

Physiology: Body

Phycology : Algae

Pedology: Soil

Palaeontology : FossilsIchthyology: Fishes

Taxonomy : Classification

Selenography : Moon

Botany : Plants

Mycology: Fungi

Haematology: Blood

Nephrology: Kidney

Herpetology: Amphibians

Eccrinology: Secretions

14. Word and Intensity :

Anger: Rage

Rage is of higher intensity than Anger.

Some more examples are given below :

Wish: Desire	Touch: Push
Sink: Drown	Quarrel: War
Famous: Renowned	Unhappy: Sad
crime : Sin	Moisten: Drench
Kindle: Burn	Error: Blunder
Refuse: Deny	Speak: Shout

15. Product and Raw Material :

Prism : Glass

Prism is made of glass.

Butter: Milk

Cloth : Fibre

Wine : Grapes

Fabric: Yarn

Road : Asphalt

Furniture: Wood

Shoes : Leather

Pullover: Wool

Omelette: Egg

Metal : Ore

Rubber: Latex

Linen: Flax

Oil : Seed

Paper: Pulp

Wall : Brick

Book: Paper

Sack : Jute

Jewellery: Gold

Jaggery : Sugarcane

RELATION ANALOGY

DIRECTIONS (ILLUSTRATION 7-8) : *There is a certain relation between two given words on one side of : : and one word is given on another side of : : while another word is to be found from the given alternatives, having the same relation with this word as the given pair has. Select the best alternative.*

ILLUSTRATION 7 :

Pigeon : Peace : : White flag : ?

(a) Enmity

(b) Victory

(c) Surrender

(d) War

***Sol.* (c)** Pigeon is a symbol of peace and white flag is a symbol of surrender.

ILLUSTRATION 8 :

Mature : Regressed : : Varied : ?

(a) Rhythmic

(b) Monotonous

(c) Decorous

(d) Obsolete

***Sol.* (b)** The words in each pair are opposites of each other.

SIMPLE ANALOGY

DIRECTIONS (EXAMPLE 9-10) : *For the following questions, choose the best option.*

ILLUSTRATION 9:

Cyclone is related to Anticyclone in the same way as Flood is related to .... ? ....

(a) Devastation (b) Havoc

(c) River (d) Drought

***Sol.* (d)** Both words are opposite to each other.

ILLUSTRATION 10 :

Accident is related to Carefulness in the same way as Disease is related to .... ?

(a) Sanitation (b) Treatment

(c) Medicine (d) Doctor

***Sol.* (a)** Lack of second results in the first.

CHOOSING A SIMILAR WORD

DIRECTIONS (ILLUSTRATION 11-12) : *In each of the following questions, a group of three interrelated words is given. Choose a word from the given alternatives that belongs to the same group.*

ILLUSTRATION 11 :

Potato : Carrot : Raddish

(a) Tomato (b) Spinach

(c) Sesame (d) Groundnut

***Sol.* (d)** All grow underground.

ILLUSTRATION 12 :

Patna : Mumbai : Dispur

(a) Cochin (b) Trombay

(c) Udaipur (d) Chennai

***Sol.* (d)** All are Capitals of states

DETECTING ANALOGIES

DIRECTIONS (ILLUSTRATION 13-14) : *In each question three words in bold letters are given which have something in common among themselves. Out of the four given alternatives, choose the most appropriate description about these three words.*

ILLUSTRATION 13 :

Mars : Mercury : Venus :

(a) They have no opposite motion

(b) They are evil planets

(c) They are the planets nearest to the earth

(d) They have no corresponding lucky stone.

Sol. **(c)**

ILLUSTRATION 14 :

Canoe : Yacht : Dinghy

(a) These are tribal people

(b) These are famous clubs

(c) These are names of boats

(d) These are rest houses

Sol. **(c)**

THREE WORD ANALOGY

DIRECTIONS (ILLUSTRATION 15-16) : *In each of the following questions, some words are given which are related in some way. The same relationship is obtained among the words in one of the four alternatives given under it. Find the correct alternative.*

ILLUSTRATION 15:

Evaporation : Cloud : Rain

(a) Sneezing : Cough : Cold

(b) Accident : Injury : Pain

(c) Tanning : Leather : Purse

(d) Bud : Flower : Fragrance

Sol. **(b)** First causes the second and second leads to the third.

ILLUSTRATION 16:

Lizard : Reptile : Insects

(a) Fox : Wolf : Forest

(b) Fly : Insect : Bee

(c) Man : Mammals : Meat

(d) Tiger : Mammal : Deer

Sol. **(c)** Second denotes the class to which the first belongs. Also, first feeds on the third.

NUMBER ANALOGY

DIRECTIONS (ILLUSTRATION 17-18) : *In the following question, there is a certain relation between two given numbers on one side of : : and one number is given on another side of : : while another number is to be found from the given alternatives, having the same relation with this number as the numbers of the given pair. Choose the best alternative:*

ILLUSTRATION 17 :

583 : 293 : : 488 : ?

(a) 777 (b) 945

(c) 1155 (d) 324

Sol. **(b)** Sum of digits of the first number is 2 more than the sum of digits of the second number.

ILLUSTRATION 18 :

5 : 35 : : ?

(a) 7 : 77 (b) 9 : 45

(c) 11 : 55 (d) 3 : 24

***Sol.* (a)** The first number is multiplied by the next prime number to obtain the second number.

ALPHABET ANALOGY

DIRECTIONS (ILLUSTRATION 19-20) : *In each of the following questions, there is some relationship between the two terms to the left of : : and the same relationship holds between the two terms to its right. Also, in each question, one term either to the right of : : or to the left of it is missing. This term is given as one of the alternatives below each question. Find out this term.*

ILLUSTRATION 19 :

ACE : FHJ: : OQS : ?

(a) PRT (b) RTU

(c) TVX (d) UWY

***Sol.* (c)** Each letter of the first group is moved five steps forward to obtain the corresponding letter of the second group.

ILLUSTRATION 20:

BUCKET : ACTVBDJLDFSU : : BONUS : ?

(a) ACMNMOTVRT

(b) SUNOB

(c) ACNPMOTVRT

(d) ACMNMOTURT

***Sol.* (c)** Each letter of the first group is replaced by two letters - one that comes after it and one that comes before it, in the second group.

PYRAMIDS :

Brief review of concepts : The questions in this unit are based on the pyramid of numbers from 1 to 100, as given below.

```
                              1
                           2  3  4
                        9  8  7  6  5
                    10 11 12 13 14 15 16
                 25 24 23 22 21 20 19 18 17
              26 27 28 29 30 31 32 33 34 35 36
           49 48 47 46 45 44 43 42 41 40 39 38 37
        50 51 52 53 54 55 56 57 58 59 60 61 62 63 64
     81 80 79 78 77 76 75 74 73 72 71 70 69 68 67 66 65
  82 83 84 85 86 87 88 89 90 91 92 93 94 95 96 97 98 99 100
```

Many types of questions are possible based on the above pattern. For instance, formation of parallel lines, perpendicular lines, triangles, squares etc. by taking numbers in order.

ILLUSTRATION 21 :

Fill the blanks from the choice given below.

129 : 145 : : 3811 : ?

(a) 3713 (b) 328

(c) 346 (d) 3615

***Sol.* (d)** There are two groups of numbers. The numbers on the right hand side must have the same relation as the numbers on the left hand side. 129 and 145, in the above pyramid, from a pattern.

Hence, the number in the blank on the right hand side must form same pattern with 3811. Therefore, the answer is 3615 which forms the pattern.

ILLUSTRATION 22 :

Fill the blank from the choice given below.

2812 : 765 : : 91123: ?

(a) 121110 (b) 121314

(c) 122132 (d) 303132

***Sol.* (b)** The two numbers on the left hand side from perpendicular line in the pyramid . Therefore, the numbers on the right hand side must be of the same pattern .The answer to the above question should be (2) 121314 to satisfy the same relation.

LEVEL 1

DIRECTIONS (Qs. 1-4): *Choose the odd one out:*

1. (a) Seismograph
   (b) Earthquake
   (c) Cyclone
   (d) Tsunami
2. (a) 145 (b) 120
   (c) 90 (d) 105
3. (a) Flourine (b) Bromine
   (c) Chromium (d) Chlorine
4. (a) Titan (b) Eris
   (c) Urenus (d) Haumea
5. 6 : 18 :: 4 : ?
   (a) 2 (b) 6
   (c) 8 (d) 16
6. 583 : 293 :: 488 : ?
   (a) 291 (b) 378
   (c) 487 (d) 581
7. 8 : 28 :: 27 : ?
   (a) 8 (b) 28
   (c) 64 (d) 65
8. Oxygen : Burn : : Carbon dioxide : ?
   (a) Isolate (b) Foam
   (c) Extinguish (d) Explode
9. Major : Battalion :: Colonel : ?
   (a) Company (b) Regiment
   (c) Army (d) Soldiers
10. Shout : Whisper :: Run : ?
    (a) Stay (b) Stand
    (c) Walk (d) Hop
11. 'JKLM' is related to 'XYZA' in the same way as 'NOPQ' is related to
    (a) RSTU (b) YZAB
    (c) DEFG (d) BCDE

DIRECTIONS (Qs.12-16): *Choose one number which is similar to the numbers in the given set of three numbers.*

12. Given set: 363, 489, 579
    (a) 562 (b) 471
    (c) 382 (d) 281
13. Given set: 282, 354, 444
    (a) 453 (b) 417
    (c) 336 (d) 255
14. Given set: 134, 246, 358
    (a) 372 (b) 460
    (c) 572 (d) 684
15. Given set: (6, 13, 22)
    (a) (6, 13, 27) (b) (10, 16, 28)
    (c) (11, 18, 27) (d) (13, 19, 27)
16. Given set: (12, 20, 4)
    (a) (5, 10, 15) (b) (13, 18, 5)
    (c) (17, 27, 5) (d) (20, 15, 25)

DIRECTION (Q. 17): *The following questions, a group of three interrelated words is given. Choose a word from the given alternative, that belongs to same group.*

17. Ohm : Watt: Volt:?
    (a) Light (b) Electricity
    (c) Hour (d) Ampere

DIRECTION (Qs. 18) : *In the following questions there is a specific relationship between the first and. second term. The same relationship exists between the third and fourth term which will replace the question mark (?). Select the correct term from the alternatives given :*

18. 531 : 99 :: ? : ?
    (a) 451 : 55 (b) 321 : 44
    (c) 642 : 66 (d) 212 : 11

DIRECTIONS (Qs. 19-21) : *In each question below there are two words separated by ':' in the upper row. Below that there are some words on each side of the symbol ':'. Find the relation between two upper words and select one word from the right side of ':' below which have the same relation as above.*

19. Octopus : Mollusca
    Spider : ?
    (a) Arthropoda (b) Clean
    (c) Porifera (d) Genus
20. Pituitary : Brain
    Thymus : ?
    (a) Throat (b) Chest
    (c) Spinal Cord (d) Larynx
21. Eye : Myopia
    Teeth : ?
    (a) Cataract (b) Trachoma
    (c) Pyorrhoea (d) Eczema
22. In a certain way 'Diploma' is related to 'Education'. Which of the following is related to 'Trophy' in a similar way?
    (a) Sports (b) Athlete
    (c) Winning (d) Prize
23. 'Necklace' is related to 'Jewellery' in the same way as 'Shirt' is related to
    (a) Cloth (b) Cotton
    (c) Apparel (d) Thread
24. 'Hospital' is related to 'Nurse' in the same way as 'Court'is related to
    (a) Justice (b) Lawyer
    (c) Judgement (d) Trial

DIRECTIONS (Qs. 25-27) : *Choose the right answer and write the answer in the answer box.*

25. Uncle is to Aunt as Cook is to ....
    (a) Fowl (b) Hen
    (c) Chicken (d) Duck
26. Wood is to table as .... is to coat
    (a) Shirt (b) Wear
    (c) Trouser (d) Cloth
27. Boy is to Girl as nephew is to ....
    (a) Uncle (b) Niece
    (c) Brother in law (d) Aunt

DIRECTIONS (Qs. 28-29) : *In the questions given below one term is missing. Based on the relationship of the two given words/ numbers find the missing term from the given options.*

28. Physicist : Physics : : ? : Anatomy
    (a) Botany (b) Botanist
    (c) Body (d) Biologist
29. Frequently : Always : : Selden : ?
    (a) Often (b) Rarely
    (c) Occasionally (d) Never

DIRECTIONS (Qs. 30-31) : *In the questions given below one term is missing. Based on the relationship of the two given words/ letters/ numbers find the missing term from the given options.*

30. ACE : FGH : : LNP : ?
    (a) QRS (b) PQR
    (c) QST (d) MOQ
31. EIGHTY : GIEYTH : : OUTPUT : ?
    (a) UTOPTU (b) UOTUPT
    (c) TUOUTP (d) TUOTUP
32. Find the missing numbevr that has same relation to 289 as 13 has to 169.
    169 : 13 : : 289 : ?
    (a) 19 (b) 17
    (c) 27 (d) 23
33. Choose the word which is least like the other words in the group?
    (a) Ladder (b) Staircase
    (c) Bridge (d) Escalator

34. Choose the alternative that has the same relationship to 16 has 12 as with 168.
12 : 168 :: 16 : ?
(a) 232 (b) 256
(c) 224 (d) 208

35. Sword, arrow, dagger, trident
(a) sword (b) arrow
(c) dagger (d) trident

36. Man, drone, bison, bull
(a) man (b) drone
(c) bison (d) bull

37. Army, corps, brigade, division, company
(a) army
(b) corps
(c) brigade
(d) company

38. Dermatologist, neurologist, obstetrician, dentist, oculist
(a) oculist
(b) neurologist
(c) obstetrician
(d) dermatologist

39. Viable, feasible, ample, dirigible
(a) viable
(b) feasible
(c) ample
(d) dirigible

40. Select the odd one out.
(a) 415 (b) 165
(c) 325 (d) 247

41. There is a certain relationship between the numbers on the left pair. Establish the same relationship in the right pair and find the missing number.
14 : 72 : : ? : 82
(a) 12 (b) 14
(c) 16 (d) 18

42. Select the odd one out.
(a) RTW (b) KMP
(c) ACE (d) QSV

43. If 346 is related to 8 in some way, then in the same way 592 is related to ?.
(a) 4 (b) 7
(c) 10 (d) 6

44. There is a certain relationship between the terms on the either side of : :. Identify the relationship on the left pair and find the missing term.
LNQ : MOP : : TVY : ?
(a) UVX (b) SVX
(c) UWX (d) UWZ

45. There is a certain relationship between the pair of letters on the either side of ::. Identify the given relationship and select the term which will replace the '?'. **[2020]**
PLEH : SOHK :: ? : GURZ
(a) DSPX (b) DRPV
(c) EROV (d) DROW

46. Choose the number pair/group which is different from others. **[2022]**
(a) 65 : 82
(b) 145 : 170
(c) 37 : 50
(d) 120 : 143

LEVEL 2

DIRECTIONS (Qs.1-18): *In each of the following questions, four words, letters/ numbers have been given, out of which three are alike in some manner and one is different. Choose out the odd one.*

1. (a) Nephrology (b) Entomology (c) Astrology (d) Mycology
2. (a) NEERG (b) DER (c) KNIP (d) DLEIF
3. (a) Rival (b) Opponent (c) Foe (d) Ally
4. (a) POCG (b) KLIZ (c) BUDX (d) FQMV
5. (a) 36 - 48 (b) 56 - 44 (c) 78 - 66 (d) 33 - 64
6. (a) Morning (b) Noon (c) Evening (d) Night
7. (a) Liberty (b) Society (c) Equality (d) Fraternity
8. (a) DWFU (b) EVHS (c) HSKP (d) KQNN
9. (a) CBEF (b) EDGH (c) IHKL (d) GFHJ
10. (a) 4025 (b) 7202 (c) 6023 (d) 5061
11. (a) 96 : 80 (b) 64 : 48 (c) 80 : 60 (d) 104 : 78
12. (a) Sirius
    (b) Proximacentauri
    (c) Deimos
    (d) Alpha centauri
13. (a) Ornithology : Birds
    (b) Mycology : Fungi
    (c) Biology : Botany
    (d) Phycology : Algae
14. (a) PON (b) SRQ (c) XYZ (d) VUT
15. (a) 1919 (b) 5656 (c) 6761 (d) 7760
16. (a) 2890 (b) 3375 (c) 1728 (d) 1331
17. (A) TSR (B) LKJ (c) PQO (d) HGF
18. (a) DfH (b) MoQ (c) UwY (d) lnO

DIRECTION (Q.19): *Find the odd-one-out from the alternatives*

19. (a) 25, 5, 5 (b) 51, 3, 17 (c) 96, 6, 16 (d) 75, 5, 25
20. Find the odd one out of the following terms : EF22, JK42, GH24, VW90, IJ38
    (a) EF22 (b) GH24 (c) IJ38 (d) VW90
21. Which one of the following differs from the rest?
    (a) MGDLFC
    (b) JQVIPU
    (c) ZUBXTA
    (d) DYSCXR
22. Which group of letters is different from others?
    (a) CBAED
    (b) IJHGK
    (c) SRQPT
    (d) TVWYX

DIRECTIONS (Qs. 23-29) : *Out of the four choices given for each question, you have to select one that will maintain the relationship on the two sides of the sign : : the same if it is substituted for the question mark '?'*

23. A b c : pQr : : ? : x Y z
    (a) LMN (b) Mno
    (c) uvw (d) BCD
24. 25 : 15 : : 7 : ?
    (a) 4 (b) 5
    (c) 6 (d) 7
25. ? : WPJ : : MHZ : ?
    (a) YRL, KFX (b) VOI, NIB
    (c) XQK, LGY (d) WRJ, MIZ
26. FLO : MOC :: RDP : ?
    (a) NGO (c) MGP
    (b) GMP (d) MPG
27. CJDL : FMGR :: IKJR: ?
    (a) OQPT (b) RSTU
    (c) LSMT (d) KRMO
28. A : X : : B : ....
    (a) W (b) V
    (c) Y (d) Z
29. KLM : PON : : NOP : ....
    (a) LMK (b) MLK
    (c) NML (d) KLN
30. B E J Q : A C G M U : : F I N U : ?
    (a) E H L R Z (b) E G K Q Y
    (c) F H K R Z (d) E H L Q W
31. B D G K : O K H F : : K M P T : ?
    (a) X T O Q (b) X O T Q
    (c) X T Q O (d) O X T Q
32. Guitar : Music :: Book : ?
    (a) Pages (b) Writer
    (c) Publisher (d) Knowledge
33. Select the option that is related to the third word in the same way as the second word is related to the first word.
    Thermometer : Temperature :: Hygrometer : ?
    (a) Pressure (b) Density
    (c) Stress (d) Humidity
34. Find the odd one out.
    (a) 68 – 43 (b) 74 – 40
    (c) 85 – 60 (d) 103 – 78
35. In a certain code language, if 'POPULAR' is coded as 'QPQVMBS', then which word will be coded as 'GBNPVT'?
    (a) FAMOUS (b) FCMOUS
    (c) FARMES (d) FARMER

DIRECTIONS (ILLUSTRATION 36-39) : *In each question three words in bold letters are given which have something in common among themselves. Out of the four given alternatives, choose the most appropriate description about these three words.*

36. **Prakrit : Pali : Sanskrit**
    (a) They are classical languages of Asia and Europe
    (b) The Vedas are written in these languages
    (c) They are old languages of India
    (d) They are dead languages
37. **Vinci : Angelo : Raphael**
    (a) They were Italian engineers
    (b) They were European painters
    (c) They were dictators
    (d) They were famous politicians
38. **India : Pakistan : Bangladesh**
    (a) Japan : China : Turkey
    (b) Sri Lanka : Japan : India
    (c) Iraq : Kuwait : Iran
    (d) Canada : California : Mexico
39. **Morning : Evening : Dusk**
    (a) Triangle : Quadrilateral : Pentagon
    (b) Happy : Gay : Excited
    (c) Summer : Winter : Autumn
    (d) Botany : Zoology : Physiology

DIRECTIONS (Qs. 40-46): *In the following questions, there is a relationship between the letter terms on the left of the sign (: :). The some relationship exists to the right of the sign (: :), of which one is missing. Find the missing term from the alternatives.*

40. N O V A : O V O N : : O Z O N : ?
(a) O Z O Z (b) Z O Z O
(c) N O N O (d) Z N Z N

41. B E F C : E D B F : : V Y Z W : ?
(a) Y X V Z (b) X Y V Z
(c) Y X Z V (d) V Y X Z

42. Choose the correct alternatives. Famine : Hunger : : War : __________
(a) Enmity (b) Insecurity
(c) Destruction (d) Infantry

43. Stimulant : Activity : : ?
(a) Symptom : Disease
(b) Food : Hunger
(c) Fertilizer : Growth
(d) Diagnosis : Treatment

44. Choose appropriate option from given alternatives such that the relationship defined by ':' is preserved.PNLJ : LIFC and VTRP : ________
(a) ROLI (b) SOLH
(c) RPOM (d) DMEN

45. If MENTAL : SMXFOB then ABILITY : ______
(a) GJSXWJQ (b) GSXWJJQ
(c) SGXWJJQ (d) SJXQJWG

46. As JAISALMER is to JAILSARME, as HYDERABAD is to __________.
(a) HYDAERDBA
(b) HYDRBEDAA
(c) HYDBDREAA
(d) HYDEADRAB

47. Select the odd one out. **[2019]**
(a) AEFJ (b) KOPT
(c) EHIL (d) QUVZ

48. If there is a certain relationship between the pair of numbers on either side of : :. Identify the relationship between the given pair and find the missing number. **[2020]**
8 : 56 : : 9 : ?
(a) 90 (b) 81
(c) 72 (d) 89

49. Select the pair of words which are related in the same way as 'Current' is related to 'Ampere'. **[2022]**
(a) Power : Energy
(b) Pressure : Time
(c) Force : Newton
(d) Mass : Metre

50. To establish the same relationship between two pairs of terms on either side of '::', choose the option that will replace the question mark(?). **[2022]**
16 : 20 :: 49 : ?
(a) 64 (b) 40
(c) 81 (d) 56

ANSWER KEY

LEVEL-1

1	(a)	**6**	(b)	**11**	(d)	**16**	(b)	**21**	(c)	**26**	(d)	**31**	(d)	**36**	(c)	**41**	(c)	**46**	(d)
2	(a)	**7**	(d)	**12**	(b)	**17**	(d)	**22**	(a)	**27**	(b)	**32**	(b)	**37**	(a)	**42**	(c)		
3	(c)	**8**	(c)	**13**	(a)	**18**	(c)	**23**	(c)	**28**	(d)	**33**	(c)	**38**	(a)	**43**	(c)		
4	(c)	**9**	(b)	**14**	(b)	**19**	(a)	**24**	(b)	**29**	(c)	**34**	(c)	**39**	(d)	**44**	(c)		
5	(c)	**10**	(c)	**15**	(c)	**20**	(b)	**25**	(b)	**30**	(a)	**35**	(b)	**40**	(d)	**45**	(d)		

LEVEL-2

1	(c)	**6**	(d)	**11**	(a)	**16**	(a)	**21**	(c)	**26**	(a)	**31**	(c)	**36**	(c)	**41**	(a)	**46**	(a)
2	(c)	**7**	(b)	**12**	(c)	**17**	(c)	**22**	(d)	**27**	(c)	**32**	(d)	**37**	(b)	**42**	(c)	**47**	(c)
3	(d)	**8**	(a)	**13**	(c)	**18**	(d)	**23**	(b)	**28**	(a)	**33**	(d)	**38**	(c)	**43**	(c)	**48**	(c)
4	(d)	**9**	(d)	**14**	(c)	**19**	(d)	**24**	(c)	**29**	(b)	**34**	(b)	**39**	(c)	**44**	(a)	**49**	(c)
5	(d)	**10**	(d)	**15**	(b)	**20**	(b)	**25**	(c)	**30**	(b)	**35**	(a)	**40**	(b)	**45**	(a)	**50**	(d)

CHAPTER 2 Coding-Decoding

CODING

The word 'coding' stands for converting a **word from English language** into a certain pattern or expression.

Therefore, **code** is a sequence of letters/numbers, which is used in place of the original **word/series of numbers** that is coded.

Coding can be done for a group of letters (a word), a series of numbers or an **alphanumeric series** (*i.e.,* a series having both alphabets as well as numerals).

There are 7 types of coding methods :

1. **Simple Arrangement.**
2. **Direct Coding**
3. **Letter coding**
4. **Alphanumeric Coding.**
5. **Substitution Coding**
6. **Decephering message word/Number/ Symbol Coding.**
7. **Jumbled Coding.**

I. **Simple Arrangement Method :** This is the most common & the simplest kind of coding. These codes are generally obtained by simply re-aligning the given alphabets in a word.

ILLUSTRATION 1 :

In a code language, if TRAINS is coded as RTIASN, how will FLOWER be coded in the same language ?

(a) LFOWER (b) LFWORE
(c) WORELF (d) ERFLOW

Sol. (b) TRAINS ⟶ RTIASN

In the above code, we can clearly observe that the code is obtained simply by interchanging the positions of 2 **consecutive alphabets** *i.e.,* TR becomes RT, AI becomes IA and NS becomes SN similarly,

FLOWER will be coded as (FL becomes LF, OW becomes WO and ER becomes RE) LFWORE.

FLOWER ⟶ LFWORE

Therefore, correct answer is option (b).

ILLUSTRATION 2 :

In a certain code language, the word 'PARTNER' is coded as 'TRAPREN', how will 'FOUNDER' be coded in the same language.

(a) NUOFDER (b) NUOFRED
(c) FOUNRED (d) OFNUEDR

Sol. (b) When we divide letters of the word 'PARTNER' in two group.

First group of first 4 letters and second group of last 3 letters, *i.e.,* PART and NER and then reverse the order of the letters in these two groups.

PART ⟶ TRAP ⎤
⇒ TRAPREN
NER ⟶ REN ⎦

Similarly, we divide the letters of the word 'FOUNDER' in two group.

First group with first 4 letters (FOUN) and second group with last 3 letters (DER) & then reverse the order of the letters in the 2 groups.

FOUN ⟶ NUOF DER ⟶ RED

∴ the code for FOUNDER is NUOFRED

Therefore, correct answer is option (b).

Quick Tips

Notes for simple arrangement :

(i) Number of characters (letters / numbers / symbols) in the code should be same as that of the original word, otherwise coding is not possible.

(ii) Pay attention to the alignment of the word, *i.e,* if the letter/ number has changed its position from first to last & vice versa, a swap coding is possible.

For e.g. : in ***e.g.* 3**, first group had 4 letters — 'FOUN' & there was a swap between letters at first & last position.

Swap coding

II. Direct Coding : When the characters, *i.e.,* letters of a word or numerals of a series are substituted by a coded character, *i.e.,* an alphabet, a numeral or a symbol & are placed in the coded word at similar positions as in the given / original word, it is known as direct substitution method.

These codes (substitutions) may either be in a direct fashion or in a jumbled fashion in order to make the questions tricky.

ILLUSTRATION 3 :

In a code language, if SUGAR is coded as ZNMDB and TEA is coded as FLD, how would you code GRATE in the same code language.

(a) BNDFL (b) MBDFL
(c) LDZMN (d) FLDZB

Sol. (b)

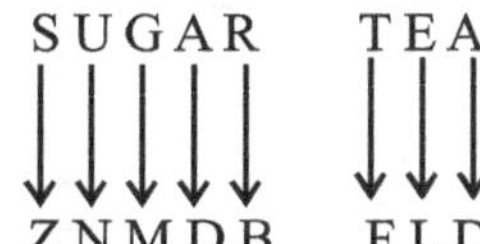

First we write the original words SUGAR & TEA and is corresponding alignment to these, we write down their codes respectively.

Therefore, we see that Z is coded for S, N for U, M for G, D for A and B for R, in the word SUGAR. While in the word TEA, F is substituted for T, L for E & D for A.

This implies that this code is in direct fashion as in both the words 'D' is coded for A.

Therefore, code for GRATE will be MBDFL.

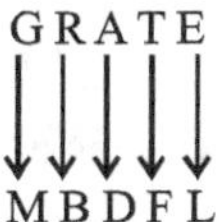

So, correct answer option is (b).

ILLUSTRATION 4 :

If in a certain code language, TWENTY is coded as 863985 and ELEVEN is coded as 323039, how will TWELVE be coded?

(a) 863903 (b) 863650
(c) 863203 (d) 683583

Sol. (c)

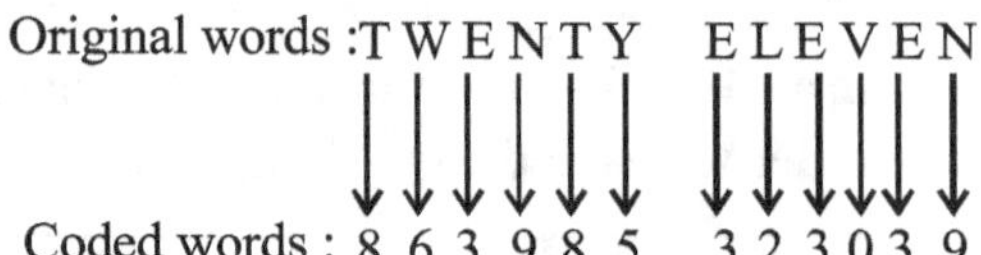

Therefore, in the word TWELVE, 8 will be the code for T, 6 will be the code for W, 3 for E, 2 for L, and 0 for V.

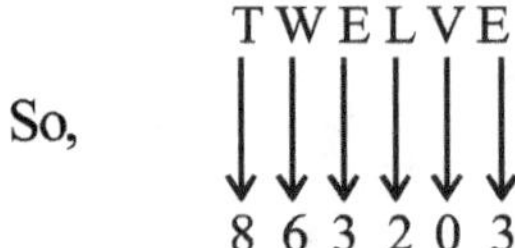

Hence, answer option (c) is the correct answer.

Quick Tips

__Notes for direct substitution :__

(i) If there are 2 words in the question for which codes are given and these 2 words have 1 or more same alphabets, then the codes for these alphabets will be the same as well.

(ii) In case of confusion, note (a), *i.e.*, same codes in both the words for same alphabet, will help us identify that the question belongs to the category of **direct substitution.**

III. Letter Coding : This method involves the use of the alphabet series (A B C D E F ....X Y Z).

A certain word will be coded as certain other letters from the alphabet series following a certain pattern. It is further explained by examples.

ILLUSTRATION 5 :

In a certain code language, the word 'RECTANGLE' is coded as TGEVCPING, then how is the word 'RHOMBUS' coded ?

(a) TJOQDWV (b) UVWTJQN
(c) TJQODWU (d) JTQOEWN

Sol. (c) Each letter of the word RECTANGLE is moved two steps forward to obtain the corresponding letters of the code, *i.e.*,

R E C T A N G L E
+2 +2 +2 +2 +2 +2 +2 +2 +2
T G E V C P I N G

Similarly, we have :

R H O M B U S
+2 +2 +2 +2 +2 +2 +2
T J Q O D W U

So, the desired code is 'TJQODWU'. So, option (3) is the correct answer.

IV. Alpha-Numeric Series Coding : Out of the entire alphabet series numbered 1 to 26, *i.e.*,

A B C D E F G H I J K
1 2 3 4 5 6 7 8 9 10 11
L M N O P Q R S T U
12 13 14 15 16 17 18 19 20 21
V W X Y Z
22 23 24 25 26

it is difficult to remember each and every alphabets' numeric value, therefore, we just have to remember.

E = 5, J = 10, O = 15, T = 20 and Y = 25 which are multiples of 5.

In alphanumeric coding, the alphabets of the word are given and we code them in terms of their numeric value or some pattern according to their numeric values.

ILLUSTRATION 6 :

If in a certain code language, 'MIRROR' is coded as '13918181518', how will 'APPLE' be coded in the same language ?

(a) 11616125 (b) 3984145
(c) 1162254 (d) 11213147

Sol. (a) As we can see from the alphabet series, numeric values for the alphabets M is 13, I is 9, R is 18 and O is 15.
Similarly, for the word APPLE, A = 1, P = 16, P = 16, L = 12 & E = 5. So, the code is 11616125. Therefore, option (a) is the correct answer.

V. Substitution Coding: In this type of questions, some particular words are assigned certain substituted names. Then a question is asked that is to be answered in the substituted code language.

ILLUSTRATION 7:

If white is called blue, blue is called red, red is called yellow, yellow is called green, green is called black, black is called violet and violet is called orange, what would be the colour of human blood?

(a) Red (b) Green
(c) Yellow (d) Violet

Sol. (c) Yellow
The colour of the human blood is 'red' ans as given, 'red' is called 'yellow.'
So, the colour of human blood is 'yellow.'

VI. Deciphering Message Word Codes: In this type of questions, some messages are given in the coded language and the code for a particular word or message is asked. To analyse such codes, any two messages bearing a common word are picked up. The common code-word will thus represent that word. Proceeding similarly by picking up all possible combinations of two, the entire message can be decoded and the codes for individual words found.

ILLUSTRATION 8:

In a certain code, 'bi nie pie' means 'some good jokes': 'nie bat lik' means 'some real stories'; and 'pie lik tol' means 'many good stories.' Which word in that code means 'jokes'?

(a) bi (b) nie
(c) pie (d) Can't be determined

Sol. (a) bi In the first and second statements, the common code word is 'nie' and the common word is 'some'.
So, 'nie' means 'some'.
In the first and third statements, the common code word is 'pie' and the common word is 'good'.
So, 'pie' means 'good'.

VII. Deciphering Number and Symbol Codes for Messages

In this type of questions, a few groups of numbers/symbols, each coding a certain message, are given. Through a comparison of the given coded messages, taking two at a time, the candidate is required to find the number/symbol code for each word and them formulate the code for the given message.

ILLUSTRATION 9:

In a certain code language, '743' means 'mangoes are good', '657' means 'eat good food and '934' means 'mangoes are ripe.' Which digit means 'ripe' in the that language?

(a) 9 (b) 4
(c) 5 (d) 7

Sol. (a) 9 In the first and third statements, the common code digits are '4' and '3' and the common words are 'mangoes' and 'are'.
So, '4' and '3' are the codes for 'mangoes' and 'are'.
Thus, in the third statements, '9' means 'ripe'.

VIII. Jumbled Coding: In this type of questions, certain sample words are given along with their codes. The candidate is required to decipher individual codes for different letters by comparing, taking two words at a time, and then answer the given questions accordingly.

DECODING

The word decoding stands for converting a certain pattern or expressions, *i.e.,* the code, to a word from English language or a certain series of numbers.
In other words, decoding refers to the process of converting the code back to the original word.

Similar to coding, there are 4 types of Decoding Methods :

I. Simple Arrangement

II. Direct Decoding

III. Letter Decoding

IV. Alphanumeric Decoding

We would first like you to go back and revise the four types of CODING methods before we move on.

I. Simple Arrangement Method : Under this, the code will be obtained simply by re-arrangement of the alphabets of the word. The questions will test you on decoding these codes.

ILLUSTRATION 1 :

In a certain language, 'SIMPLE' is written as 'ISPMEL' and 'CHAPTER' is written as 'HCPARET'. Then 'LFWORE' stands for which word ?

(a) LOWFER (b) FLOREW
(c) FLOWER (d) WORFEL

Sol. (c) SIMPLE ⟶ ISPMEL

The word 'SIMPLE' is of 6 letters and so is the code given in the question. Therefore, we have to follow the pattern of the word 'SIMPLE'.

In the above code, we can clearly observe that the code is obtained simply by inter changing the positions of consecutive alphabets, *i.e.*,

Similarly,

Hence, option (c) is the correct answer. 'FLOWER' is the word for which the code is given.

ILLUSTRATION 2 :

In a certain language, if 'CARROM' is written as 'MORRAC', then what is the word coded as 'TIBBAR'.

(a) RIBBAT (b) RABBIT
(c) BARTIB (d) BITRAB

Sol. (b) The code for the word 'CARROM', is obtained by reversing the order of the alphabets of the word *i.e.,*

C A R R O M

⟵ reverse the order

M O R R A C

Similarly, the word for code 'TIBBAR' will be an outcome of the same pattern as followed for the word 'CARROM', *i.e.,* the code TIBBAR will also be written in reverse order.

T I B B A R

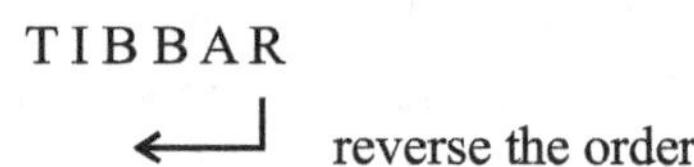

R A B B I T

Hence, 'RABBIT' is the word, making option (2) the correct answer.

Note for Decoding : Solve by options, *i.e.,* by taking one option at a time into consideration.

II. Direct Decoding : In these kind of questions, there will be one or more words given in the question for which codes will be given either in direct fashion or in jumbled up fashion. We'll discuss both.

We will be asked to find out the original word (s) for the given code(s).

Command data for Illustration 3 & 4 :

In a certain code language, if P O U R I N G is written as x f n p l o m, S A M P L E is written as z e h x c j and W H I T E N E R is written as a t l k j o j p.

ILLUSTRATION 3 :

Then which word is written as 'hjecz' ?

(a) LEAMS (b) SMEAL

(c) MEALS (d) MALES

Sol. **(c)** The codes for the three words are direct substitution of the small alphabets for the capital ones, because 'N' & 'I' are codes as 'o' & 'l' respectively in both POURING as well as WHITENER, while 'E' is written as 'j' both the times in the word WHITENER and also in the word SAMPLE.

Words	P	O	U	R	I	N	G	S	A	M	P	L	E	W	H	I	T	E	N	E	R
Codes	x	f	n	p	l	o	m	z	e	h	x	c	j	a	t	l	k	j	o	j	p

Letter	P	O	U	R	I	N	G	S	A	M	L	E	W	H	T
Codes :	x	f	n	p	l	o	m	z	e	h	c	j	a	t	k

Therefore, the code 'h j e c z' stands for MEALS.

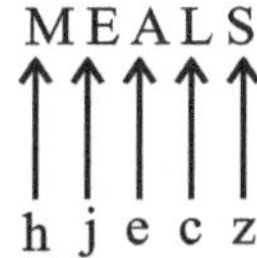

deriving the word from the code (see arrows)

Hence, option (3) is the correct answer.

ILLUSTRATION 4 :

Which word is coded as 'ajlmtk' ?

(a) WAISTE (b) WEIGHT

(c) WASTES (d) HEIGHT

Sol. (b) Following the same concept as in example 5, the code 'ajlmtk' represents

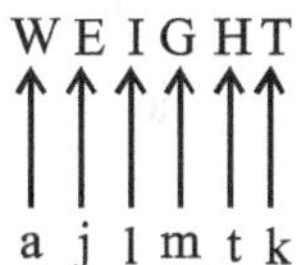

deriving the word from the code.

Hence, option (b) 'WEIGHT' is the correct answer.

Quick Tips

(i) Spot out the common letters in the words and try to find the code for the common letters first.

(ii) As soon as you find the codes for some letters, tick those letters as well as codes so you don't keep checking them again & again. This will save your time & save you from any kind of confusion while solving the questions.

III. Letter Decoding

Under this method, a code will be given to you, you will have to recognize the pattern the code is following.

The pattern may be moving a few alphabets forward, a few alphabets backward or alternate forward & backward.

ILLUSTRATION 5 :

If, in a certain language, POWERFUL is coded as QQZIWLBT, then which word is coded as ECQGJXZ ?

(a) DANCERS (b) HARMLESS

(c) PRACTISE (d) DANGERS

Sol. **(a)** The pattern followed by the code is moving up in an increasing order.

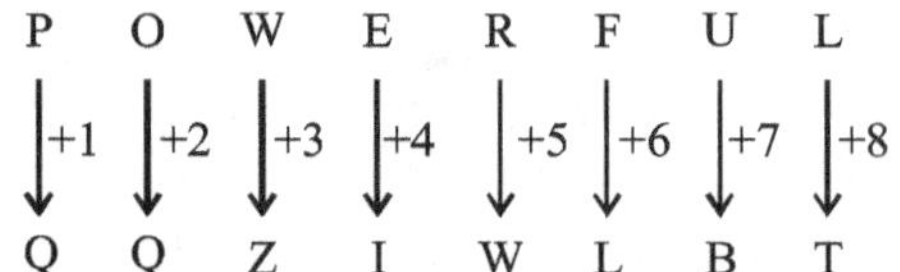

First method : similarly, the code given will also follow the same pattern. Therefore, we subtract or move the alphabets of the code backwards to form the word.

E C Q G J X Z

↓−1 ↓−2 ↓−3 ↓−4 ↓−5 ↓−6 ↓−7

D A N C E R S

Second method : We can also go by the options, *i.e.,* check each option one by one and see if it forms the code given in the questions using the same pattern as coded in the word 'POWERFUL'.

IV. Alpha-Numeric Decoding

This is similar to alpha-numeric coding, with the only difference that we have to derive the code from a given word in case of alpha-numeric coding. While in decoding, we have to derive the word from the code following the alphabet series (ABCDEFG. ……. PQRSTUVWXYZ).

ILLUSTRATION 6 :

If the code in a certain language, for PAPER = 56 and SHEET = 57, then for which of the following words is the code 88 ?

(a) IRON (b) PUPPET

(c) HELMETS (d) PARROT

Sol. (d) As we know the values of each alphabet in the alphabet series, so we can unlock the codes.

PAPER ⟶ P = 16, A = 1, P = 16, E = 5, R = 18

$16+1+16+5+18=56$

SHEET ⟶ S = 19, H = 8, E = 5, E = 5, T = 20

$19+8+5+5+20=57$

Now, to find the word for the code 88, we have to check all the options.

Option (a)

IRON ⟶ I = 9, R = 18, O = 15, N = 14

$9+18+15+14=56$

Option (b)

PUPPET → P = 16, U = 21, P = 16, P = 16, E = 5, T = 20,

$16+21+16+16+5+20=94$

Option (c)

HELMETS → H = 8, E = 5, L = 12, M = 13, E = 5, T = 20, S = 19

$8+5+12+13+5+20+19=82$

Option (d)

PARROT → P = 16, A = 1, R = 18, R = 18, O = 15, T = 20

$16+1+18+18+15+20=88$

The required word.

Therefore, option (d) PARROT is the answer.

LEVEL 1

1. If VISHAL is coded as 22102111517, then what will be the code for SACHIN ?
   (a) 1925311191 (b) 1295111319
   (c) 1925111319 (d) 1952111319
2. In a certain code, APPLE is XNNZM and BAT is HXC, then BATTLE will be coded as ?
   (a) XHCCZH (b) HXCCZM
   (c) HXCCMZ (d) HXMCCZ
3. In a certain code, RADIO is XZOPL and SHEET is NBGGI, then HEATER is coded as?
   (a) BNGZIX (b) BGZGIX
   (c) BGZIGX (d) GZBIXZ
4. If VISHAL is coded as 22102111517, then what will be the code for SACHIN ?
   (a) 1925311191 (b) 1295111319
   (c) 1925111319 (d) 1952111319
5. In a certain code, APPLE is XNNZM and BAT is HXC, then BATTLE will be coded as ?
   (a) XHCCZH (b) HXCCZM
   (c) HXCCMZ (d) HXMCCZ
6. In a certain code, RADIO is XZOPL and SHEET is NBGGI, then HEATER is coded as ?
   (a) BNGZIX (b) BGZGIX
   (c) BGZIGX (d) GZBIXZ
7. If in a certain language, SHIFT is coded as RFFBO, which word would be coded as LKUMB?
   (a) MMXQG (b) MLVNC
   (c) KJVLS (d) MJVLC

DIRECTIONS (Qs. 8-12) : *DELHI is coded as WVOSR, choose the right code for the following :*

8. ORNRG
   (a) LIMIT (b) PEARL
   (c) BEARS (c) LAPEL
9. NZCRNFN
   (a) NININUM (b) MAXIMUM
   (c) MINIMAL (d) MINUTES
10. NRMRNFN
    (a) MINIMUM (b) MAXIMUM
    (c) MINIMAL (d) MINUTES
11. XSZKVO
    (a) CHAPTS (b) CHITES
    (c) CHORES (d) CHAPEL
12. If in a certain language 'how can you go' is written as 'je de ke pe', 'you come here' is written as 'ne ke se' and 'come and go' as 're pe se', then how will 'here' be written in the language?
    (a) je (b) pe
    (c) me (d) ke

DIRECTIONS (Qs. 13-15): *Following alphabets are written in a special coded language like:*

B L A C K	W H I T E
0 1 2 3 4	5 6 7 8 9

13. Then code 62830 will be written as
    (a) HATCB (b) HATEC
    (c) HATBC (d) HATCE
14. 'BHICK' will be coded as
    (a) 06734 (b) 67340
    (c) 67430 (d) 06743

15. If 'SKY WAS BLUE' is 123
'SEA IS BLUE' is 245
'PEOPLE SWIMMING IN SEA' is 4678
'PEOPLE LIKE SKY' is 801and
'BIRDS IN SKY' IS 169. Then 'PEOPLE LIKE BIRDS' will have the number.
(a) 809
(b) 104
(c) 036
(d) 806

16. In a certain code language, 'PAPER' is written as 'OZODQ'. How will 'BIOLOGY' be written in that language? **[2018]**
(a) AHNKNFY
(b) FOBHMX
(c) ADMDJFX
(d) AHNKNFX

17. If in a certain code language, ACNE is coded as 35167 , then how will PAIR be coded in the same language? **[2018]**
(a) 1831120 (b) 1831125
(c) 1341118 (d) 1541927

18. If in a certain code language, men are very busy' is written as '1234', 'busy persons need encouragement' is written as '4567', 'encouragement is very important' is written as '3589' and 'important persons are rare' is written as '2680', then how will 'encouragement' be written in that language? **[2018]**
(a) 5 (b) 6
(c) 8 (d) 9

19. If 'CIGARETTE' is coded as 'GICERAETT', then 'DIRECTION' will be coded as: **[2022]**
(a) NOIETCRID (b) RIDTCENOI
(a) IRDCTIONE (d) NORTECDII

LEVEL 2

DIRECTIONS (Qs.1-4): *In the following questions the words are coded but are not in their respective position. Study them carefully and answer the questions that follow:*

'Mohan Wants Car' is 1, 2, 3
'Car Is Good' is 1, 4, 5
'Mohan Has Good Scooters' is 2, 4, 6, 7
'Amit Has Car' is 7, 1, 8 and
'Car Is Precious' is 1, 5, 9

1. Which digit stands for 'Good'?
(a) 1 (b) 4
(c) 6 (d) 7

2. What will be the code for 'Amit Wants Precious Scooter'?
(a) 2, 3, 6, 9 (b) 8, 3, 9, 6
(c) 8, 6, 5, 9 (d) 8, 7, 9, 1

3. If RIR is coded as IRI then MUM is coded as
(a) NFN (b) UMU
(c) UNU (d) MFM

4. A coding language writes English words in the coded form as:
S T A T θ δ θ γ
R A T δ θ β
S A Y ε γ δ
The code does not appear in the same order of the letters in the English words. On this basis, which of the following will be the code of the word T R A Y?
(a) ε β θ γ (b) β γ δ ε
(c) β θ δ ε (d) θ δ γ ε

DIRECTIONS (Qs. 5-6) : *Read the following information and answer the question that follows:*

Code :	Z	A	X	B	Y	O	T	W	C	M	I
Original alphabet	B	U	E	T	F	A	I	R	V	L	D

5. AFRAID
   (a) OYTWOI (b) OYWTOI
   (c) OWYOTI (d) OYWOTI
6. BULLET
   (a) BAMMXZ (b) ZAMMXI
   (c) OWYOTI (d) OYWOTI

DIRECTIONS (Qs. 7-12) : *Letters A to Z are coded using the following cells in diagram I and sectors in diagram II. The first letter in each cell is coded by its shape while the second letter includes a dot in it. for example.*

A is coded as ⌋; M is coded as •⌋

K is coded as  >; P is coded as •>

Diagram I

AM	NF	CO
BU	TV	DG
EW	IZ	XY

Diagram II

7. How SUGAR will be coded?
   (a) 
   (b) 
   (c) 
   (d) 
8. How SPICE will be coded?
   (a) 
   (b) 
   (c) 
   (d) 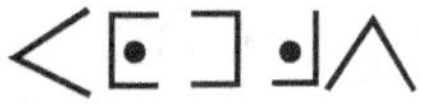
9. How PATCH will be coded?
   (a) 
   (b) 
   (c) 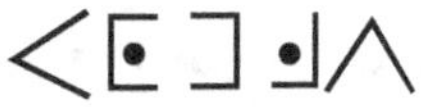
   (d) 
10. If in a certain code, STUDENT is written as RSTEDMS, then how would TEACHER be written in the same code?
    (a) SZZDGEQ (b) SZDDGEQ
    (c) SDZDGDQ (d) SDZCGDQ
11. If RAJASTHAN = 9R17J8L19H13 in a coded language, then what is the encrypted form of the MANIPUR in the same language ?
    (a) 14R13H11G9
    (b) 13M14W11B9
    (c) 13R14J11F9
    (d) 14M13V11J9
12. If FAST is coded as 798 and LAST is coded as 906 then BUSY is coded as
    (a) 17599 (b) 1431
    (c) 952 (d) 948

DIRECTIONS (Qs. 13-26) : *A coding language is used to write English words in coded form given below:*

TENNIS	%#$@$&
TRUE	@+#*
PRIME	* = ?#%
SPINE	#$%?&

The codes do not appear in the same order of the letters in English words. Decode the language and based on these codes identify the code for English word given in each question from the alternatives provided.

13. MINT
    (a) % = & * (b) = # ? %
    (c) @ % = $ (d) * @ ? +
14. RINSE
    (a) = ? + * @
    (b) % * $ # &
    (c) * $ # @ +
    (d) $ & # = ?
15. INTEREST
    (a) = ? * + % & = *
    (b) ? # = ? + # * $
    (c) + $ @ + $ = * %
    (d) @ # * # @ $ % &

16. Some translated words in an artificial Language (in which the word order is not necessarily same) are given below

mie pie sie	good person sing
pie sie rie	sing good lyrics
tie rie sie	love good lyrics

What is the translation for "person love lyrics"?
(a) pie tie rie (b) tie rie sie
(c) rie mie tie (d) sie mie pie

17. In a certain language IMPHAL is coded as JLRFDI. How will MYSURU be coded in the same language?
(a) NXUSUR (b) RUSUXN
(c) NXSUUR (d) NXTTUR

18. If in a code language STAR = 50 and CIRUS = 65 then PLANET will be
(a) 68 (b) 78
(c) 84 (d) 94

19. If in a coded language.
'Busy bees' are coded as 'Cpu cff'
'Busy crows' are code as 'cpu hup'
"Bright crows' are coded "Csj Hup'
Then Busy crows are clever will be coded as ________
(a) Cpu Hup Bsf Dmf
(b) Cpu hup bsf Dmf
(c) cpu Hup Baf Dmf
(d) cpu hup bsf Dmf

20. What is the code used for 'Blue' derived from the given coded statements as per a code language?
I. 'Flower Blue Red White' is coded as Sa Ra Ga Ma'
II. 'Take Red Pink Flower' is coded as 'Sa Ha Ma Pa'
III. 'Take Blue Red Buds' is coded as 'Pa Da Ma Ga'
IV. 'Bring Red Take White' is coded as Ma Na Pa Ra'
(a) Sa (b) Ga
(c) Pa (d) Ra

21. In a certain code 'TOME' is written as '@$*?' and 'ARE' is written as '! & ?'. How can 'REMOTE' be written in that code?
(a) & ? $ @ ? (b) & ? * $ @ ?
(c) @ ? * $ @ ? (d) * @ $ * ? !

22. In a certain code language, 'REPAIR' is written as 'FSBQSJ'. How is 'EXAMINATIONS' written in the same language?
(a) YFNBOUJBPJOT
(b) YFNBOJUBPJTO
(c) YFNBOJUBJPTO
(d) YFNBOJBUJPOT

23. If in a certain code language,'546' is written as 'you are best','538' is written as 'you can do' and '692' is written as 'all are good', then which digit is written as 'best'?
(a) 5
(b) 4
(c) 6
(d) Can't be determined

24. In a coding language, the digits 0, 1, 2, 3, 4, 5, 6, 7. 8 and 9 are substituted by a, b, c, d, e, f, g, h, i and j. If 10 is written as ba, then (cd + ef) × bc is equal to ________.
(a) 684 (b) 816
(c) 916 (d) 1564

25. In a certain code language, DISTANCE is written as FDOBUTJE. How will DONATION be written in that language?
(a) POJUBPQE (b) OPJUBPQE
(c) OPJUBOPE (d) POJUCOPE

26. In a certain code language, if SCIENTIST is written as VFJHQULVU, then how will EDUCATION be coded in that language?
(a) FEVDBUJPO
(b) HGVFDULRO
(c) HGUCDULRO
(d) FGVGEVLPO

27. If 11529 is related to 72135 in some way, then in the same way 152943 is related to________. **[2018]**

(a) 163044 (b) 162034
(c) 213549 (d) 203448

28. In a certain code language, "what else can you do for me Mr Ajay' is written as 'you Mr what can Ajay else do me for'. How will 'anyone else who can do such favour to me' be written in that language? **[2018]**
(a) can to who anyone me else do favour such
(b) can favour anyone who me else do to such
(c) can to anyone who me else do favour such
(d) can to anyone who me do else favour such

29. In a certain code language, DISTANCE is written as FEQEYYPL. How will CHARCOAL be written in that code language? **[2019]**
(a) LOGWGRCM
(b) MCRGWGOL
(c) KOGWGRCM
(d) MCRGWGOK

30. In a certain code language, if 'MYSTERIOUS' is coded as 'FUTZNUWQKT', then how will PRODUCTIVE' be coded in the same language? **[2019]**
(a) FWJUDVEPSQ
(b) QSPEVDUJWF
(c) VEPSQGXKVE
(d) VEPSQFWJUD

31. In a certain code language, ORDINARY is written as TWINJWNU. How will PRECIOUS be written in the same language? **[2021]**
(a) SUHFLFNP (b) TVIGKEOQ
(c) VXKIEKQO (d) UWJHEKQO

32. In a certain code language, PHILOSOPHY is written as SFLJRQRNKW. How will PSYCHOLOGY be written in the same language? **[2021]**
(a) SQBALNPMJW
(b) SVBFKRORJB
(c) SQBAKMOMJW
(d) SBVFKPSKSC

33. In a certain code language, if DEFENSIVE is coded as FCHCPQKTG, then how will PROTECTED be coded in the same code language? **[2022]**
(a) TORPEDETIC
(b) RTQUDARCB
(c) RPQRGAVCF
(d) EFUDFUPSQ

34. In a certain code language, '3a 2b 7c' means 'Truth is Eternal', '7c 9a 8b 3a' means 'Enmity is not Eternal' and '9a 4b 2b 6b' means 'Truth does not Perish'. **[2022]**
Which one of the following means 'enmity' in that language?
(a) 3a (b) 7c
(c) 8b (d) 9a

ANSWER KEY																			
LEVEL-1																			
1	(c)	**2**	(b)	**3**	(c)	**4**	(c)	**5**	(b)	**6**	(c)	**7**	(a)	**8**	(a)	**9**	(b)	**10**	(a)
11	(d)	**12**	(*)	**13**	(a)	**14**	(a)	**15**	(a)	**16**	(d)	**17**	(a)	**18**	(a)	**19**	(b)		
LEVEL-2																			
1	(b)	**5**	(d)	**9**	(b)	**13**	(c)	**17**	(a)	**21**	(b)	**25**	(c)	**29**	(d)	**33**	(c)		
2	(b)	**6**	(b)	**10**	(c)	**14**	(b)	**18**	(d)	**22**	(b)	**26**	(b)	**30**	(c)	**34**	(c)		
3	(b)	**7**	(c)	**11**	(d)	**15**	(d)	**19**	(b)	**23**	(b)	**27**	(c)	**31**	(d)				
4	(c)	**8**	(a)	**12**	(b)	**16**	(c)	**20**	(b)	**24**	(b)	**28**	(c)	**32**	(c)				

CHAPTER 3

Series Completion and Inserting

NUMBER SERIES

In this type of series, the set of given numbers in a series are related to one another in a particular pattern or manner. The relationship between the numbers may be

(i) consecutive odd/even numbers,

(ii) Consecutive prime numbers,

(iii) Squares/cubes of some numbers with/without variation of addition or subtraction of some number,

(iv) Sum/product/difference of preceding number(s),

(v) Addition/subtraction/multiplication/division by some number, and

(vi) Many more combinations of the relationships given above.

ILLUSTRATION 1 :

Find the missing term in the following sequence.

5, 11, 24, 51, 106, ...

(a) 216 (b) 217

(c) 215 (d) 212

Sol. (b) Double the number and then add to it 1, 2, 3, 4 etc.

Thus the next term is $2 \times 106 + 5 = 217$.

ILLUSTRATION 2 :

Complete the series 4, 9, 16, 25, ...

(a) 32 (b) 42

(c) 55 (d) 36

Sol. **(d)** Each number is a whole square.

ILLUSTRATION 3:

Find the wrong term in the series

3, 8, 15, 24, 34, 48, 63.

(a) 15 (b) 12

(c) 34 (d) 63

Sol. **(c)** $8 - 3 = 5$

$15 - 8 = 7$

$24 - 15 = 9$

$34 - 24 = 10$

$48 - 34 = 14$

$63 - 48 = 15$

Obviously difference should be 11 & 13 instead of 10 & 14.

Therefore, 34 is the wrong term.

ALPHABET SERIES

In this type of question, a series of single, pairs or groups of letters or combinations of letters and numbers is given. The terms of the series form a certain pattern as regards the position of the letters in the English alphabet.

In the following questions, various terms of a letter series are given with one term missing as shown. Choose the missing term out of the options.

ILLUSTRATION 4 :

AZ, GT, MN, ..., YB

(a) KF (b) RX

(c) SH (d) TS

Sol. **(c)** The logic is +6 and –6.

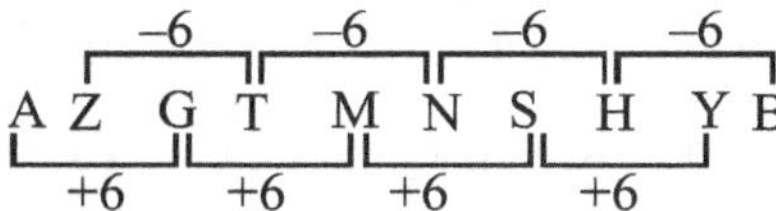

DIRECTIONS (ILLUSTRATION 5) : In the following question, various terms of an alphabet series are given with one or more terms missing as shown by '?'. Choose the missing terms out of the given alternatives.

ILLUSTRATION 5 :

UPI, ?, ODP, MBQ, IAW

(a) RHJ (b) SHJ

(c) SIJ (d) THK

Sol. **(b)**

1st letter : U $\xrightarrow{-2}$ (S) $\xrightarrow{-4}$ O $\xrightarrow{-2}$ M $\xrightarrow{-4}$ I

2nd letter : P $\xrightarrow{-8}$ (H) $\xrightarrow{-4}$ D $\xrightarrow{-2}$ B $\xrightarrow{-1}$ A

3rd letter : I $\xrightarrow{+1}$ (J) $\xrightarrow{+6}$ P $\xrightarrow{+1}$ Q $\xrightarrow{+6}$ W

CONTINUOUS PATTERN SERIES

This type of question usually consists of a series of small letters which follow a certain pattern. However, some letters are missing from the series. These missing letters are then given in a proper sequence as one of the alternatives.

DIRECTIONS (ILLUSTRATION 6) : In the following letters series, some of the letters are missing which are given in that order as one of the alternatives below it. Choose the correct alternative.

ILLUSTRATION 6 :

.... bcc .... ac .... aabb .... ab cc

(a) aabca (b) abaca

(c) bacab (d) bcaca

Sol. **(c)** The series is b b c c a a / c c a a b b / a a b b c c.

The letter pairs move in a cyclic order.

ALPHA - NUMERIC SERIES

A series in which both alphabets and numbers are used is called Alpha numeric.

DIRECTIONS (ILLUSTRATION 7) : In the following question, a letter number series is given with one or more terms missing as shown by (?). Choose the missing term out of the given alternatives.

ILLUSTRATION 7 :

D-4, F-6, H-8, J-10, ? ?

(a) K-12, M-13 (b) L-12, M-14

(c) L-12, N-14 (d) K-12, M-14

Sol. **(c)** The letters in the series are alternate and the numbers indicate their position in the English alphabet from the beginning.

MISSING CHARACTER

In such type of questions, a figure, a set of figures, an arrangement or a matrix is given, each of which bears certain characteristics, be it numbers, letters or a group/ combination of letters/ numbers, following a certain pattern.

The candidate has to find a missing character in the figure out of the given options.

Let us develop the ability to identify missing character with the help of following examples.

ILLUSTRATION 8 :

11	3	49
5	19	?
7	13	100

(a) 96 (b) 120

(c) 144 (d) 100

Sol. **(c)** In a row the third term is the square of the average of the first two numbers.

$$\therefore ? = \left(\frac{5+19}{2}\right)^2 = 12^2 = 144.$$

ILLUSTRATION 9 :

1	4	9	?
1	2	3	4
2	4	6	?

(a) 16, 8

(b) 49, 7

(c) 36, 4

(d) 25, 5

Sol. **(a)** I st row : $1^2, 2^2, 3^2, 4^2$,

Third row : 2, 4, 6, 8

$\therefore$ The missing numbers = 16, 8

ILLUSTRATION 10 :

3C	24D	8E
7I	21 K	3M
4D	?	7J

(a) 11 E (b) 28 G

(c) 351 (d) 48 F

Sol. **(b)** In the first row, letters are consecutive CDE.In the 2nd row, letters are one step forward I-K-M

In the third row, the letters are + 2 forward i.e

D – – G – – J.

Number is the product of the two numbers.

Hence, $4 \times 7 = 28$

ILLUSTRATION 11 :

Figure 1: top 9, left 4, inside 58, right 8, bottom 10

Figure 2: top 15, left 9, inside ?, right 8, bottom 10

(a) 117 (b) 100

(c) 78 (d) 63

Sol. **(c)** In the first figure $9 \times 10 - 4 \times 8 = 58$

$\therefore$ The missing figure $= 15 \times 10 - 9 \times 8 = 78$

ILLUSTRATION 12 :

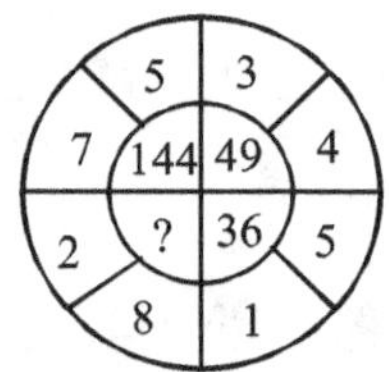

(a) 82 (b) 100

(c) 68 (d) 64

Sol. **(b)** Required number $= (2 + 8)^2 = 100.$

ILLUSTRATION 13 :

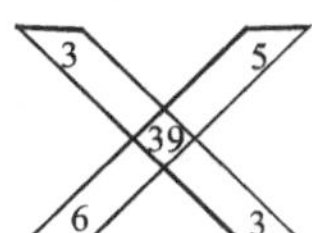
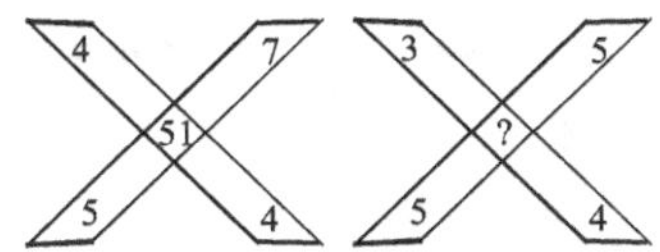

(a) 47 (b) 45

(c) 37 (d) 35

***Sol.* (c)** Fig 1 : $3 \times 3 + 6 \times 5 = 39$

Fig 2 : $4 \times 4 + 5 \times 7 = 51$

$\therefore$ So ? = $3 \times 4 + 5 \times 5 = 37$

ILLUSTRATION 14 :

Find the number in place of question mark (?) in the following matrix

3	5	7	9	11	13
8	26	48	82	?	170

(a) 121 (b) 120

(c) 119 (d) 111

***Sol.* (b)** The numbers are according to the rule $n^2 \pm 1$.

i.e, $3^2 - 1$, $5^2 + 1$, $7^2 - 1$, $9^2 + 1$. $11^2 - 1$ and $13^2 + 1$.

$\therefore$ the missing number is 120.

ILLUSTRATION 15 :

Find the missing number

(a) 52 (b) 36

(c) 117 (d) 81

***Sol.* (b)** The rule is : In the figure : $5 \times 4 = 20$, $5 + 4 = 9$

In the second figure : $3 \times 8 = 24$ and $3 + 8 = 11$

$\therefore$ In the third figure $9 \times 4 = 36$.

LEVEL 1

DIRECTIONS (Qs. 1-9) : *Complete the series.*

1. EJO, TYD, INS, XCH, ?
   (a) NRW (b) MRW
   (c) MSX (d) NSX
2. J2Z, K4X, I7V, ?, H16R, M22P
   (a) I11T (b) L11S
   (c) L12T (d) L11T
3. 3, 8, 35, 48, ?, 120
   (a) 64 (b) 72
   (c) 80 (d) 99
4. 5, 9, 21, 37, 81, ...
   (a) 153 (b) 150
   (c) 158 (d) 151
5. 240, ? 120, 40, 10, 2
   (a) 120 (b) 240
   (c) 40 (d) 10
6. A ......BBC......AAB .....CCA........BBCC
   (a) BACB (b) ABBA
   (c) CABA (d) ACBA
7. C.......BCCD....CCDB ....CDBCC ......BC
   (a) DBCD (b) DBDD
   (c) BDAA (d) BDCD

8. 16, 33, 67, 135, ...
   (a) 251 (b) 259
   (c) 271 (d) 289
9. ab – – a – d c a cb – a c d –
   (a) d c b d b (b) c d b b d
   (c) d a b d b (d) c d b d b

DIRECTIONS (Qs. 10-19) : *Complete the series.*

10. 1, 2, 10, 4, 3, 14, 9, 5, ...
    (a) 19 (b) 20
    (c) 17 (d) 18
11. ZYYZR, ABVUM, ?, BCUTL, XWABT, CDTSK
    (a) YXZAS (b) ZYABT
    (c) XWYZR (d) YXZAB
12. Z, S, W, O, T, K, Q, G, ..., ...
    (a) N, C (b) N, D
    (c) S, E (d) O, D
13. A L W B M X C N ?
    (a) V (b) W
    (c) Y (d) X
14. 1, 2, 9, ? , 65, 126
    (a) 28 (b) 82
    (c) 99 (d) 108
15. 41, 31, ?, 17, 11, 5
    (a) 9 (b) 21
    (c) 23 (d) 27
16. 8, 15, 28, 53, ?
    (a) 106 (b) 98
    (c) 100 (d) 102
17. 336, 210, 120, ?, 24, 6, 0
    (a) 40 (b) 50
    (c) 60 (d) 70
18. 2, 9, 28, ?, 126, 217
    (a) 36 (b) 42
    (c) 56 (d) 65
19. 24, 6, 18, 9, 36, 9, 24, ?,
    (a) 24 (b) 12
    (c) 8 (d) 6

DIRECTIONS (Qs. 20-22): *In each of the following number series, a wrong number is given. Find out that number.*

20. 3 2 3 6 12 37.5 115.5
    (a) 37.5 (b) 12
    (c) 6 (d) 2
21. 2 3 11 38 102 229 443
    (a) 11 (b) 229
    (c) 120 (d) 38
22. 3 7. 5 15 37.5 75 167.5 375
    (a) 167.5 (b) 75
    (c) 37.5 (d) 15

DIRECTION (Q. 23) : *Find out the missing one from the given alternatives.*

23. 08 : 28 : : (?) : 65
    (a) 9 (b) 12
    (c) 15 (d) 18

DIRECTIONS (Qs. 24-25) : *Questions are based on number/figure series. In each series missing term is mentioned by question mark (?). Find out the missing term in given alternatives.*

24. 16, 19, 28, 43, 64, ?
    (a) 91 (b) 86
    (c) 97 (d) 76
25. 8, 48, 16, 96, 32, ?
    (a) 192 (b) 150
    (c) 58 (d) 288
26. Find the missing number which will complete the given series.

    8, 14, 26, ?, 68, 98

    (a) 32 (b) 44
    (c) 52 (d) 48
27. Find the missing number to continue the given number pattern.

    3, 8, 15, 24, 35, 48, ?

    (a) 53 (b) 54
    (c) 63 (d) 62

28. Find the missing number to continue the given number pattern.
21, 25, 33, 49, 81, ?
(a) 144 (b) 133
(c) 154 (d) 145

29. A series is given with one term missing. Choose the correct alternative from the given options that will complete the series.
AZ, GT, MN, ? , YB
(a) SK (b) JH
(c) SH (d) TS

30. Select the term from the options which will continue the given series.
J12M, L15K, N181, P21G, ?
(a) Q23D (b) R23D
(c) R24E (d) Q24E

31. Which of the following options will continue the given series?
BEH, CGK, DIN, EKQ, ?
(a) FNR (b) GLU
(c) FMT (d) None of there

32. Select the missing letters for the given letter series from the given options.
a_bc_bb_ab_c_bbc
(a) a b c b a (b) b a c b a
(c) a b b c a (d) b a c c a

33. Find the missing term in the series given below.
7, 6, 12, 9, 17, 15, 22, 24, ?
(a) 36 (b) 32
(c) 24 (d) 27

34. Find the missing number, if a certain rule is followed either row-wise or column-wise. **[2020]**

5	6	8
6	9	10
121	?	324

(a) 225 (b) 384
(c) 216 (d) 289

35. Find the missing number, if a certain rule is followed either row-wise or column-wise. **[2021]**

15	7	12
4	18	20
3	5	?
57	125	64

(a) 4 (b) 2
(c) 6 (d) 7

LEVEL 2

DIRECTIONS (Qs. 1-3) : *Complete the series*

1. 1, 1, 2, 4, 7, 11, 16, ?,
(a) 20 (b) 21
(c) 22 (d) 23

2. abc – c – c –ba – – bca
(a) abacb (b) babac
(c) baabc (d) bacba

3. ab – –a – dcacb – acd –
(a) dcbdb (b) cdbbd
(c) dabdb (d) cdbdb

DIRECTIONS (Qs. 4-14) : *Complete the series*

4. $\frac{1}{81}, \frac{1}{54}, \frac{1}{36}, \frac{1}{24}, ?$
(a) $\frac{1}{52}$ (b) $\frac{1}{9}$
(c) $\frac{1}{16}$ (d) $\frac{1}{18}$

5. Q 1 F S 2 E U 6 D W 21 C ?
(a) Y 66 B (b) Y 88 B
(c) Z 88 B (d) Y 44 B

6. 1, 1, 2, 4, 3, 27, 4 —, —
(a) 5, 64 (b) 64, 81
(c) 64, 5 (d) 16, 5

7. 8, 15, 24, 35, ...
   (a) 42 (b) 52
   (c) 48 (d) None of these
8. 1, 1, 4, 2, 9, 3, 16, 4, ...
   (a) 18 (b) 15
   (c) 25 (d) 32
9. Find the correct group of letters in place of '?' in the following series.
   FNHLJ, WOUQS, BNEKH, ?, DTHPL
   (a) N B K E H (b) N V P T R
   (c) N F L H J (d) N D R Z V
10. Certain blank spaces are left in the following sequence. Which is the group of letters given below, will complete the sequence?
   c_bba_cab_ac_ab_ac
   (a) acbcb (b) bcacb
   (c) babec (d) abebe
11. Complete the series
   D3Y104, G9U91, J27Q78, M8IM65, ____
   (a) P243139 (b) Q243I52
   (c) P243I52 (d) Q162J39
12. In the following sequence, one number is wrong. Find the wrong number.
   9, 23, 51, 106, 219, 643
   (a) 23 (b) 51
   (c) 106 (d) 219
13. Which of the following alternatives will fit in place of 'M'?
   255, 3610, 4915, M, 8125
   (a) 5100 (b) 5420
   (c) 6420 (d) 6422
14. What is the number in place of '?' ?
   6,15,35, ? , 143, 221
   (a) 45 (b) 65
   (c) 77 (d) 93
15. Find the missing number, if same rule is followed in all the three figures.

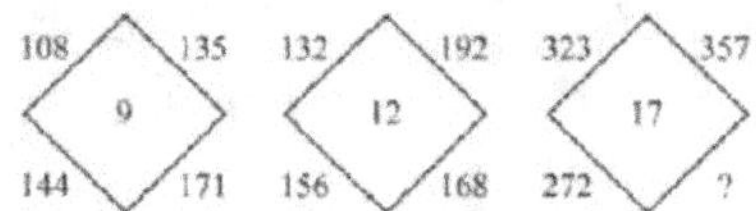

   (a) 392 (b) 382
   (c) 374 (d) 375
16. Find the missing character, if same rule is followed in all the three figures.

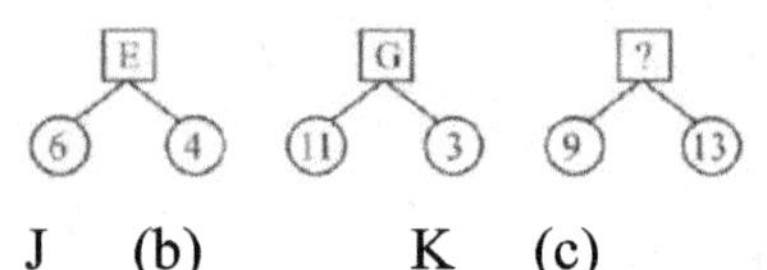

   (a) J (b) K (c) V
   (d) M
17. Find the missing number.

   (a) 190 (b) 221
   (c) 136 (d) 131
18. Find the missing character, if a certain rule is followed either row-wise or column-wise.

B	G	N
D	J	R
H	P	?

   (a) Z (b) V
   (c) W (d) X
19. Find the missing number, if a certain rule is followed either row-wise or column-wise.

42	28	38
28	35	23
39	?	37

   (a) 7 (b) 21
   (c) 14 (d) 18
20. Find the missing number, if same rule is followed in all the three figures.

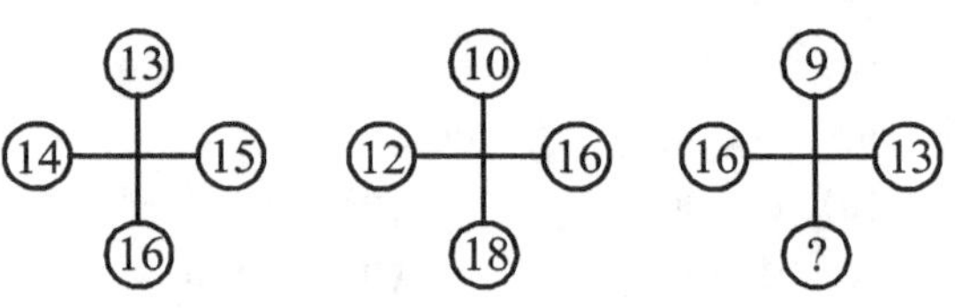

   (a) 20 (b) 21
   (c) 22 (d) 24

21. Select a letter-number pair from the given options to replace the question marks and complete the series.

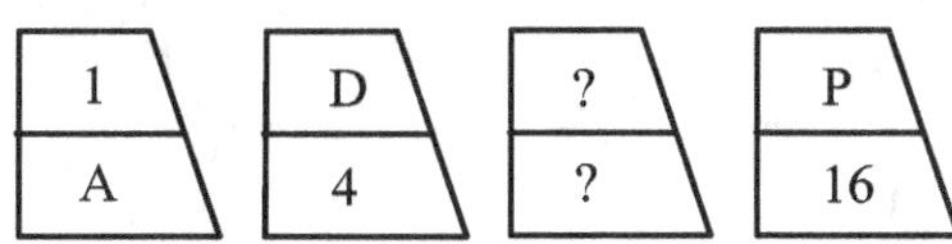

(a) $\frac{J}{10}$ (b) $\frac{9}{I}$

(c) $\frac{M}{16}$ (d) $\frac{P}{11}$

22. Find the missing character, if same rule is followed in all the three figures.

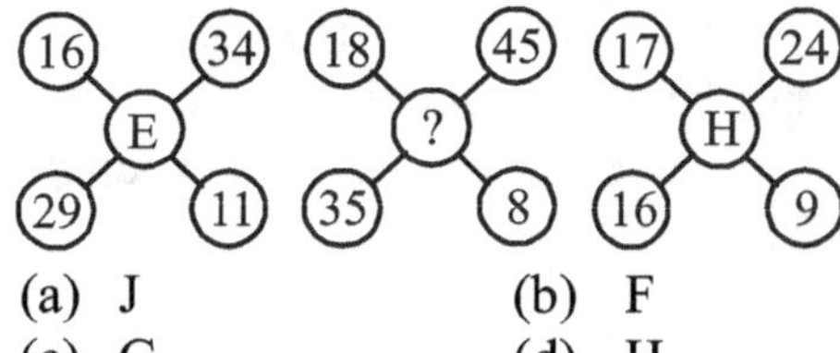

(a) J (b) F
(c) G (d) H

23. Find the missing number, if same rule is followed in all the three figures.

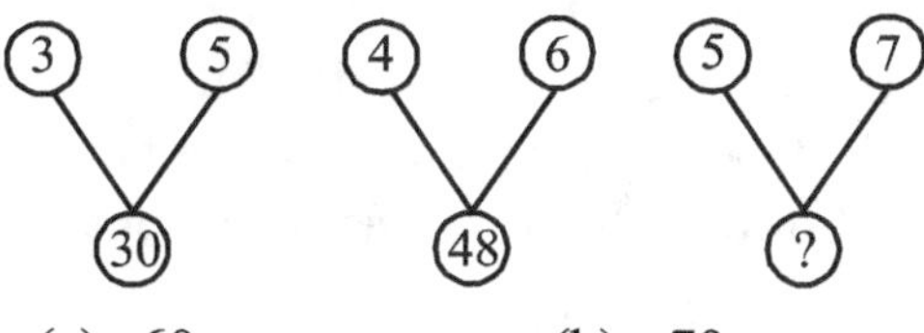

(a) 60 (b) 70
(c) 80 (d) 35

24. Which one of the following terms will replace the question mark(?) in the pattern given below?
?, W40M, U38P, S36S, Q34V, O32Y
(a) X39K (b) Y42J
(c) J42Y (d) Y44K

25. A series is given with one term missing. Choose the correct alternative from the given ones that will complete the series.
1, 9, 17, 33, 49, 73, ____?
(a) 100 (b) 99
(c) 97 (d) 89

26. Which one of the following terms will replace the question mark(?) in the pattern given below?

?	C13P	F17K	H19G	K23D	M25B

(a) A9V (b) B12U
(c) A11V (d) A12X

27. Find the missing number.

12	8	24
16	9	36
24	11	?

(a) 66 (b) 44
(c) 36 (d) 28

28. Which one of the following numbers will replace the question mark(?) in the number pattern given below?\

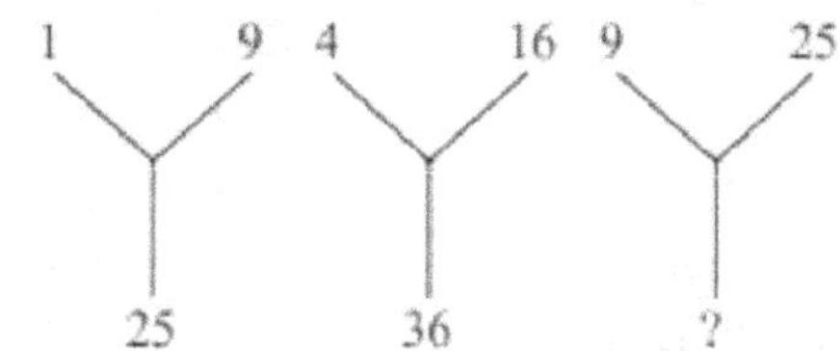

(a) 57 (b) 50
(c) 49 (d) 47

29. Select the option which will continue the given series.
A50G, I3060, Q818W, Y650E, ?
(a) H245J (b) G245M
(c) G218M (d) M218G

30. Which of the following options will complete the given letter series?
MOT, SRV, XVX, ?, EGB
(a) BZZ (b) BAZ
(c) BAX (d) ABZ

31. Find the missing number, if a certain rule is followed either row-wise or column-wise. **[2018]**

6	7	3
3	7	?
3	3	4
42	102	50

(a) 4 (b) 5
(c) 6 (d) 7

32. Find the missing number, if same rule is followed in all the three figures. **[2018]**

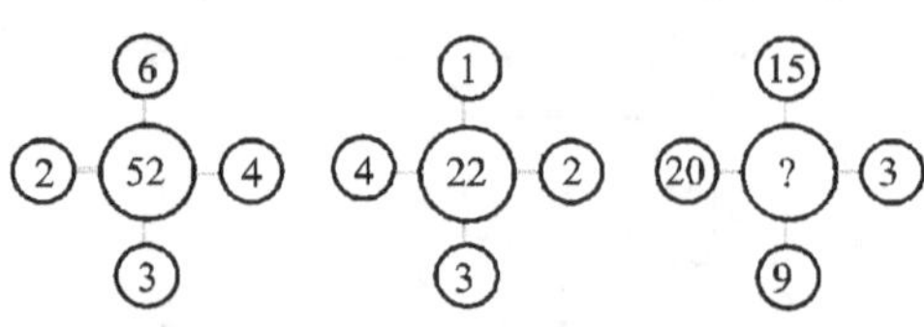

(a) 390 (b) 205
(c) 104 (d) 208

33. Find the missing number, if same rule is followed in all the three figures. **[2018]**

(a) 35 (b) 25
(c) 28 (d) 30

34. Find the missing term in the given series.
ayd, bvf, drh, ? kgl **[2019]**
(a) FMI (b) GMJ
(c) GLJ (d) HLK

35. Find the missing number, if a certain rule is followed either row-wise or column-wise.

3	?	5
5	9	7
4	4	6
30	72	105

[2019]

(a) 4 (b) 6
(c) 9 (d) 8

36. Find the missing number, if a certain rule is followed either row-wise or column-wise.

5	6	7
3	4	5
9	10	11
289	?	529

[2019]

(a) 200 (b) 600
(c) 900 (d) 400

37. Find the missing number, if same rule is followed in all the three figures. **[2020]**

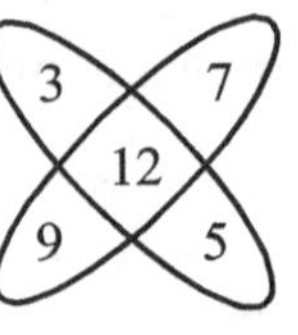

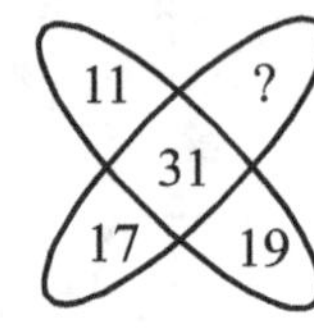

(a) 14 (b) 13
(c) 15 (d) 18

38. Find the missing number, if same rue is followed in all the three figures. **[2020]**

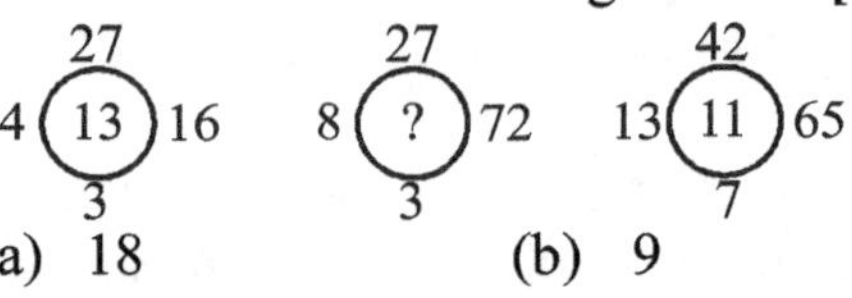

(a) 18 (b) 9
(c) 15 (d) 12

39. Find the missing number, if a certain rule is followed either row-wise or column-wise.

18	21	16
17	23	14
12	24	?
23	20	9

[2021]

(a) 18 (b) 19
(c) 20 (d) 21

40. Find the missing number, if a certain rule is followed either row–wise or column–wise.

4	5	3
0	1	2
3	4	6
343	1000	?

[2022]

(a) 1331 (b) 121
(c) 1150 (d) 1911

41. A series is given with one term missing. Choose the correct alternative from the given options that will complete the series.
MES, LDR, ? , JBP, IAO **[2022]**
(a) KCQ (b) KBQ
(c) JCQ (d) KCO

42. Find the missing term in the given series.
625, 606, 580, 540, ?, 390 **[2022]**
(a) 524 (b) 500
(c) 492 (d) 479

43. Find out the missing number on the basis of a certain trend. **[2022]**

106	64	14
98	62	12
84	45	?

(a) 36 (b) 24 (c) 13 (d) 48

44. Find out the missing number on the basis of a certain pattern. **[2022]**

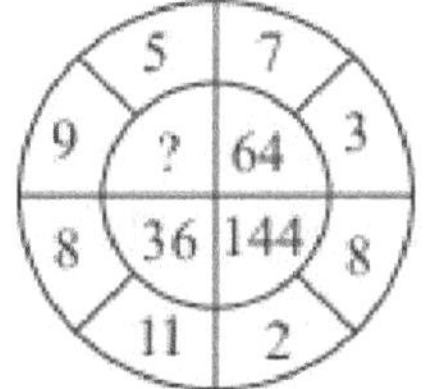

(a) 81 (b) 100 (c) 64 (d) 16

45. Select the option that will replace the question mark (?) in the number series given below. **[2022]**

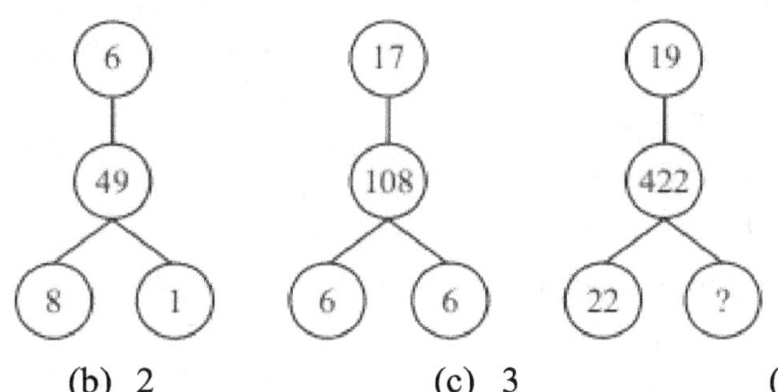

(a) 0 (b) 2 (c) 3 (d) 4

ANSWER KEY																	
LEVEL-1																	
1	(b)	**5**	(b)	**9**	(d)	**13**	(c)	**17**	(c)	**21**	(b)	**25**	(a)	**29**	(c)	**33**	(d)
2	(d)	**6**	(d)	**10**	(d)	**14**	(a)	**18**	(d)	**22**	(a)	**26**	(b)	**30**	(c)	**34**	(b)
3	(d)	**7**	(a)	**11**	(a)	**15**	(c)	**19**	(b)	**23**	(c)	**27**	(c)	**31**	(c)	**35**	(a)
4	(a)	**8**	(c)	**12**	(a)	**16**	(d)	**20**	(b)	**24**	(a)	**28**	(d)	**32**	(b)		
LEVEL-2																	
1	(c)	**6**	(d)	**11**	(c)	**16**	(b)	**21**	(a)	**26**	(c)	**31**	(d)	**36**	(a)	**41**	(c)
2	(c)	**7**	(c)	**12**	(c)	**17**	(d)	**22**	(a)	**27**	(a)	**32**	(a)	**37**	(a)	**42**	(d)
3	(d)	**8**	(c)	**13**	(c)	**18**	(a)	**23**	(b)	**28**	(c)	**33**	(a)	**38**	(d)	**43**	(c)
4	(c)	**9**	(a)	**14**	(c)	**19**	(c)	**24**	(b)	**29**	(c)	**34**	(d)	**39**	(b)	**44**	(c)
5	(b)	**10**	(a)	**15**	(c)	**20**	(a)	**25**	(c)	**30**	(b)	**35**	(d)	**40**	(a)	**45**	(d)

CHAPTER 4

Blood Relations

While attempting questions on blood relations, one should be clear of all the relation patterns that can exist between any two individuals.

These type of questions are given mainly to test one's relationship ability.

Mother's or father's son	Brother
Mother's or father's daughter	Sister
Mother's or father's brother	Uncle
Mother's or father's sister	Aunt
Mother's or father's father	Grandfather
Mother's or father's mother	Grandmother
Son's wife	Daughter-in-law
Daughter's husband	Son-in-law
Husband's or wife's sister	Sister-in-law
Husband's or wife's brother	Brother-in-law
Brother's son	Nephew
Brother's daughter	Niece
Uncle or aunt's son or daughter	Cousin
Sister's husband	Brother-in-law
Brother's wife	Sister-in-law
Grandson's or Grand daughter's daughter	Great granddaughter

A relation on the mother's side is called maternal while that on the father's side is called paternal.

Thus, mother's brother is maternal uncle while father's brother is paternal uncle.

To solve problems on relationship you can construct family tree.

To build a family tree, certain standard notations are used to indicate a relationship between the members of the family. It is not necessary to follow them implicity; you can formulate your own notations to draw the family tree quickly and accurately

1. A is male 

2. A is a female (A)

3. Sex of A not known A

4. A and B are married to each other A = B

5. A and B are siblings A ↔ B

6. A and C are B's children 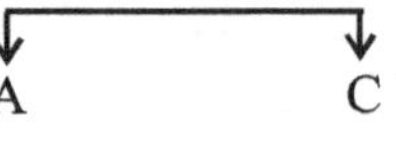

7. A is the uncle/ aunt of B 

8. A is the only child of B 

A

To make a family tree from the given data, we will first identify the males and the females in the family and then try to put each member in their respective position in the tree. For example A, B, C, D, E and F are related to each other as given here, B is F' s daughter-in-law. D is A's only grand child. C is D's only uncle. A has only 2 children F and C, one male and one female (not necessarily in the same order). E is the father of C.

(i) Who is the grandmother of D ?

(ii) Who is the mother-in-law of B?

(iii) When a girl G is married into the family, what is the relationship between G and D?

Step I : Identify the elements A, B, C, D, E and F,

From the given conditions we can determine who are the males/ females in the above group.

(1) B is F's daughter-in-law (B)

(2) C is D's only uncle [C]

(3) A has 2 children F and C, one male (F) and one female, Since C is male, F is Female.

Step II : Try to identify the positions of the members in the family tree. For this , determine the number of generations involved from the statements. D is A's only grand child. Thus, we know that there are three generations.

Step III : Use the conditions to arrange A , B , C, D, E and F in these three generations.

(a) B is F 's daughter-in-law,

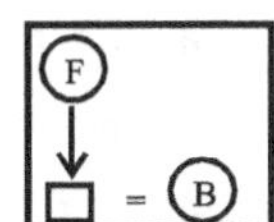

(b) D is A 's only grandchild

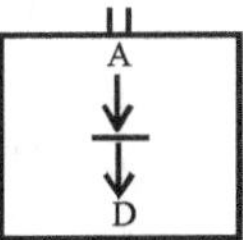

(c) C is D's uncle.

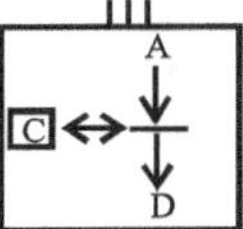

(d) A has only two children

F and C, one male and one female.

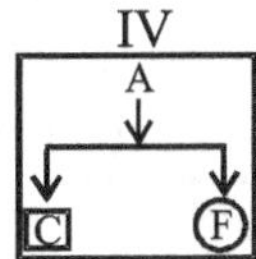

(e) E is C's father.

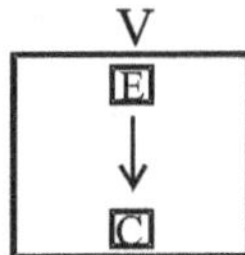

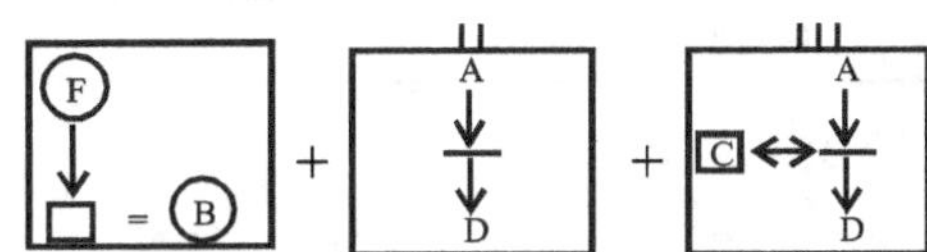

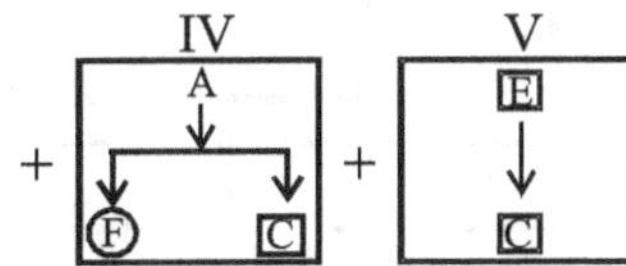

Level- I

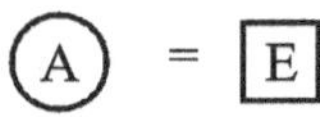

Level - II

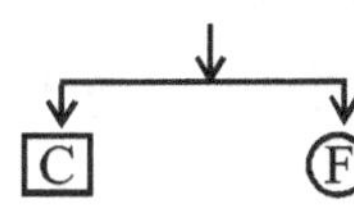

Level- III

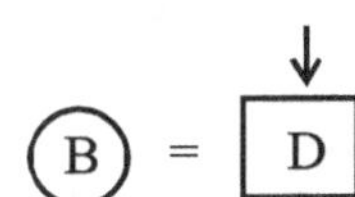

Question (i) and (ii) can be answered easily by looking at the family tree. A is the grandmother of D and F is the mother-in - law of B. For question (iii), C is the only male in the family who is unmarried. G will be married to C and hence she will be D's aunt.

DIRECTIONS (ILLUSTRATION 1-3) : Abra is Rambo's daughter. Shintu is Rambo's sister. Shintu's daughter is called Cabra and son is called Dabra. Limba is Cabra's maternal Aunt.

ILLUSTRATION 1 :

Abra is Limba's

(a) Aunt (b) Nephew

(c) Uncle (d) None of these

Sol. **(d)** Abra can be Limba's niece or daughter.

ILLUSTRATION 2 :

Cabra is Rambo's;

(a) Nephew (b) Niece

(c) Uncle (d) Cannot say

Sol. **(b)** Cabra is Rambo's niece.

ILLUSTRATION 3 :

Dabra is Limba's

(1) Niece (b) Aunt

(c) Nephew (d) None of these

Sol. **(c)** Dabra is Limba's nephew.

For answers to examples 1 to 3 :

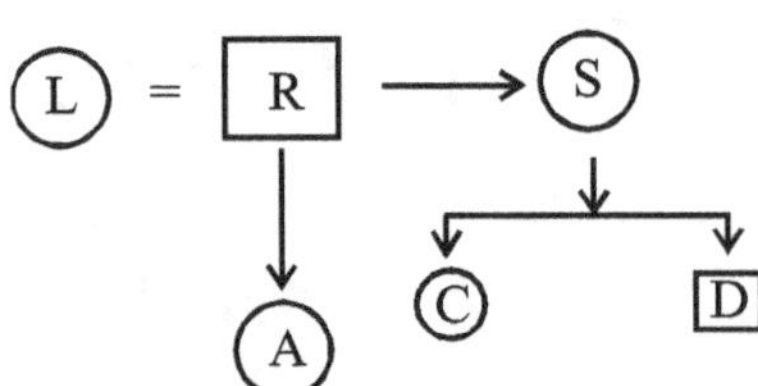

or

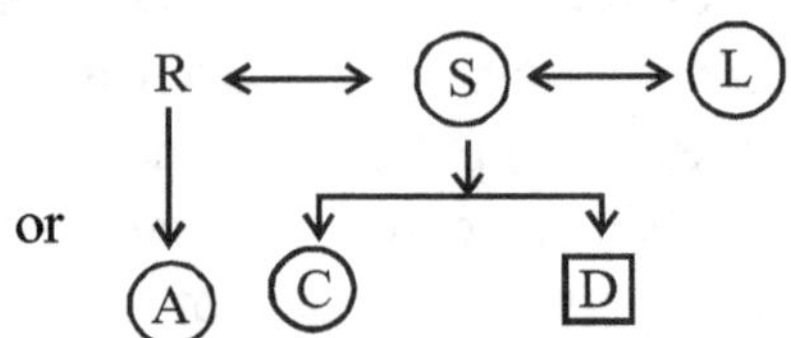

PROBLEMS IN DECIDING RELATIONSHIP

TYPE 1 :

In this type of question, a roundabout description is given in the form of certain small relationships and you are required to analyse the whole chain of relations and decipher the direct relationship between the persons concerned.

ILLUSTRATION 4:

Anil introduces Rohit as the son of the only brother of his father's wife. How is Rohit related to Anil ?

(a) Cousin (b) Son

(c) Uncle (d) Son-in-law

Sol. **(a)** The relations may be analysed as follows.

Father's wife– mother, Mother's brother — Uncle; Uncle's son— Cousin.

So, Rohit is Anil's cousin. Hence, the answer is (a)

TYPE 2 :

In this type of question, mutual blood relations of more than two persons are mentioned. The candidate is required to analyse the given information, work out a family chart and then answer the given questions.

DIRECTIONS (ILLUSTRATION 5-8) : Read the following information carefully and answer the questions given below.

There are six children playing football, namely A,B,C,D, E and F. A and E are brothers. F is the sister of E. C is the only son of A's uncle. B and D are the daughter of the brother of C's father.

ILLUSTRATION 5 :

How is C related to F ?

(a) Cousin (b) Brother son

(c) Son (d) Uncle

Sol. **(a)** F is E's and hence A's sister. So, C is also the son of F's uncle and is, therefore, F's Cousin.

ILLUSTRATION 6 :

How many male players are there ?

(a) One

(b) Three

(c) Four

(d) Five

Sol. **(b)** As given, A and E are brothers. Hence both are males. F is the sister of E and hence female. C is the son and hence male. B and D are daughters and hence female. Thus, there are three males. So, the answer is (b)

ILLUSTRATION 7 :

How many female players are there ?

(a) One (b) Two

(c) Three (d) Four

Sol. **(c)** Clearly, from the solution of 2, we find that there are three females. So, the answer is (c).

ILLUSTRATION 8 :

How is D related to A?

(a) Uncle (b) Sister

(c) Niece (d) Cousin

Sol. **(d)** Clearly, D's father is the brother of C's father and C's father is A's uncle. So D is A's sister. Hence the answer is (d).

TYPE 3 :

Coded Relations

In such questions, the relationships are represented by certain specific codes or symbols. The candidate is then required to analyse some given codes to determine the relationship between a set of persons, or to express a given relationship in the coded form.

DIRECTIONS (ILLUSTRATION 9-12) : Study the information given below and answer the questions that follow :

A + B ' means 'A is the daughter of B; A – B ' means ' A is the husband of B'. A × B means A is the brother of B.

ILLUSTRATION 9 :

If P + Q – R, which of the following is true ?

(a) R is the mother of P.

(b) R is the sister in -law of P.

(c) R is the aunt of P.

(d) R is the mother in- law of P.

Sol. **(a)** P + Q – R means P is the daughter of Q who is the husband of R i.e, R is the mother of P.

ILLUSTRATION 10 :

If P × Q + R, which of the following is true ?

(a) P is the brother of R.

(b) P is the uncle of R.

(c) P is the son of R.

(d) P is the father of R.

Sol. **(c)** $P \times Q + R$ means P is the brother of Q, who is the daughter of R i.e, P is the son of R.

ILLUSTRATION 11 :

If $P + Q \times R$ which of the following is true ?

(a) P is the niece of R.

(b) P is the daughter of R.

(c) P is the cousin of R.

(d) P is the daughter-in law of R.

Sol. **(a)** $P + Q \times R$ means P the daughter of Q, who is the brother of R i.e, P is the niece of R.

ILLUSTRATION 12 :

If P + Q means P is the son of Q and

P = Q means P is the sister of Q.

Then what does $P = R + Q$ means ?

Sol. $P = R + Q \Rightarrow P = R$ which mean P is the sister of R.

R + Q means R is the son of Q.

$\therefore$ P is the daughter of Q.

Useful Tips

1. The only son of your father — Yourself
2. Wife of the father —Mother
3. The only son of grand father or grand mother – father
4. The only daughter-in-law of grand father or grand mother – Mother
5. Mother-in-law of mother –Grand mother
6. Father-in-law of mother – Grand father
7. The only daughter of the father –Sister
8. Son of the father of the sister – Brother
9. Son of the only son of the father –son
10. Son of the only son of grand father – Brother
11. Daughter of the only son of Grand father – Sister

LEVEL 1

1. Given that
   1. A is the mother of B
   2. C is the son of A
   3. D is the brother of E
   4. E is the daughter of B.

   The grandmother of D is
   (a) A (b) B
   (c) C (d) E
2. Deepak said to Nitin, " That boy playing football is the younger of the two brothers of the daughter of my father's wife " How is the boy playing football related to Deepak ?
   (a) Son (b) Brother
   (c) Cousin (d) Niece

DIRECTIONS (Qs. 3-7) : *Read the following information carefully to answer the questions.*
(i) 'A $ B' means 'A' is mother of 'B'
(ii) A' # B' means 'A' is father of 'B'
(iii) 'A @ B' Means 'A' is husband of 'B'
(iv) 'A % B' means 'A' is daughter of 'B'

3. P @ Q $ M # T indicates what relationship of P with T
   (a) Paternal grandmother
   (b) Maternal grandmother
   (c) Paternal grandfather
   (d) Maternal grandfather
4. Which of the following expressions indicates 'R is the sister of H'?
   (a) H $ D @ F # R (b) R % D @ F $ H
   (c) R $ D @ F # H (d) H % D @ F $ R
5. If F @ D % K # H, then how is F related to H?
   (a) Brother-in- law
   (b) Sister
   (c) Sister-in-law
   (d) Cannot be determined
6. Which of the following expressions indicates 'H is the brother of N'?
   (a) H # R $ D $ N
   (b) N % F @ D $ H # R
   (c) N% F @ D $ H
   (d) N% F @ D % H
7. If G $ M @ K, how is K related to G?
   (a) Daughter-in-law (b) Mother-in-law
   (c) Daughter (d) Aunt
8. A lady said, ' The person standing there is my grandfather's only son's daughter' How is the lady related to the standing person?
   (a) Sister (b) Mother
   (c) Aunt (d) Cousin
9. Pointing out to a lady, a girl said " she is the daughter-in-law of the grandmother of my father's only son." How is the lady related to the girl ?
   (a) Sister-in-law (b) Mother
   (c) Aunt (d) Mother-in-law
10. Pointing out to a photograph, a man tells his friend, " she is the daughter of the only son of my father's wife. How is the girls related to the man in the photograph?
    (a) Daughter (b) Cousin
    (c) Mother (d) Sister
11. A man pointing to a photograph says. " The lady in the photograph is my nephew's maternal grandmother" How is the lady in the photograph related to the man's sister who has no other sister.
    (a) Cousin (b) Sister-in-law
    (c) Mother (d) Mother-in-law
12. Pointing to Kapil, shilpa said, His mothers's brother is the father of my son Ashish" How is Kapil related to shilpa
    (a) Sister-in-law
    (b) Nephew
    (c) Niece
    (d) Aunt

DIRECTION (Q. 13) : *Study the following information and answer the questions given below.*

'P = Q' means Q is the father of P'
*'P * Q' means 'P' is the sister of Q'*
'P ? Q' means Q is the mother of P'
'P $ Q means P is the brother of Q'
'P ς Q' means Q is the son of P'
'P x Q' means 'P is the daughter of Q'

13. Which of the following is not correct ?
    (a) R × S ? T means R is the granddaughter of T.
    (b) P = Q ? R means R is the grandmother of P.
    (c) L $ M * O means O is the sister of L.
    (d) M * O ς P = Q means Q and O are husband and wife.
14. If P $Q means P is the father of Q, P # Q means P is mother Q and P * Q means P is the sister of Q then how is Q related to N if N # L $ P * Q
    (a) grandson
    (b) grand daughter
    (c) nephew
    (d) data inadequate
15. Pointing towards a man in the photograph, lady said the father of his brother is the only son of my mother " How is the man related to lady ?
    (a) Brother (b) Son
    (c) Cousin (d) Nephew
16. Soni, who is Dubey's daughter, says to Preeti, "Your mother Shyama is the yougest sister of my father, Dubey's Father's child is Prabhat". How is Prabhat related to Preeti?
    (a) Uncle
    (b) Father
    (c) Grandmother
    (d) Father in law

DIRECTION (Q. 17): *Read the information given below carefully and answer the question.*

x + y means x is the sister of y.
x – y means x is the son of y.
x × y means x is the mother of y
x ≠ y means x is the father of y
x ÷ y means x is the brother of y
x = y means x is daughter of y

17. Which of the following alternative means 'F is father of J'?
    (a) F ÷ G ≠ H × I – J
    (b) J = I + H ≠ G ÷ F
    (c) F + G – H × I – J
    (d) J + I – H × G – F
18. Pointing towards a woman in the photograph, Rajesh said "the only daughter of her grandfather (Paternal) is my wife". How is Rajesh related to that woman
    (a) Uncle (Fufa) (b) Father
    (c) Maternal uncle (d) Brother
19. Sailesh introduces Mahipal as the son of the only brother of his father's wife. How is Mahipal related to Sailesh?
    (a) Cousin
    (b) Son
    (c) Maternal uncle
    (d) Son-in-law
20. Ram is the husband of Reenu. Reena is the sister of Raju and Raju is the a son of Hemant. How is Ram related to Hemant?
    (a) Father (b) Brother-in-law
    (c) Father-in-law (d) Son-in-law
21. Pointing to Aanya, Rohit says, "She is the only daughter of my father's mother-in-law". How is Aanya related to Rohit? **[2019]**
    (a) Mother (b) Aunt
    (c) Sister (d) Sister-in-law

LEVEL 2

DIRECTIONS (Qs. 1-2) : Study the following information and answer the questions given below.

'P = Q' means 'Q' is the father of P'
'P * Q' means 'P' is the sister of Q'
'P ? Q' means 'Q' is the mother of P'
'P $ Q means 'P' is the brother of Q'
'P ς Q' means 'Q' is the son of P'
'P x Q' means 'P' is the daughter of Q.

1. Which of the following is correct ?
   (a) V × T * P means P is the maternal uncle of V.
   (b) D ? V × T means D is the granddaughter of T.
   (c) L ς M $ R means R is the paternal uncle of L.
   (d) M $ R * D ? V means M is the son of V.
2. Which of the following indicates 'A' is the grandfather of B' ?
   (a) M × A = N = B (b) B $ L × Q × A
   (c) B × L × A (d) L * B = S $ Q = A

DIRECTIONS (Qs. 3-5) : Read the information given below to answer these questions:

Rani and Shreshtha are a married couple having two daughters, Medha and Deepti. Deepti is married to Anurag who is the son of Garima and Tarun. Nidhi is the daughter of Anurag. Komal, who is Anurag's sister, is married to Harshit and has two sons, Aman and Prem. Prem is the grandson of Garima and Tarun.

3. What is the relationship between Aman and Nidhi?
   (a) Cousins (b) Husband-Wife
   (c) Father-Daughter (d) Uncle-Niece
4. How is Komal related to deepti ?
   (a) Aunt (b) Sister-in -law
   (c) Sister (d) None of these
5. Which of the following is true?
   (a) Tarun is Deepti's maternal uncle
   (b) Aman is the son of Medha.
   (c) Garima is Harshit's mother-in law
   (d) Nidhi is the cousin of Komal.
6. P + Q means P is the father of Q; P – Q means P is the wife of Q; P × Q means P is the brother of Q. Which of the following means A is the maternal uncle of D ?
   (a) A × B – C + D
   (b) D × C – B × A
   (c) A × C + B – D
   (d) A – C × B + D
7. A + B means A is the daughter of B, A × B means A is the son of B and A – B means A is the wife of B. If T – S × B – M, which of the following is NOT true?
   (a) M is the husband of B
   (b) B is the mother of S
   (c) S is the daughter of B
   (d) T is the wife of S
8. In a family of 6 (A, B, C, D, E and F) members, there is one married couple with equal number of male and female members. Read the following relations and find out the one from the alternatives. Which is not true for the given family.
   Relations:
   A and E are sons of F.
   D is the mother of a boy and a girl.
   B is the son of A.
   (a) A, E, B are males
   (b) C is the granddaughter of F
   (c) C is the daughter of E
   (d) D is the wife of A
9. If P + Q means P is husband of Q, $\frac{P}{Q}$ means P is sister of Q, P*Q means P is the son of Q. How is D related to A in D*B+ $\frac{C}{A}$?

(a) Son (b) Nephew
(c) Sister (d) Couple

10. Afsana was walking in a desert. Anwar was passing by riding on a camal. Afsana requested for a lift. Anwar said he will give lift only to those who are related to him.
At this, Afsana told him that Anwar's mother-in-law is the mother of her mother-in-law.
How is Anwar related to Afsana?
(a) Father
(b) Maternal uncle
(c) Brother-in-law
(d) Father-in law

11. How many male members are there in the family?
(a) Two (b) Three
(c) Four (d) Five

12. Harsh is the father of Santosh, Preeti is the daughter of Beena and Beena is the wife of Harsh. Santosh is not the daughter of Beena. Find out the relationship of Santosh and Preeti.
(a) Father – daughter
(b) Brother – sister
(c) Husband – wife
(d) Mother – daughter

13. A family consists of six members P,Q,R,X,Y,Z.
Q is the son of R but R is not mother of Q.
P and R are a married couple.
Y is the brother of R, X is the daughter of P.
Z is the brother of Q.
Which symbol represents all the children of P ?
(a) QXYZ (b) QXZ
(c) XZR (d) QZ

14. Pointing to a girl, Rahul said, "She is the daughter of my grandfather's only son". How is the girl related to Rahul?
(a) Father (b) Brother
(c) Sister (d) Mother

15. There are six children P, Q, R, S, T and U playing football. P and T are brothers. U is the sister of T. R is the only son of P's uncle. Q and S are the daughters of the brother of R's father. How many female players are there?
(a) 1 (b) 2
(c) 3 (d) 4

16. P, Q, R, S, T and U are sitting around a circle facing the centre. Q is second to the right of P and third to the left of S. Q is not a neighbour of R who is third to the right of T. Who are the neighbours of S?
(a) PT (b) PQ
(c) RP (d) RU

17. M, N, O, P, Q and R are six family members. Q is the sister of P. N is the daughter-in-law of R, who is not the grandfather of P. If M and N are a married couple, then who are the children of M and N?
(a) O, P
(b) P, Q
(c) Q, R
(d) Data inadequate

18. Ajay is the brother of Vijay. Mili is the Sister of Ajay. Sanjay is the brother of Rahul and Mehul is the daughter of Vijay. Who is Sanjay's uncle?
(a) Rahul
(b) Ajay
(c) Mehul
(d) Data inadequate

19. If 'P + Q' means 'P is the daughter of Q', 'P % Q' means 'P is the brother of Q', 'P % Q', means 'P is the father of Q, and 'P × Q' means 'P is the sister of Q', then which of the following means 'I is the niece of J'? **[2018]**
(a) J " N% C × I
(b) I × C – N% J
(c) I × C + N " J
(d) J + M × C% I

20. If 'A x B' means that 'A is the sister of B', 'A ÷ B' means that 'A is the daughter of B', 'A — B' means that 'A is the son of

B', then how is P related to S in relationship P – Q × R ÷ S ? **[2018]**

(a) Brother (b) Son
(c) Grandson (d) None of these

21. Saksham is the nephew of Karan. Karan's father is Ajay. Sadhna is Ajay's mother. Sadhna's husband is Atul. Ankita is the mother-in-law of Atul. How is Karan related to Atul? **[2019]**
(a) Son
(b) Great grandson
(c) Grandson
(d) Father

22. If X – Y means X is the brother of Y, X + Y means X is the mother of Y, X ÷ Y means X is the daughter of Y, then who is the father of B in A + B – C ÷ D? **[2020]**
(a) C
(b) D
(c) A
(d) Data inadequate

23. Pointing to a girl in a photograph, Ajay says, "She is the daughter of my grandfather's only son's daughter". How is the girl related to Ajay? **[2021]**
(a) Wife (b) Sister
(c) Niece (d) Cousin

24. Study the given information carefully and answer the following question. **[2021]**
'A # B' means 'A is the mother of B'.
'A % B' means 'A is the husband of B'.
'A @ B' means 'A is the father of B'.
'A © B' means 'A is the sister of B'.
Which of the following indicates S is the mother of Q?
(a) Q@S%T#U©R
(b) R@S%Q#T© U
(c) T@U%S#R© Q
(d) S@R%Q#T© U

25. If 'M × N' means 'M is the daughter of N', 'M + N' means 'M is the father of N', 'M ÷ N' means 'M is the mother of N' and 'M – N' means 'M is the brother of N', then in the expression 'P ÷ Q + R – T × K', how is P related to K?
(a) Daughter–in–law
(b) Mother–in–law
(c) Aunt
(d) Mother

26. A is B's sister. C is B's mother. D is C's father. E is D's mother. How is D related to A? **[2022]**
(a) Grandmother (b) Grandfather
(c) Daughter (d) Granddaughter

27. Pointing to a lady, a girl said, "she is the daughter-inlaw of the grandmother of my father's only son." How is the lady related to the girl? **[2022]**
(a) Sister-in-law (b) Mother
(c) Aunt (d) Mother-in-law

ANSWER KEY

LEVEL-1

1	(a)	4	(b)	7	(a)	10	(a)	13	(c)	16	(a)	19	(a)
2	(b)	5	(a)	8	(a)	11	(c)	14	(d)	17	(d)	20	(d)
3	(c)	6	(b)	9	(b)	12	(b)	15	(d)	18	(a)	21	(a)

LEVEL-2

1	(d)	4	(b)	7	(c)	10	(d)	13	(b)	16	(c)	19	(c)	22	(b)	25	(b)
2	(d)	5	(c)	8	(c)	11	(b)	14	(c)	17	(b)	20	(c)	23	(c)	26	(b)
3	(a)	6	(a)	9	(b)	12	(b)	15	(c)	18	(d)	21	(c)	24	(c)	27	(b)

CHAPTER

Direction Sense Test

DIRECTION SENSE TEST :

There are four directions North, South, East and West. The word NEWS came from North, East, West and South. There are four regions :

North-East (I); South-East (IV); North-West (II); South-West (III). The directions OP, OS, OQ and OR are North East direction; North-West direction; South-West and South-East direction.

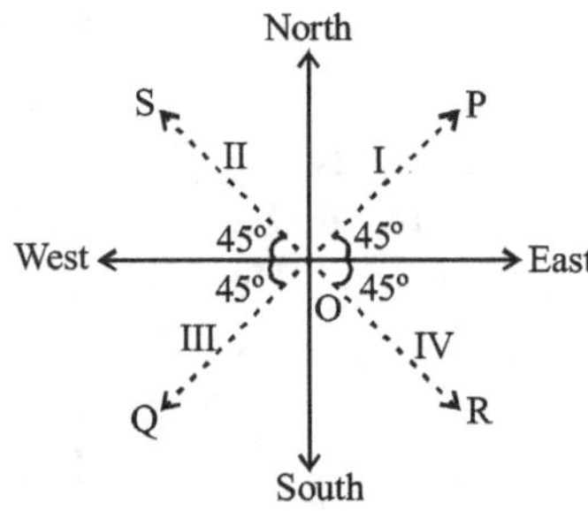

The candidate must distinguish between the regions and directions i.e. between North-East region and North-East direction.

If you move with your face east-wards, your left hand is towards north and your right hand is towards south. Similarly the positions of the directions of the hands can be fixed when you move in any of the other three directions.

To solve the question, first draw the direction figure

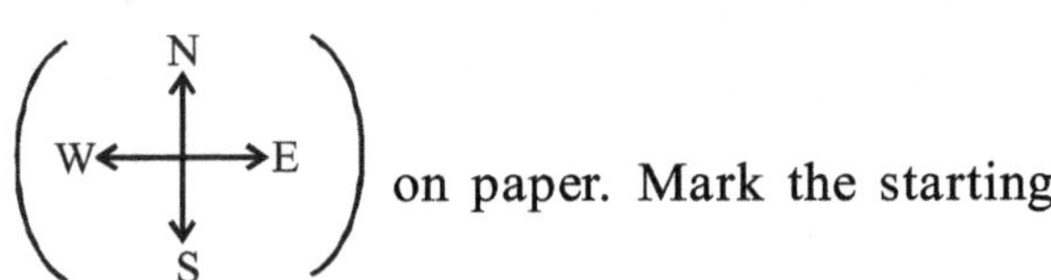

on paper. Mark the starting point. After that move carefully according to the directions given in the question.

DIRECTIONS (ILLUSTRATION 1-3) : Read the information given below to answer these questions.

a, b, c, d, e, f, g, h and i are nine houses. c is 2 km east of b. a is 1 km north of b and h is 2 km south of a, g is 1 km west of h while d is 3 km east of g and f is 2 km north of g. i is situated just in the middle of b and c while e is just in middle of h and d.

ILLUSTRATION 1:

Distance between e and g is :

(a) 2 km (b) 1 km

(c) 5 km (d) 1.5 km

ILLUSTRATION 2:

Distance between a and f is :

(a) 1.41 km

(b) 3 km

(c) 2 km

(d) 1 km

ILLUSTRATION 3:

Distance between e and i is :

(a) 4 km (b) 2 km
(c) 1 km (d) 3 km

Sol. **(1-3) :**

From the information given, positions of houses are as follows :

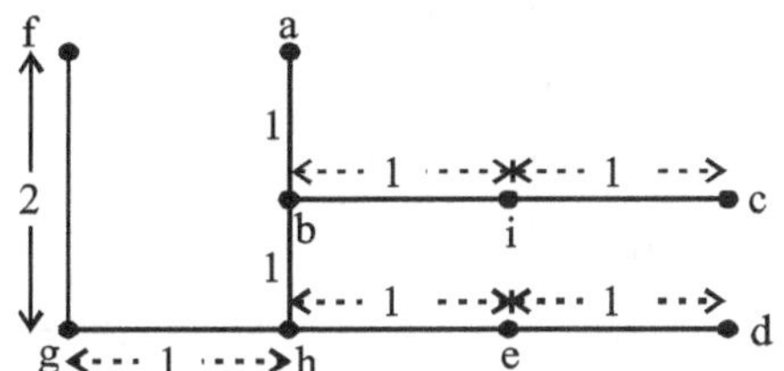

Sol. **1 : (a)** Clearly, the distance between e and g is 2 km.

Sol. **2 : (d)** From the above diagram, the distance between a and f is 1 km.

Sol. **3 : (c)** Clearly, the distance between e and i is 1 km.

ILLUSTRATION 4:

In the given figure, P is 300 km eastward of O and Q is 400 kms North of O, R is exactly in the middle of Q and P. The distance between Q and R is :

(a) 250 kms

(b) $250\sqrt{2}$ kms

(c) 300 kms

(d) 350 kms

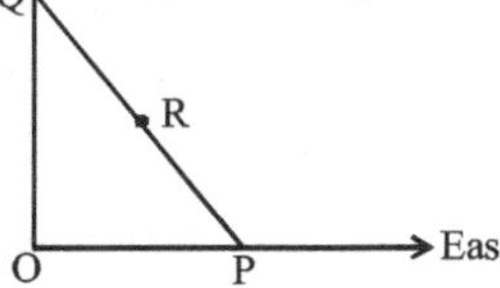

Sol. **(a)** $PQ = \sqrt{OP^2 + OQ^2}$

$= \sqrt{(300)^2 + (400)^2} = \sqrt{100^2(3^2 + 4^2)}$

$= \sqrt{100^2 \times 5^2} = (100 \times 5)$ i.e., 500 km.

R being in the midway of PQ, so QR = 250 kms.

ILLUSTRATION 5:

Four persons stationed at the four corners of a square piece as shown in the diagram. P starts crossing the field diagonally. After walking half the distance, he turns right, walks some distance and turns left.

Which direction is P facing now ?

(a) North-east

(b) North-west

(c) North

(d) South-east

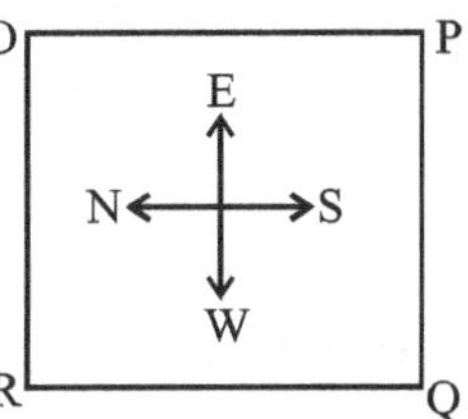

Sol. **(b)** The route of P is shown in the diagram.

Clearly the direction of P is North-west.

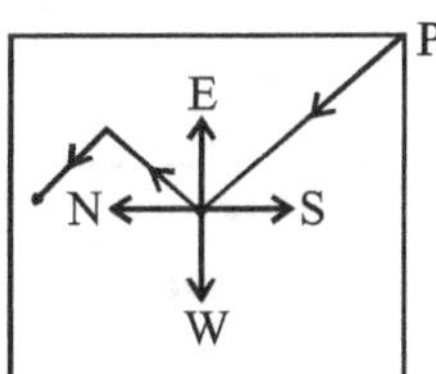

ROTATION OF ANGLES

To solve angle movement questions. It is necessary to know about the rotations of angles which are given below.

i) For right direction movement (Clockwise)

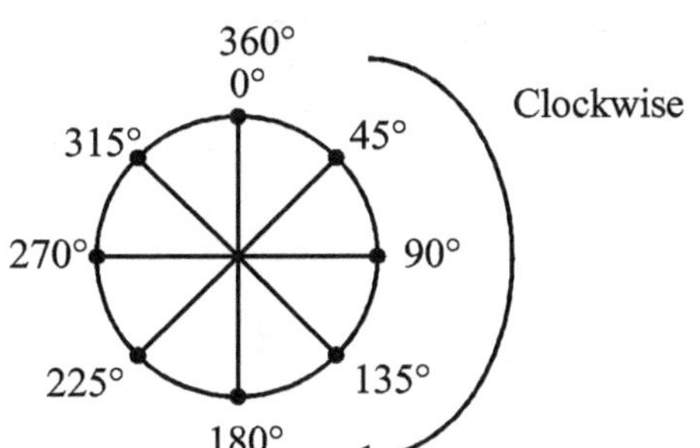

ii) For left direction movement (Anti-clockwise)

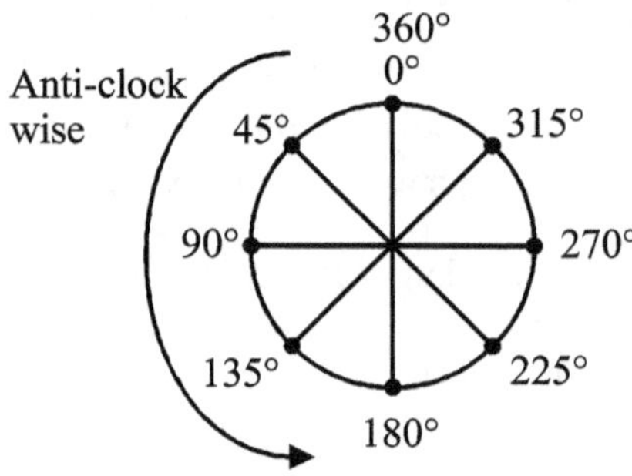

Left turn Anti-clockwise direction

Right turn Clockwise direction

The Change in Direction when a Person or Vehicle Takes A Right or a Left Turn

Direction before taking	Direction in which the person or vehicle will be moving after taking	
the turn	**the turn**	
	Right	**Left**
North	East	West
South	West	East
East	South	North
West	North	South

Pythogoras Theorem

While solving the distance related question, one must be through with the Pythagorean Theorem to be able to solve most of the questions, The Pythagorean Theorem is used calculate the shortest path traveled, the minimum distance between two points, etc.

It states that, in **a right angled triangle** the length of the **hypotenuse** is equal to the **square root of the sum of squares of the other two sides.**

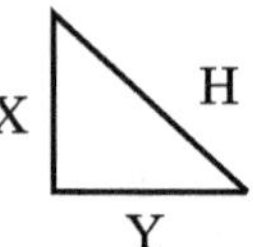

Where, H = Hypotenuse

X = Height

Y = Base

Therefore, according to the theorem $H^2 = X^2 + Y^2$

i.e., $H = \sqrt{(X^2 + Y^2)}$

Shadow Case

In morning/Sunrise time

a) If a person facing towards Sun, the shadow will be towards his back or in west.

b) If a person facing towards South, the shodow will be towards his right.

c) If a person facing towards West, the shadow will be towards his front.

d) If a person facing towards North, the shadow will be towards his left.

In evening/Sunset time

a) If a person facing towards Sun, the shadow will be towards his back or in East

b) If a person facing towards North, the shadow will be towards his right.

c) If a person facing towards East, the shadow will be towards his front.

d) If a person facing towards South, the shadow will be towards his left.

LEVEL 1

1. A child is looking for his father. He went 90 metres in the East before turning to his right. He went 20 metres before turning to his right again to look for his father at his uncle's place 30 metres from this point. His father was not there. From here he went 100 metres to the North before meeting his father in a street. How far did the son meet his father from the starting point ?
   (a) 80 metres (b) 100 metres
   (c) 140 metres (d) 260 metres
2. A,B,C and D are playing cards. A and B are partners. D faces towards North. If A faces towards west, then who faces towards south?
   (a) B (b) C
   (c) D (d) Data inadequate
3. Deepak starts walking straight towards east. After walking 75 metres, he turns to the left and walks 25 metres straight. Again he turns to the left, walks a distance of 40 metres straight, again he turns to the left and walks a distance of 25 metres. How far is he from the starting point ?
   (a) 25 metres (b) 50 Metres
   (c) 115 Metres (d) 35 Metres
4. One morning after sunrise, Gopal was facing a pole. The shadow of the pole fell exactly to his right. Which direction was he facing?
   (a) South (b) East
   (c) West (d) Data inadequate
5. A man leaves for his office from his house. He walks towards East. After moving a distance of 20 m, he turns south and walks 10 m. Then he walks 35 m towards the west and further 5 m towards the North. He then turns towards east and walks 15 m. What is the straight distance (in metres) between his initial and final positions ?
   (a) 0
   (b) 5
   (c) 10
   (d) Cannot be determined
6. Aman starts walking in south and walks for 7 km, then turns left and walks for 2 km, Then, once again turns left and walks for 12 km, turns left one more time and walks for 2 km. How much distance he has to cover to reach the starting point?
   (a) 7 km (b) 12 km
   (c) 4 km (d) 5 km
7. I am facing East. I turn 100° in the clockwise direction and the 145° in anticlockwise direction. Which direction am i facing now?
   (a) East (b) North-East
   (c) North (d) South-East
8. Yash starts moving towards South and walks for 12 m. Then he takes the left turn and walks for 8 m. Again he takes a right turn and walks for 24 m. Now he takes a turn to North-east direction and walks 25 m. From that he takes a turn towards North and walks 20 m. Find the distance between the start point and the finishing point of his movement.
   (a) 12 m (b) 15 m
   (c) 17 m (d) 25 m
9. At 12 : 30 the hour hand of a clock faces north and the minute hand faces south. At 2 : 45 the minutes hand will be in which direction?
   (a) North-West (b) West
   (c) South-East (d) East
10. A man leaves for his office from his house. He walks towards East. After moving a distance of 20 m, he turns south and walks 10 m. Then he walks 35 m towards the west

and further 5 m towards the North. He then turns towards east and walks 15 m. What is the straight distance (in metres) between his initial and final positions?

(a) 0
(b) 5
(c) 10
(d) Cannot be determined

11. Shrikant from a certain place went 4 km to East. He turned left and went 1 km. Then he turned right and went 2 km. Again he turned right and walked a distance of 9 km. Then at what distance is he from his original position ?

(a) 4 km (b) 10 km
(c) 9 km (d) 6 km

12. A man is facing North-West. He turns 90° in clockwise direction and then 135° in the anticlockwise direction. Which direction is he facing now ?

(a) East (b) West
(c) North (d) South

13. A and B starts moving towards each other from two places 200 m apart. After walking 60 m, B turns left and goes 20 m, then he turns right and goes 40 m. He then turns right again and comes back to the road on which he had started walking. If A and B walk with the same speed, what is the distance between A and B now ?

(a) 20 m (b) 30 m
(c) 40 m (d) 50 m

14. Aman starts walking in south and walks for 7 km, then turns left and walks for 2 km, Then, once again turns left and walks for 12 km, turns left one more time and walks for 2 km. How much distance he has to cover to reach the starting point?

(a) 7 km (b) 12 km
(c) 4 km (d) 5 km

15. I am facing East. I turn 100° in the clockwise direction and the 145° in anticlockwise direction. Which direction am i facing now?

(a) East (b) North-East
(c) North (d) South-East

16. At 12 : 30 the hour hand of a clock faces north and the minute hand faces south. At 2 : 45 the minutes hand will be in which direction?

(a) North-West (b) West
(c) South-East (d) East

17. Komal goes 3 m towards South, then she takes a left turn and goes 5 m. Again she turns left and goes 3 m. How far is she now from her starting point?

(a) 3 m (b) 4 m
(c) 5 m (d) 8 m

18. P is 600 km eastward of O and Q is 800 km north of O. R is exactly in the middle of Q and P. The distance between Q and R is

(a) 1000 km (b) 500 km
(c) 400 km (d) 300 km

19. Ahika is standing to the North of Sumit. Priyanka is standing to the East of Ahika. Puneet is to the West of Sumit. What is the position of Puneet with respect to Priyanka?

(a) West (b) South-West
(c) South (d) North-West

20. Sonal walked 8 metres towards East, took a right turn and walked 12 metres and again took a left turn and walked 5 metres and stopped. In which direction is she now with respect to her starting point? **[2019]**

(a) South (b) South-West
(c) South-East (d) North-East

21. Pranav walks 20 m towards East. Then he turns left and walks 9 Then he again turns left and walks 32 m. In which direction and how far is he now from his starting position? **[2019]**

(a) 15 m, North-East
(b) 15 m, North-West
(c) 15 m, South-West
(d) 15 m, South-East

22. Anamika walks 6 km towards North. Then she turns to West and walks 10 km. After this, she turns to North and walks 9 km.

Again she turns towards West and walks 10 km. How far is she now from her starting point? **[2019]**

(a) 10 km (b) 23 km
(c) 15 km (d) 25 km

23. Mayank went 50 m South from his house, then turned left and went 20 m, then turning to North he went 30 m. In which direction is his home with respect to the final point? **[2020]**

(a) North–East (b) South–East
(c) North–West (d) South–West

LEVEL 2

1. While facing East, Rohit turns to his left and walks 10 metres, then he turns left and walks 10 meters. Now he turns 45° towards his right and goes straight to cover 25 meters. In which direction is he from his starting point ?
(a) North-east (b) North-west
(c) South-west (d) South-east
2. Rasik walks 20 m North. Then, he turns right and walks 30 m. Then he turns right and walks 35 m. Then he turns left and walks 15 m. Then he again turns left and walks 15 m. In which direction and how many metres away is he from his original position?
(a) 15 metres West (b) 30 metres East
(c) 30 metres West (d) 45 metres East

DIRECTIONS (Qs. 3-5) : *These questions are based on the following information.*

Farmer Batuk Singh has a larger square field divided into nine smaller square fields, all equal, arranged in three rows of three fields each. One side of the fields runs exactly east-west. The middle square must be planted with rice because it is wet. The wheat and barley should be continuous so that they can be harvested all at once by the mechanical harvester. Two of the field should be planted with soyabeans. The north westernmost field should be planted with peanuts and the southern third of the field is suitable only for vegetables.

3. If Batuk Singh decides to plant the wheat next to the peanuts, in which square will the barley be ?
(a) The square immediately north of the rice.
(b) The square immediately east of the rice.
(c) The square immediately west of the rice.
(d) The square immediately north east of the rice.
4. Which square cannot be planted with wheat?
(a) The square immediately north of the rice.
(b) The square immediately east of the rice.
(c) The square immediately west of the rice.
(d) The square immediately north east of the rice.
5. Which square cannot be planted with soyabeans?
(a) The square immediately north of the rice.
(b) The square immediately east of the rice.
(c) The square immediately west of the rice.
(d) The square immediately north east of the rice.

DIRECTIONS (Qs. 6-10) : *These questions are based on the diagram given below showing four persons stationed at the four corners of a square piece of a plot as shown.*

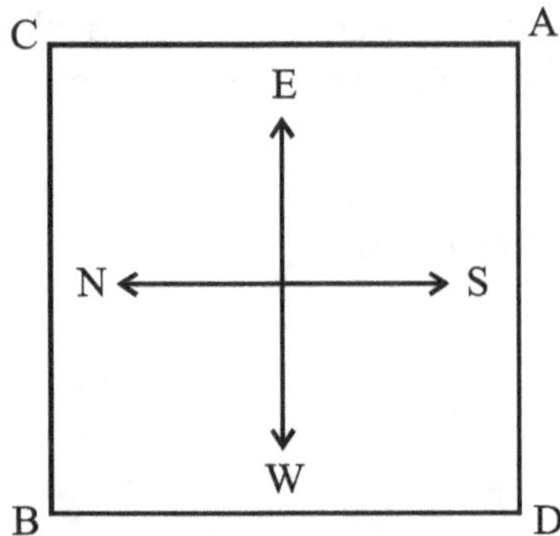

6. A starts crossing the plot diagonally. After walking half the distance, he turns right, walks some distance and turns left. Which direction is A facing now ?
   (a) North-east (b) North
   (c) North-west (d) South-east
7. From the original position given in the above figure, A and B move one arm length clockwise and then cross over to the corners diagonally opposite; C and D move one arm length anti-clockwise and cross over to the corners diagonally opposite. The original configuration ABCD has now changed to
   (a) CDAB (b) DACB
   (c) BDAC (d) ACBD
8. From the original position, B and D move one and a half length of sides clockwise and anti-clockwise respectively. Which one of the following starements is true ?
   (a) B and D are both at the mid point between A and C.
   (b) B is at the midpoint between A and C, and D is at the corner originally occupied by A.
   (c) D is at the midpoint between A and C, and B is at the corner originally occupied by C.
   (d) B and D are both at the midpoint between A and D.
9. From the positions in the original figure. C and A move diagonally to opposite corners and then one side each clockwise and anti-clockwise respectively. B and D move two sides each clockwise and anti-clockwise respectively. Where is A now ?
   (a) At the north-west corner
   (b) At the south-east corner
   (c) At the north-east corner
   (d) At the south-west corner
10. After the movements given in the above question, who is at the north-west corner ?
   (a) A (b) C
   (c) B (d) D
11. A girl is facing towards East. She turns 225° in the anticlockwise direction and then 90° in the clockwise direction. Which direction is she facing now?
   (a) North (b) South
   (c) North-West (d) South-East
12. Shreya is facing South-West. She wants to go to her friend's house, so she turns through 135° in clockwise direction. In which direction is she facing now?
   (a) North-West (b) South-East
   (c) North (d) South
13. Ali starts walking towards North. He walked a distance of 20 m and then took a right turn and walked a distance of 30 m. Then he took a right turn again and walked a distance of 20 m. How far and in which direction is Ali now from the starting point?
   (a) 30 m, East
   (b) 20 m, North
   (c) 30 m, South-East
   (d) 10 m, North-West
14. Meena walks 3 km North, then turns West and walks 4 km, then turns South and walks 7 km, then turns to her left and walks 4 km. Where is she now from her starting position?
   (a) 10 km North (b) 4 km South
   (c) 10 km South (d) 4 km North
15. Raj walked 55 m towards South, then he took a left turn and walked 38 m. After that,

he turned 270° clockwise and walked 55 m. How far is Raj from the starting point?

(a) 55 m (b) 93 m
(c) 17 m (d) None of these

16. Kirti walks 10 km towards North. From there, she walks 6 km towards South. Then, she walks 3 km towards East. How far and in which direction is she now with respect to her starting point?
(a) 5 km North-West
(b) 7 km South-West
(c) 7 km West
(d) 5 km North-East

17. Kritika faces towards West. Turning to her left, she walks 30 metres. She then turns to her right and walks 25 metres. Next, she moves 30 metres to her right. Finally, she turns to the left and moves 20 metres. How far and in which direction is she now from her starting point?
(a) 45 m, East (b) 45 m, West
(c) 45 m, North (d) 40 m, West

18. Ritika faces towards South. Turning to her right, she walks 20 metres. She then turns to her left and walks 35 metres. Next, she walks 25 metres to her right. She then turns to her right again and walks 55 metres. Finally, she turns to the right and walks 25 metres. In which direction is she now from her starting point?
(a) South-West (b) South
(c) North-West (d) South-East

19. Abhinav started walking straight towards South. He walked a distance of 10 metres and then took a right turn and walked a distance of 20 metres. He again took a right turn and walked a distance of 45 metres. In which direction is he now from his starting point?
(a) North-East (b) South
(c) North-West (d) South-West

20. Vandana walks 25 m towards North. Then she turns towards her left and walks 20 m. She then turns to her right and walks 25 m. She again turns towards her left and walks 15 m. Which direction is Vandana facing now?
(a) East (b) West
(c) North (d) South

21. A bus is moving towards West. It moves 7 km towards West, then turn right and covers 5 km distance. The bus takes a right turn again and covers 19 km. How far is the bus now from its starting point?
(a) 12 km (b) 10 km
(c) 13 km (d) 16 km

22. A girl is facing South. She turns 135° in the anticlockwise direction and then 180° in the clockwise direction. Which direction is the girl facing now?
(a) North-East (b) South-East
(c) South-West (d) North-West

23. A person starts from a point A and travels 3 km eastwards to B and then turns left and travels thrice that distance to reach C. He again turns left and travels five times the distance he covered between A and B and reaches his destination D. The shortest distance between the starting point and the destination is
(a) 12 km (b) 15 km
(c) 16 km (d) 18 km

24. Lokesh's school bus is facing North when it reaches his school. After starting from Lokesh's house, it turns right twice and then left before reaching the school. What direction was the bus facing when it left the bus stop in front of Lokesh's house?
(a) North (b) South
(c) East (d) West

25. A watch reads 4.30 If the minute hand points East, in what direction will the hour hand point ?

(a) North (b) North-west
(c) South-east (d) North-east

26. A pilgrim started from a shrine. After walking straight for 100 m, he again moved to his right and then after 500 m, he again moved to his right. After walking a distance of 100 m, he moved to his left and then walked 200 m. He again moved to his right and walked 700 m. In the end he turned to his left two times.
What is the distance of his location from the shrine?
(a) 1100 m (b) 1300 m
(c) 1400 m (d) 2100 m

27. A sprinter goes off the starting block for 100m run and at that instant the second-hand of a stopwatch had pointed towards North. He touches the finishing line exactly after 12 seconds. In which direction did the second hand point when he just crossed the finishing line?
(a) 18° North of East
(b) 18° East of North
(c) 72° North of East
(d) 82° East of North

28. Amita is standing at point A facing north direction. She walks for 5 kilometres in the north east direction. Then she turns at an angle of 90° at her right and once again travels the same distance. She reaches at Point B. Now she takes a turn at 90° to her left and walks for 3 kilometres and once again takes right turn at 90° and travels 3 kilometres and reaches at Point C. What is the direction of Point B and C respectively with respect to Point A?
(a) East , East
(b) East, North-East
(c) North -East, East
(d) North-East, North-East

29. Just before sunset Veena and Zeba were talking to each other standing face-to-face. If Veena sees Zeba's shadow to be exactly towards the right of Zeba, which direction was Veena facing?
(a) South (b) North
(c) East (d) North-East

30. Danish starts walking straight towards East. After walking 75 m, he turns to the left and walks 25 m straight. Again he turns to the left, walks a distance of 40 m straight again he turns to the left and walks a distance of 25 m.
How far is he from starting point
(a) 30 m (b) 35 m
(c) 40 m (d) 50 m

31. In a city, all the roads are either parallel to the East-West or North-South irection. Every $\frac{1}{8}$th of a kilometre from each road there is a crossing and the square area covered beween four crossings is called a block. Staring from a crossing. if I travel four blocks north. take left and then travel three blocks west. I reach another crossing. What is the distance between these two crossings?

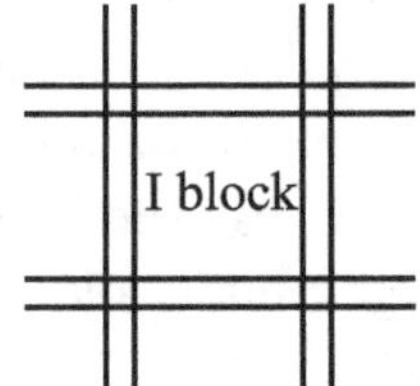

(a) 5 km (b) 7 km
(c) 7/8 km (d) 5/8 km

32. A person walked 100m straight from the point 'A' in the North-East direction, walked 200m in South- West direction from there, 100m in North-East direction again, walked 100m eastward, 200m southward and 100m westward to reach at the point 'B'. Choose the right answer from the following to find out his/her distance and direction from 'A'.
(a) 100m, North (b) 100m, South
(c) 200m, North (d) 200m, South

33. Pankaja puts her alarm clock on the table in such a way that at 6 pm the hour hand points to North. In which direction will the minute hand point at 9 : 15 pm?
    (a) South-East (b) South
    (c) North (d) West

34. One evening before sunset two friends Rajni and Sanjiv were talking face to face. If Sanjiv's.s shadow was exactly to his right side, to which direction Rajni was facing?
    (a) North (b) North east
    (c) South (d) South east

35. Samay travels 12 km towards West, turns right and travels 5 km and then turns left and travels another 3 km and then again turns left and travels another 5 km. How far and in which direction is he now from his starting point? **[2019]**
    (a) 11 km, West (b) 11 km East
    (c) 15 km, West (d) 15 km, East

36. Arpita left her home and walked 10 m towards South. She then turned right and walked 5 m and again after turning to her right, she walked 10 m. She then turned left and walked 10 m. How far does she now from her home? **[2020]**
    (a) 25 m (b) 10 m
    (c) 15 m (d) 30 m

37. Sudhir was facing South. He turned to right and walked 20 m. Then he turned right again and walked 10 m. Then after turning to left he walked 10 m. He then turned right and walked 20 m. Again after turning to right he walked 60 m. Which direction is he now with respect to the starting point? **[2021]**
    (a) North (b) North-West
    (c) South-East (d) North-East

38. After walking 6 km, Mohit turned right and covered a distance of 2 km, then turned left and covered a distance of 10 km. If in the end, he was facing towards the North, then towards which direction did Mohit start his journey? **[2022]**
    (a) North (b) South
    (c) East (d) West

39. Ankit left for his office in his car. He drove 15 km towards the north and then 10 km towards the west. He then turned to the south and covered 5 km. Further, he turned to the east and moved 8 km. Finally, he turned right and drove 10 km. How far and in which direction is he from his starting point? **[2022]**
    (a) 2 km west (b) 5 km East
    (c) 3 km north (d) 6 Km south

ANSWER KEY																			
LEVEL-1																			
1	(b)	**2**	(b)	**3**	(d)	**4**	(a)	**5**	(b)	**6**	(d)	**7**	(b)	**8**	(c)	**9**	(b)	**10**	(b)
11	(b)	**12**	(b)	**13**	(c)	**14**	(d)	**15**	(b)	**16**	(b)	**17**	(c)	**18**	(c)	**19**	(b)	**20**	(c)
21	(b)	**22**	(d)	**23**	(c)														
LEVEL-2																			
1	(b)	**5**	(d)	**9**	(d)	**13**	(a)	**17**	(b)	**21**	(c)	**25**	(d)	**29**	(a)	**33**	(d)	**37**	(d)
2	(d)	**6**	(c)	**10**	(b)	**14**	(b)	**18**	(c)	**22**	(c)	**26**	(c)	**30**	(b)	**34**	(c)	**38**	(a)
3	(d)	**7**	(a)	**11**	(c)	**15**	(d)	**19**	(c)	**23**	(b)	**27**	(c)	**31**	(d)	**35**	(c)	**39**	(a)
4	(c)	**8**	(a)	**12**	(c)	**16**	(d)	**20**	(b)	**24**	(d)	**28**	(a)	**32**	(d)	**36**	(c)		

CHAPTER 6

Alpha-Numeric Sequence

TYPE I : WORD-FORMATION

In these types of questions, certain words are given. The candidate is required to arrange them in the order in which they are asked.

ILLUSTRATION 1 :

If it is possible to make a meaningful word with the 3rd, 4th and 11th letters the of word 'CONTROVERSIAL', write the first letter of the word. Write M if more than one word can be made, otherwise write X.

(a) M (b) T

(c) N (d) X

***Sol.* (b).** The 3rd, 4th and 11th, letters of the word 'CONTROVERSIAL' are N, T and I respectively. With these three letters, the following word can be formed : TIN. Therefore, Answer is T.

TYPE II : LETTER WORD PROBLEM

In these type of questions, a word is given and candidates are required to find out the Number of pairs of letters that matches the same sequence as in the English Alphabets.

ILLUSTRATION 2 :

How many letters are there in the word BACKLASH, each of which is as far away from the beginning of the word as it is from the beginning of the English alphabet ?

(a) None (b) One

(c) Two (d) Three

***Sol.* (c)** Clearly, C and H are respectively the third and eighth letters in the word BACKLASH as well as in the English alphabet. Thus, there are two such letters.

TYPE III : ALPHABETICAL QUIBBLE

In this type of question, generally a letter series is given, be it the English alphabets from A to Z or a randomised sequence of letters. The candidate is required to trace the letters satisfying certain given conditions as regards their position in the given sequence or the sequence obtained by performing certain given operations on the given sequence.

DIRECTIONS (ILLUSTRATION 3-4) : Each of the following questions is based on the following alphabet series : A B C D E F G H I J K L M N O P Q R S T U V W X Y Z

ILLUSTRATION 3 :

Which letter will be the eighth to the right of the third letter of the second half of the English alphabet ?

(a) V (b) W
(c) X (d) Y

***Sol.* (c)** Clearly, the first half of English alphabet has letters from A to M, and the second half has letters from N to Z.
The third letter of the second half is P, and the eighth letter to the right of P is X.

ILLUSTRATION 4 :

If only the last ten letters of the alphabet are written in the reverse order, which of the following will be the sixth to the right of the thirteenth letter from the left end ?

(a) U (b) V
(c) W (d) X

***Sol.* (d)** The new alphabet series is :
A B C D E F G H I J K L M N O P Z Y X W V U T S R Q
The thirteenth letter from the left is M.
The sixth letter to the right of M is X.

ILLUSTRATION 5 :

If every alternative letter of English alphabet from B onwards (including B) is written in lower case (small letters) and the remaining letters are capitalized, then how will the first month of the second half of the year be written ?

(a) JuLy (b) AuGuSt
(c) jUlY (d) AugUSt

Sol. (c) The new letter series becomes :
A b C d E f G h I j K l M n O p Q r S t U v W x Y z
The first month of the second half of the year is July, which shall be written as jUlY.

TYPE IV : ALPHABETICAL ORDER

Arranging words in alphabetical order implies 'to arrange them in the order as they appear in a dictionary', i.e., as per the order in which the beginning letters of these words appear in the English alphabet.
First consider the first letter of each word. Arrange the words in the order in which these letters appear in the English alphabet.
In some cases, two or more words begin with the same letter. Such words should be arranged in the order of second letters in the alphabet.

DIRECTIONS (ILLUSTRATION 6-8): In each of the following questions, four words are given. Which of them will be the last if all of them are arranged alphabetically as in a dictionary?

ILLUSTRATION 6 :

(a) Praise (b) Practical
(c) Prank (d) Prayer

***Sol.* (d)** Practical, Praise, Prank, Prayer.

ILLUSTRATION 7 :

(a) Nature (b) Native
(c) Narrate (d) Nascent

***Sol.* (a)** Narrate, Nascent, Native, Nature.

ILLUSTRATION 8 :

(a) Relieve (b) Ringlet
(c) Rightful (d) Rigour

***Sol.* (b)** Relieve, Rightful, Rigour, Ringlet

LEVEL 1

1. If the first three letters of the word COMPREHENSION are reversed, then the last three letters are added and then the remaining letters are reversed and added, then which letter will be exactly in the middle.?
   (a) H (b) N
   (c) R (d) S
2. If the first and second letters in the word DEPRESSION were interchanged, also the third and the fourth letters, the fifth and the sixth letters and so on, which of the following would be the seventh letter from the right?
   (a) R (b) O
   (c) S (d) None of these
3. Select the combination of numbers so that letters arranged accordingly will form a meaningful word.
   R A C E T
   1 2 3 4 5
   (a) 1, 2, 3, 4, 5 (b) 3, 2, 1, 4, 5
   (c) 5, 2, 3, 4, 1 (d) 5, 1, 2, 3, 4

DIRECTIONS (Qs. 4-5) : *Arrange the given words in the sequence in which they occur in the dictionary and then choose the correct sequence.*

4. 1. Wrinkle 2. Wriggle
   3. Writhe 4. Wretch
   5. Wrath
   (a) 4, 5, 1, 2, 3 (b) 5, 4, 2, 1, 3
   (c) 4, 2, 5, 1, 3 (d) 5, 2, 1, 3, 4
5. 1. Brook 2. Bandit 3. Boisterous
   4. Baffle 5. Bright
   (a) 4, 2, 3, 5, 1 (b) 2, 4, 3, 1, 5
   (c) 2, 4, 3, 5, 1 (d) 4, 2, 3, 1, 5

DIRECTIONS (Qs. 6-8) : *Find which one word cannot be made from the letters of the given word.*

6. INTERNATIONAL
   (a) ORIENTAL (b) TERMINAL
   (c) LATTER (d) RATIONALE
7. CONTEMPORARY
   (a) PARROT (b) COMPANY
   (c) CARPENTER (d) PRAYER
8. REFRIGERATE
   (a) REFER (b) REGRET
   (c) REGENERATE (d) FREE

DIRECTIONS (Qs. 9-12) : *Read the data carefully and answer the questions.*

LAP BUT CAR SON HID

(New words to be formed may or may not necessarily be meaningful English words.)

9. If the positions of the 1st and the 3rd alphabets of each of the word are interchanged, which of the following would form meaningful words with the mew arrangement?
   (a) HID (b) SON
   (c) TUB (d) CAR
10. If the given words are arranged in the order as they would appear in a dictionary from the left to right, which of the following will be 4th from the left?
    (a) LAP (b) BUT
    (c) CAR (d) SON
11. Which alphabet is on same place in two words given in the question?
    (a) u (b) i
    (c) a (d) n
12. If second alphabet in each of the words is changed to next alphabet in the English

alphabetical order, how many words having no vowels will be formed?

(a) One (b) Two
(c) Three (d) More than three

13. If two is subtracted from each of the following numbers, then which of the following is the sum of the second digit of the second highest number and the second digit of the highest number?

486 441 634 932 873

(a) 8 (b) 3
(c) 7 (d) 10

14. How many consonants are there in the given series which is immediately preceded by a vowel?

V E T R V T E S B A W R I P V O T

(a) Two (b) Three
(c) Four (d) Five

15. Arrange the following words in a meaningful sequence and select the correct option.

1. Word 2. Chapter
3. Book 4. Sentence
5. Paragraph

(a) 2, 3, 4, 1, 5 (b) 3, 2, 5, 4, 1
(c) 3, 5, 2, 1, 4 (d) 2, 4, 3, 5, 1

16. Rahul ranks eleventh from the top in a class of 40 students. What will be his rank from the bottom?

(a) 29th (b) 30th
(c) 31st (d) 32nd

17. What is the smallest number of ducks that could swim in this formation - two ducks in front of three ducks, two ducks behind three ducks?

(a) 6 (b) 5
(c) 4 (d) 3

18. Sumit is fourteenth from the right end in a row of 35 boys. If first two boys from the left end leave the row, then what is Sumit's position from the left end?

(a) 20th (b) 19th
(c) 21st (d) 18th

19. In a row of girls, if Arpita is twelfth from the left end and fifth from the right end, then how many girls should join the row such that there are 30 girls in the row?

(a) 12 (b) 13
(c) 14 (d) 20

20. Which of the following will be the middle digit of the middle number formed after adding 1 to each of the given numbers and then arranged in ascending order?

642, 378, 894, 546, 692

(a) 2 (b) 3
(c) 4 (d) 5

21. In a class of 45 students, Harshit is at 7th position from the top and Nitin is at 9th position from the bottom. If Priyanka is placed exactly between them, then find the position of Priyanka from the top.

(a) 21st (b) 22nd
(c) 23rd (d) 32nd

22. Some letters are given which are numbered 1, 2, 3, 4 and 5. Find the combination of numbers from the options so that the letters are arranged accordingly to form a meaningful English word.

O	S	A	T	R
1	2	3	4	5

(a) 1, 2, 3, 4, 5 (b) 2, 4, 1, 3, 5
(c) 5, 1, 3, 4, 2 (d) 5, 1, 3, 2, 4

23. How many 8 's are there in the given series, which are immediately preceded by a number which does not divide it but followed by a number which divides it? **[2018]**

4 8 2 8 2 8 3 8 5 8 8 5 3 2 8 2 3 8 4 7 1 5 8 3 8 2 8 6 8 8 6

(a) 1 (b) 2
(c) 3 (d) 4

24. How many pairs of letters are there in the word 'CONTEMPORARY' which have as many letters between them in the word as in the English alphabets? **[2018]**

(a) Three (b) Two
(c) Four (d) More than four

25. How many pairs of letters are there in the word DEPARTMENT which have as many letters between them in the word as in the English alphabets? **[2019]**
(a) Three (b) Two
(c) Four (d) More than four

26. How many 6's are there in the given arrangement, each of which is immediately preceded by an odd number and immediately followed by an even number? **[2019]**
8 7 6 7 8 6 7 5 6 7 9 7 6 1 6 7 7 6 8 8 6 9 7 6 8 7
(a) None (b) One
(c) Two (d) Three

27. If the first and second digits from the left of each of the given numbers are interchanged and one is subtracted from the third digit, then what is the sum of digits of the third highest number thus formed? **[2020]**
375 463 567 728 639
(a) 12 (b) 17
(c) 16 (d) 15

28. How many even numbers are there is the given series each of which is immediately preceded by an even number and immediately followed by an odd number? **[2020]**
8 6 7 6 8 9 3 2 7 5 3 4 2 2 3 5 5 2 2 8 1 1 9
(a) 1 (b) 3
(c) 5 (d) 4

29. Arrange the words given below in a meaningful sequence and select the correct option. **[2021]**
1. Town 2. District
3. Street 4. Room
5. Home
(a) 2, 1, 3, 4, 5 (b) 2, 3, 1, 4, 5
(c) 2, 1, 3, 5, 4 (d) 2, 1, 4, 5, 3

30. If the positions of the first and the third digits of each of the following numbers are interchanged, then which of the following will be the third digit of the second highest number formed? **[2021]**
468 945 869 247 369 127
(a) 8 (b) 3
(c) 5 (d) 7

LEVEL 2

1. How many such pairs of letters are there in the word CORPORATE each of which has as many letters in the same sequence between them in the word as in the english alphabet?
(a) None (b) One
(c) Two (d) Three

2. How many letters are there in the following series which are immediately followed by B as well as immediately proceded by Z?
A M B Z A N A A B Z A B
A Z B A P Z A B A Z A B
(a) Nil (b) One
(c) Two (d) Three

3. If the alphabet series is written in the reverse order, which letter will be fifth to the left of the fourteenth letter from the left ?
(a) R (b) I (c) S (d) V

4. If the letters of the word 'BLUE' are arranged according to dictionary, what is the position of the word 'UBLE'?
(a) 19 (b) 20
(c) 21 (d) 22

DIRECTIONS (Qs. 5-6) : *Each of the following questions is based on the following alphabet series.*
A B C D E F G H I J K L M N O P Q R S T U V W X Y Z

5. Which letter is midway between 22nd letter from the left and 21st letter from the right?
   (a) L (b) M
   (c) O (d) N
6. Which letter should be ninth letter to the left of ninth letter from the right, if the first half of the given alphabet is reversed?
   (a) D (b) E
   (c) F (d) I
7. The letters of the word NUMKIPP are in disorder. If they are arranged in proper order, the name of a vegetable is formed. What is the last letter of the word so formed?
   (a) K (b) M
   (c) N (d) P
8. If by arranging the letters of the word NABMODINT, the name of a game is formed, what are the first and the last letters of the word so formed?
   (a) B, T (b) B, N
   (c) N, D (d) M, T

DIRECTIONS (Qs. 9-14) : *Each of the following questions is based on the following alphabet series.*

A B C D E F G H I J K L M N O P Q R S T U V W X Y Z

9. Which letter is eighth to the left on sixteenth letter from the right end?
   (a) B (b) S
   (c) C (d) H
10. Which letter is exactly midway between H and S in the given alphabet?
   (a) No such letter (b) L
   (c) M (d) O
11. If the english alphabet are divided into two equal halves – from A to M and N to Z, which letter in the later half would be corresponding to letter J?
   (a) Q (b) V
   (c) X (d) W
12. Which letter is midway between 22nd letter from the left and 21st letter from the right?
   (a) L (b) M
   (c) O (d) N
13. Which letter should be ninth letter to the left of ninth letter from the right, if the first half of the given alphabet is reversed?
   (a) D (b) E
   (c) F (d) I
14. If the first and the second letters interchange their positions and similarly the third and the fourth letters, the fifth and the sixth letters and so on, which letter will be the seventeenth from your right?
   (a) F (b) H
   (c) I (d) J
15. Which alphabet comes immediately before the sixth alphabet from the right extreme of the given alphabets ?
   (a) E (b) F
   (c) G (d) U
16. If every even letter beginning from B is replaced by odd number starting with 3, which letter/number will be the third to the right of the tenth number/letter counting from your right.
   (a) M (b) S
   (c) 11 (d) 21
17. If the positions of the fifth and twelfth letters of the word GLORIFICATIONS are interchanged, and likewise the positions of the fourth and fourteenth letters, the third and tenth letters, the second and eleventh letters and the first and thirteenth letters are interchanged, which of the following will be the twelfth letter from the right end ?
   (a) I (b) O
   (c) R (d) T
18. Five boys took part in a race. Raj finished before Mohit but behind Garv. Avinash

finished before Sumit but behind Mohit. Who finished the race at second position?
(a) Raj (b) Garv
(c) Mohit (d) Sumit

19. In the English alphabetical series, if A interchanges its position with B, C with D, E with F and so on up to Y and Z, then will be the seventh letter from the right end.
(a) S (b) T
(c) G (d) H

20. How many such 4's are there in the following sequence of numbers, each of which is immediately preceded by a prime number and immediately followed by an odd number?
9 2 4 4 5 4 7 4 2 9 8 7 4 7 3 4 5 2 1 4 1 3 4 4 8 4 7 3 3 9 1 1 4 2 1
(a) 2 (b) 3
(c) 5 (d) 4

21. If it is possible to make only one meaningful word with the second, fifth, seventh and tenth letters of the word ENTHUSIASTIC using each letter only once, then which of the following will be the second letter of the word formed? If no such word can be formed, then give ' Z ' as the answer and if more than one such word can be formed, then give ' Q ' as the answer.
(a) N (b) I
(c) Z (d) Q

22. In a row of 40 boys, Satish is 10th to the right of Rohan and Kewal is 10th to the left of Vilas. If Vilas is twenty-sixth from the left end and there are three boys between Kewal and Satish, then what is the position of Rohan in the row?
(a) 10th from the right end
(b) 10th from the left end
(c) 39th from the right end
(d) Data inadequate

23. If the middle digit of the smallest number is subtracted from the middle digit of the greatest number after adding three to each of the given numbers, then which of the following numbers will be obtained?
534 469 337 264 875
(a) 1 (b) 5
(c) 2 (d) None of these

24. Arrange the given words in the sequence in which they occur in the dictionary and select the correct option.
1. Tissues 2. Tisane
3. Tissular 4. Trial
5. Tricky
(a) 2, 4, 1, 5, 3 (b) 5, 3, 1, 4, 2
(c) 2, 1, 3, 4, 5 (d) 1, 5, 4, 3, 2

25. How many 7's are there in the given arrangement which is immediately followed by a symbol and immediately preceded by N?
M ? N 7 % M @ N 7 # N ? M 7 © 7 N M @ N M 7 # M % N
(a) 5 (b) 4
(c) 3 (d) 2

26. How many such pairs of letters are there in the word MATHEMATICS each of which has as many letters between them in the word as there are in the English alphabet?
(a) Three (b) Four
(c) Two (d) One

27. Arrange the letters to form a meaningful word.

A	C	T	I	R	E	N
1	2	3	4	5	6	7

(a) 2635417 (b) 2653147
(c) 2645137 (d) 2561473

28. In a queue, the position of Rinki from the left is 15th and the position of Meena is 18th from the right. If there are 4 girls in between these two girls, then find the minimum number of girls in the queue.
(a) 26 (b) 27 (c) 35 (d) 36

29. Today is Wednesday. What will be the day after 98 days?
(b) Sunday (b) Monday
(b) Wednesday (d) Friday

30. If all the vowels are removed after reversing the English alphabetical series, then which will be the 8th letter from the right end? **[2018]**
(a) L (b) H
(c) K (d) J

31. Dilip's position from the left in a row of students is 10th and Jagdish's position is 20th from the right. Both of them interchange their positions and Jagdish becomes 23rd from the right. How many students are there in the row? **[2018]**
(a) 33 (b) 44
(c) 32 (d) 42

32. How many 7 's are there in the given number sequence which are immediately preceded by an even number and immediately followed by an odd number? **[2019]**
4 7 5 5 9 4 5 7 6 4 5 9 8 7 5 6 7 6 4 3 2 5 6 7 8
(a) One (b) Two
(c) Three (d) Four

33. In the given arrangement, if all the digits are arranged in descending order from left to right and all the vowels are dropped, then which of the following will be 5th to the right of 12th element from the right end? **[2019]**
A E C B % 7 D $ E B 5 C ? 3 D E 9 @ 2 #
(a) ? (b) 5
(c) C (d) 7

34. In the given Venn diagram, triangle represents the students who like cricket, rectangle represents the students who like football and circle represents the students who like swimming. **[2019]**

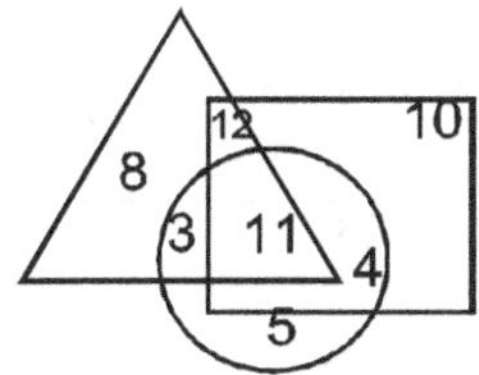

Which of the following numbers represents the students who like swimming and football but not cricket?
(a) 3 (b) 5
(c) 4 (d) 11

35. How many 6's are there in the given number arrangement each of which are immediately preceded by an even number and immediately followed by 9? **[2020]**
9 6 2 6 9 4 7 6 2 5 6 4 6 7 8 3 2 6 9 2 2 6 5 6 2
(a) 3 (b) 2
(c) 4 (d) 5

36. Each vowel in the word 'GAMBLE' is substituted by the next letter of the English alphabet and each consonant is substituted by the previous letter of the English alphabet. If new letters are then rearranged in alphabetical order, then which of the following will be the fourth letter from the right end. **[2020]**
(a) B (b) A
(c) L (d) F

37. How many such symbols are there in the given arrangement each of which is immediately preceded by a letter and immediately followed by a number? **[2021]**
P @ R 1 A × 2 3 B P $ 7 Q / 9 P + 6 C D – E F ÷ 8 5
(a) 4 (b) 3
(c) 5 (d) 6

38. If it is possible to make only one meaningful English word with 1st, 2nd, 5th and 8th letters of the word TECHNOLOGY (using each letter only once), then first letter of the word formed would be the answer. If more than one such word can be formed, then give Z as the answer and if no such word can be formed, then give Y as the answer. **[2021]**
(a) N (b) Y
(c) Z (d) T

39. Some students are sitting in a row facing North. Akhil is sitting 15th from the left end. Vivek is sitting 12th to the right of Akhil. If

Vivek's position is 4th from the right end, then how many students are sitting in that row? **[2021]**
(a) 18 (b) 20
(c) 25 (d) 30

40. How many such symbols are there in the given arrangement each of which is immediately preceded by a number and immediately followed by a letter? **[2021]**
5 8 # B F L ? 4 * M 7 9 G H 2 M 3 + 8 4 ? $ P Q 6 R 7 * H T
(a) 2 (b) 3
(c) 4 (d) 5

41. In the following question, two rows of numbers are given. The resultant number in each row is to be worked out separately based on the following rules and the question below the rows of numbers is to be answered. The operations on numbers progress from left to right. **[2021]**
Rules:
(i) If an odd number is followed by an even number, then the even number is subtracted from the odd number.
(ii) If an even number is followed by an odd number, then they are to be added.
(iii) If a two digit even number is followed by another two digit even number, then they are to be added.
(iv) If two digit even number is followed by single digit even number, then the two digit even number is divided by single digit even number.
16 14 2
8 7 12
What is the quotient when the resultant of first row is divided by the resultant of second row? **[2021]**
(a) 6 (b) 5
(c) 4 (d) 2

42. How many 3's are there in the given sequence, each of which is immediately preceded by an odd digit but not immediately followed by an even digit? **[2022]**
4 5 8 3 4 6 2 5 3 7 9 8 1 0 2 3 4 9 6 8 1 3 5 5
(a) None (b) One
(c) Two (d) Three

43. Prem is 7 ranks ahead of Raj in a class of 39. If Raj's rank is seventeenth from the last, then what is Prem's rank from the start? **[2022]**
(a) 14th (b) 15th (c) 16th (d) 17th

ANSWER KEY																			
LEVEL-1																			
1	(d)	**4**	(b)	**7**	(c)	**10**	(a)	**13**	(d)	**16**	(b)	**19**	(c)	**22**	(d)	**25**	(d)	**28**	(d)
2	(d)	**5**	(a)	**8**	(c)	**11**	(c)	**14**	(d)	**17**	(b)	**20**	(c)	**23**	(c)	**26**	(c)	**29**	(c)
3	(d)	**6**	(b)	**9**	(c)	**12**	(d)	**15**	(b)	**18**	(a)	**21**	(b)	**24**	(d)	**27**	(a)	**30**	(b)
LEVEL-2																			
1	(c)	**6**	(b)	**11**	(d)	**16**	(d)	**21**	(a)	**26**	(c)	**31**	(c)	**36**	(d)	**41**	(b)		
2	(d)	**7**	(c)	**12**	(d)	**17**	(d)	**22**	(b)	**27**	(b)	**32**	(b)	**37**	(c)	**42**	(c)		
3	(a)	**8**	(b)	**13**	(b)	**18**	(a)	**23**	(c)	**28**	(b)	**33**	(a)	**38**	(c)	**43**	(c)		
4	(b)	**9**	(c)	**14**	(c)	**19**	(a)	**24**	(c)	**29**	(c)	**34**	(c)	**39**	(d)				
5	(d)	**10**	(a)	**15**	(a)	**20**	(b)	**25**	(d)	**30**	(c)	**35**	(b)	**40**	(b)				

CHAPTER 7 Logical Venn Diagrams

The best method of solving the problems based on inference or deduction is Venn diagram.

Venn diagram is a way representing sets pictorially.

Various cases of Venn diagram

Case I :

An object is called a subset of another object, if the former is a part of the latter and such relation is shown by two concentric circles.

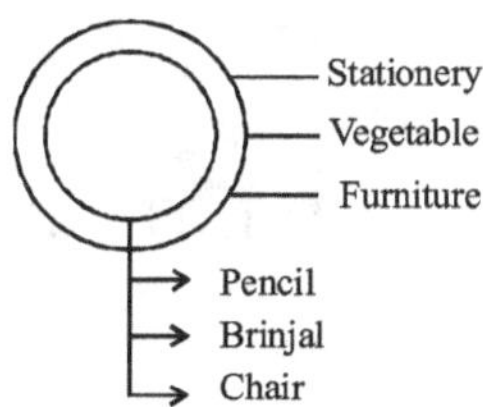

(i) Pencil, Stationery

(ii) Brinjal, Vegetable

(iii) Chair, Furniture It is very clear from the above relationship that one object is a part of the other, and hence all such relationships can be represented by the figure shown.

Case II :

An object is said to have an intersection with another object that share some things in common.

(i) Surgeon, Males

(ii) Politicians, Indian

(iii) Educated, Unemployed

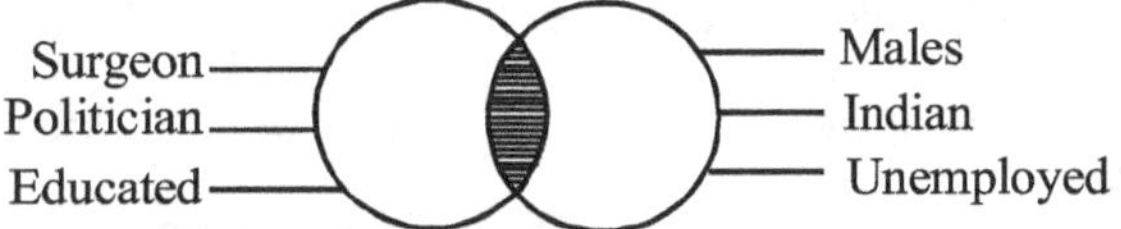

All the three relationships given above have something in common as some surgeons can be male and some female, some politicians may be Indian and some may belong to other countries, educated may be employed and unemployed as well and all the three relationships can be represented by the figure shown.

Case III :

Two objects are said to be disjoint when neither one is subset of another and nor do they share anything in common. In other words, totally unrelated objects fall under this type of relationship.

(i) Furniture, Car (ii) Copy, Cloth

(iii) Tool, Shirt

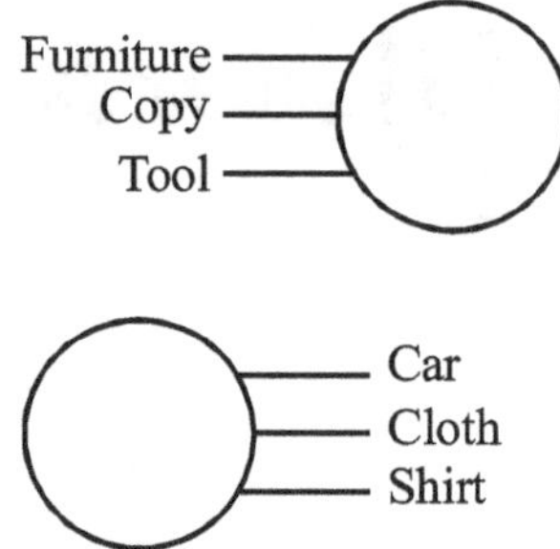

It is clear from the above relationships that both the objects are unrelated to each other, and hence can be represented diagrammatically as shown in figure above.

From the above discussion we observe that representation of the relationship between two objects is not typical if students follow the above points. But representation of three objects diagrammatically pose slight problems before the students.

ANALYTICAL METHOD :

Try to understand these type of questions using analytical method.

A statement always has a subject and a predicate:

All politicians are liars.

(subject) (predicate)

Basically, there are four types of sentences.

A - type ⇒ All politicians are liars.

I-type ⇒ Some politicians are liars

O-type ⇒ Some politicians are not liars

E-type ⇒ No politicians are liars

Conclusions can be drawn by taking two of the above statements together. The rules of conclusion are :

A + A = A A + E = E I + A = I

I + E = O E + A = O* E + I = O*

Conclusion can only be drawn from the two statements if the predicate of the first statement is the subject of the second statement. The common term disappears in the conclusion and it consists of subject of the first statement and predicate of the second statement. For examples

A + A = A

(i) All boys are girls. (ii) All girls are healthy

Conclusion : All boys are healthy.

A + E = E

(i) All boys are girls. (ii)No girls are healthy

Conclusion : No boys are healthy.

I + A = I

(i) Some boys are girls. (ii) All girls are healthy

Conclusion : Some boys are healthy.

I + E = O

(i) Some boys are girls. (ii) No girls are healthy

Conclusion : Some boys are not healthy.

E + A = O*

(i) No boys are girls. (ii)All girls are healthy

Conclusion : Some healthy are not boys.

I + I = O*

(i) No boys are girls. (ii)Some girls are healthy

Conclusion : Some healthy are not boys.

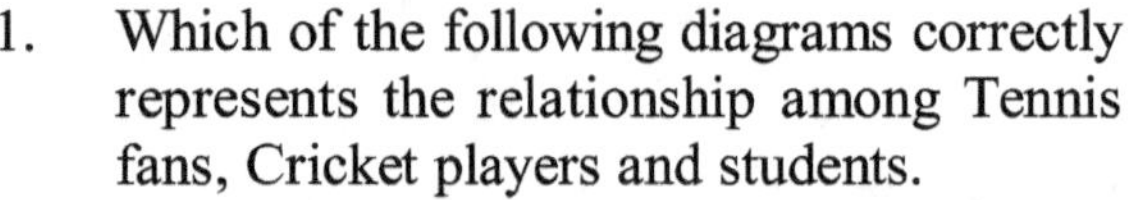

1. Which of the following diagrams correctly represents the relationship among Tennis fans, Cricket players and students.

(a)  (b) 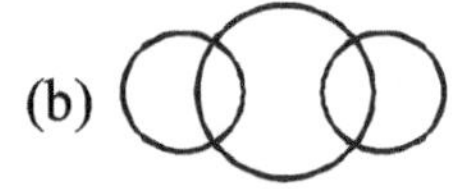

(c) 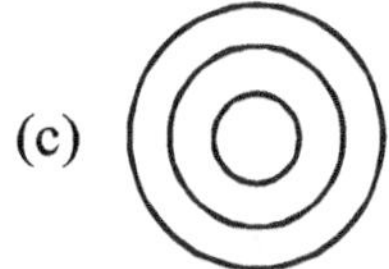 (d) 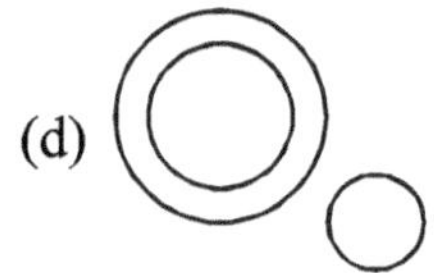

2. In a dinner party both fish and meat were served. Some took only fish and some only meat. There were some vegetarians who did not accept either. The rest accepted both fish and meat. Which of the following logic diagrams correctly reflects this situations ?

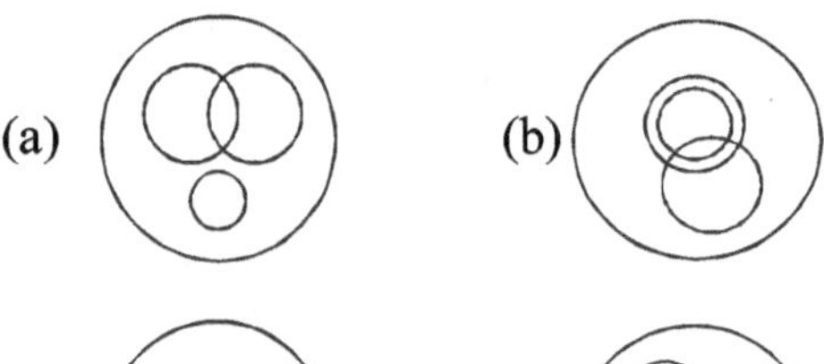

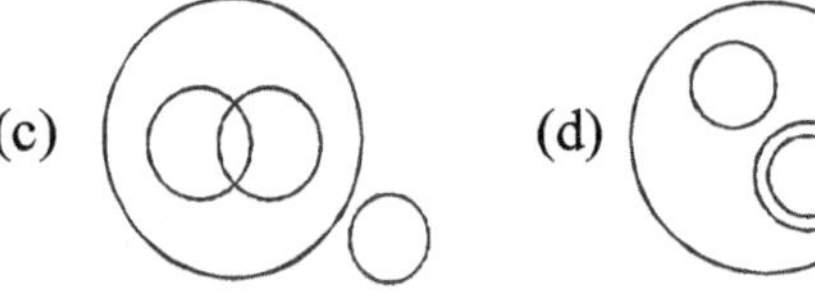

DIRECTIONS (Qs. 3-6) : *Refer to the following Venn diagram :*

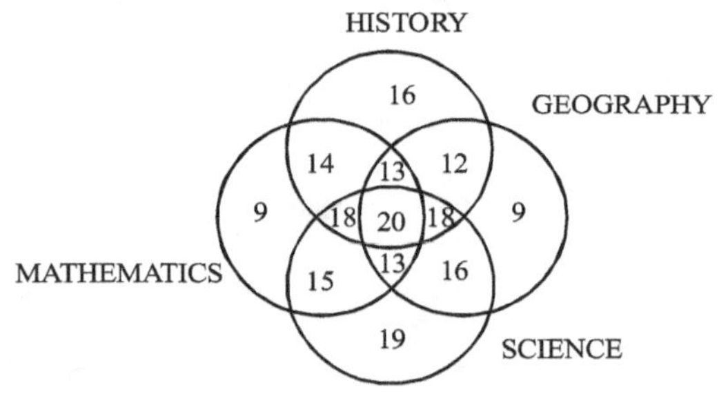

3. The number of students who took any three of the above subjects was
   (a) 62 (b) 63
   (c) 64 (d) 66
4. The number of students in total, who took History or Mathematics or Science, was
   (a) 183 (b) 190
   (c) 424 (d) 430
5. The number of students who took both History and Geography among other subjects was
   (a) 62 (b) 63
   (c) 65 (d) 66
6. Which subject was taken by the largest number of students?
   (a) Mathematics (b) Science
   (c) Geography (d) History
7. In a class of 46 students, 18 played football, 17 played cricket including 6 who played football. 16 students played hockey including 4 who played cricket, but not football. Five students played carrom but no outdoor games. Which of the following figure represents these facts ?

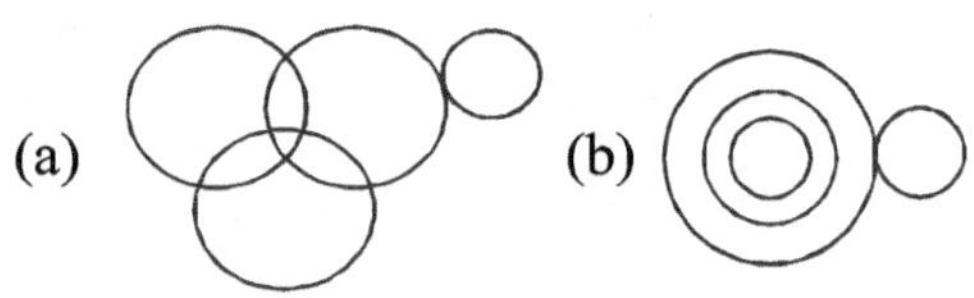

(c) 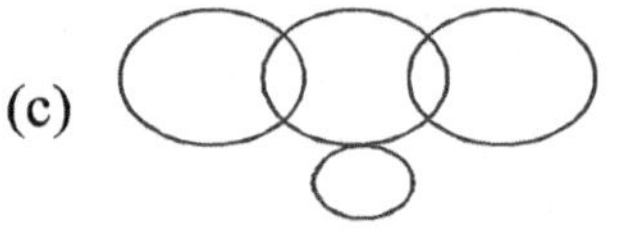

(d) 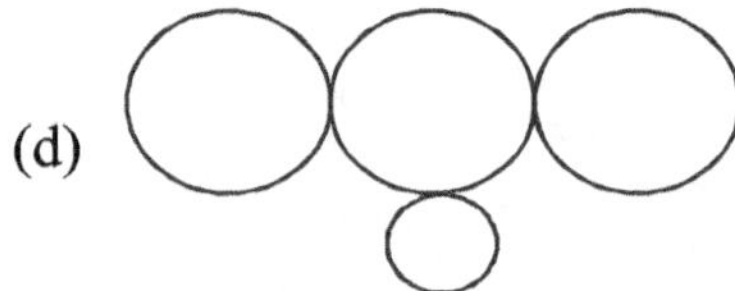

DIRECTIONS (Qs. 8– 10) : *In the diagram given below △ big triangle represents writer, □ rectangle represents poet, △small triangle represents dramatician and ○circle represents essay writer. Study the diagram and choose the correct answers of the given questions.*

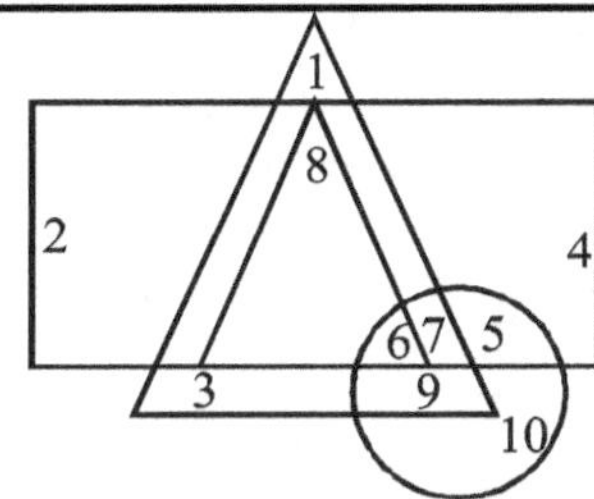

8. Which number denotes the poets who are essay writer, dramatician and writer also ?
   (a) 7 (b) 5
   (c) 6 (d) 8
9. Which numbers only denotes writers who are not poets neither dramatician nor essay writer?
   (a) 2 & 3 (b) 1 & 3
   (c) 4 & 5 (d) 8 & 6
10. Which numbers only denotes, poets who are not writers neither essay writer nor dramatician?
    (a) 2 & 4 (b) 8 & 3
    (c) 7 & 9 (d) 5 & 1
11. Which of the following Venn diagrams correctly represents female, mother and doctor?

    (a) 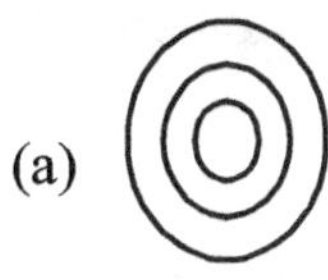 (b) 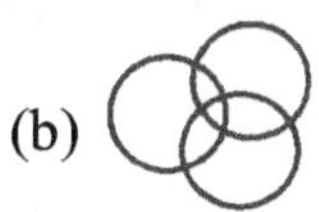

    (c) 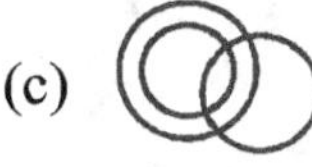 (d) 

12. Which diagram represents language, English and Hindi?

    (a) (b) (c) (d)

13. Choose the correct alternative that represents the relationship among illiterates, poor people and unemployed.

    (a)  (b) 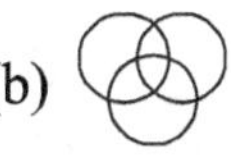

    (c) (d) 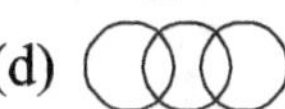

14. Which of the following Venn diagrams best represents the relationship amongst, "Polygons, Quadrilaterals and Triangles"?

    (a) 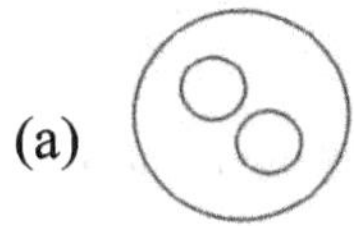 (b) 

    (c) 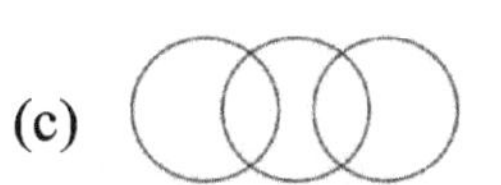 (d) 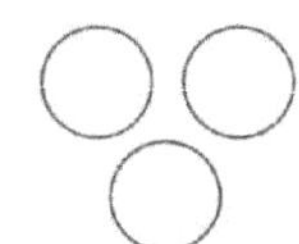

15. Which of the following Venn diagrams best depicts the relationship amongst, 'India, Asia and Australia'?

    (a) 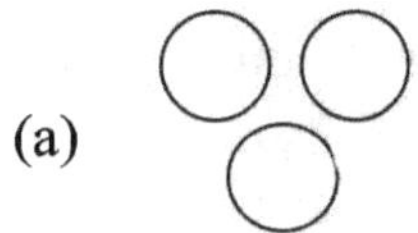 (b) 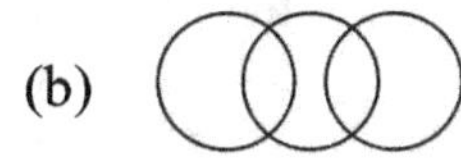

    (c) 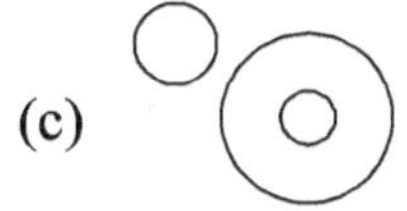 (d) 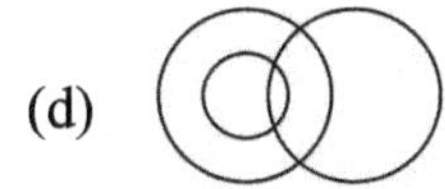

16. Which of the following Venn diagrams best represents the relationship amongst, "Teachers, Youths and Females"?

    (a) 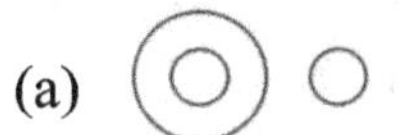 (b) 

    (c) 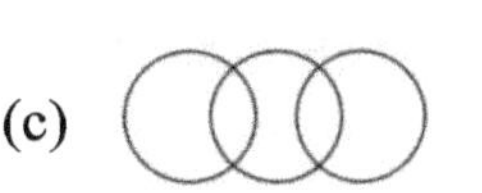 (d) 

17. Which of the following Venn diagrams best represents the relationship amongst, "Mobile phones, Washing machines and Electronic devices"?

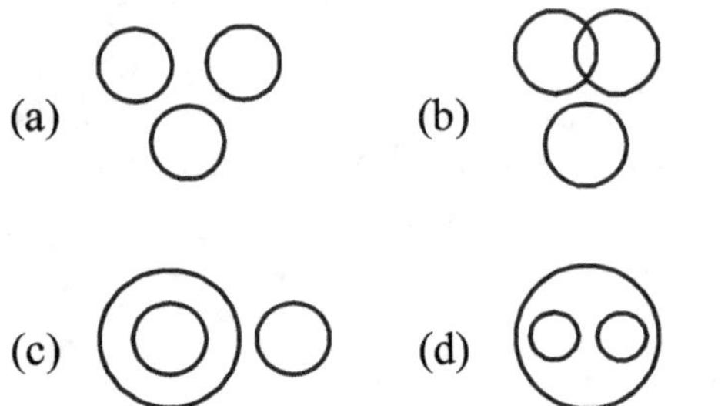

18. Which of the following Venn diagrams best represents the relationship amongst, "Liquid, Sand and Water"?

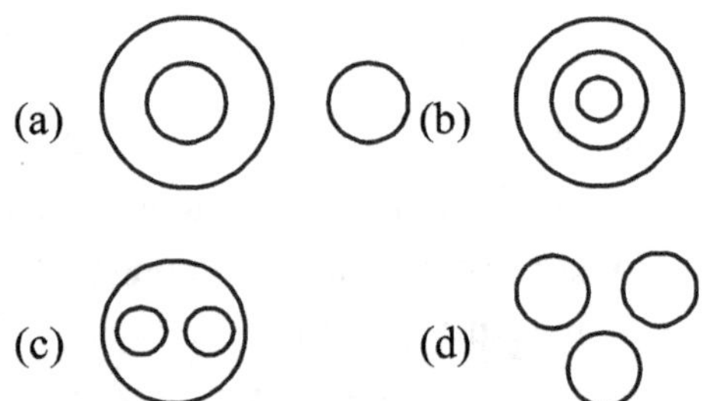

19. Which of the following Venn diagrams best represents the relationship amongst, "Paper, Stationery, Pen"?

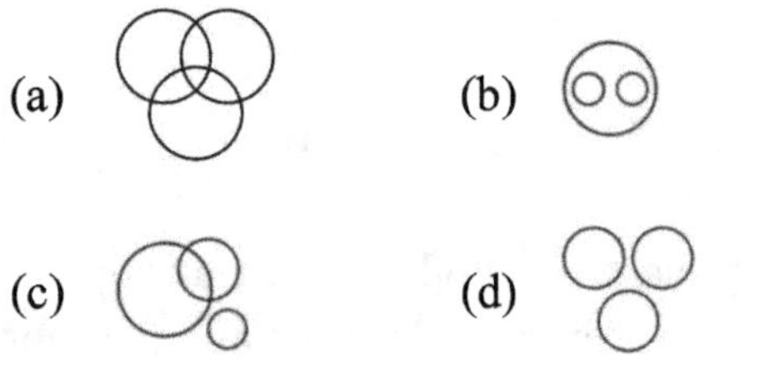

20. Which of the following Venn diagrams best represents the relationship amongst, "Stationery, Pen, Scale"?

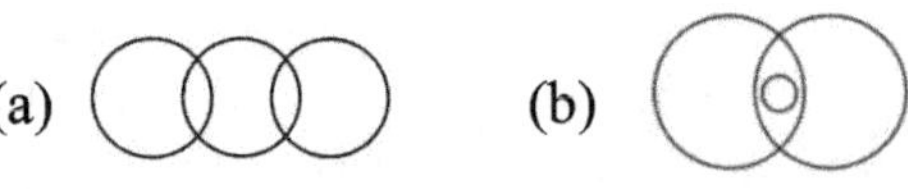

21. Which of the following Venn diagrams best represents the relationship amongst, "Cars, Houses and Vehicles" ?

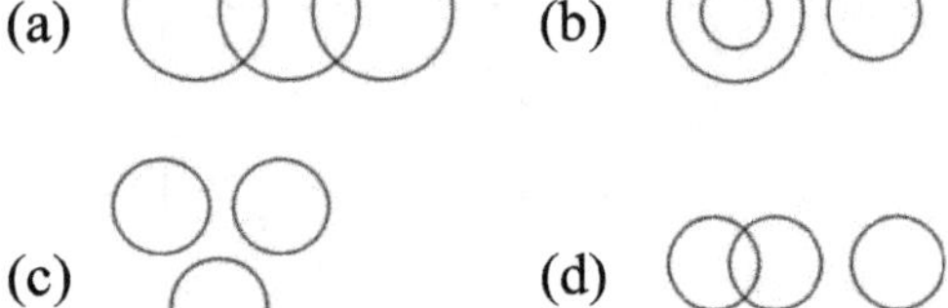

22. Which of the following Venn diagrams best represents the relationship amongst, "Mobile phones, Ceiling fans and Electronic devices"? **[2020]**

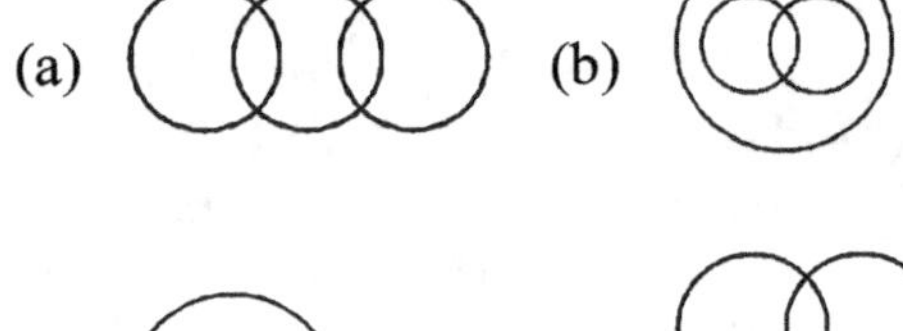

23. Which of the following Venn diagrams best represents the relationship amongst, "Women, Engineers and Mothers"? **[2021]**

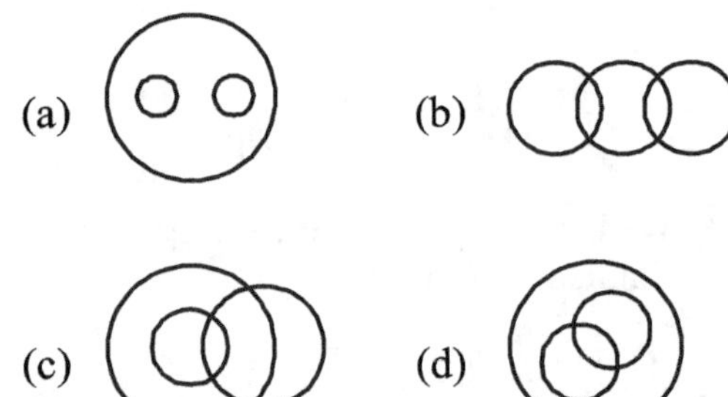

LEVEL 2

DIRECTIONS (Qs. 1-5) : *In the following figure, rectangle, square, circle and triangle represent the regions of wheat, gram, maize and rice cultivation respectively. On the basis of the above figure, answer the following questions.*

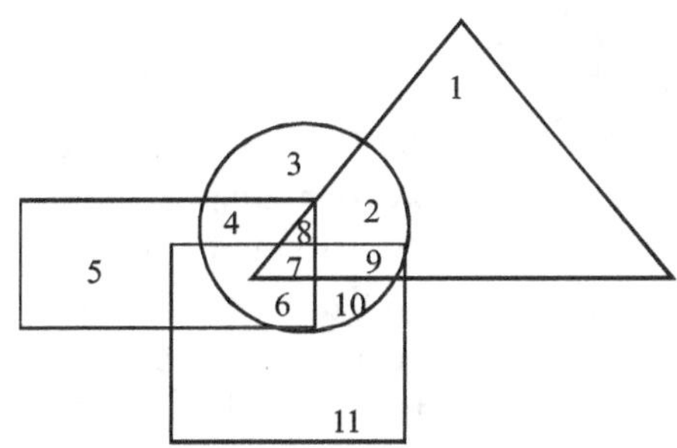

1. Which area is cultivated by all the four commodities ?
   (a) 7 (b) 8
   (c) 9 (d) 2
2. Which area is cultivated by wheat and maize only?
   (a) 8 (b) 6
   (c) 5 (d) 4
3. Which area is cultivated by rice only ?
   (a) 5 (b) 1
   (c) 2 (d) 11
4. Which area is cultivated by maize only ?
   (a) 10 (b) 2
   (c) 3 (d) 4
5. Which area is cultivated by rice and maize and nothing else?
   (a) 9 (b) 8
   (c) 2 (d) 7
6. In the figure, the circle represents youth, the triangle represents footballers and the rectangle represents athletes. Which letter(s) represent(s) athletes among youths who are not footballers?

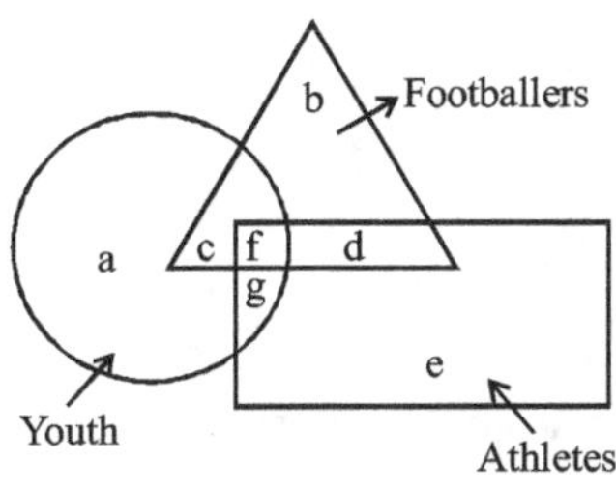

   (a) g (b) g and c
   (c) f (d) f and d
7. Four diagrams marked A, B, C and D are given below. The one that best illustrates the relationship among three given classes: Women, Teachers, Doctors

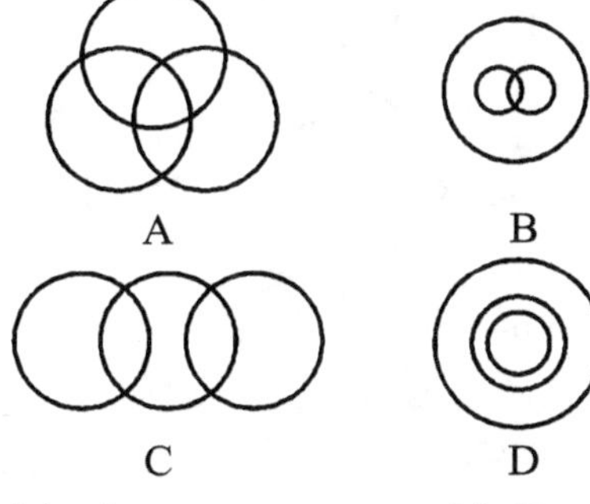

   (a) A (b) B
   (c) C (d) D
8. Which of the following diagrams indicates the best relation among men, fathers and teachers?

(a)  (b) 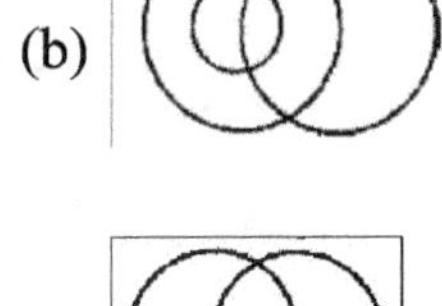

(c) 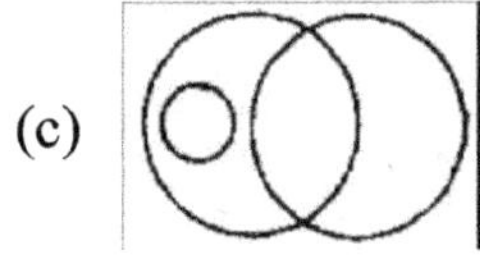 (d) 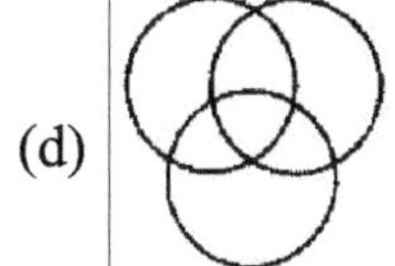

9. Study the given Venn diagram carefully and answer the following question.

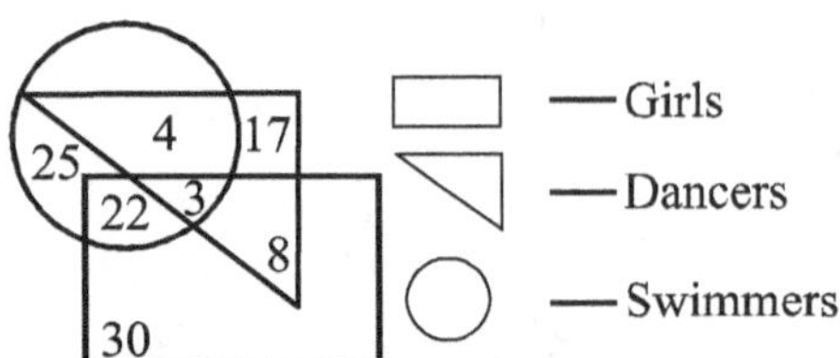

Which of the following numbers represents girls who are dancers but not swimmers?

(a) 3 (b) 22
(c) 8 (d) 4

10. Which of the following elements satisfies the given Venn diagram?

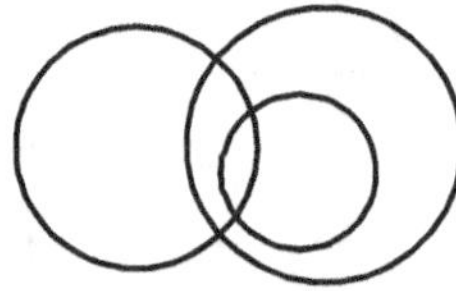

(a) Stationery items, Pen, Pencil
(b) Father, Mother, Male
(c) Football player, Cricket player, Student
(d) Sisters, Teachers, Females

11. Which of the following Venn diagrams best represents the relationship amongst, 'Triangles, Quadrilaterals and Rectangles?

(a) 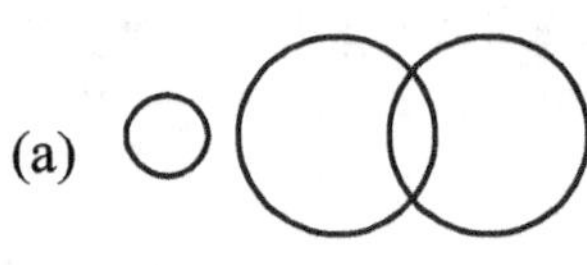

(b) 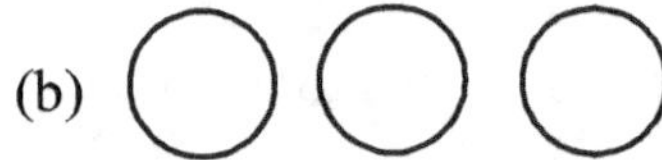

(c) 

(d) 

12. Study the given Venn diagram carefully.

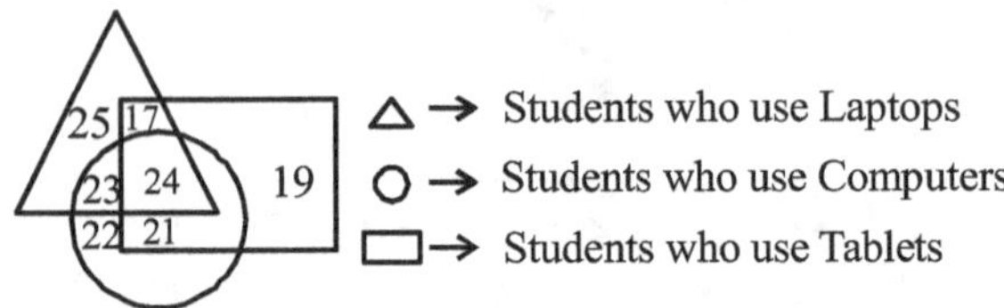

Which of the following number will represent the number of students using Laptops, Computers and Tablets for study?

(a) 24 (b) 23
(c) 22 (d) 21

13. In the given question, two statements are followed by two conclusions numbered I and II. You have to consider the given statements to be true even if they seem to be at variance from the commonly known facts. Then decide which of the given conclusions logically follow from the given two statements, disregarding the commonly known facts. **[2018]**

Statements : All books are clocks.
All clocks are pens.

Conclusions: I. All books are pens.
II. Some pens are books.

(a) Only I (b) Only II
(c) Both I and II (d) Neither I nor II

14. Study the given Venn diagram and identify the number representing youth who are employed but not educated. **[2018]**

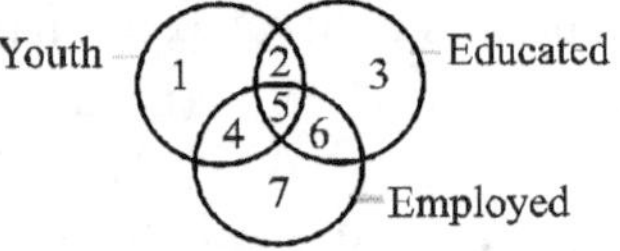

(a) 4 only (b) 5, 6
(c) 1, 4, 7 (d) 4, 7

15. In the question below, two statements followed by two conclusions numbered I and II are given. You have to take the two given statements to be true even if they seem to be at variance of commonly known facts and decide which of the conclusion(s)

logically follow(s) from the two given statements, disregarding commonly known facts. **[2018]**

Statements : Some books are papers.
Some papers are notebooks.

Conclusions :

I. Some papers are books.
II. Some notebooks are papers.

(a) Only conclusion I follows
(b) Only conclusion II follows
(c) Neither I nor II follows
(d) Both I and II follow

16. In the given Venn diagram, circle represents the boy child, triangle represents the girl child and square represents twin child born in a day in a particular hospital. Which of the following number represents the twin girl child born in a day in that hospital? **[2021]**

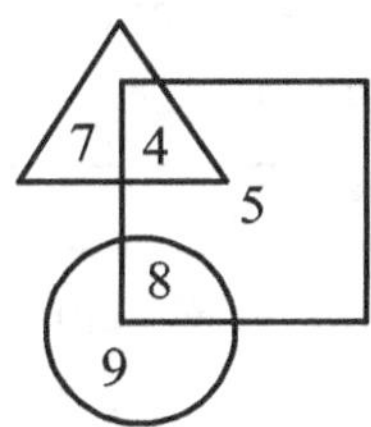

(a) 8
(b) 4
(c) 9
(d) 5

17. In the given Venn diagram, square represents persons who like banana, triangle represents persons who like strawberry and circle represents persons who like apple. **[2022]**

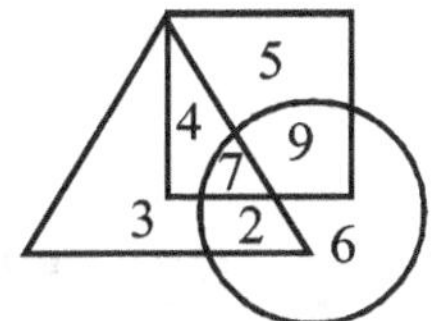

How many persons like banana and strawberry but not apple?

(a) 4
(b) 5
(c) 9
(d) 2

ANSWER KEY																			
LEVEL-1																			
1	(a)	**4**	(a)	**7**	(c)	**10**	(a)	**13**	(b)	**16**	(d)	**19**	(b)	**22**	(c)				
2	(a)	**5**	(b)	**8**	(c)	**11**	(c)	**14**	(a)	**17**	(d)	**20**	(d)	**23**	(c)				
3	(a)	**6**	(b)	**9**	(b)	**12**	(a)	**15**	(c)	**18**	(a)	**21**	(b)						
LEVEL-2																			
1	(a)	**2**	(d)	**3**	(b)	**4**	(c)	**5**	(c)	**6**	(a)	**7**	(c)	**8**	(b)	**9**	(c)	**10**	(d)
11	(c)	**12**	(a)	**13**	(c)	**14**	(a)	**15**	(d)	**16**	(b)	**17**	(c)						

CHAPTER

Mathematical Operations

MATHEMATICAL OPERATIONS

This section deals with questions on simple mathematical operations. There are four fundamental operations, namely :

Additions i.e, + ; Subtraction i.e, – ;

Multiplication i.e, × ; and Division i.e. , ÷

There are also statements such as Less than i.e. <, greater than i.e. >, and equal to i.e =, not equal to i.e ≠ , etc.

Such operations are represented by symbols different from the usual ones. The questions involving these operations are coded using artificial symbols. The candidate has to make a substitution of the real signs and solve the equation accordingly.

We always, while solving a mathematical expression, proceed according to the rule B O D M A S.

i.e, B for Brackets ; O for ' of (literally multiplication),

D for division ; M for multiplication , A for additions and S for subtraction in sequence.

DIFFERENT TYPES OF PROBLEMS

TYPE 1 : Problem-solving By Substitution

In this type, you are provided with substitutes for various mathematical symbols or numbers. Followed by a question involving calculation of an expression or choosing the correct/ incorrect equations. The candidate is required to put in the real signs or numerals in the given equation and then solve the questions as required.

ILLUSTRATION 1:

If L stands for +, M stands for –, N stands for ×, P stands for ÷, then 14 N 10 L 42 P 2 M 8 = ?

(a) 153 (b) 216

(c) 248 (d) 251

Sol. **(a)** Using the proper signs, we get

Given expression

$= 14 \times 10 + 42 \div 2 - 8 = 14 \times 10 + 21 - 8$

$= 140 + 21 - 8 = 161 - 8 = 153.$

DIRECTIONS (ILLUSTRATION 2) : In each of the following examples which one of the four interchanges in signs and numbers would make the given equation correct ?

ILLUSTRATION 2:

$6 \times 4 + 2 = 16$

(a) + and ×, 2 and 4 (b) + and ×, 2 and 6

(c) + and ×, 4 and 6 (d) None of these

***Sol.* (c)** On interchanging + & × and 4 and 6, we get the equation as

$4 + 6 \times 2 = 16$ or $4 + 12 = 16$ or $16 = 16$, which is true

MATHEMATICAL LOGIC

Consider the statement "5 is greater than 3".

Now consider which of the following statements are true and which are false.

" 5 is not greater than 3 " (False)

" 5 is equal to 3 " (False)

" 5 is less than 3 " (False)

" 5 is not equal to 3" (True)

" 5 is not less than 3 " (True)

In general, between any two numbers a and b, only one of the following relations can exist at a time

$a > b$ or $a < b$

or $a = b$

If $a > b$, then $a \nless b$ and $a \neq b$

If $a < b$, then $a \ngtr b$ and $a \neq b$

If $a = b$, then $a \ngtr b$ and $a \nless b$

DIRECTIONS (ILLUSTRATION 3-4): *Let the following symbols denote some relationships between numbers.*

O = greater than   ϕ = not greater than

+ = equal to   Δ = not equal to

÷ = less than   x = not less than

In the examples below, find the correct answer.

ILLUSTRATION 3:

If p ÷ q O r, it is possible that

(a) p ϕ q ÷ r (b) p ϕ q × r

(c) p + q × r (d) p Δ q ϕ r

Sol. (b) ÷ (less than ⇒ Δ (Not equal to or ϕ (not greater than)

O (greater than) ⇒ Δ (Not equal to) or × (not less than)

For p, and q, option (a), (b), (d) are possible.

For q and r, options (b), (c) are possible.

Hence the answer is (b)

ILLUSTRATION 4:

If p Δ q O r, it is possible that

(a) p × q × r (b) p × q ÷ r

(c) P ÷ q ϕ r (d) p ϕ q ϕ r

***Sol.* (a)** Δ = not equal to

Hence, Δ ⇒ O (greater than)

or Δ ⇒ ÷ (Less than)

Δ ⇒ ϕ (not greater than)

or Δ ⇒ × (not less than)

Similarly, O ⇒ Δ and O ⇒ ×

hence P Δ q ⇒ p O q or p ÷ q or p ϕ q or p × q

and q O r ⇒ q Δ r or q × r

All four options are possible so far as p and q are concerned.

Between q and r, only the first is correct.

TYPE II

DIRECTIONS (ILLUSTRATION 5-6) : *In each of the following questions, an equation becomes incorrect due to the interchange of* *two signs. One of the four alternatives, specifies the interchange of sign in the equations, which when made, will make the equation correct. Find the correct alternative.*

ILLUSTRATION 5:

$16 - 8 \div 4 + 5 \times 2 = 8$

(a) $\div$ and $\times$ (b) $-$ and $\div$

(c) $\div$ and $+$ (d) $-$ and $+$

***Sol.* (b)** On interchanging $-$ and $\div$ we get :

Given expression $= 16 \div 8 - 4 + 5 \times 2$
$= 2 - 4 + 10 = 8$

ILLUSTRATION 6:

$121 \div 11 - 3 \times 13 + 2 = 22$

(a) $-$ and $\times$ (b) $-$ and $\div$

(c) $\div$ and $-$ (d) $+$ and $-$

***Sol.* (a)** On interchanging $-$ and $\times$ we get

Given expression $= 121 \div 11 \times 3 - 13 + 2$

$= \frac{121}{11} \times 3 - 13 + 2 = 11 \times 3 - 13 + 2 = 22$

TYPE III

DIRECTION (ILLUSTRATION 7) : *In the following question, three statements of numbers following same rules are given. Find the rule and accordingly find the value of the number ?*

ILLUSTRATION 7:

If $32 \times 41 = 15$; $51 \times 34 = 47$; $41 \times 52 = 37$, then $87 \times 53 = ?$

(a) 68 (b) 64

(c) 85 (d) 18

Sol. (d) The logic is $32 \times 41 = (3 - 2)(4 + 1) = 15$;

$51 \times 34 = (5 - 1)(3 + 4) = 47$ etc.

$\therefore 87 \times 53 = (8 - 7)(5 + 3) = 18$

DIRECTIONS (ILLUSTRATION 8) : *In each of the following questions, three statements of numbers following same rules are given. Find the rule and accordingly find the value of the number.*

ILLUSTRATION 8:

If $2 \times 1 = 81$; $3 \times 2 = 278$; $2 \times 5 = 8125$, then $1 \times 3 =$

(a) 127 (b) 271

(c) 126 (d) 129

Sol. (a) The rule is $a \times b = a^3 b^3$

$2 \times 1 = 2^3 1^3 = 81$ etc. So, $1 \times 3 = 1^3 3^3 = 127$

LEVEL 1

1. In the following questions which one of the four interchanges in signs and numbers would make the given equation correct ?
   $(3 \div 4) + 2 = 2$
   (a) + and ÷, 2 and 3
   (b) + and ÷, 2 and 4
   (c) + and ÷, 3 and 4
   (d) No interchanges, 3 and 4
2. If A stands for +, B stands for –, C stands for ×, then what is the value of (10 C4) + (4 C 4) B 6 = ?
   (a) 60 (b) 56
   (c) 50 (d) 20

DIRECTIONS (Qs. 3–4) : *In each of the following questions, three statements of numbers following same rules are given. Find the rule and accordingly find the value of the number?*

3. If $84 \oplus 72 = 45; 63 \oplus 41 = 33, 25 \oplus 52 = 33,$ then $94 \oplus 82 = ?$
   (a) 45 (b) 59
   (c) 56 (d) 65
4. If $5 \times 9 = 144$; $7 \times 8 = 151$: $4 \times 6 = 102$, then $2 \times 5 = ?$
   (a) 73 (b) 77
   (c) 37 (d) 97
5. If × stands for' addition', < for 'substraction', + stands for 'division', > for 'multiplication', – stands for 'equal to', ÷ for 'greater than' and = stands for 'less than', then which of the following is true ?
   (a) $3 \times 2 < 4 \div 16 > 2 + 4$
   (b) $5 > 2 + 2 = 10 < 4 \times 2$
   (c) $3 \times 4 > 2 - 9 + 3 < 3$
   (d) $5 \times 3 < 7 \div 8 + 4 \times 1$
6. Of '×' Stands for ' addition' '<' for subtraction' '+' for division' > for multiplication' '–' for equal to' '+' for ' greater than' and '=' for ' less than' state which of the following is true. ?
   (a) $3 \times 4 > 2 - 9 + 3 < 3$
   (b) $5 \times 3 < 7 \div 8 + 4 \times 1$
   (c) $5 > 2 + 2 = 10 < 4 \times 8$
   (d) $3 \times 2 < 4 \div 16 > 2 + 4$
7. If the given interchanges namely : signs + and ÷ and numbers 2 and 4 are made in signs and numbers, which one of the following four equations would be correct ?
   (a) $2 + 4 \div 3 = 3$ (b) $4 + 2 \div 6 = 1.5$
   (c) $4 \div 2 + 3 = 4$ (d) $2 + 4 \div 6 = 8.$
8. It being given that × denotes ' greater than', ϕ denote ' equal to', < denotes ' not less than', $\perp$ denotes 'not equal to, Δ denotes ' less than' and + denotes ' not greater than', choose the correct statement from the following
   If $a \times b \Delta c$, it follows that
   (a) $a \phi c \Delta b$ (b) $b < a \times c$
   (c) $a < b + c$ (d) $b < a \phi c$
9. If $A + B = C + D$ and $A + D > B + C$, then which one of the following is definitely wrong >
   (a) $A > B$ (b) $A < C$
   (c) $C > D$ (d) $B > D$
10. If $3 + 5 = 16$; $7 + 9 = 64$; $10 + 12 = 121$, then $11 + 3 = ?$
    (a) 56 (b) 48
    (c) 49 (d) 196
11. If '+' stands for multiplication, '–' stands for division, 'X' stands for subtraction and '÷' stands for addition then
    $\frac{(36 \times 4) - 8 \times 4}{4 + 8 \times 2 + 16 \div 1}$. Which of the interchange of sign/signs would make the equations correct?
    (a) 0 (b) 8
    (c) 12 (d) 16

DIRECTIONS (Qs. 12-14) : *In the following questions some relations are written by particular indicators as shown below:*

O	=	Greater than
+	=	Equal to
Δ	=	Not equal to
∅	=	Not greater than
×	=	Not less than
□	=	Less than

12. If p Δ q O r, it is possible that :
    (a) p × q × r (b) p × q □ r
    (c) p □ q ∅ r (d) p ∅ q ∅ r
13. If p □ q Δ r, it is not possible that :
    (a) p Δ q ∅ r (b) p □ q Δ r
    (c) p ∅ q □ r (d) p + q × r
14. If p × q ∅ r, it is not possible that :
    (a) p Δ q □ r (b) p × q + r
    (c) p Δ q O r (d) p O q + r
15. Which one of the following equations is NOT meaningful by substituting the set of given mathematical signs (÷, + =, ×) sequentially in the given equations?
    (a) 80 ÷ 5 + 4 = 5 × 4
    (b) 30 ÷ 2 + 5 = 2 × 10
    (c) 40 ÷ 10 + 4 = 10× 6
    (d) 60 ÷ 3 + 10 = 6 × 5
16. If '–' stand for division, '+' for multiplication, '÷' for subtraction and '×' for addition, which one of the following equation is correct?
    (a) 6 ÷ 20 × 12 + 7 – 1 = 70
    (b) 6 + 12 – 12 ÷ 7 × 1 = 62
    (c) 6 – 20 ÷ 12 × 7 + 1 = 57
    (d) 6 + 20 – 12 ÷ 7 + 1 = 38
17. If 54 + 43 = 2
    60 + 51 = 10
    Then 62 + 72 = ?
    (a) 30 (b) 18
    (c) 20 (d) 9
18. If M denotes ÷, L denotes –, P denotes × and J denotes +, then find the value of 25 M 5 L 10 P 2 J 15.
    (a) 10 (b) 0
    (c) 5 (d) 15
19. If 'P' denotes '×', 'Q' denotes '+', 'R' denotes '÷' and 'S' denotes '–', then find the value of 34 P 2 Q 14 R 7 S 8.
    (a) 64 (b) 63
    (c) 62 (d) 60
20. If L stand for '+', M stands for '–', N stands for '×' and P stands for '÷', then value of 14 N 10 L p 2 M 8 is
    (a) 90 (b) 103
    (c) 153 (d) 212
21. If 'K' denotes '×', 'B' denotes '÷', 'T' denotes '–' and 'M' denotes '+', then 40 B 8 T 6 M 3 K 4 = ?
    (a) 19 (b) 11
    (c) " 31 (d) 23
22. If '@' denotes '×', '$' denotes '÷', '©' denotes '–' and '£' denotes '+', then find the value of 52 © 4 @ 5 £ 8 $ 2.
    (a) 36 (b) 30
    (c) " 36 (d) " 28
23. If '÷' stands for 'subtraction', '×' stands for 'addition', '–' stands for 'division' and '+' stands for 'multiplication', then what is the value of 2 + 14 – 4 ÷ 11 × 5 ?
    (a) 5 (b) 8 (c) 1 (d) 4
24. If 'S' denotes '÷', 'T' denotes '×', 'U' denotes '+' and 'V' denotes '–', then find the value of 16 U 12 S 4 T 9 V 3.
    (a) 36 (b) 38 (c) 40 (d) 42
25. Which of the following interchanges in signs would make the given equation true? **[2019]**
    16 – 8 ÷ 4 + 5 × 2 = 8
    (a) " and ÷ (b) " and ×
    (c) ÷ and + (d) ÷ and ×
26. If the signs '×' and '—'are interchanged in each of the following options, then which of the following options will be incorrect? **[2019]**
    (a) 26 × 5 – 4 = 6 (b) 18 – 6 × 7 = 100
    (c) 24 × 6 – 3 = 6 (d) 9 – 6 × 2 = 52
27. Which of the following two signs must be interchanged to make the given equation correct? **[2021]**
    1 ÷ 14 × 30 + 20 – 10 = 12
    (a) – and + (b) × and –
    (c) ÷ and × (d) + and ÷

LEVEL 2

1. If P denotes +, Q denotes –, R denotes × and S denotes ÷, which of the following statements is correct?
(a) 36 R 4 S 8 Q 7 P 4 = 10
(b) 16 R 12 P 49 S 7 Q 9 = 200
(c) 32 S 8 R 9 = 160 Q 12 R 12
(d) 8 R 8 P 8 S 8 Q 8 = 57

2. If P denotes +, Q denotes –, R denotes × and S denotes ÷, which of the following statements is correct?
(a) 36 R 4 S 8 Q 7 P 4 = 10
(b) 16 R 12 P 49 S 7 Q 9 = 200
(c) 32 S 8 R 9 = 160 Q 12 R 12
(d) 8 R 8 P 8 S 8 Q 8 = 57

3. If × stands for –, ÷ stands for +, + stands for ÷ and – stands for × , which one of the following equations is correct ?
(a) 15 – 5 ÷ 5 × 20 + 10 = 6
(b) 8 ÷ 10 – 3 + 5 × 6 = 8
(c) 6 × 2 + 3 ÷ 12 – 3 = 15
(d) 3 ÷ 7 – 5 × 10 + 3 = 10

4. Which one of the four interchanges in signs and numbers would make the given equation correct?
3 + 5 – 2 = 4
(a) + and –, 2 and 3
(b) + and –, 2 and 5
(c) + and –, 3 and 5
(d) None of these

5. Select from the alternatives two signs which need to be interchanged to make the following equation correct.
36 ÷ 12 × 6 + 9 – 6 = 38
(a) – and × (b) ÷ and ×
(c) – and + (d) ÷ and +

6. According to a certain code, '=' means '>' '–' means '+' and '+' means '–'. If a, b and c are positive integers and a = b = c, then which of the following is true?
(a) b = a + c (b) ac = b^2
(c) a – c = 2b (d) ab = c^2

7. With what operators, should the symbols @ and < be replaced so that the following expression is valid.
100 – 81 ÷ 27 @ 3 < 6 = 115
(a) + and – (b) × and ÷
(c) + and × (d) ÷ and –

8. If 'Σ' means '×', 'δ' means '÷', 'σ' means '+' and '∝' means '–' then evaluate the following expression usuing standard operator precedence.
56δ (6σ8) Σ4∝1
(a) 52 (b) 24
(c) 15 (d) 43

9. Which interchange in signs and number would make the equation correct?
96 ÷ 128) + 64 = 2
(a) + and ÷, 64 and 96
(b) + and ÷, 64 and 128
(c) + and ÷, 96 and 128
(d) ÷ and +, 94 and 128

10. If in a certain code
23 × 26 = 42 and, 11 × 15 = 19
Then,
32 × 16 = ?
(a) 40 (b) 41
(c) 44 (d) 48

11. If M denotes +, N denotes –, O denotes × and P denotes ÷, then find the value of 125 P 25 N 36 P 18 M 35.
(a) 38 (b) 42
(c) 49 (d) 80

12. If '÷' stands for' 'greater than', '×' stands for' 'addition', '+' stands for division', '–' stands for 'equal to', '>' stands for 'multiplication', '=' stands for 'less than', '<' stands for 'subtraction', then which of the following options is correct? **[2018]**

(a) $3 + 2 < 4 \div 6 > 3 \times 2$
(b) $3 \times 2 < 4 \div 6 + 3 < 2$
(c) 3 > 2 < 4 “ 6 × 3 × 2
(d) $3 \times 2 \times 4 = 6 + 3 < 2$

13. Which of the following interchanges in signs makes the given statement true? **[2018]**
$5 \times 15 \div 7 - 20 + 4 = 77$
(a) – and + (b) + and ×
(c) ÷ and + (d) ÷ and ×

14. If ‘ Δ ’ denotes ‘equal to’; ‘ %’ denotes ‘not equal to’; ‘+’ denotes ‘greater than’; ‘—’ denotes ‘less than’; ‘×’ denotes ‘not greater than’; ‘÷’ denotes ‘not less than’ then a – b – c implies ________. **[2018]**
(a) a – b + c (b) b + a – c
(c) c x b + a (d) None of these

15. If X stands for subtraction, Y stands for addition, Z stands for division and W stands for multiplication, then find the value of 13 Z 13 X 13 Y 13 W 13. **[2020]**
(a) 170 (b) 157
(c) 150 (d) 118

16. If a # b = a ÷ b, a % b = a × b, a δ b = a + b and a $ b = a – b, then the value of (7 % 6) + (16 # 8) + (4 δ 3) is **[2021]**
(a) 41 (b) 51
(c) 42 (d) 52

17. If '–' stands for '+', '+' stands for '–', '×' stands for '÷' and '÷' stands for '×', then which of the following is correct? **[2022]**
(a) $40 - 10 + 20 \times 10 \div 4 = 40$
(b) $10 - 8 \div 4 \times 8 + 9 = 5$
(c) $31 + 5 \times 3 \div 4 - 9 = 21$
(d) $40 - 30 \times 10 + 5 \div 7 = 10$

18. If ‘–’ stand for division, ‘+’ stands for multiplication, ‘÷’ stands for subtraction and ‘×’ stands for addition **[2022]**
Which one of the following equations is correct?
(a) $18 + 14 - 24 \times 12 \div 16 = 12$
(b) $16 \times 14 - 24 \div 18 + 12 = -24$
(c) $24 - 12 + 12 \div 16 \times 18 = 26$
(d) $18 \div 16 + 12 \times 18 \div 12 = 24$

ANSWER KEY

LEVEL-1

1	(a)	**4**	(a)	**7**	(d)	**10**	(c)	**13**	(d)	**16**	(a)	**19**	(c)	**22**	(a)	**25**	(a)		
2	(c)	**5**	(b)	**8**	(c)	**11**	(a)	**14**	(c)	**17**	(d)	**20**	(c)	**23**	(d)	**26**	(d)		
3	(c)	**6**	(c)	**9**	(d)	**12**	(a)	**15**	(c)	**18**	(b)	**21**	(b)	**24**	(c)	**27**	(d)		

LEVEL-2

1	(d)	**2**	(d)	**3**	(b)	**4**	(c)	**5**	(d)	**6**	(a)	**7**	(c)	**8**	(c)	**9**	(a)	**10**	(b)
11	(a)	**12**	(b)	**13**	(c)	**14**	(d)	**15**	(b)	**16**	(b)	**17**	(b)	**18**	(c)				

CHAPTER

9

Time Sequence (Clock and Calendar)

TO SOLVE PROBLEMS BASED ON CALENDAR

REMEMBER FOLLOWING POINTS :

We are supposed to find the day of the week on a given date.

For this, we use the concept of odd days.

(i) Odd Days : In a given period, the number of days more than the complete weeks are called odd days.

(ii) Leap Year :

(1) Every year divisible by 4 is a leap year, if it is not a century.

(2) Every 4th century (i.e., divisible by 400) is a leap year and no other century is a leap year.

Note : A leap year has 366 days.

Examples.

1. Each of the years 1948, 2004, 1676 etc. has been a leap year.

2. Each of the years 400, 800, 1200, 1600, 2000 etc. is a leap year.

3. None of the years 2001, 2002, 2003, 2005, 1800, 2100 is a leap year.

(iii) Ordinary Year :

The year which is not a leap year is called an ordinary year. An ordinary year has 365 days.

(iv) Counting of odd days :

(1) 1 ordinary year = 365 days
= (52 weeks + 1 day)
$\therefore$ 1 ordinary year has 1 odd day.

(2) 1 leap year = 366 days = (52 weeks + 2 days).
$\therefore$ 1 leap year has 2 odd days.

(3) 100 years = 76 ordinary years + 24 leap years
= $(76 \times 1 + 24 \times 2)$ odd days = 124 odd days.
= (17 weeks + 5 days) $\equiv$ 5 odd days.

$\therefore$ Number of odd days in 100 years = 5
Number of odd days in 200 years
= $(5 \times 2) \equiv 3$ odd days.
Number of odd days in 300 years
= $(5 \times 3) \equiv 1$ odd day.
Number of odd days in 400 years
= $(5 \times 4 + 1) \equiv 0$ odd days.
Similarly, each one of 800 years, 1200 years, 1600 years, 2000 years etc. has 0 odd days.

(v) First January 1 AD was Monday. Therefore, we must count days from Sunday, i.e. Sunday for 0 odd days, Monday for 1 odd day, Tuesday for 2 odd days and so on.

(vi) February in an ordinary year gives no odd day, but in a leap year gives one odd day.

ILLUSTRATON 1:

What was the day of the week on 15th August, 1947 ?

(a) Friday (b) Saturday

(c) Thursday (d) Monday

***Sol.* (a)** 15th August, 1947 = (1946 years + Period from 1.1.1947 to 15.8.1947)

Odd days in 1600 years = 0

Odd days in 300 years = (5×3)

$= 15 \equiv 1$

46 years = (11 leap years + 35 ordinary years)

$= (11 \times 2 + 35 \times 1)$ odd days

= 57 odd days

= (8 weeks + 1 day) = 1 odd day.

$\therefore$ Odd days in 1946 years = $(0 + 1 + 1)$

= 2.

Jan. Feb. March April May June July Aug.

$(31 + 28 + 31 + 30 + 31 + 30 + 31 + 15)$

= 227 days.

227 days = (32 weeks + 3 days) $\equiv$ 3 odd days.

Total number of odd days = $(2 + 3)$

= 5.

Hence, the required day is Friday.

ILLUSTRATON 2:

What day of the week was 20th June 1837 ?

(a) Monday (b) Tuesday

(c) Wednesday (d) Sunday

***Sol.* (b)** 20th June 1837 means 1836 complete years + first 5 months of the year 1837 + 20 days of June.

1600 years give no odd days.

200 years give 3 odd days.

36 years give (27 + 9) or 3 odd days.

1836 years give 6 odd days.

From 1st January to 20th June there are 3 odd days.

Odd days :

January	:	3
February	:	0
March	:	3
April	:	2
May	:	3
June	:	6

		17

Therefore, the total number of odd days = (6 + 3) or 2 odd days.

This means that the 20th of June fell on the 2nd day commencing from Monday. Therefore, the required day was Tuesday.

TO SOLVE PROBLEMS BASED ON CLOCKS,

REMEMBER THE FOLLOWING POINTS :

The face of the dial of a watch is a circle whose circumference is divided into 60 equal parts, called minute spaces.

A clock has two hands, the smaller one is called the hour hand or short hand while the larger one is called the minute hand or long hand.

(i) In 60 minutes, the minute hand gains 55 minutes on the hour hand.

(ii) 1 minute space = $\frac{360^\circ}{60}$.

(As 360° of the circle is divided into 60 minutes).

(iii) In one minute, the hour hand moves $\frac{360}{12 \times 60}$

$= \frac{360}{720} = \frac{1^\circ}{2}$

(As there are 12 hours of 60 minutes each) Thus, in one minute the minute hand gains

$5\frac{1^{\circ}}{2}$ over the hour hand.

(iv) In every hour, both the hands coincide once.

(v) The hands are in the same straight line when they are coincident or opposite to each other.

(vi) When the two hands are at right angles, they are 15 minute spaces apart.

(vii) The hands coincide 11 times in every 12 hours (between 11 and 1 O'clock there is a common position at 12 O'clock). Hence, the hands coincide 22 times in a day.

(viii) The hands of a clock are at right angles twice in every hour, but in 12 hours they are at right angles 22 times since there are two common positions in every 12 hours.

(ix) When the hands are in opposite directions, they are 30 minute spaces apart.

(x) Angle traced by hour hand in 12 hrs = 360°.

(xi) Angle traced by minute hand in 60 min. = 360°.

(xii) Interchangeable positions of minute hand and hour hand occur when the original interval between the two hands is $\frac{60}{13}$ minute spaces or a multiple of this.

$$\frac{\text{True time interval}}{\text{Time interval in incorrect clock}}$$

$$= \frac{1}{1 \pm \text{hour gained / lost in 1 hour by incorrect clock}}$$

(+) when incorrect clock gains time

(–) when incorrect clock loses time

In a correct (true) clock, both hands coincide at a interval of $65\frac{5}{11}$ minutes.

But, if both hands coincide at an interval of x minutes $\left(\neq 65\frac{5}{11}\right)$ of correct time, then the clock is incorrect and, total time gained

$\therefore$ lost $= 60T \times \frac{65\frac{5}{11} - x}{x}$ min. (in T hours of correct time).

Too Fast and Too Slow : If a watch or a clock indicates 8.15, when the correct time is 8, it is said to be 15 minutes too fast.

On the other hand, if it indicates 7.45, when the correct time is 8, it is said to be 15 minutes too slow.

Clock image : Sum of the actual time and time observed in image $= 23^{H}59^{M}60^{S}$ (railway timing) or $11^{H}59^{M}60^{S}$

LEVEL 1

1. At what time between 9 and 10 will the hands of a watch be together ?
   (a) 45 minutes past 9
   (b) 50 minutes past 9
   (c) $49\frac{1}{11}$ minutes past 9
   (d) $48\frac{2}{11}$ minutes past 9
2. Between 2 O'clock to 10 O'clock, how many times the hands of a clock are at right angle ?
   (a) 14 (b) 12
   (c) 16 (d) 15
3. The year next to 1988 having the same calendar as that of 1988 is –
   (a) 1990 (b) 1992
   (c) 1993 (d) 1995
4. The first republic day of India was celebrated on 26th January, 1950. It was –
   (a) Monday (b) Tuesday
   (c) Thursday (d) Friday
5. On January 12, 1980, it was Saturday. The day of the week on January 12, 1979 was –
   (a) Saturday (b) Friday
   (c) Sunday (d) Thursday
6. The number of odd days in a leap year is –
   (a) 1 (b) 2
   (c) 3 (d) 4
7. Monday falls on 4th April, 1998. What was the day 3rd November, 1987 ?
   (a) Monday (b) Sunday
   (c) Tuesday (d) Wednesday
8. Smt. Indira Gandhi died on 31st October, 1984. The day of the week was –
   (a) Monday (b) Tuesday
   (c) Wednesday (d) Friday
9. How many times in a day, the two hands of a clock coincide ?
   (a) 11 (b) 12
   (c) 22 (d) 24
10. When the time is 4.20, the angle between the hands of the clock is –
    (a) 20° (b) 15°
    (c) 12 ½° (d) 10°
11. At 12 O'clock, the minute hand is point East. At 4:30, in which direction will the hour hand point?
    (a) North-West (b) South-East
    (c) South (d) South-West
12. What will be the acute angle between hands of a clock at 2 : 30?
    (a) 105° (b) 115°
    (c) 95° (d) 135°
13. What will be the day of the week on 1st January, 2010 ?
    (a) Friday (b) Saturday
    (c) Sunday (d) Monday
14. The calendar for the year 2005 is the same as for the year :
    (a) 2010 (b) 2011
    (c) 2012 (d) 2013
15. How many times in a day, the two hands of a clock coincide?
    (a) 11 (c) 12
    (b) 22 (d) 24

16. When the time by the watch is 20 minutes past 7, the angle between the hands of the watch is:
(a) 100° (c) 90°
(b) 80° (d) 95°

LEVEL 2

1. How many times between 4 a.m. and 5 a.m.The minute and hour hands of a clock will be at right angle ?
(a) 2 (b) 3
(c) 4 (d) 1
2. If it was Saturday on 17th December, 2002 what was the day on 22nd December, 2004 ?
(a) Monday (b) Tuesday
(c) Wednesday (d) Sunday
3. Find the day of the week on 16th July, 1776.
(a) Tuesday (b) Wednesday
(c) Monday (d) Thursday
4. At what time between 4 and 5 will the hands of a watch point in opposite directions ?
(a) 45 min. past 4
(b) 40 min. past 4
(c) $50\frac{4}{11}$ min. past 4
(d) $54\frac{6}{11}$ min. past 4
5. A clock is set right at 1 p.m. If it gains one minute in an hour, then what is the true time when the clock indicates 6 p.m. in the same day?
(a) $55\frac{5}{61}$ minutes past 5
(b) 5 minutes past 6
(c) 5 minutes to 6
(d) $59\frac{1}{64}$ minutes past 5
6. Two clocks were set right at noon on Sunday. One gains 2 min and the other loses 3 min in 24 hours. What will be the true time when the first clock indicates 3 pm on Wednesday?
(a) 2:38 pm (b) 2:54 pm
(c) 2:23 pm (d) 2:48 pm
7. At what time between 9'O clock and 10'O clock will the hands of a clock point in the opposite directions?
(a) $16\frac{4}{11}$ minutes past 9
(b) $16\frac{4}{11}$ minutes past 8
(c) $55\frac{5}{61}$ minutes past 7
(d) $55\frac{5}{61}$ minutes to 8
8. A clock gains 15 minutes per day. It is set right at 12 noon. What time will it show at 4.00 am, the next day?
(a) 4 : 10 am (b) 4 : 45 am
(c) 4 : 20 am (d) 5 : 00 am
9. What is the angle between the 2 hands of the clock at 8:24 pm?
(a) 100° (b) 107°
(c) 106° (d) 108°
10. In a watch, the minute hand crosses the hour hand for the third time exactly after every 3 hrs., 18 min., 15 seconds of watch

time. What is the time gained or lost by this watch in one day?
(a) 14 min. 10 seconds lost
(b) 13 min. 50 seconds lost
(c) 13min. 20 seconds gained
(d) 14 min. 40 seconds gained

11. The first Republic Day of India was celebrated on 26th January, 1950. It was :
(a) Tuesday (b) Wednesday
(c) Thursday (d) Friday

12. What will be the day of the week on 1st January, 2010 ?
(a) Friday (b) Saturday
(c) Sunday (d) Monday

13. The calendar for the year 2005 is the same as for the year :
(a) 2010 (b) 2011
(c) 2012 (d) 2013

14. If 09/12/2001 happens to be Sunday, then 09/12/1971 would have been at
(a) Wednesday (b) Tuesday
(c) Saturday (d) Thursday

15. What was the day of the week on 15th August, 1947 ?
(a) Wednesday (b) Tuesday
(c) Friday (d) Thursday

16. The last day of a century cannot be :
(a) Monday (b) Wednesday
(c) Friday (d) Tuesday

ANSWER KEY

LEVEL-1

1	(c)	2	(a)	3	(c)	4	(c)	5	(b)	6	(b)	7	(c)	8	(c)	9	(c)	10	(d)
11	(d)	12	(a)	13	(a)	14	(c)	15	(c)	16	(a)								

LEVEL-2

1	(a)	2	(d)	3	(a)	4	(d)	5	(a)	6	(b)	7	(a)	8	(a)	9	(d)	10	(b)
11	(c)	12	(c)	13	(c)	14	(d)	15	(c)	16	(d)								

CHAPTER

Seating (Linear) Arrangement & Puzzle

In Linear arrangement problems we are generally given a set of information about positioning of different elements with respect to other elements. From the given set of information we have to use the given information systematically to find the actual arrangement of the elements. The arrangements can be in a straight line, on chair, in rooms in a row. Another type of arrangement is arrangement in two rows parallel to each other.

Left & Right: We can use Left and Right as per Information that generally is given and its interpretation is as follows:

- **Left & Right:** We can use Left and Right as per our convenience. Generally (and in this book) we will use as follow:

Left End									Right End

- **A is 2 places right of B:** Generally students used to get confuse that how many gaps are there between A and B. Here in this case there is only 1 gap between A and B. As it is explained in the diagram below.

Left End	1st Place	2nd Place	3rd Place	Right End
	B		A	

- **A is 3 places left of B:** Here in this case there is only 2 gaps between A and B. As it is explained in the diagram below. If B is at 1st place then A ia at 4th place.

Left End	1st Place	2nd Place	3rd Place	4th place	Right End
	B			A	

- **A stays 2 places away of B:** Here in this case it is not given who is in right and who is in left so we have two different cases:

Left End	1st Place	2nd Place	3rd Place	Right End
	B/A		A/B	

- **A stays 2 places away of B who is 3 place left of C:** In this case, we can assume that B is at 3rd place then C is at 6th place,

Left End	1st Place	2nd Place	3rd Place	4th place	5th place	6th place	Right End
			B			C	

Example 1. Six friends A, B, C, D, E and F are sitting in a row facing towards North. C is sitting between A and E. D is not at the end. B is sitting immediate right to E. F is not at the right end.

1. Who is on the extreme right?

   (a) B (b) E

   (c) F (d) G

2. Who is exactly in between F and A?

   (a) A

   (b) C

   (c) E

   (d) D

Solution: B is to the immediate right of E i.e E, B. C is between A and E i.e A, C, E, B. as, D is not at the ends and f is not inn right end, so sequence in the row becomes:

F D A C E B N

1. So, extreme right is B, option (a)
2. So, exactly in between F & A, is D, option (d).

Example 2. A,B,C,D,E,F and G are sitting on a wall and all of them are facing east. C is on the immediate right of D. B is at an extreme end and has E as his neighbour. G is between E and F. D is sitting third from the south end.

3. Who is sitting to the right of E?

   (a) A (b) C

   (c) D (d) G

4. Which of the following pairs are sitting at the extreme ends?

   (a) AB (b) AE

   (c) CB (d) FB

Solution: The arrangement is :

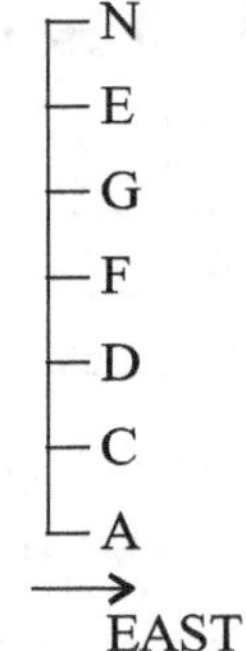

3. Option (d). G is right of E
4. Option (a) AB

PUZZLE TEST :

This chapter comprises questions given in the form of puzzles, involving certain number of items, persons or things. You are required to analyse the given information or clues and answer the questions accordingly.

HINTS FOR HANDLING THE QUESTIONS :

1. Generally, several conditions in the form of information are given with the question. So, do not make hurry to mix all the given information, instead go step by step.
2. To avoid confusion while solving such questions, you should symbolize persons, items by dot, lines etc. If sitting arrangement is a circular one, then draw a circle.

ILLUSTRATION 1 :

On a shelf are placed six volumes side by side labelled A, B, C, D, E and F; B, C, E and F have green covers while others have yellow covers. A, D, B are new volumes while the rest are old volumes. A, C, B, are law reports while the rest are medical extracts. Which two volumes are old medical extracts and have green covers ?

(a) B, C

(b) C, D

(c) C, E

(d) E, F

Sol. **(d)**

	Green cover	Yellow cover	New volume	Old volume	Law reports	Medical extracts
A		√	√		√	
B	√		√		√	
C	√			√	√	
D		√	√			√
E	√			√		√
F	√			√		√

Clearly, E and F are old volumes which have green covers and are medical extracts.

ILLUSTRATION 2 :

Mr. A, Miss. B, Mr. C and Miss. D are sitting around a table and discussing their trades

(A) Mr. A sits opposite to cook

(B) Miss B sits right to the barber

(C) The washerman is on the left of the tailor

(D) Miss D sits opposite Mr. C

What are the trades of A and B?

(a) Tailor and Barber

(b) Tailor and cook

(c) Barber and cook

(d) Washerman and cook

Sol. **(b)** Clearly, C and D sit opposite to each other. So, if A sits opposite to cook, B shall be the cook. Now B is to the right of barber, so, one of the rest, say C will be barber. Clearly, then D on the opposite side shall be washerman or tailor. But washerman is left of tailor and D is to the left of A. So, D is washerman and A is tailor. Thus A and B are tailor and cook.

ILLUSTRATION 3 :

A worker may claim ₹. 15 for each km which he travels by taxi and ₹. 5 for each km when he drives his own car. If in one week he claimed ₹. 500 for travelling 80 kms, how many kms did he travel by taxi ?

(a) 10 (b) 20

(c) 30 (d) 40

Sol. **(a)** The problem can be solved by considering the options one by one.

Option (a) implies 10 km by taxi and 70 km by own car. Total charges

= ₹ 10 × 15 + ₹ 5 × 70

= ₹ 500 which is true.

ILLUSTRATION 4 :

There are five persons P, Q, R, S and T. One is football player, one is chess player and one is hockey player. P and S are unmarried ladies and do not participate in any game. None of the ladies plays chess or football. There is a married couple in which T is the husband. Q is the brother of R and is neither a chess player nor a hockey player.

(i) Who is the football player ?

(a) P (b) Q

(c) R (d) S

(ii) Who is the hockey player ?

(a) P (b) Q

(c) R (d) S

(iii) Who is the chess player ?

(a) P

(b) Q

(c) R

(d) T

(iv) Who is the wife of T ?

(a) P (b) Q

(c) R (d) S

(v) The three ladies are :

(a) P, Q, R

(b) Q, R, S

(c) P, Q, S

(d) P, R, S

Sol. Q is neither a hockey player nor a chess player. So, Q must be a football player and thus cannot be a lady. T is a husband (not a lady) and so must be a chess player. Hence, R must be a hockey player, and therefore she must be a lady and T's wife. So, the information can be summarised as follows :

Person	Sex	Interest in Games	Relationships
P	Female	No	Unmarried
Q	Male	Football	Brother of R
R	Female	Hockey	Wife of T
S	Female	No	Unmarried
T	Male	Chess	Husband of R

(i) (a) Q is the foot ball player.

(ii) (c) R is the hockey player.

(iii) (d) T is the chess player.

(iv) (c) R is the wife of T.

(v) (d) The three ladies are P, R and S.

LEVEL 1

DIRECTIONS (Qs. 1-5): *Study the following information carefully and answer the questions given below.*

A, B, C, D, E, F and G are travelling in three different vehicles. There are at least two passengers in each vehicle– I, II and III and each vehicle has passengers of both the sexes. There are two engineers, two doctors and three teachers among them. C is a lady doctor and she does not travel with the pair of sisters A and F. B, a male engineer, travels with only G, a teacher in vehicle I. D is a male doctor. Two persons belonging to same profession do not travel in the same vehicle. A is not an engineer and travels in vehicle II.

1. In which vehicle does C travel?
   (a) I (b) II
   (c) III (d) II and III
2. How many lady members are there among them?
   (a) Three
   (b) Four
   (c) Three or Four
   (d) Data inadequate
3. What is F's profession?
   (a) Doctor
   (b) Engineer
   (c) Teacher
   (d) Data inadequate
4. Which of the following is not correct?
   (a) A - Female - Teacher
   (b) B - Male - Engineer
   (c) E - Male - Teacher
   (d) F - Female - Teacher
5. Which of the following represents the three teachers?
   (a) AEG
   (b) EFG
   (c) AEG or EFG
   (d) Data inadequate

DIRECTIONS (Qs. 6-7) : *Answer the following questions based on the information given below:*

(1) Bhanudas, Gopal, Amar, Akhil and Chaitanya each practice one of the professions. Farmer, Lawyer, Doctor, Teacher, Photographer. (2) Akhil who is richer than Amar and Chaitanya, is a lawyer. (3) Farmer is the richest of all. (4) Occupation of the poorest is photography. (5) Amar is a doctor and Gopal is a photographer. (6) Akhil is more richer than Amar but less richer than Bhanudas. Then:

6. What is the occupation of Chaitanya?
   (a) Lawyer (b) Doctor
   (c) Farmer (d) Teacher
7. Who among the following is farmer?
   (a) Akhil (b) Bhanudas
   (c) Gopal (d) Chaitanya
8. In a classroom, there are 5 rows, and 5 children A, B, C, D and E are seated one behind the other in 5 seperate rows as follows :
   A is sitting behind C, but in front of B.
   C is sitting behind E, D is sitting in front of E.
   The order in which they are sitting from the first row to the last is
   (a) DECAB
   (b) BACED
   (c) ACBDE
   (d) ABEDC
9. (i) A and B can speak Tamil and Malayalam.
   (ii) C and D can speak English and Hindi.
   (iii) B and D can speak Malayalam and Hindi.
   (iv) A and C can speak Tamil and English.

One who speaks English, Hindi and Malayalam is

(a) A (b) B
(c) C (d) D

10. Five coaches P, L, R, M, O are in a row. R is to the right of M and left of P. L is to the right of P and left of O. Which coach is in the middle?
(a) P (b) L
(c) R (d) O

11. Five boys A, B, C, D and E are standing in a row. D is on the right of E. B is on the left of E, but on the right of A. D is on the left of C, who is standing on the extreme right. Who is standing in the middle ?
(a) D (b) E
(b) B (d) C

12. Five policemen are standing in a row facing south. Shekhar is to the immediate right of Dhanush. Bala is between Basha and Dhanush. David is at the extreme right end of the row. Who is standing in the middle of the row?
(a) Bala (b) Basha
(c) Shekhar (d) Dhanush

13. Seven persons A, B, C, D, E, F and G are standing in a straight line.
D is to the right of G.
C is between A and B.
E is between F and D.
There are three persons between G and B.
Who is on the extreme left?
(a) A (b) B
(c) D (d) G

14. Five boys A, B, C, D and E are standing in a line. A is taller than E but shorter than D. B is shorter than E and C is the tallest. Who is in the middle?
(a) A (b) C
(c) D (d) E

15. In an automobile showroom, seven two-wheelers of seven different companies, viz. H, M, T, V, Y, B and S are displayed in a row, facing east such that:
(A) The H vehicle is to the immediate right of the S vehicle.
(B) The S is fourth to the right of T.
(C) The V is between the M and the B.
(D) The T, which is third to the left of the M, is at one of the ends.
Which vehicle is second to the left of the M?
(a) V (b) S
(c) B (d) T

16. Eight persons A, B, C, D, E, F, G and H are sitting in a straight line facing the north. C is between B and A. D is between B and H. E is third to the left of A. B is second to the right of A. G is between A and F. H is at one of the corners. Who is sitting at the other corner?
(a) E (b) G
(c) B (d) F

17. Parents of a bride go to a jeweller's shop to buy a diamond ring. The jeweller shows them 5 different rings D, E, F, G and H. The difference in their prices is as follows: **[2018]**
(i) D costs twice as much as E.
(ii) E costs four and a half times as much as F.
(iii) F costs half as much as G.
(iv) G costs half as much as H.
(v) H costs less than D but more than F.
Which of the following represents the rings in ascending order of their prices?
(a) E, G, H, D, F
(b) D, E, G, H, F
(c) H, F, G, D, E
(d) F, G, H, E, D

18. B, M, T, R, K, H and D are sitting around a circle facing the centre. H is third to the left of T, who is second to the left of B. M is second to the right of K, who is third to the right of D. H is sitting between R and D. What is the position of T with respect to R ? **[2019]**
(a) Third to the left
(b) Second to the left
(c) Third to the right
(d) Second to the right

LEVEL 2

DIRECTIONS (Qs. 1-2) : *These questions are based on the following information.*

Five men A, B, C, D and E read a newspaper. The one who reads first gives it to C. The one who reads last had taken from A. E was not the first or last to read. There were two readers between B and A.

1. B passed the newspaper to whom ?
   (a) A (b) C
   (c) D (d) E
2. Who read the newspaper last ?
   (a) A (b) B
   (c) C (d) D

DIRECTIONS (Qs. 3-4) : *These questions are based on the following information.*

Five men A, B, C, D and E read a newspaper. The one who reads first gives it to C. The one who reads last had taken from A. E was not the first or last to read. There were two readers between B and A.

3. B passed the newspaper to whom ?
   (a) A (b) C
   (c) D (d) E
4. Who read the newspaper last ?
   (a) A (b) B
   (c) C (d) D
5. Six students A, B, C, D, E and F are sitting in the field. A and B are from Delhi while the rest are from Bangalore. D and F are tall while others are short A. C and D are girls while others are boys. Which is the tall girl from Bangalore?
   (a) C (b) D
   (c) E (d) F
6. In a group of six women, there are four dancers, four vocal musicians, one actress and three violinists. Girija and Vanaja are among the violinists while Jalaja and Shailja do not know how to play on the violin. Shailja and Tanuja are among the dancers. Jalaja, Vanaja, Shailja and Tanuja are all vocal musicians and two of them are also violinist. If Pooja is an actress who among the following is both a dancer and a violinist?
   (a) Jalaja (b) Shailja
   (c) Tanuja (d) Pooja

DIRECTIONS (Qs. 7-11) : *The following questions are based on the following information:*

α, β, γ, δ, $\in$, ϕ, Ψ, η are sitting on a merry-go-round facing at the centre. δ is second to the left on η who is third to the left of α. β is fourth to the right of γ who is immediate neighbour of η. Ψ is not a neighbour of β or γ. ϕ is not a neighbour of β.

7. Who is third to the left of β?
   (a) α (b) γ
   (c) ϕ (d) Ψ
8. In which of the following pairs is the first person sitting to the immediate right of the second person?
   (a) δ, Ψ (b) $\beta, \in$
   (c) η, β (d) Ψ, η

9. What is ϕ's position with respect to Ψ?
   (a) Third towards right
   (b) Third towards left
   (c) Second towards right
   (d) Second towards left

10. Who is sitting between α and β?
    (a) Both $\in$ and η
    (b) Both ϕ and γ
    (c) Only $\in$
    (d) Only ϕ

11. How many of them are sitting between γ and β?
    (a) 0 or 6 (b) 1 or 5
    (c) 2 or 4 (d) 3

DIRECTIONS (Qs. 12-14) : *Study the following information and answer the questions given below it.*

Six boys Prem, Kamal, Ramesh, Shyam, Tarun and U mesh go to University Sports Centre and play a different game of football, cricket, tennis, kabaddi, squash and volleyball.

A. Tarun is taller than Prem and Shyam
B. The tallest among them plays kabaddi
C. The shortest one plays volleyball
D. Kamal and Shyam neither play volleyball nor kabaddi
E. Ramesh plays volleyball
F. If all six boys stand in order of their height then Tarun is in between Kamal and Prem; and Tarun plays football

12. Who among them plays kabaddi?
    (a) Kamal (b) Ramesh
    (c) Shyam (d) Umesh

13. Who will be at fourth place if they are arranged in the descending order of their heights ?
    (a) Prem (b) Kamal
    (c) Tarun (d) Shyam

14. Who plays tennis?
    (a) Kamal
    (b) Prem
    (c) Tarun
    (d) Information insufficient

DIRECTIONS (Qs. 15-18) : *A group of students is sitting in such a way that each occupies a corner of a hexagonal table . Ninong is sitting opposite to Yaangba, Ribiya is sitting next to Silva, Nazelii is sitting opposite to Silva, but not next to Ninong, one person is sitting between Talyang and Yaangba.*

15. Who is sitting opposite to Ribiya ?
    (a) Yaangba (b) Silva
    (c) Talyang (d) Nazeli

16. Who is sitting between Ribiya and Ninong?
    (a) Yaangba (b) Nazeli
    (c) Talyang (d) Silva

17. Who is sitting between Talyang and Yaangba?
    (a) Nazeli (b) Ribiya
    (c) Ninong (d) Silva

18. If Talyang sits to the right of Ninong, who is on the left of Ninong?
    (a) Ribiya (b) Nazeli
    (c) Yaangba (d) Silva

19. P, Q, R, S and T are to be seated in a row facing East, but R and S cannot be together. Also, Q cannot be at third place. If P and Q

are together and R is at the first place, then which of the following cannot be true?

(a) S is at the second place.

(b) S is at the third place.

(c) P is at the third place.

(d) None of these

20. Five boys are sitting in a circular table, Amit is left side of Shyam and Radhey is sitting between Miraj and Pankaj. Pankaj is sitting left side of Amit.

Who is sitting left of Miraj?

(a) Radhey (b) Pankaj

(c) Amit (d) Shyam

21. Study the following information carefully and answer the question that follows.

Eight friends P, Q, R, S, T, U, V and W are sitting in a circle facing the centre.

(i) P, who is sitting between V and R, is just opposite to U.

(ii) T is sitting between W and R. Also, T is second to the right of P and second to the left of U,

(iii) S is sitting second to the left of V.

Who is sitting between W and S?

(a) Q (b) R
(c) P (d) U

22. Read the given information carefully and answer the question that follows. **[2019]**

Five ships J, K, L, M and N are to be unloaded on 5 consecutive days beginning from Monday to Friday.

I. Each ship takes exactly one day to unload.

II. K must be unloaded before (not necessarily immediately before) the days on which M and N are unloaded.

III. L cannot be unloaded on Tuesday.

IV. M is the second ship to be unloaded after J is unloaded.

If M is unloaded on Friday, then which of the following is definitely true?

(a) J is unloaded on Wednesday

(b) K is unloaded on Tuesday

(c) L is unloaded on Monday

(d) L is unloaded on Thursday

23. Eight friends P, Q, R, S, T, U, V and W are sitting around a circular table facing the centre. P is opposite to W. S is between U and W. T is to the immediate right of P. U is the neighbour of R. Q is between V and W. Who is to the immediate right of U? **[2020]**

(a) S (b) P

(c) T (d) R

24. P, Q, R, S, T and U are sitting in a circle facing the centre. S is between R and U. Q is between T and P. R and T are opposite to each other. Q is second to the right of R. Who is third to the left of Q? **[2020]**

(a) U (b) S

(c) P (d) T

25. P, Q, R, S, T and U are six persons travelling together in a boat. Q, R and T are women and the rest are men. However P, Q, R and T are all vegetarian and S and U are non-vegetarian. Finally Q, T and U knows swimming while the test do not know how to swim.

Which of the following is the vegetarian female who knows swimming? **[2021]**

(a) R (b) Q

(c) P (d) U

26. A, B, C, D, E, F, G and H are eight friends sitting around a circular table facing the centre. A sits second to the left of D, who is third to the left of E. C sits third to the right of G, who is not an immediate neighbour of E. H sits third to the right of B, who sits second to the right of G. Who sits between D and C? **[2022]**

    (a) B (b) H

    (c) G (d) E

DIRECTIONS (Qs. 27-28): *Read the following information and answer the questions given below.* **[2022]**

i. A, B, C, D, E, F, G and H are sitting in a line facing towards the east.

ii. A is fourth to the right of E.

iii. H is fourth to the left of D.

iv. C and F are not at the ends and are neighbours

of B and G, respectively.

v. H is next to the left of A and A is the neighbour of B.

27. Which one of the following statements is definitely true about the position of F?

    (a) F is to the right of E

    (b) F is to the right of H

    (c) Next to the right of D

    (d) Between A and H

28. Which of the following statements is true?

    (a) G is the neighbour of H and A

    (b) D is next to the right of A

    (c) E is at left end

    (d) D is next to the left of B

ANSWER KEY																					
LEVEL-1																					
1	(c)	**2**	(b)	**3**	(b)	**4**	(d)	**5**	(a)	**6**	(d)	**7**	(b)	**8**	(a)	**9**	(d)	**10**	(a)	**11**	(b)
12	(d)	**13**	(d)	**14**	(a)	**15**	(c)	**16**	(a)	**17**	(d)	**18**	(d)								
LEVEL-2																					
1	(b)	**4**	(d)	**7**	(c)	**10**	(c)	**13**	(a)	**16**	(d)	**19**	(a)	**22**	(c)	**25**	(b)	**28**	(c)		
2	(d)	**5**	(b)	**8**	(b)	**11**	(d)	**14**	(a)	**17**	(a)	**20**	(d)	**23**	(d)	**26**	(a)				
3	(b)	**6**	(c)	**9**	(a)	**12**	(d)	**15**	(c)	**18**	(d)	**21**	(d)	**24**	(c)	**27**	(a)				

CHAPTER

Analytical Reasoning (Diagrammatic Puzzle)

FIGURE PARTITION :

The problems on figure partition are based on counting the number of figures generated due to partition lines.

1. If a square is subdivided into n parts on each side, then the total number of squares formed is given by

$$\frac{n(n+1)(2n+1)}{6}$$

2. Total no. of rectangles (including squares) in a rectangular figure of size n × m

$$= \frac{n(n+1)}{6}\frac{m(m+1)}{2}$$

ILLUSTRATION 1 :

What is the number of straight lines in the following figure?

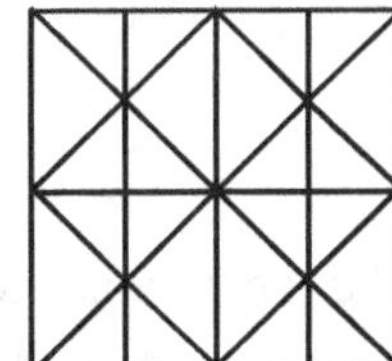

(a) 11 (b) 14
(c) 16 (d) 17

Sol. **(b)** The figure is labelled as shown.

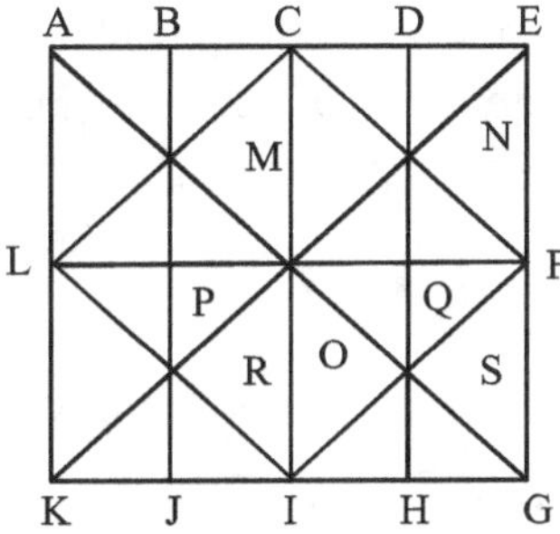

Clearly, there are 3 horizontal lines namely AE, LF and KG.
There are 5 vertical lines : AK, BJ, CI, DH and EG.
There are 6 slanting lines : LC, KE, IF, LI, AG and CF.
Thus, there are 3 + 5 + 6 = 14 straight lines in the figure.

ILLUSTRATION 2 :

How many squares does the figure have ?

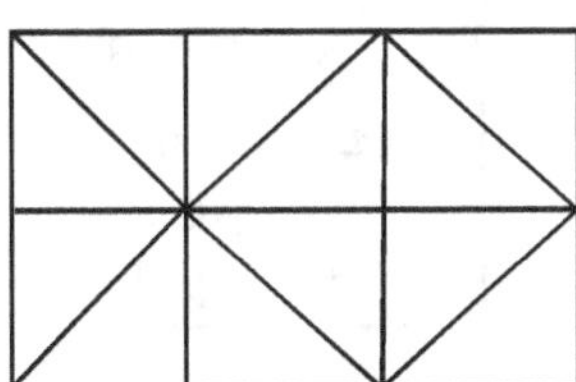

(a) 6 (b) 7
(c) 9 (d) 10

Sol. **(c)** The figure may be labelled as shown :

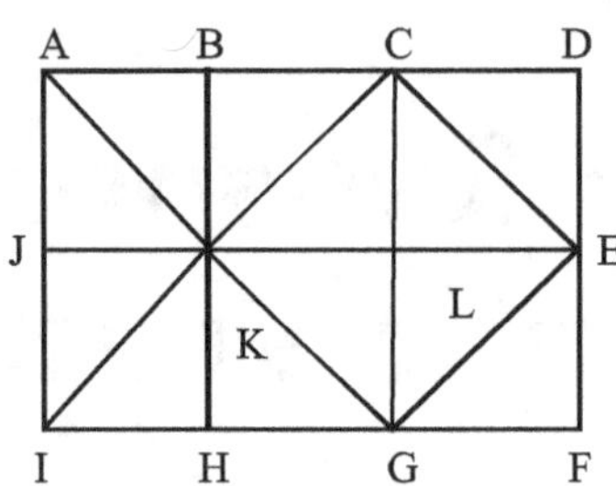

The squares composed to two components each, are ABKJ, BCLK, CDEL, LEFG, KLGH, JKHI. Thus, there are 6 such squares. Only one square, KCEG is composed of four components. Two squares namely, ACGI and BDFH are composed of eight components each. Thus, there are 2 such squares.

∴ There are 6 + 1 + 2 = 9 squares in the figure

ILLUSTRATION 3 :

What is the number of rectangles in the following figure ?

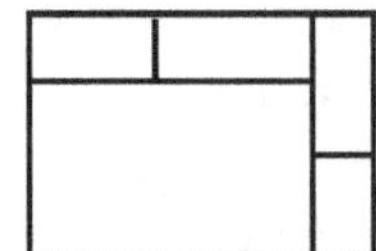

(a) 5 (b) 7

(c) 8 (d) 9

Sol. (d) The figure is labelled as shown :

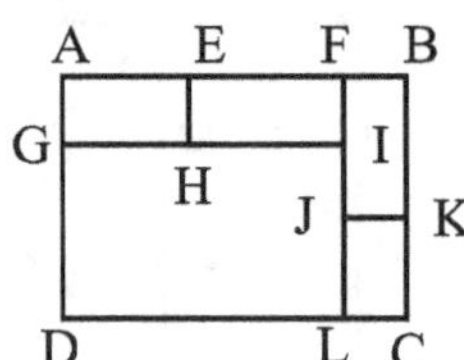

Simplest rectangles are AEHG, EFIH, FBKJ, JKCL and GILD. i.e. there are 5 such rectangles. The rectangles composed of two components each are AFIG and FBCL. Thus, there are 2 such rectangles. Only one rectangle, namely AFLD is composed of 3 components and only one rectangle, namely ABCD is composed of 5 components.

Thus, there are 5 + 2 + 1 + 1 = 9 rectangles in the figure.

ILLUSTRATION 4 :

Determine the number of pentagons in the following figure:

(a) 5 (b) 6

(c) 8 (d) 10

Sol. **(d)** The figure is labelled as shown. In this case, six pentagons have been formed by the combination of three triangles and two rhombuses-
ADFHJ, CFHJL, EHJLB, GJLBD, ILBDF and KBDFH.

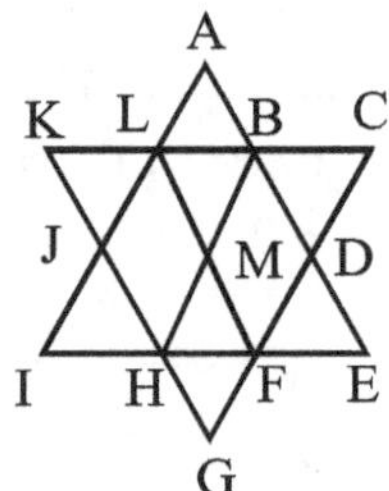

Four other pentagons are formed by the combination of three triangles and one rhombus -LCFHM, LBEHM, BKFHM and BLIFM. Thus, there are 10 pentagons in the figure.

LEVEL 1

1. What is the number of squares in fig ?
   (a) 12
   (b) 13
   (c) 15
   (d) 17
2. What is the number of triangles in figure ?
   (a) 24
   (b) 32
   (c) 48
   (d) 52

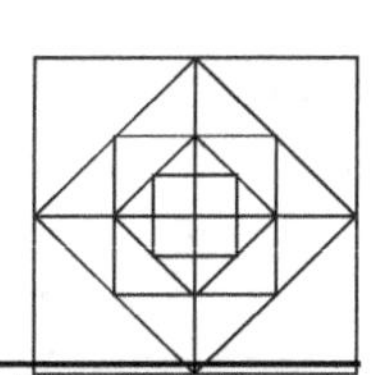

DIRECTION (Q. 3) : *In the following question, there is a diagram marked (X), with one or more dots placed in it. The diagram is followed by four other figures, marked (a), (b), (c) and (d) only one of which is such as to make possible the placement of the alternative in each these.*

3. 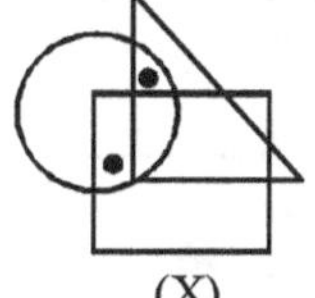

(X)

(a)  (b) 

(c)  (d) 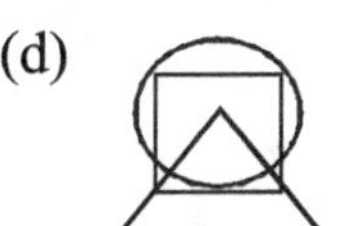

4. In the following question there is a diagram marked in which one or more dots have been placed in certain positions. Examine the placement of these dots carefully. From the four choices given below dots, select the one in which the placement of dots is similar to that in the diagram marked (X).

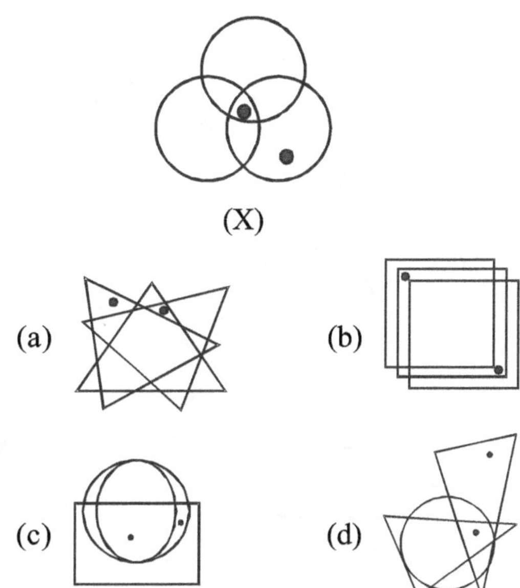

DIRECTIONS (Qs. 5-6) : *In each of the following questions there is a diagram (X) in which one or more dots have been placed in certain positions. Examine the placement of these dots carefully. From the four choices, select the one in which the placement of dots is similar to that in the diagram.*

5. 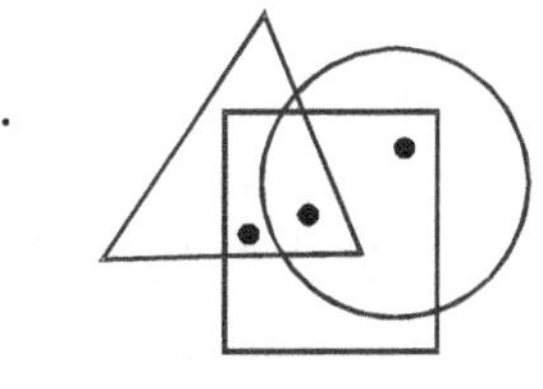

(X)

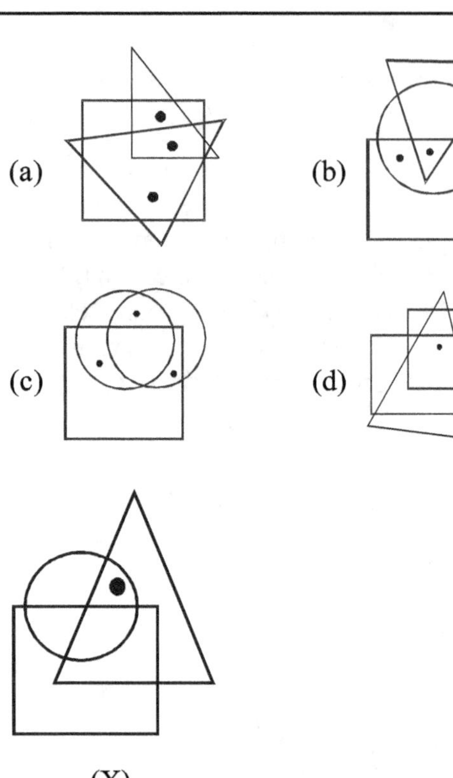

6.

(X)

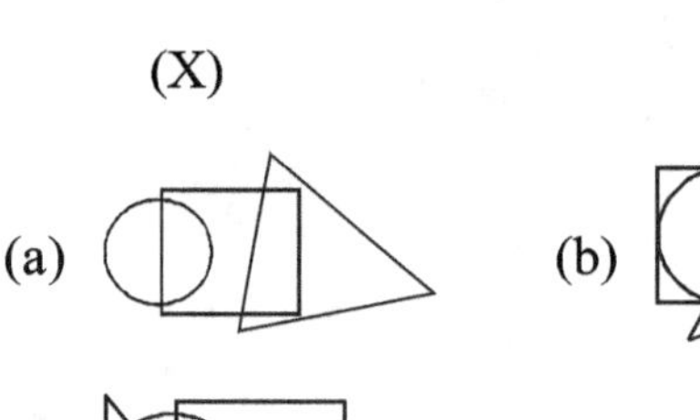

7. What will be the number of Parallelograms in the given figure ?

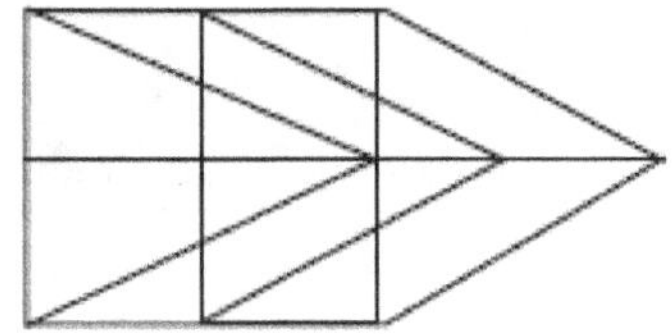

(a) 15 (b) 17
(c) 13 (d) 16

DIRECTION (Q. 8): *Identify the number of specified geometric shapes in the given diagram and mark the correct answer.*

8. How many triangles are in the given figure?

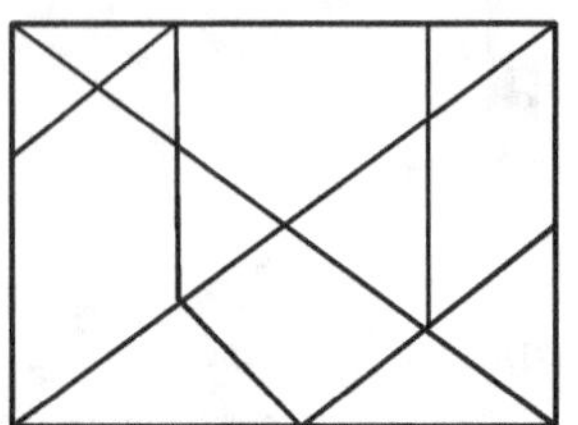

DIRECTIONS (Qs. 9-10): *Observe the following figure and answer the following questions by choosing the correct alternative given below.*

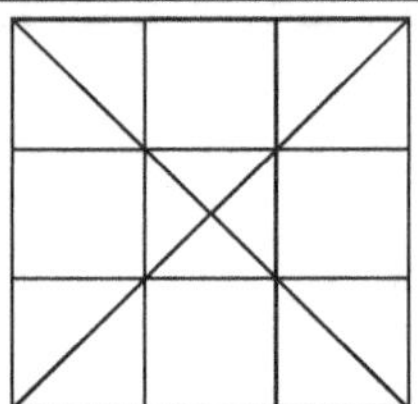

9. Find the number of equilateral triangles in the given figure.
(a) 32 (b) 18
(c) 5 (d) 0

10. Find the number of parallelograms which are not rectangles from the given figure.
(a) 4 (b) 6
(c) 8 (d) 10

DIRECTION (Q. 11): *Find the number of triangles in the given figure.*

11.

(a) 18 (b) 20
(c) 24 (d) 27

12. Count the number of triangles in the given figure. **[2018]**

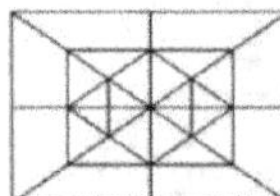

(a) 10 (b) 12
(c) 16 (d) None of these

13. Count the number of triangles in the given figure. **[2018]**

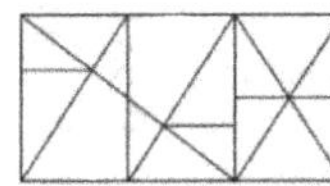

(a) 15 (b) 18
(c) 20 (d) None of these

14. Count the number of triangles in the given figure. **[2018]** 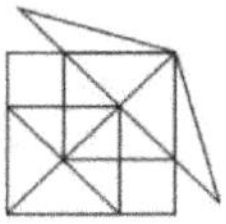
(a) 25
(b) 23
(c) 27
(d) None of these

15. Court the number of triangles formed in the given figure. **[2021]**

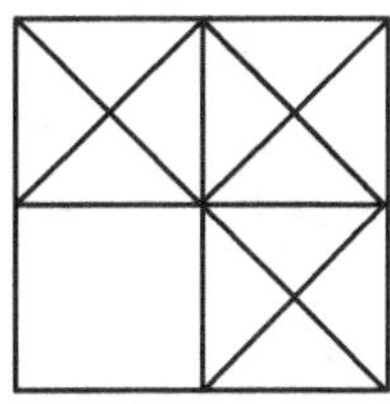

(a) 15 (b) 16
(c) 17 (d) More than 17

16. Find the number of triangles formed in the given figure. **[2022]**

(a) 13 (b) 14
(c) 15 (d) More than 15

LEVEL 2

1. 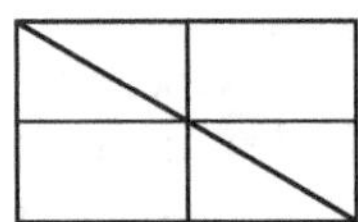

   How many triangles and quadrilaterals are there in this figure?

   (a) 7 and 6 (b) 6 and 7
   (c) 6 and 8 (d) 6 and 9

2. 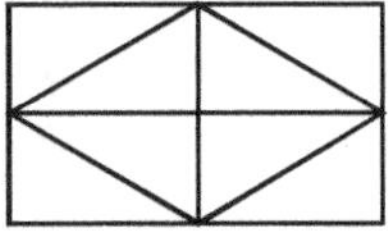

   How many quadrilaterals are there in this figure?

   (a) 8 (b) 9
   (c) 10 (d) 11

DIRECTION (Q. 3-4): *Identify the number of specified geometric shapes in the given diagram and mark the correct answer.*

3. How many triangles are in the given figure?

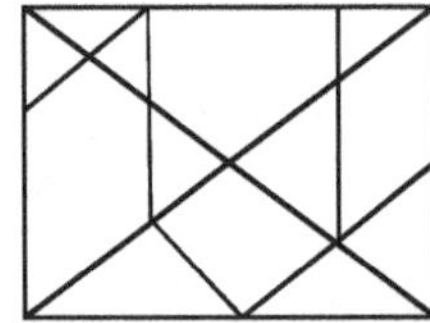

   (a) 19 (b) 20
   (c) 21 (d) 22

4. Find the number of squares/rectangles in the given figure.

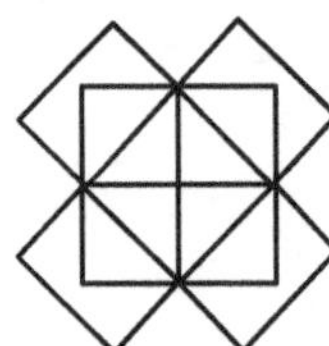

   (a) 20 (b) 18
   (c) 16 (d) 15

5. Find the total number of squares formed in figure?

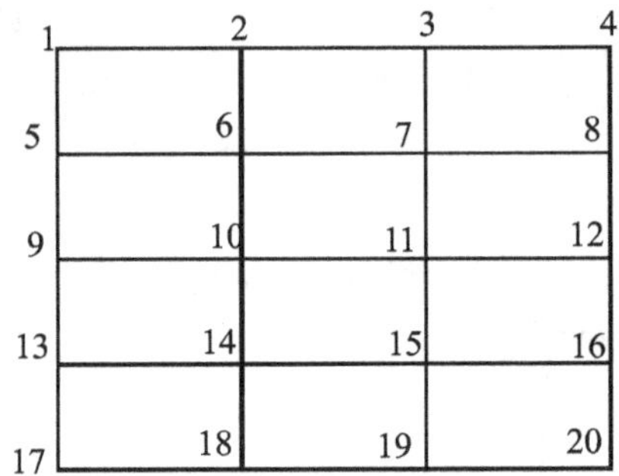

   (a) 22 (b) 18
   (c) 20 (d) 30

6. What is the number of parallelogram in figure?

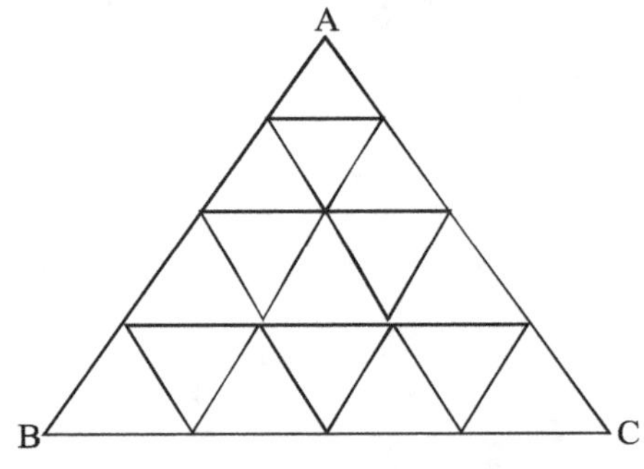

   (a) 27 (b) 33
   (c) 34 (d) 42

7. What is the number of triangles in figure ?

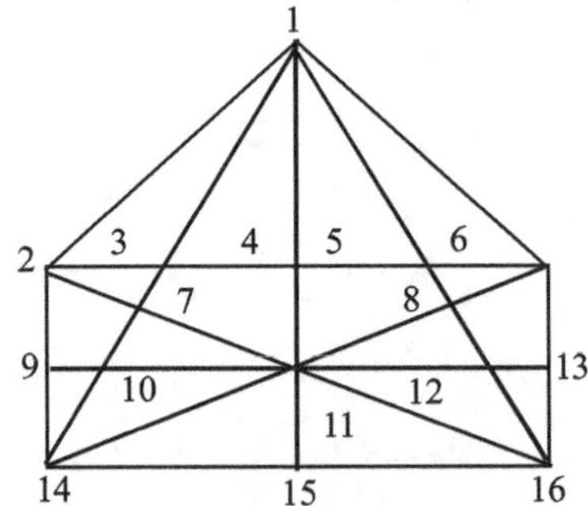

(a) 32
(b) 39
(c) 46
(d) 60

DIRECTIONS (Qs. 8-13) : *In each of the following questions, from amongst the figures marked (1), (2), (3) and (4), select the one which satisfies the same conditions of placement of the dot as in fig. (X).*

8.     

(X) (a) (b) (c) (d)

9. 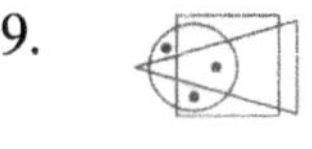 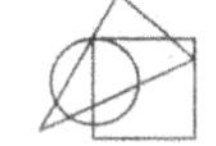 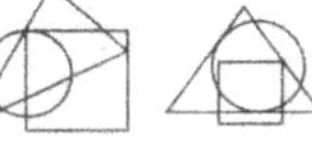  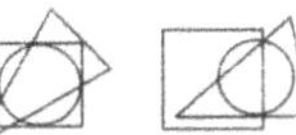

(X) (a) (b) (c) (d)

10. 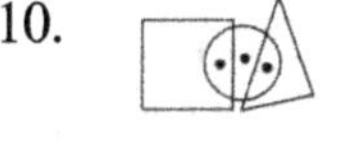    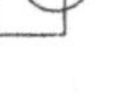 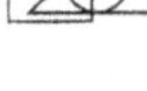

(X) (a) (b) (c) (d)

11. 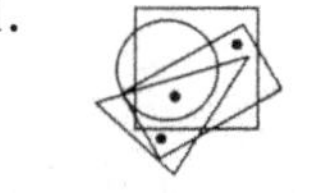    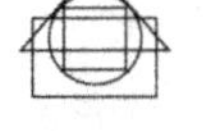   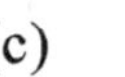

(X) (a) (b) (c) (d)

12. 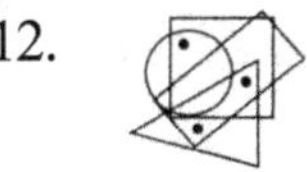 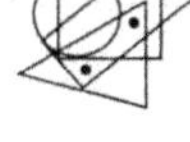 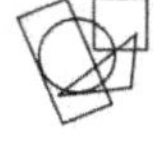     

(X) (a) (b) (c) (d)

13. 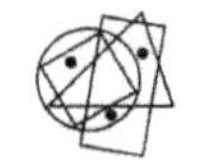    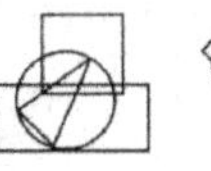

(X) (a) (b) (c) (d)

14. Count the number of triangles in the given figure.

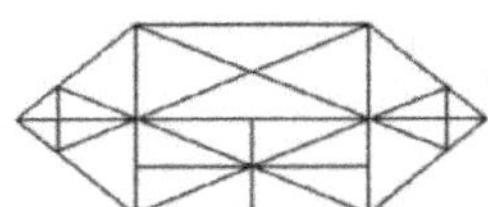

(a) 25 (b) 26
(c) 28 (d) None of these

15. Count the number of squares in the given figure.

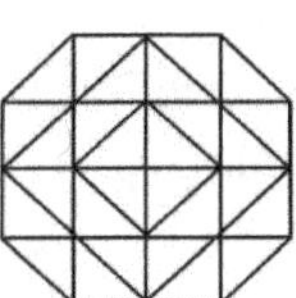

(a) 25 (b) 26
(c) 20 (d) None of these

16. How many triangles are there in the given figure?

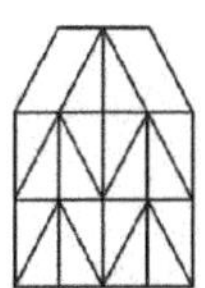

(a) 28 (b) 26
(c) 25 (d) None of these

17. How many squares are there in the given figure?

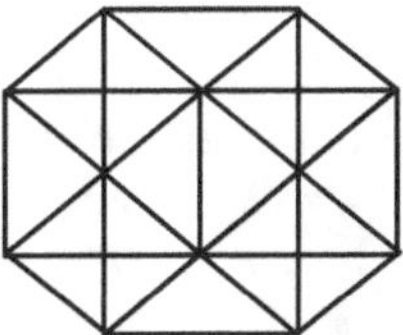

(a) 8 (b) 7
(c) 6 (d) 10

18. How many squares are there in the given figure?

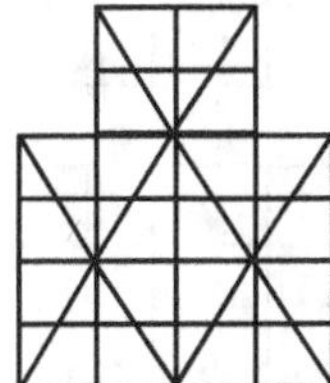

(a) 35 (b) 32
(c) 37 (d) 36

19. Find the total number of triangles in the figure given below.

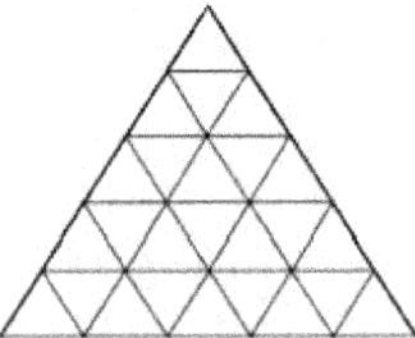

(a) 19
(b) Less than 18
(c) More than 30
(d) Between 20 to 30

20. Count the number of triangles in the given figure. **[2018]**

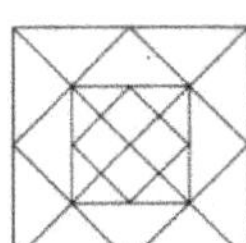

(a) 43 (b) 46
(c) 42 (d) None of these

21. How many triangles are formed in the given figure? **[2019]**

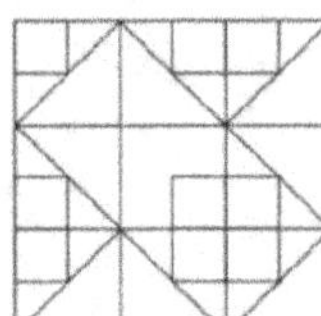

(a) 24 (b) 26
(c) 20 (d) None of these

22. How many triangles are there in the given figure? **[2020]**

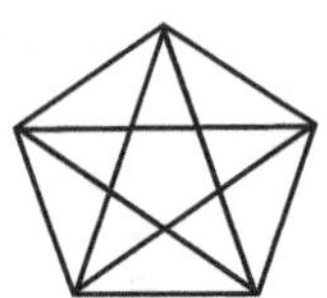

(a) 25 (b) 27
(c) 26 (d) More than 27

23. How many triangles are there in the given figure? **[2021]**

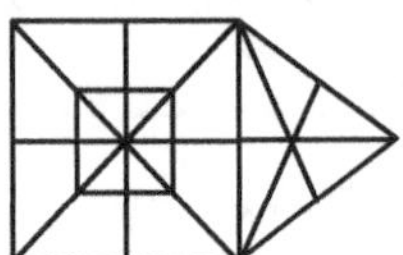

(a) 26 (b) 28
(c) 27 (d) More than 28

24. How many triangles are there in the given figure? **[2021]**

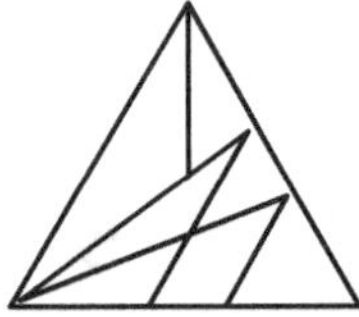

(a) 10 (b) 11
(c) 12 (d) More than 12

25. How many triangles are there in the adjoining figure? **[2022]**

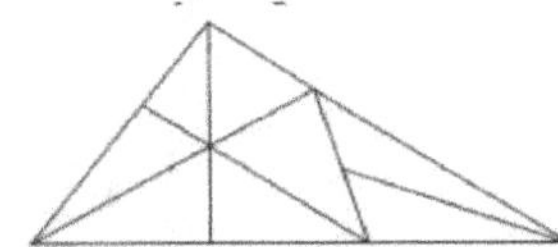

(a) Between 14 to 28 (b) Less than 10
(c) 11 (d) More than 28

ANSWER KEY																			
LEVEL-1																			
1	(d)	**2**	(c)	**3**	(b)	**4**	(d)	**5**	(a)	**6**	(c)	**7**	(b)	**8**	(d)	**9**	(d)	**10**	(d)
11	(d)	**12**	(d)	**13**	(d)	**14**	(d)	**15**	(d)	**16**	(d)								
LEVEL-2																			
1	(d)	**4**	(a)	**7**	(d)	**10**	(c)	**13**	(d)	**16**	(d)	**19**	(c)	**22**	(d)	**25**	(a)		
2	(c)	**5**	(c)	**8**	(b)	**11**	(a)	**14**	(d)	**17**	(b)	**20**	(d)	**23**	(d)				
3	(b)	**6**	(d)	**9**	(a)	**12**	(d)	**15**	(d)	**18**	(c)	**21**	(d)	**24**	(a)				

CHAPTER

Mirror and Water Images

Mirror Images

In this category questions are based on the criteria that a few figures are given and you have to find out which one is the exact image of the given figure in a mirror placed in front of it. This image formation is based on the principle of 'lateral inversion' which implies that size of the image is equal to the size of the object but both sides are interchanged. The left portion of the object is seen on the right side and right portion of the object is seen on the left side. For example, mirror image of ABC = ƆꓭA

Note : There are '11' letters in English Alphabet which have identical mirror images: A, H, I, M, O, T, U, V, W, X, Y.

Characteristics of Reflection by plane mirror

1. Perpendicular distance of object from mirror = Perpendicular distance of image from mirror.
2. The image is laterally inverted.

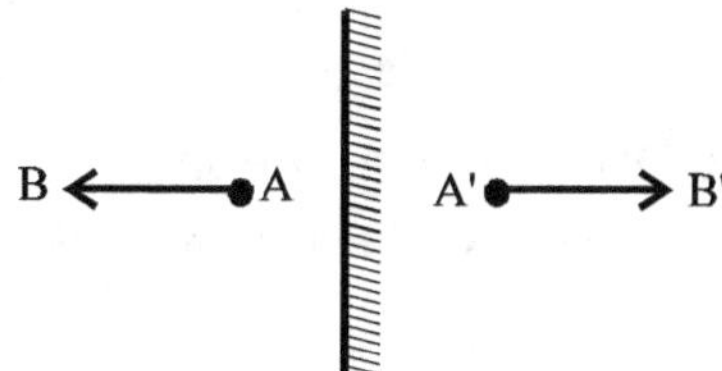

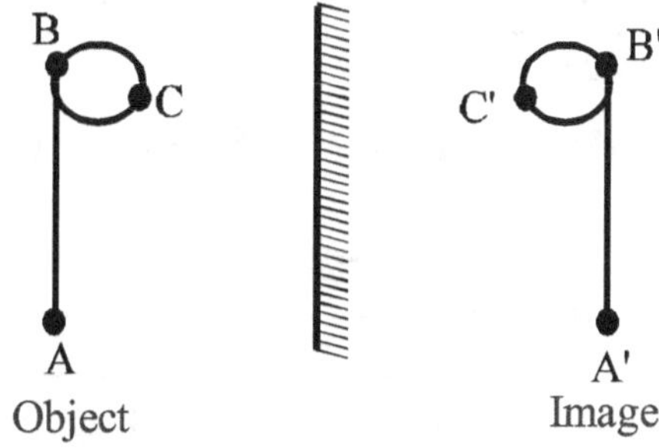

3. The line joining the object point with its image is normal to the reflecting surface.
4. The size of the image is the same as that of the object.

***E.g* -1:** Mirror-images of certain words are given below :

(1) F U N : И U ꟻ

(2) GOLKONDA : AᗡИOꓘ⅃Oᘓ

***E.g* -2:** Mirror-image of certain combinations of alphabets and numbers are given below :

(1) BMC49JN2317 : ᒣ1ƐƧИႱϱ4ƆMꓭ

(2) 15bg82XQh : dϘXƧ8gdƧ1

I. Mirror Images of Capital Letters

A	A
B	ꓭ
C	Ɔ
D	ᗡ
E	Ǝ
F	ꟻ
G	Ә
H	H
I	I
J	Ⴑ
K	ꓘ
L	⅃
M	M

N	И
O	O
P	ꟼ
Q	Ϙ
R	Я
S	Ƨ
T	T
U	U
V	V
W	W
X	X
Y	Y
Z	Ƹ

II Mirror Images of Small Letters

a	ɒ
b	d
c	ɔ
d	b
e	ɘ
f	ʇ
g	ǫ
h	ʜ
i	i
j	ᒑ
k	ʞ
l	l
m	m

n	n
o	o
p	q
q	p
r	ɿ
s	ƨ
t	ɟ
u	υ
v	v
w	w
x	x
y	γ
z	ƹ

III. Mirror Images of Numbers

0	0
1	I
2	ς
3	Ɛ
4	ᔦ
5	ƨ

6	∂
7	Ꞁ
8	8
9	ɘ
10	0I

Examples of lateral inversion of few figures and words are given below :

IV. Mirror Images of Various Objects :

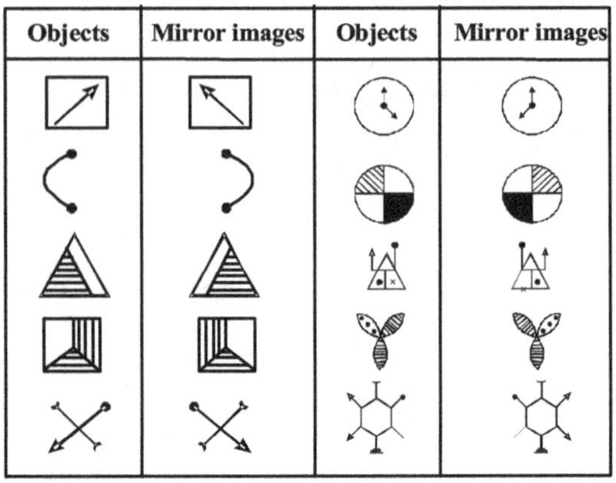

Objects	Mirror images	Objects	Mirror images

V. Mirror Images of Certain Words and Numbers:

Words	Mirror images	Numbers	Mirror images
PREDICTION	NOITƆIDƎЯꟼ	32596	∂9ƧςƐ
HOSPITAL	⅃ATIꟼƧOH	8932	ςƐɘ8
DARPAN	NAꟼЯAᗡ	868	8∂8
STRIDENT	TNƎᗡIЯTƧ	786	∂8Ꞁ
OPULENT	TNƎ⅃UꟼO	10190	0ɘI0I
SARCASM	MƧAƆЯAƧ	5693	Ɛɘ∂Ƨ
LIBERAL	⅃AЯƎꓭI⅃	8964	ᔦ∂ɘ8
OFFENCE	ƎƆNƎꟻꟻO	7362	ς∂ƐꞀ
ADVANCE	ƎƆNAVᗡA	5893	Ɛɘ8Ƨ
IMAGES	ƧƎӘAMI	7839	ɘƐ8Ꞁ

VI. Mirror Images of Clock:

There are certain questions in which the position of the hour-hand and the minute-hand of a clock as seen in a mirror are given. On the basis of the time indicated by the mirror-image of the clock we have to detect the actual time in the clock. In the solution of such questions we use the fact that if an object A is the mirror-image of another object B then B is the mirror-image of A.

Time of image in plane mirror

(a) Real time = X^H, Image time = $12^H - X^H$ (H = hours)

(b) Real time = X^HY^M, Image time = 11^H60^M – X^HY^M (M = minutes)

(c) Real time = $X^HY^MZ^S$, Image time = $11^H59^M60^S$ – $X^HY^MZ^S$ (S = seconds)

(d) if $X^HY^MZ^S > 11^H59^M60^S$, image time = $23^H59^M60^S$ – $X^HY^MZ^S$

Quick Tip

Whenever you have to solve a mirror image question, imagine a mirror placed in front of the object and then try to find its inverted image. The portion of the object that is near the mirror will now be the portion of the image near to the mirror in the inverted form.

ILLUSTRATION 1 :

By looking in a mirror, it appears that it is 6 : 30 in the clock. What is the real time ?

(a) 6 : 30 (b) 5 : 30

(c) 6 : 00 (d) 4 : 30

Sol. **(b)**

(Fig A) (Fig B)

Clearly, fig (A) shows the time (6 : 30) in the clock as it appears in a mirror. Then its mirror-image i.e. Fig (B) shows the actual time in the clock i.e. 5 : 30. You can solve it quickly if you remember that the sum of actual time and image time is always 12 hours.

DIRECTIONS (ILLUSTRATION 2) :

Find the correct option for the mirror image for the following examples.

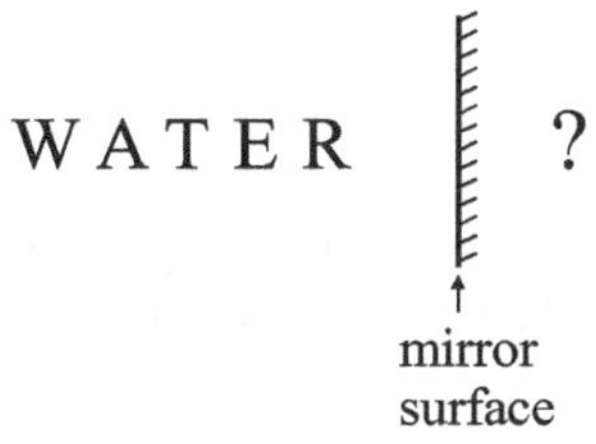

(a) W A T Ǝ Я

(b) Я Ǝ T Ǝ W

(c) W A Я Ǝ T

(d) Я Ǝ T A W

Sol. (d) We have to find the correct mirror image for the word 'WATER' for which we need to find the mirror image for each letter separately and then arrange it, like the mirror image for the letters W is W, A is A, T is T, E is Ǝ and R is Я.

Since, the word ends with R, i.e., where the mirror is placed, therefore the mirror image will start from the mirror images of R, i.e.; Я. Thus the mirror image for water is Я Ǝ T A W

WATER | ЯƎTAW

Thus option (4) is the correct answer.

ILLUSTRATION 3 :

8 6 9 5 2 | ?

(a) 8 ∂ 9 ꙅ ꙅ

(b) 8 9 ∂ 5 ꙅ

(c) 8 ∂ ꙅ ꙅ ℮

(d) ꙅ ꙅ ℮ ∂ 8

Sol. (d) Mirror image for '8' is '8', '6' is '∂', '9' is '℮', '5' is 'ꙅ' and '2' is 'ꙅ'.

8 6 9 5 2 | ꙅ ꙅ ℮ ∂ 8

Thus, option (d) is the answer.

ILLUSTRATION 4 :

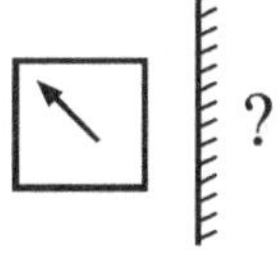

(a)  (b) 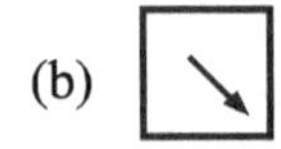

(c) 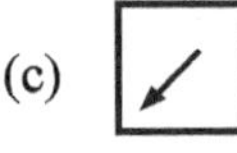 (d)

Sol. (a) The mirror image of a square remains a square while the arrow inside it will be changed.

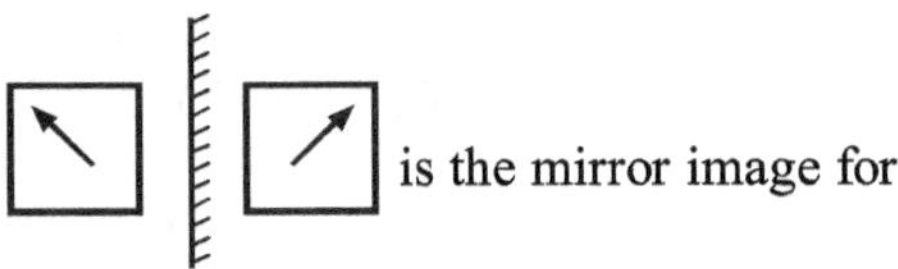 is the mirror image for the given image. Thus opiton (a) is the correct answer.

ILLUSTRATION 5 :

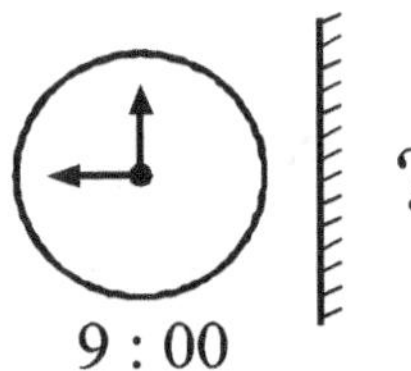

(a) 12 : 00 (b) 5 : 00
(c) 3 : 00 (d) 6 : 00

Sol. (c) The mirror image of circle remains a circle, and the arrow facing north also remains the same but the arrow facing will face East in its mirror image.

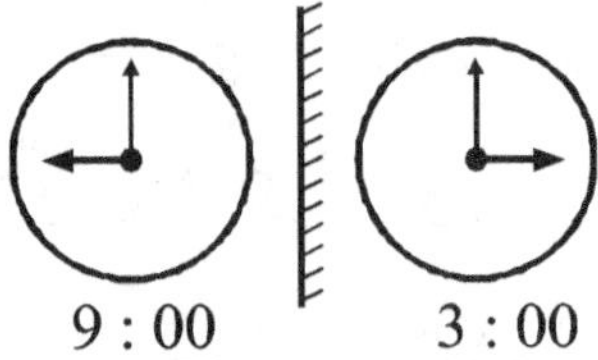

Thus, answer is 3 : 00, i.e., option (c).

Water Image

The reflection of an object as seen in water is called its water image. It is the inverted image obtained by turning the object upside down.

Water-images of capital letters

Letters	A	B	C	D	E	F	G	H	I	J	K	L	M
Water-image	∀	B	C	D	E	Ⅎ	ɢ	H	I	ſ	K	Γ	W
Letters	N	O	P	Q	R	S	T	U	V	W	X	Y	Z
Water-image	И	O	Ь	Ó	ʁ	S	⊥	∩	Λ	M	X	⅄	Z

Water-images of small letters

Letters	a	b	c	d	e	f	g	h	i	j	k	l	m
Water-image	ɐ	p	c	q	ǝ	ɟ	ƃ	ɥ	ᴉ	ɾ	ʞ	l	ɯ
Letters	n	o	p	q	r	s	t	u	v	w	x	y	z
Water-image	u	o	b	d	ɹ	s	ʇ	n	ʌ	ʍ	x	ʎ	z

Water-images of numbers

Letters	0	1	2	3	4	5	6	7	8	9
Water-image	0	I	Ƨ	Ɛ	ㄣ	ϛ	9	ㄥ	8	6

Note :

1. The letters whose water-images are identical to the letter itself are : C, D, E, H, I, K, O, X
2. Certain words which have water-images identical to the word itself are : KICK, KID, CHIDE, HIKE, CODE, CHICK

Quick Tip

Whenever we have to analyze the water image of an object, imagine a mirror or a surface that forms an image just under the given object. The portion of the object that is near the water surface will be inverted but will be near the water surface in the image as well.

DIRECTIONS (ILLUSTRATION 6-8) :
Find the correct option for the water images for the following examples.

ILLUSTRATION 6 :

STORE
←water surface
?

(a) S⊥ORE (b) S⊥OᴚE
(c) S⊥OʁE (d) Ƨ⊥OʁE

Sol. (d) In case of water image, the water reflection will usually be formed under the object / word.
In this case, the water image of the word will be an outcome of the water images of each of the letters like, the water images of S is Ƨ, T is ⊥, O is O, R is ꓤ and E is E . Thus the water image of the word 'STORE' is 'Ƨ ⊥ O ꓤ E.'

STORE
/////////////
Ƨ⊥OꓤE

ILLUSTRATION 7 :

1 6 8 9 2
/////////////
?

(a) 1 ɐ 8 ә Ƨ (b) ↿ ɐ 8 ә Ƨ
(c) ↿ ɐ 8 ә 5 (d) ↿ ɐ 8 6 Ƨ

Sol. (b) The water image of '1' is ↿, '6' is 'ɐ', '8' is 8, '9' is 'ә' and '2' is 'Ƨ'.
Thus, the water image of 1 6 8 9 2 is ↿ ɐ 8 ә Ƨ

ILLUSTRATION 8 :

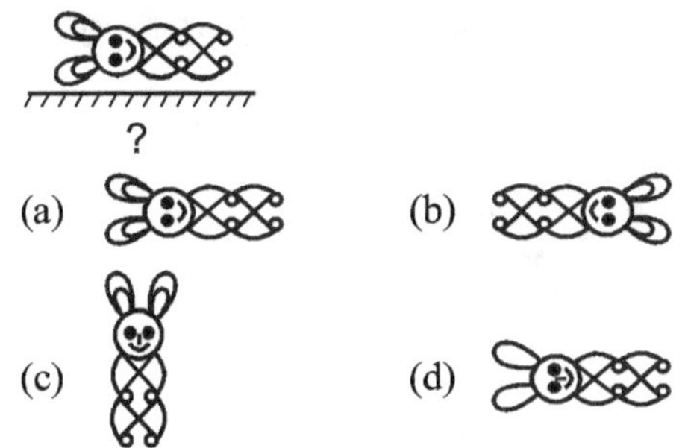

Sol. (a) Since, the teddy bear is facing west, in its water image also it will face west. Therefore, options (b) & (c) are ruled out. Now among options (a) & (d) check the ears and nose of the bear in the actual diagram, it does not have a nose, but the image in option (d) has a nose. Therefore, option (a) is the correct representation.

Quick Tips

(i) While solving a question, try eliminating some options and solving the questions will become easier.
To eliminate options, keep in mind the pattern used in the object (given diagram whose image is to be formed) as well as the position of mirror or water such that the portion of the object near to the mirror / water will produce the same portion near the mirror / water in an inverted form.

(ii) Images are images, be it water or mirror, in both the cases an inverted image of the alphabets / numerals / clocks / any other object are formed by inverting the object. Inverting of the object solely depends upon the position of mirror or water surface w.r.t. the object.

LEVEL 1

DIRECTIONS (Qs. 1–6) : *Find the correct option for the mirror images for the following questions.*

1. DREAM | ?

(a) MAEЯD (b) ᗡЯƎAM
(c) MAƎЯᗡ (d) MAƎЯD

2. NEWS | ?

(a) ƧWƎИ (b) ИƎWƧ
(c) NƎWƧ (d) SWƎИ

3. jealous | ?

(a) ꞁɘɒlouƨ (b) ꞁɘɒlous
(c) soulɒɘj (d) ƨuolɒɘꞁ

4. 312568 | ?

(a) 3ƖƧƼ68 (b) 86ƼƧƖƐ
(c) 895ƧƖƐ (d) 89ƼƧƖƐ

5. Rotate the mirror image 90° clockwise.

B | ꓭ

(a) ϖ (b) ɯ
(c) B (d) ꓭ

6. Rotate the mirror image 90° anticlockwise.

72 | ƧΓ

(a) 27 (b) ƧΓ
(c) ƧΓ (d) ƧL

DIRECTIONS (Qs. 7-13) : *In each of the following questions, choose the correct mirror-image of the Fig. (X) from amongst the four alternatives (a), (b), (c) and (d) given along with it.*

7.

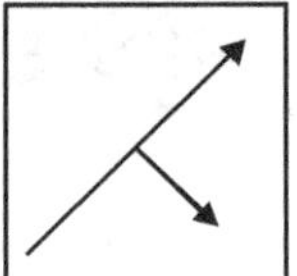

(X)

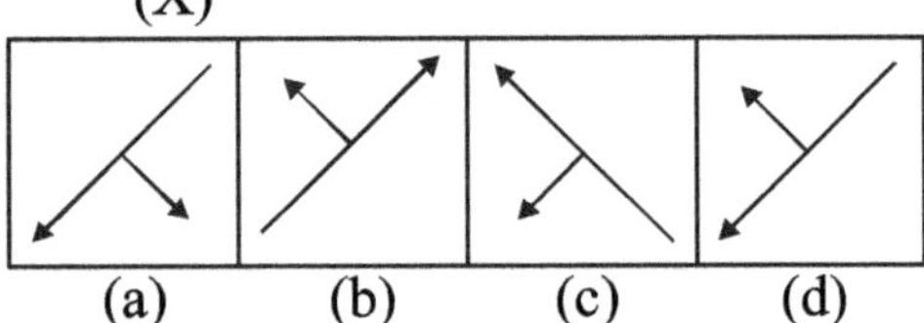

(a) (b) (c) (d)

8.

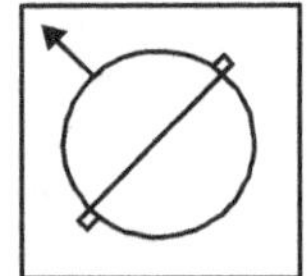

(X)

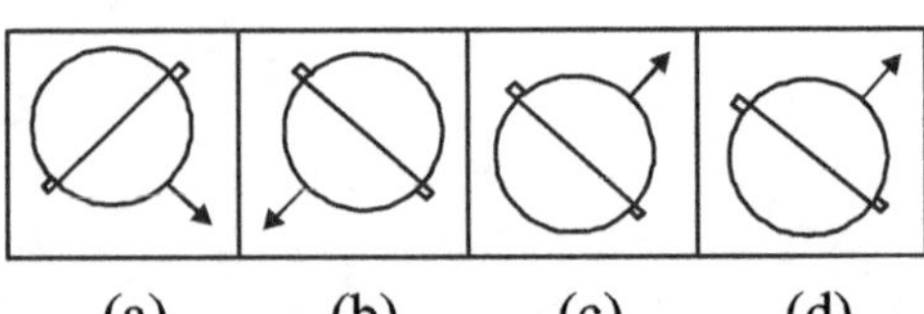

(a) (b) (c) (d)

9.

(X)

(a) (b) (c) (d)

10.

(X)

(a) (b) (c) (d)

11.

(X)

(a) (b) (c) (d)

12.

M N

(X)

(a) (b) (c) (d)

13.

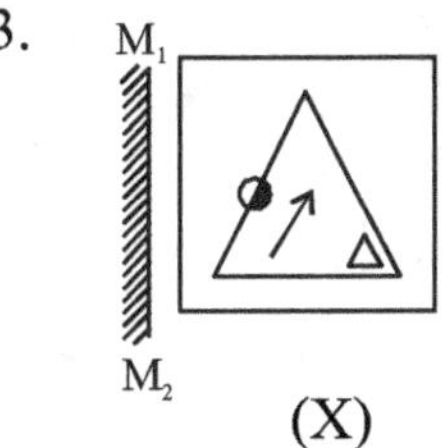

(X)

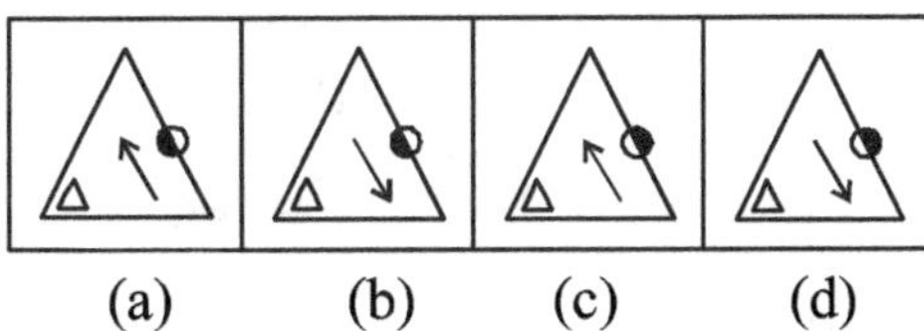

(a) (b) (c) (d)

14. Looking into a mirror, the clock shows 9 : 30 as the time. The actual time is
(a) 2 : 30 (b) 3 : 30
(c) 4 : 30 (d) 6 : 30

15. A clock seen through a mirror shows quarter to three. What is the correct time shown by the clock ?
(a) 8 : 15 (b) 9 : 12
(c) 8 : 17 (d) 9 : 15

DIRECTIONS (Qs. 16-19) : *In each of the following questions, you are given a combination of alphabets and/or numbers followed by four alternatives (a), (b), (c) and (d). Choose the alternative which most closely resembles the mirror-image of the given combination.*

16. WHITE
(a) ƎꓕIHW (b) ƎTIHM
(c) ƎTIHW (d) ETIHW

17. TERMINATE
(a) TƎЯMIИATƎ
(b) ƎTAИIWЯƎT
(c) ƎTAИIMЯƎT
(d) ETAИIMЯƎT

18. REASONING
(a) ꓤEꓯSOИIИ⅁
(b) ƏИIИOƨAƎЯ
(c) ЯƎꓯSOИIИ⅁
(d) ƏИIИOSAƎЯ

19. BR4AQ16HI
(a) IH∂1QA4ЯB (b) IH61QA4ЯB
(c) IH∂1QA4ЯB (d) IH91QA4ЯB

DIRECTIONS (Qs. 20-22) : *In each of the following questions, choose the correct mirror-image of the Fig. (X) from amongst the four alternatives (a), (b), (c) and (d) given along with it.*

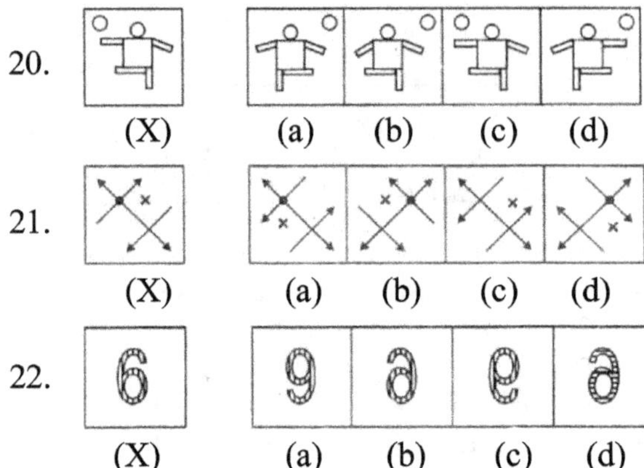

23. The following figure is rotated in anticlockwise direction through 90° and its mirror image is obtained. Select the correct mirror image from four alternatives given.

Question figure :

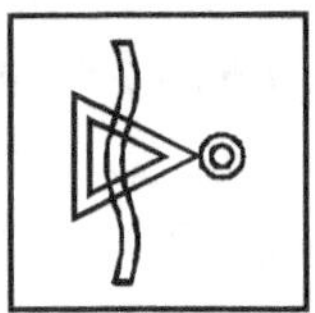

(a) 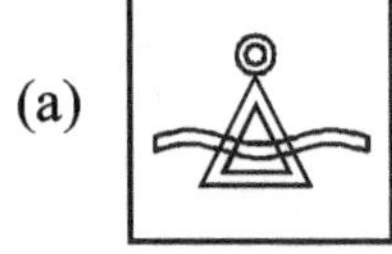 (b) 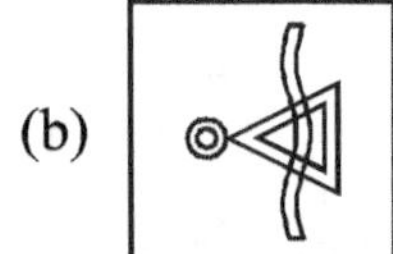

(c) 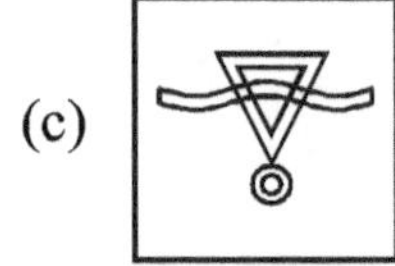 (d) 

24. **Question Figure**

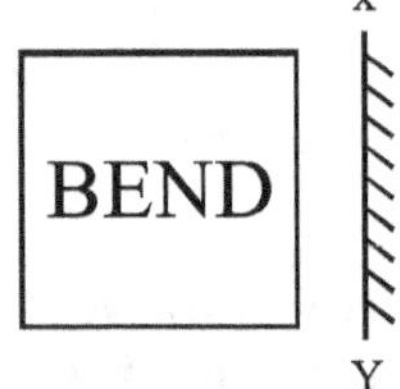

Answer Figures

(a)  (b) 

(c)  (d) 

25. **Question Figure**

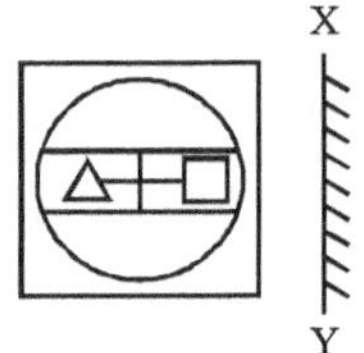

Answer Figures

(a) 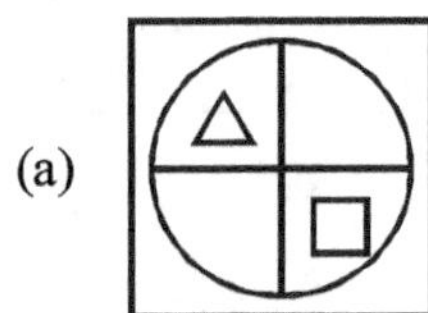 (b) 

(c) 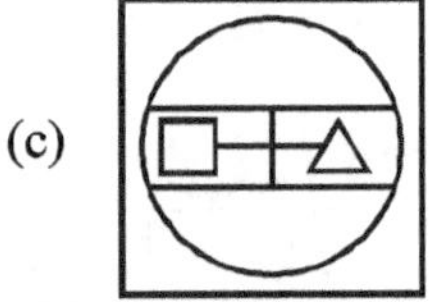 (d) 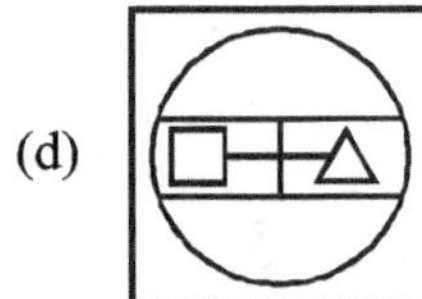

26. Select the correct water image of the given combination of letters.

S W I M M I N G

(a) Ƨ WIM MIN G
(b) Ƨ ꟽI ꟽ ꟽI И G
(c) S ꟽI ꟽ ꟽI И G
(d) G И I ꟽ ꟽI ꟽƧ

27. Select the mirror image of the given figure.

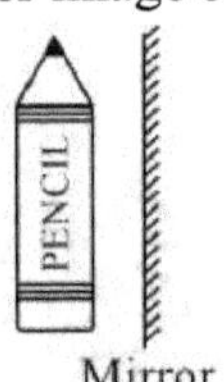

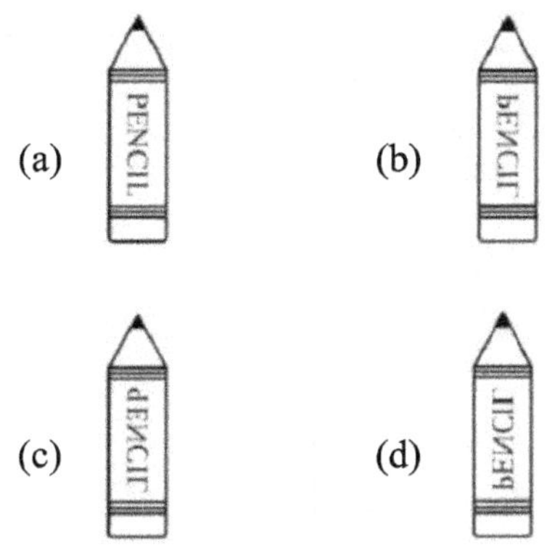

28. Select the correct water image of the given combination of letters.

INDIANAIRFORCE

(a) IИDIVИVIꓤℲOꓤCE

(b) IИDIVИVIꓤℲOCꓤE

(c) IDИVIVИIꓤℲOꓤEC

(d) IDИVIVИIꓤOℲEꓤC

29. Find the mirror image of the given figure, if the mirror is placed vertically to the left.

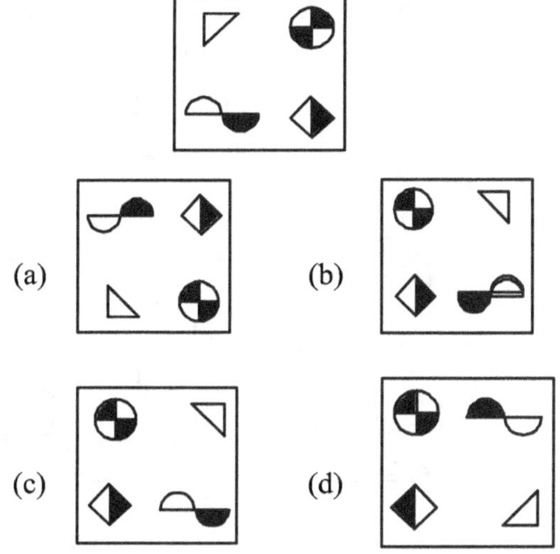

30. Find the correct water image of the given figure.

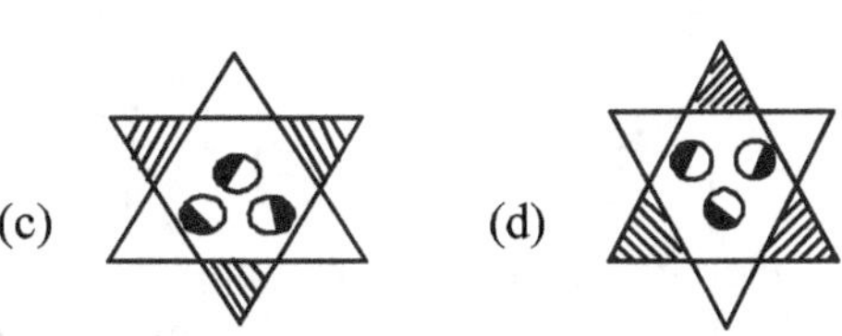

31. Select the correct water image of the given figure.

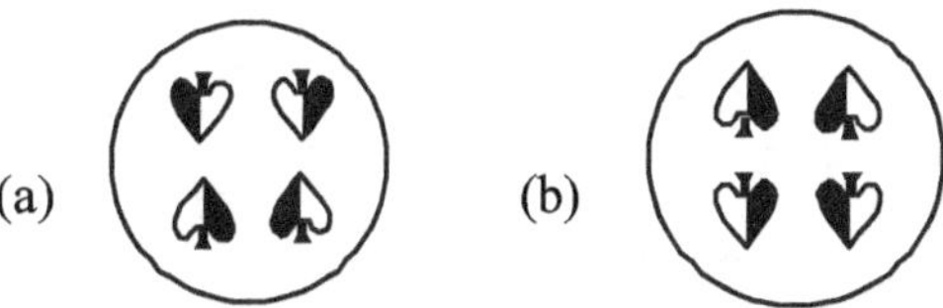

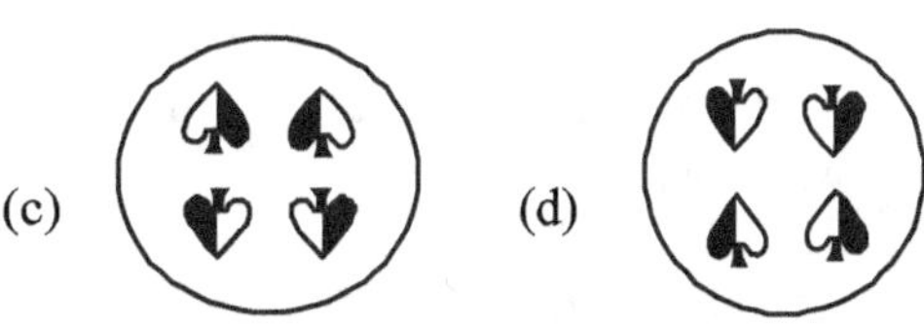

32. Find the mirror image of the given word, if mirror is placed vertically to the left.

PLAY

(a) YAJꟼ (b) YAJP

(c) YAPL (d) YALꟼ

33. Select the correct mirror image of the given word, if mirror is placed vertically to the right.

HINDI

(a) IᗡNIH (b) IᗡИIH

(c) IᗡNIH (d) IᗡИIH

34. Select the correct mirror image of the given figure. **[2018]**

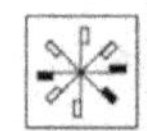

(a) 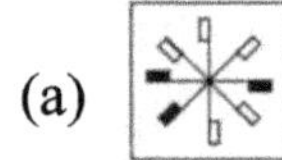 (b) 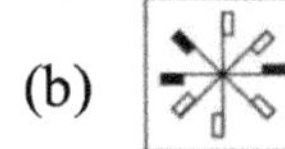

(c) 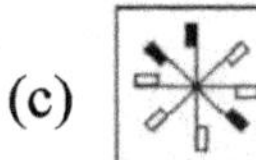 (d) 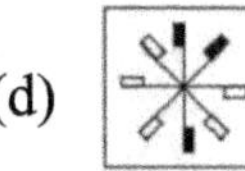

35. Select the correct water image of the given combination of letters and numbers. **[2018]**

US91Q4M5W3

(a) ∩Sə1Ó4W2W3
(b) ∩Sə1Ó4W2W3
(c) EW2M4Q19SU
(d) ∩S91Ó4W2W3

36. Select the correct water image of the given figure.

[2018]

(a) 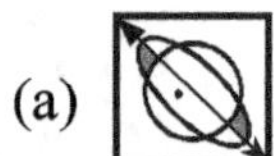 (b) 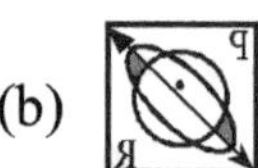

(c) 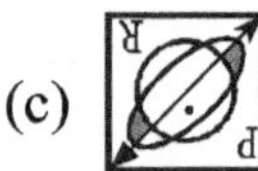 (d) 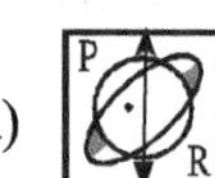

37. Select the correct water image of the given combination of letters, numbers and symbols.

HR26DA$20?@90 **[2019]**

(a) HꓤƧ9DV$Ƨ0¿@60
(b) HRƧ9DV$Ƨ0¿@90
(c) HꓤƧ9DA$Ƨ0¿@60
(d) Hꓤ29DV$Ƨ0¿@60

38. Find the correct water image of the given figure. **[2020]**

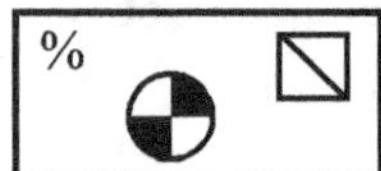

(a) 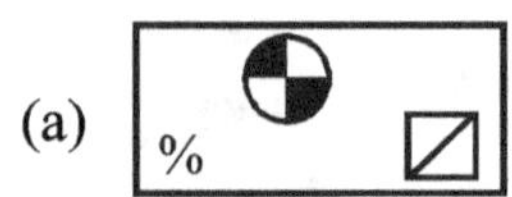

(b) 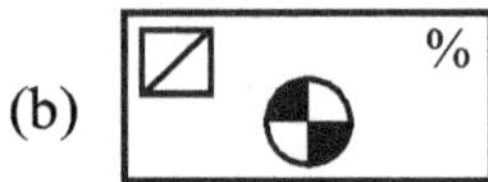

(c) 

(d) 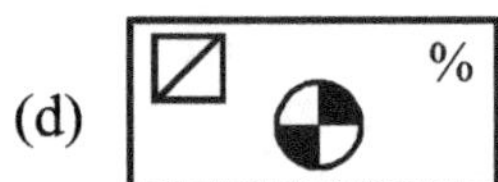

39. Select the correct mirror image of the given combination of letters and numbers. **[2021]**

(a) ꓘꓶ0Sə4ИWOᗡ (b) ꓘꓶ0Sə4NWOᗡ
(c) ꓘꓶ0Sə4ИWOᗡ (d) ꓘL0Sə4ИWOᗡ

40. Select the correct water image of the given figure.

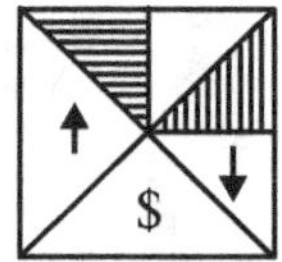

[2021]

(a) 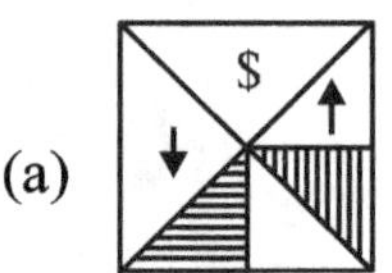

(b) 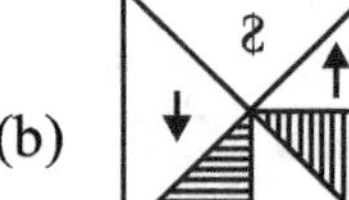

(c) 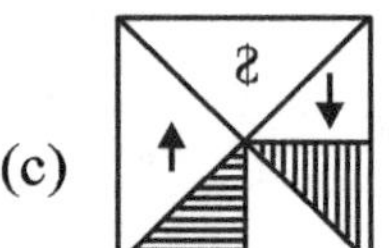

(d) 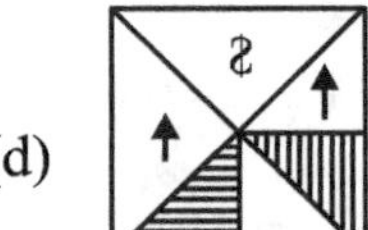

LEVEL 2

DIRECTIONS (Qs. 1-4) : *In each of the following questions, choose the correct water image of the figure (X) from amongst the four alternatives (a), (b), (c) and (d) given along with it.*

1. 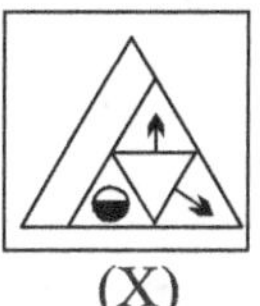

(X)

(a) (b)

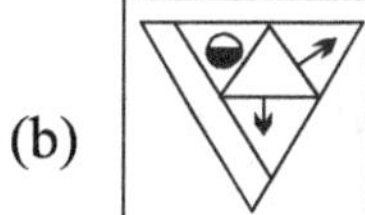

(c) (d)

2. 

(X)

(a) (b)

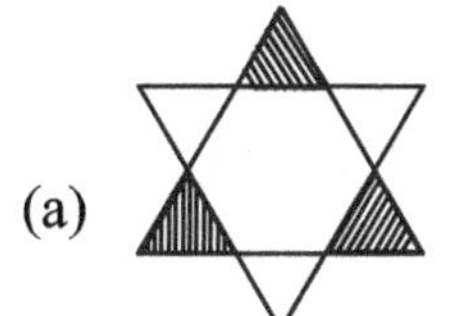

(c) (d)

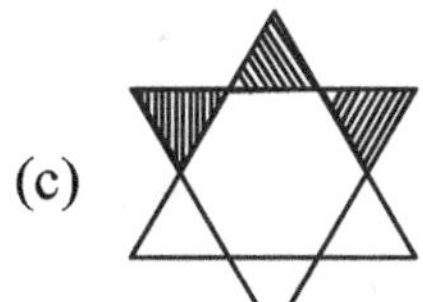

3. 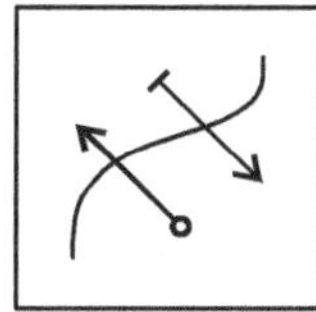

(X)

(a) 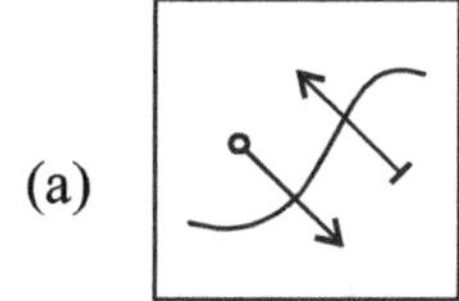

(b) 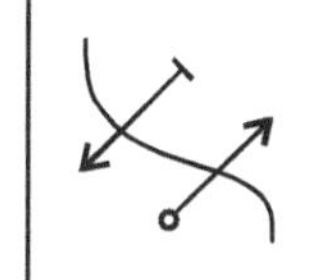

(c) 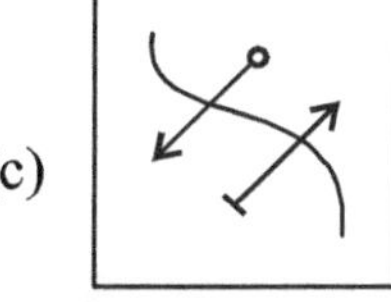

(d) 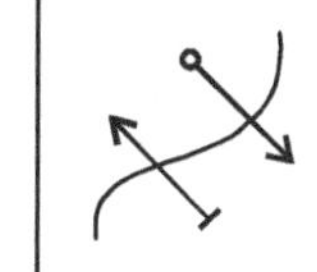

4. 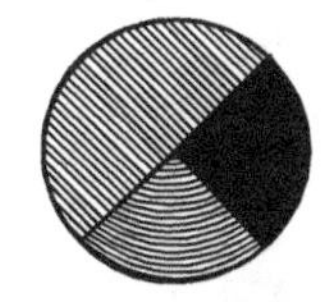

(X)

(a) 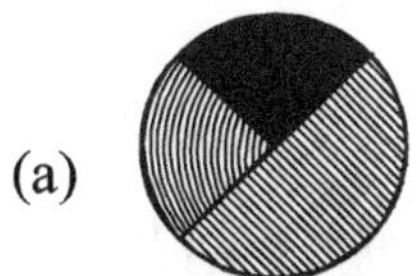

(b) 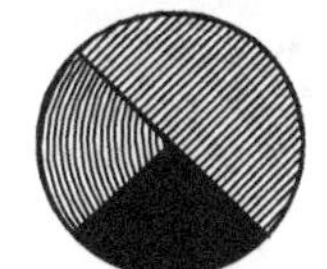

(c) 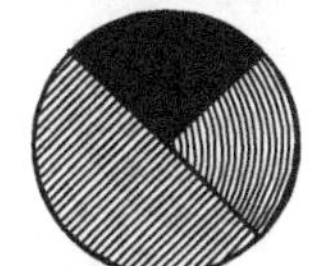

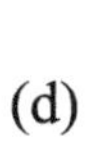

(d) 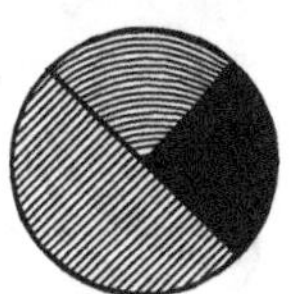

DIRECTIONS (Qs. 5-12) *Find the correct option for the water images for the following questions.*

5. 918423 (above the water line) ?

(a) ∂⇃8ᔭ53 (b) ∂⇃8ᔦ53

(c) ∂↿8ᔦ23 (d) ∂⇃8ᔦ53

6. What will be the water image of given diagram?

? (above the water line)

(a) ¿ (b) ʖ̇

(c) ·ɔ (d) ᴖ·

7. gLad (above the water line) ?

(a) ∂Γɐq (b) ∂˥ɘq

(c) ∂Γɘq (d) ∂Γɘp

8. SNOW (above the water line) ?

(a) ƧИOM (b) SИOM

(c) SИOM (d) SИOW

9. drain (above the water line) ?

(a) qɾɐ!u (b) qɾɘ!u

(c) qɾa!u (d) qɹɘ!u

10. ZEBRA (above the water line) ?

(a) ƸƎBꓤ∀ (b) ƸEBꓤ∀

(c) ƸEBꓤ∀ (d) ƸEBꓤ∀

11. 671 (above the water line) ?

(a) 9˩⇃ (b) ɘ˩⇃

(c) ɘ˩⇃ (d) ɘ˩↾

12. 9283 (above the water line) ?

(a) ∂Ƨ8Ɛ (b) ∂Ƨ8Ɛ

(c) ∂Ƨ83 (d) 6Ƨ83

DIRECTIONS (Qs. 13-20) : *In each of the following questions, choose the correct **water image** of the figure (X) from amongst the four alternatives (a), (b), (c), (d) given alongwith it.*

13. 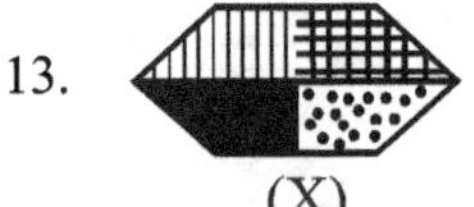

(X)

(a) 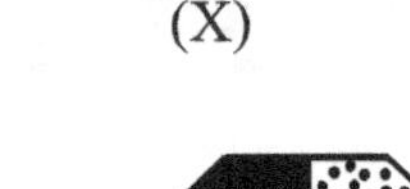 (b) 

(c) 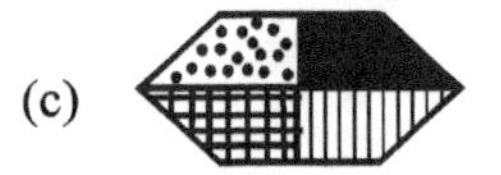 (d) 

14. 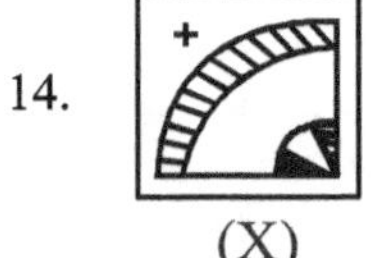

(X)

(a) 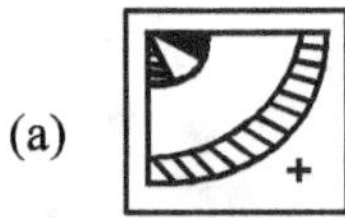 (b) 

(c) 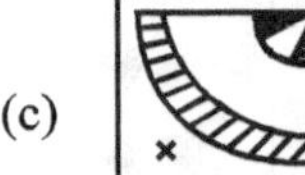 (d) 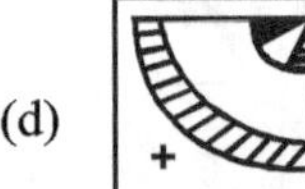

15.

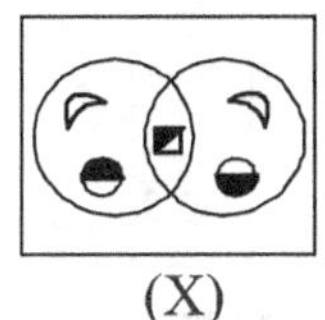

(X)

(a)  (b) 

(c) 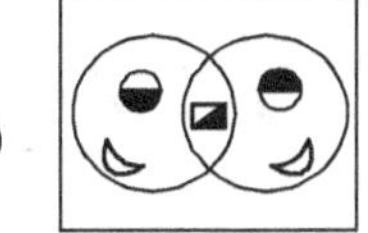 (d) 

16.

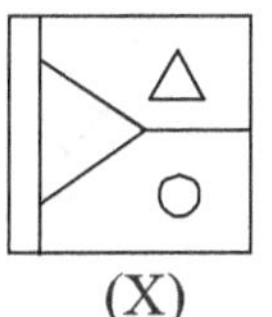

(X)

(a) 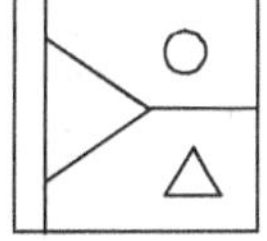 (b) 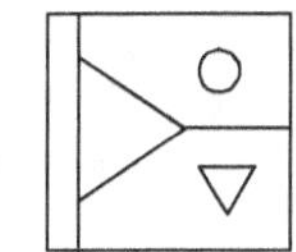

(c) 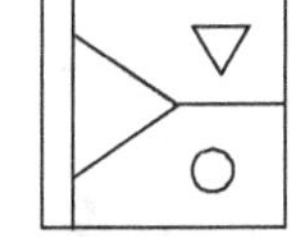 (d) 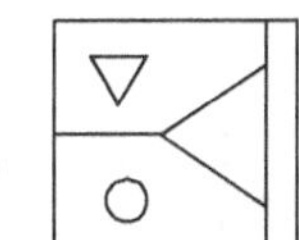

17.

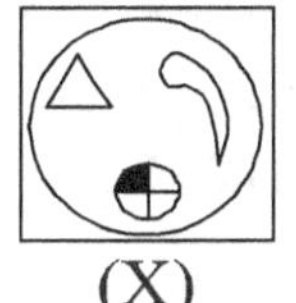

(X)

(a) 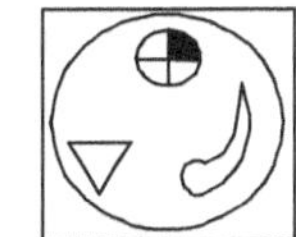 (b) 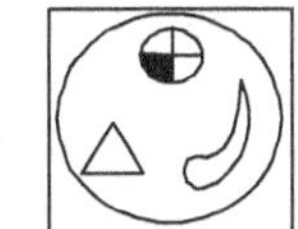

(c) 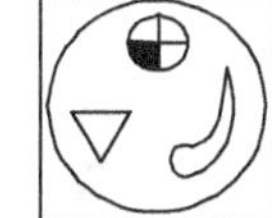 (d) 

18.

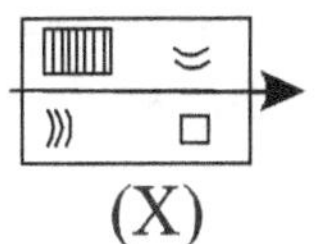

(X)

(a) 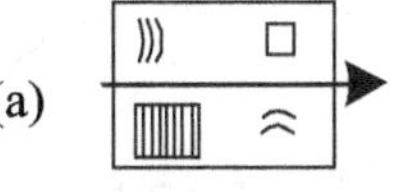 (b) 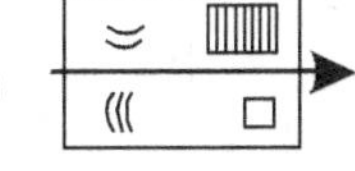

(c) 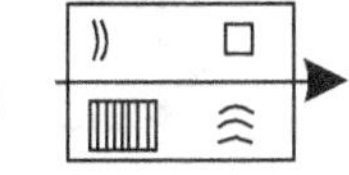 (d) 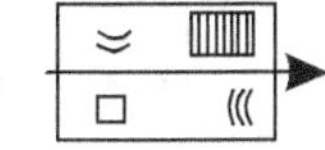

19.

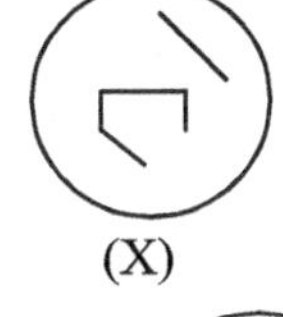

(X)

(a) 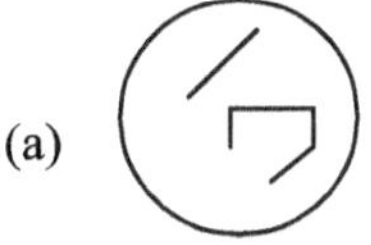 (b) 

(c)  (d) 

20.

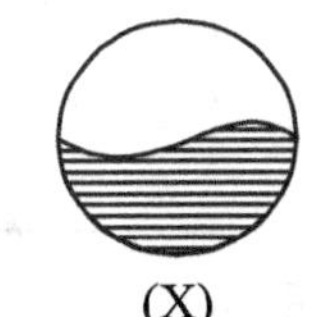

(X)

(a) 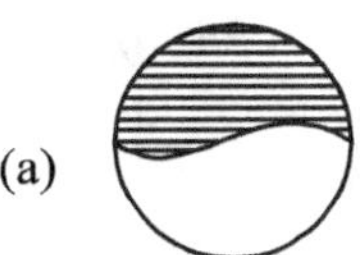 (b) 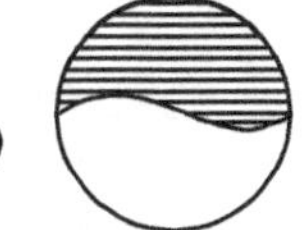

(c)  (d) 

21. Observe the figures below :

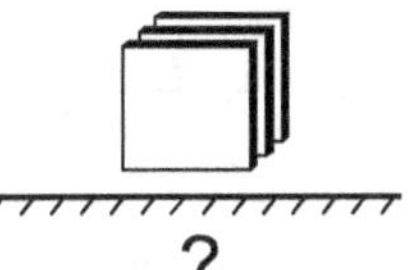

First rotate the figure by 90° in clock-wise direction and find out its water reflection from the given alternatives

(a)  (b) 

(c)  (d) 

22. Directions - Choose the water image of the 'Question Figure' from the given alternatives.

Question Figure:

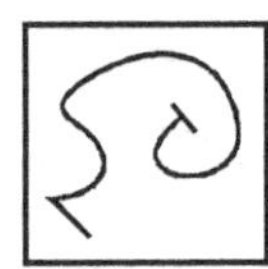

Answer Figures:

(a) 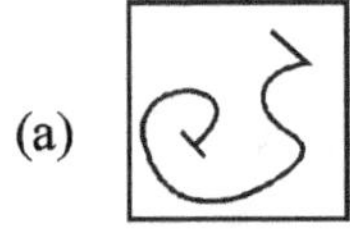 (b) 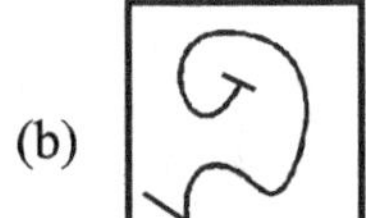

(c) 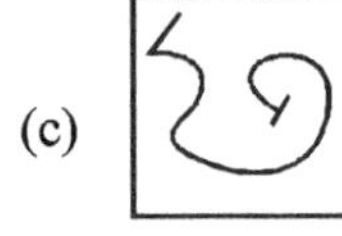 (d) 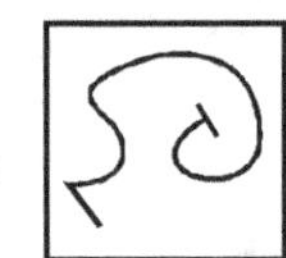

DIRECTIONS (Q. 23): *In this question, out of the four figures marked (a), (b), (c) and (d), three are similar in a certain manner. Howerer one figure is not like the other three. Choose the figure wchic is diffence from the rest.*

23.

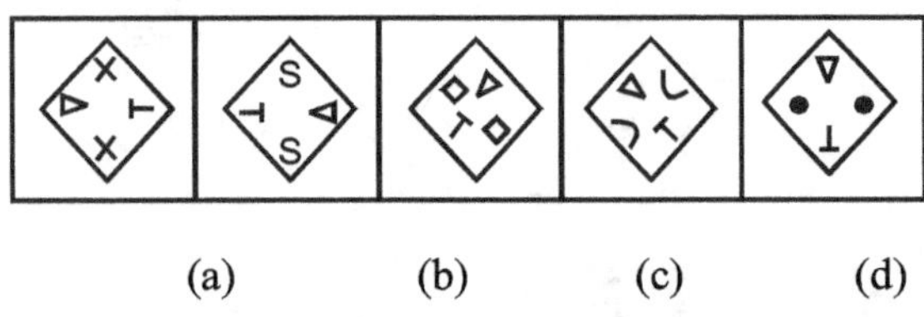

(a) (b) (c) (d)

DIRECTIONS: *In questions 24 to 26, four figures (a), (b), (c), (d) have been given in each question. Of these four figures three figures are similar in some way and one figure is different. Select the figure which is different.*

24. (a) 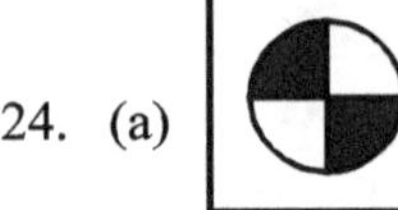  (b) 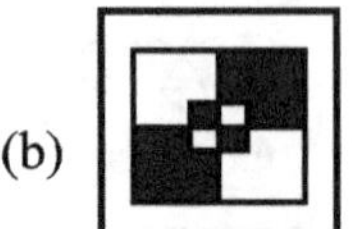

(c) 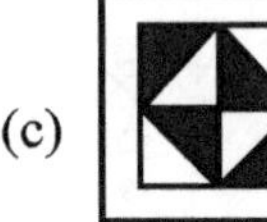 (d) 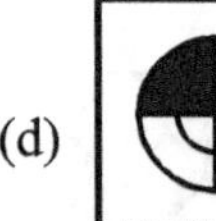

25. (a) 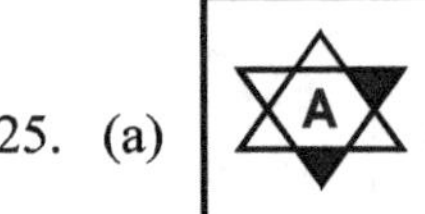 

(b) 

(c) 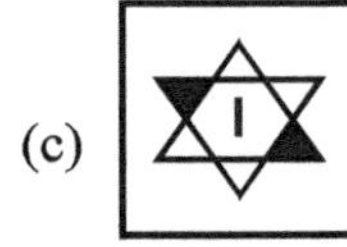

(d) 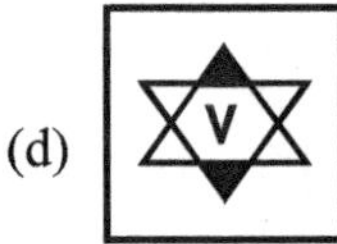

26. (a) 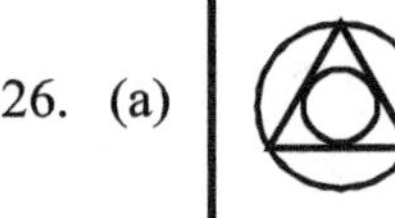 (b) 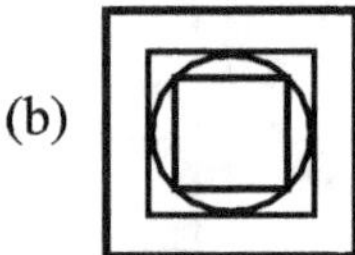

(c) 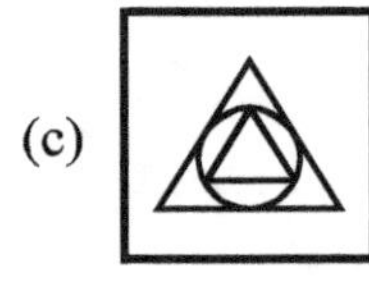 (d) 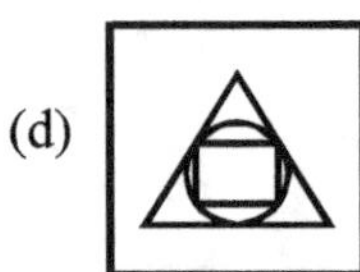

27. Select the correct mirror image of the given combination of letters and numbers.

(a) 0ƧИ8Я9U4T
(b) 0ƧИ8ЯeU4T
(c) 0ƧИ8ReU4T
(d) 0ƧN8ReU4T

28. Select the correct water image of the given figure.

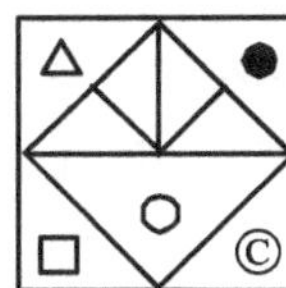

(a) 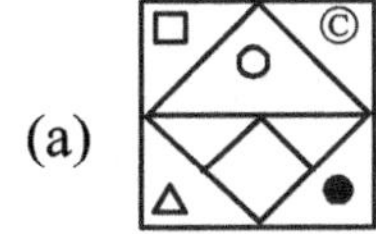 (b) 

(c) 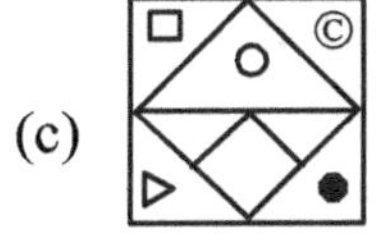 (d) 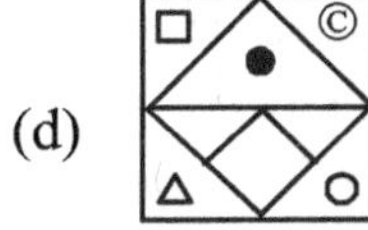

29. Select the correct mirror image of the given figure, if mirror is placed vertically to the left.

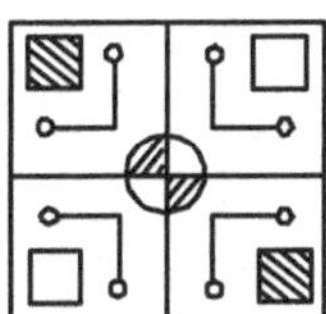

(a) 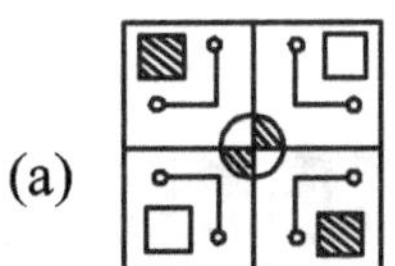 (b) 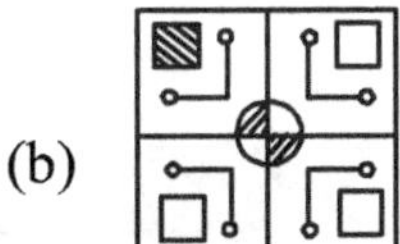

(c) 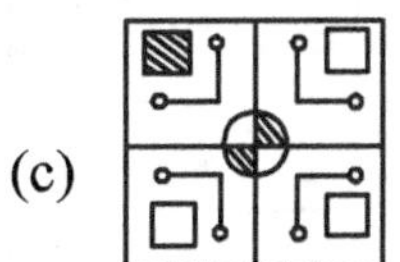 (d) 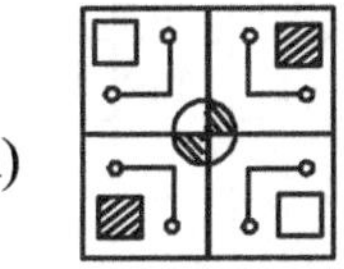

30. Select the correct water image of the given figure. **[2018]**

(a) 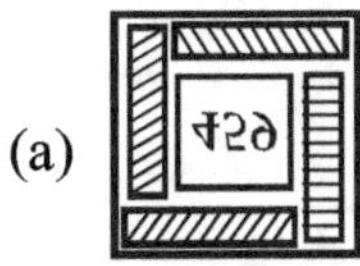 (b) 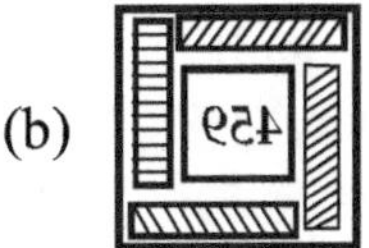

(c) 

(d) 

31. Select the correct mirror image of the given figure. **[2019]**

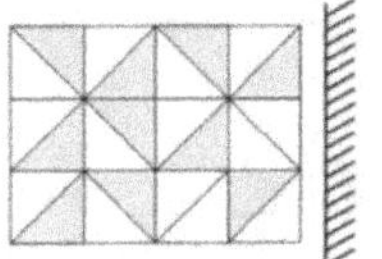

(a) 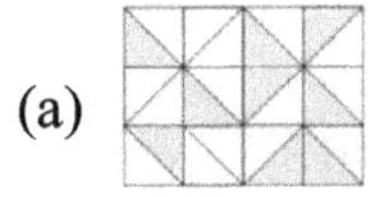 (b) 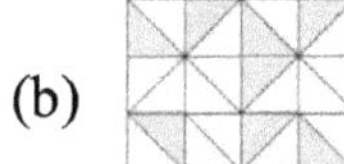

(c) 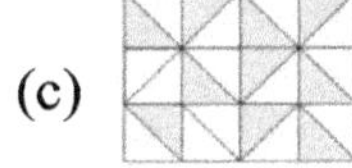 (d) 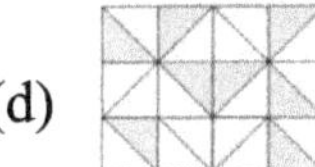

32. Find the correct mirror image of the given figure. **[2019]**

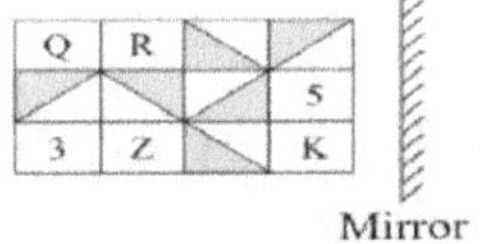

(a) 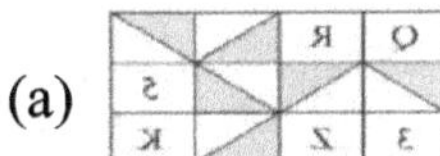

(b) 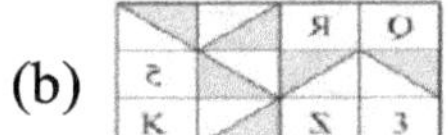

(c) 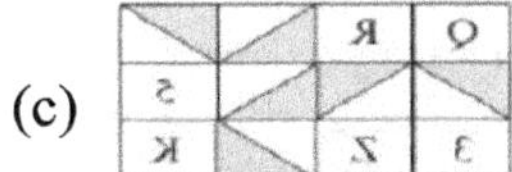

(d) 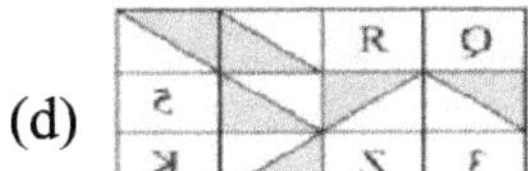

33. Select the correct water image of the given figure. **[2020]**

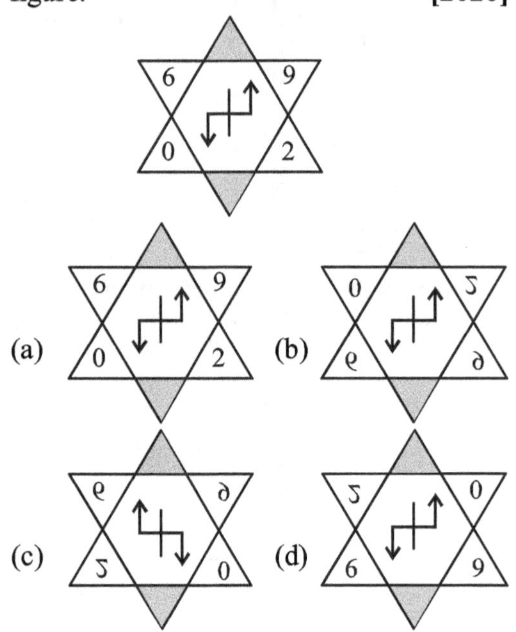

34. Choose the correct mirror image of the given figure, if mirror is placed vertically to the left. **[2021]**

(a)  (b) 

(c)  (d) 

35. Select the correct water image of the given combination of letters, numbers and symbols. **[2021]**

@7M5#∆RJ

(a) ſꓤ∇#ϛWL@ (b) @⅃W2#∆Ꞅ⅂

(c) @⅃W2#∇ꓤ⅂ (d) @⅃W2#∇Ꞅ⅂

36. Select the correct mirror image of the given combination of letters and numbers, if mirror is placed vertically to the left. **[2022]**

SO73CC22ER

(a) ЯƎƧƧƆƆƐOΓƧ

(b) ЯƎƧƧƆƆƐΓOƧ

(c) ЯƎƧƧƆƐƆΓOƧ

(d) ЯƎƧƧƆƐƆΓƧO

ANSWER KEY

LEVEL-1

1	(c)	**5**	(b)	**9**	(c)	**13**	(a)	**17**	(c)	**21**	(b)	**25**	(c)	**29**	(b)	**33**	(b)	**37**	(a)
2	(a)	**6**	(c)	**10**	(d)	**14**	(a)	**18**	(b)	**22**	(b)	**26**	(b)	**30**	(a)	**34**	(a)	**38**	(a)
3	(d)	**7**	(c)	**11**	(a)	**15**	(d)	**19**	(a)	**23**	(c)	**27**	(d)	**31**	(a)	**35**	(b)	**39**	(a)
4	(d)	**8**	(c)	**12**	(d)	**16**	(c)	**20**	(d)	**24**	(a)	**28**	(a)	**32**	(a)	**36**	(a)	**40**	(b)

LEVEL-2

1	(d)	**5**	(d)	**9**	(b)	**13**	(a)	**17**	(c)	**21**	(b)	**25**	(a)	**29**	(d)	**33**	(b)		
2	(d)	**6**	(b)	**10**	(c)	**14**	(d)	**18**	(a)	**22**	(b)	**26**	(d)	**30**	(a)	**34**	(d)		
3	(c)	**7**	(c)	**11**	(b)	**15**	(d)	**19**	(d)	**23**	(d)	**27**	(b)	**31**	(c)	**35**	(d)		
4	(d)	**8**	(a)	**12**	(c)	**16**	(b)	**20**	(b)	**24**	(d)	**28**	(b)	**32**	(a)	**36**	(b)		

CHAPTER

Paper Folding & Paper Cutting

PAPER FOLDING :

The problems on paper folding involve the process of selecting a figure which would most nearly match the pattern that would be formed when a transparent sheet carrying designs on either side of a dotted line is folded along this line. The figure has to be selected from a set of four alternatives (answer or response figures).

DIRECTION : In each one of the following examples, find from amongst the four response figures, the one which resembles the pattern formed when the transparent sheet, carrying a design, is folded along the dotted line.

ILLUSTRATION 1 :

Transparent Sheet

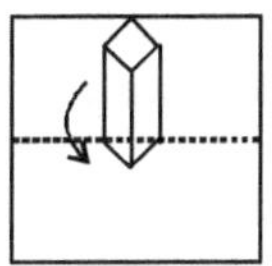

Response Figures

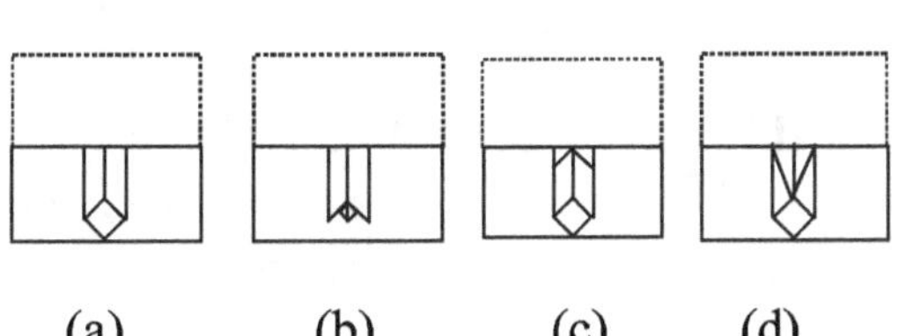

(a) (b) (c) (d)

Sol. **(d)** Clearly, the upper half of the square sheet has been folded over the lower half. The combination of the design in the lower half and the water image of the design in the upper half will appear as the resultant design when the sheet is folded. Visualising this combination we get the design shown in fig. (d). Hence, fig. (d) is the answer.

ILLUSTRATION 2 :

Transparent Sheet

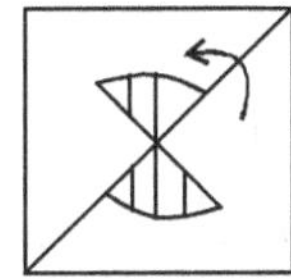

Response Figures

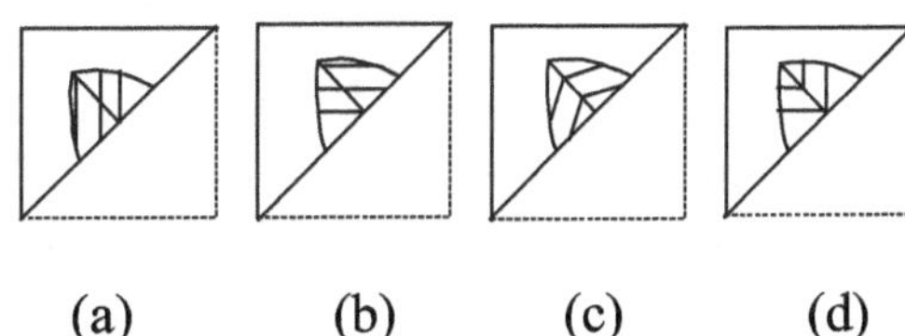

(a) (b) (c) (d)

Sol. **(d)** Here, the sheet has been folded diagonally and design on either side of the dotted line combine to from fig .(d). Hence, fig.(d) is the answer.

PAPER CUTTING :

The problems on paper cutting contain a set of three figures showing the manner in which a piece of paper has been folded. In each of the first two figures, a dotted line together with an arrow on it has been given indicating the line along which the paper is to be folded and the direction of the fold respectively. In the third figure, there are marks showing the position and nature of the cut made in the folded sheet. The candidate has to select one of the figures from the set of four answer figures (1), (2), (3) and (4), that would most nearly match the pattern when the paper is unfolded. It will be interesting to see that the designs of the cut will appear on each fold made in the paper.

ILLUSTRATION 3 :

Consider the three figures, marked X, Y, and Z showing one fold in X, another in Y and cut in Z. From amongst the four alternative figures (a), (b), (c) and (d), select the one showing the unfolded position of Z.

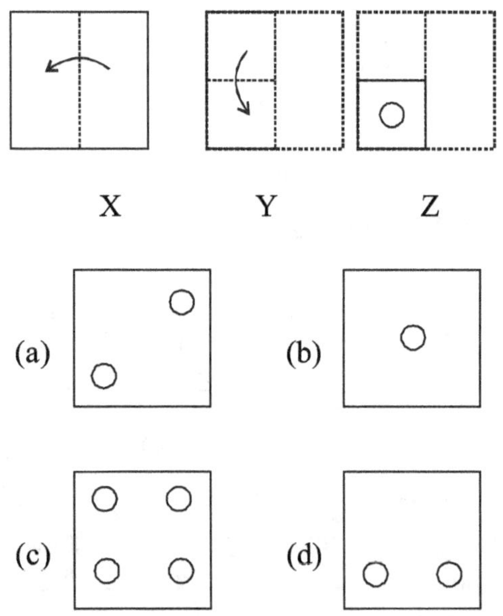

***Sol.* (c)** In fig. (X), the square sheet of paper has been folded along the vertical line of symmetry so that the right half of the sheet overlaps the left half.

In fig. (Y), the sheet is folded further to a quarter.

In fig.(Z), a circle has been punched in the folded sheet.

Clearly, the punched circle will be created in each quarter of the paper .

Thus, when the paper is unfolded, four circles will appear symmetrically over it and the paper will then appear as shown in fig. (c). Hence, fig. (c) is the answer.

ILLUSTRATION 4 :

Find from amongst the four response figures, the one that resembles the pattern formed when the transparent sheet, carrying a design is folded along the dotted line.

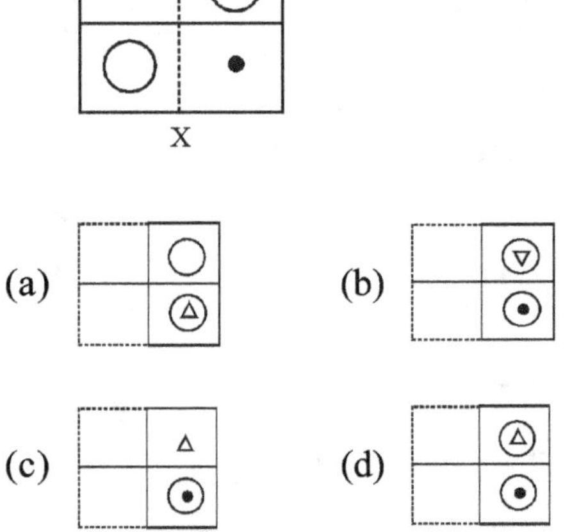

***Sol.* (b)** Clearly left half is folded on the right half. Hence triangle is in side the circle and circle is surrounding the dot. The answer is (b).

ILLUSTRATION 5 :

Consider the figures X and Y showing a rectangular sheet of paper folded in fig. (X) and punched in fig. (Y). From amongst the answer figures (a), (b), (c), (d), select the figure which will most closely resemble the unfolded position of figure (Y).

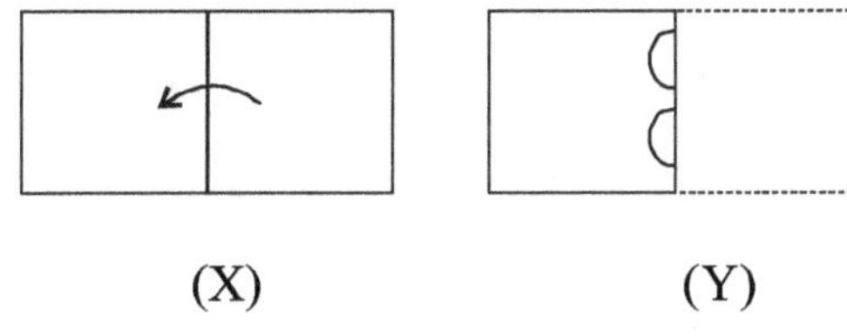

(X) (Y)

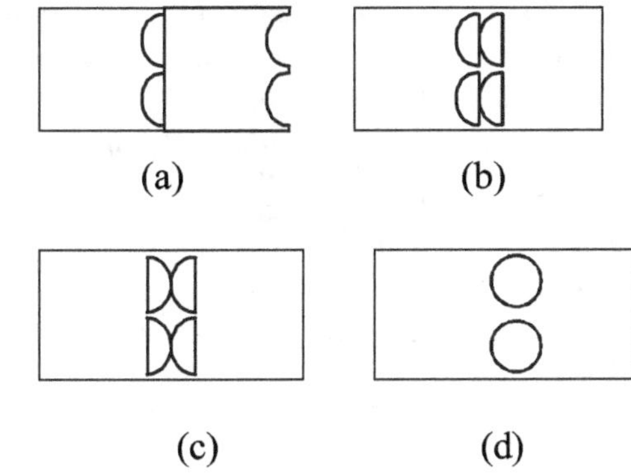

(a) (b)

(c) (d)

***Sol.* (d)** In fig. (X), the rectangular sheet of paper has been folded along a line that divides the sheet into two equal halves. In figure (Y), two semicircular holes are punched close at the centre of the sheet as shown figure (d).

LEVEL 1

DIRECTION (Q.1): *In each one of the following questions, find from amongst the four response figures, the one which resembles the pattern formed when the transparent sheet, carrying a design, is folded along the dotted line.*

1. **Transparent Sheet**

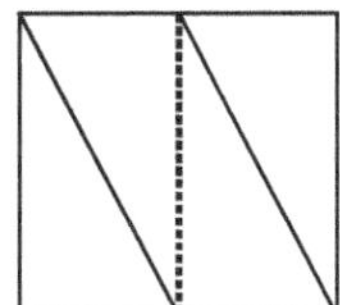

Response Figures

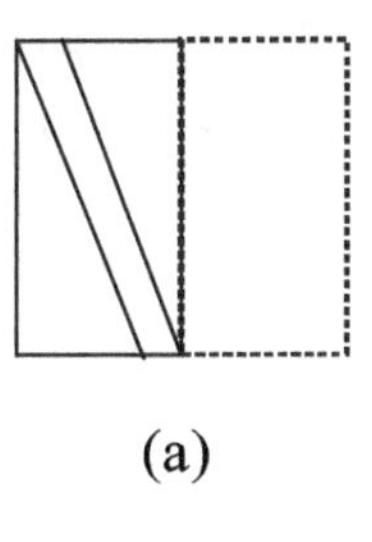

(a)

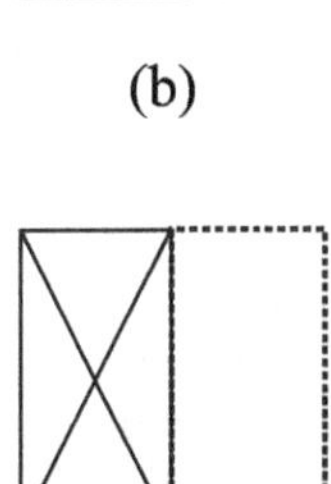

(b)

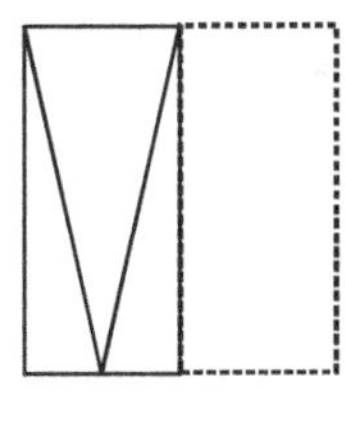

(c)

(d)

DIRECTIONS (Qs. 2-3) : *In each of the following questions a set of three figures A, B and C showing a sequence of folding of a piece of paper. Fig. (C) shows the manner in which the folded paper has been cut. These three figures are followed by four answer figures from which you have to choose a figure which would most closely resemble the unfolded form of fig. (C).*

2.
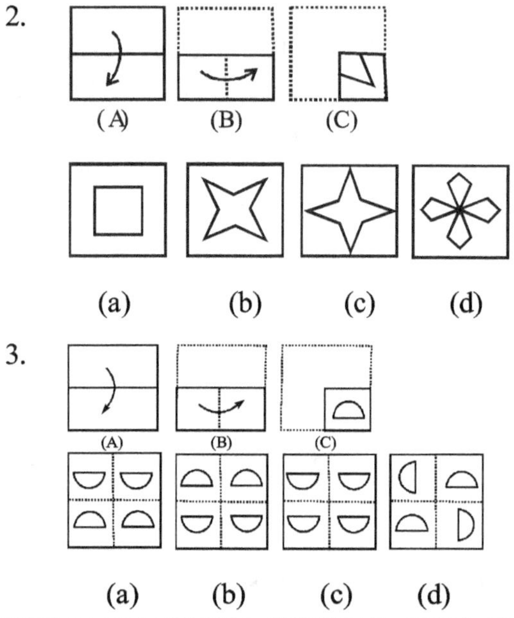

DIRECTIONS (Qs. 4-5): *The following questions are related to paper cutting. The questions that follow contain a set of three figures X, Y and Z, showing a sequence of folding of a piece of paper. Fig. (Z) shows the manner in which the folded paper has been cut. These three figures are followed by four answer figures 1, 2, 3 and 4 (IInd Set) from which you have to choose a figure which would most closely resemble the unfolded form of fig. (Z).*

4. Sequence of folding the paper

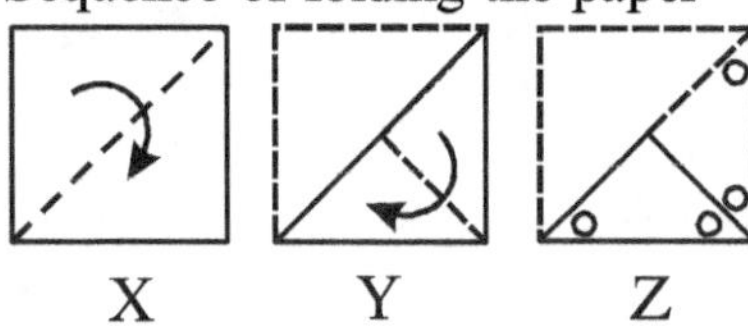

Answer-Figures

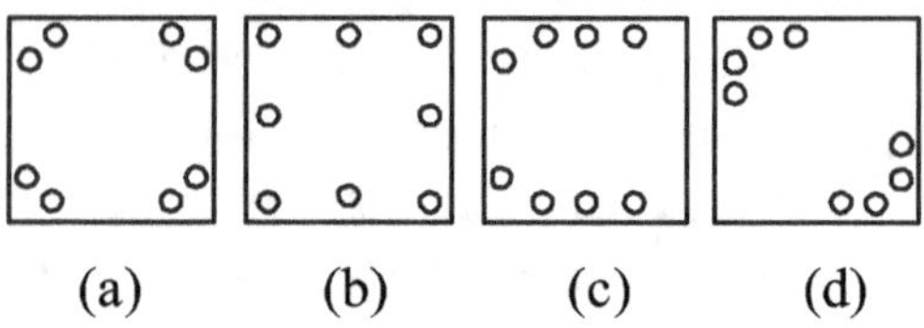

5. Sequence of folding the paper

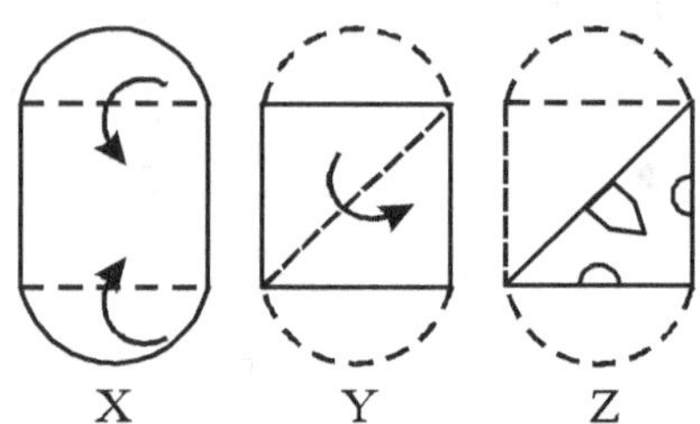

Answer-Figures

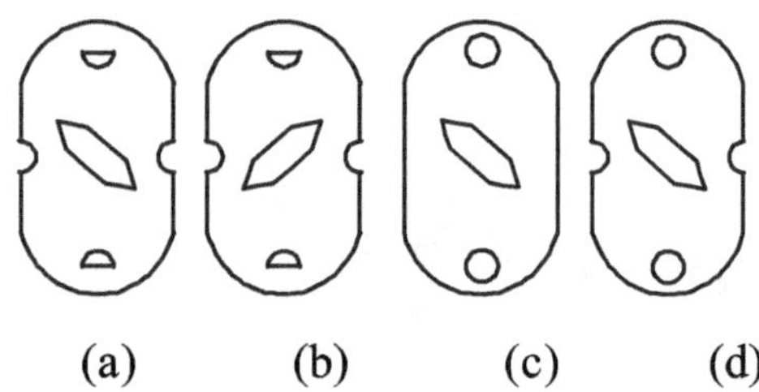

DIRECTIONS (Qs. 6-7) : *A paper is folded and a cut is made. Select the alternative which correctly depicts how the paper will appear when it is opened?*

6.
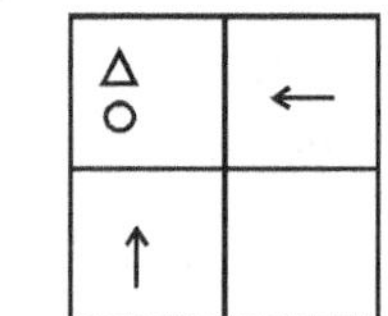

(a) (b)

(c)
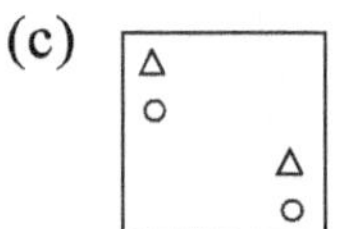

(d)
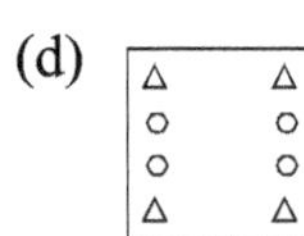

7. 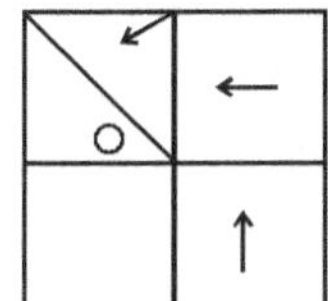

(a) 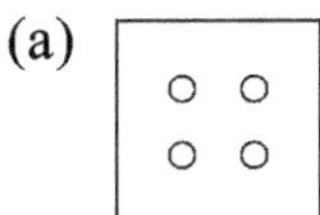

(b) 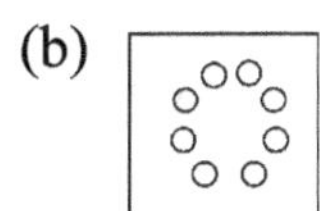

(c) 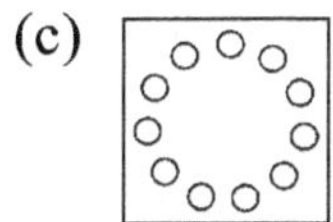

(d) 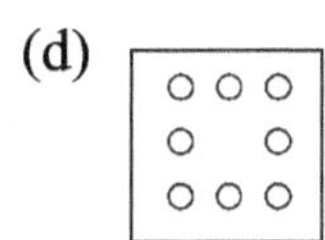

8. A square piece of paper is folded and cut at specific spots as shown in the figure. The paper when unfolded will look as shown in one of the alternatives. Select the correct alternative.

Question figure:

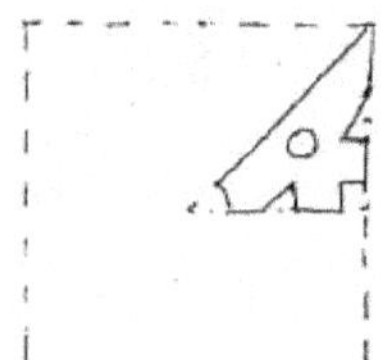

Answer Figures:

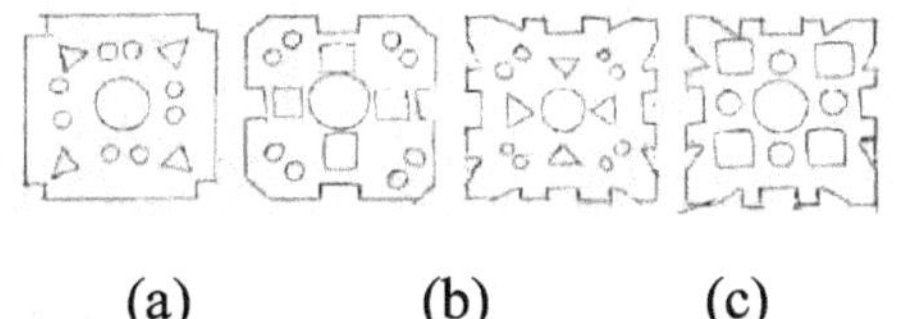

(a) (b) (c) (d)

DIRECTION (Q. 9) : *In the following question, figures showing a sequence of folding and cutting a paper are given. Which could resemble the figure in the Answer figure?*

9. **Problem Figures**

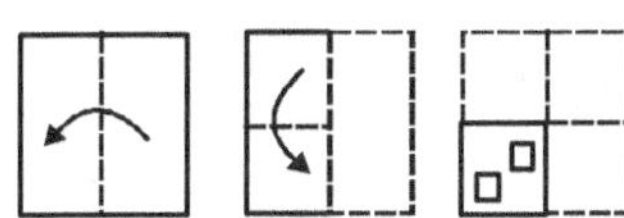

Answer Figures

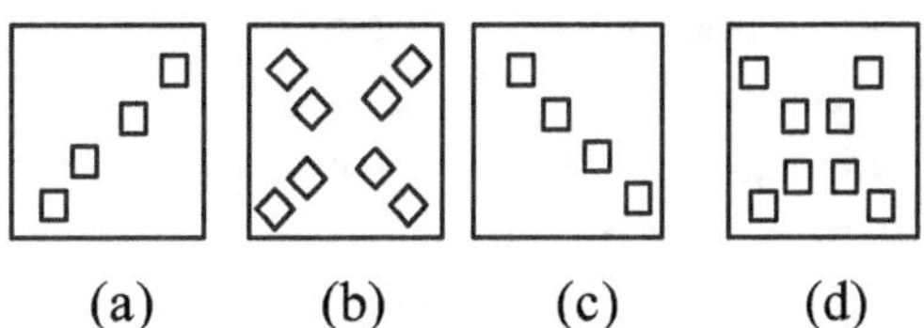

(a) (b) (c) (d)

10. A square piece of paper is folded and cut at specific spot as shown in the figure. The paper when unfolded will look like as shown in one of the alternatives. Select the correct alternative.

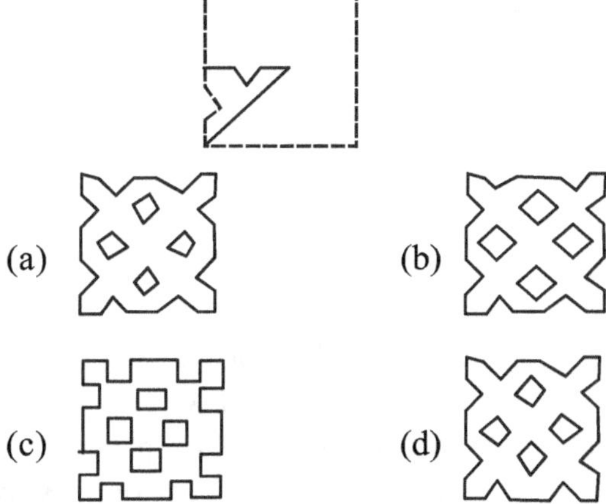

11. Given question consists of a set of three figures X, Y and Z showing a sequence of folding of a piece of paper. Fig. (Z) shows the manner in which the folded paper has been cut. Select a figure from the options which would most closely resemble the unfolded form of Fig. (Z).

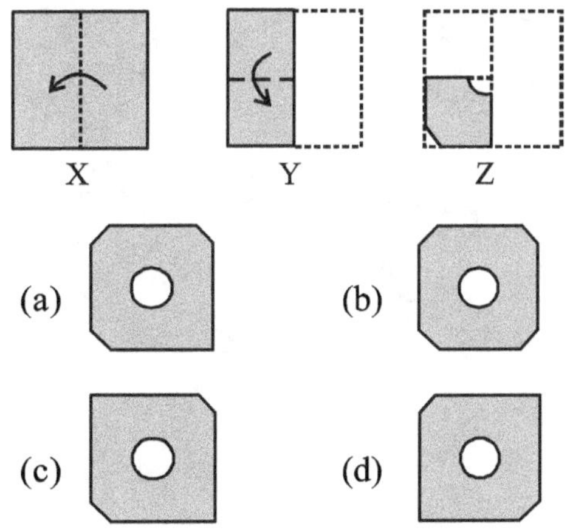

12. A square transparent sheet with a pattern and a dotted line on it is given. Select a figure from the options as to how the pattern would appear when the transparent sheet is folded along the dotted line.

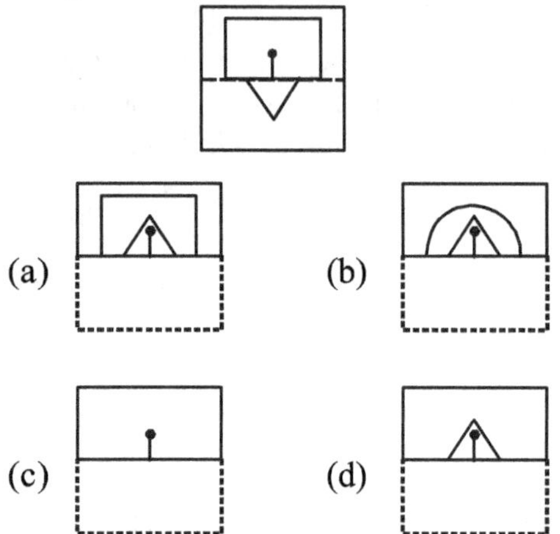

13. The given question consists of a set of three figures X, Y and Z which shows the folding of a piece of paper. Fig. (Z) shows the manner in which the folded paper has been cut. Select a figure from the options which shows the unfolded form of Fig. (Z).

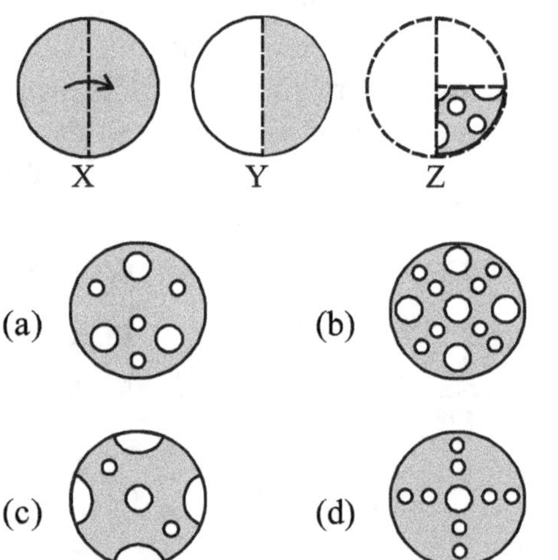

14. The question consists of a set of three figures X, Y and Z showing a sequence of folding of a piece of paper. Fig. (Z) shows the manner in which the folded paper has been cut. Select a figure from the options which would most closely resemble the unfolded form of Fig. (Z).

[2019]

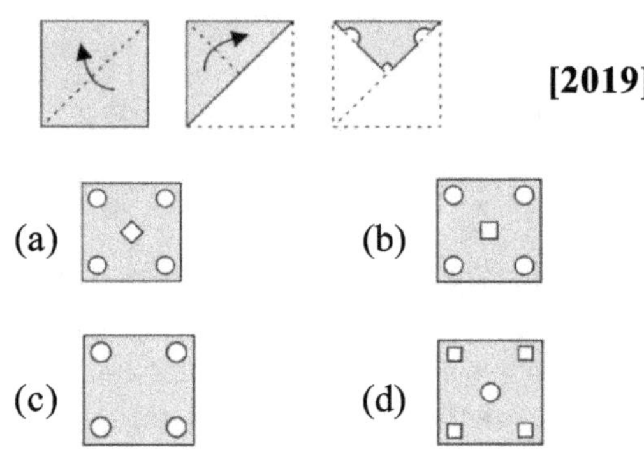

15. Select a figure from the options as to how the pattern would appear when the transparent sheet is folded along the dotted line. **[2021]**

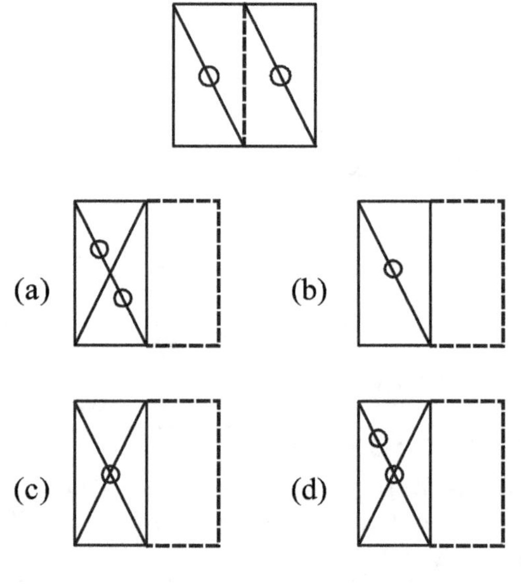

LEVEL 2

DIRECTIONS (Qs. 1-4) : *In the following questions, a square sheet of paper is folded along the dotted lines and then cuts are made on it. How would the sheet look when opened? Select the correct figure from the given choices.*

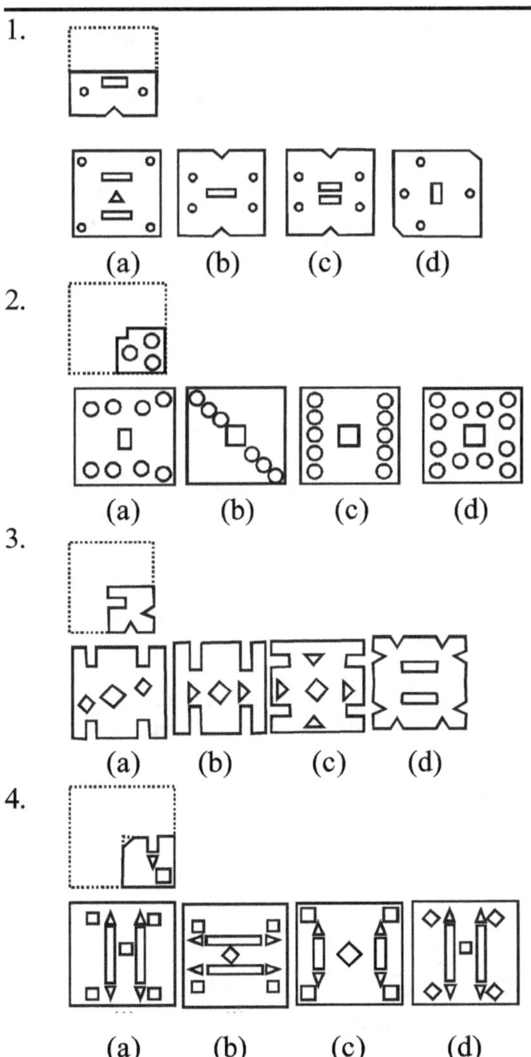

5.

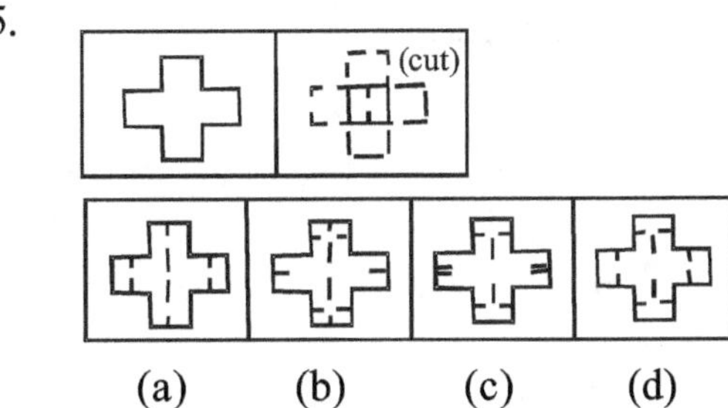

6. A square paper is folded in a particular manner and a punch is made. When unfolded the paper appears as given below:

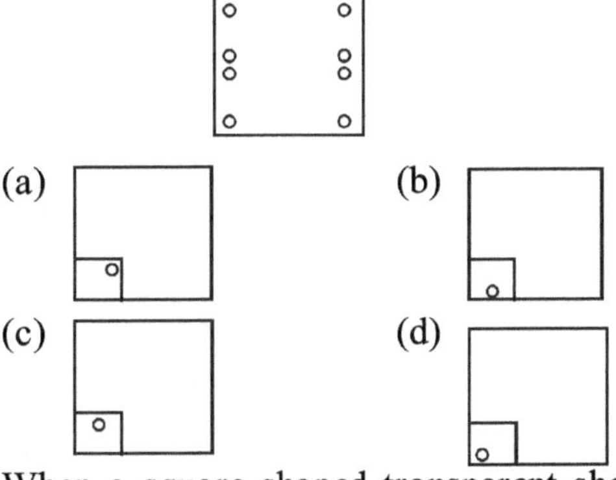

7. When a square shaped transparent sheet with the pattern shown in the figure is folded along the dotted along the dotted line which pattern would appear?

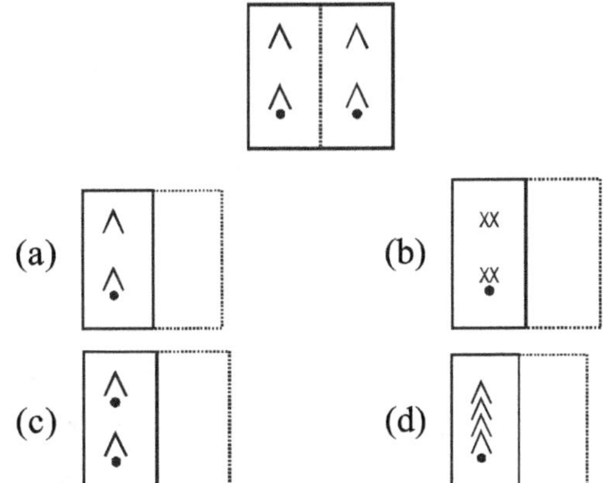

DIRECTIONS (Qs. 8-10) : *Consider the three figures, marked X, Y and Z showing one fold x another in Y and cut in Z. From amongst the four alternative Figures 1, 2, 3 and 4. Select the one showing the unfolded position of Z.*

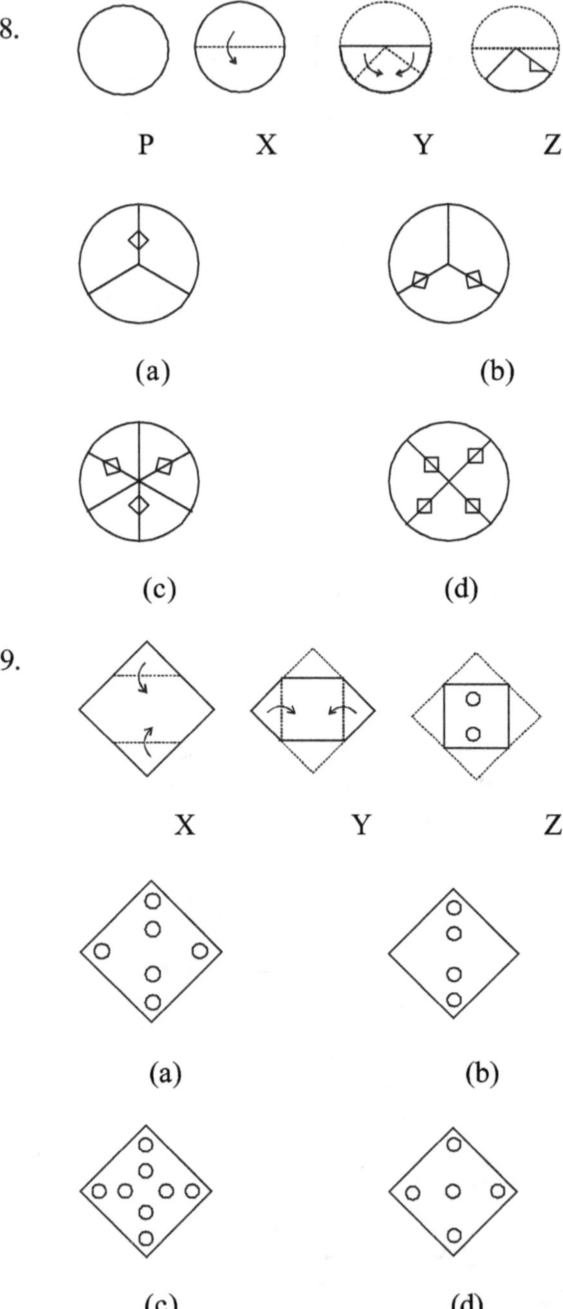

10.

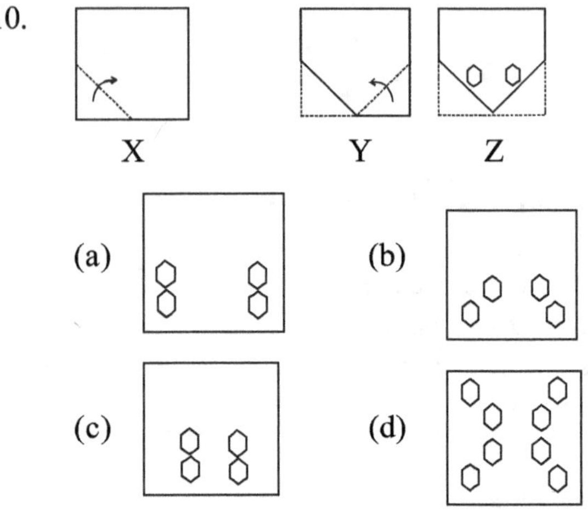

DIRECTIONS (Qs. 11-15) : *In the following questions, a square sheet of paper is folded along the dotted lines and then cuts are made on it. How would the sheet look when opened? Select the correct figure from the given choices.*

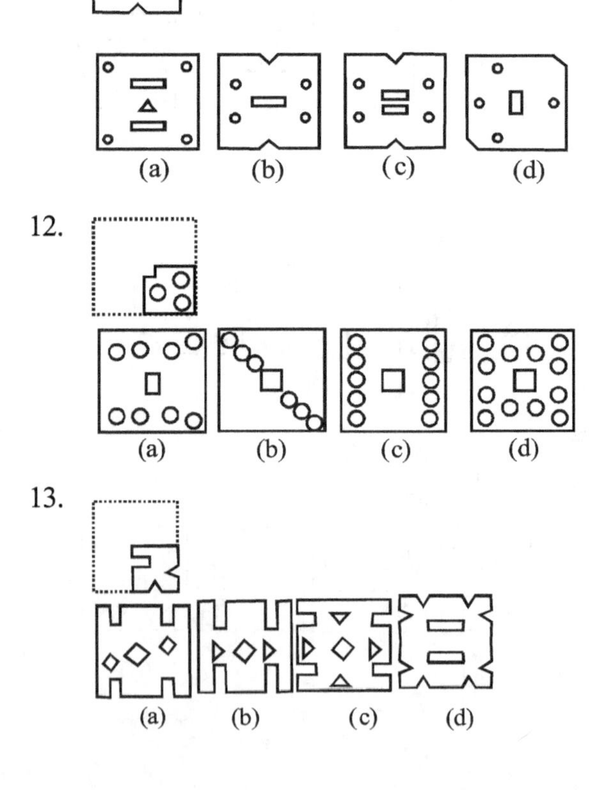

14.

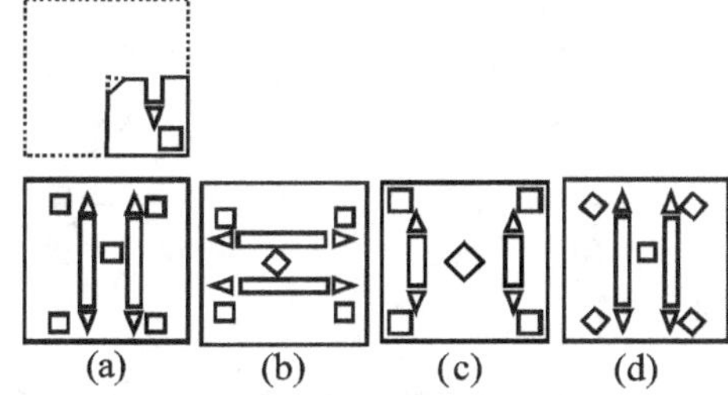

15.

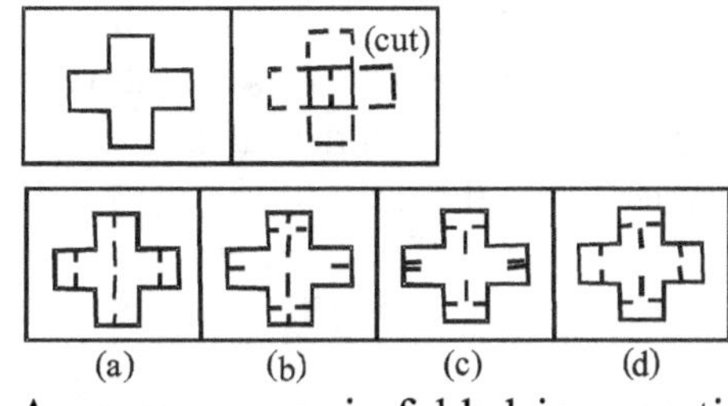

16. A square paper is folded in a particular manner and a punch is made. When unfolded the paper appears as given below:

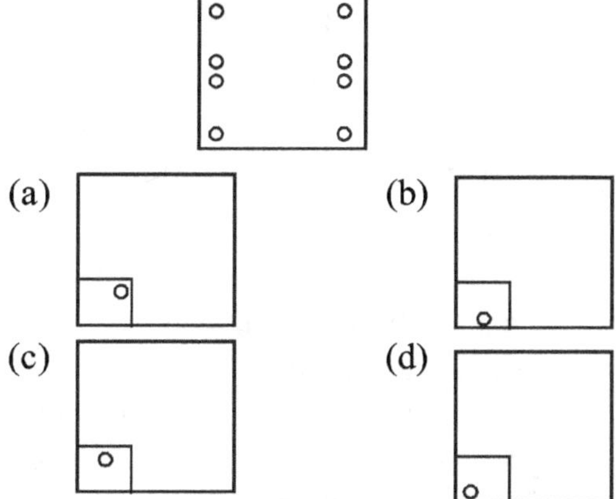

17. When a square shaped transparent sheet with the pattern shown in the figure is folded along the dotted along the dotted line which pattern would appear?

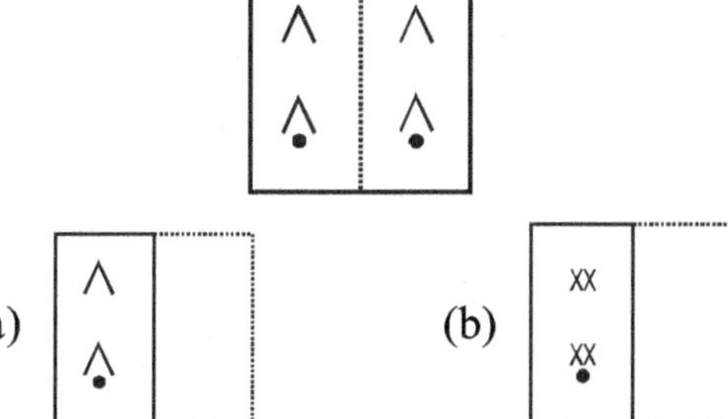

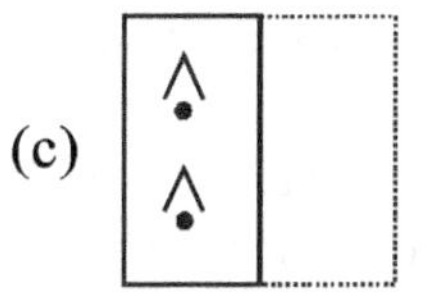

18. The given question consists of a set of three figures X, Y and Z showing a sequence of folding of a piece of paper. Fig. (Z) shows the manner in which the folded paper has been cut. Select a figure from the options which would most closely resemble the unfolded form of Fig. (Z).

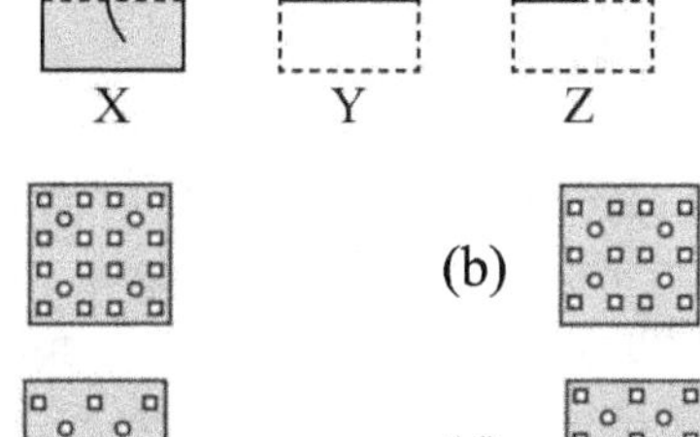

19. The question consists of a set of three figures X, Y and Z showing a sequence of folding of a piece of paper. Fig. (Z) shows the manner in which the folded paper has been cut. Select a figure from the options which would most closely resemble the unfolded form of Fig. (Z).

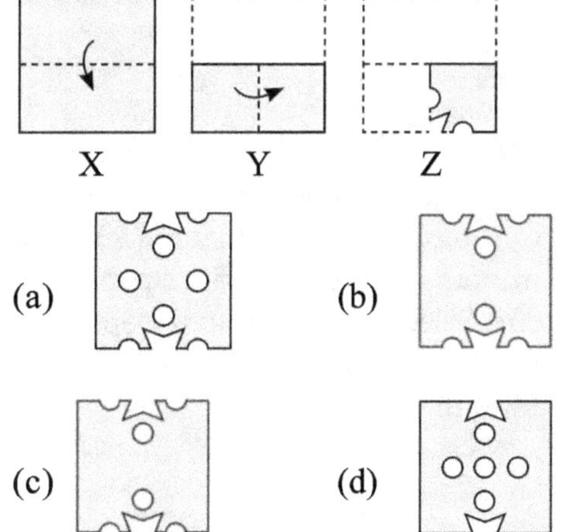

20. The given question consists of a set of three figures P, Q and R showing a sequence of folding of a piece of paper. Fig. (R) shows the manner in which the folded paper has been cut. Select a figure from the options which would most closely resemble the unfolded form of Fig. (R). [2019]

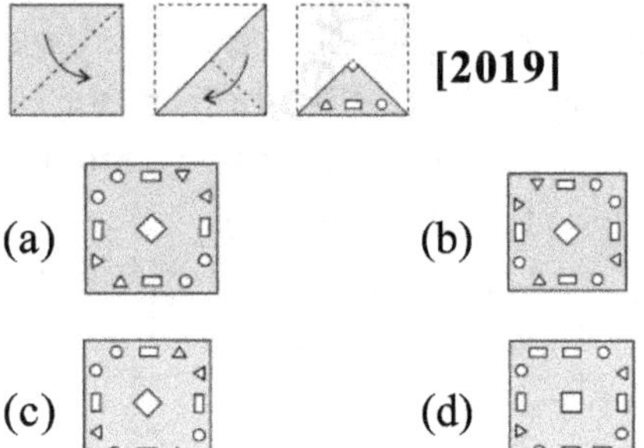

21. The given question consists of a set of three figures X, Y and Z showing a sequence of folding of a piece of paper. Fig. (Z) shows the manner in which the folded paper has been cut. Select a figure from the options which would most closely resemble the unfolded form of Fig. (Z). [2019]

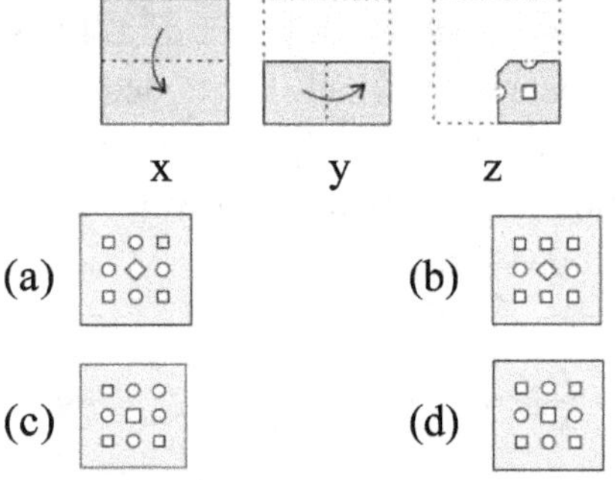

22. The given question consists of three figures P, Q and R showing a sequence of folding of a piece of paper. Figure (R) shows the manner in which the folded paper has been cut. Select a figure from the options which would most closely resembles the unfolded form of figure (R). [2020]

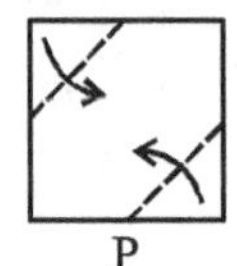
P

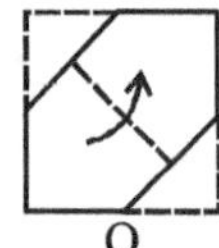
Q

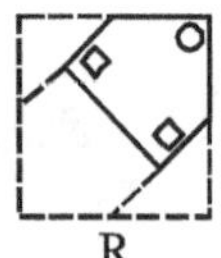
R

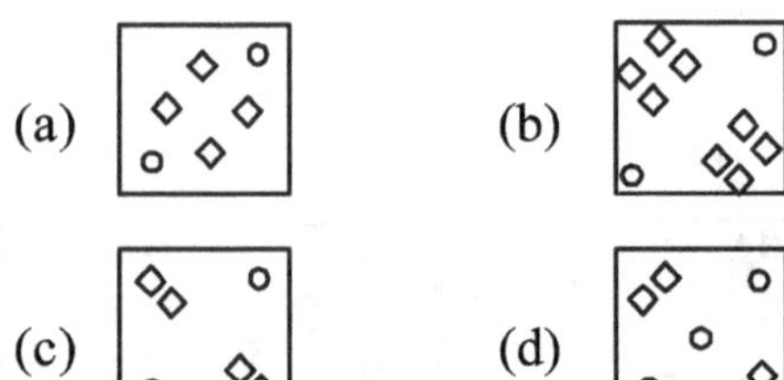

23. A square transparent sheet with a pattern and a dotted line on it is shown here. Select a figure from the options as to how the pattern would appear when the transparent sheet is folded along the dotted line. [2020]

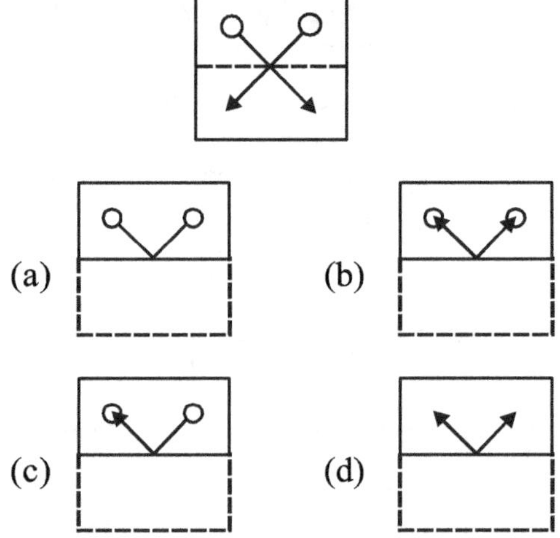

24. A square transparent sheet with a pattern and a dotted line on it is given. Select a figure from the options as to how the pattern would appear when the transparent sheet is folded along the dotted line. [2020]

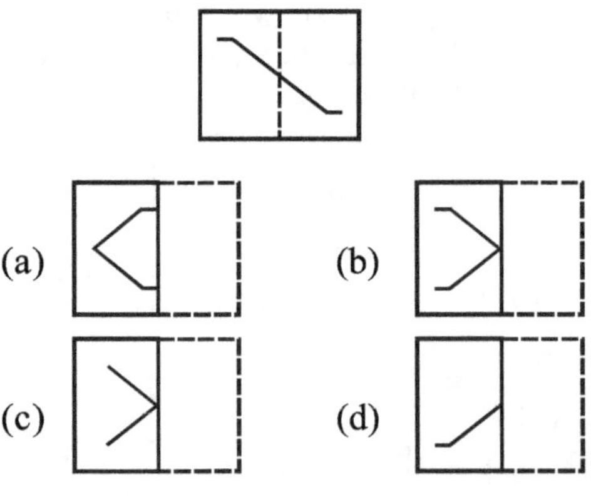

25. Three figures X, Y and Z showing a sequence of folding of a piece of paper. Fig. (Z) shows the manner in which the folded paper has been cut. Select a figure from the options which represents the unfolded form of Fig. (Z). **[2021]**

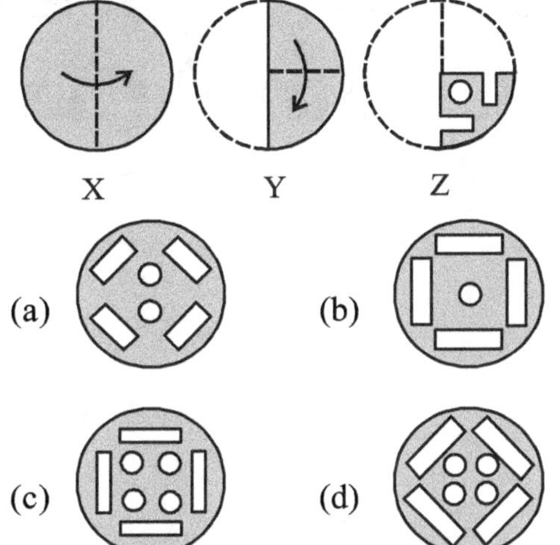

26. A square transparent sheet with a pattern and a dotted line on it is given. Select a figure from the options as to how the pattern would appear when the transparent sheet is folded along the dotted line. **[2022]**

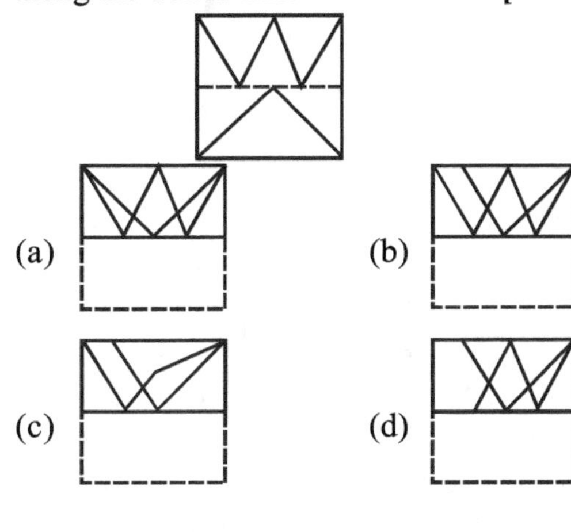

ANSWER KEY																			
LEVEL-1																			
1	(d)	**2**	(a)	**3**	(b)	**4**	(a)	**5**	(d)	**6**	(d)	**7**	(b)	**8**	(c)	**9**	(d)	**10**	(a)
11	(b)	**12**	(a)	**13**	(b)	**14**	(a)	**15**	(c)										
LEVEL-2																			
1	(c)	**3**	(d)	**5**	(a)	**7**	(a)	**9**	(b)	**11**	(c)	**13**	(d)	**15**	(a)	**17**	(a)	**19**	(c)
2	(d)	**4**	(c)	**6**	(d)	**8**	(d)	**10**	(b)	**12**	(d)	**14**	(c)	**16**	(d)	**18**	(a)	**20**	(a)
21	(a)	**22**	(b)	**23**	(b)	**24**	(b)	**25**	(c)	**26**	(a)								

CHAPTER

Embedded Figures, Figure Completion

A figure (X) is said to be embedded in a figure Y, if figure Y contains figure (X) as its part. Thus problems on embedded figures contain a figure (X) followed by four complex figures in such a way that fig (X) is embedded in one of these. The figure containing the figure (X) is your answer.

DIRECTIONS (ILLUSTRATIONS 1 & 2) : In each of the following examples, fig (X) is embedded in any one of the four alternative figures (a), (b), (c) or (d). Find the alternative which contains fig. (X) as its part.

ILLUSTRATION 1 :

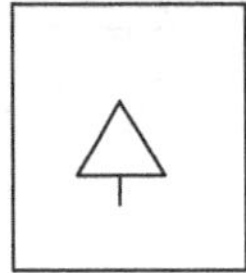

(X)

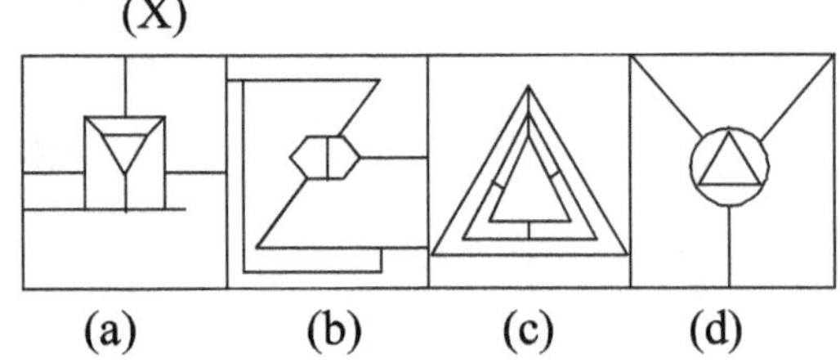

(a) (b) (c) (d)

***Sol.* (c)** On close observation, we find that fig. (X) is embedded in fig. (c) as shown below :

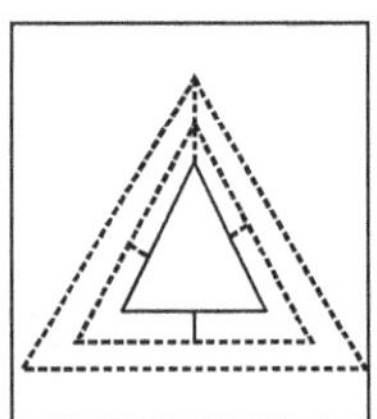

Hence, the answer is (c)

ILLUSTRATION 2 :

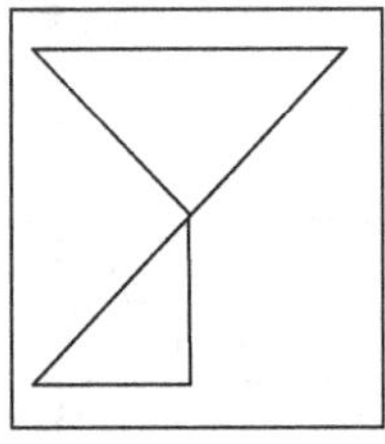

(X)

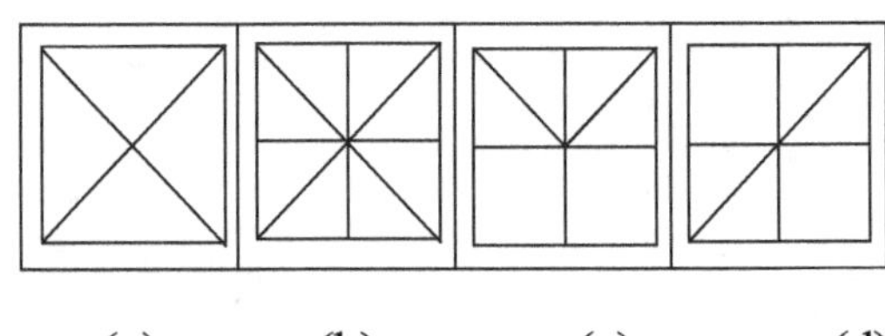

(a) (b) (c) (d)

***Sol.* (b)** Clearly, fig. (X) is embedded fig. (b) as shown below :

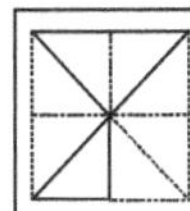

Hence, the answer is (b)

ILLUSTRATION 3 :

Find amongst the four alternatives (a), (b), (c) and (d), the figure which most nearly contains the figure (X).

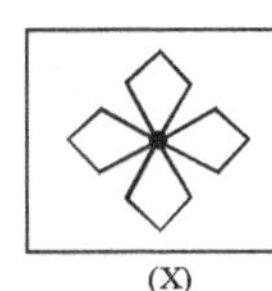

(X)

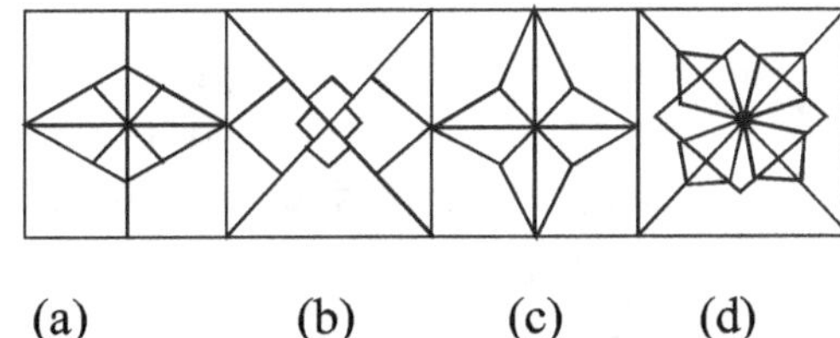

(a) (b) (c) (d)

Sol. (d) Figure (X) is not contained in (a), nor in (b) nor in (c) but in (d), (X) is embedded. Thus answer is (d).

COMPLETION OF INCOMPLETE PATTERN:

In such problems, a figure following a particular sequence or pattern is given, in which a part, usually one-fourth, is left blank. This problem figure is followed by four alternative figures. One is required to choose the one which best fits into the blank space of problem figure so as to complete the original pattern.

COMPLETION OF A SQUARE

Each problem in this topic contains five different parts numbered 1, 2, 3, 4 and 5. A square is to be constructed by selecting three parts out of five parts. The steps given below can help the candidate to do the needful:

(i) Select a piece which contains a right angle between two adjacent outer edges.

(ii) Try to fit another piece in its vacant spaces. If it does not fit, try another piece.

(iii) Repeat this system with different sets of such pieces till you are sure that the two pieces fit in each other.

(iv) Find the third piece out of the remaining three pieces to get the square complete.

ILLUSTRATION 4 :

Select a figure from the four alternatives, which when placed in the blank space of figure (X) would complete the pattern.

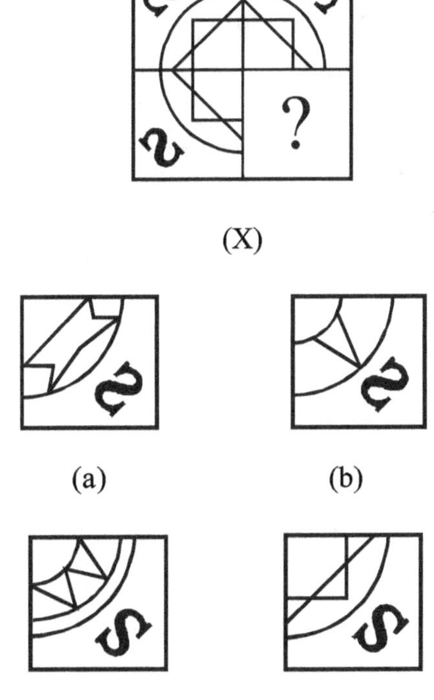

(X)

(a) (b)

(c) (d)

Sol. **(d)** Clearly, figure (d) will complete the pattern when placed in the blank space of figure (X) as shown below. Hence, the answer is (d).

ILLUSTRATION 5 :

Find out which of the figures (a), (b), (c) and (d) can be formed from the pieces given in figure (X)

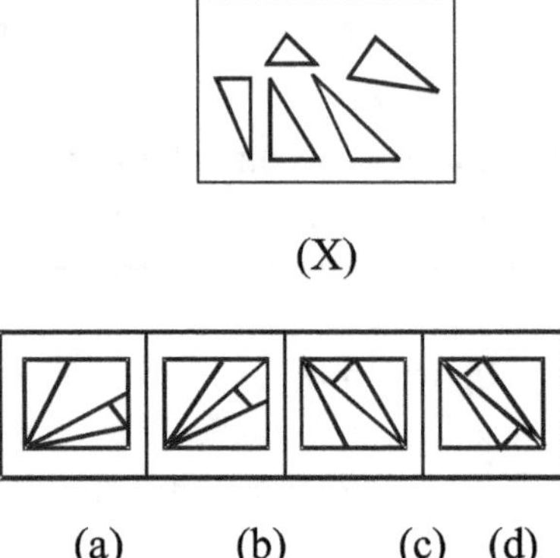

(a) (b) (c) (d)

Sol. **(c)** Clearly the pieces in the figure (X) are in the figure (c).

The answer is therefore (c).

ILLUSTRATION 6 :

Find three figures out of the following five figures a, b, c, d and e which when fitted into each other would form a complete square.

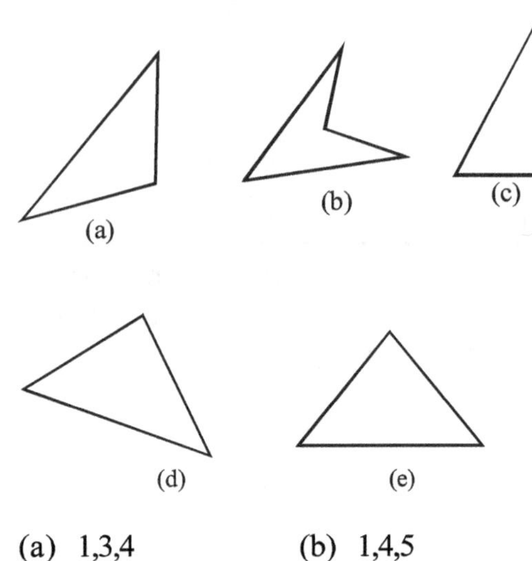

(a) 1,3,4 (b) 1,4,5

(c) 1,2,5 (d) 1,2,4

Sol. **(b)** We begin with choosing a figure having a right angle. Out of the five figures (b) seems to be having two equal sides including a right angle. Fitting along (d) with it, we have a figure as now. Looking into a vacant space, we find that out of the remaining three figures (a), (b) and (c) only fig. (a) will fit, hence the answer is (b).

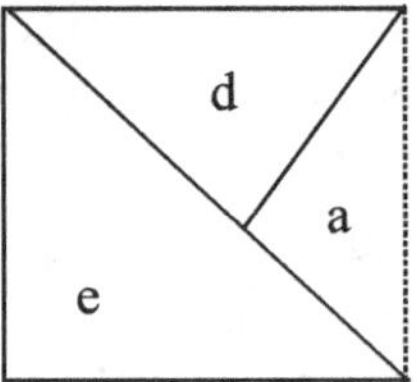

LEVEL 1

DIRECTIONS (Qs. 1-4) : *In each of the following questions, you are given a figure (X) followed by four alternative figures (a), (b), (c) and (d) such that fig. (X) is embeded in one of them. Trace out the alternative figure which contains fig. (X) as its part.*

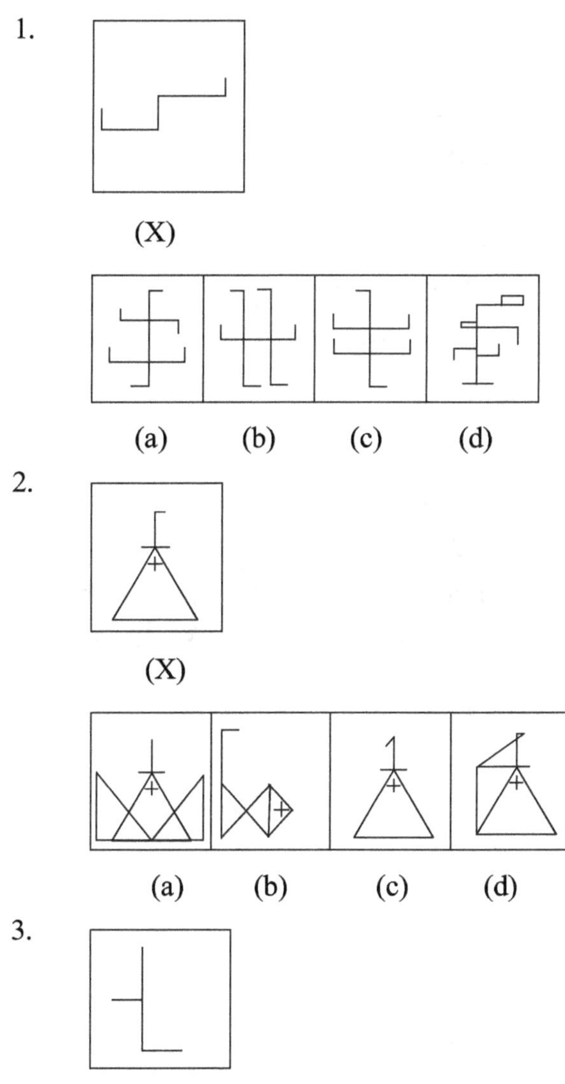

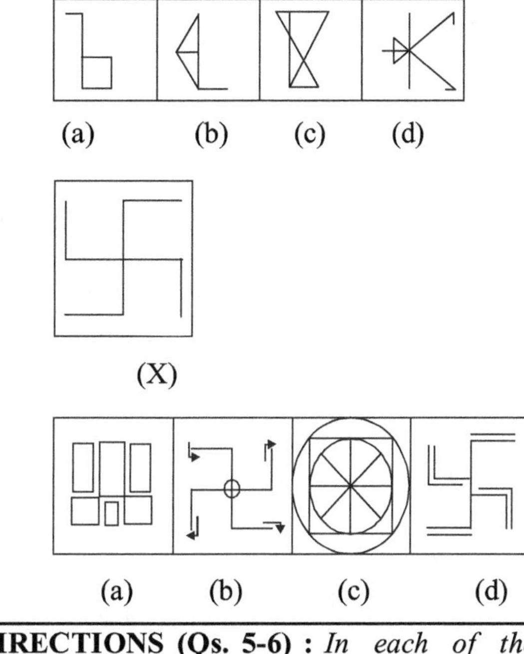

DIRECTIONS (Qs. 5-6) : *In each of the questions, a part of the figure is given. Select one from the given four figures in which that part is embedded.*

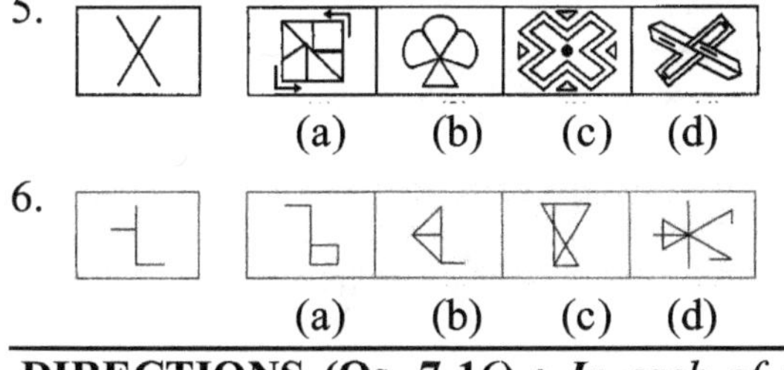

DIRECTIONS (Qs. 7-16) : *In each of the following questions, select a figure from amongst the four alternatives, which when placed in the blank space of fig. (X) would complete the pattern.*

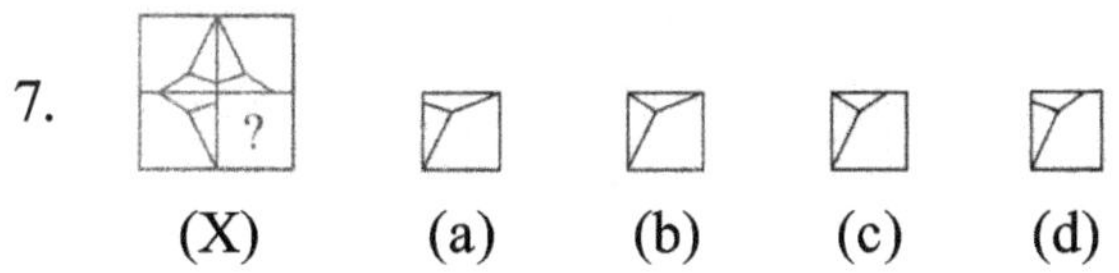

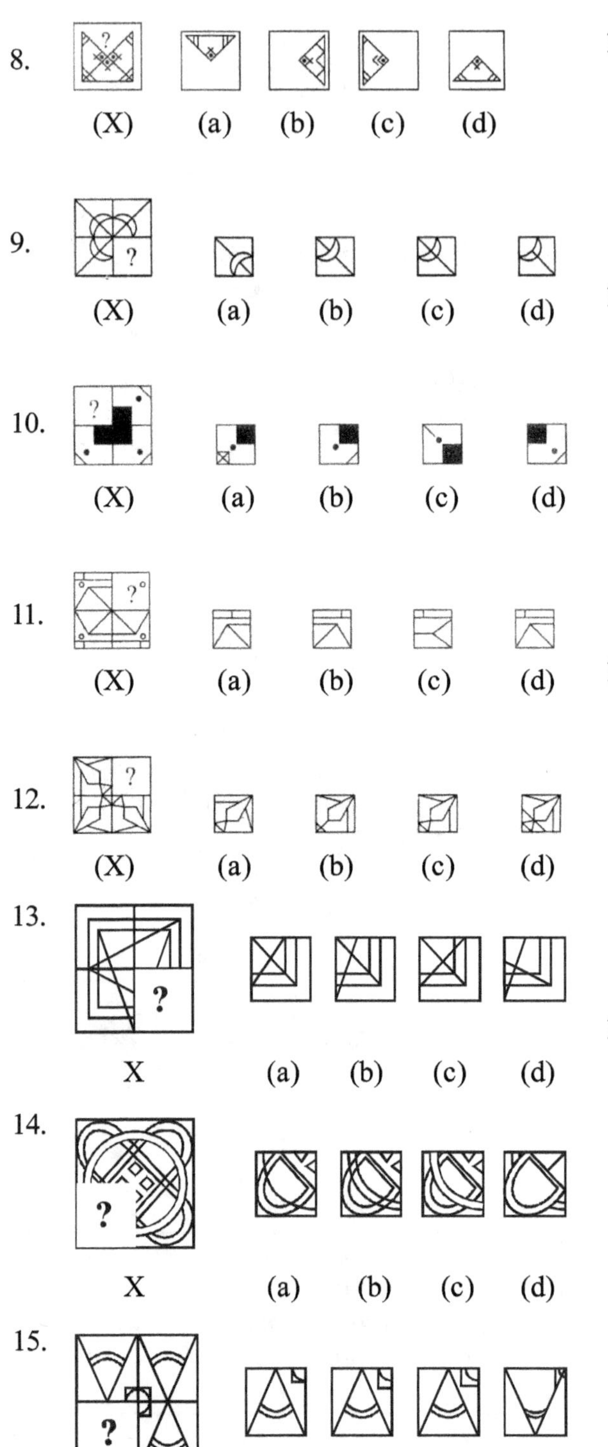

16. 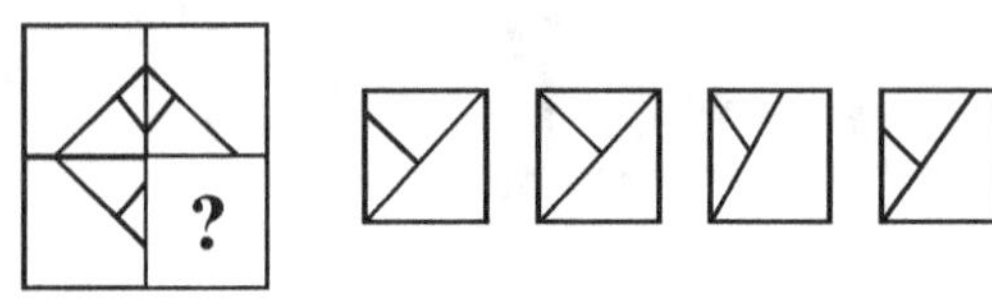

X (a) (b) (c) (d)

17. 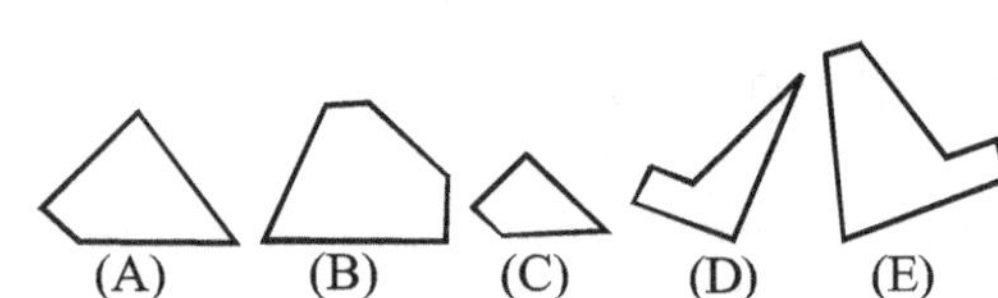

(a) ABD
(b) BCD
(c) BDE
(d) ADE

18. 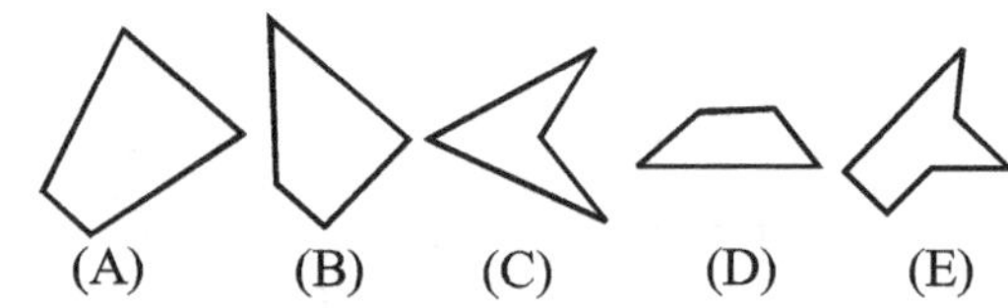

(a) ABC
(b) BCE
(c) BDE
(d) ADE

19. Select a figure from the options which is exactly embedded in the given figure as one of its parts.

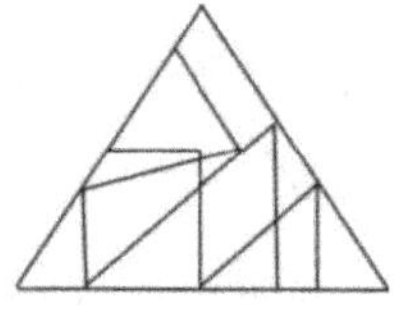

(a) 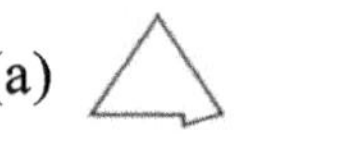 (b) 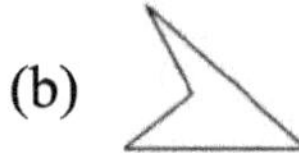

(c)  (d) 

20. Which of the following figures is exactly embedded in the given figure as one of its parts?

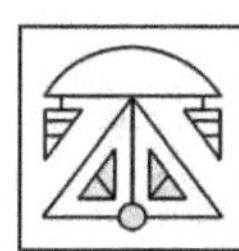

(a) 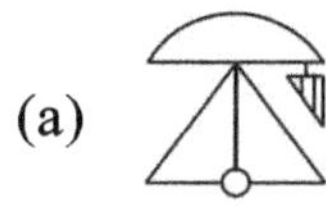 (b) 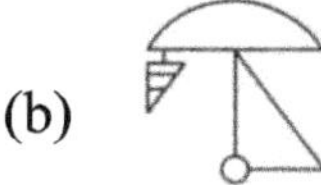

(c) 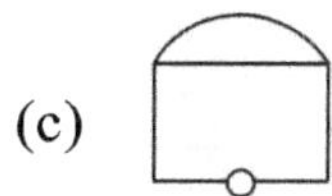 (d) 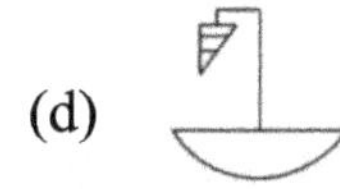

21. Select a figure from the options which is exactly embedded in the given figure as one of its parts.

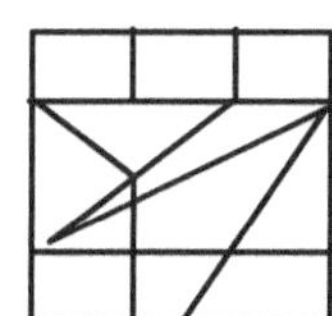

(a)  (b) 

(c)  (d) 

22. In which of the following figures, the given figure is exactly embedded as one of its parts? **[2018]**

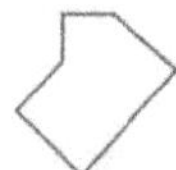

(a) 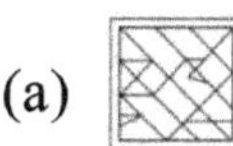 (b) 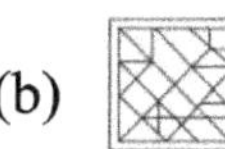

(c) 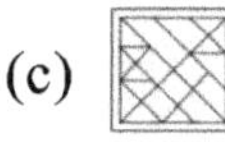 (d) 

23. Which of the following figures is not exactly embedded in the given figure as one of its parts? **[2019]**

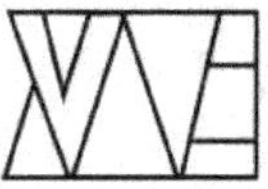

(a) 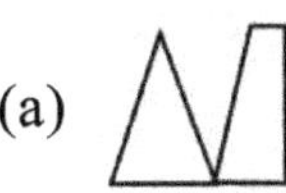 (b) 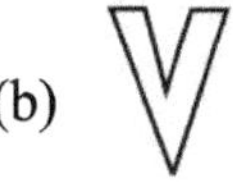

(c)  (d) 

24. Select a figure from the options which when placed in the blank space of the given figure would complete the pattern. **[2019]**

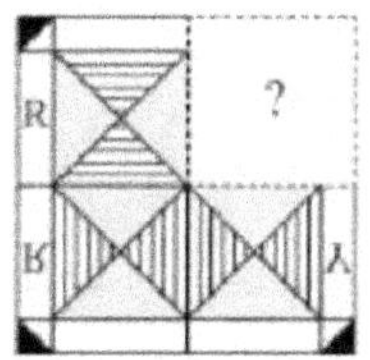

(a) 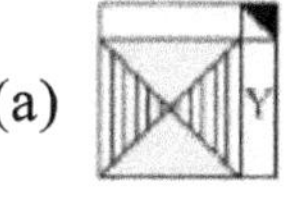 (b) 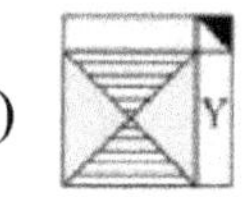

(c) 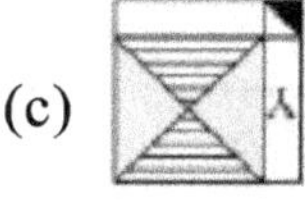 (d) 

25. Which of the following figures will complete the pattern in the given figure? **[2020]**

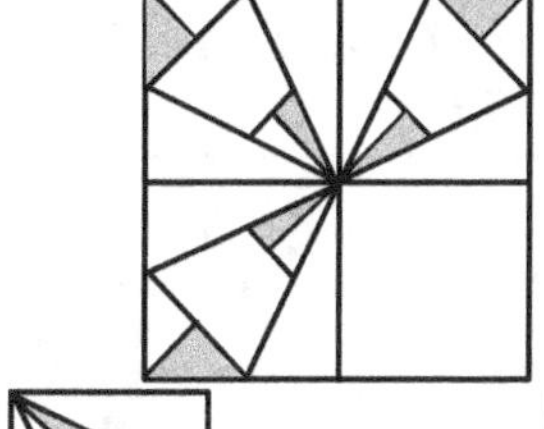

(a) 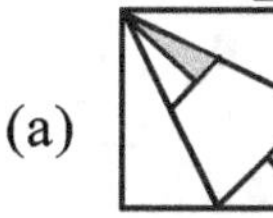 (b) 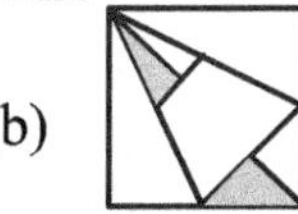

(c) 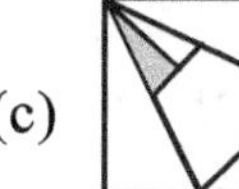 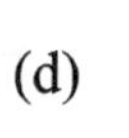 (d) 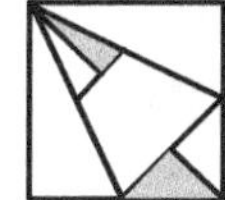

26. Select a figure from the options which when placed in the blank space of given figure would complete the pattern. **[2021]**

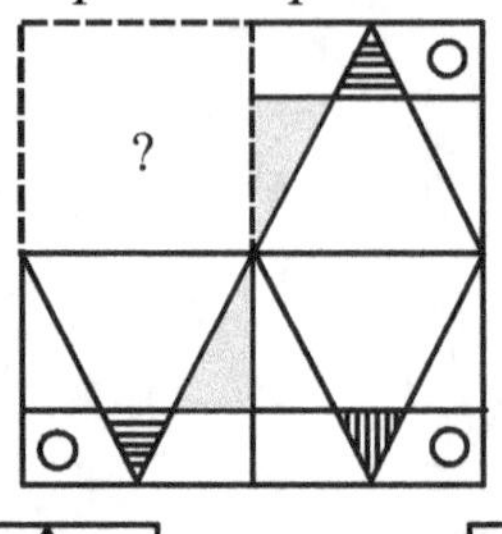

(a) 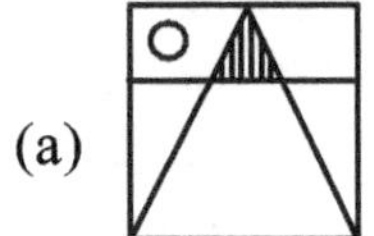 (b) 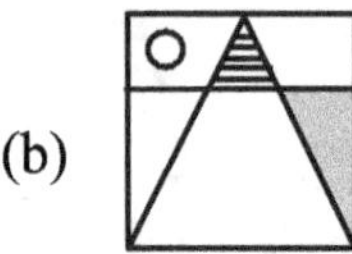

(c) 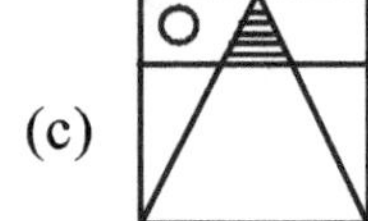 (d) 

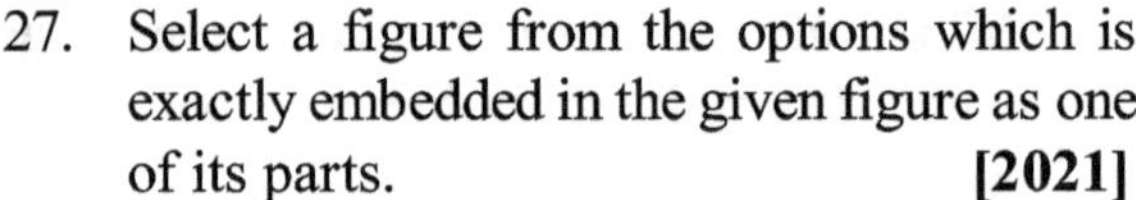

27. Select a figure from the options which is exactly embedded in the given figure as one of its parts. **[2021]**

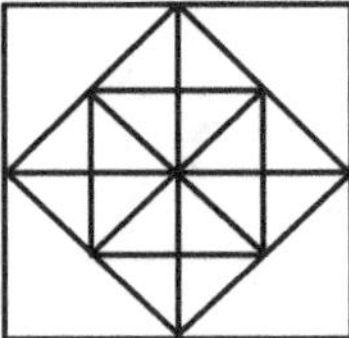

(a)  (b) 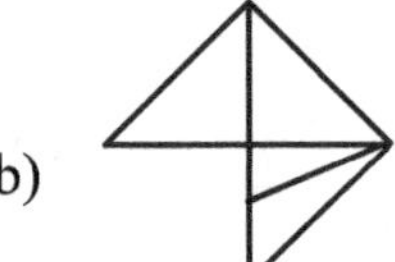

(c) 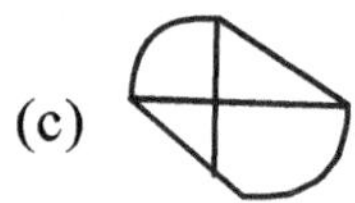 (d) 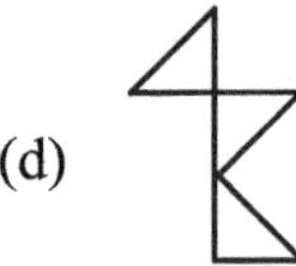

LEVEL 2

DIRECTIONS (Qs. 1-5) : *In each of the following questions, you are given a fig. (X) followed by four alternative figures (a), (b), (c) and (d) such that fig. (X) is embedded in one of them. Trace out the alternative figure which contains fig. (X) as its part.*

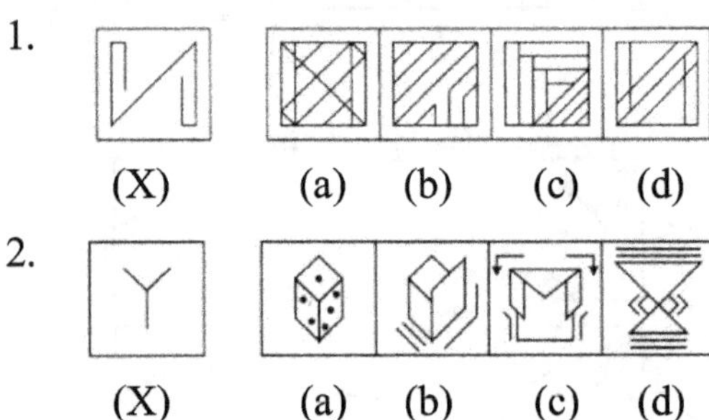

1\. (X) (a) (b) (c) (d)

2\. (X) (a) (b) (c) (d)

3\.

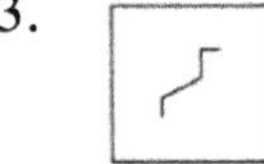 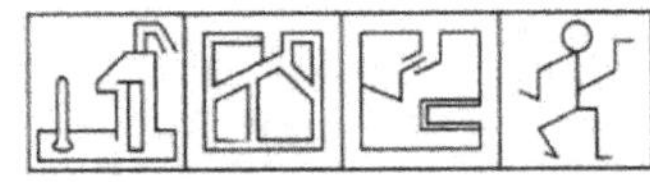

(X) (a) (b) (c) (d)

4\.

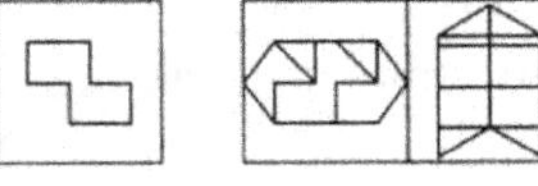 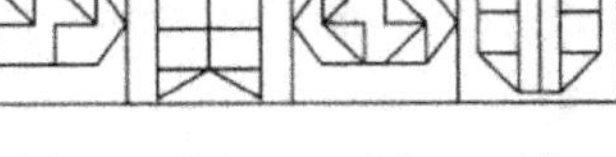

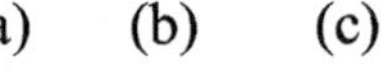

(X) (a) (b) (c) (d)

5\.

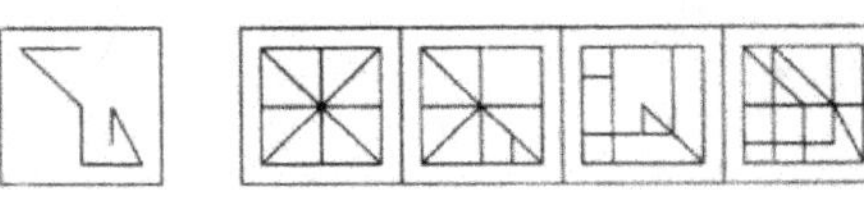

(X) (a) (b) (c) (d)

DIRECTIONS (Qs. 6-7) : *In each of the following questions, select a figure from amongst the four alternatives, which when placed in the blank space of fig. (X) would complete the pattern.*

6.

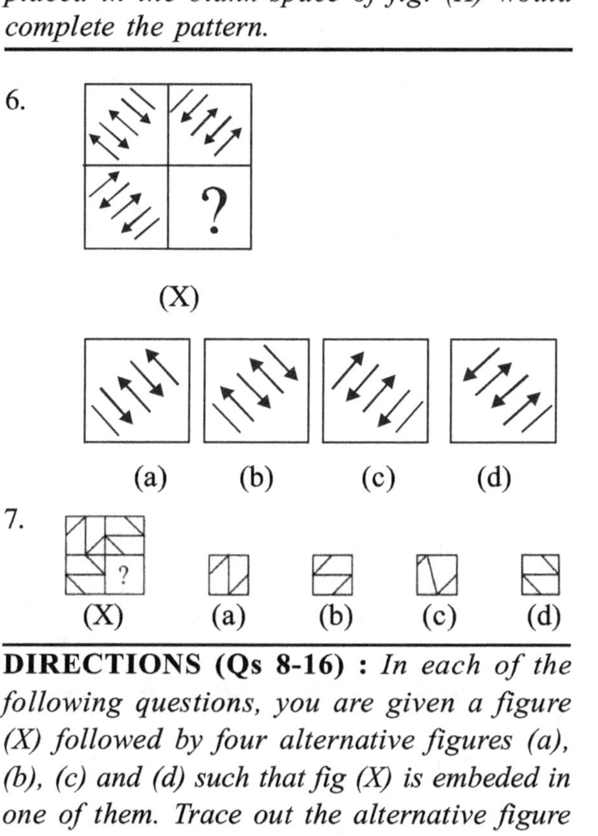

7.

DIRECTIONS (Qs 8-16) : *In each of the following questions, you are given a figure (X) followed by four alternative figures (a), (b), (c) and (d) such that fig (X) is embeded in one of them. Trace out the alternative figure which contains fig (X) as its part.*

8.

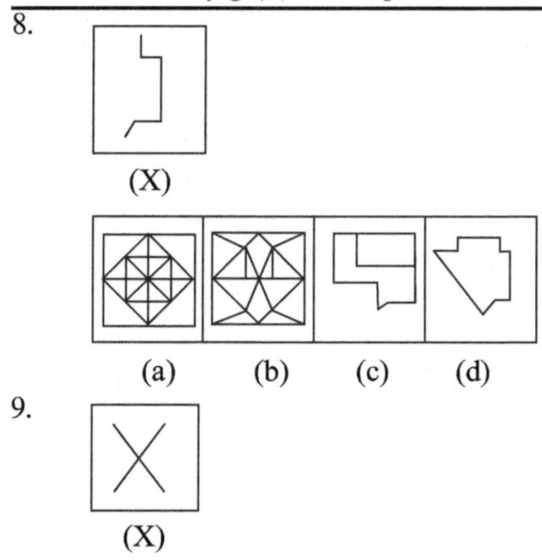

9.

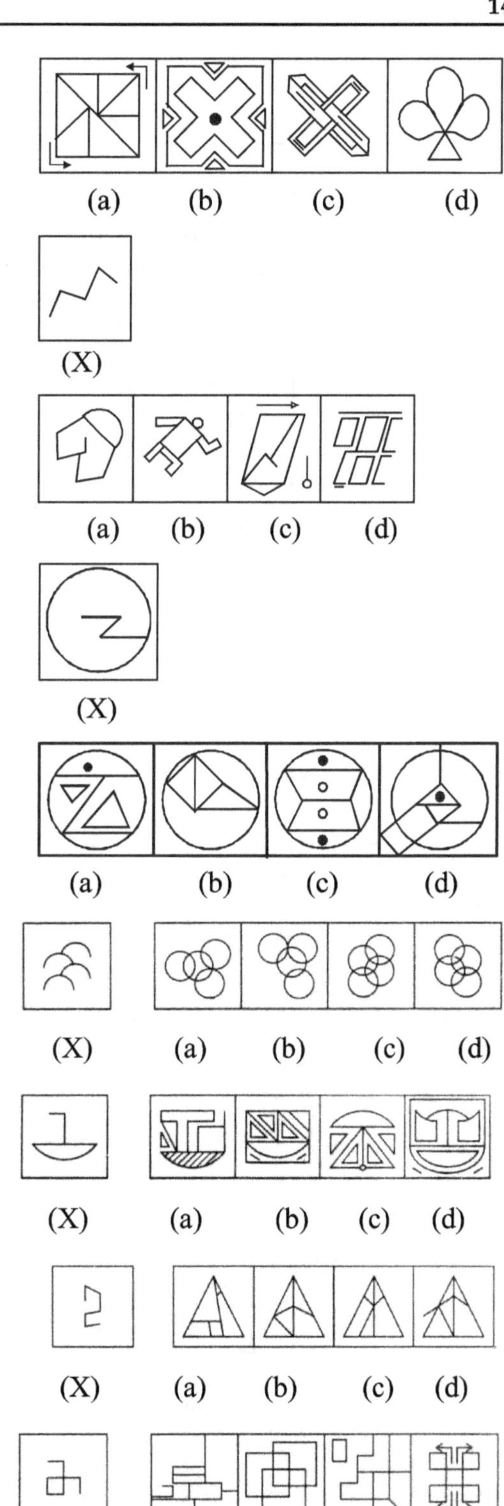

10.

11.

12.

13.

14.

15.

16.

(X) (a) (b) (c) (d)

17. A problem figure is given. Find out which of the figures given as alternatives is embedded in the given problem figure.

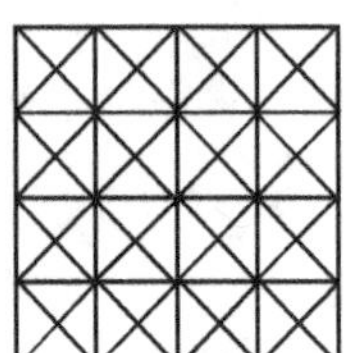

(a) 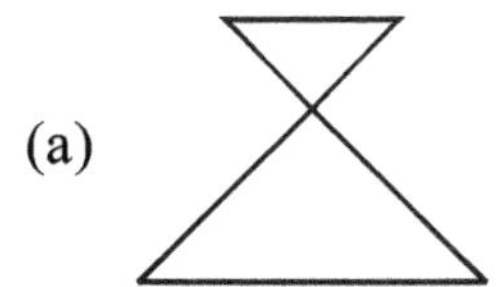

(b) 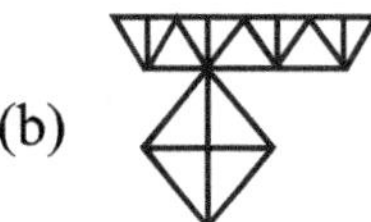

(c) 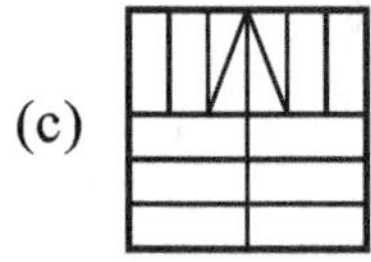

(d) 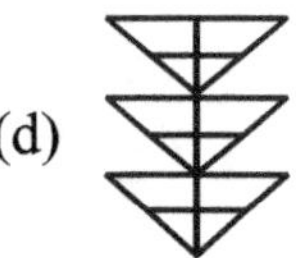

18. A pattern is given below. You have to identify which among the following pieces will not be required to complete the pattern.

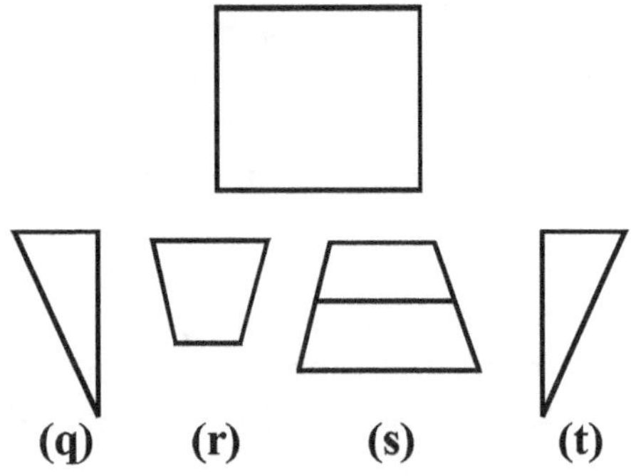

(a) q (b) r

(c) s (d) t

19. Identify the figure that completes the pattern.

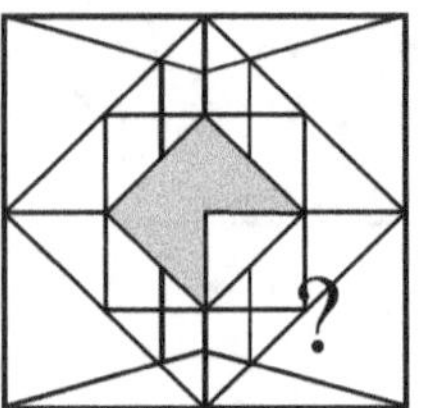

(a) 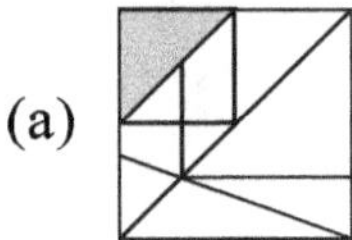

(b) 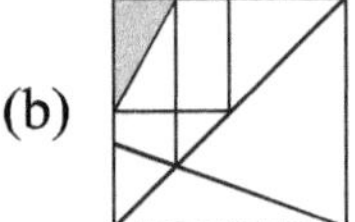

(c) 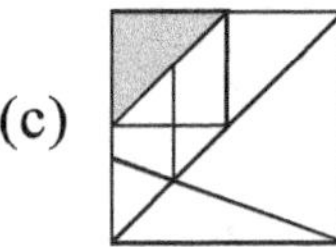

(d) 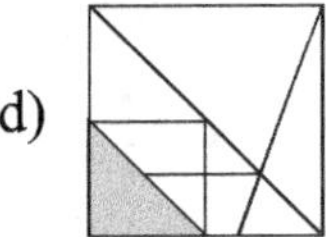

DIRECTIONS (Qs.20-23): *In each question, out of the four figures marked (a), (b), (c) and (d), three are similar in a certain manner. Howerer one figure is not like the other three. Choose the figure wchic is diffence from the rest.*

20.

21.

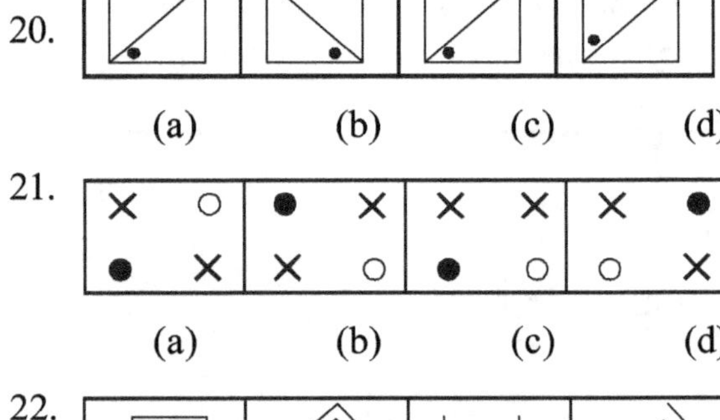

(a) (b) (c) (d)

22.

23.

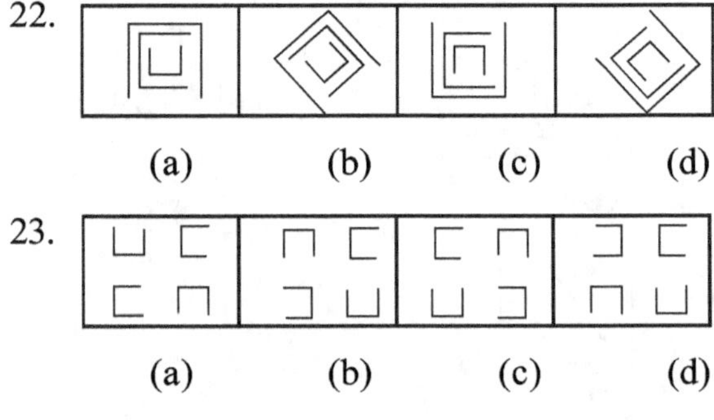

(a) (b) (c) (d)

DIRECTIONS: *In questions 24 to 27, four figures (a), (b), (c), (d) have been given in each question. Of these four figures three figures are similar in some way and one figure is different. Select the figure which is different.*

24. (a) (b) (c) (d)

25. (a) A (b) O (c) U (d) W

26. (a) (b) (c) (d)

27. (a) (b) (c) (d)

DIRECTIONS (Qs. 28-31) : *There is a question figure, a part of which is missing. Observe the answer figures (a), (b), (c) and (d) and find out the answer figure which,* ***without changing the direction****, fits in the missing part of the question figure in order to complete the pattern in the question figure.*

28. **Question Figure**

Answer Figures

(a)

(b) 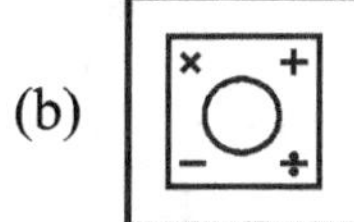

(c)

(d) 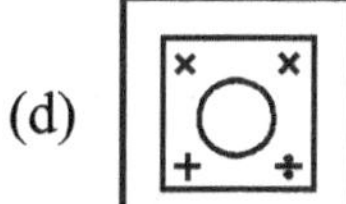

29. **Question Figure**

Answer Figures

(a)

(b)

(c)

(d) 

30. **Question Figure**

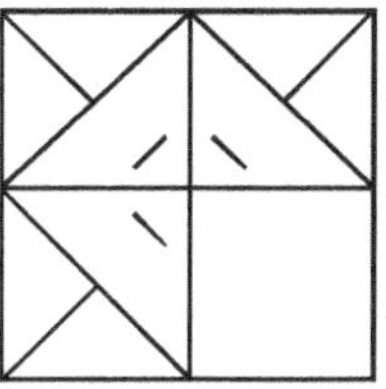

Answer Figures

(a) 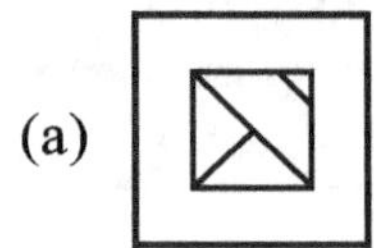 (b) 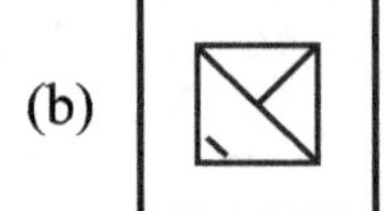

(c) 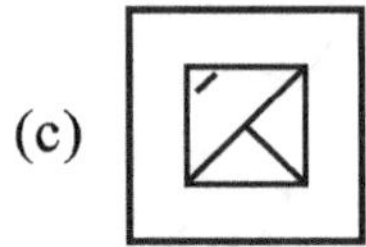 (d) 

31. **Question Figure**

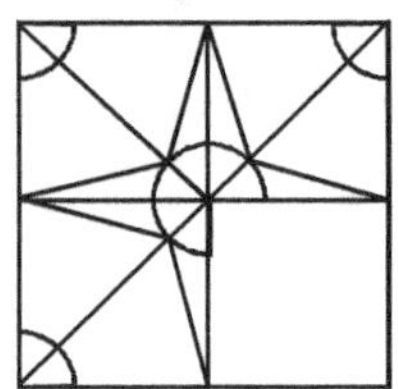

Answer Figures

(a) 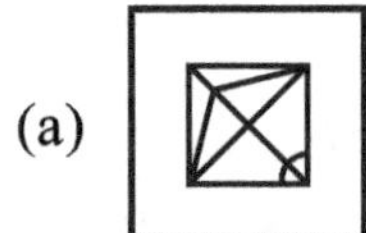 (b) 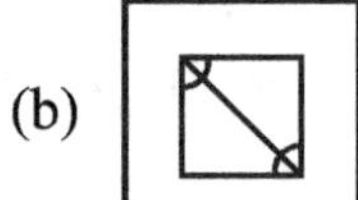

(c) 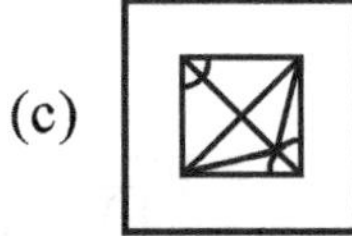 (d) 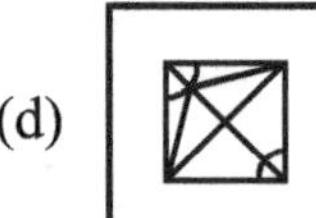

32. Select a figure from the options which is exactly embedded in the given figure as one of its parts.

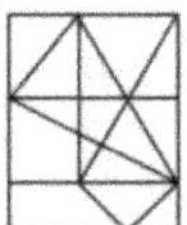

(a) 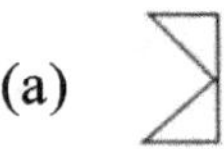 (b) 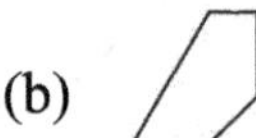

(c) 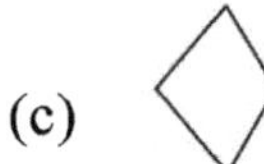 (d) 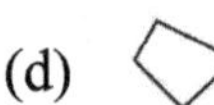

33. In which of the following figures, the given figure is exactly embedded as one of its parts?

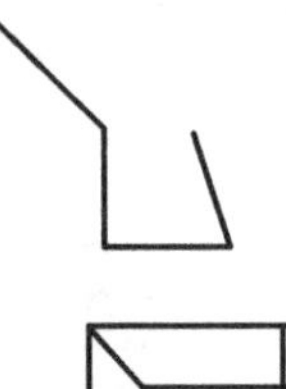

(a) 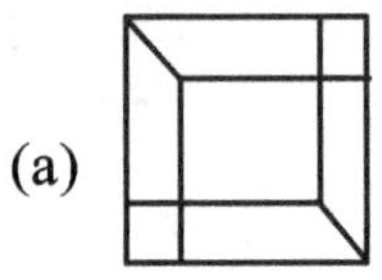 (b) 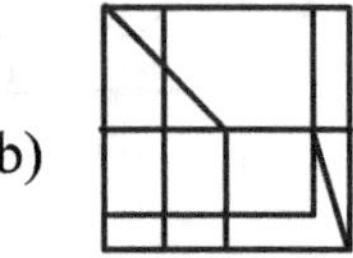

(c) 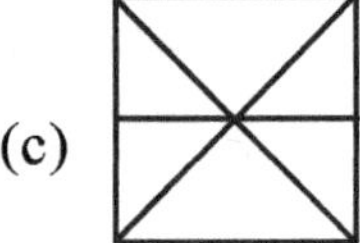 (d) 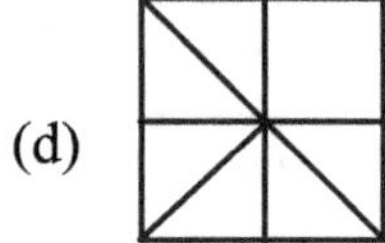

34. Select a figure from the options in which the given figure is exactly embedded as one of its parts.

(a) 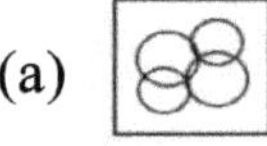 (b) 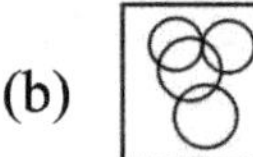

(c) 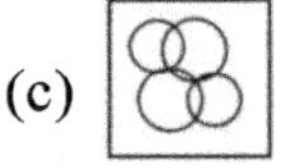 (d) 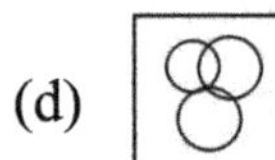

35. Select a figure from the options in which the given figure is exactly embedded as one of its parts.

(a) 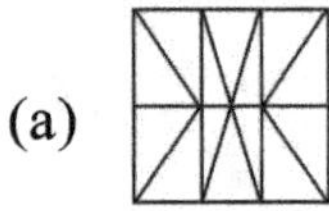 (b) 

(c) 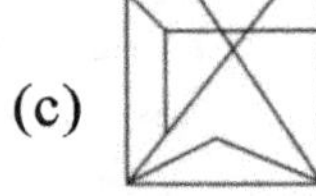 (d) 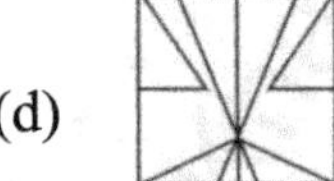

36. Select a figure from the options which when placed in the blank space of given figure would complete the pattern.

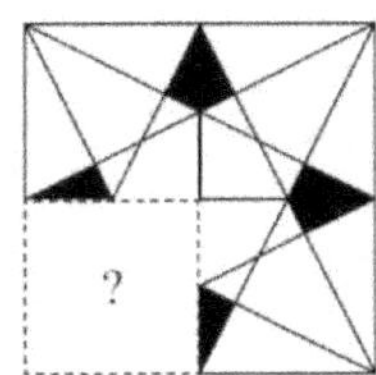

(a) 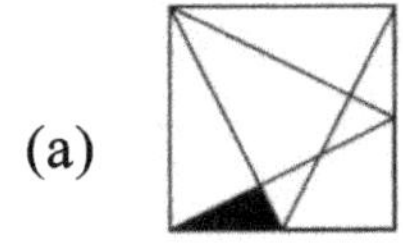 (b) 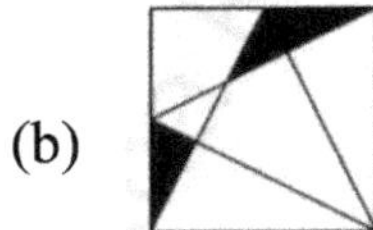

(c) 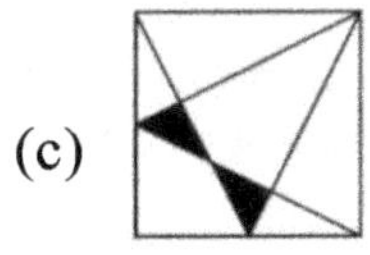 (d) 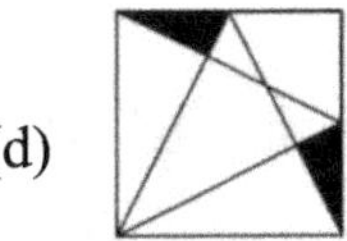

37. Which of the following options will complete the pattern in the given figure?

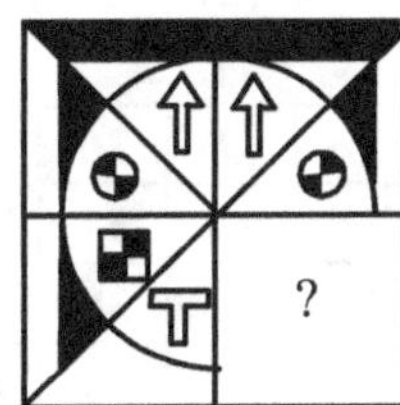

(a) 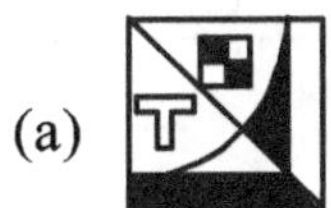 (b) 

(c) 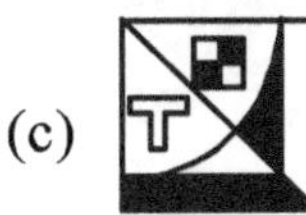 (d) 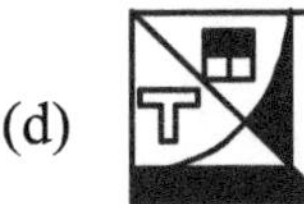

38. Select a figure from the options which is exactly embedded in the given figure as one of its parts.

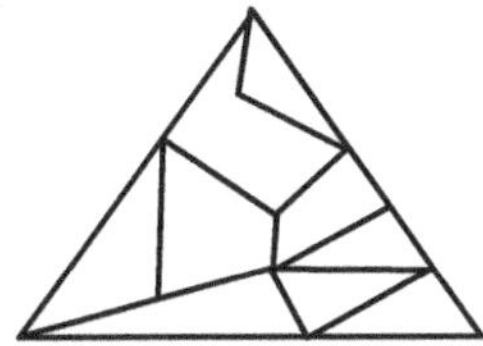

39. Which of the following options will complete the pattern in the given figure?

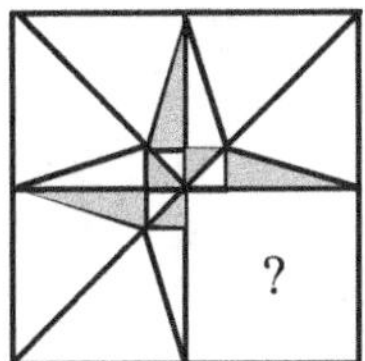

(a) 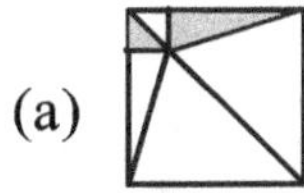 (b) 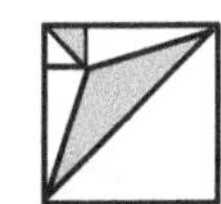

(c) 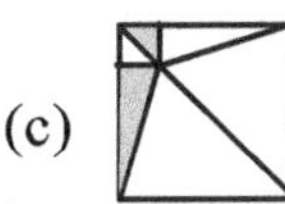 (d) 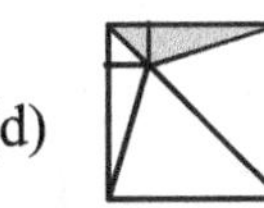

40. Select the figure from the options which will complete the pattern in Figure (x).

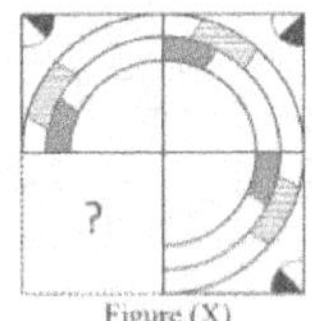

(a) 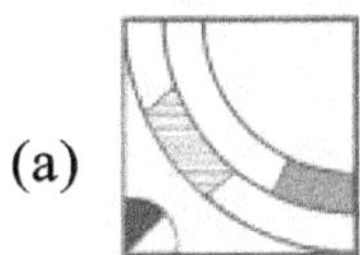 (b) 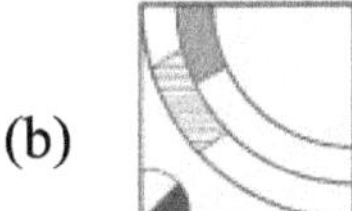

(c) 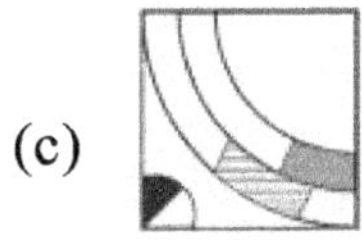 (d) 

41. Select a figure from the options which will complete the given figure. **[2018]**

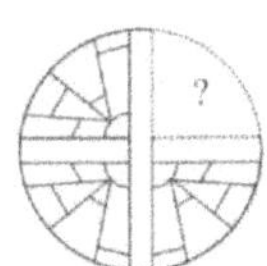

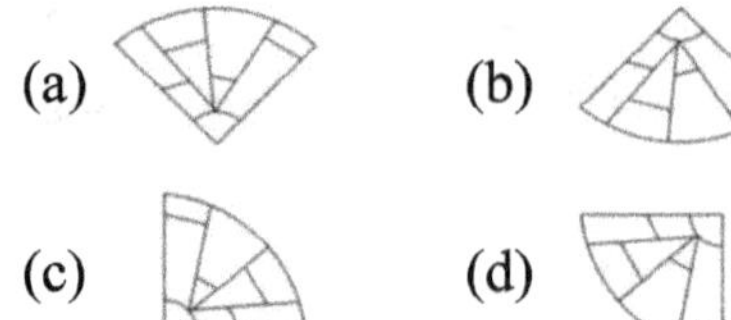

42. Which of the following figures is not exactly embedded in the given figure as one of its parts? **[2019]**

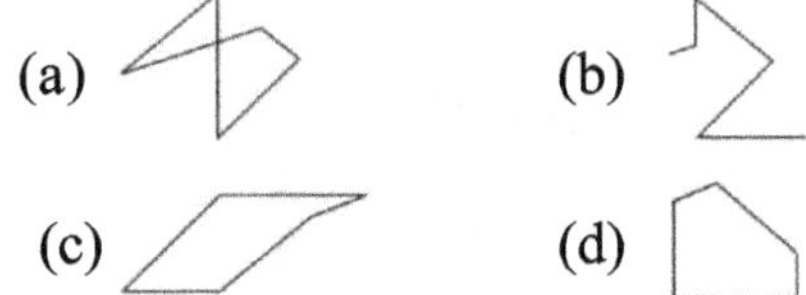

43. Select a figure from the options which is exactly embedded in the given figure as one of its parts. **[2020]**

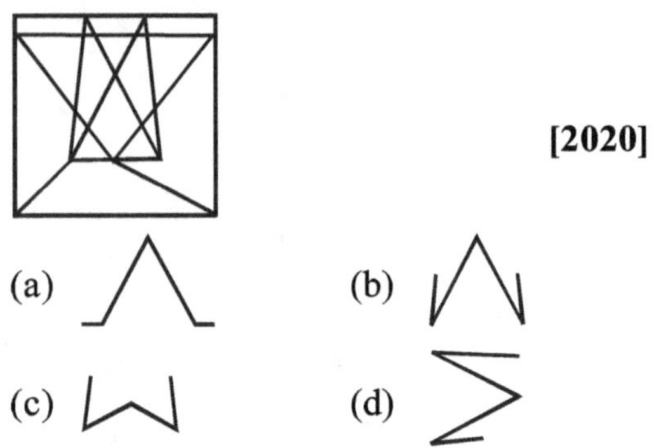

ANSWER KEY																	
LEVEL-1																	
1	(c)	**4**	(c)	**7**	(d)	**10**	(d)	**13**	(d)	**16**	(d)	**19**	(a)	**22**	(b)	**25**	(c)
2	(d)	**5**	(b)	**8**	(d)	**11**	(b)	**14**	(c)	**17**	(b)	**20**	(b)	**23**	(c)	**26**	(a)
3	(b)	**6**	(b)	**9**	(c)	**12**	(c)	**15**	(a)	**18**	(c)	**21**	(d)	**24**	(b)	**27**	(d)
LEVEL-2																	
1	(d)	**6**	(a)	**11**	(d)	**16**	(d)	**21**	(c)	**26**	(d)	**31**	(d)	**36**	(d)	**41**	(c)
2	(a)	**7**	(a)	**12**	(c)	**17**	(a)	**22**	(a)	**27**	(d)	**32**	(d)	**37**	(a)	**42**	(d)
3	(d)	**8**	(d)	**13**	(c)	**18**	(c)	**23**	(a)	**28**	(b)	**33**	(b)	**38**	(d)	**43**	(b)
4	(c)	**9**	(d)	**14**	(a)	**19**	(c)	**24**	(a)	**29**	(b)	**34**	(a)	**39**	(c)		
5	(d)	**10**	(b)	**15**	(b)	**20**	(d)	**25**	(d)	**30**	(c)	**35**	(a)	**40**	(c)		

CHAPTER 15 Figure Matrix

In such type of problems, a 2×2 or 3×3 grid is given. Each cell of this grid has some design or symbols, on the basis of some specific rule. But a cell of the grid is left empty. A student is required to fill up the cell. For it one needs to analyse the grid and identify the rule along row-wise or column-wise in the grid.

EXAMPLE

Find out which figure in given option completes the figure matrix.

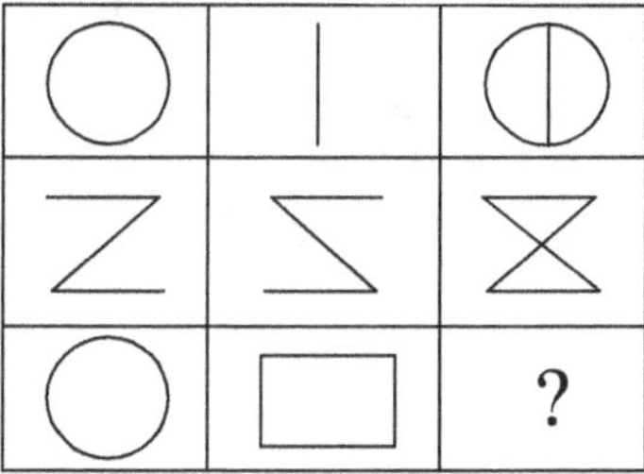

(a) 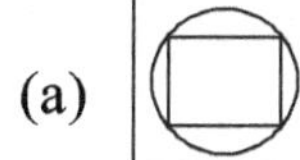 (b) 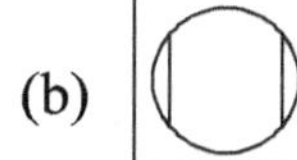 (c) 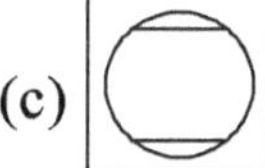 (d)  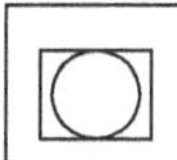

Sol. **(a)** In each row, the third figure is the combination of the first and second figure.

LEVEL 1

1. Select a suitable figure from the four alternatives that would complete the figure matrix.

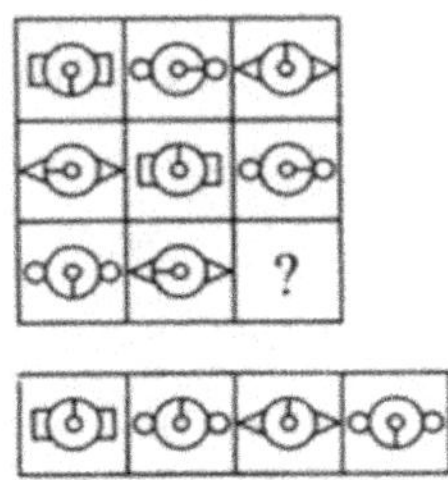

(a) (b) (c) (d)

(a) 1
(b) 2
(c) 3
(d) 4

2. Select a suitable figure from the four alternatives that would complete the figure matrix.

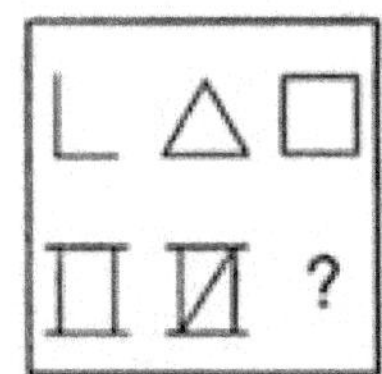

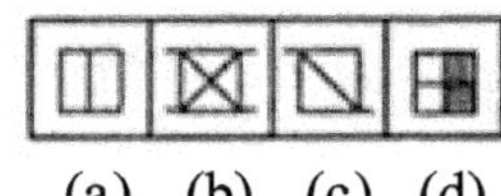

(a) (b) (c) (d)

(a) 1
(b) 4
(c) 3
(d) 2

3. Find out which of the answer figures (a), (b), (c), and (d) completes the figure matrix?

(a) (b) (c) (d)

(a) 1 (b) 2
(c) 3 (d) 4

4. Find out which of the answer figures (a), (b), (c), and (d) completes the figure matrix?

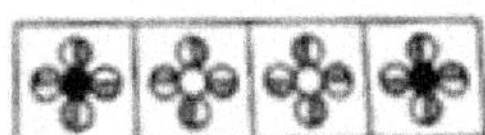

(a) (b) (c) (d)

(a) 1 (b) 2
(c) 3 (d) 4

5. In the following question, find out which of the answer figures (a), (b), (c) and (d) completes the figure matrix?

Problem Figures **Answer Figures**

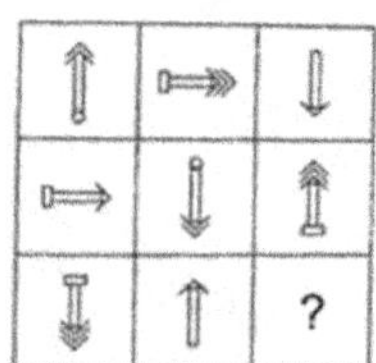

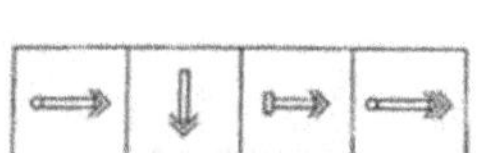

(a) (b) (c) (d)

(a) 2 (b) 1
(c) 4 (d) 3

6. In the following question, find out which of the answer figures (a), (b), (c), (d) and (e) completes the figure matrix?

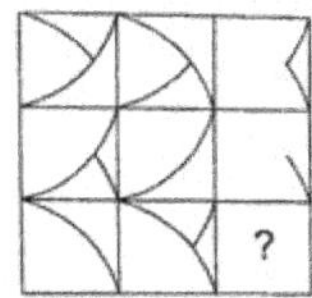
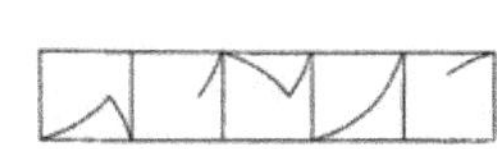

(a) (b) (c) (d) (e)

(a) 2
(b) 3
(c) 4
(d) 1

7. In the following questions, find out which of the answer figures (a), (b), (c), (d) and (e) completes the figure matrix?

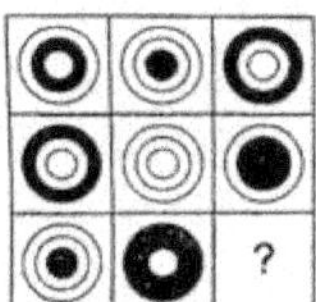
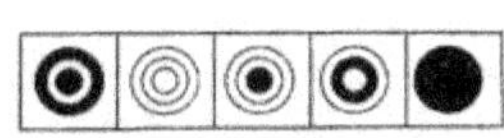

(a) (b) (c) (d) (e)

(a) 2
(b) 3
(c) 4
(d) 1

8. In the following question, find out which of the answer figures (a), (b), (c), and (d) completes the figure matrix?

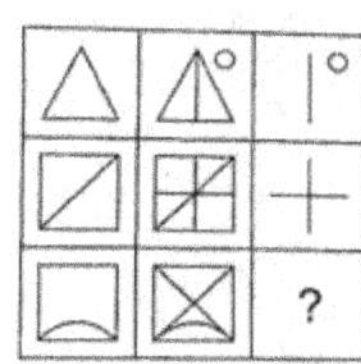
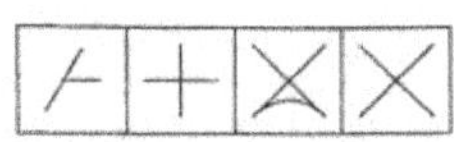

(a) (b) (c) (d)

(a) 2
(b) 3
(c) 1
(d) 4

9. Select a suitable figure from the four alternatives that would complete the figure matrix.

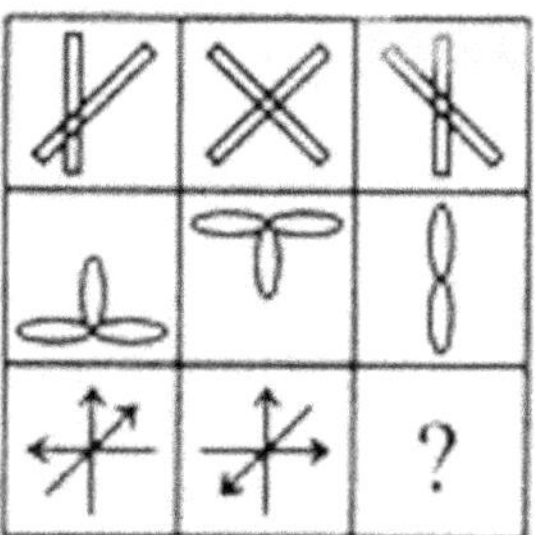
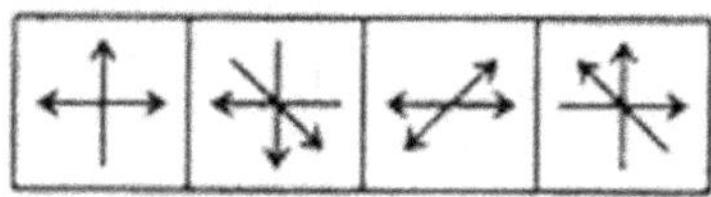

(a) (b) (c) (d)

(a) 1
(b) 2
(c) 3
(d) 4

10. Select a suitable figure from the four alternatives that would complete the figure matrix.

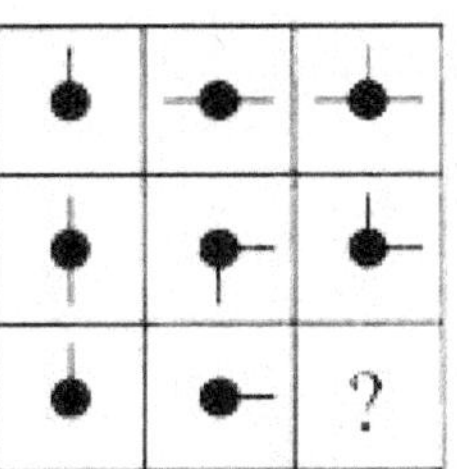
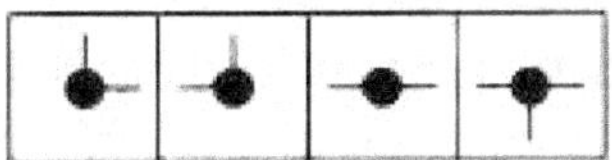

(a) (b) (c) (d)

(a) 1 (b) 2
(c) 3 (d) 4

11. Select the option in which all the components of the key figure (X) are available.

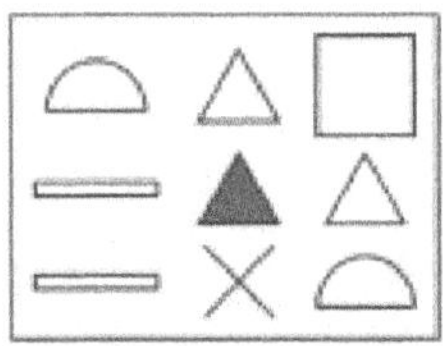
Figure (X)

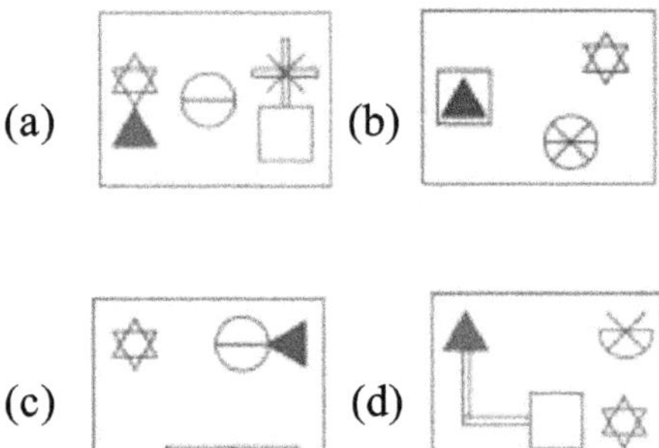

12. Group the given figures into three classes on the basis of their identical properties using each figure only once.

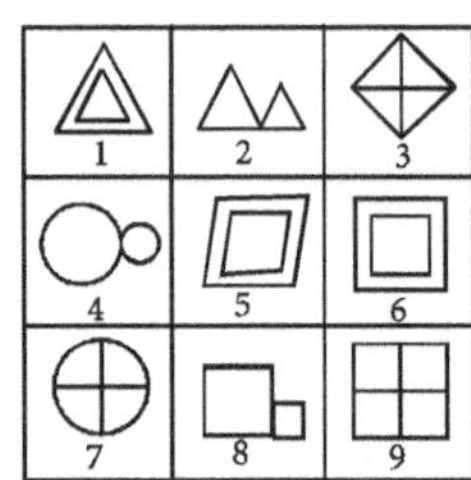

(a) 1, 6, 7; 2, 4, 8; 3, 5, 9
(b) 1, 5, 6; 2, 4, 8; 3, 6, 9
(c) 1, 4, 7; 2, 5, 8; 3, 6, 9
(d) 1, 7, 9; 3, 5, 8; 2, 4, 6

13. Group the given figures into three classes on the basis of their identical properties using each figure only once. **[2020]**

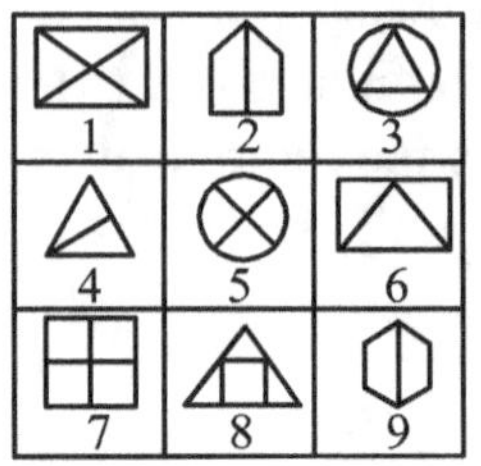

(a) 1, 5, 3 ; 2, 8, 9 ; 4, 6, 7
(b) 1, 5, 7 ; 2, 4, 9 ; 3, 6, 8
(c) 1, 5, 6 ; 2, 4, 9 ; 3, 7, 8
(d) 1, 5, 6 ; 2, 8, 9 ; 3, 4, 7

14. Group the given figures into three classes on the basis of their identical properties using each figure only once. **[2020]**

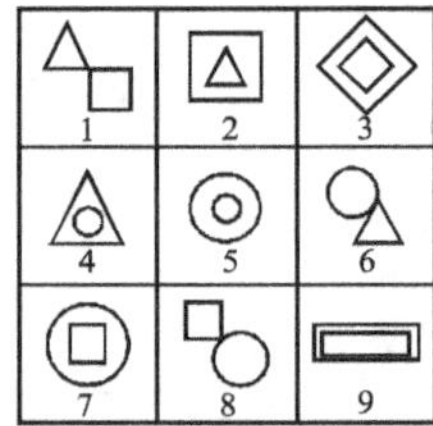

(a) 1, 6, 8 ; 2, 3, 9 ; 4, 5, 7
(b) 1, 6, 8 ; 2, 4, 7 ; 3, 5, 9
(c) 1, 6, 7 ; 2, 4, 8 ; 3, 5, 9
(d) 1, 6, 8 ; 2, 5, 7 ; 3, 4, 9

15. Group the given figures into three classes on the basis of their identical properties using each figure only once. **[2021]**

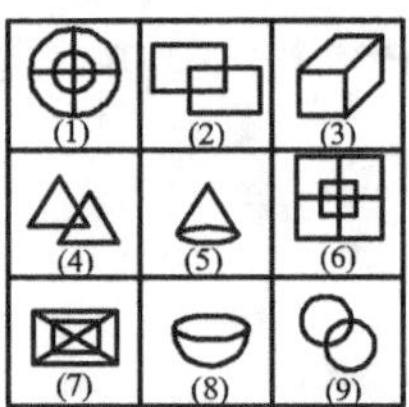

(a) 1, 6, 7; 2, 4, 8; 3, 5, 9
(b) 1, 6, 7; 2, 4, 9; 3, 5, 8
(c) 1, 6, 7; 2, 3, 5; 4, 8, 9
(d) 1, 2, 6; 3, 4, 5; 7, 8, 9

LEVEL 2

1. Select a suitable figure from the four alternatives that would complete the figure matrix.

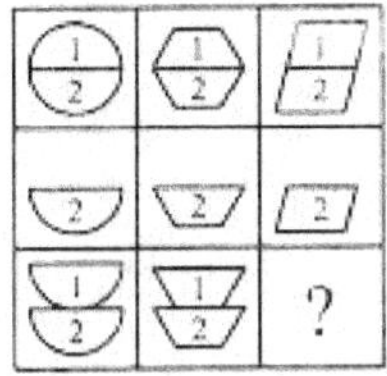

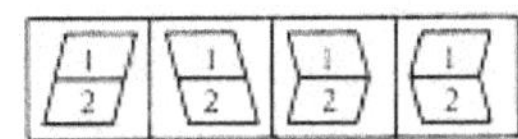

(a) (b) (c) (d)

(a) 1 (b) 2
(c) 3 (d) 4

2. Select a suitable figure from the four alternatives that would complete the figure matrix.

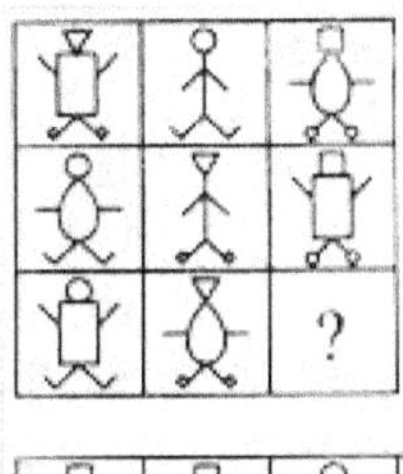

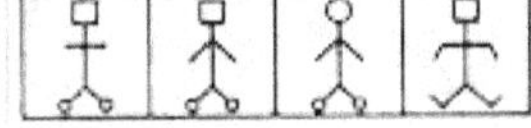

(a) (b) (c) (d)

(a) 1
(b) 2
(c) 3
(d) 4

3. Select a suitable figure from the four alternatives that would complete the figure matrix.

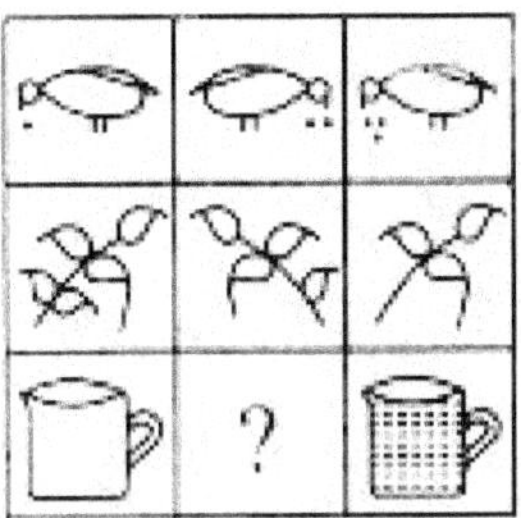

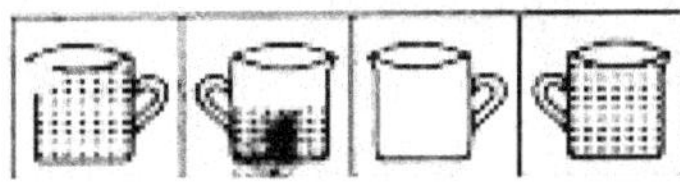

(a) (b) (c) (d)

(a) 1
(b) 2
(c) 3
(d) 4

4. Find out which of the answer figures (a), (b), (c) and (d) completes the figure matrix ?

(a) (b) (c) (d)

(a) a (b) b
(c) c (d) d

5. Select a suitable figure from the four alternatives that would complete the figure matrix.

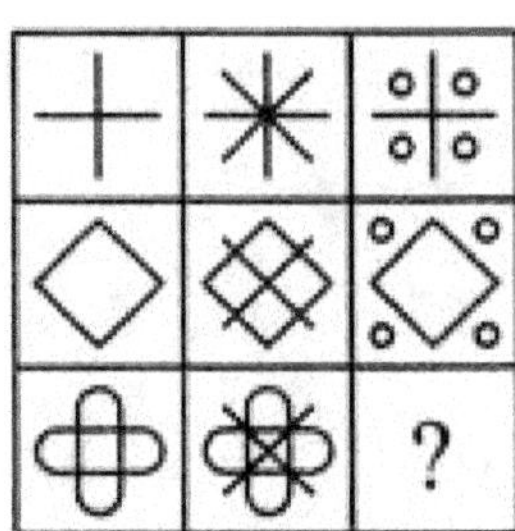

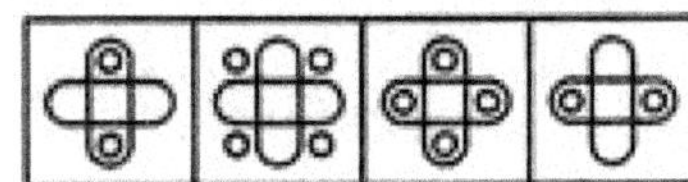

(a) (b) (c) (d)

(a) 2
(b) 4
(c) 3
(d) 1

6. Select a suitable figure from the four alternatives that would complete the figure matrix.

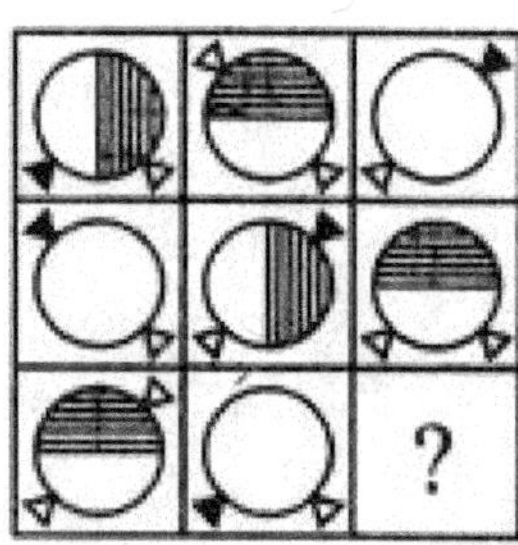

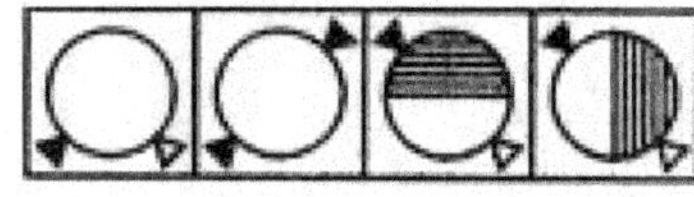

(a) (b) (c) (d)

(a) 1
(b) 2
(c) 3
(d) 4

7. Select a suitable figure from the four alternatives that would complete the figure matrix.

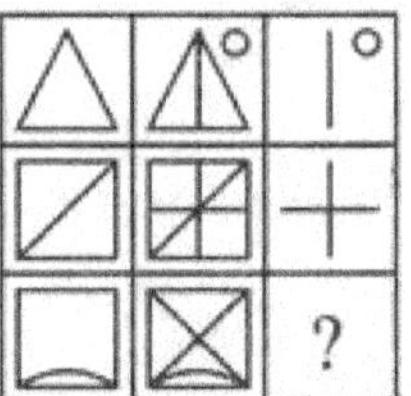

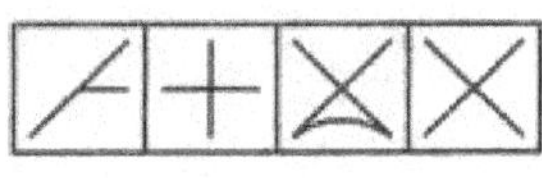

(a) (b) (c) (d)

(a) 1 (b) 2
(c) 3 (d) 4

8. Select one from the four alternative figures which one replace it?

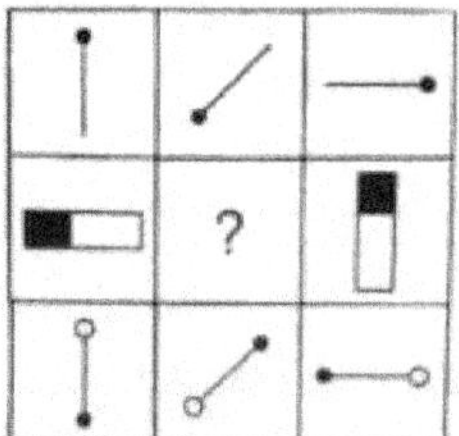

Answer Figures

(a) (b) (c) (d)

(a) a (b) b
(c) c (d) d

9. Select a figure from the four alternatives that would complete the figure matrix.

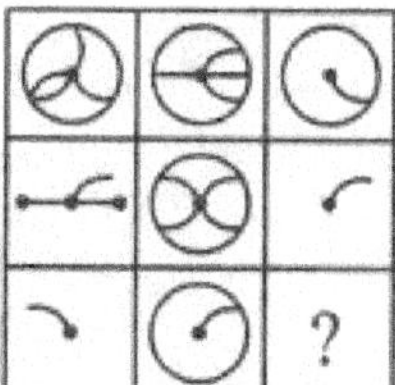

(a) (b) (c) (d)

(a) a (b) b
(c) c (d) d

10. Select a suitable figure from the four alternatives that would complete the figure matrix.

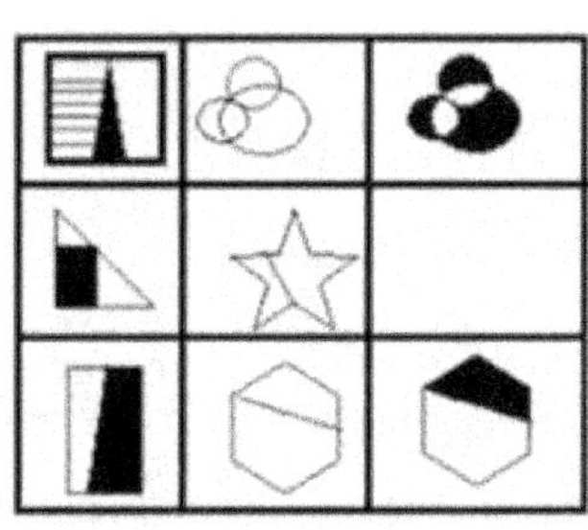

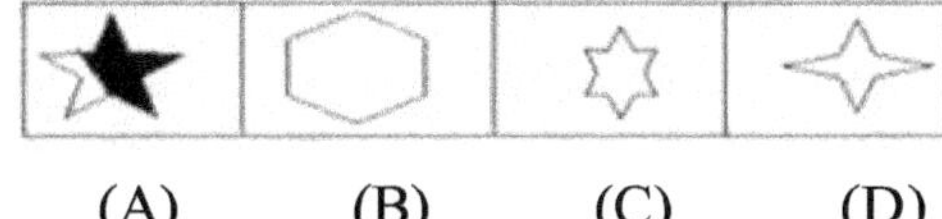

(A) (B) (C) (D)

(a) B (b) D
(c) A (d) C

11. Select a figure from the options which will complete the given figure matrix.

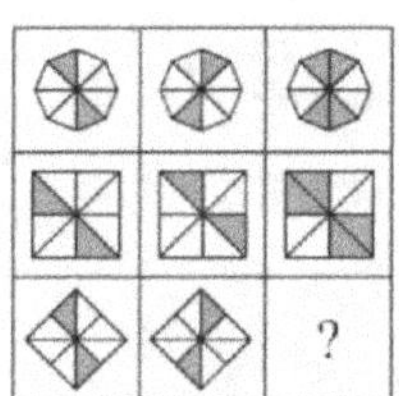

(a) 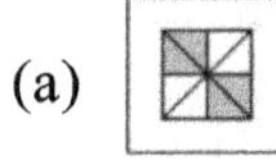 (b) 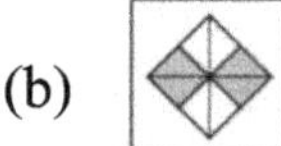

(c) 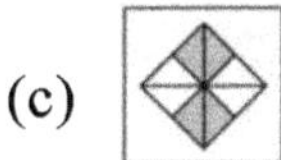 (d) 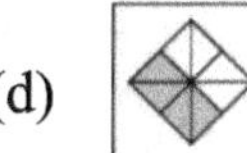

12. Group the given figures into three classes on the basis of their identical properties using each figure only once.

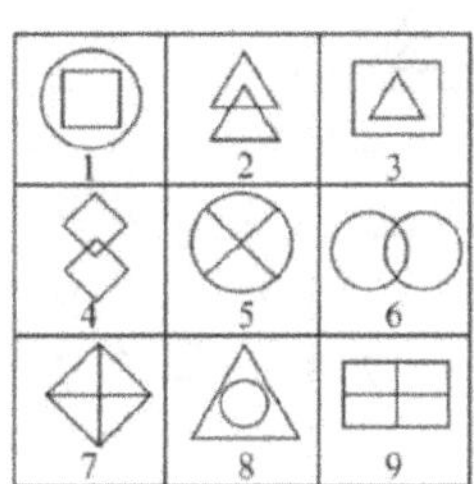

(a) 1, 2, 8; 3, 4, 5; 6, 7, 9
(b) 1, 3, 8; 2, 4, 6; 5, 7, 9
(c) 1, 3, 8; 2, 5, 7; 4, 6, 9
(d) 1, 3, 5; 2, 4, 8; 6, 7, 9

13. Select a figure from the options which will complete the given figure matrix.

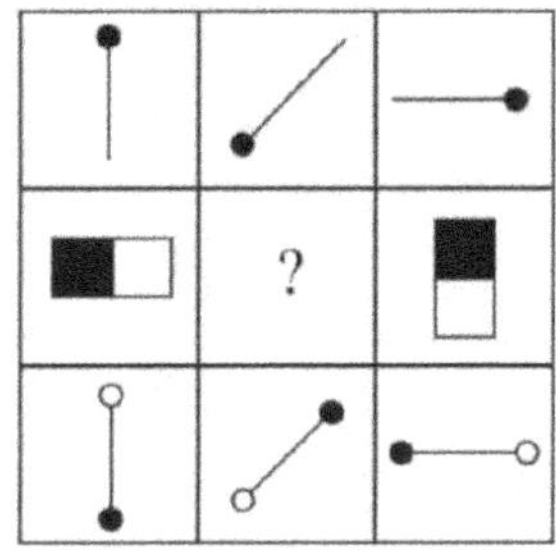

(a)  (b) 

(c) 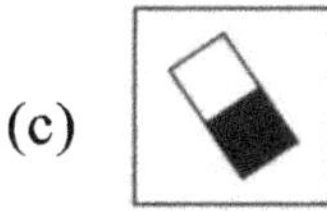 (d) 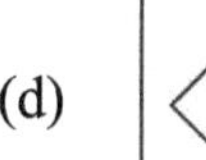

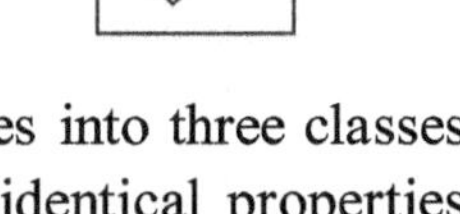

14. Group the given figures into three classes on the basis of their identical properties using each figure only once.

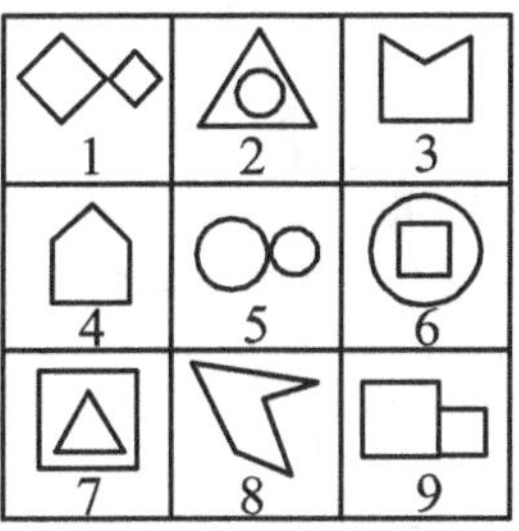

(a) 1, 5, 9 ; 2, 4, 8 ; 3, 6, 7
(b) 1, 4, 8 ; 2, 6, 7 ; 3, 5, 9
(c) 1, 6, 7 ; 2, 5, 9 ; 3, 4, 8
(d) 1, 5, 9 ; 2, 6, 7 ; 3, 4, 8

15. Select a figure from the options which will complete the given figure matrix.

(a) U (b) T

(c) 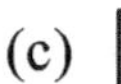 (d) J

16. Group the given figures into three classes on the basis of their identical properties using each figure only once.

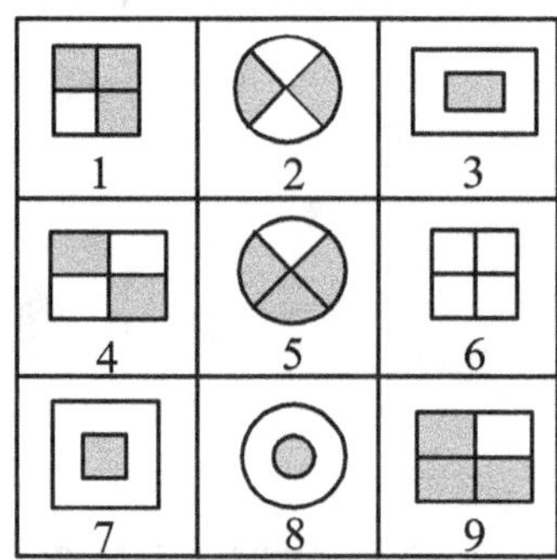

(a) 1, 4, 6; 2, 5, 9; 3, 7, 8
(b) 1, 7, 8; 2, 4, 6; 3, 5, 9
(c) 1, 6, 9; 2, 4, 5; 3, 7, 8
(d) 1, 5, 9; 2, 4, 6; 3, 7, 8

17. Select a figure from the options which will complete the given figure matrix.

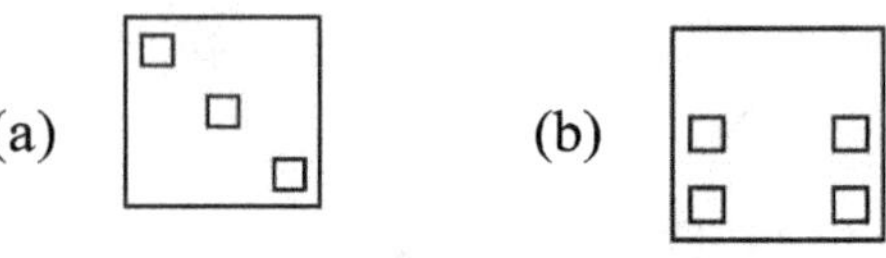

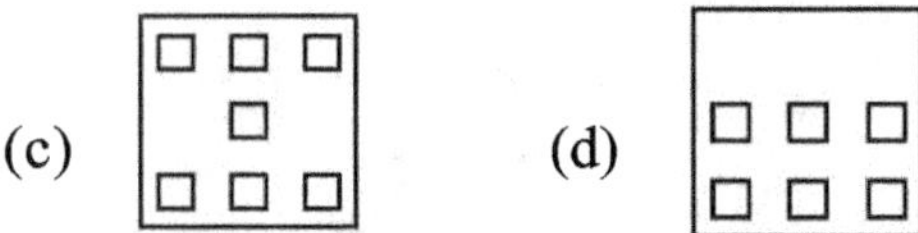

18. Group the given figures into three classes on the basis of their identical properties using each figure only once.

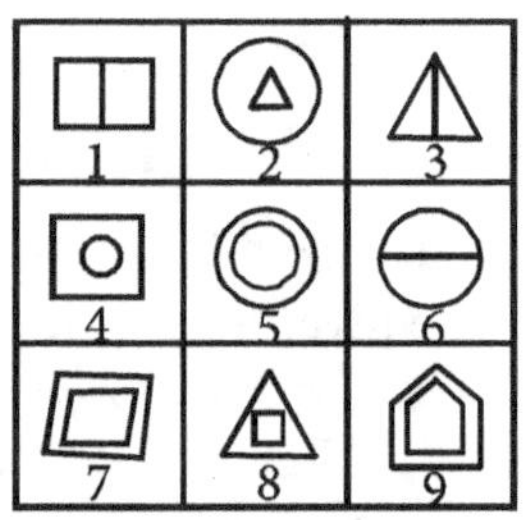

(a) 1, 3, 6; 2, 4, 7; 5, 8, 9
(b) 1, 3, 7; 2, 4, 8; 5, 6, 9
(c) 1, 5, 7; 4, 9, 8; 2, 3, 6
(d) 1, 3, 6; 2, 4, 8; 5, 7, 9

19. Group the given figures into three classes on the basis of their identical properties using each figure only once.

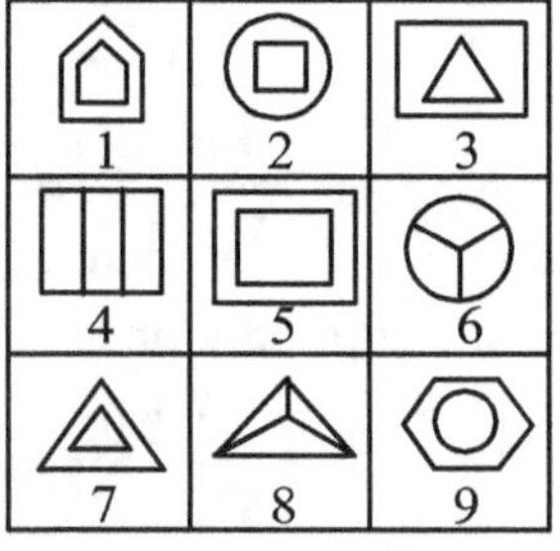

(a) 1, 5, 7 ; 2, 3, 9 ; 4, 6, 8
(b) 1, 5, 6 ; 2, 3, 9 ; 4, 7, 8
(c) 1, 6, 8 ; 2, 3, 9 ; 4, 5, 7
(d) 1, 6, 9 ; 2, 5, 8 ; 3, 4, 7

20. Select a figure from the options which will replace the (?) to complete the given figure matrix. **[2019]**

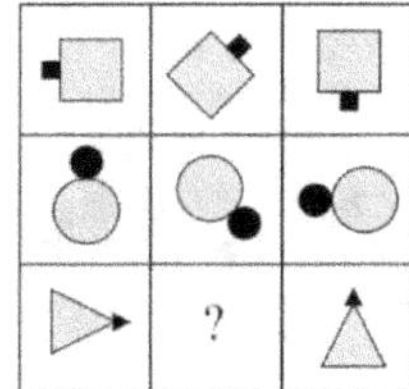

(a) 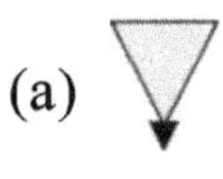 (b) 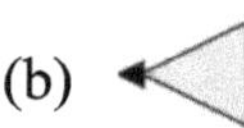

(c) 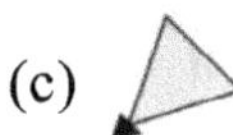 (d) 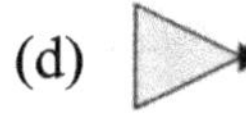

21. Group the given figures into three classes on the basis of their identical properties using each figure only once. **[2019]**

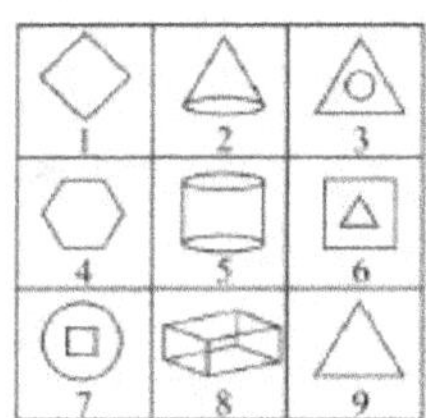

(a) 1, 4, 7; 2, 5, 8; 3, 6, 9
(b) 1, 4, 7; 2, 5, 9; 3, 6, 8
(c) 1, 4, 9; 2, 5, 8; 3, 6, 7
(d) 1, 4, 9; 2, 5, 7; 3, 6, 8

22. Select a figure from the options which completes the given figure matrix. **[2021]**

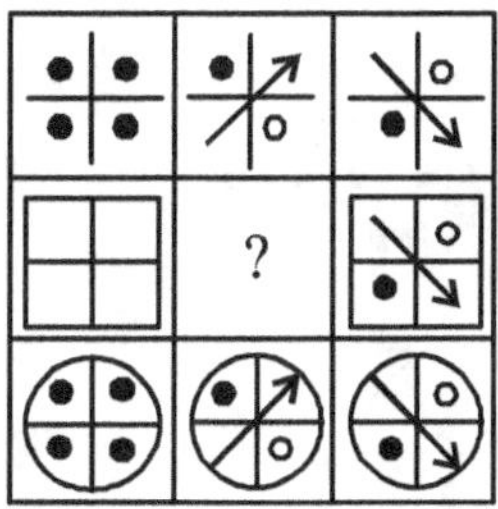

(a) 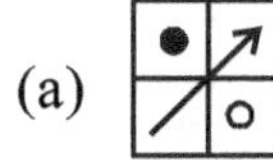 (b) 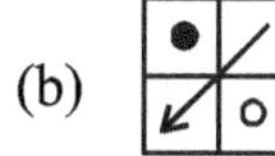

(c) 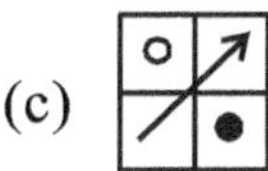 (d) 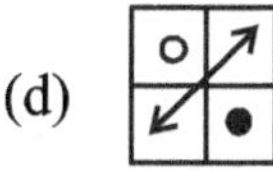

23. Select a figure from the options which will complete the given figure matrix. **[2022]**

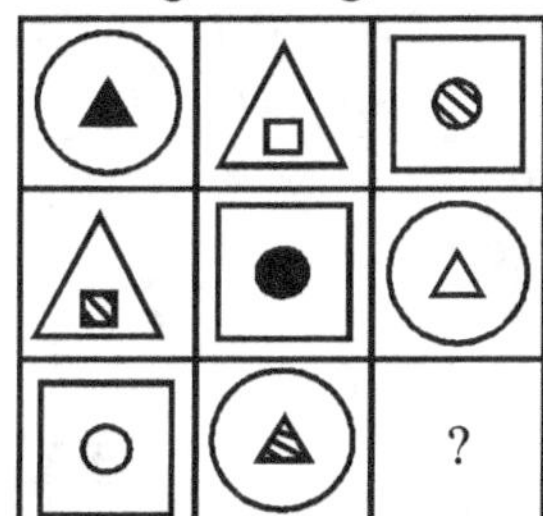

(a)  (b) 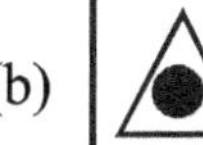

(c) 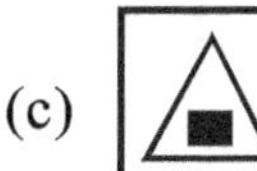 (d) 

ANSWER KEY																			
LEVEL-1																			
1	(a)	**2**	(d)	**3**	(c)	**4**	(d)	**5**	(b)	**6**	(a)	**7**	(a)	**8**	(d)	**9**	(c)	**10**	(a)
11	(a)	**12**	(b)	**13**	(b)	**14**	(b)	**15**	(b)										
LEVEL-2																			
1	(c)	**2**	(b)	**3**	(b)	**4**	(a)	**5**	(a)	**6**	(d)	**7**	(d)	**8**	(d)	**9**	(c)	**10**	(c)
11	(c)	**12**	(b)	**13**	(c)	**14**	(d)	**15**	(c)	**16**	(d)	**17**	(b)	**18**	(d)	**19**	(a)	**20**	(c)
21	(c)	**22**	(a)	**23**	(c)														

CHAPTER

Cube and Dice

Cube

A cube is a three dimensional figure, having 8 corners, 6 surfaces and 12 edges. If a cube is painted on all of its surfaces with any colour and further divided into various smaller cubes, we get the following results.

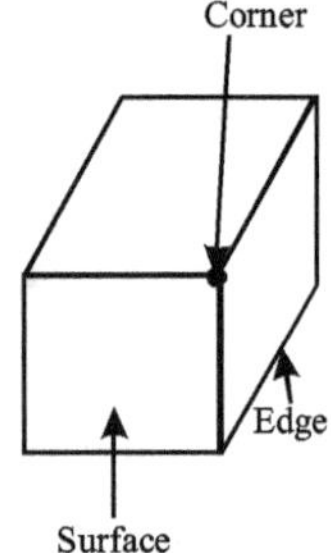

(a) Smaller cubes with three surfaces painted will be present on the corners of the big cube.

(b) Smaller cubes with two surface painted will be present on the edges of the big cube.

(c) Smaller cubes with one surface painted will be present on the outer surfaces of the big cube.

(d) Smaller cubes with no surface painted will be present inside the big cube.

If a cube is painted on all of its surfaces with a colour and then divided into smaller cubes of equal size, then after separation, number of smaller cubes so obtained will be calculated as under :

Number of smaller cubes with three surfaces painted = 8

Number of smaller cubes with two surfaces painted

$$= (n - 2) \times 12$$

Number of smaller cubes with one surface painted

$$= (n - 2)^2 \times 6$$

Number of smaller cubes with no surfaces painted = $(n - 2)^3$

Where n = No. of divisions on the surfaces of the bigger cube

$$= \frac{\text{length of edge of big cube}}{\text{length of edge of one smaller cube}}$$

TYPE-I : A cube is painted on all of its surfaces with a single colour and then divided into various smaller cubes of equal size.

DIRECTIONS : A cube of side 4 cm. is painted black on all of its surfaces and then divided into various smaller cubes of side 1 cm. each. The smaller cubes so obtained are separated.

$$\text{Total cubes obtained} = \frac{4 \times 4 \times 4}{1 \times 1 \times 1} = 64$$

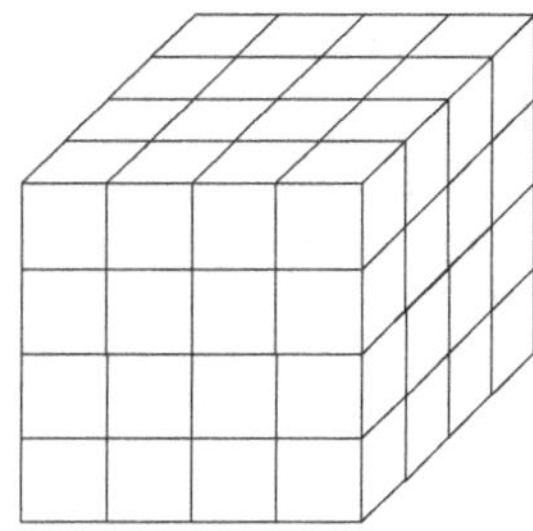

$$\text{Here,} \quad n = \frac{\text{side of big cube}}{\text{side of small cube}} = \frac{4}{1} = 4$$

1. Number of smaller cubes with three surfaces painted = 8

2. Number of smaller cubes with two surfaces painted

$= (n - 2) \times 12 = (4 - 2) \times 12 = 24$

3. Number of smaller cubes with one surface painted

$= (n - 2)^2 \times 6 = (4 - 2)^2 \times 6 = 24$

4. Number of smaller cubes with no surface painted

$= (n - 2)^3 = (4 - 2)^3 = (2)^3 = 8$

TYPE-II : A cube is painted on its surfaces with different colours and then divided into various smaller cubes of equal size.

DIRECTIONS : A cube of side 4 cm. is painted black on pair of opposite surfaces, blue on another pair of opposite surfaces and red on the remaining pair of opposite surfaces. The cube is divided into smaller cubes of equal side of 1 cm each.

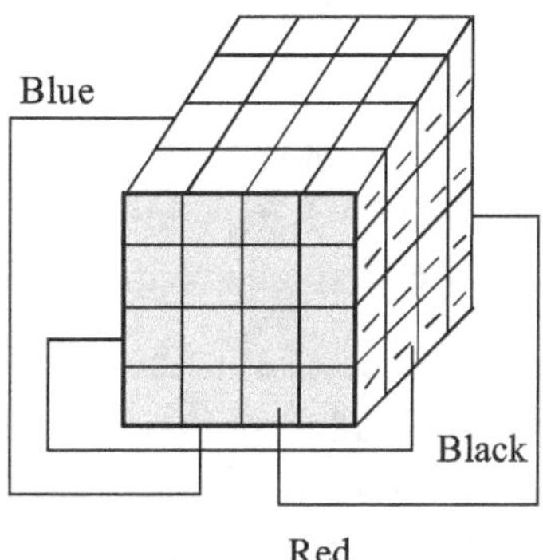

1. Number of smaller cubes with three surfaces painted = 8

(These smaller cubes will have all three surfaces painted with different colours blue, black and red)

2. Number of smaller cubes with two surfaces painted = 24.

And out of this

(1) Number of cubes with two surfaces painted with black and blue colour = 8

(2) Number of cubes with two surfaces painted with blue and red colour = 8

(3) Number of cubes with two surfaces painted with black and red colour = 8

3. Number of smaller cubes with one surface painted = 24. And out of this

(1) Number of cubes with one surface painted with black colour = 8

(2) Number of cubes with one surface painted with blue colour = 8

(3) Number of cubes with one surface painted with red colour = 8

TYPE-III : A cube is painted on its surfaces in such a way that one pair of opposite surfaces is left unpainted.

DIRECTIONS : A cube of side 4 cm. is painted red on one pair of opposite surfaces, green on another pair of opposite surfaces and one pair of opposite surfaces is left unpainted. Now the cube is divided into 64 smaller cubes of side 1cm. each.

1. Number of smaller cubes with three surfaces painted = 0 (Because each smaller cube at the corner is having a surface which is not painted)
2. Number of smaller cubes with two surfaces painted

   = Number of cubes present at the corners + Numbers of cubes present at the 4 edges = $8 + (n - 2) \times 4 = 8 + 8 = 16$

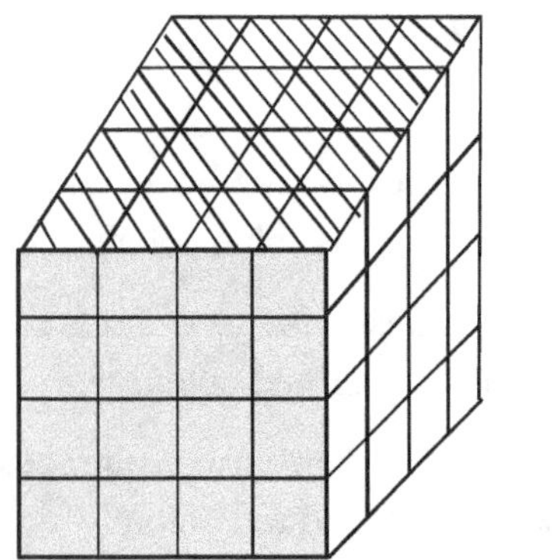

3. Number of smaller cubes with one surface painted.

   = Number of cubes present at 8 edges + number of cubes present at the four surfaces

   $= (n - 2) \times 8 + (n - 2)^2 \times 4 = 2 \times 8 + 4 \times 4 = 32$

4. Number of smaller cubes with no side painted.

   = Number of cubes on the two unpainted surfaces + number of cubes present inside the cube

   $= (n - 2)^2 \times 2 + (n - 2)^3 = 2 \times 4 + 8 = 16$

TYPE-IV : A cube is painted on its surfaces in such a way that one pair of adjacent surfaces is left unpainted.

DIRECTIONS : A cube of side 4 cm. is painted red on one pair of adjacent surfaces, green on the other pair of adjacent surfaces and two adjacent surfaces are left unpainted. Now the cube is divided into 64 smaller cubes of side 1 cm. each.

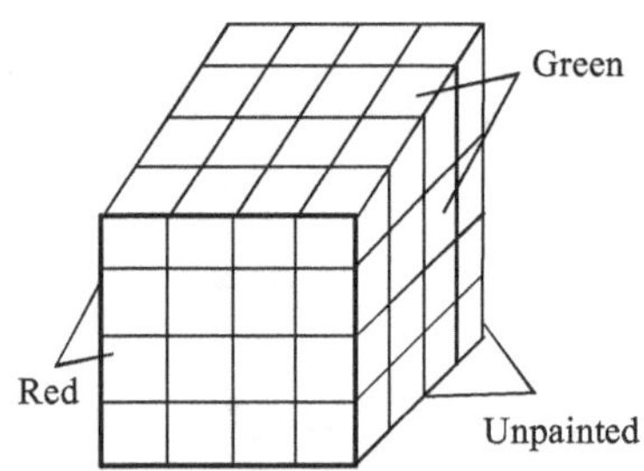

1. Number of smaller cubes with three surfaces painted = Number of smaller cubes at two corners = 2
2. Number of smaller cubes with two surface painted = Number of smaller cubes at four corners + Numbers of smaller cubes at 5 edges

   $= 4 + (n - 2) \times 5 = 4 + 2 \times 5 = 4 + 10 = 14$

3. Number of smaller cubes with one surface painted

   = Number of smaller cubes at four surfaces

   + Number of cubes present at 6 edges

+ Number of smaller cubes at two corners

$= (n-2)^2 \times 4 + (n-2) \times 6 + 2$

$= 4 \times 4 + 2 \times 6 + 2 = 16 + 12 = 28 + 2 = 30$

4. Number of smaller cubes with no surfaces painted = Number of smaller cubes from inside the big cube +

Number of cubes at two surfaces + Number of cubes at one edge = $(n-2)^3 + (n-2)^3 \times 2 + (n-2)$

$= (2)^3 + (2)^2 + 2 = 8 + 8 + 2 = 18$

ILLUSTRATION 1 :

Count the number of cubes in the given figure.

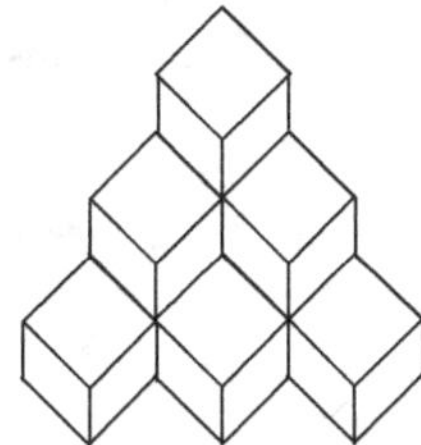

(a) 6

(b) 8

(c) 10

(d) 12

***Sol.* (c)** Clearly, there is 1 column containing 3 cubes , 2 columns containing 2 cubes each and 3 columns containing 1 cube each.

ILLUSTRATION 2 :

Select from the alternatives the box that can be formed by folding the sheet shown in figure (X) :

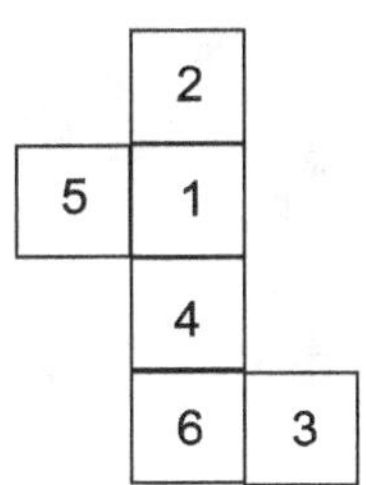

(X)

(a) 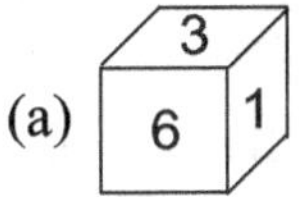

(b) 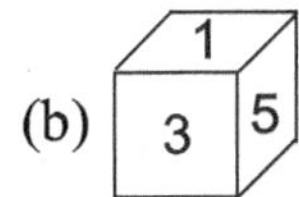

(c) 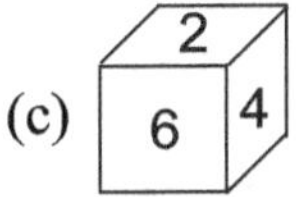

(d) 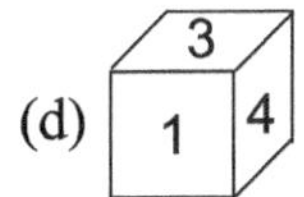

***Sol.* (d)** When the sheet in fig.(X) is folded to from a box (cube) then

The number 2 will lie opposite the number 4; the number 1 will lie opposite the number 6 and the number 5 will lie opposite the number 3. Fig. (a) has the numbers 1 and 6 on adjacent face, fig.(b) has number 3 and 5 on adjacent faces and the fig. (c) has the numbers 2 and 4 on the adjacent face. So, these three alternatives are not possible. Since, the numbers 1, 3 and 4 can appear on adjacent face, so fig.(d) is possible.

Hence, only the box shown in fig. (d) can be formed by folding fig. (X).

ILLUSTRATION 3 :

Count the number of cubes in the given figure.

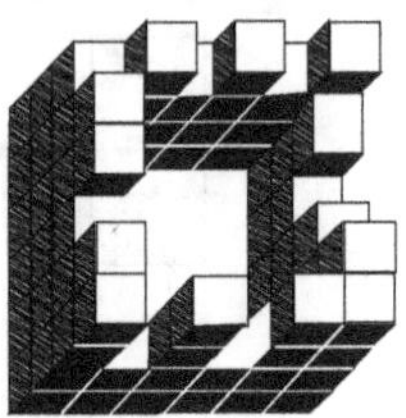

(a) 68 (b) 69
(c) 70 (d) 71

***Sol.* (b)** In the figure, there are 11 columns containing 4 cubes each , 7 columns containing 3 cubes each and 2 columns containing 2 cubes each .

$\therefore$ Total number of cubes

$= (11 \times 4) + (7 \times 3) + (2 \times 2) = 44 + 21 + 4 = 69.$

ILLUSTRATION 4 :

The figures given below show the two different positions of a dice. Which number will appear opposite to number 2.

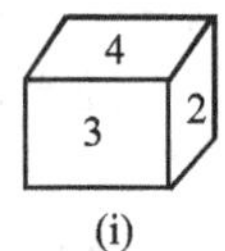

(i)

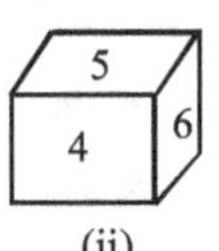

(ii)

(a) 3

(b) 4

(c) 5

(d) 6

***Sol.* (c)** The above question, where only two positions of a dice are given, can easily be solved with the following method.

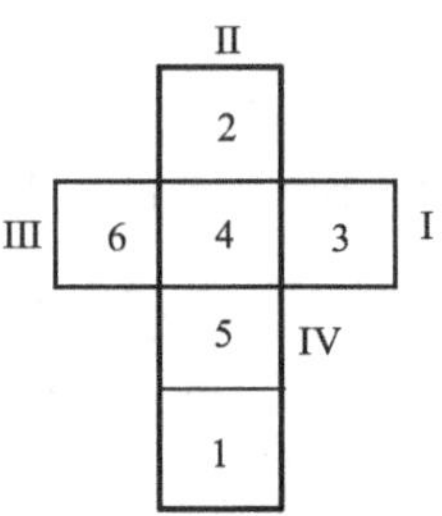

Step I : The dice, when unfolded, will appear as shown in the figure given on the right side.

Step II : Write the common number to both the dice in the middle block. Since common number is 4, hence number 4 will appear in the central block.

Step III : Consider the figure (i) and write the first number in the anti-clockwise direction of number 4, (common number) in block I and second number in block II. Therefore, numbers 3 and 2 being the first and second number to 4 in anticlockwise directions respectively, will appear in block I and II respectively.

Step IV : Consider figure (ii) and write first and second number in the anticlockwise direction to number 4, (common number) in block (III) and (IV). Hence numbers 6 and 5 will appear in the blocks III and IV respectively.

Step V : Write remaining number in the remaining block. Therefore, number 1 will come in the remaining block. Now, from the unfolded figure we find that number opposite to 6 is 3, number opposite to 2 is 5 and number opposite to 4 is 1. Therefore, option (c) is our answer.

LEVEL 1

1. Count the number of cubes in the given figure.

(a) 80 (b) 87
(c) 89 (d) 90

2. Select from the alternative, the box that can be formed by folding the sheet shown in figure (X) :

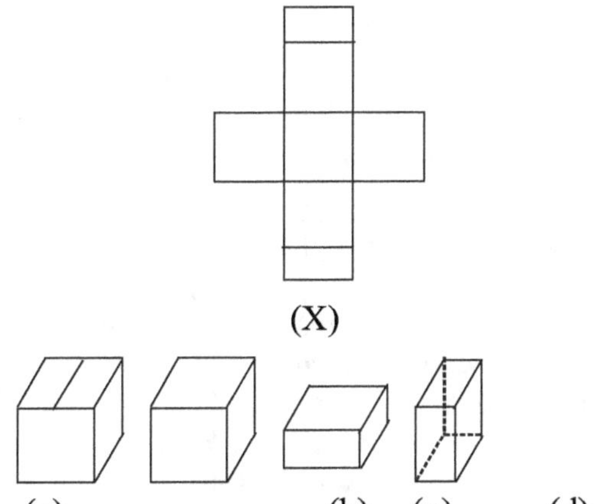

(X)

(a) (b) (c) (d)

3. Select from the alternative, the box that can be formed by folding the sheet shown in figure (X) :

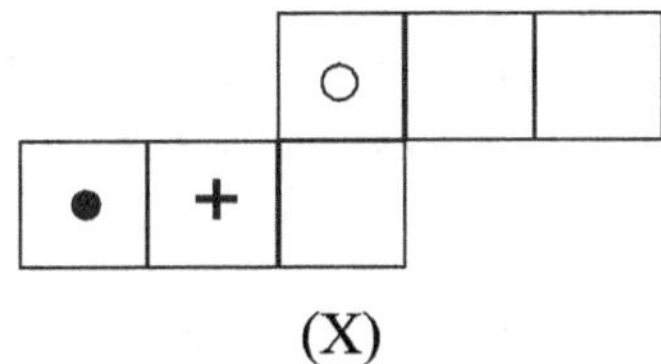

(X)

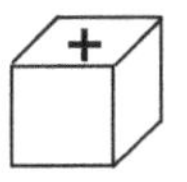
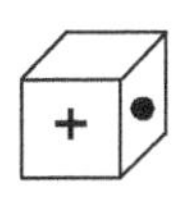
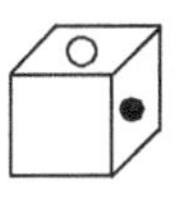
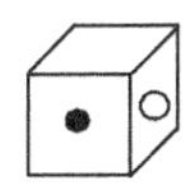

(a) (b) (c) (d)

(a) A only
(b) A, B, and C only
(c) B and C only
(d) A, B, C and D

4. How many dots are their on the dice face opposite the one with three dots ?

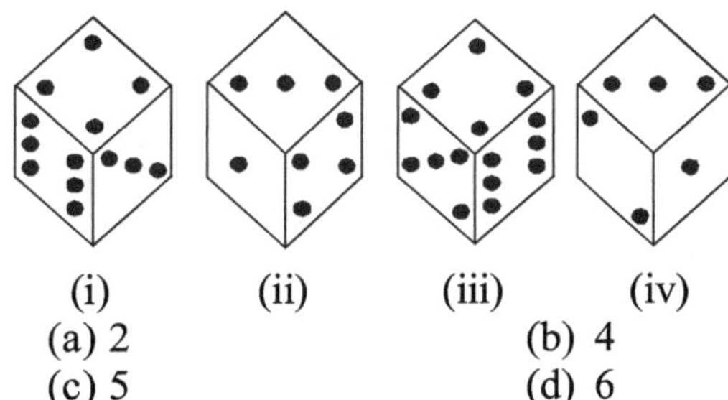

(i) (ii) (iii) (iv)

(a) 2 (b) 4
(c) 5 (d) 6

5. When the following figure is folded to form a cube, how many dots would lie opposite the face bearing five dots ?

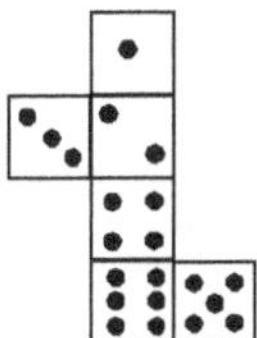

(a) 1 (b) 2
(c) 3 (d) 4

6. Which number lies opposite the face 4, if the four different positions of a dice are as shown in the figures given below.

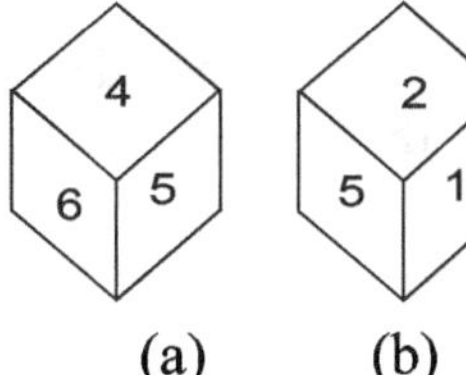

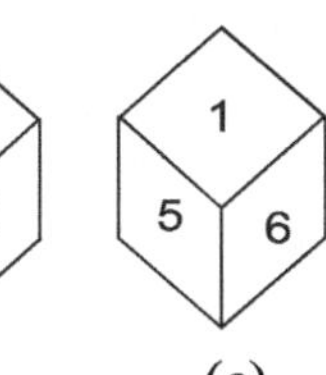

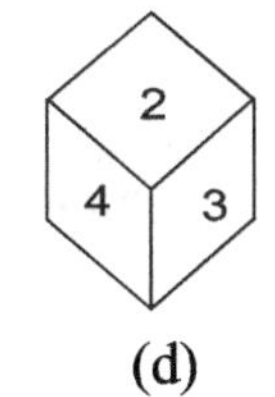

(a) (b) (c) (d)

(a) 5 (b) 3
(c) 2 (d) 1

7. What should be the number opposite 3 ?

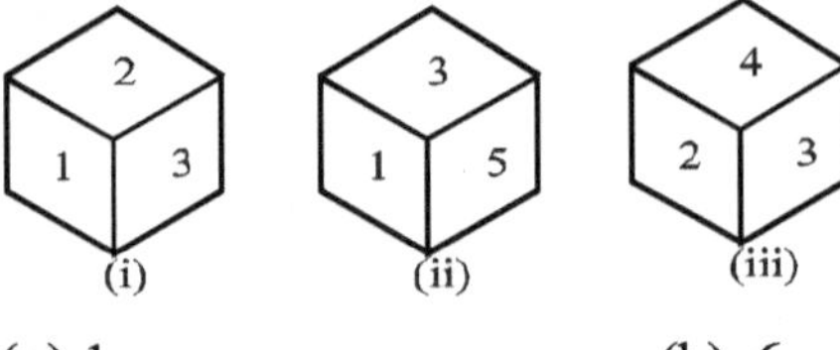

(a) 1 (b) 6
(c) 5 (d) 4

8. From the following positions of dice, find which number will come in place of "?"

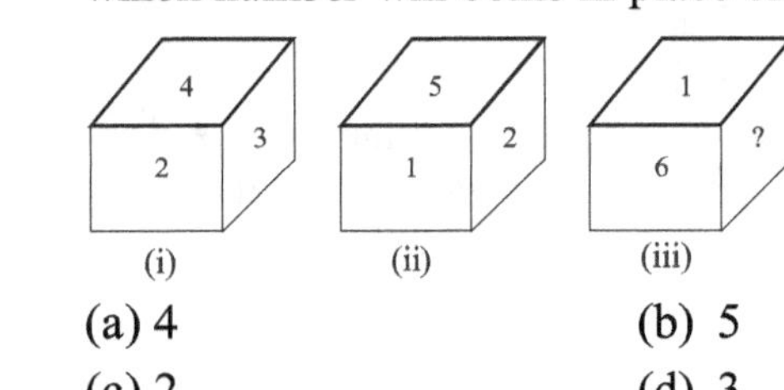

(a) 4 (b) 5
(c) 2 (d) 3

9. The following figure is converted into a cube. Its correct shape will be:–

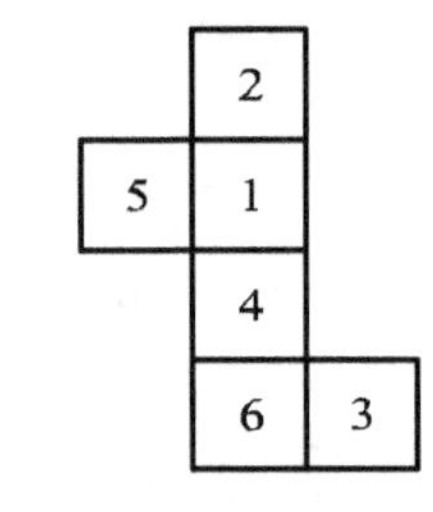

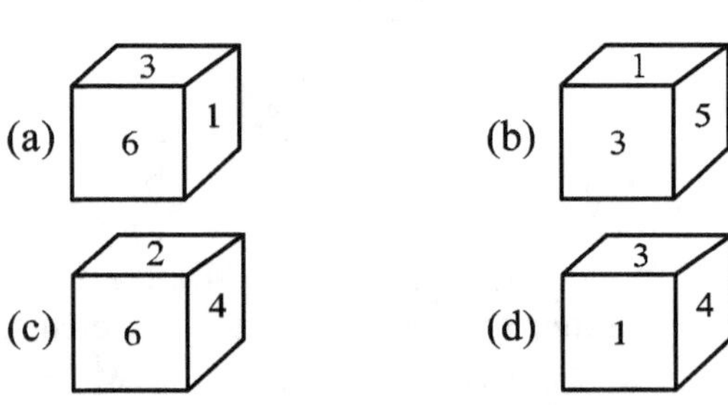

10. The following figure is converted into a cube. Its four positions (a), (b), (c), and (d) are shown. On the basis of these select correct alternative.

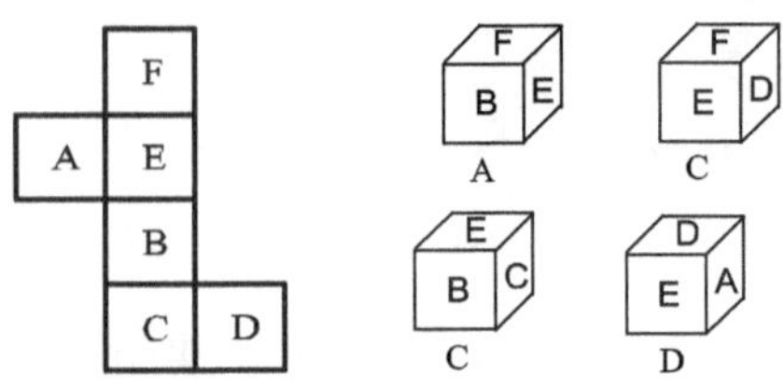

(a) A only (b) B only
(c) A and C only (d) A,B,C&D

11. Select from the alternative, the box that can be formed by folding the sheet shown in figure (X) :

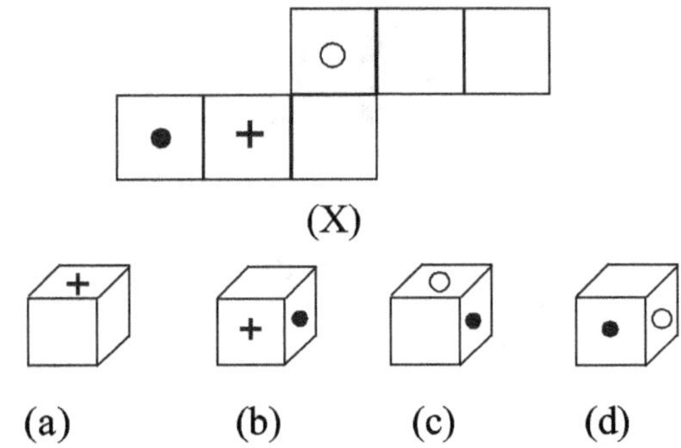

(a) A only
(b) A, B, and C only
(c) B and C only
(d) A, B, C and D

DIRECTIONS (Qs. 12– 15) : *A wooden cube is painted Blue on all four adjoining sides and Green on two opposite sides i.e. top and bottom. It is then cut at equal distances at right angles four times vertically (top to bottom) and two times horizontally as shown in the figure where dotted lines represent the cuts made. Study the diagram and answer the questions that follow.*

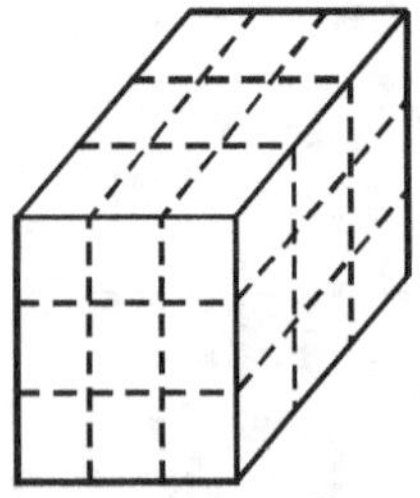

12. How many cubes will have one face painted only in Blue?
(a) 1 (b) 2
(c) 3 (d) 4
13. How many cubes will have one face painted only in Green?
(a) 1 (b) 2
(c) 3 (d) 4
14. How many cubes will have at least three sides painted?
(a) 8 (b) 6
(c) 3 (d) 2
15. How many cubes will have no side painted at all?
(a) 1 (b) 2
(c) 3 (d) 4
16. The following figure is converted into a cube. Its correct shape will be:–

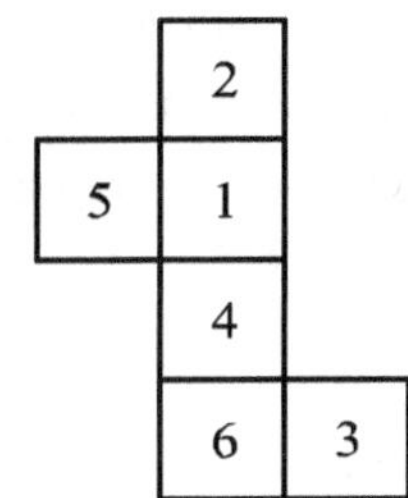

(a) 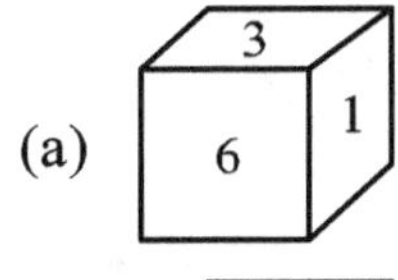

(b) 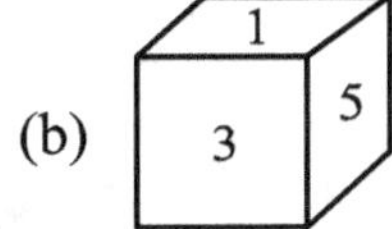

(c) 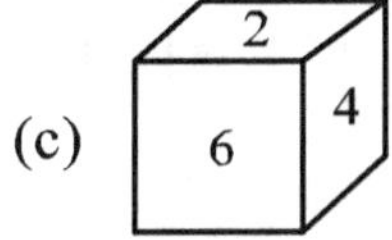

(d) 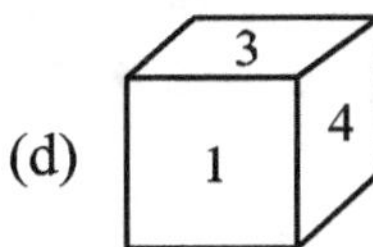

17. The two positions on a dice are shown below. If 1 is at the bottom then what will be on the top?

(a) 2 (b) 3
(c) 4 (d) 5

DIRECTIONS (Qs. 18-19) *Read the information carefully and answer the question given below:*

A cube is cut into two equal parts along a plane parallel to one of its faces. One piece is coloured orange on the two largest faces and yellow on the remaining. The other piece is coloured yellow on two small adjacent faces and orange on the remaining. Each is then cut into 32 cubes of the same size. These 64 cubes are mixed up. Then:

18. How many cubes have no coloured face at all?
(a) 0 (b) 4
(c) 8 (d) 16
19. How many cubes have only one coloured face?
(a) 8 (b) 16
(c) 20 (d) 24
20. Two positions of a dice are given. What number will be on the face opposite to the face having number 5? **[2018]**
(a) 1
(b) 3
(c) 4
(d) 2

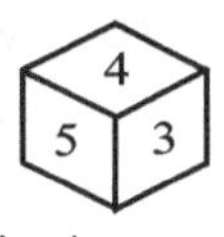

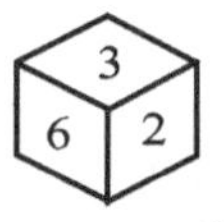

21. Three positions of a dice are given below. When 6 is at the top, which number will be at the bottom? **[2020]**

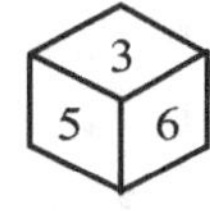

(a) 1 (b) 4
(c) 2 (d) 5
22. Which of the following symbol will be on the face opposite to the face having symbol ★, if the given net is folded to form a cube? **[2020]**

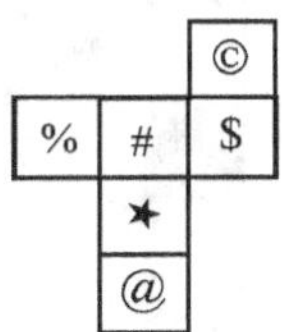

(a) % (b) ©
(c) $ (d) #

LEVEL 2

1. Count the number of blocks in the given figure.

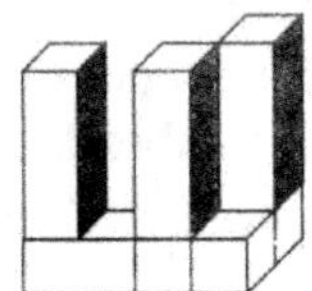

(a) 6 (b) 7
(c) 8 (d) 9

DIRECTIONS (Qs. 2-5): *Count the number of cubes in each of the following figures:*

2.

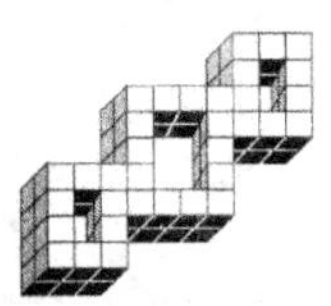

(a) 64 (b) 66
(c) 68 (d) 70

3.

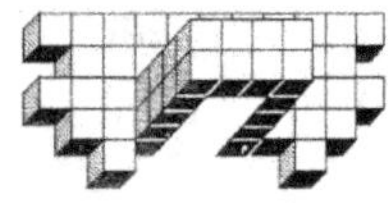

(a) 57 (b) 58
(c) 60 (d) 62

4. Select from the alternatives the box that can be formed by folding the sheet shown in figure (X) :

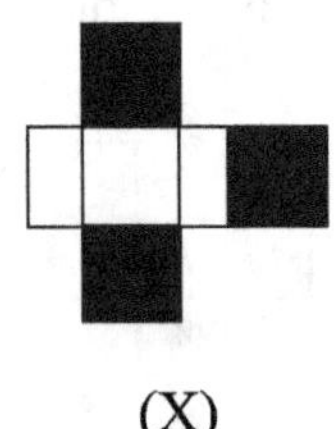

(X)

(a) 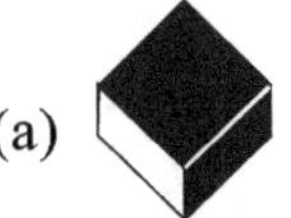 (b) 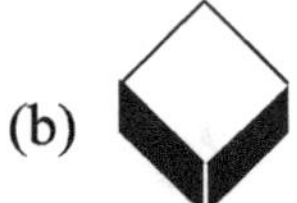

(c) 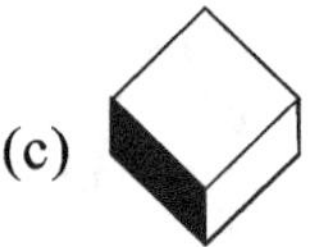 (d) 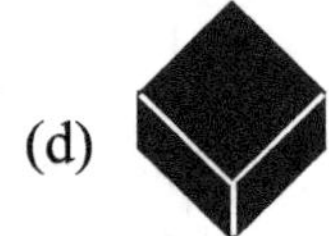

(a) A and C only
(b) B and D only
(c) C and D only
(d) A and D only

5. Amongst the following figures, find the correct one, if it is known that the total number of dots on opposite faces of cube shown is always 7.

(a) 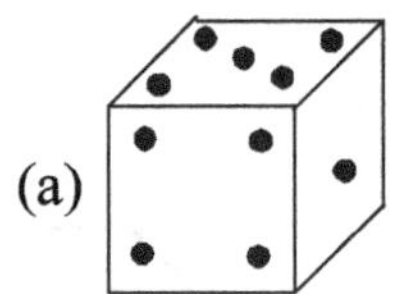 (b) 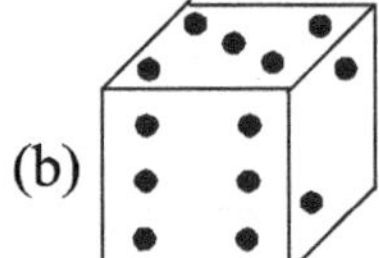

(c) 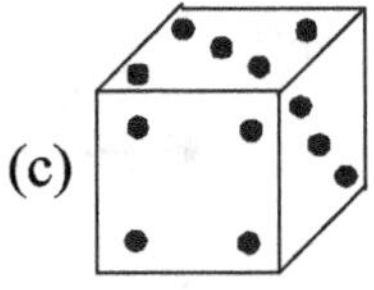 (d) 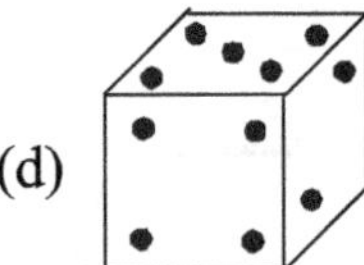

6. Two positions of a dice are shown below. When four is at the top what number will be at the bottom?

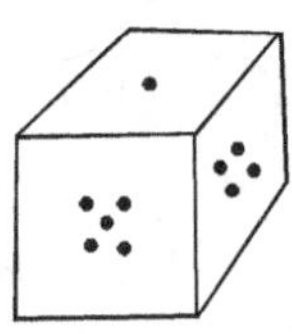 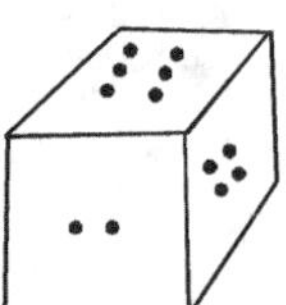

(a) 2 (b) 3
(c) 5 (d) 6

7. Four positions of a single wooden cube, having various marking on its all the six faces are shown below. Study the positions carefully.

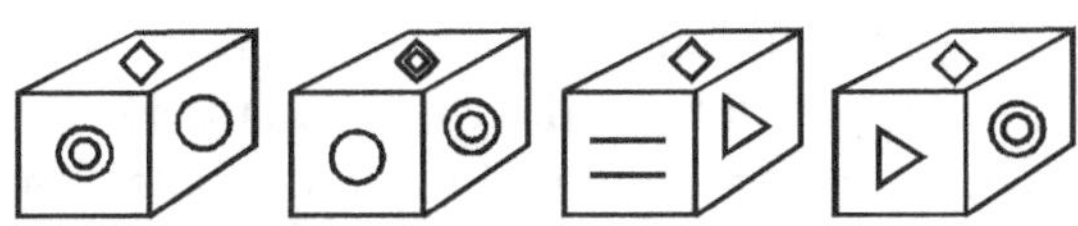

Which symbol is opposite to the symbol '=' ?

(a) △ (b) ○
(c) ◎ (d) □

DIRECTIONS (Qs. 8-9): *Count the number of cubes in each of the following figures:*

8.

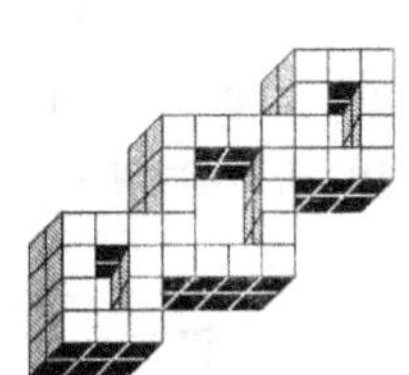

(a) 64 (b) 66
(c) 68 (d) 70

9.

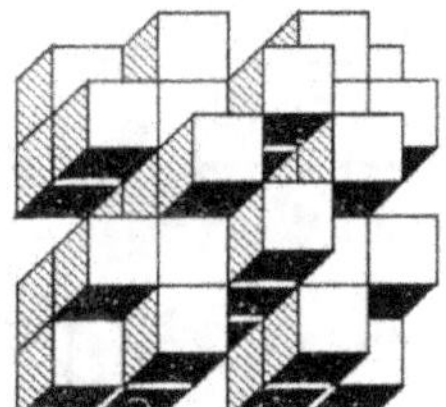

(a) 28 (b) 36
(c) 40 (d) 42

10.

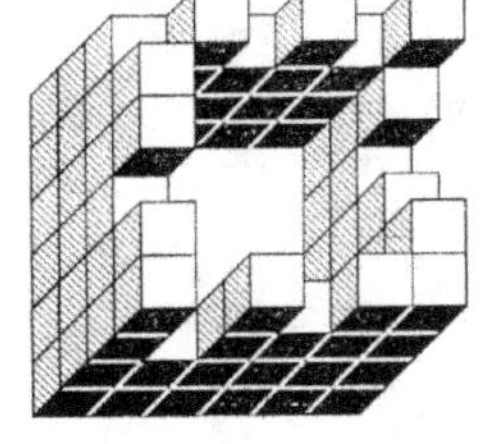

(a) 68 (b) 69
(c) 70 (d) 71

11. A Dice Is Thrown Three Times And Its Three Different Positions Are Given Below. Find The Number On The Face Opposite The Face Showing 3.

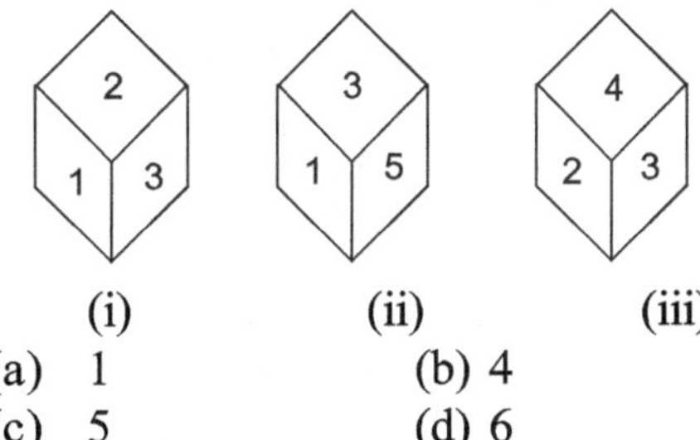

(i) (ii) (iii)

(a) 1 (b) 4
(c) 5 (d) 6

12. Select from the alternatives the box that can be formed by folding the sheet shown in figure (X) :

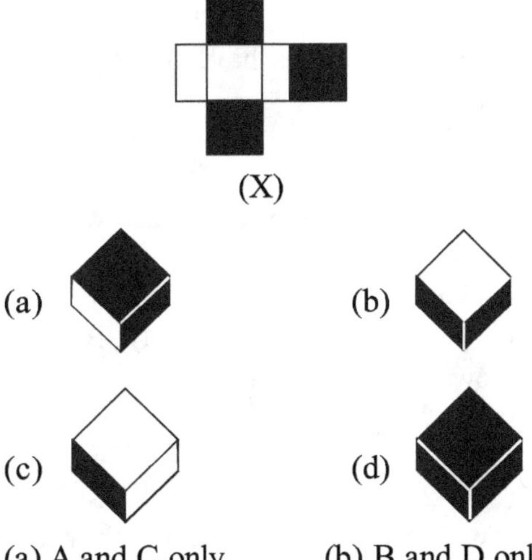

(a) A and C only (b) B and D only
(c) C and D only (d) A and D only

13. Amongst the following figures, find the correct one, if it is known that the total number of dots on opposite faces of cube shown is always 7.

(a) 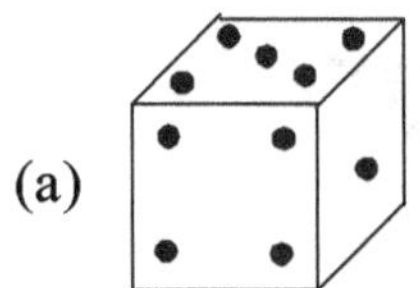 (b) 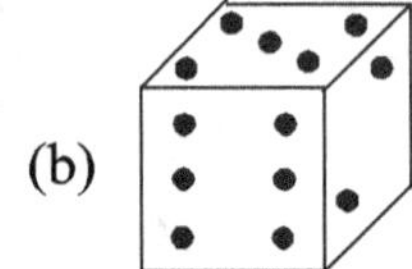

(c) 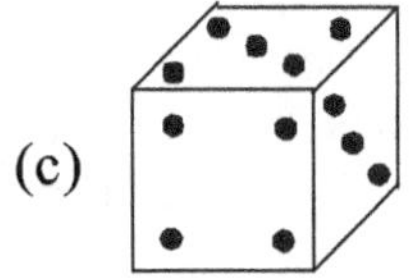 (d) 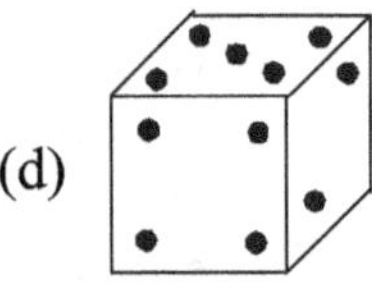

DIRECTIONS (Qs. 14-18) : *A cube is painted red on three adjacent sides and then cut into 8 small cubes. Each blank face is then painted green. Then each such cube is again cut into eight cubes. Total number of cubes after second dissection = 8 × 8 = 64.*

14. How many cubes have three red faces each?
(a) 1 (b) 2
(c) 4 (d) 8

15. How many cubes have two green faces each?
(a) 4 (b) 5
(c) 6 (d) 9

16. How many cubes have three green faces each?
(a) 8 (b) 12
(c) 24 (d) 27

17. How many cubes have at least two red faces ?
(a) 4 (b) 6
(c) 8 (d) 10

18. How many cubes have at least two blank faces ?
(a) 24 (b) 48
(c) 42 (d) 64

19. Two positions of a dice are shown below. When four is at the top what number will be at the bottom?

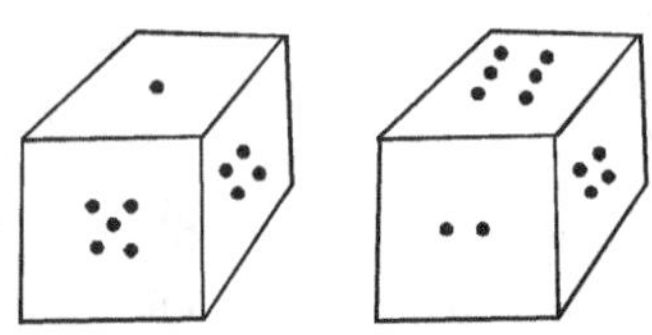

(a) 2 (b) 3
(c) 5 (d) 6

20. Four positions of a single wooden cube, having various marking on its all the six faces are shown below. Study the positions carefully.

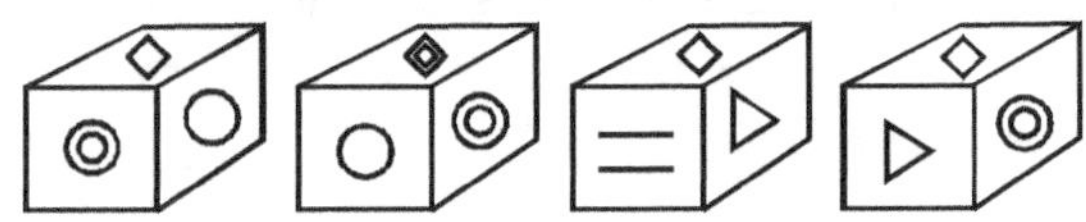

Which symbol is opposite to the symbol '='?

(a) △ (b) ○
(c) ◎ (d) □

21. If the given figure is folded to form a box, which among the boxes below will be formed?

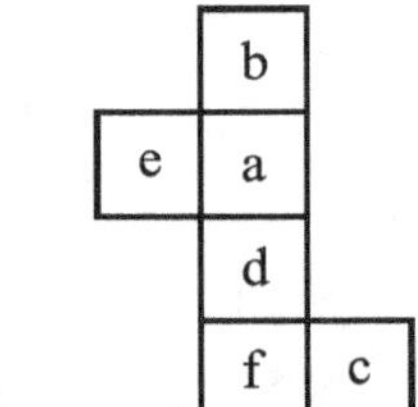

(a) 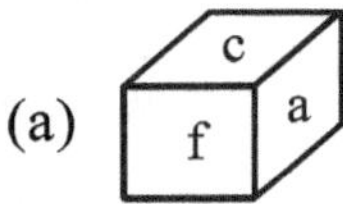

(b) 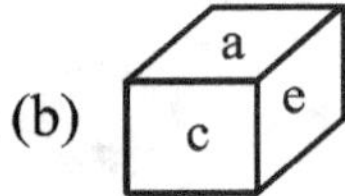

(c) 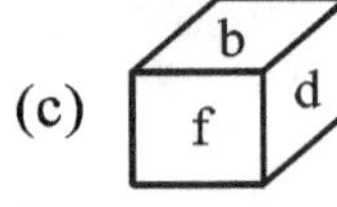

(d) 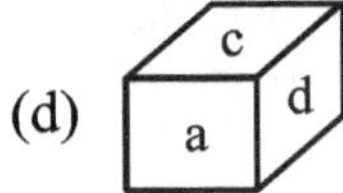

22. 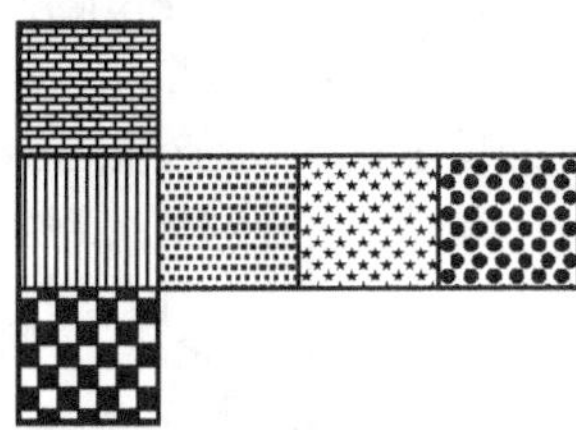

When the above is folded into a cube, which is the only cube that can be produced amongst the following?

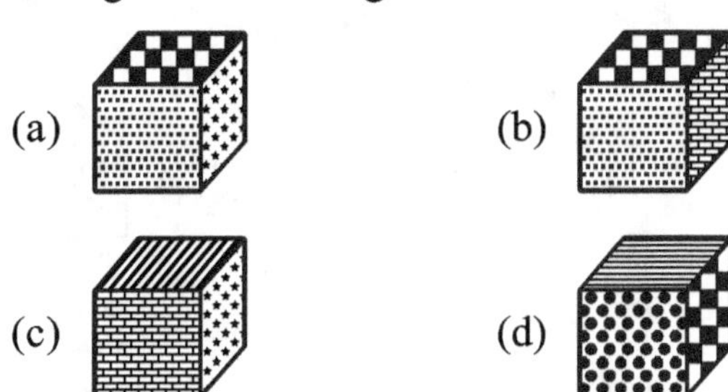

23. The given solid is painted red on all the faces.
How many cubes in the second layer from the top do not have any coloured faces? **[2018]**

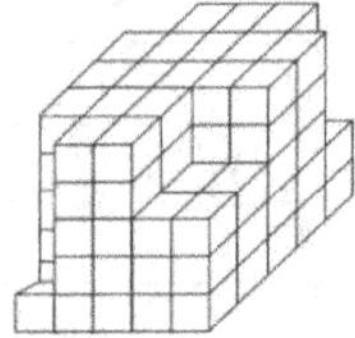

(a) 4 (b) 6
(c) 8 (d) 9

24. Choose the box that is similar to the box formed when the given Sheet (X) is folded to form a box.

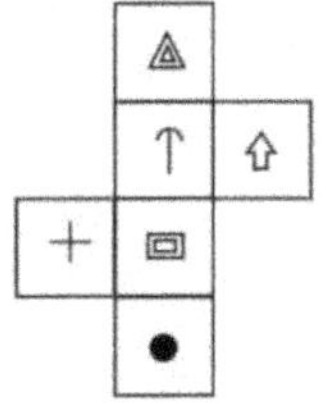

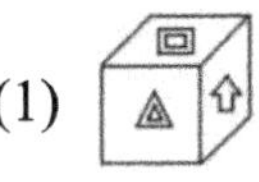

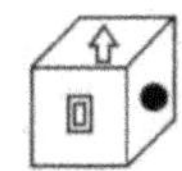
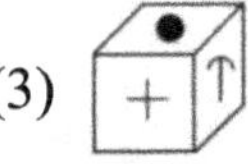

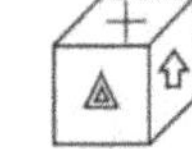

(a) (3) only
(b) (2) only
(c) (1), (2) and (4) only
(d) (1), (2), (3) and (4)

25. Two different positions of a dice are shown below. Find the number on the face opposite to the face having number 5. **[2019]**

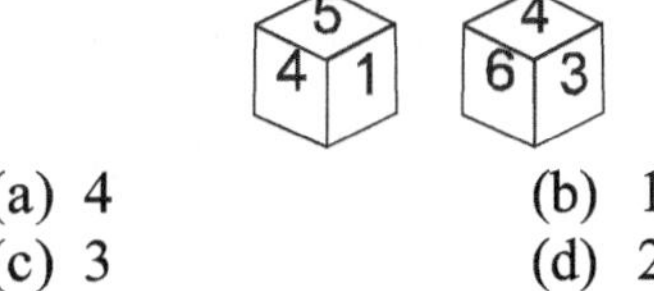

(a) 4 (b) 1
(c) 3 (d) 2

26. How many dots lie on the face opposite to the face having three dots, when the given sheet of paper is folded to form a dice? **[2020]**

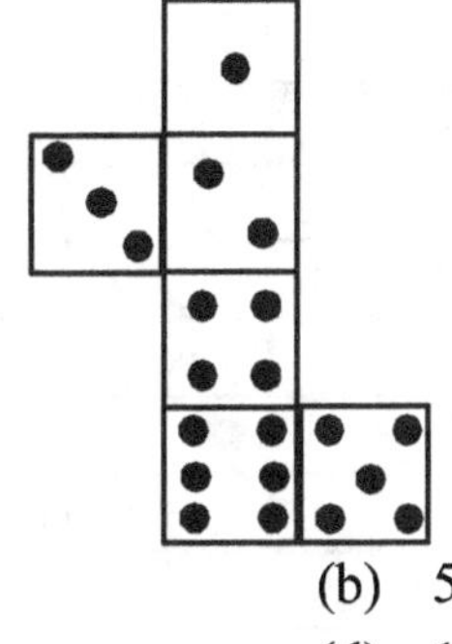

(a) 6 (b) 5
(c) 4 (d) 1

27. Choose the box that is similar to the box formed when the given sheet of paper is folded to form a box. **[2021]**

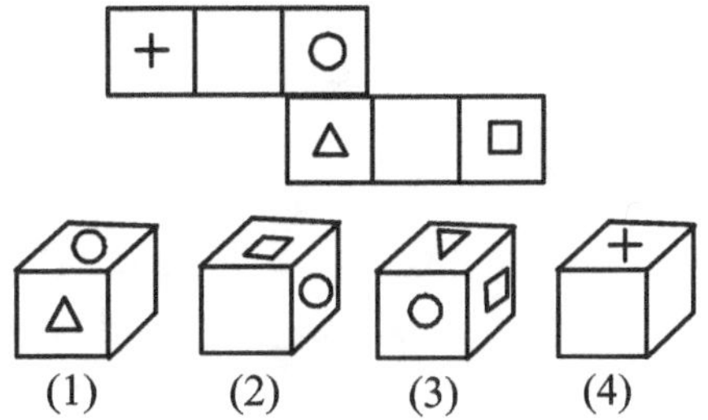

(a) (1), (3) and (4) only
(b) (2), (3) and (4) only
(c) (1) and (2) only
(d) (2) and (3) only

28. Count the number of cubes in the given figure. [2021]

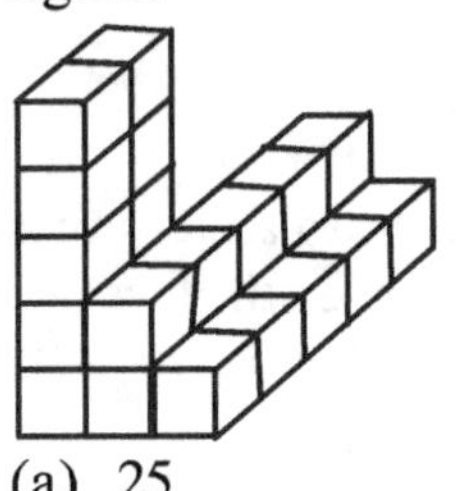

(a) 25 (b) 24
(c) 22 (d) 26

29. Select a box from the options that is similar to the box formed when the given sheet of paper is folded to form a box. [2022]

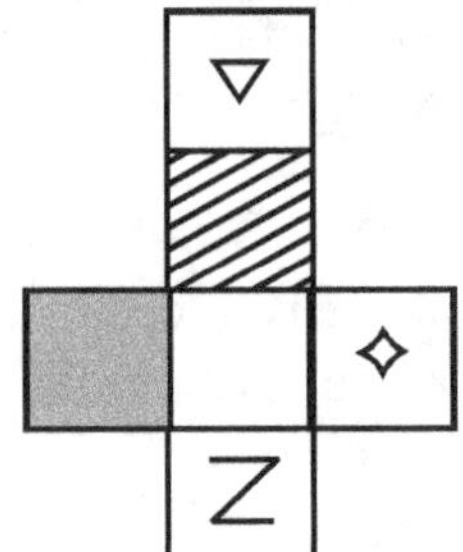

(a) 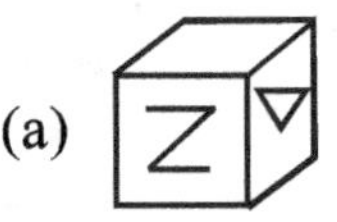 (b) 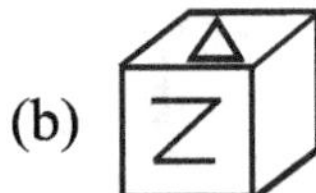

(c) 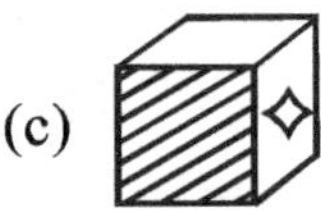 (d) 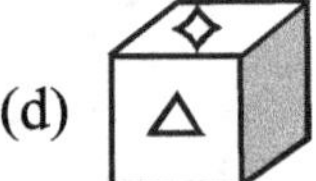

ANSWER KEY																					
LEVEL-1																					
1	(c)	**3**	(d)	**5**	(c)	**7**	(b)	**9**	(d)	**11**	(d)	**13**	(b)	**15**	(a)	**17**	(b)	**19**	(b)	**21**	(b)
2	(a)	**4**	(c)	**6**	(d)	**8**	(d)	**10**	(b)	**12**	(d)	**14**	(a)	**16**	(d)	**18**	(a)	**20**	(c)	**22**	(b)
LEVEL-2																					
1	(b)	**4**	(a)	**7**	(c)	**10**	(b)	**13**	(a)	**16**	(d)	**19**	(b)	**22**	(d)	**25**	(c)	**28**	(a)		
2	(c)	**5**	(a)	**8**	(c)	**11**	(d)	**14**	(a)	**17**	(d)	**20**	(c)	**23**	(b)	**26**	(b)	**29**	(c)		
3	(b)	**6**	(b)	**9**	(c)	**12**	(a)	**15**	(d)	**18**	(d)	**21**	(d)	**24**	(b)	**27**	(c)				

CHAPTER 17 Dot Situation

DOT SITUATION :

The problems on dot situation involve the search of similar conditions in the alternative figures as indicated in the problem figure. The problem figure contains dots placed in the spaces enclosed between the combinations of square, triangle, rectangle and circle. Selecting one of these dots we observe the region in which this dot is enclosed i.e. to which of the four figures (circle, square, rectangle and triangle) is this region common. Then we look for such a region in the four alternatives. Once we have found it we repeat the procedure for other dots, if any. The alternative figure which contains all such regions is the answer.

DIRECTIONS (ILLUSTRATION 1-4) : *In each of the following examples, there is a diagram marked (X), with one or more dots placed in it. The diagram is followed by four other figures, marked (a), (b), (c) and (d) only one of which is such as to make possible the placement of the dot. Select this alternative as the answer.*

ILLUSTRATION 1 :

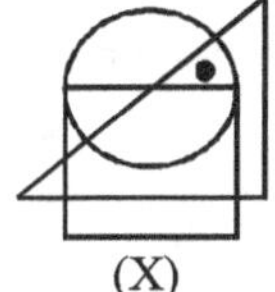

(X)

(a) 

(b) 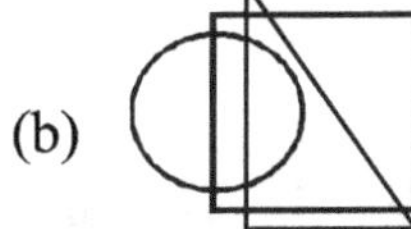

(c) 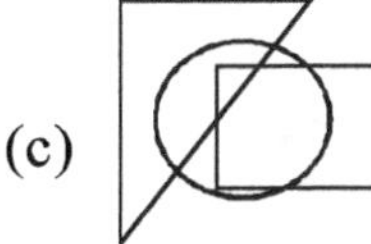

(d) 

***Sol.* (c)** In figure (X), the dot lies in the region common to the circle and the triangle only. Such a region is present in figure (c) only.

ILLUSTRATION 2 :

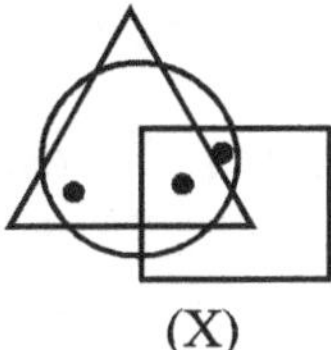

(X)

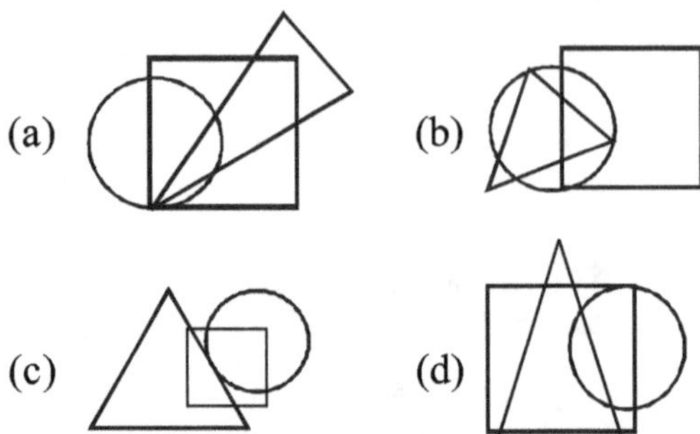

***Sol.* (b)** Figure (X) contains one dot in the region common to the circle and the triangle, another dot in the region common to all the three figures and the third dot in the region common to the square and the circle only. In figures (a) and (d), the region common to the circle and the triangle lies within the square. In figure (c), there is no region common to the circle and the triangle. Only figure (b) contains all the three types of regions.

ILLUSTRATION 3 :

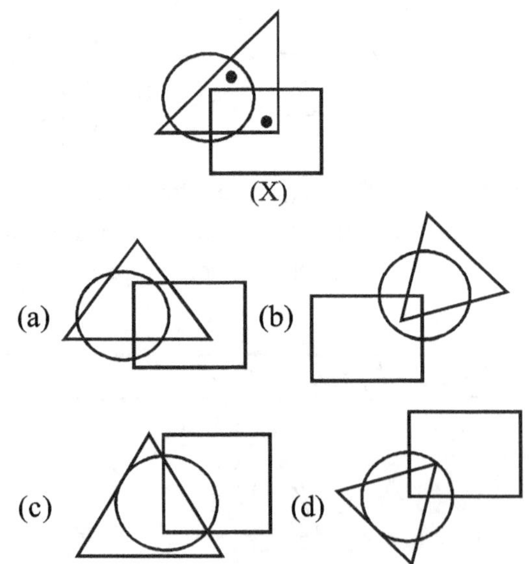

***Sol.* (1)** In figure (X), one of the dots is placed in the region common to the circle and the triangle and the other dot is placed in the region common to the triangle and the square. From amongst the figures (a), (b), (c) and (d), only figure (1) has both the regions, one common to circle and triangle and the other common to triangle and square.

ILLUSTRATION 4 :

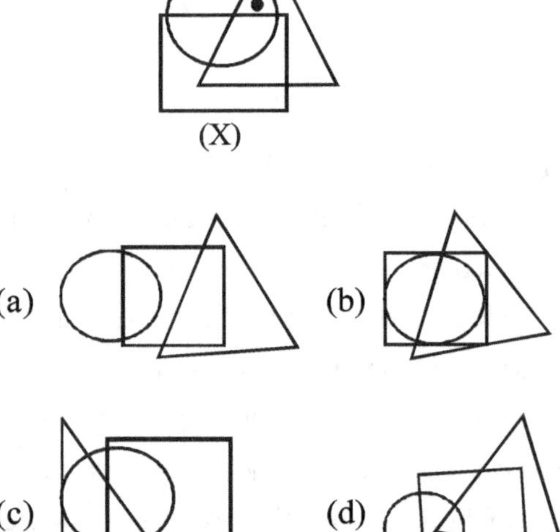

***Sol.* (c)** In figure (X), the dot lies in the region common to the circle and the triangle only. Such a region is present in figure (c) only.

ILLUSTRATION 5 :

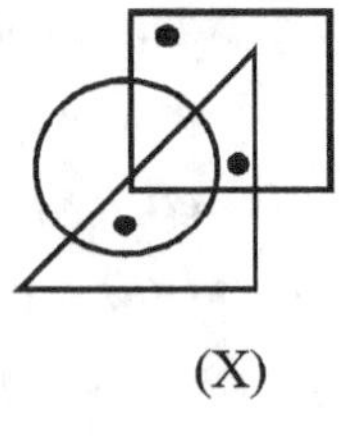

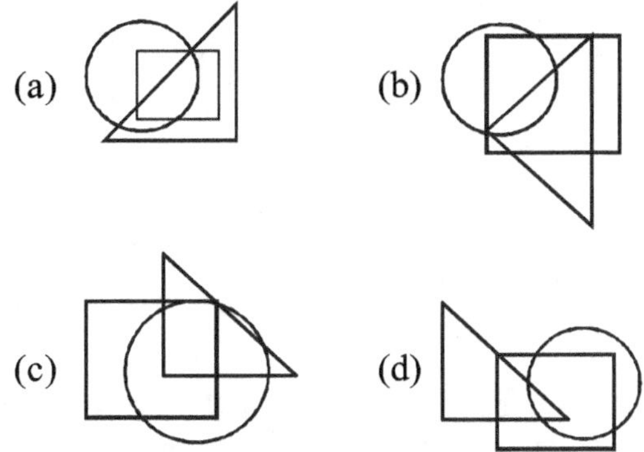

***Sol.* (c)** Figure (X), contains one dot in the square only, another dot in the region common to the square and the triangle only and the third dot in the region common to the circle and the triangle. Figure (a) does contain a region which lies in the square alone. Figures (b) & (d) do not contain any region common to the circle & the triangle. Only figure (c) contains all the three types of regions.

LEVEL 1

DIRECTION (Q. 1) : *In the following question, there is a diagram marked (X), with one or more dots placed in it. The diagram is followed by four other figures, marked (a)z, (b), (c) and (d) only one of which is such as to make possible the placement of the alternative in each these.*

1\.

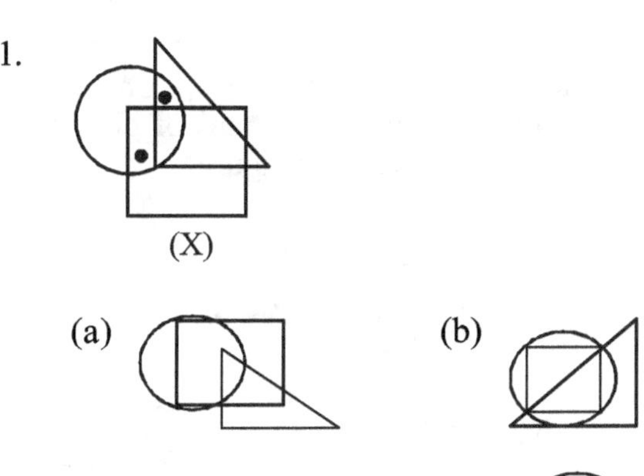

2\. From amongst the figures marked (a), (b), (c) and (d), select the figure which satisfies the same conditions of placement of dots as in figure (X).

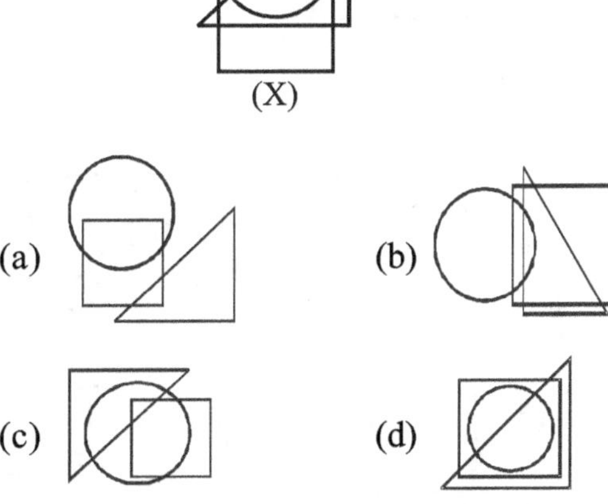

DIRECTIONS (Qs. 3-4) : *In each of the following questions there is a diagram (X) in which one or more dots have been placed in certain positions. Examine the placement of these dots carefully. From the four choices, select the one in which the placement of dots is similar to that in the diagram.*

3.

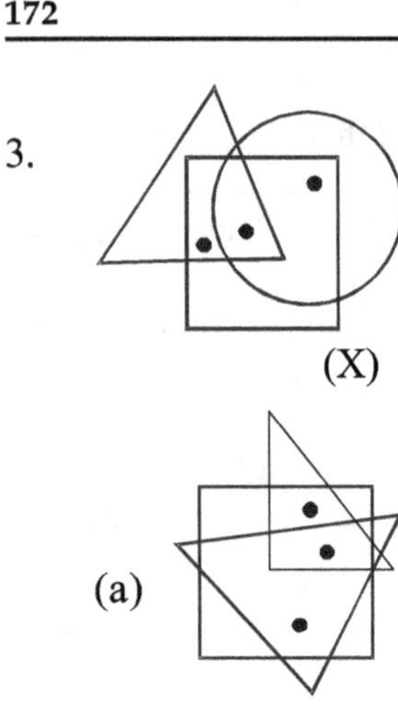

(X)

(a)

(b)

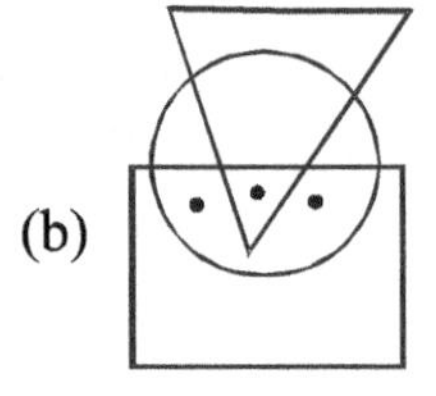

(c)

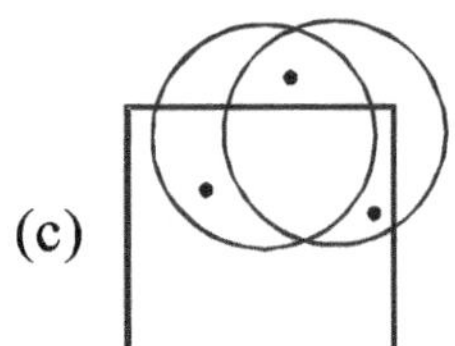

(d)

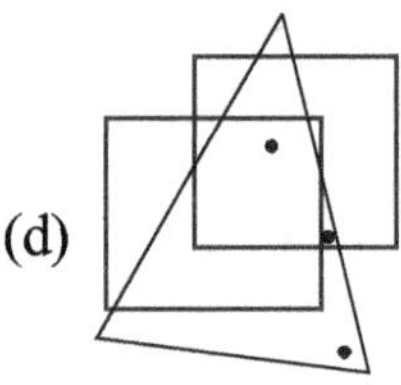

4.

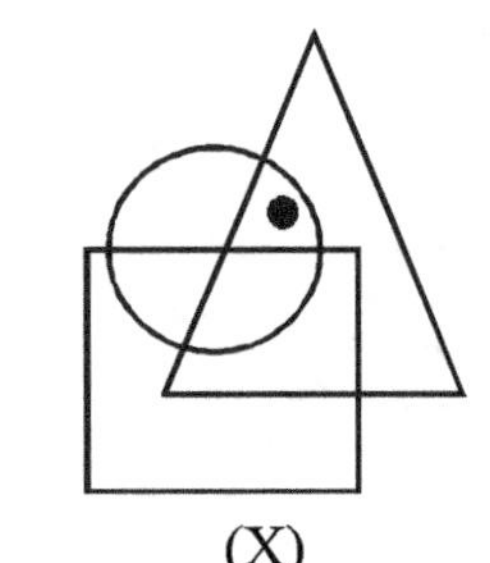

(X)

(a)

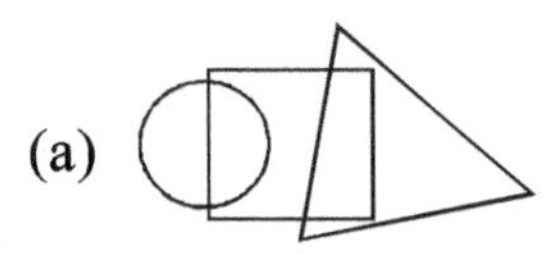

(b)

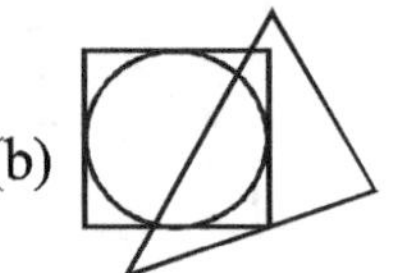

(c)

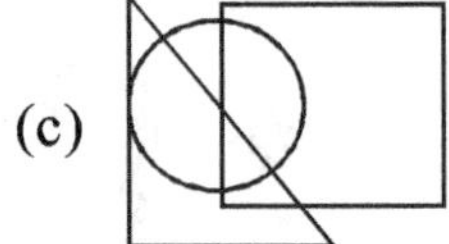

(d)

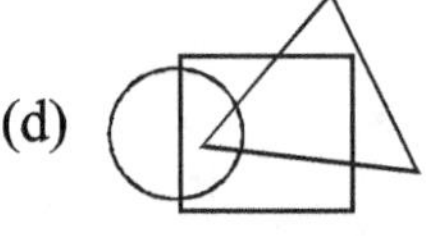

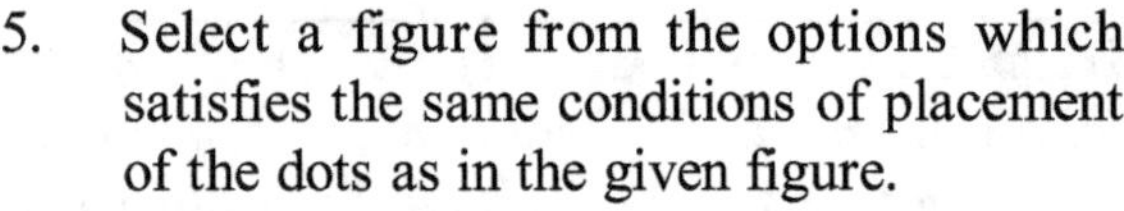

5. Select a figure from the options which satisfies the same conditions of placement of the dots as in the given figure.

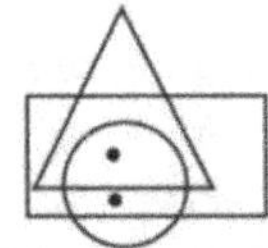

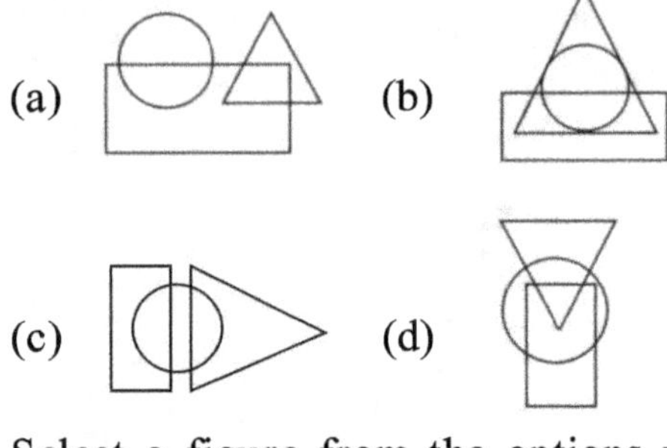

(a) (b)

(c) (d)

6. Select a figure from the options which satisfies the same conditions of placement of the dots as in the given figure.

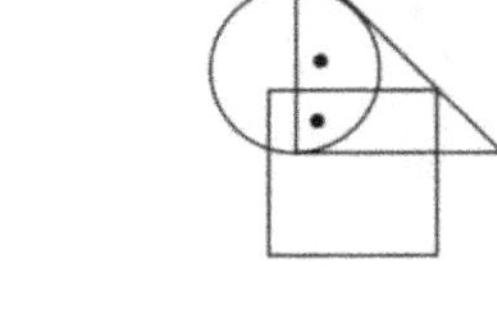

(a)

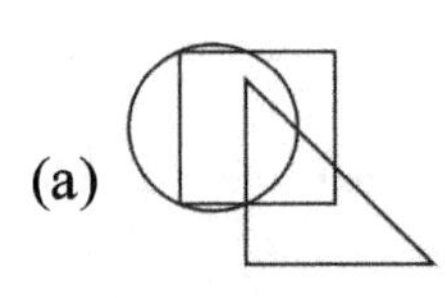

(b)

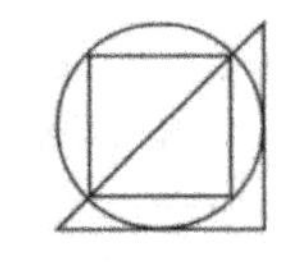

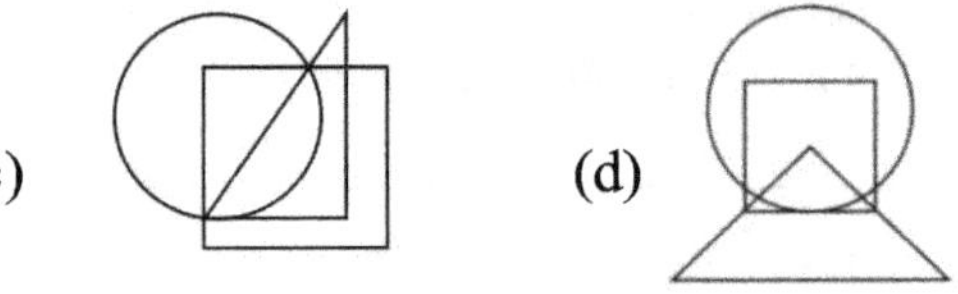

(c) (d)

7. Select a figure from the options which satisfies the same conditions of placement of dots as in the given figure.

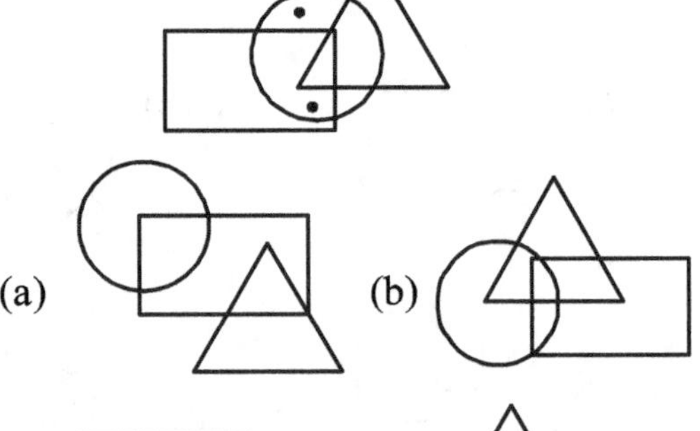

(a) (b)

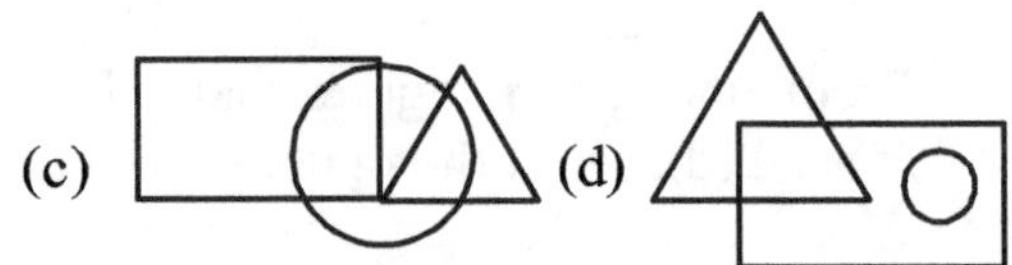

(c) (d)

8. Select a figure from the options which satisfies the same conditions of placement of dots as in the given figure.

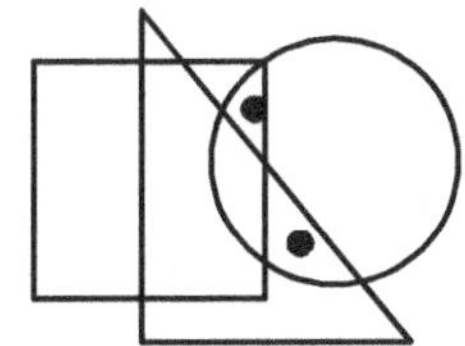

(a) 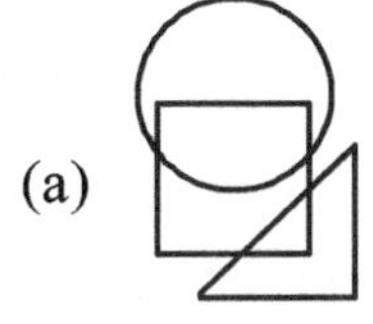 (b) 

(c) 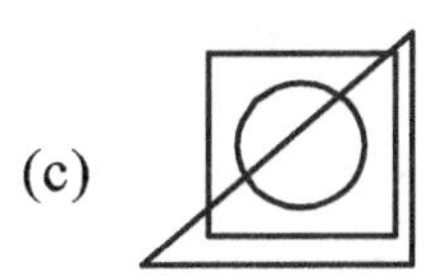 (d) 

9. Select a figure from the options which satisfies the same conditions of placement of the dots as in the given figure. **[2019]**

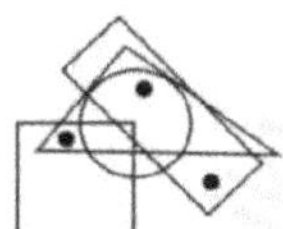

(a) 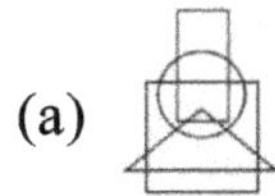 (b) 

(c) 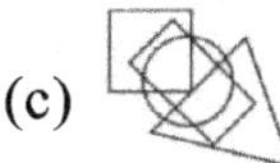 (d) 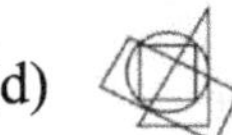

10. Select a figure from the options which satisfies the same conditions of placement of the dots as in the given figure. **[2019]**

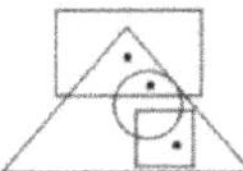

(a) 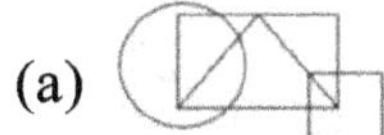 (b) 

(c) 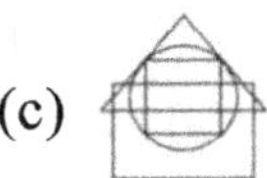 (d) 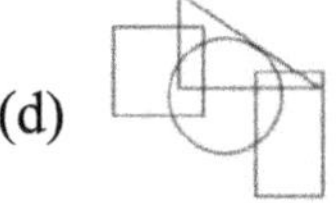

11. Which of the following options does not satisfy the same conditions of placement of dots as in the given figure? **[2020]**

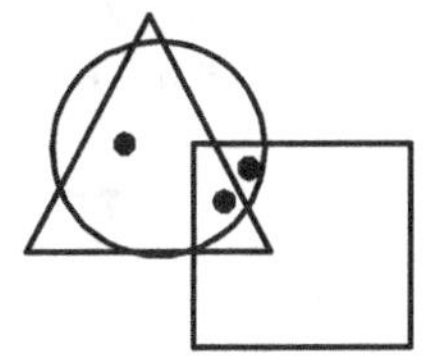

(a) 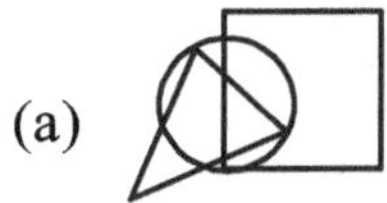 (b) 

(c) 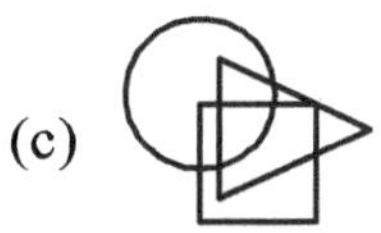 (d) 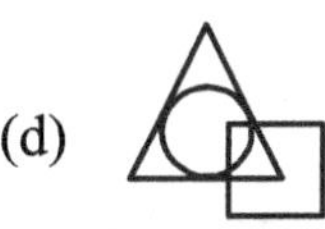

12. Which of the following options satisfies the same conditions of placement of dots as in the given figure? **[2021]**

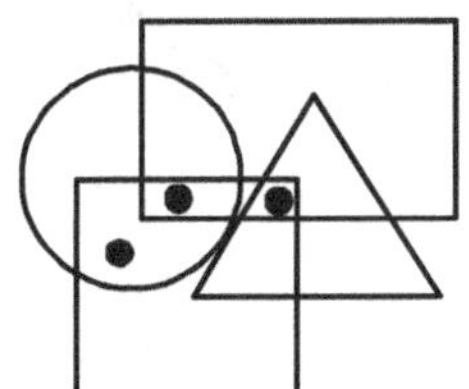

(a) (b) 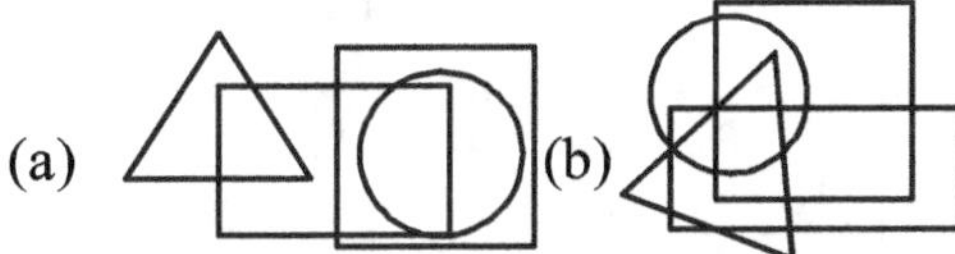

(c) 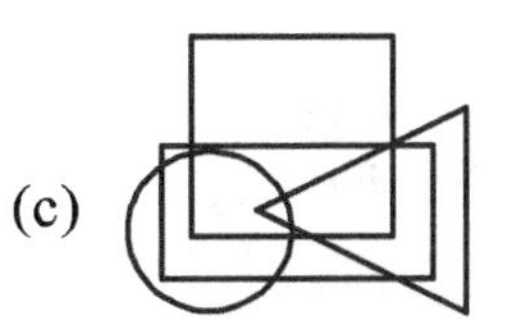 (d) 

LEVEL 2

DIRECTIONS (Qs.1-6) : *In each of the following questions, from amongst the figures marked (a), (b), (c) and (d), select the one which satisfies the same conditions of placement of the dot as in fig. (X).*

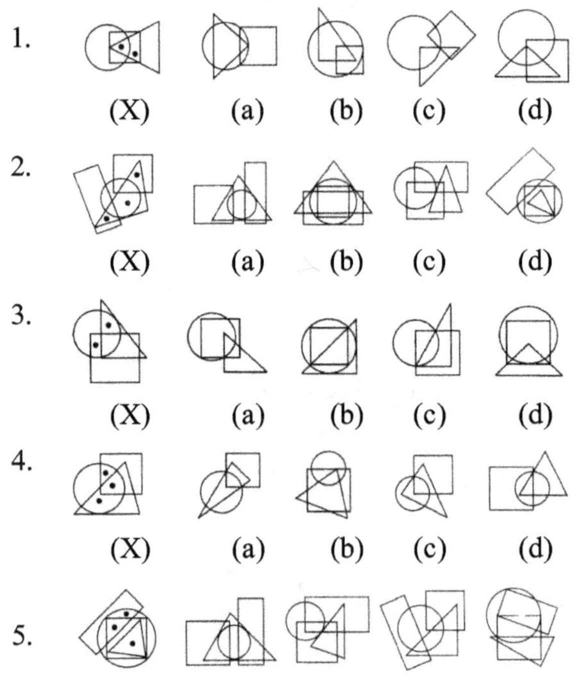

7. Select a figure from the options which satisfies the same condition of placement of the dots as in the given figure.

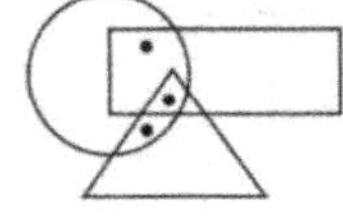

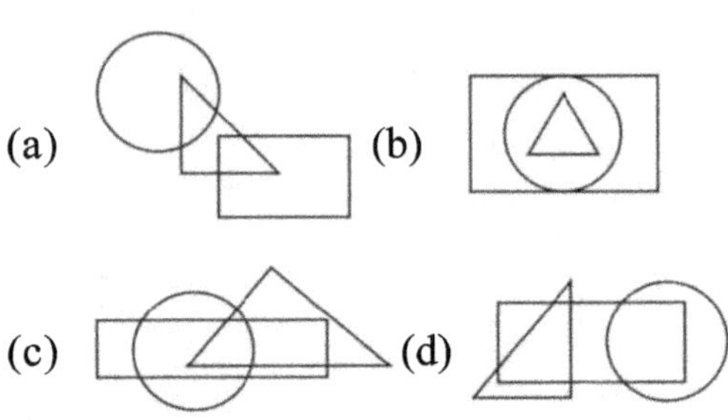

8. Select a figure from the options which satisfies the same conditions of placement of the dots as in the given figure.

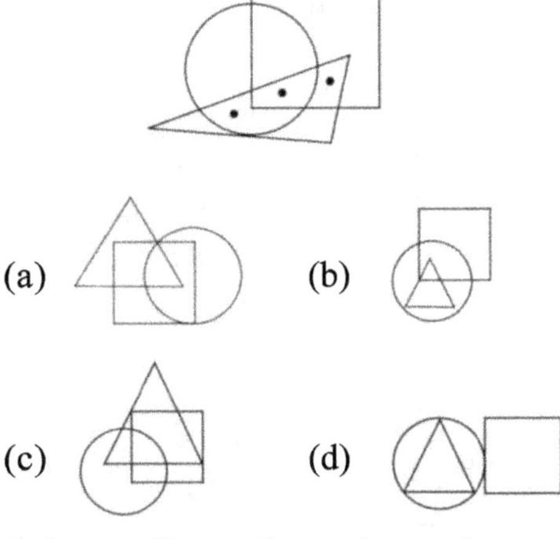

9. Select a figure from the options which satisfies the same conditions of placement of dots as in the given figure.

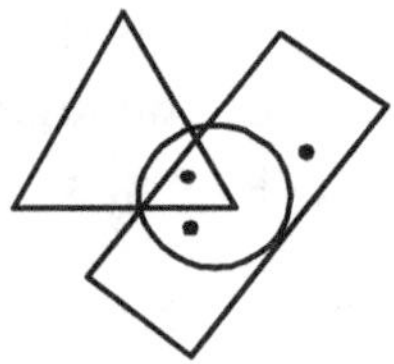

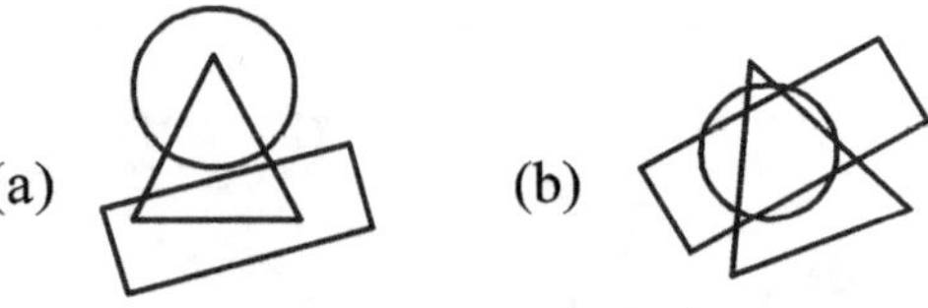

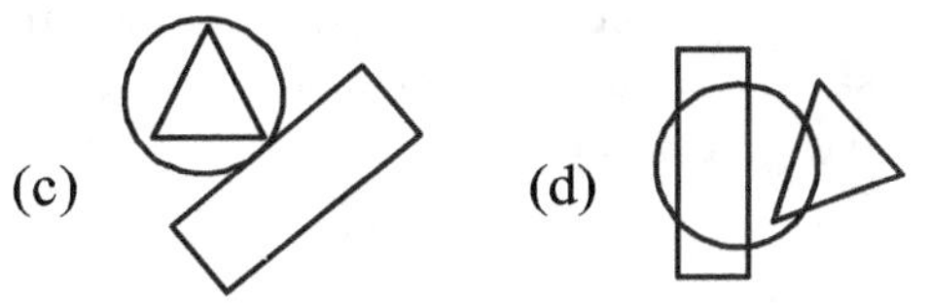

10. Select a figure from the options which satisfies the same condition of placement of the dots as in the given figure.

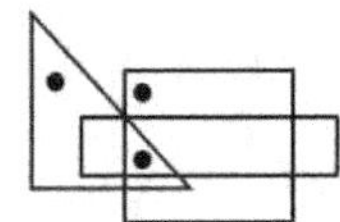

(a) 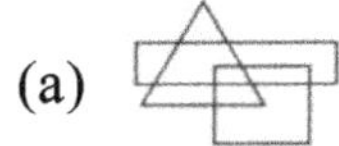 (b) 

(c) 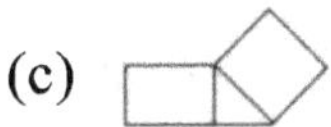 (d) 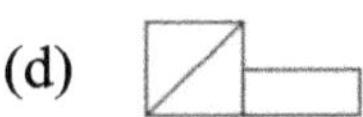

11. Select a figure from the options which satisfies the same condition of placement of the dots as in the given figure.

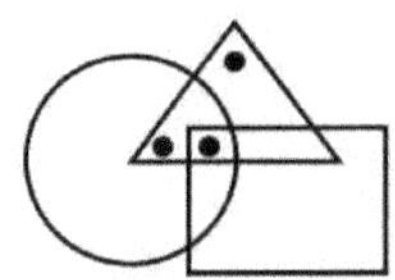

(a) 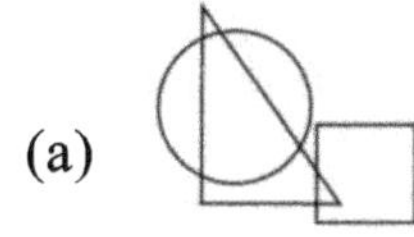 (b) 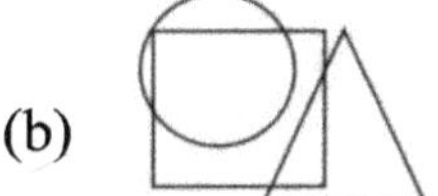

(c) 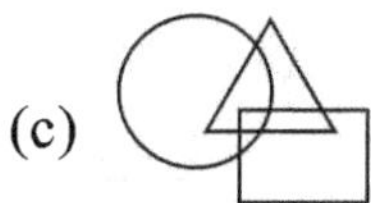 (d) 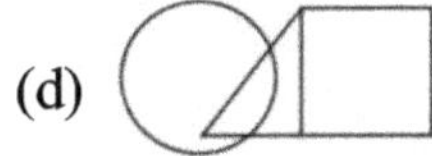

12. Select a figure from the options which satisfies the same condition of placement of the dots as in the given figure.

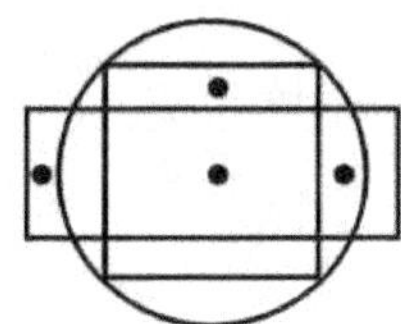

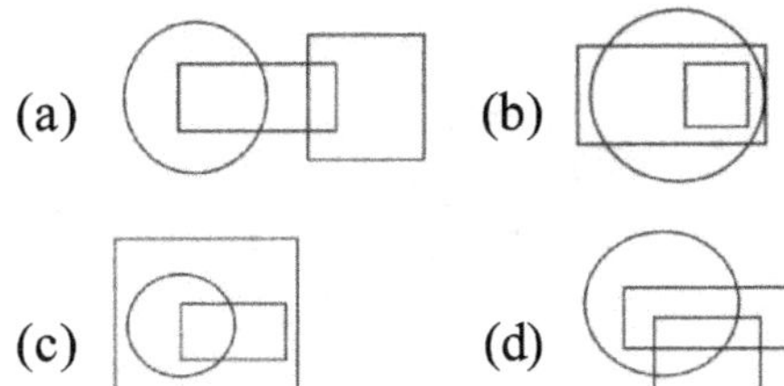

13. Select a figure from the options which does not satisfy the same condition of placement of the dots as in the given figure.

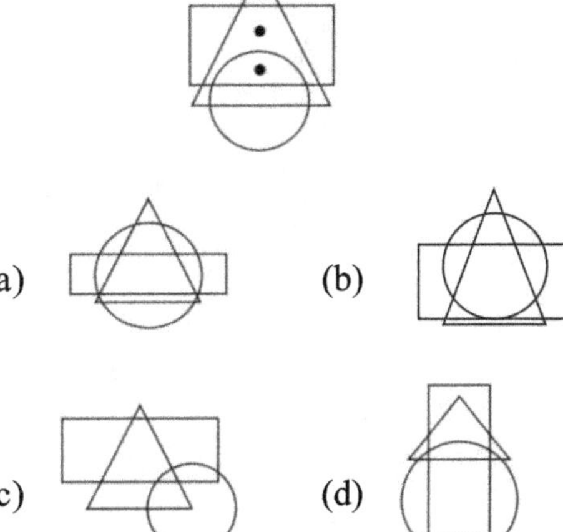

14. Which of the following options does not satisfy the same conditions of placement of the dots as in the given figure?

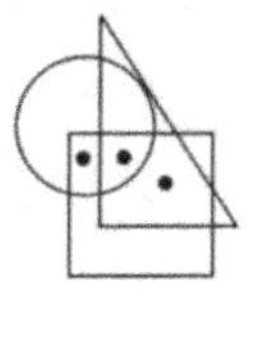

(a) 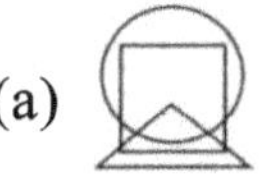 (b) 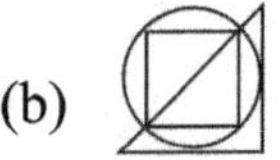

(c) 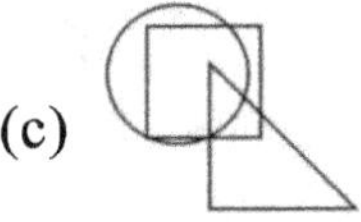 (d) 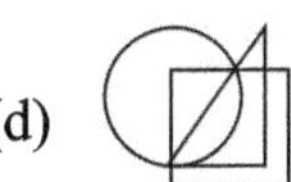

15. Which of the following figures satisfies the same conditions of placement of the dots as in the given figure?

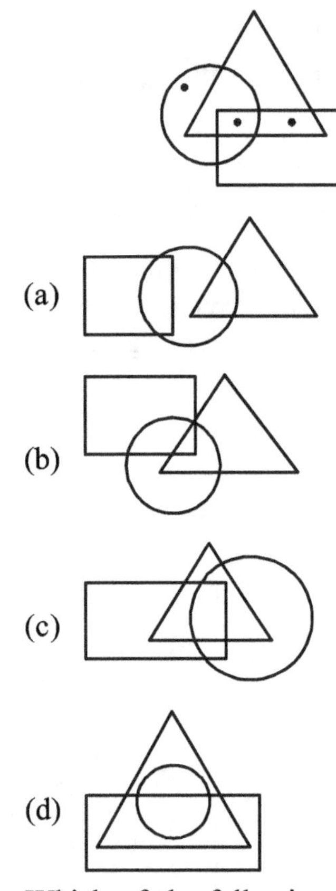

16. Which of the following options does not satisfy the same conditions of placement of the dots as in the given figure?

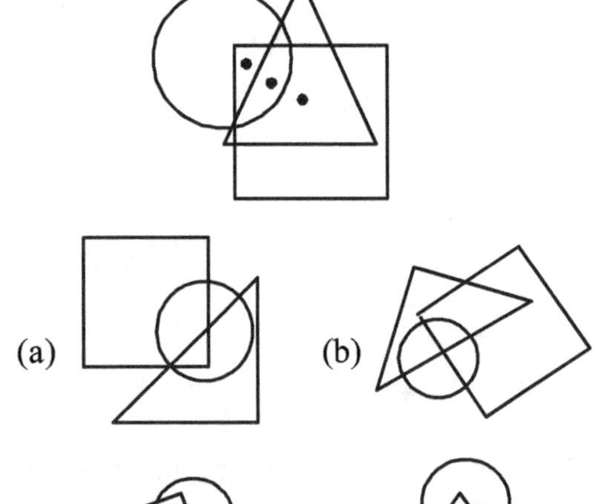

17. Which of the following options satisfies the same conditions of placement of dots as in the given figure?

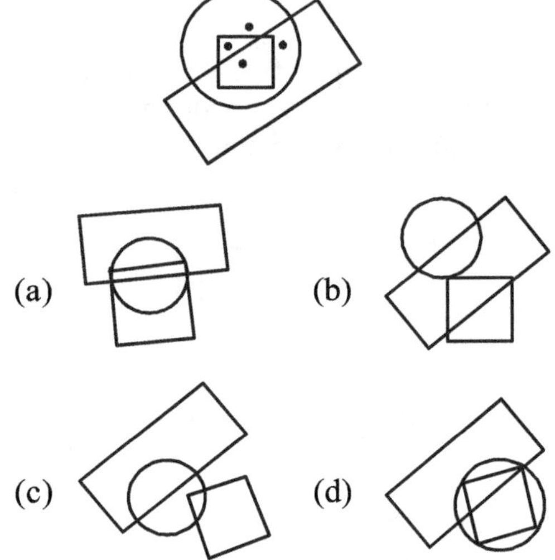

18. Select a figure from the options which does not satisfy the same conditions of placement of the dots as in the given figure. **[2019]**

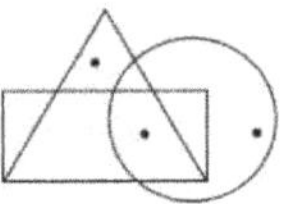

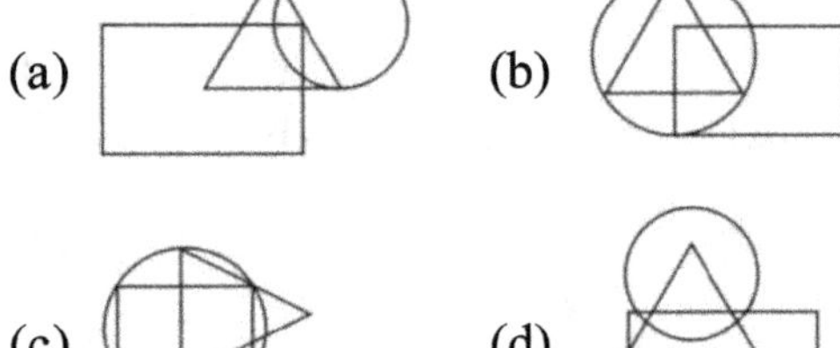

19. Select a figure from the options which satisfies the same conditions of placement of dots as in the given figure. **[2020]**

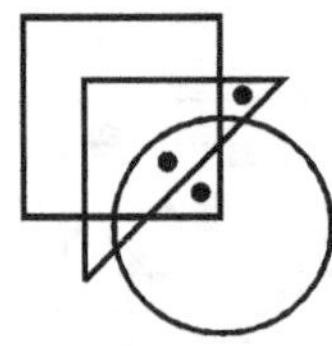

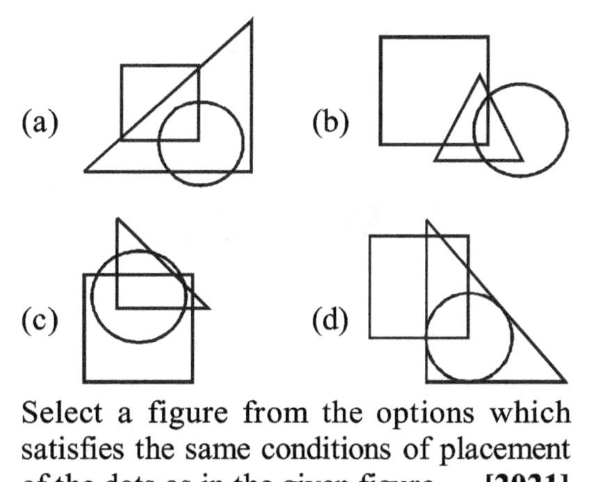

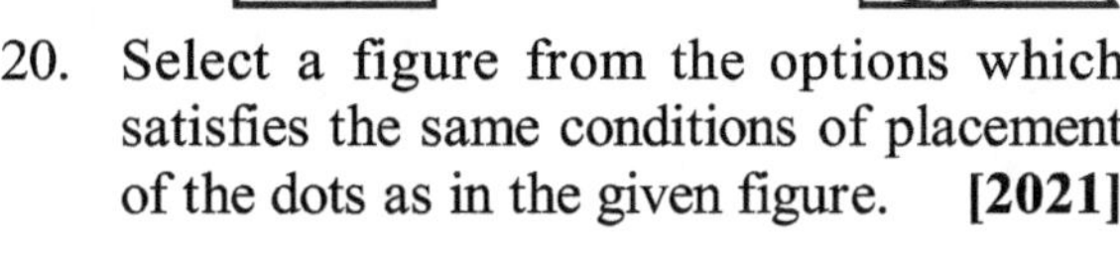

20. Select a figure from the options which satisfies the same conditions of placement of the dots as in the given figure. **[2021]**

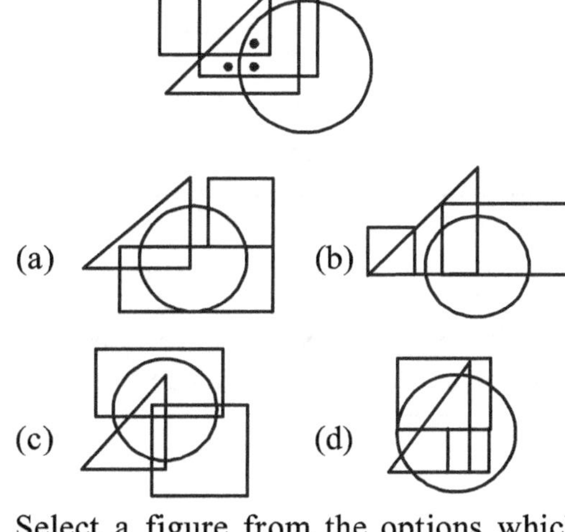

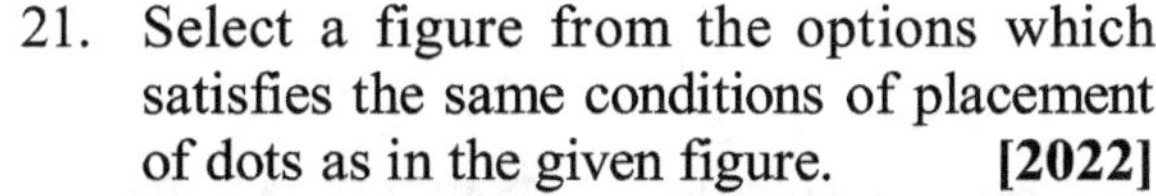

21. Select a figure from the options which satisfies the same conditions of placement of dots as in the given figure. **[2022]**

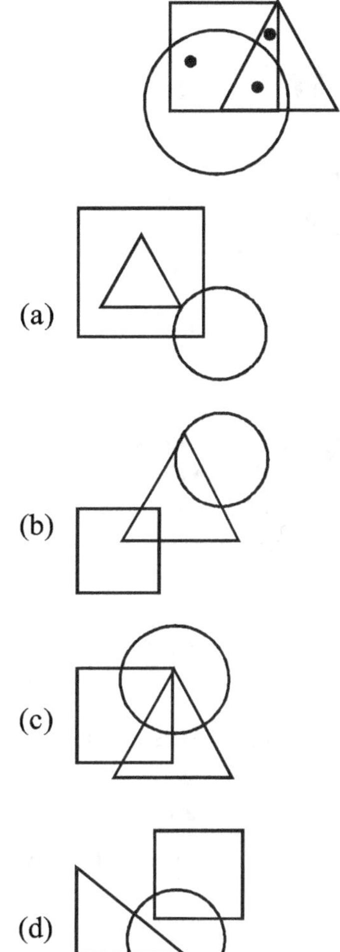

ANSWER KEY																			
LEVEL-1																			
1	(b)	**2**	(c)	**3**	(a)	**4**	(c)	**5**	(d)	**6**	(b)	**7**	(b)	**8**	(b)	**9**	(b)	**10**	(d)
11	(d)	**12**	(b)																
LEVEL-2																			
1	(d)	**2**	(a)	**3**	(b)	**4**	(d)	**5**	(d)	**6**	(b)	**7**	(c)	**8**	(c)	**9**	(b)	**10**	(a)
11	(c)	**12**	(d)	**13**	(a)	**14**	(d)	**15**	(c)	**16**	(a)	**17**	(d)	**18**	(b)	**19**	(c)	**20**	(c)
21	(c)																		

CHAPTER

Cryptography

Cryptography

The dictionary meaning of the term **'Cryptography'** is the science or study of the techniques of secret writing, especially code and cipher systems, methods and the like. In simple words, it is the procedure or the method of making & using secret codes.

And, therefore, **cryptogram** is the message or word written in a particular code or symbol, i.e., cryptogram stands for the representation.

For our study, under the section of logical reasoning, we code the digits of the number series (0 to 9) with various different alphabets and perform various arithmetic operations like addition, subtraction and multiplication on these coded digits.

For e.g.: Instead of writing $1 + 1 = 2$, we write $A + A = B$. Similarly, instead of writing $5 \times 4 = 20$, we write $A \times B = DE$.

There will be hints provided to you in the options or in some statements in the question itself.

You will understand more and more and at a deeper level once we start discussing the examples.

ILLUSTRATION 1 :

What would be the value of the code 'A' where $A + 1 = 2$.

(a) 1 (b) 2
(c) 0 (d) 3

Sol. (a) Going by the options $1 + 1 = 2$, i.e., $A = 1$.
Thus option (a) is the correct answer.

ILLUSTRATION 2 :

What would be the value of 'L' where $L + M = 3$

(a) 1 (b) 2
(c) 6 (d) either 1 or 2

Sol. (d) Since $L + M = 3$, L can either be 1 or 2 and similarly M can be either be 2 or 1 respectively.
Therefore,

$L + M = 3$
$1 + 2 = 3$
or $2 + 1 = 3$

Thus option (4) is the correct answer.

Quick Tip

All the alphabets will be a representation of a number which is an integer, i.e., the codes stand for integers.

ILLUSTRATION 3 :

Find out which number stands for AB the following operation :

$$\begin{array}{r} A\ B \\ +\ 7\ 2 \\ \hline 9\ 6 \end{array}$$

(a) 12 (b) 22
(c) 24 (d) 28

Sol. (c) A 2-digit number when added to 72 gives 96. That means 24 is the number that is added to 72. Thus AB = 24.

ILLUSTRATION 4 :

'PQ' is the representation for which number ?

```
    7  8
 +  P  Q
 -------
 1  1  2
```

(a) 24 (b) 32
(c) 34 (d) 22

Sol. (c) At the units place 8 + Q = 2, that means 4 is added to 8 to make it 12, of which 1 is the carry over.
Thus, 7 + 1 + P = 11, therefore, P should be 3.
Hence, PQ = 34, option (c).

Shortcut : Go by the options, add the numbers given in the options one by one to the given number to get the answer.

Quick Tip

Try to eliminate as many options as possible by using simple logics. This saves time and increases your accuracy.

ILLUSTRATION 5 :

```
    A  B
 -  4  3
 -------
    1  7
```

What is the value of AB ?

(a) 50 (b) 60
(c) 70 (d) 80

Sol. (b) Going by the options, AB = 60. Option (b) is the correct answer.

Common data for Illustration 6 & 7. Refer to the data below and answer the questions that follow.

ILLUSTRATION 6 :

If $A^2 = B$, then find the value of A.

(a) 1 (b) 2
(c) 4 (d) 6

Sol. (b) Given that $A + A = B \Rightarrow 2A = B$
and $A^2 = B$
Therefore, $2A = A^2$
or $A^2 - 2A = 0$
or $A(A - 2) = 0$
Hence, A = 0, 2
since, A = 0 is not an option, therefore, A = 2 option (b).

ILLUSTRATION 7 :

If $A^2 = B$, then find the value of B.

(a) 2 (b) 4
(c) 6 (d) 8

Sol. (b) In Eg. 9, we found the value of A, i.e., A = 2
Thus $A^2 = B$ or $2A = B$ will give us
$B = (2)^2 = 4$
or $B = 2 \times 2 = 4$.
Thus the value of B = 4

Let us now try some illustrations based on multiplication :

Illustration 8 & 9 : In the given Illustration , each letter stands for the same integer throught. Answer the following based on the given operation

```
        A  A
    ×   A  A
    --------
        A  A
 +  A   A  ×
    --------
    A   B  A
```

ILLUSTRATION 8 :

What is the value of A ?

(a) 2 (b) 4
(c) 7 (d) 1

Sol. (d) The given multiplication goes like
H T U ← Hundreds,
Tens and Units place

```
     A A
   × A A
   -----
     A A
 + A A ×
   -----
   A B A
```

Now, we are given an operation at the unit's place, i.e., $A \times A = A$. If we go by the options and put A's value
option (1) A = 2, then $2 \times 2 = 4$, i.e., $A \times A \neq A$. Thus this is incorrect.
Similarly, in case of options (2) & (3) $4 \times 4 \neq 4$ and $7 \times 7 \neq 7$ respectively, therefore, both these options are also discarded.
Thus option (4) $1 \times 1 = 1$ is the correct answer.

ILLUSTRATION 9 :

Which of the following could be the correct value of B ?

(a) 1 (b) 2
(c) 3 (d) 4

Sol. (b) As we know that A = 1

```
     A A            1 1
   × A A          × 1 1
   -----          -----
     A A    ⇒       1 1
 + A A ×        + 1 1 ×
   -----          -----
   A B A          1 2 1
```

Since, $A + A = B \Rightarrow 1 + 1 = B = 2$. Hence, the value of B = 2 So, option (b) is the correct answer.

Common data for Illustration 10 - 12

In the following multiplication, each of the different letters denote a different integer. Each letter stands for the same integer throughout. If 'A', stands for '2' and 'C' stands for '6'.

```
         A B C
       ×   D E
   -----------
         A B C
  +E C M A X
   -----------
   E C D M C
```

ILLUSTRATION 10 :

What is the value of E ?

(a) 1 (b) 2
(c) 3 (d) 4

Sol. (a) By logic, when ABC is multiplied with E, the product so formed is ABC, therefore, the value of E should be 1.

ILLUSTRATION 11 :

What is the value of M ?

(a) 9 (b) 7
(c) 5 (d) 8

Sol. (c) Let us write the given cryptogram again, with all the decoded integers for simplicity.

```
       A B C              2 B 6
     ×   D E            ×   7 1
   ---------          ---------
       A B C    ⇒         2 B 6
  +E C M A ×          1 6 M 2 ×
   ---------          ---------
   E C D M C          1 6 7 M 6
```

We can now see that 2 + M = 7, which means M = 7 – 2 = 5. Thus the value of M is 5. So, option (c) is correct.

Quick Tips

(i) A particular set of integers denoting a word may or may not be in the fixed order as the alphabets of the word (refer to examples 21 & 22), but it is essential only to check whether the integers that are denoted by the alphabets are present in it or not. The one which has it is the required answer.

(ii) In case all the options, have the same set of integers, look for the one that is in a fixed order as of the given word. For eg. For the word ACE (refer Eg. 22), the answer would be 261.

ILLUSTRATION 12 :

What is the remainder when D is divided by B ?

(a) 0 (b) 2
(c) 3 (d) 1

Sol. (d) As $D = 7$ and $B = 3$, therefore, when we divide D by B, i.e., 7 by 3 the remainder will be 1.

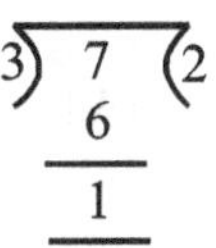

Thus option (d) 1 is the correct answer.

DIRECTIONS (Qs. 1-7): *In the following addition each of the letters denote a different integer. Each letter stands for the same integer throughout where 'P' stands for 4.*

$$\begin{array}{r} M\ N\ O\ P \\ +\ A\ Q\ R\ P \\ \hline Z\ Z\ Z\ Z \end{array}$$

1. What is the value of the letter 'Z' throughout ?
   (a) 4
   (b) 6
   (c) 8
   (d) Cannot be determined
2. If the value of N is greater than 5, then 'N' stands for :
   (a) 6 (b) 7
   (c) 8 (d) 6 or 7
3. If $M > N$ and the value of $N = 6$, then what is the value of R?
   (a) 2
   (b) 1
   (c) 3
   (d) Cannot be determined
4. If the value of N is 6 and $M > N$, then what is the value of A?
   (a) 2
   (b) 1
   (c) 3
   (d) None of these
5. If $N = 6$ and $M > N$, then which of the following numbers stand for $M\ A\ N$? If $N = 6$, $M > N$ and O = 5, then
   (a) 146 (b) 716
   (c) 356 (d) 236
6. What is the value of $POAR$?
   (a) 4513 (b) 4514
   (c) 4517 (d) 4615
7. What is the remainder when P is divided by Q ?
   (a) 3 (b) 0
   (c) 1 (d) 2

DIRECTIONS (Qs. 8-14): *Given*

$$\begin{array}{r} A\ B\ C\ D \\ +\ S\ R\ O\ P \\ \hline C\ C\ C\ C \end{array} \text{ where } C = 9.$$

8. If A is a prime number, what is the possible value of A if $A < 3$?
   (a) 0 (b) 1
   (c) 2
   (d) Cannot be determined

9. If A is a prime number less than 3, what is the value of S ?
   (a) 7 (b) 4
   (c) 2 (d) 6
10. Based on the data derived from Questions 8 & 9, what is the possible value of CAR ?
    (a) 342
    (b) 375
    (c) 923
    (d) Cannot be determined
11. If $A = 2$ and R is a prime number smaller than 5, then find. The value of $SCAR$, using all the data from above ?
    (a) 4752
    (b) 2973
    (c) 7021
    (d) Cannot be determined
12. The value of $SOAP$, using all the data from above & $D = 8$?
    (a) 7321 (b) 7021
    (c) 2379 (d) 8109
13. B ÷ 0 = ?
    (a) 0 (b) 6
    (c) 1 (d) ∞
14. What is the sum of the integers in row 1 ?
    (a) 27 (b) 25
    (c) 11 (d) 36

DIRECTIONS (Qs. 15-18): Given -

$$\begin{array}{r} T\ X\ L \\ +\ X\ T\ L \\ \hline A\ L\ T \\ \hline \end{array}$$

where L stands for '7'.

15. So, X stands for.
    (a) 2
    (b) 7
    (c) 4
    (d) 3
16. $A\ L\ T$ stands for
    (a) 467
    (b) 427
    (c) 497
    (d) 437
17. $T\ A\ X$ is represented by which of the following numbers ?
    (a) 426
    (b) 436
    (c) 476
    (d) 674
18. What is the third multiple of the sum of the second row ?
    (a) 13
    (b) 39
    (c) 26
    (d) 52
19. Read the statement and conclusions given below and decide which conclusion(s) logically follows the given statement. **[2022]**

Statement:
Money plays a vital role in politics.
Conclusions:
I. The poor can never become politicians.
II. All the rich men take part in politics.
(a) Only conclusion I follows
(b) Only conclusion II follows
(c) Either I or II follows
(d) Neither I nor II follows

LEVEL 2

DIRECTIONS (Q. 1-5): *In the following subtraction, each letter denotes a different integer. Each letter stands for the same integer throughout. If 'O' stands for 2, B for '4', L is neither prime nor composite and T, H & Y are prime numbers.*

```
  B O T H
 -O N L Y
 --------
  O O O O
```

1. Then what stands for '*BOON*' ?
   (a) 4021 (b) 4220
   (c) 4371 (d) 7242
2. Then what is the number that stands for *TOON* ?
   (a) 3900 (b) 3252
   (c) 3202 (d) 4220
3. What stands for *T H Y* ?
   (a) 375 (b) 275
   (c) 751 (d) 135
4. What is the second multiple of the product of *B*, *Y*, *T* ?
   (a) 180 (b) 60
   (c) 120 (d) 150
5. What is the fifth multiple of the product of *H*, *N*, *L*, & *T* ?
   (a) 3 (b) 21
   (c) 7 (d) 0

Common Data for (Qs. 6-9): Given

```
  B A N A
 +N A N A
 --------
  V L W L
```

where $A = 2$ and $N = 3$.

6. What will be the value of *B*, if *V* is a prime number ?
   (a) 6 (b) 4
   (c) 5 (d) 7
7. What is the probable value of *V* ?
   (a) 6 (b) 4
   (c) 7 (d) 5
8. What is the sum of all the integers denoting *BANANA?*
   (a) 21 (b) 16
   (c) 24 (d) 27
9. What is the product of the integers in the final sum, *i.e.*, product of *V*, *L*, *W* and *L* ?
   (a) 872 (b) 672
   (c) 572 (d) 472

Common Data for (Qs. 10-14):

Given -

```
  B A N A
 +N A N A
 --------
  Q B P B
```

where A = 3 and Q = 8. Now, find the values of the following:-

10. 2*B*.
    (a) 12 (b) 42
    (c) 32 (d) 16
11. 6*P*.
    (a) 48 (b) 36
    (c) 24 (d) 12
12. N^2.
    (a) 16 (b) 4
    (c) 1 (d) 9
13. $P \times Q$.
    (a) 42 (b) 64
    (c) 4 (d) 32

14. Product of all the integers of *BANANA*.
    (a) 646 (b) 648
    (c) 848 (d) 742

15. Given

$$\begin{array}{r} T\ A\ R \\ +R\ A\ T\ E \\ \hline 4\ 4\ 4\ 4 \\ \hline \end{array}$$

Find out which number from the following stands for TEA.
    (a) 103 (b) 130
    (c) 310 (d) 413

16. Choose the set of figure which follows the given rule. **[2022]**
Rule: Closed figure losing its sides and open figure gaining its sides.

(a) 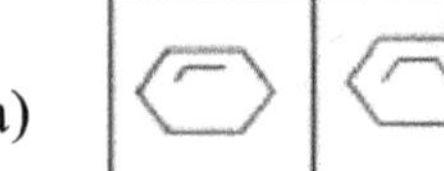 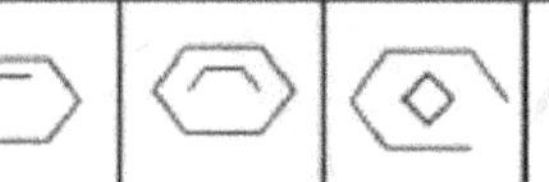

(b) 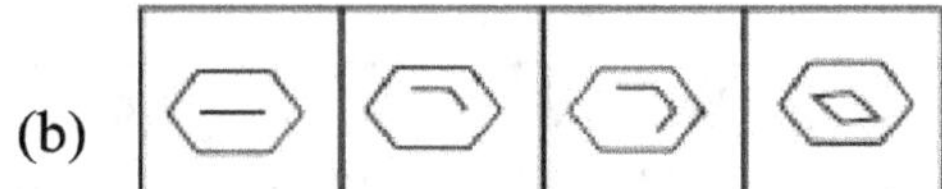

(c) 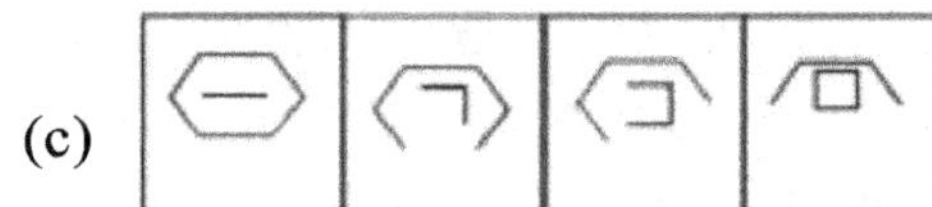

(d) 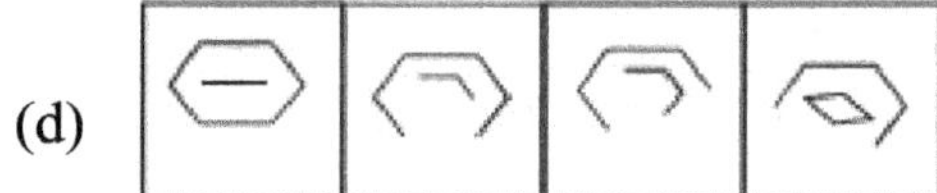

ANSWER KEY

LEVEL-1

1	(c)	**2**	(d)	**3**	(d)	**4**	(b)	**5**	(b)	**6**	(a)	**7**	(b)	**8**	(c)	**9**	(a)	**10**	(d)
11	(b)	**12**	(b)	**13**	(d)	**14**	(b)	**15**	(a)	**16**	(a)	**17**	(a)	**18**	(b)	**19**	(d)		

LEVEL-2

1	(b)	**2**	(c)	**3**	(a)	**4**	(c)	**5**	(d)	**6**	(b)	7	(c)	**8**	(b)	**9**	(b)	**10**	(a)
11	(c)	**12**	(b)	**13**	(d)	**14**	(b)	**15**	(a)	**16**	(c)								

CHAPTER

Non-verbal Series

The word "series" is defined as anything that follows or forms a specific pattern or is in continuation of a given pattern or sequence.

In this type of nonverbal test, two sets of figures pose the problem. The sets are called problem Figures and Answer Figures. Each problem figure changes in design from the preceding one. The answer figure set contains 4 figures marked 1, 2, 3, 4. You are required to choose the correct answer figure which would best continue the series.

TYPE I.

A definite relationship between elements in given figures.

ILLUSTRATION 1 :

Study the problem figures marked (A), (B) and (C) carefully and try to establish the relationship between them. From the answer figures marked a, b, c and d, pick out the figure which most appropriately completes the series.

Problem Figures

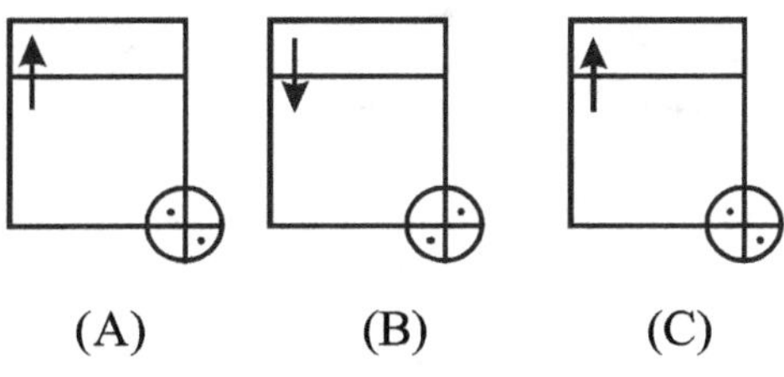

(A) (B) (C)

Answer Figures

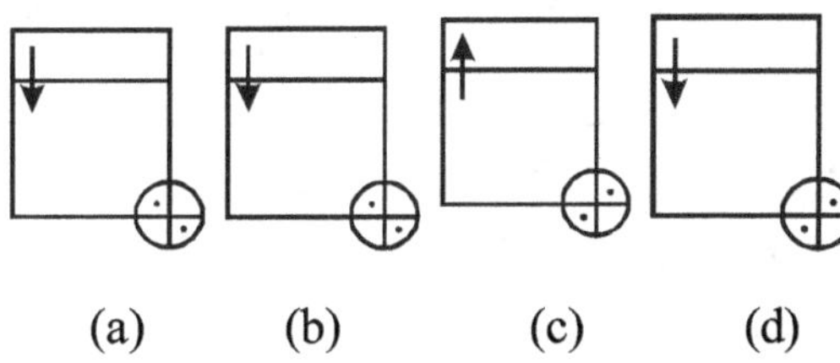

(a) (b) (c) (d)

Sol. **(d)** Note the direction of arrow which changes alternately. The dots are also changing alternately. Hence, we are looking for a figure in which the arrow points down and the dots and positioned as in figure (B).

TYPE II.

Addition of Elements : In these type of questions, each figure is obtained by either sustaining the element of preceding figure as it is or adding a part of element or one element or more than one element of the preceding figure in a systematic way.

ILLUSTRATION 2 :

Problem Figure

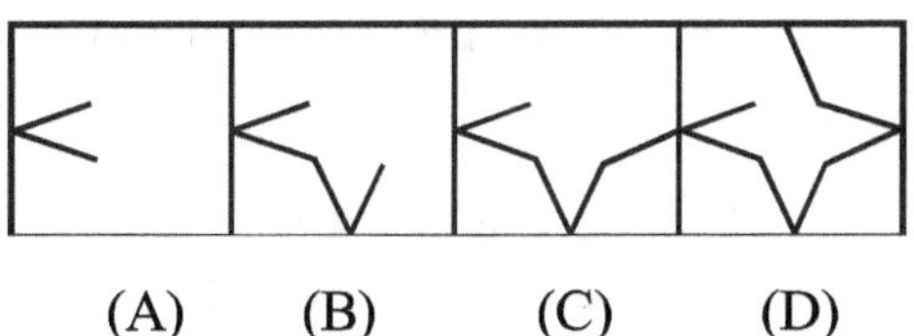

(A) (B) (C) (D)

Answer Figure

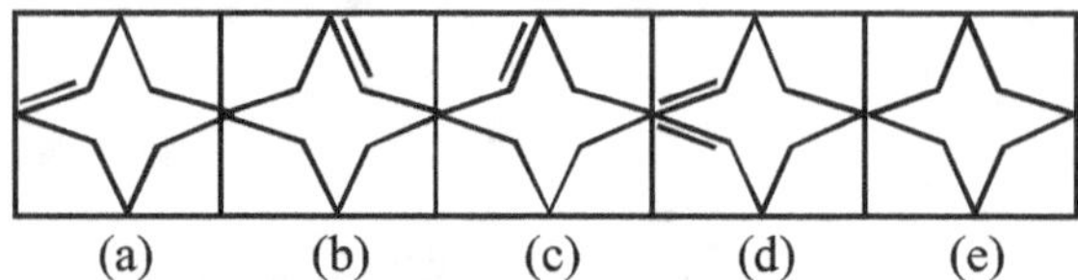

(a) (b) (c) (d) (e)

***Sol.* (e)** Two line segments are added in P1 to obtain P2 and one line segment is added in P2 to obtain P3. This process is repeated again to obtain P4. Hence, answer figure 5 continues the series.

TYPE III.

In these questions the items in the diagrams either increase or decrease in number.

ILLUSTRATION 3:

Problem Figures

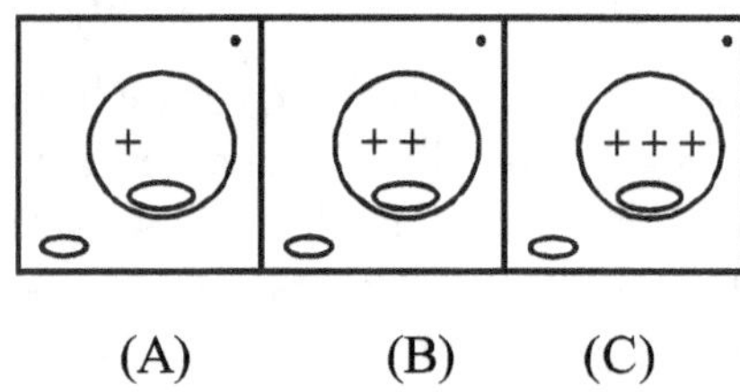

(A) (B) (C)

Answer Figures

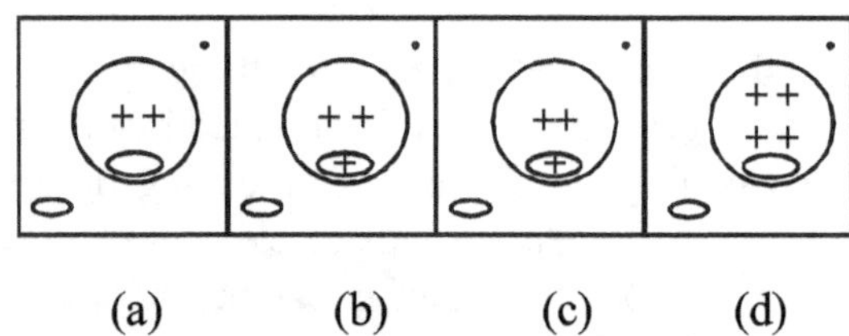

(a) (b) (c) (d)

***Sol.* (d)** Signs of Plus are adding one by one. Figure (1) has one plus sign, Figure (2) has two signs, figures (3) has three signs, the next figure should have 4 signs to keep the same pattern.

TYPE IV

Deletion of Elements : In these type of questions, each figure is obtained by either sustaining the element of preceding figure as it is or deleting a part of an element or one element or more than one element of the preceding figure in a systematic way.

ILLUSTRATION 4:

Problem Figure

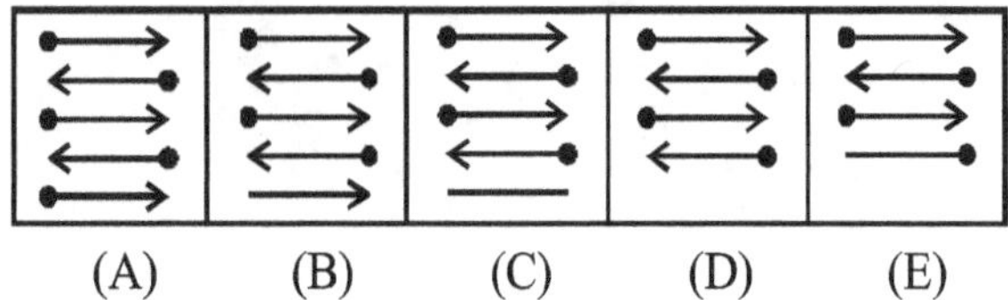

(A) (B) (C) (D) (E)

Answer Figure

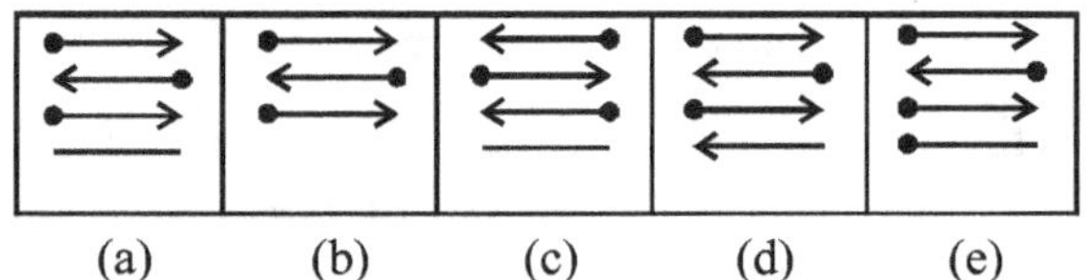

(a) (b) (c) (d) (e)

***Sol.* (a)**

TYPE V

The qualitative characteristic of various elements in the diagrams change to complete the series.

Rotation Type : The various elements in the diagrams move in a specific manner. They may rotate in clockwise or anti-clockwise direction.

ILLUSTRATION 5:

Problem Figures

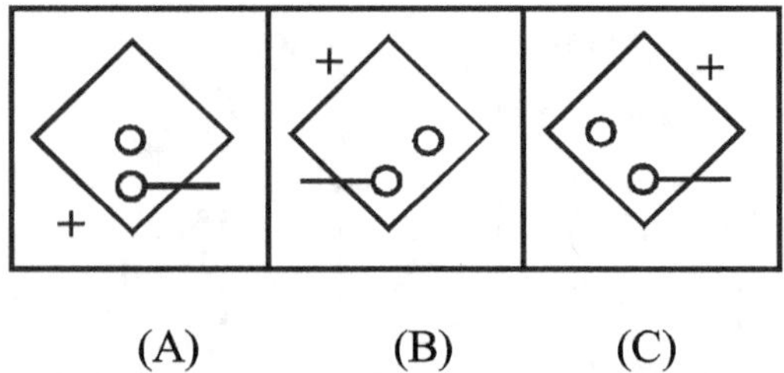

(A) (B) (C)

Answer Figures

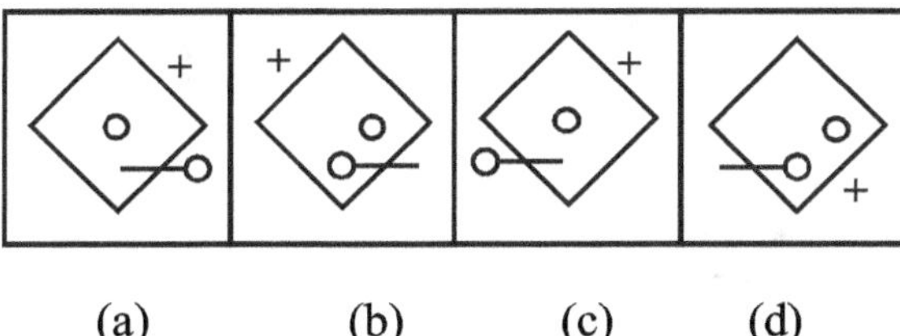

(a) (b) (c) (d)

***Sol.* (d).** The sign of plus is rotating clockwise. The pin changes direction alternately.

TYPE VI.

Replacement of Elements : In these type of questions, each figure is obtained by either sustaining the element of preceding figure as it is or replacing a part of element or one element or more than one element by a new element of the preceding figure in a systematic way.

ILLUSTRATION 6:

Problem Figure

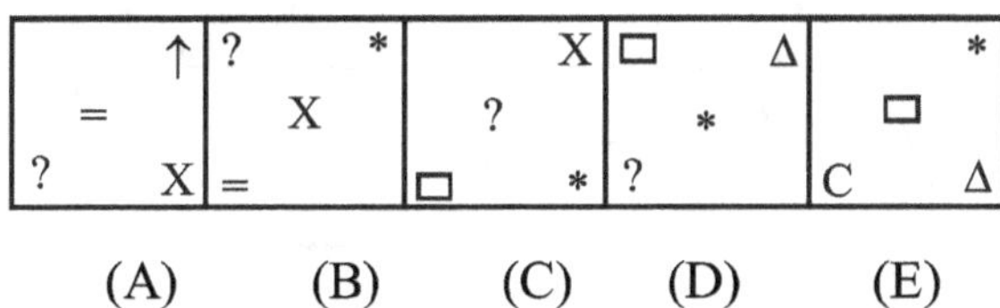

(A) (B) (C) (D) (E)

Answer figure

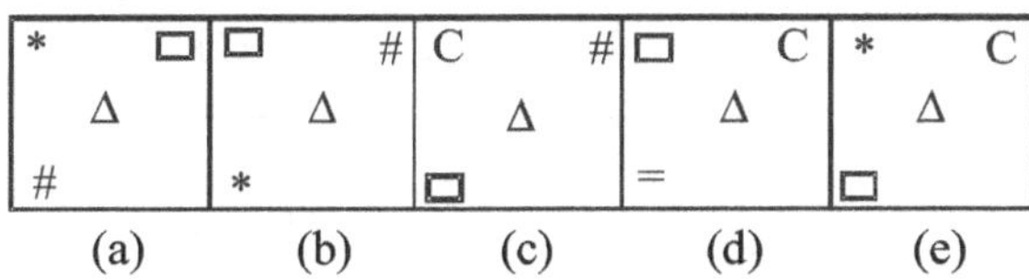

(a) (b) (c) (d) (e)

***Sol.* (c)** The elements positioned at north-east (NE) corners disappear from the odd-numbered figures. The elements positioned at the south-west (SW) corners disappear from the even-numbered figures. Therefore * should not appear in the answer figure. Hence 1, 2 and 5 cannot be the answers. Also new elements are introduced at the NE corners in even-numbered figures. Hence, answer 4 is ruled out. Therefore answer figure 3 continues the given series.

TYPE VII

Multi-Relation Series :

These are mixed series in which various elements in diagrams increase/decrease in number, change/positions in a set pattern.

ILLUSTRATION 7:

Problem Figures

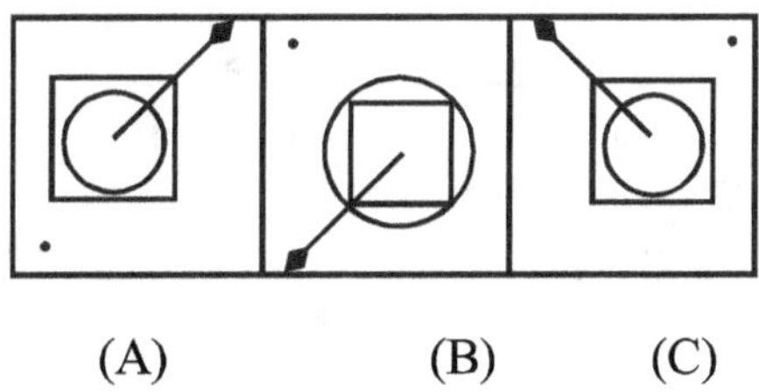

(A) (B) (C)

Answer Figures

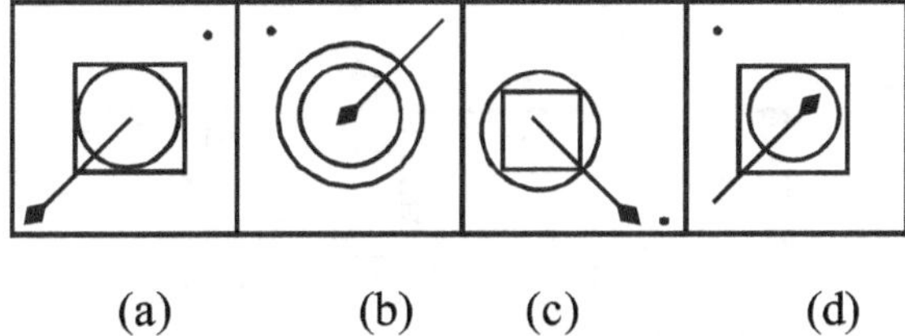

(a) (b) (c) (d)

***Sol.* (c)** Note movement of dot which is clockwise and the arrow moves in and out in opposite direction alternately. The circle and square interchange.

DIRECTIONS (Qs.1-5) : *In the Problem Figures, one figure marked by ? is missing. There is a set of answer figures also in which four alternatives are given. You have to find out the one right answer from answer figures.*

1. **Problem Figures**

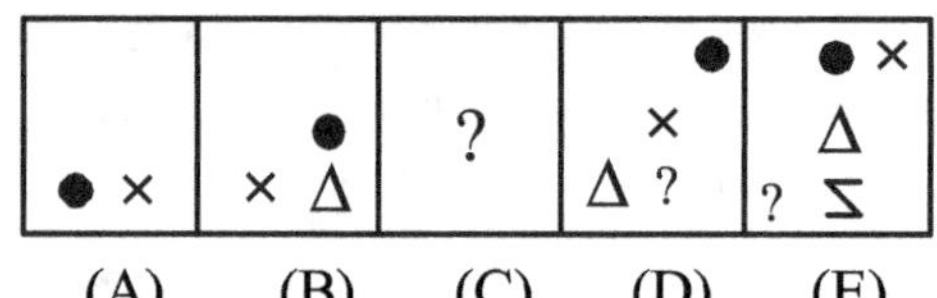

(A) (B) (C) (D) (E)

Answer Figures

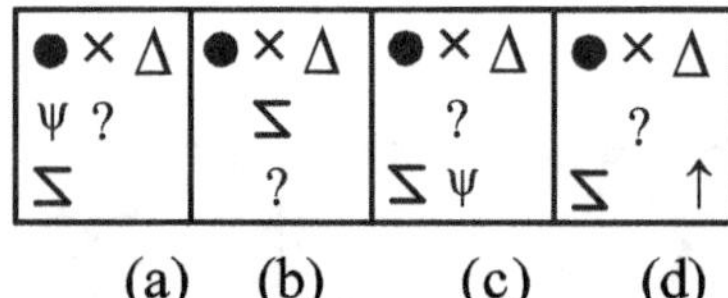

(a) (b) (c) (d)

2. **Problem Figures**

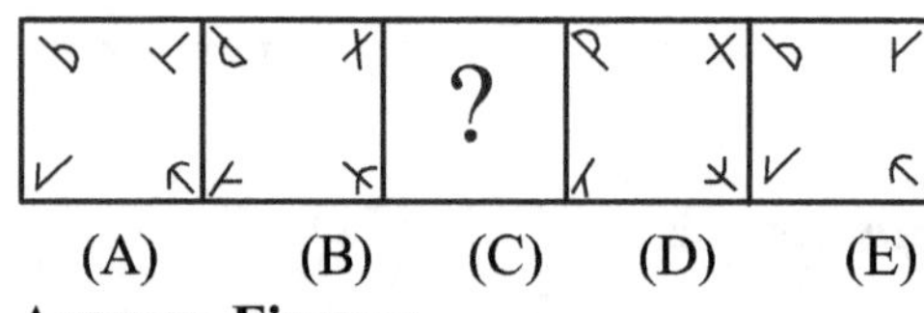

(A) (B) (C) (D) (E)

Answer Figures

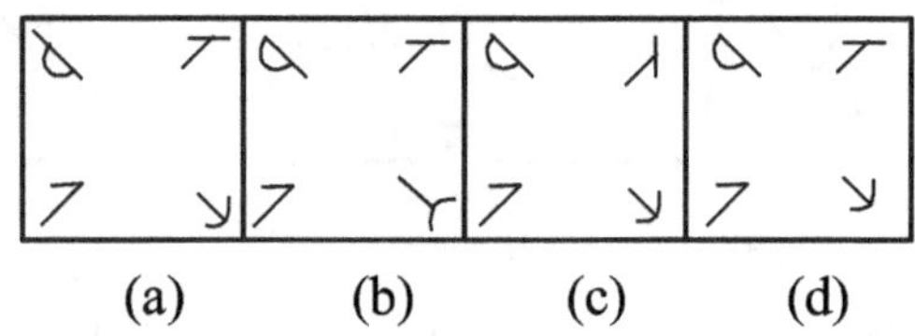

(a) (b) (c) (d)

3. **Problem Figures**

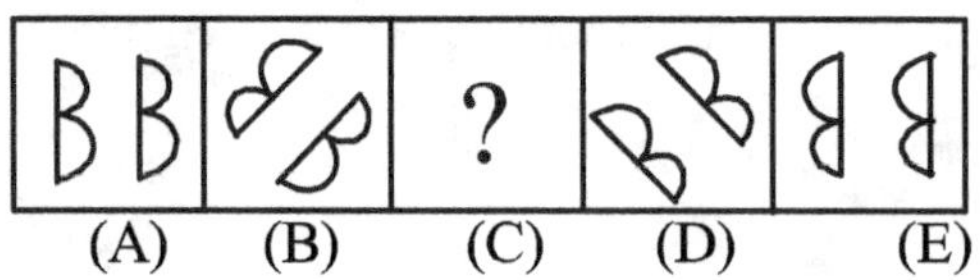

(A) (B) (C) (D) (E)

Answer Figures

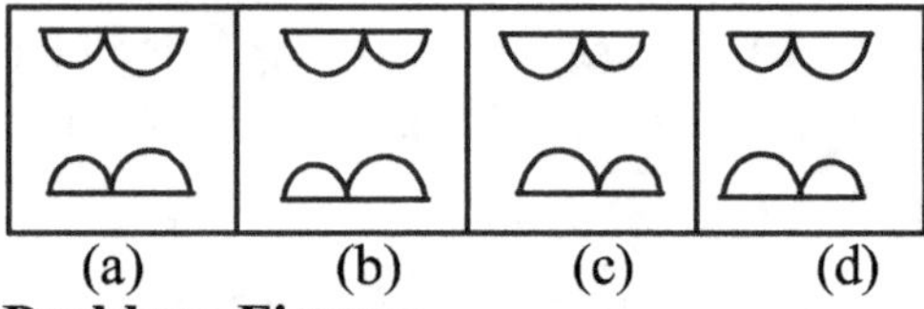

(a) (b) (c) (d)

4. **Problem Figures**

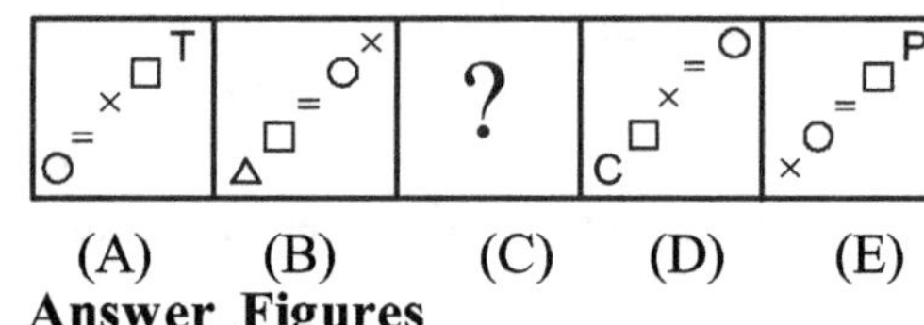

(A) (B) (C) (D) (E)

Answer Figures

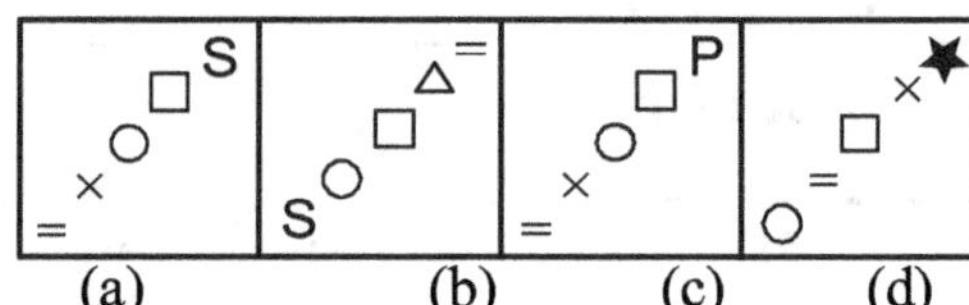

(a) (b) (c) (d)

5. **Problem Figures**

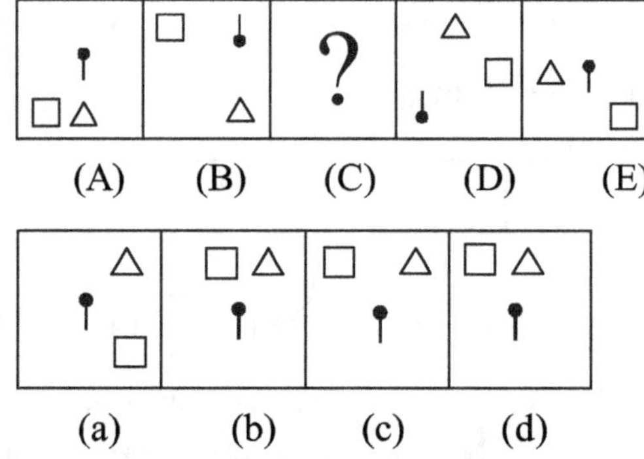

(A) (B) (C) (D) (E)

(a) (b) (c) (d)

DIRECTIONS (Qs. 6-7) : *In the Problem Figures, one figure marked by ? is missing. There is a set of answer figures also in which five alternatives are given. You have to find out the one right answer from answer figures.*

6. **Problem Figures**

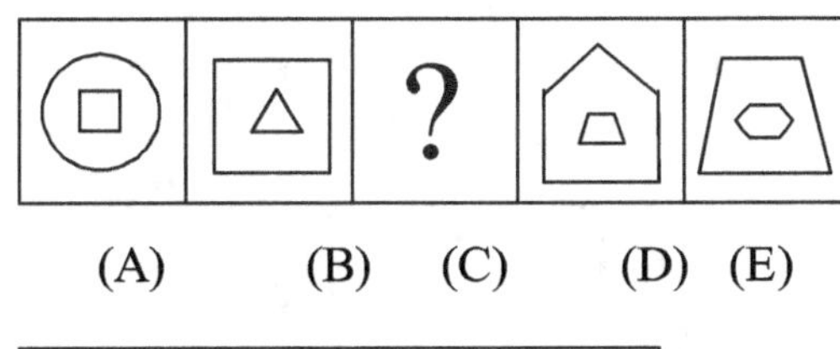

(A) (B) (C) (D) (E)

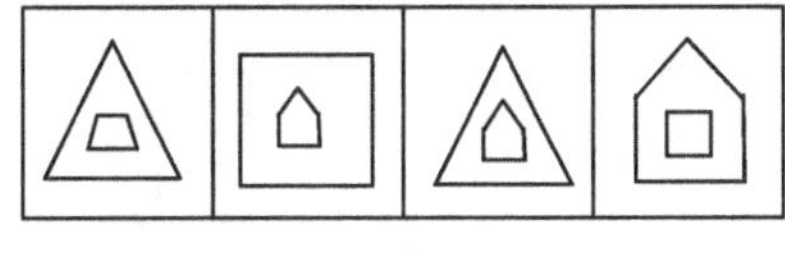

(a) (b) (c) (d)

7. **Problem Figures**

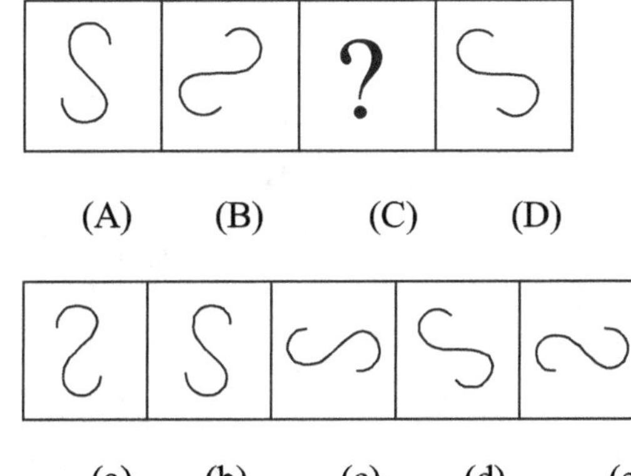

(A) (B) (C) (D)

(a) (b) (c) (d) (e)

DIRECTIONS (Qs. 8-17): *There are three problem figures and the space for the fourth figure is blank. The problem figures are in a series. Find out one figure from among the answer figures, which occupies the blank space for the fourth figure and completes the series.*

8. 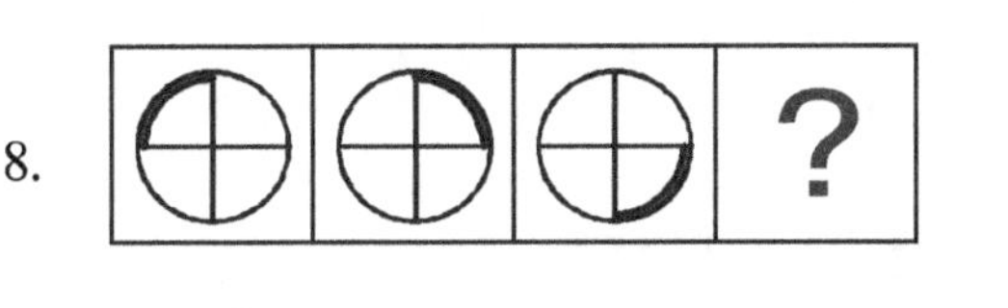

(a) 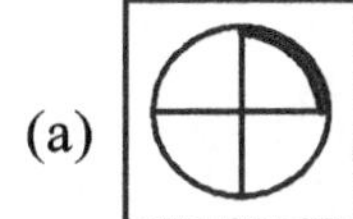

(b) 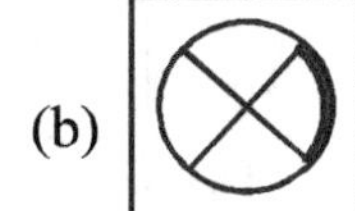

(c) 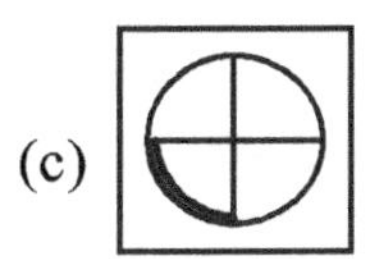

(d) 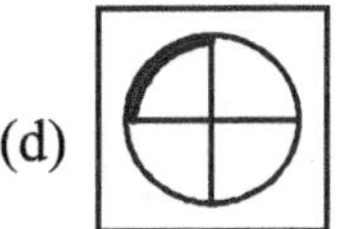

9. 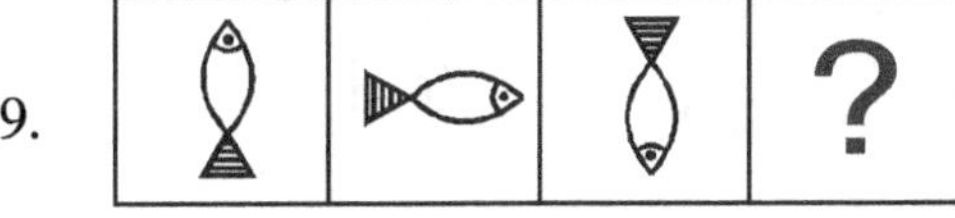

(a) 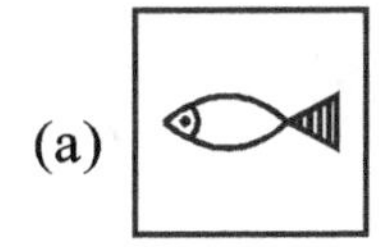

(b) 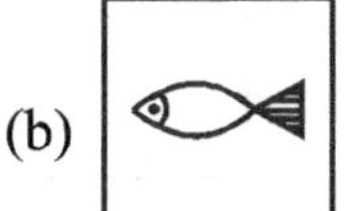

(c) 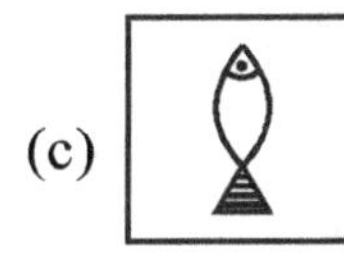

(d) 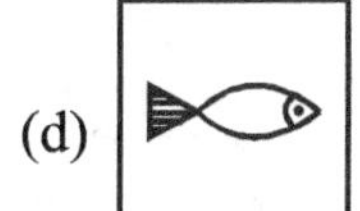

10. 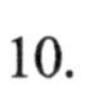

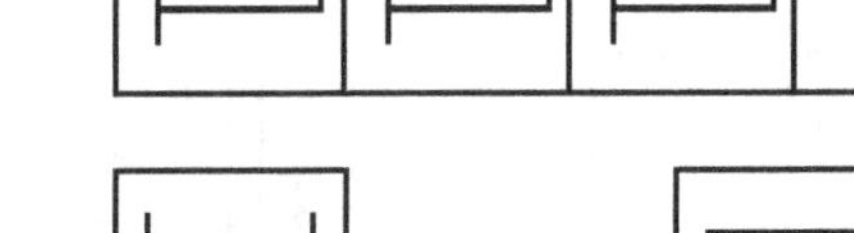

(a)

(b)

(c) 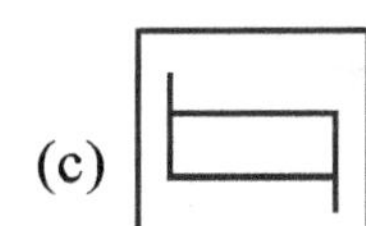

(d) 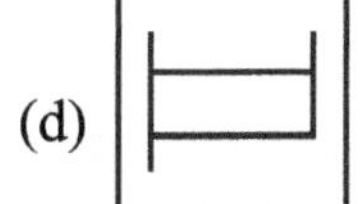

11. 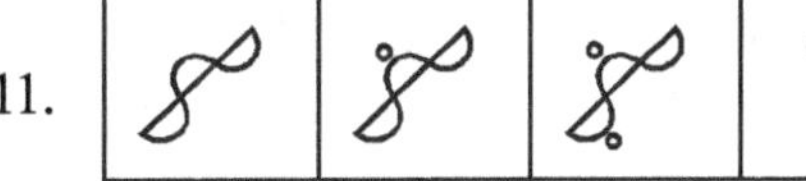

(a) 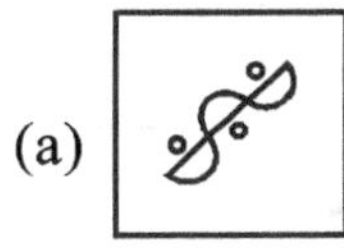

(b) 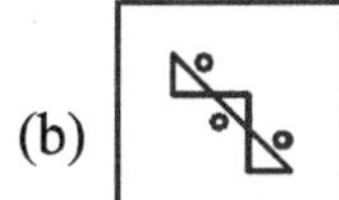

(c) 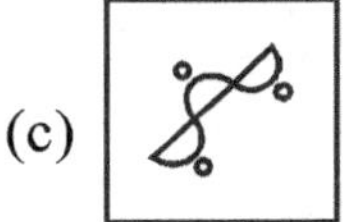

(d) 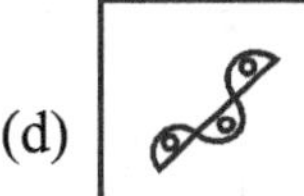

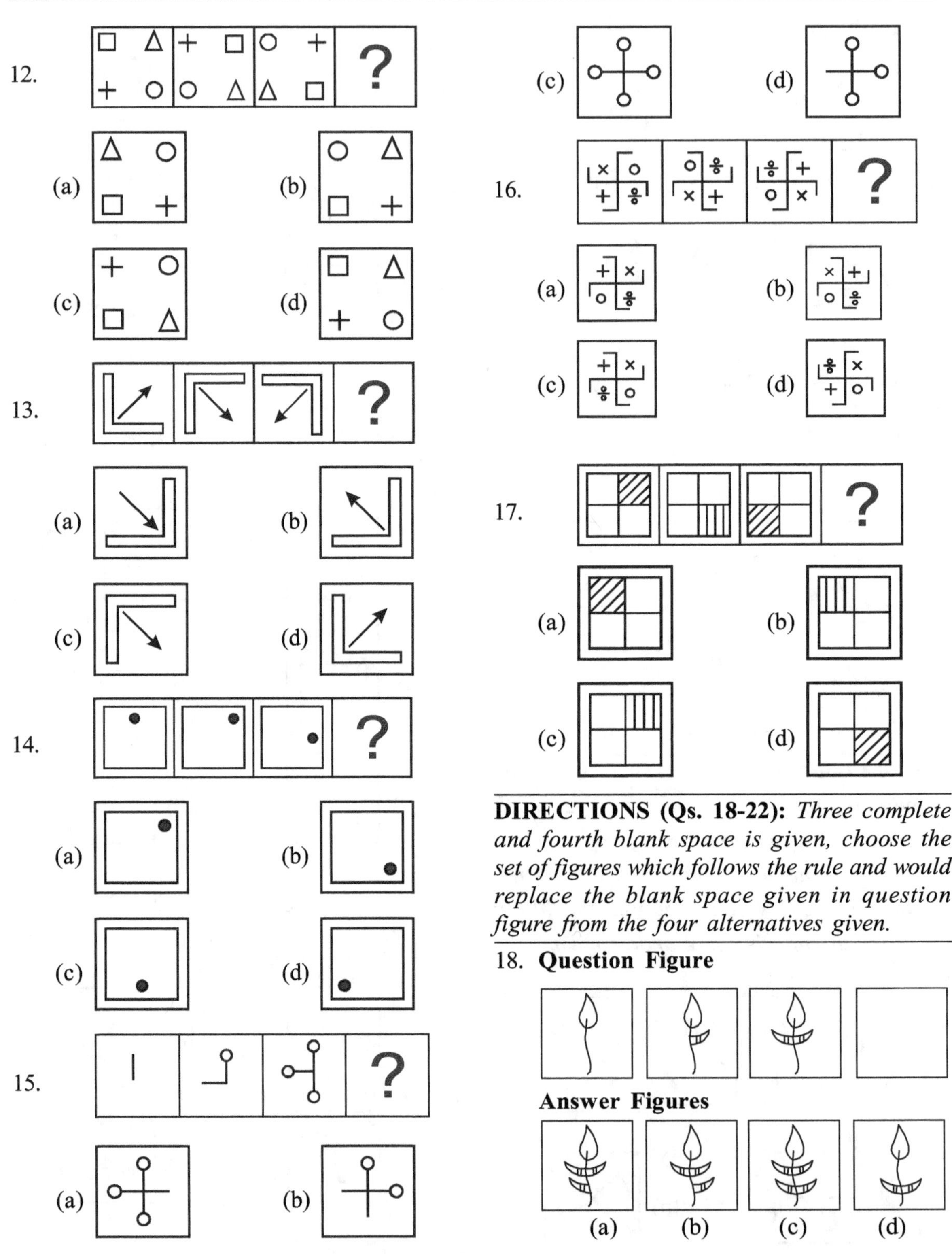

DIRECTIONS (Qs. 18-22): *Three complete and fourth blank space is given, choose the set of figures which follows the rule and would replace the blank space given in question figure from the four alternatives given.*

18. **Question Figure**

Answer Figures

(a) (b) (c) (d)

19. **Question Figure**

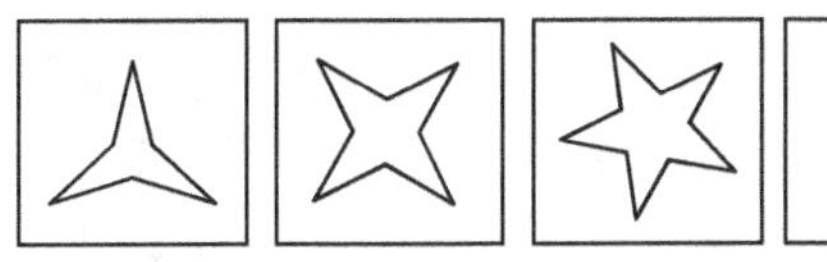

Answer Figures

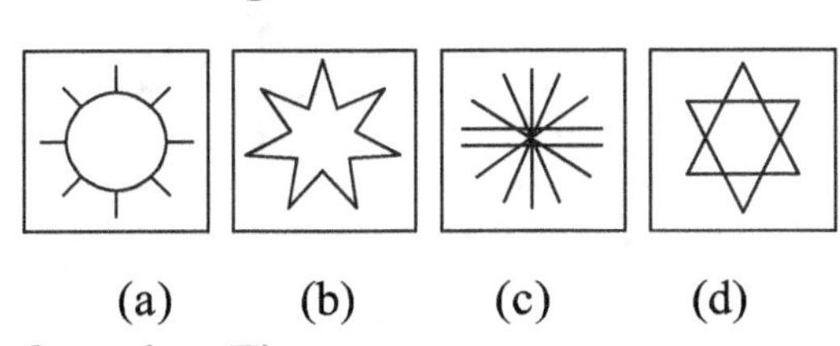

(a) (b) (c) (d)

20. **Question Figure**

Answer Figures

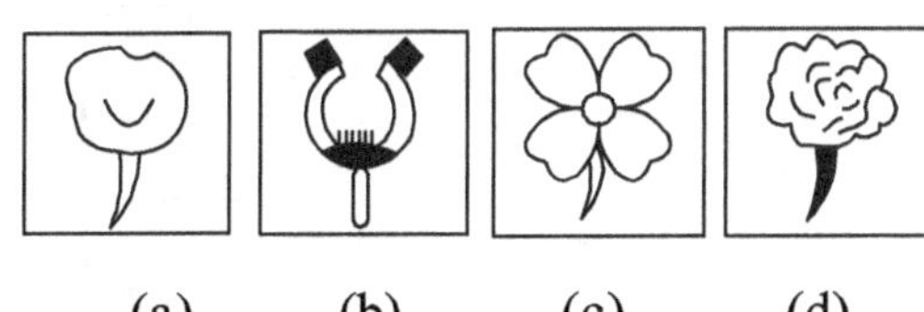

(a) (b) (c) (d)

21. **Question Figure**

Answer Figures

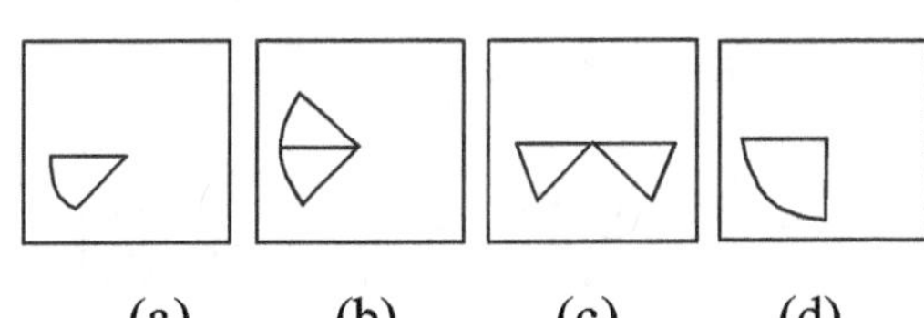

(a) (b) (c) (d)

22. **Question Figure**

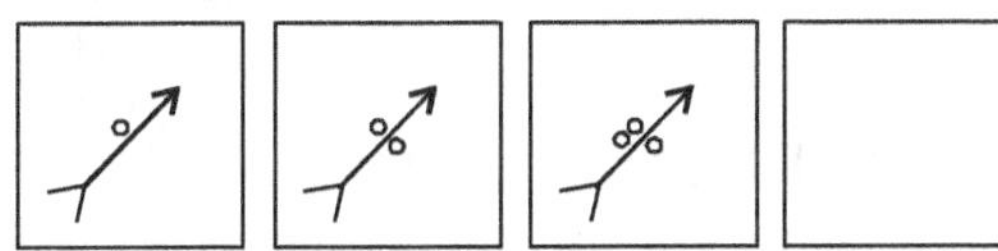

Answer Figures

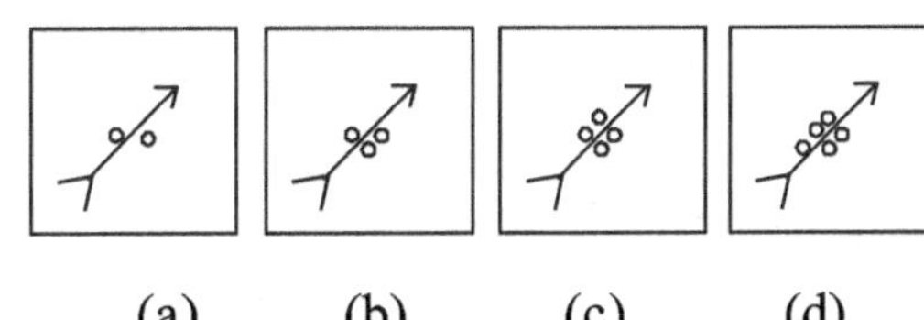

(a) (b) (c) (d)

DIRECTIONS (Qs. 23-27): *Three complete and fourth blank space is given, choose the set of figures which follows the rule and would replace the blank space given in question figure from the four alternatives given.*

23. **Question Figure**

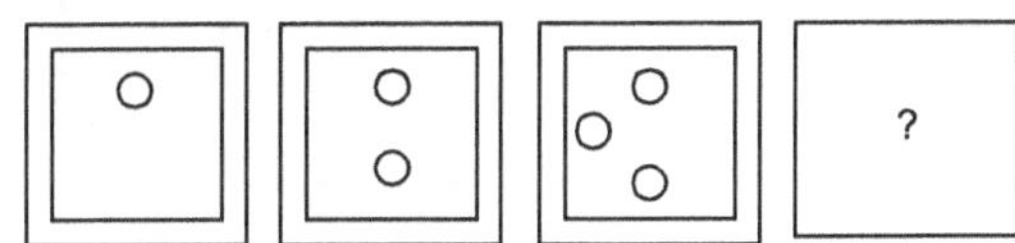

Answer Figures

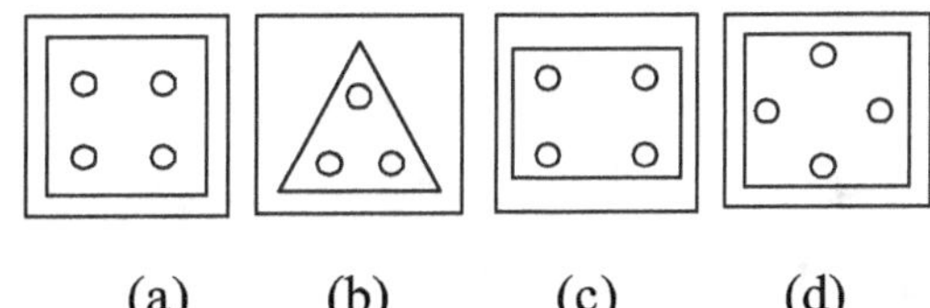

(a) (b) (c) (d)

24. **Question Figure**

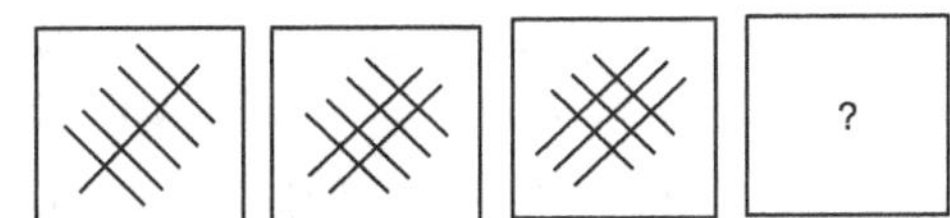

Answer Figures

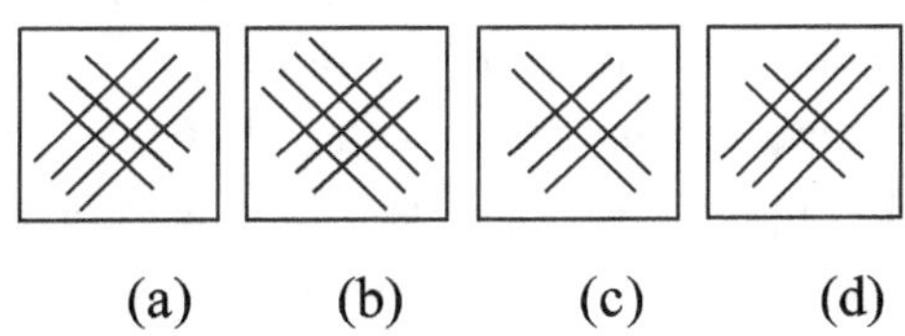

(a) (b) (c) (d)

25. **Question Figure**

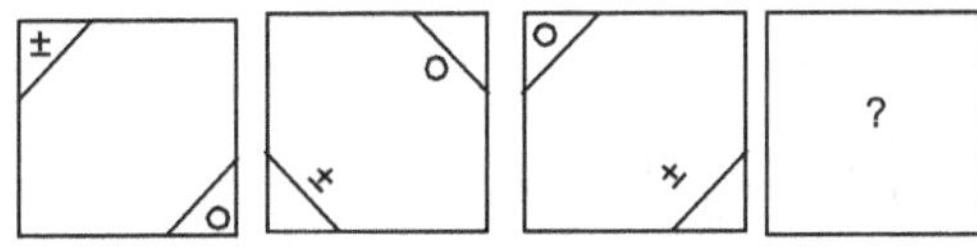

Answer Figures

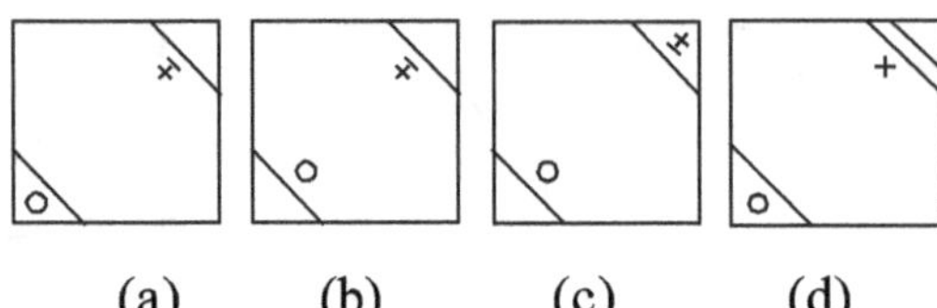

(a) (b) (c) (d)

26. **Question Figure**

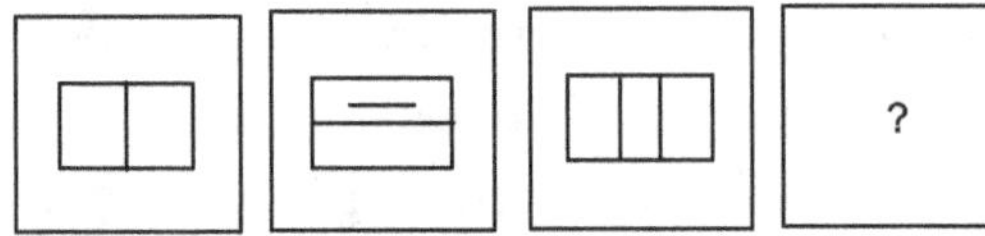

Answer Figures

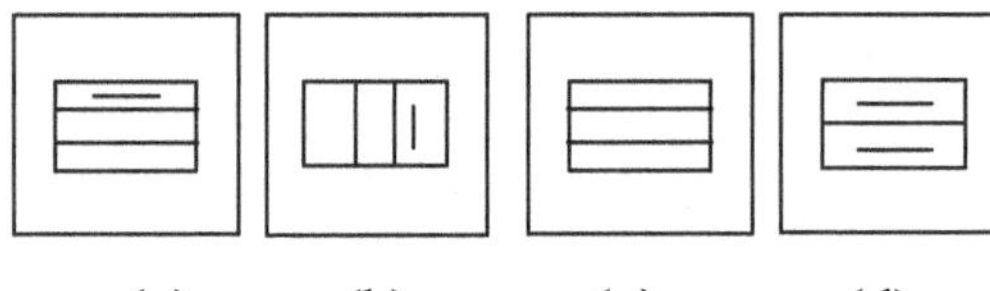

(a) (b) (c) (d)

27. **Question Figure**

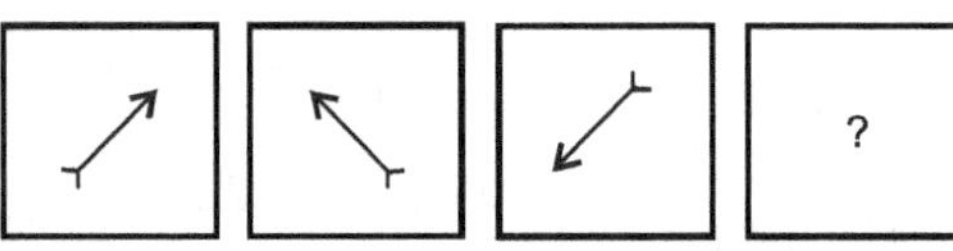

Answer Figures

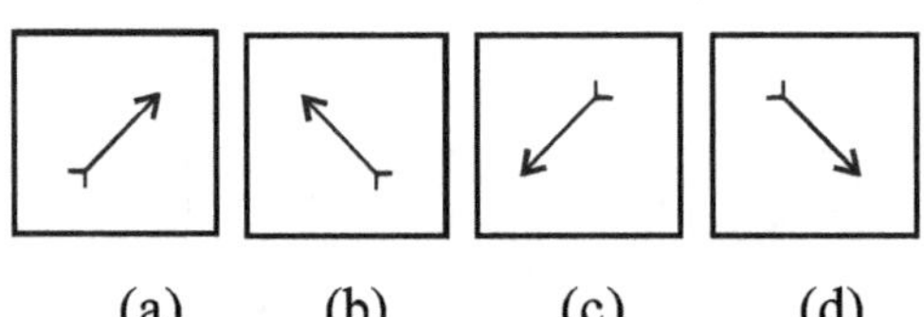

(a) (b) (c) (d)

DIRECTIONS: (Qs. 28-31): *There are three question figure and the space for the fourth figure is left blank. The question figures are in a series. Find out one figure from among the answer figures given which occupies the blank space for the fourth figure and completes the series.*

28. **Question Figures**

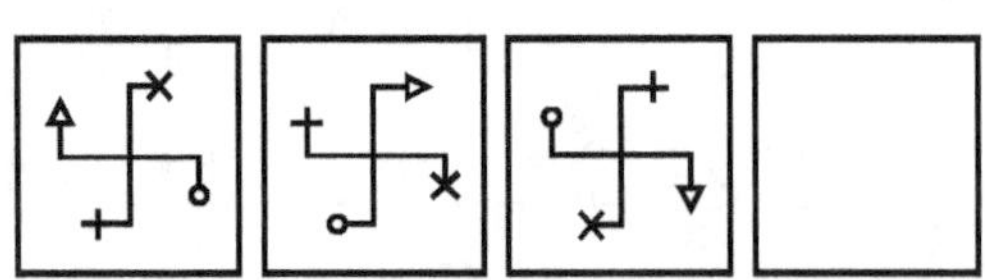

Answer Figures

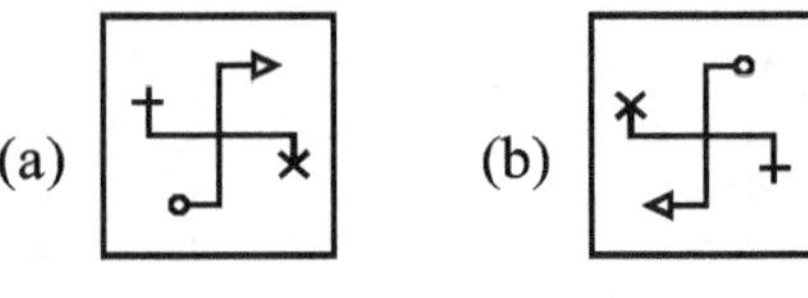

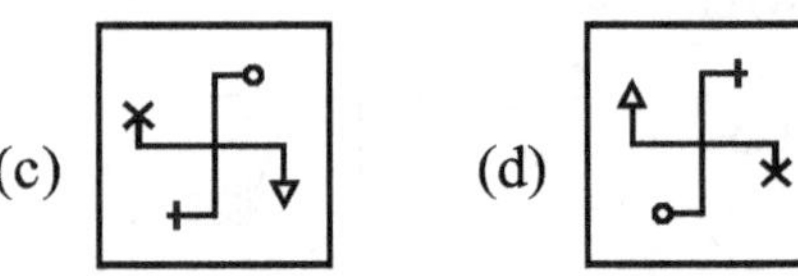

29. **Question Figures**

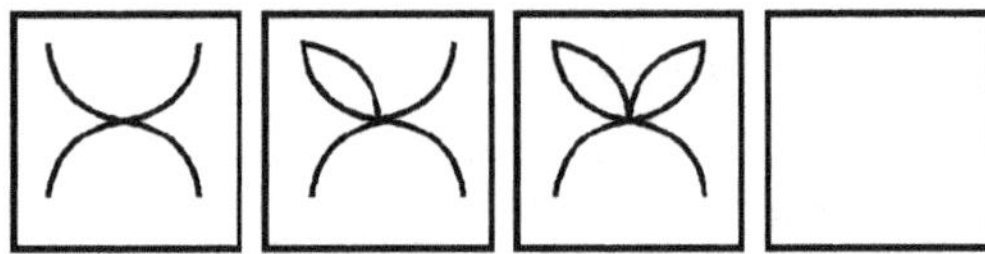

Answer Figures

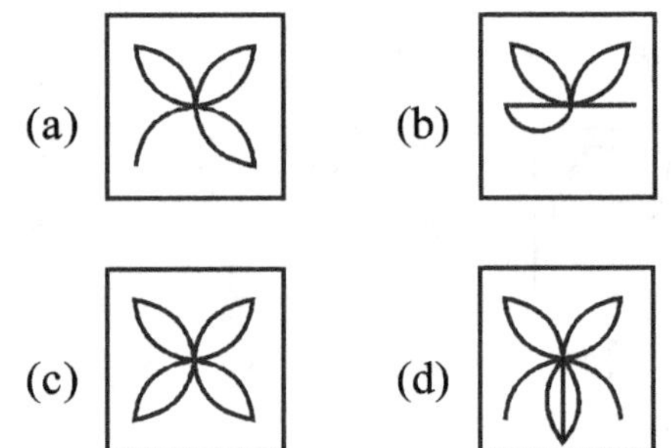

30. **Question Figures**

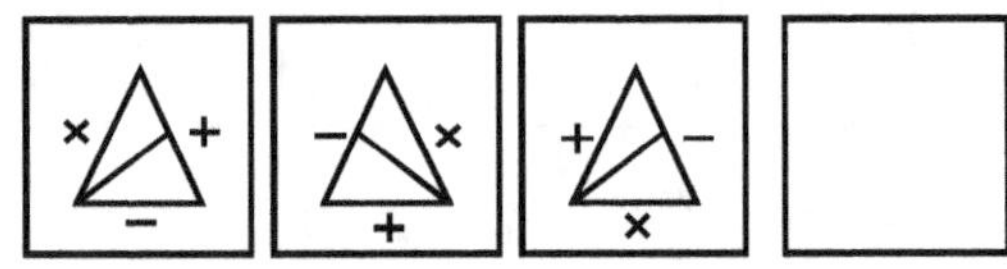

Answer Figures

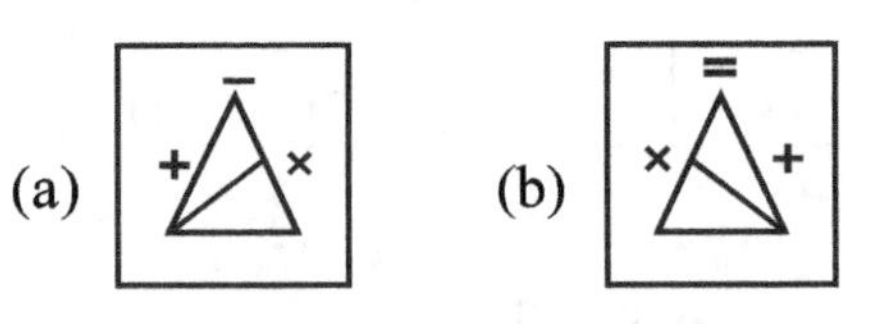

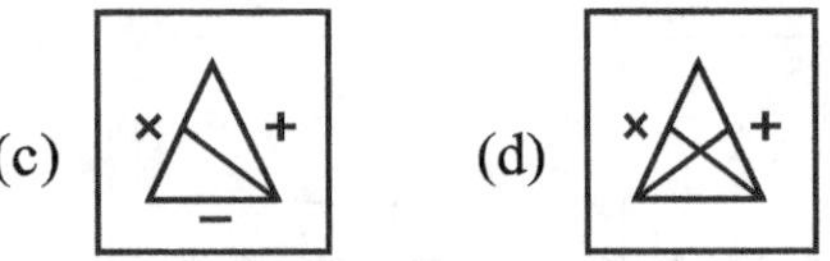

31. **Question Figures**

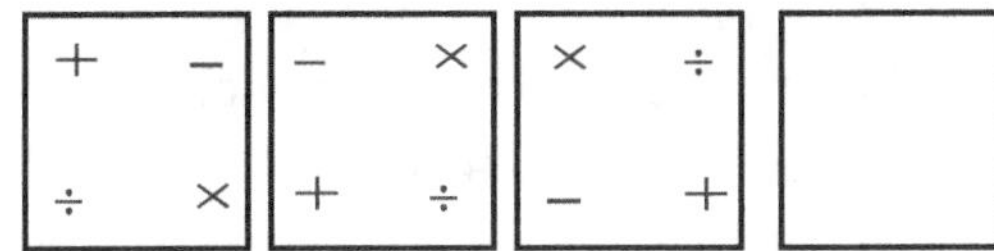

Answer Figures

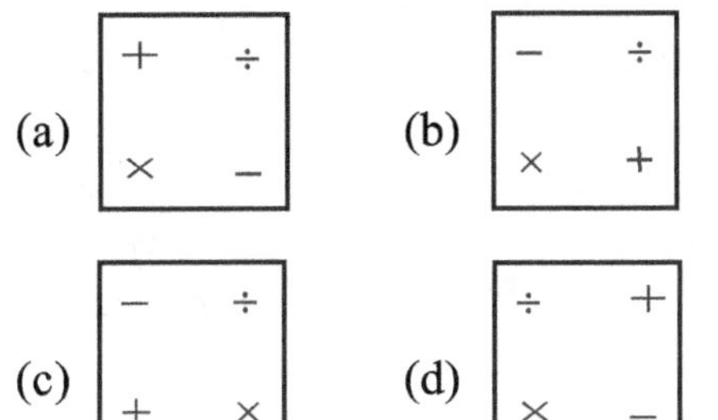

DIRECTIONS (Qs. 32 to 33) : *On there are three question figures and the space for the fourth figure is left blank. The question figures are in a series. Find out one figure from among the answer figures which occupies the blank space for the fourth figure and complete the series.*

32. **Questions Figure**

Answer Figures

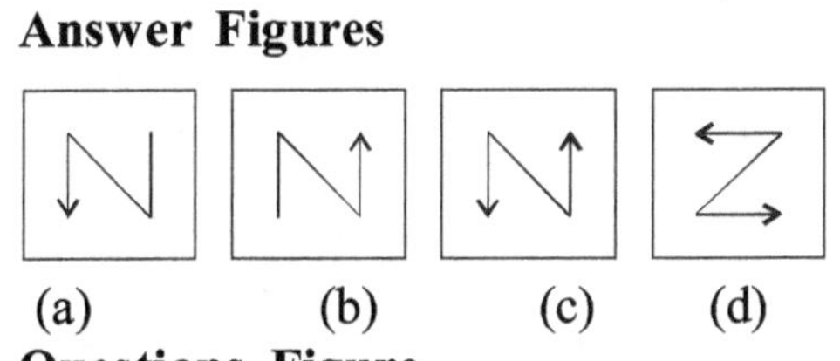

33. **Questions Figure**

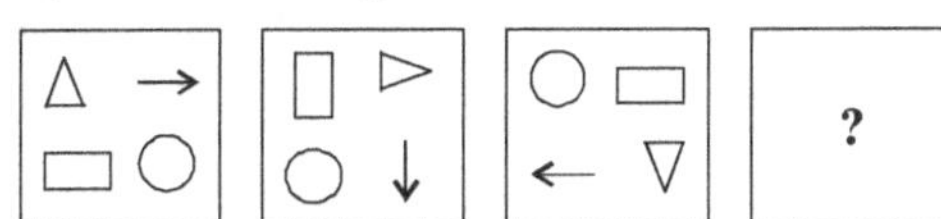

Answer Figures

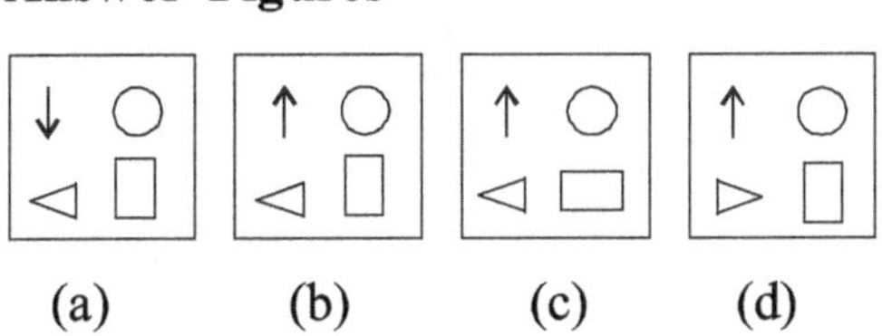

DIRECTIONS (Qs. 34-37): *There are three question figure on the left side space for the fourth figure is left blank. The question figures are in a series. Find out one figure from among the answer figures which occupies the blank space for the fourth figure and complete the series.*

34. **Question Figures**

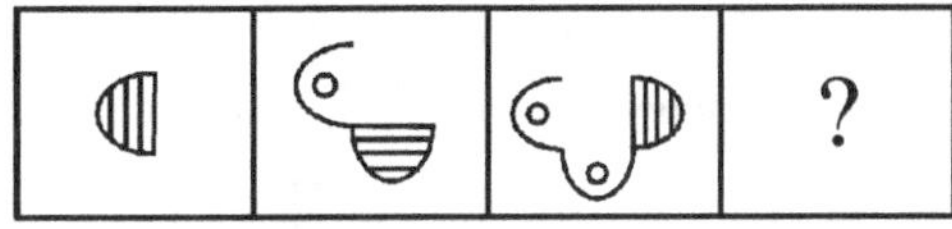

Answer Figures

35. **Question Figures**

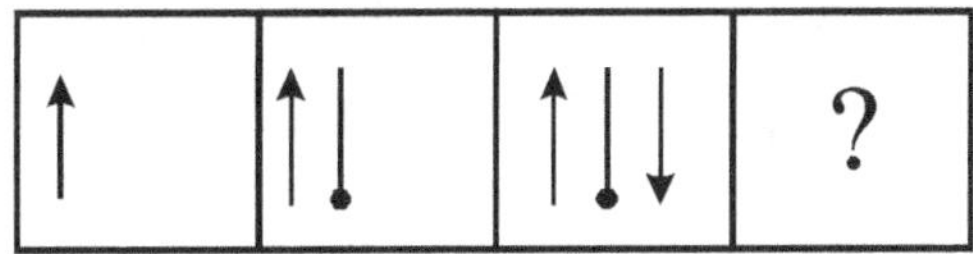

Answer Figures

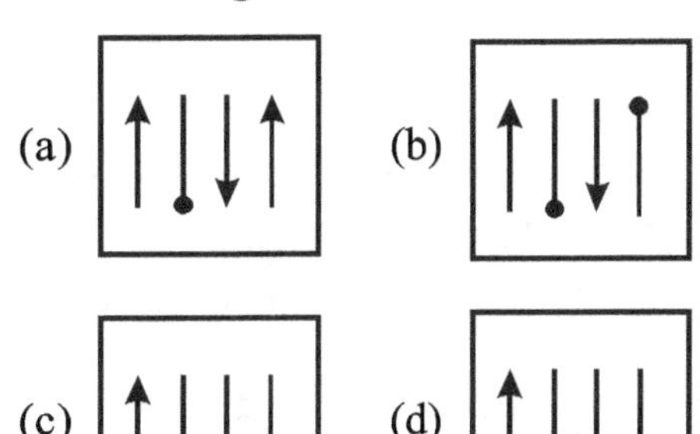

36. **Question Figures**

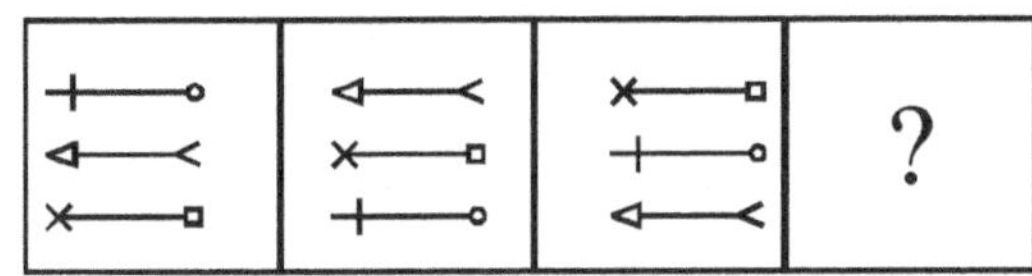

Answer Figures

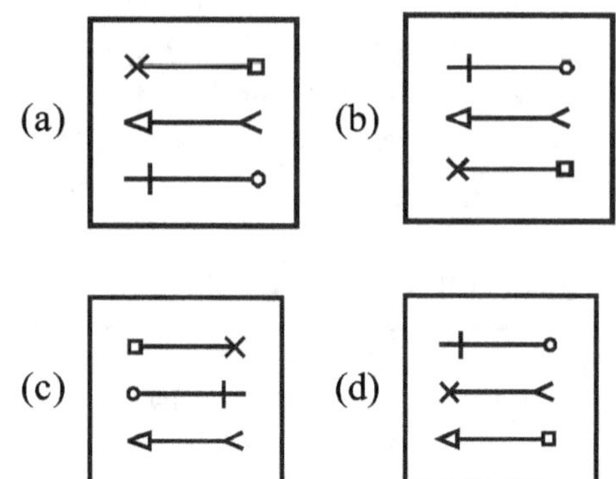

37. **Question Figure**

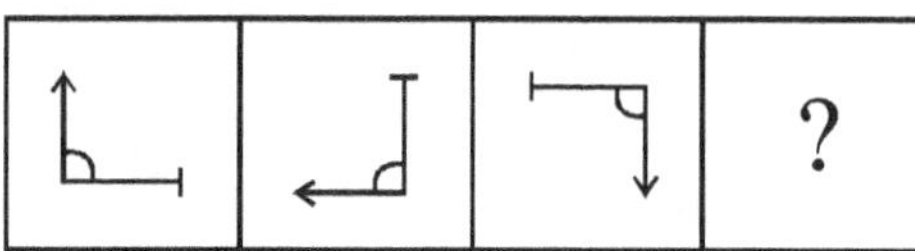

Answer Figures

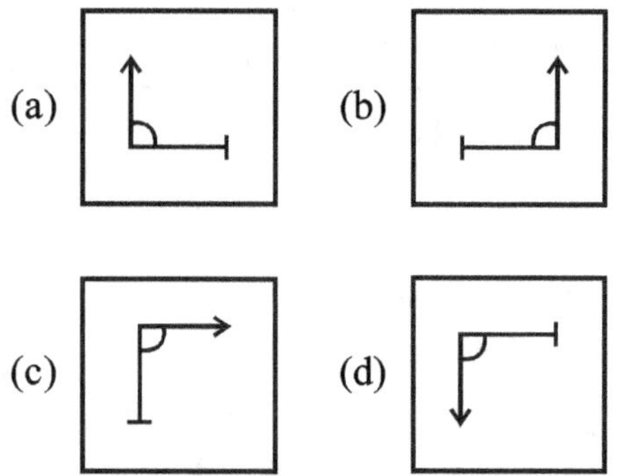

38. Which of the following numbers will replace the (?) So as to complete the given number pattern?

(a) 216 (b) 225
(c) 144 (d) 196

39. Select a figure from the options which will continue the given series.

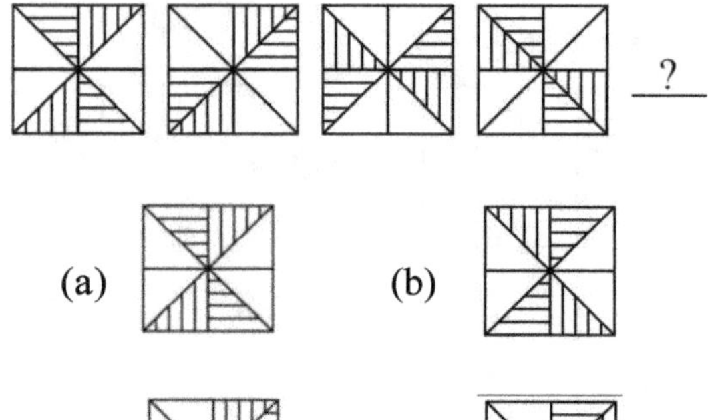

40. Find the figure from the options which will continue the same series as established by the Problem Figures. **[2020]**

Problem Figures

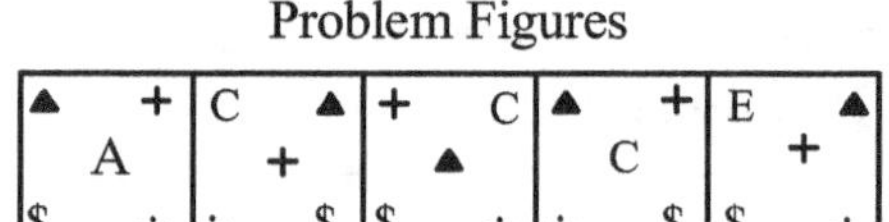

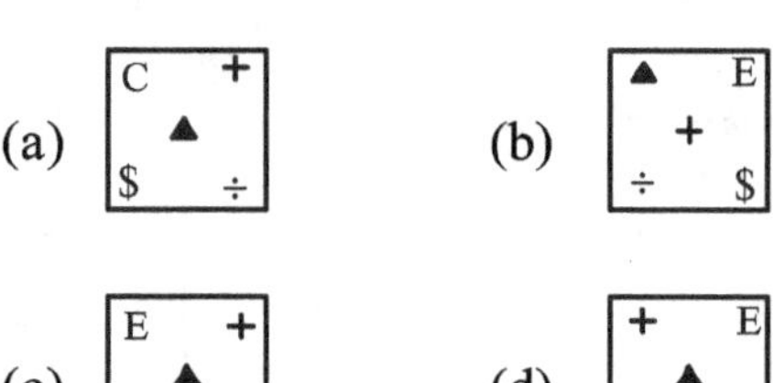

LEVEL 2

DIRECTIONS (Qs. 1-5): *Each of following questions consists of four problem figures marked A, B, C and D and five answer Figures marked a, b, c, and d. Select a figure from amongst the answer Figures which will continue the series established by the four Problem Figures.*

1. **Problem Figures**

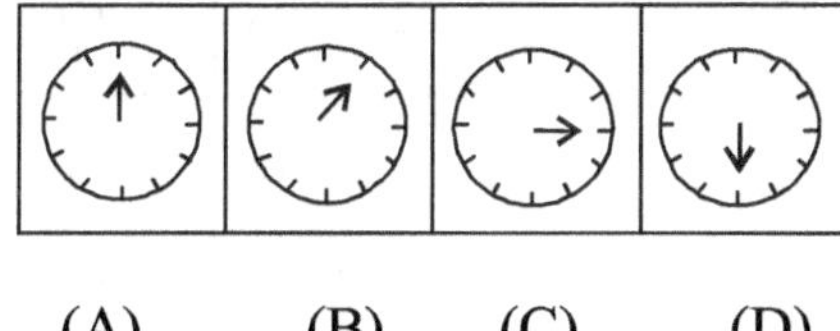

(A) (B) (C) (D)

Answer Figures

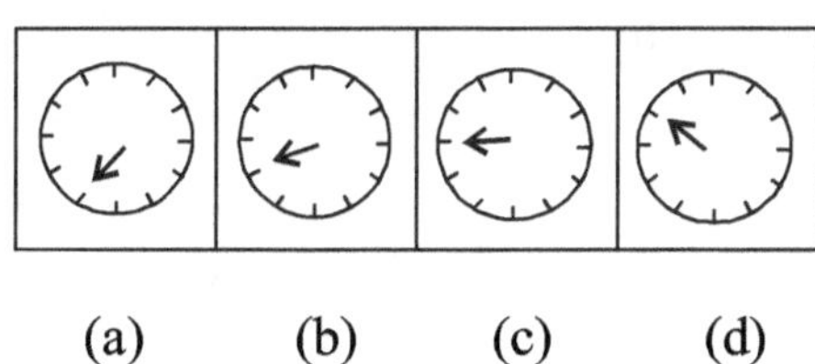

(a) (b) (c) (d)

2. **Problem Figures**

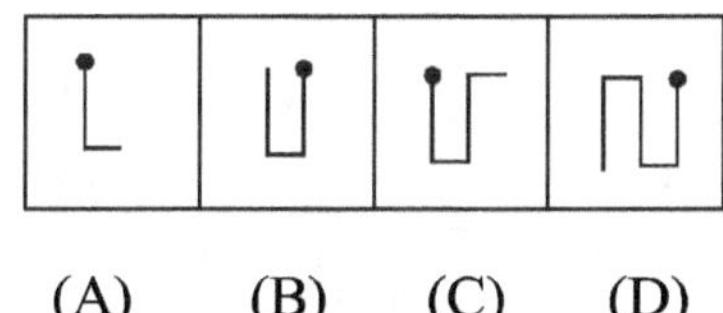

(A) (B) (C) (D)

Answer Figures

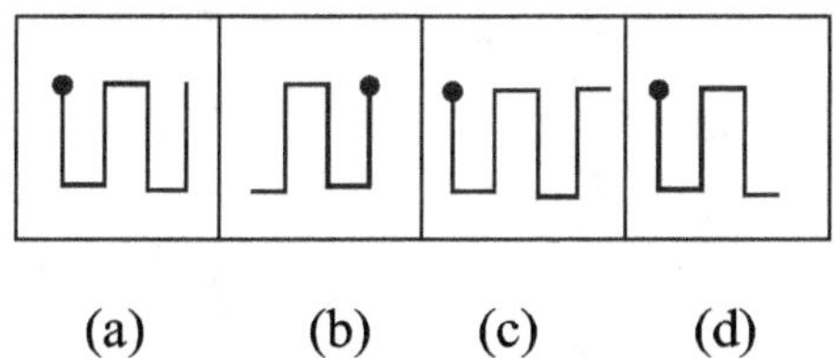

(a) (b) (c) (d)

3. **Problem Figures**

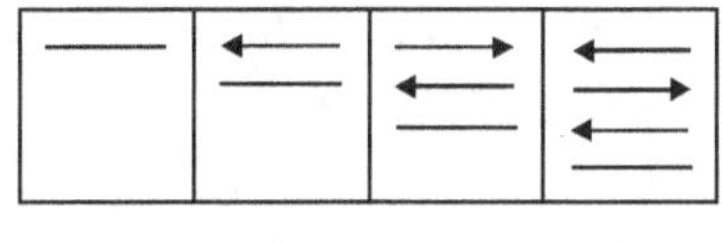

(A) (B) (C) (D)

Answer Figures

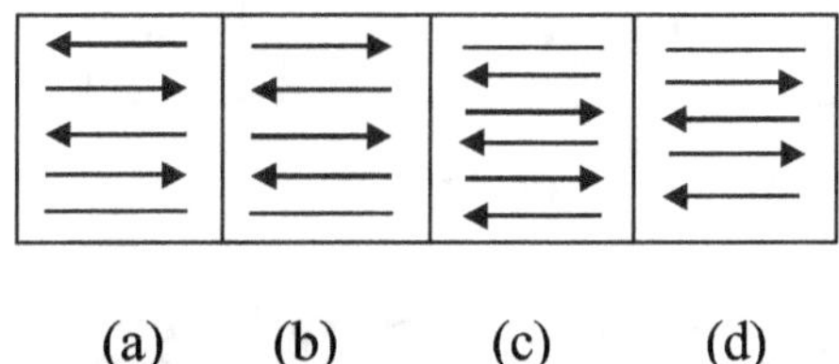

(a) (b) (c) (d)

4. **Problem Figures**

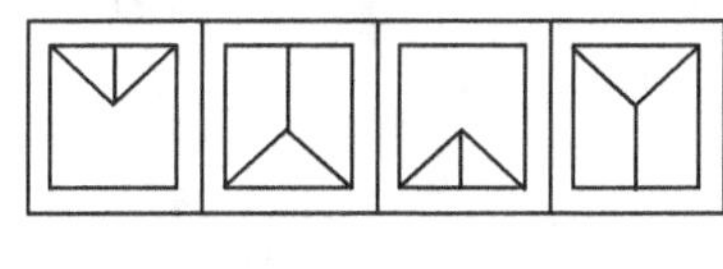

(A) (B) (C) (D)

Answer Figures

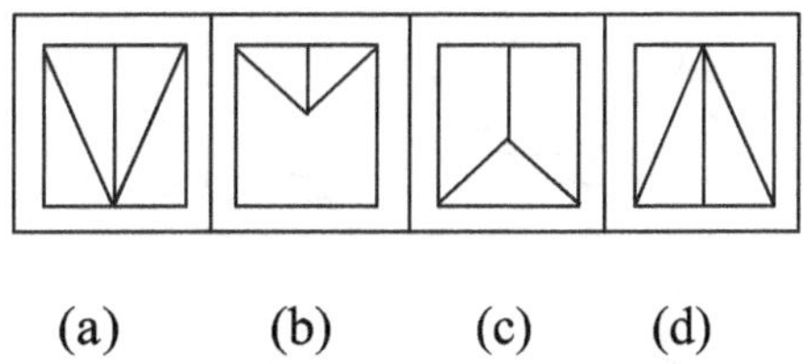

(a) (b) (c) (d)

5. **Problem Figures**

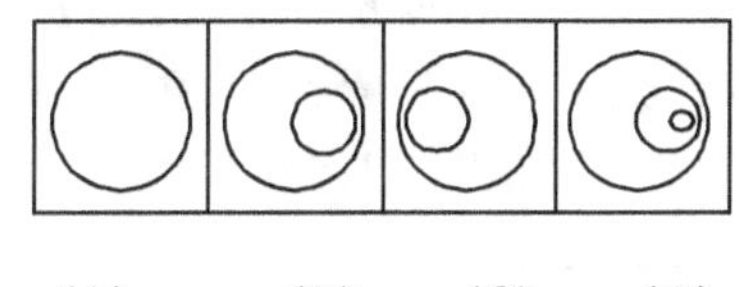

(A) (B) (C) (D)

Answer Figures

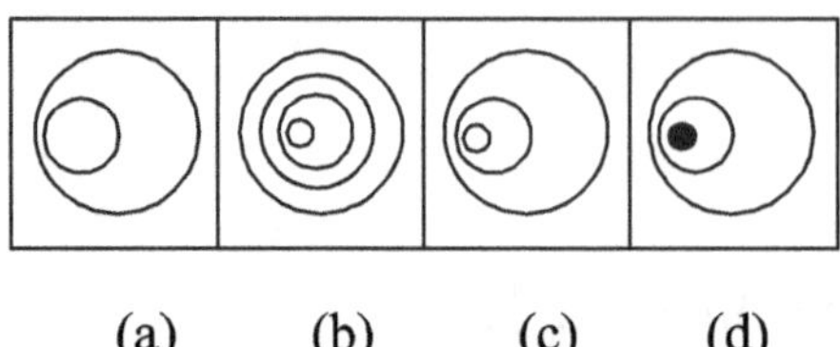

(a) (b) (c) (d)

DIRECTIONS (Qs. 6-7) : *In the following questions, which one of the answer figure would occupy the next position in the problem figure. If they continue in the same order.*

6. **Problem Figures:**

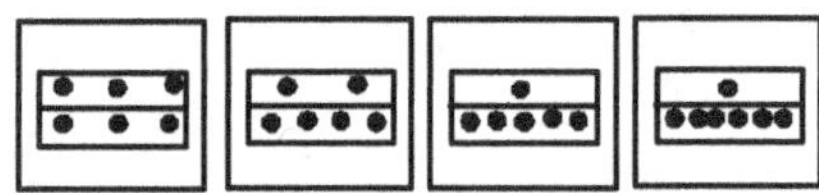

Answer Figures:

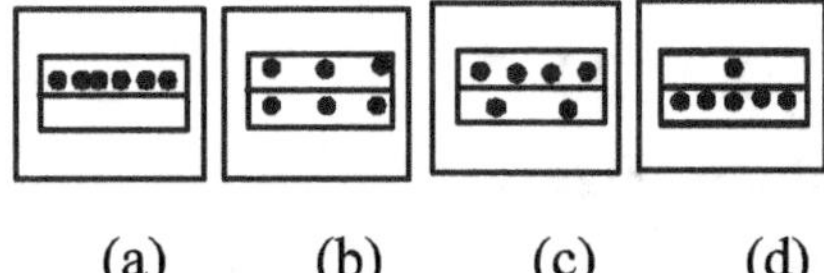

(a) (b) (c) (d)

7. **Problem Figures:**

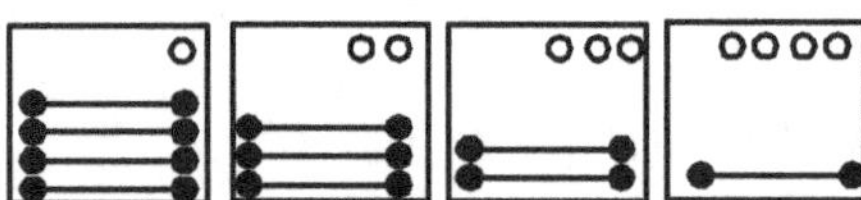

Answer Figures:

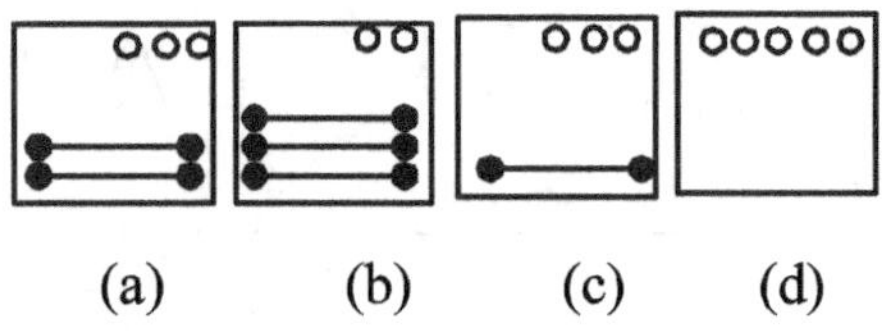

(a) (b) (c) (d)

DIRECTIONS (Qs. 8-11): *In each question, out of the four figures marked (a), (b), (c) and (d), three are similar in a certain manner. Howerer one figure is not like the other three. Choose the figure wchic is diffence from the rest.*

8.

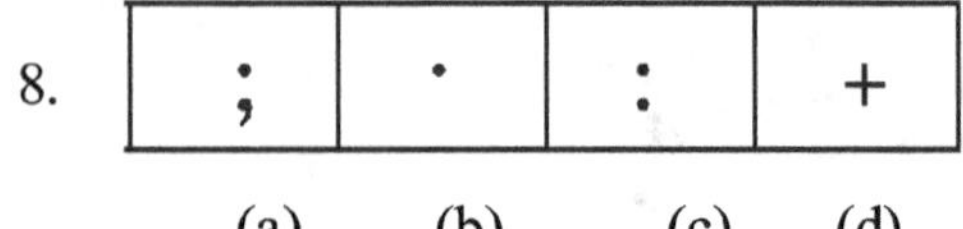

(a) (b) (c) (d)

9.

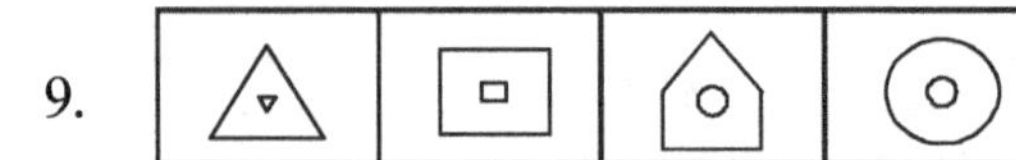

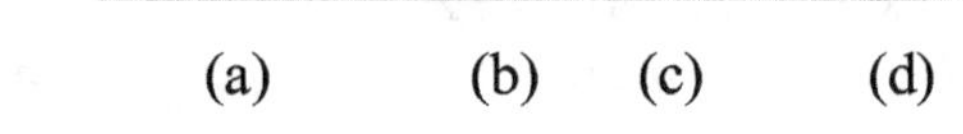

(a) (b) (c) (d)

10.

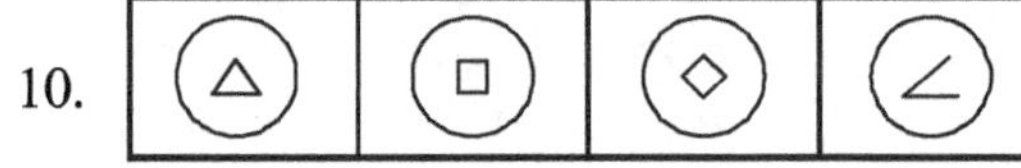

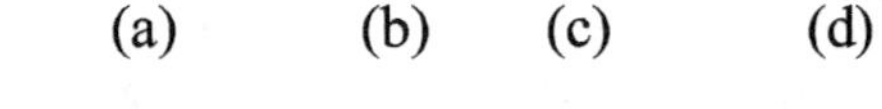

(a) (b) (c) (d)

11.

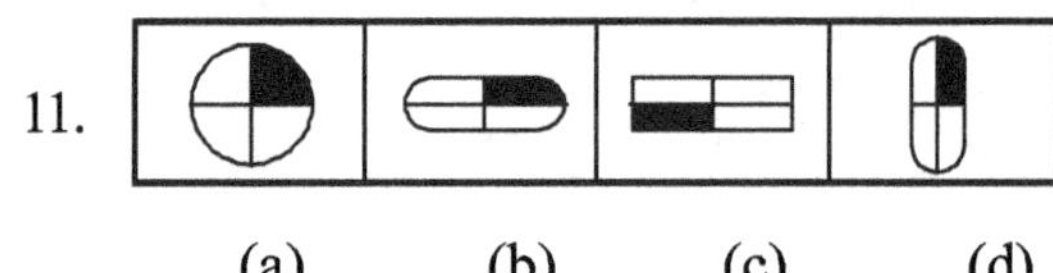

(a) (b) (c) (d)

12. Find the missing number, if same rule is followed in all the three figures.

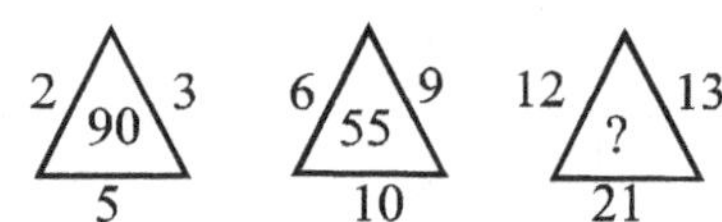

(a) 5336 (b) 1728

(c) 4339 (d) 3239

13. Select a figure from the options which will continue the same series as established by the Problem Figures.

ProblemFigures

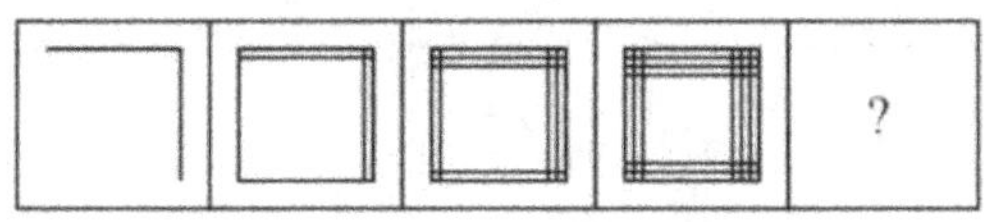

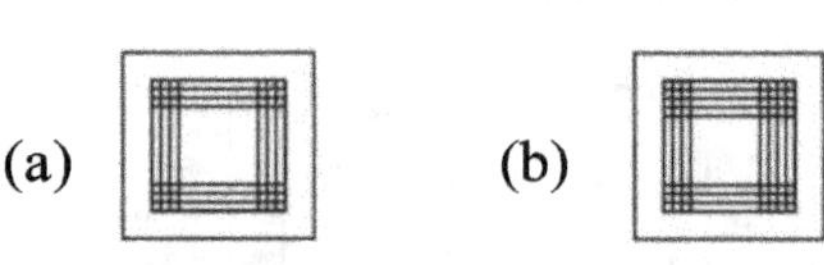

(a) (b)

(c) (d)

14. Select a figure from the options which will replace the (?) in the series as established by the Problem Figures.

ProblemFigures

(a) (b) (c) (d)

15. Which of the following figures will continue the same series as established by the Problem Figures?

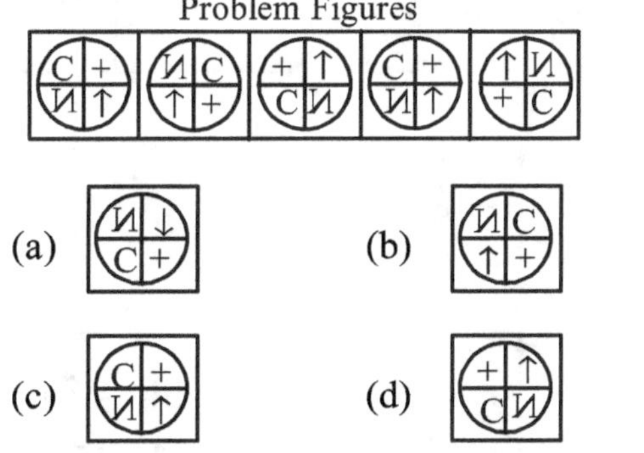

16. Select a figure from the options which will continue the same series as established by the Problem Figures.

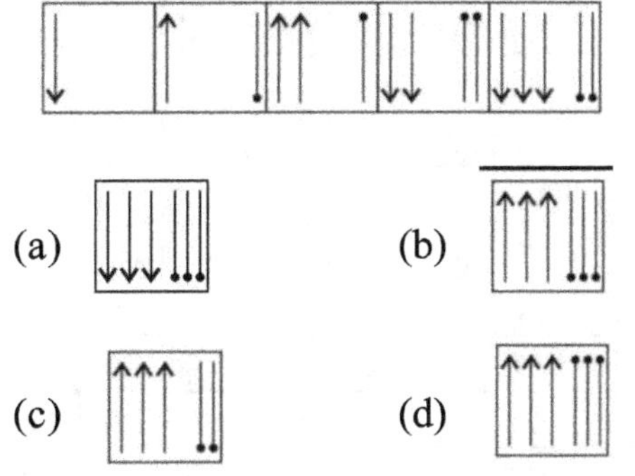

17. Select a figure from the options which will continue the same series as established by the Problem Figures.

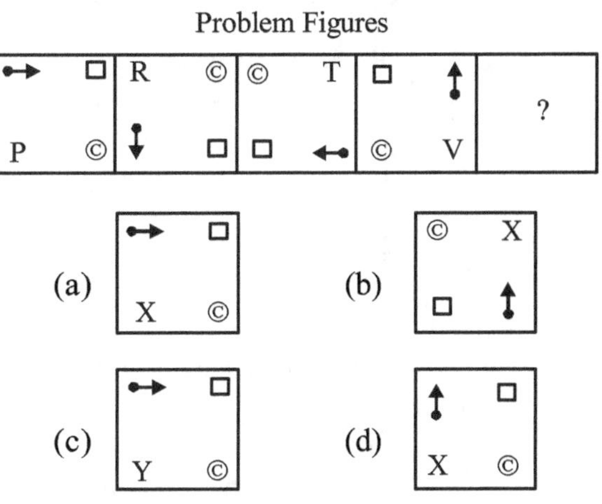

18. Select a figure from the options which will continue the same series as established by the Problem Figures. **[2018]**

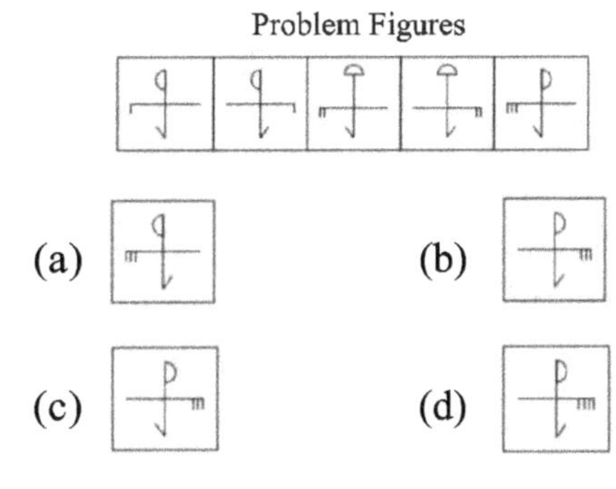

19. Select a figure from the options which will continue the same series as established by the Problem Figures. **[2018]**

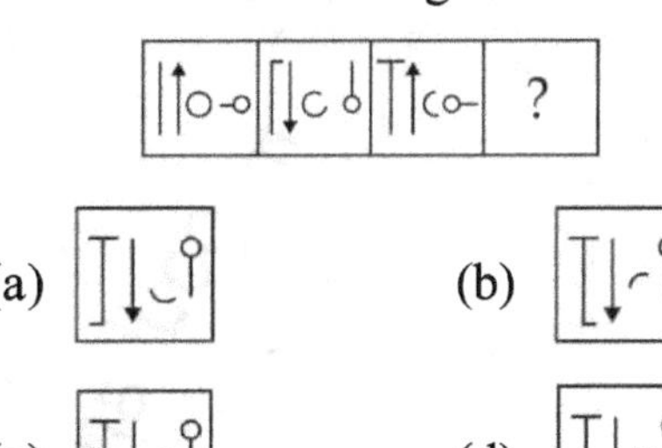

20. Select a figure from the options which will continue the series as established by the problem figures. **[2018]**

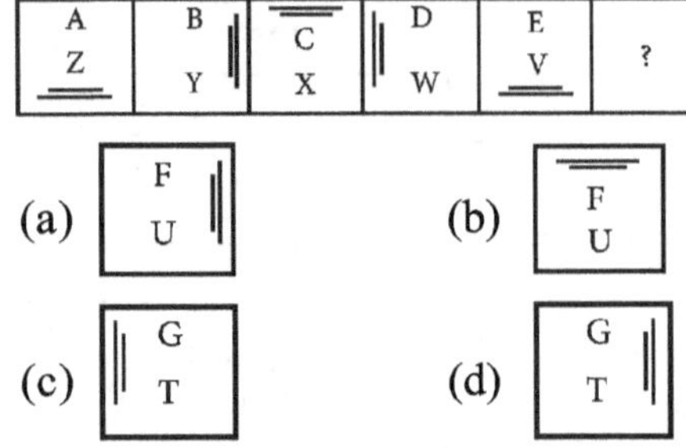

21. Find the figure from the options which will continue the same series as established by the Problem Figures **[2018]**

Problem Figure

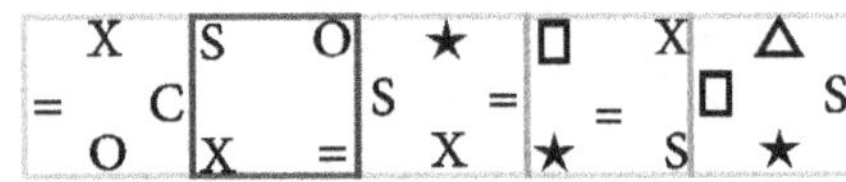

22. Which of the following figures will continue the same series as established by the Problem Figures? **[2020]**

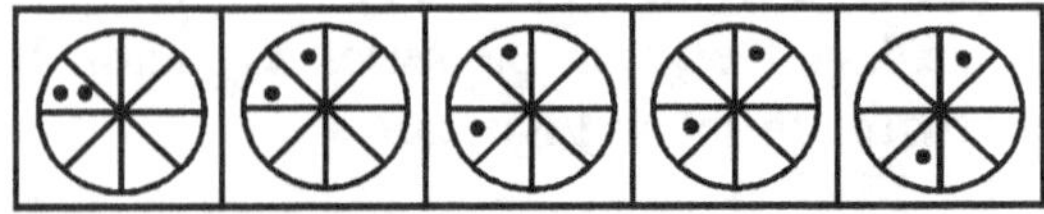

(a) 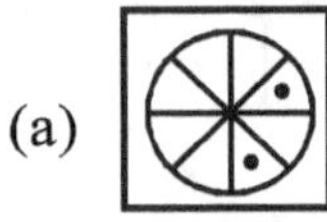 (b) 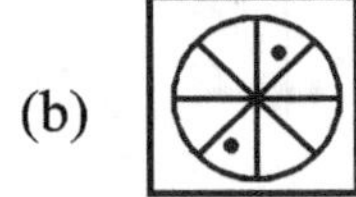

(c) 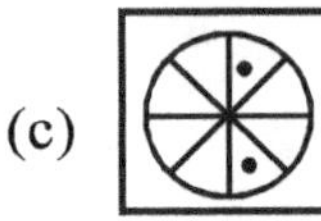 (d) 

23. Select a figure from the options which will complete the given series as established by the Problem Figures. **[2021]**

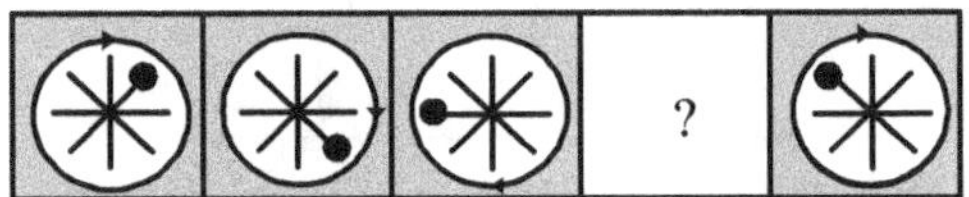

(a) 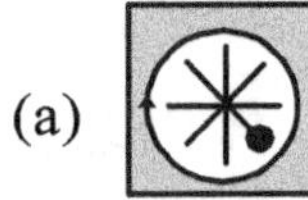 (b) 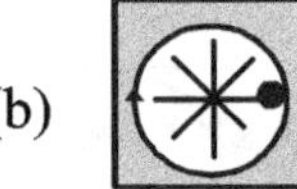

(c) 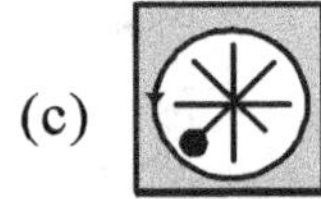 (d) 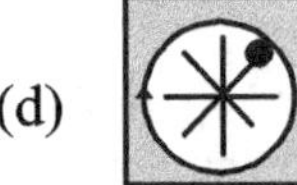

ANSWER KEY

LEVEL-1

1	(c)	**5**	(b)	**9**	(a)	**13**	(b)	**17**	(b)	**21**	(a)	**25**	(b)	**29**	(a)	**33**	(b)	**37**	(c)
2	(d)	**6**	(c)	**10**	(a)	**14**	(b)	**18**	(b)	**22**	(c)	**26**	(a)	**30**	(c)	**34**	(b)	**38**	(a)
3	(b)	**7**	(c)	**11**	(c)	**15**	(a)	**19**	(d)	**23**	(d)	**27**	(d)	**31**	(d)	**35**	(b)	**39**	(b)
4	(a)	**8**	(c)	**12**	(a)	**16**	(c)	**20**	(b)	**24**	(d)	**28**	(b)	**32**	(b)	**36**	(b)	**40**	(d)

LEVEL-2

1	(d)	**2**	(d)	**3**	(b)	**4**	(b)	**5**	(c)	**6**	(b)	**7**	(d)	**8**	(d)	**9**	(c)	**10**	(d)
11	(c)	**12**	(a)	**13**	(b)	**14**	(d)	**15**	(d)	**16**	(b)	**17**	(a)	**18**	(b)	**19**	(b)	**20**	(a)
21	(a)	**22**	(d)	**23**	(b)														

CHAPTER

Non-verbal Analogy & Classification

In these type of question, four figures (a),(b),(c), and (d) are given. These are treated both as Problem Figures as well as the Answer Figures. Out of these four figures are related to each other by way of having some common three characteristics and so form a group. Out of these four, you have to identify one figure which does not belong to the group.

Hence the problems are of odd-man-out type.

ILLUSTRATION 1 :

Choose the figure which is different from the others.

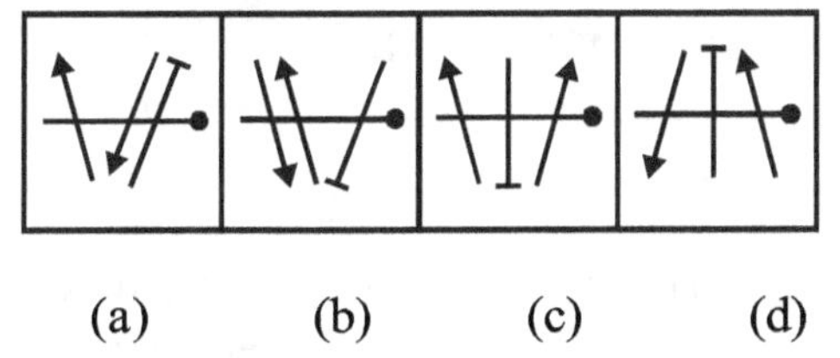

(a) (b) (c) (d)

***Sol.* (c)** Both the arrowheads are in the same direction in figure (c). In all other figures, they are in the opposite direction. Hence, (c) is the answer.

ILLUSTRATION 2 :

Choose the figure which is different from the others.

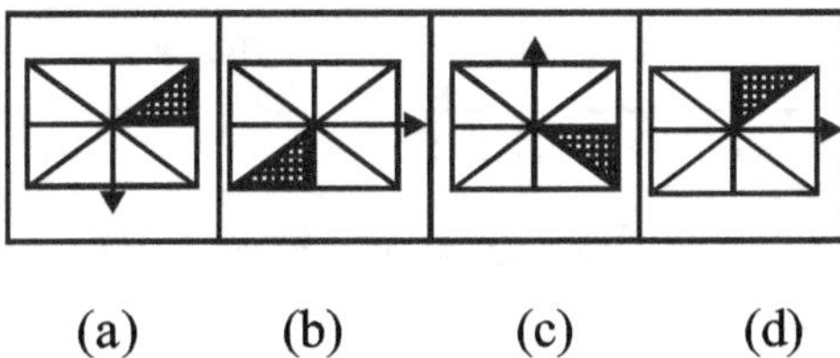

(a) (b) (c) (d)

***Sol.* (d)** Between the shaded portion and the arrow, there are two triangles in figures (a), (b), (c), and (d). Hence (d) is the answer

ILLUSTRATION 3 :

Identify the figure which is different from the remaining.

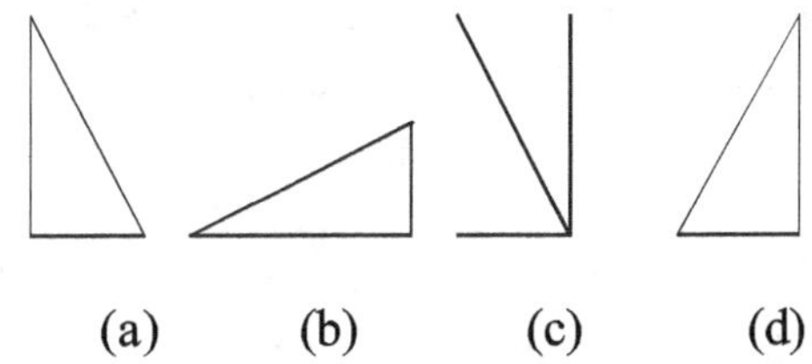

(a) (b) (c) (d)

***Sol.* (d)** Figures (a) to (d) can be obtained from one another by rotating suitably in the clockwise or anticlockwise direction.

Figure no. (d) cannot be obtained by rotation.

ILLUSTRATION 4 :

Choose the figure which is different from the others.

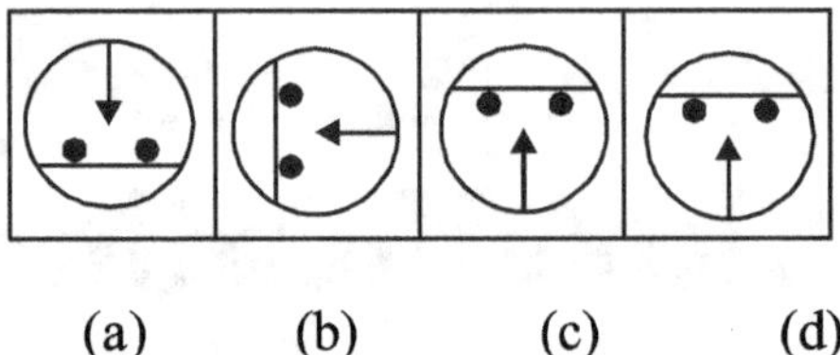

(a) (b) (c) (d)

***Sol.* (d)** The figures form a series. The complete figure rotates 90° CW in each step. Fig. (d) does not fit in the series as it is the same as fig. (c).

Hence fig. (d) is the answer.

ILLUSTRATION 5 :

Choose the figure which is different from the others.

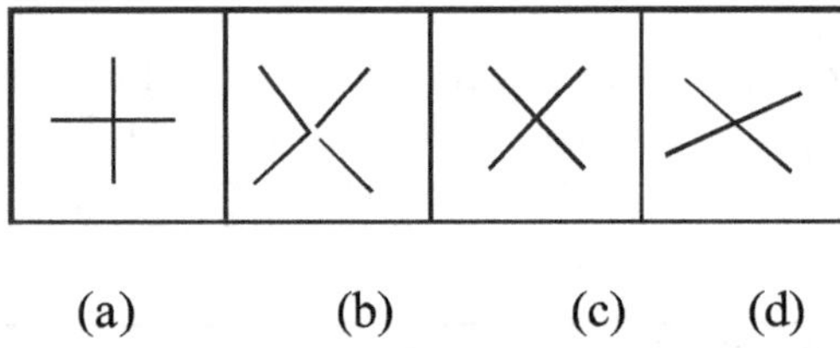

(a) (b) (c) (d)

***Sol.* (d)** The two lines cut at right angles in all the figures except (d).

The dictionary defines 'analogy' as a process of reasoning from parallel cases. These are also called relationship tests. The figures are presented in two sets ; one is called problem figure and the other answer figure. The problem figure consists of two sets. The first set has two units marked A and B. [Sometimes separated by the sign of colon (:)] and the second set (which is sometimes separated by the sign :) also has two units marked C and D. The figures in the first set bear a certain analogy or relationship with each other. The same relationship is reflected in the third figure of the second set. The fourth unit is either blank or contains a question mark (?). You have to choose from the set of answer figures marked A, B, C and D (sometimes E also) one figure bearing the same analogy in the first unit to fill the blank column or to replace the question mark.

DIRECTIONS (ILLUSTRATION 28-31) :

Each of the following examples consists of two sets of figures. Figures a, b, c and d constitute the problem set while figures (a), (b), (c), (d) and (e) constitute the answer set. There is a definite relationship between figures a and b. Establish a similar relationship between figures c and d and choose the one figure from answer set as the correct answer.

ILLUSTRATION 6 :

Problem Figures

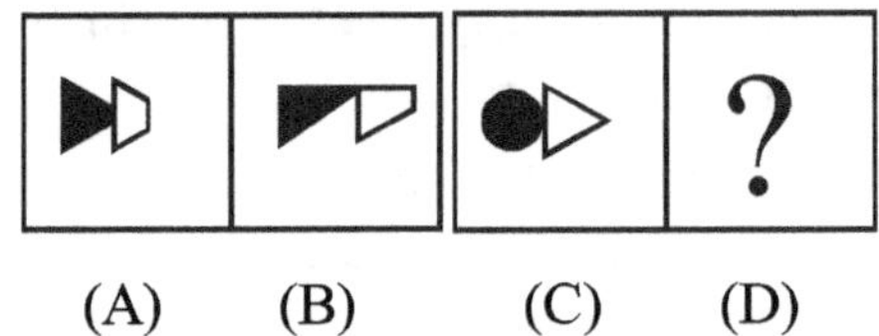

(A) (B) (C) (D)

Answer Figures

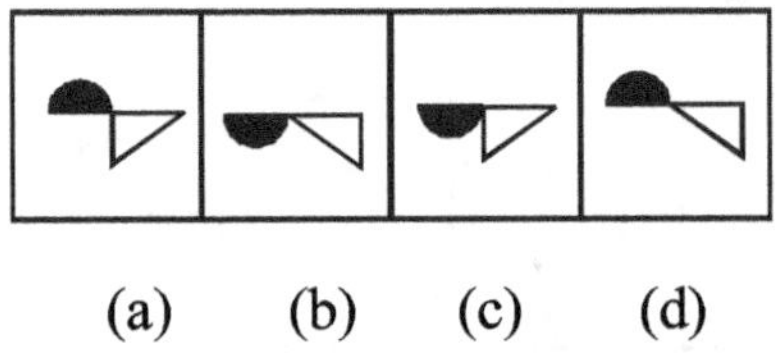

(a) (b) (c) (d)

***Sol.* (c)** (B) contains the lower half of (A). Answer figure (c) replaces the question mark.

ILLUSTRATION 7 :

is to as is to

(a) 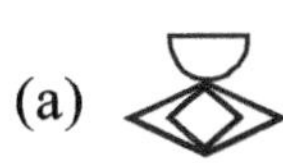 (b) 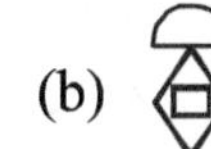

(c) 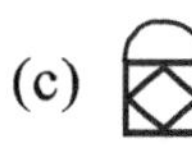 (d) 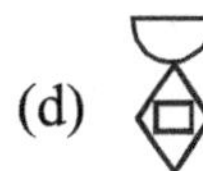

***Sol.* (d)** The diamond rotates 90°. The square goes inside the diamond. The semicircle rotates 180° and moves to the top.

ILLUSTRATION 8 :

Problem Figures

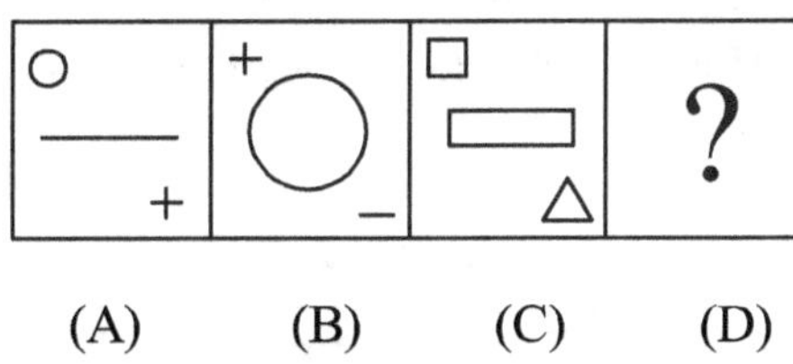

(A) (B) (C) (D)

Answer Figures

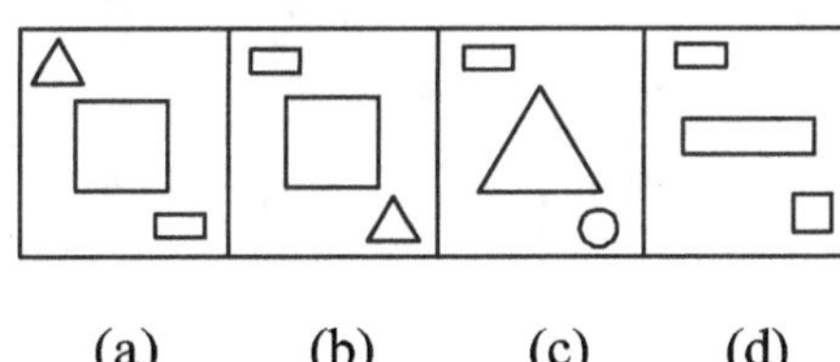

(a) (b) (c) (d)

***Sol.* (a)** The upper element gets enlarged and becomes the central element. The central element reduces in size and becomes the lower element. The lower element becomes the upper element.

ILLUSTRATION 9 :

Problem Figures

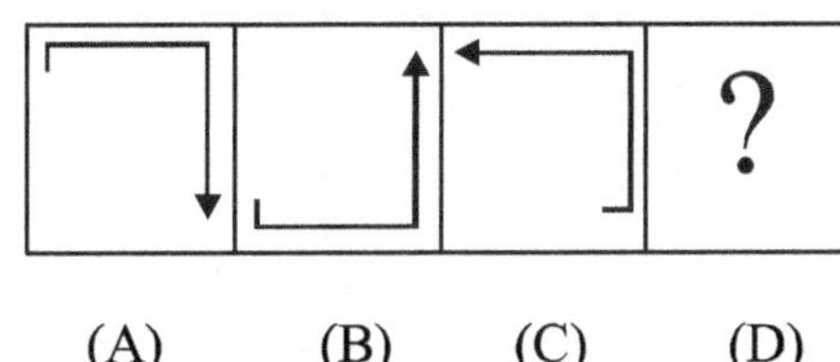

(A) (B) (C) (D)

Answer Figures

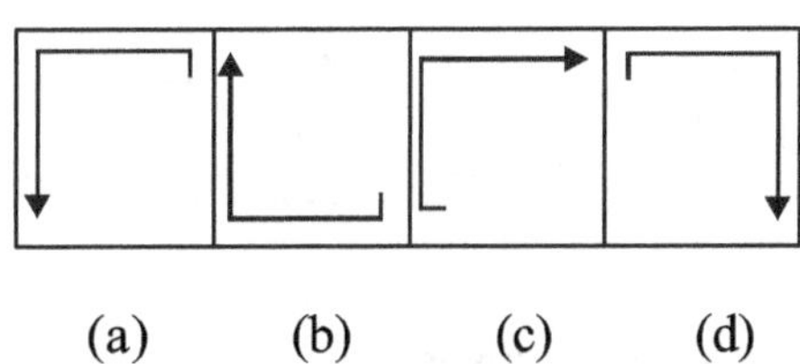

(a) (b) (c) (d)

***Sol.* (c)** The figure gets turned to the other side by rotating about the main line joining the arrow with the small line segment.

Directions (Qs. 1-2) : *In each of the following sets of figures, select the one that is different from the rest.*

1.    

(a) (b) (c) (d)

2.     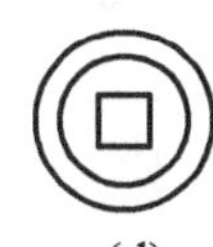

(a) (b) (c) (d)

Directions (Qs. 3-5) : *The second figure in the first unit of the Problem Figures bears a certain relationship to the first figure. Similarly, one of the figures in the Answer Figures bears the same relationship to the first figure in the second unit of the Problem Figures. Locate the figure which would fit the question mark.*

3. **Problem Figures**

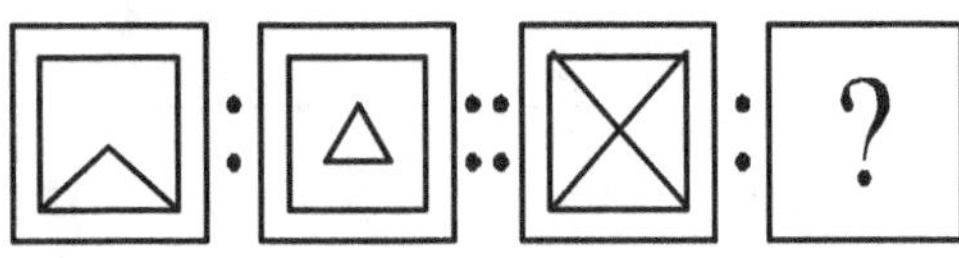

Answer Figures

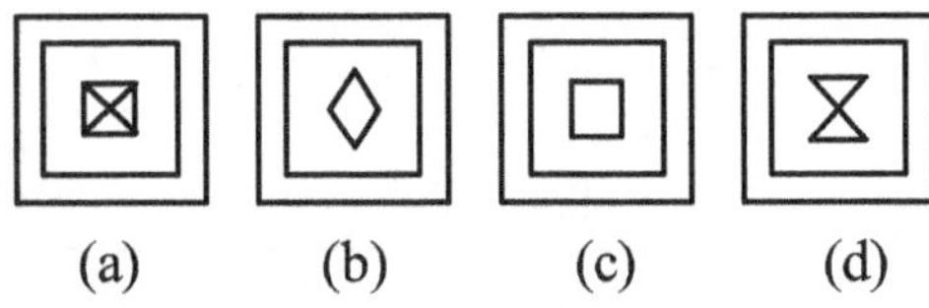

(a) (b) (c) (d)

4. **Problem Figures**

Answer Figures

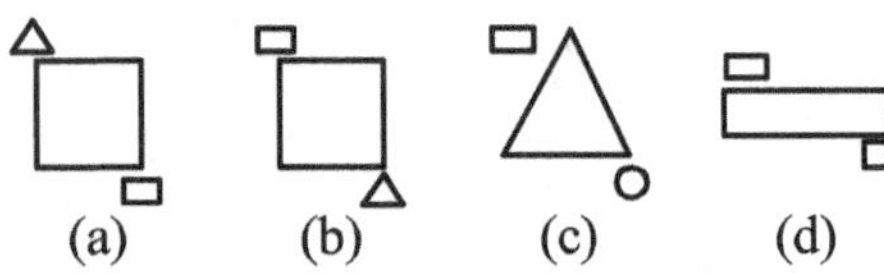

5. **Question Figures**

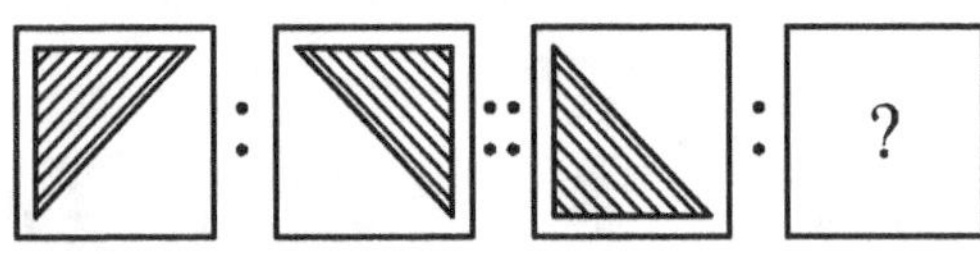

Answer Figures

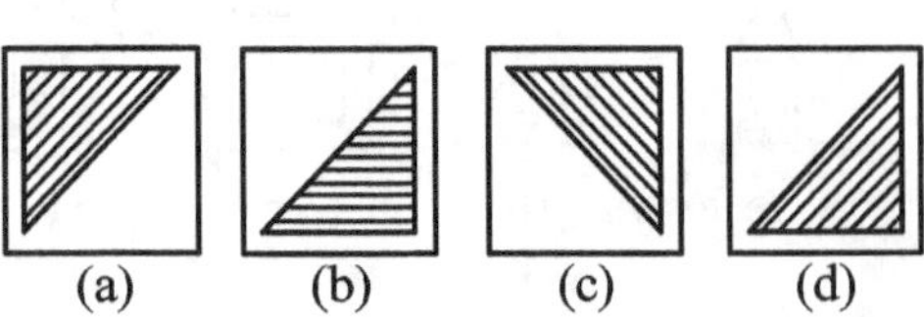

6. Select the odd one out.

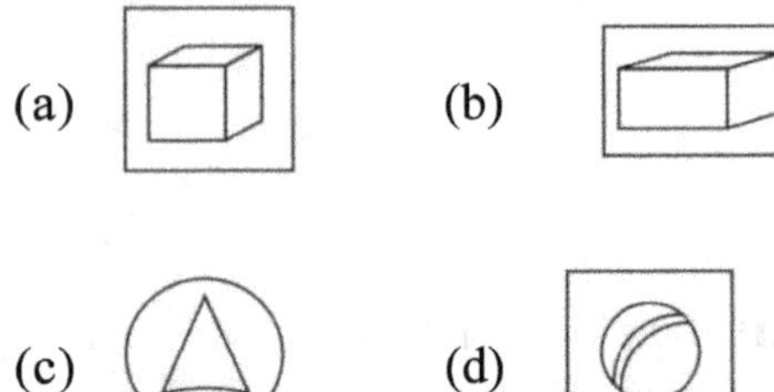

7. There is a certain relationship between figures (i) and (ii). Establish a similar relationship between figures (iii) and (iv) by selecting a suitable figure from the given options which will replace the (?) in figure (iv).

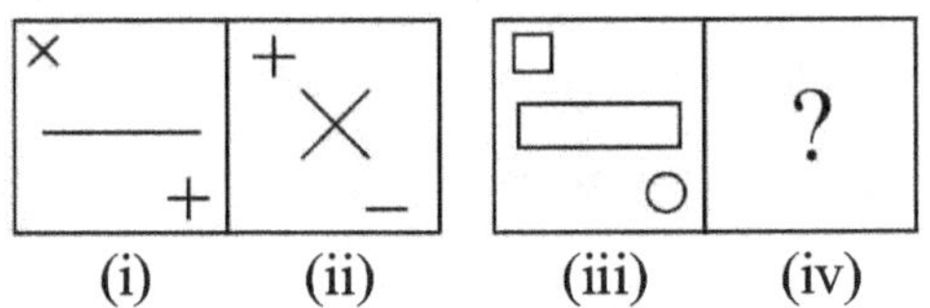

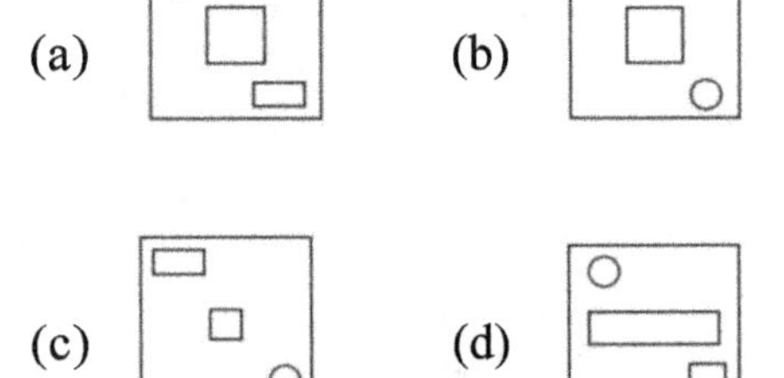

8. Find the odd one out.

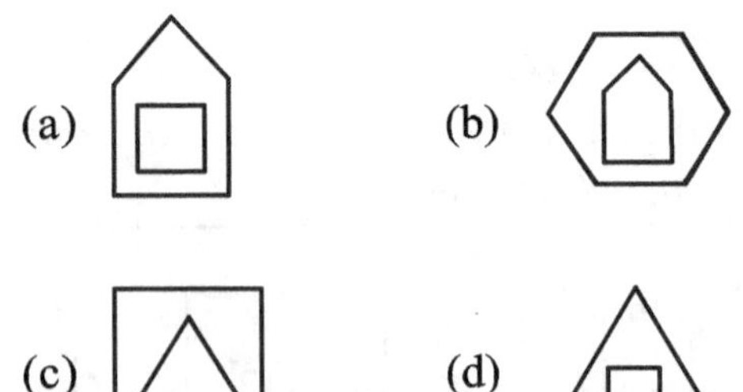

9. Select the odd one out.

(a) 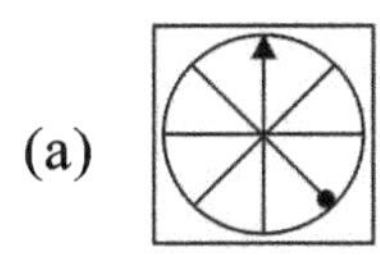
(b) 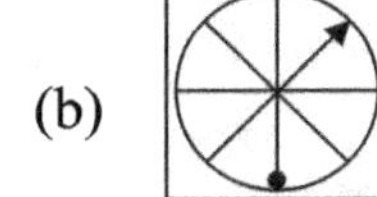

(c) 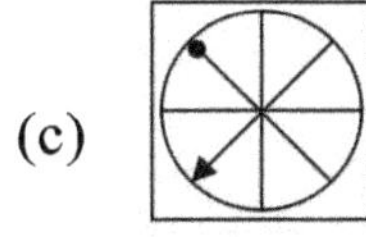
(d) 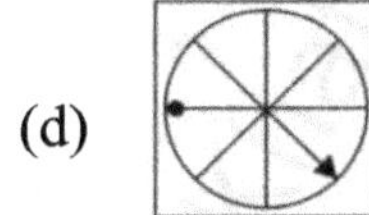

10. There is a certain relationship between figures (i) and (ii). Establish a similar relationship between figures (iii) and (iv) by selecting a suitable figure from the options which will replace the '?' in figure (iv).

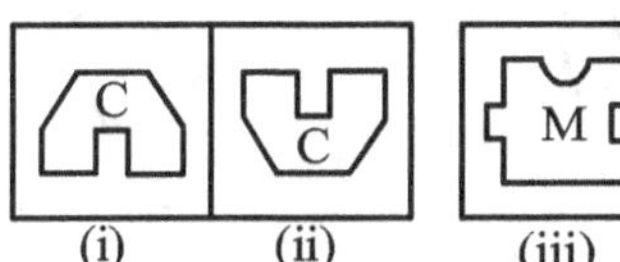
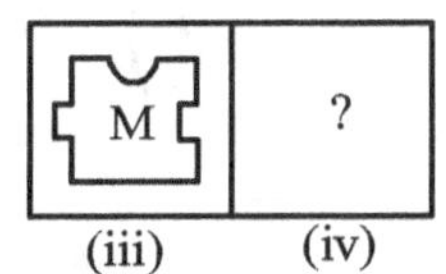

(i) (ii) (iii) (iv)

(a) 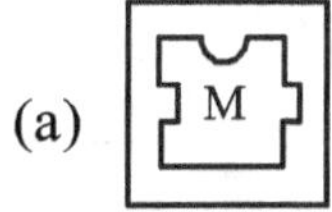
(b) 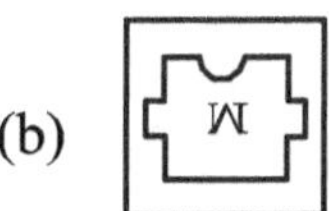

(c) 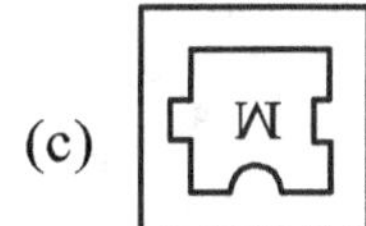
(d) 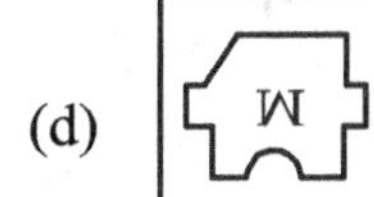

11. There is a certain relationship between the figures (i) and (ii). Establish the same relationship between figures (iii) and (iv) by selecting a suitable figure from the given options which will replace the (?) in fig. (iv). **[2018]**

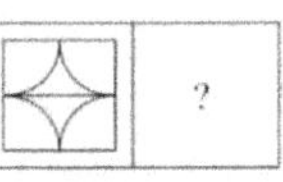

(i) (ii) (iii) (iv)

(a) 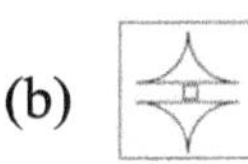
(b)

(c)
(d)

12. There is a certain relationship between the figures (i) and (ii). Establish the same relationship between the figures (iii) and (iv) by selecting a suitable figure from the options which will replace the (?) in figure (iv). **[2018]**

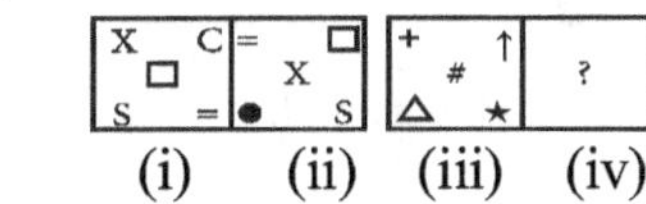

(i) (ii) (iii) (iv)

(a)
(b)

(c)
(d)

LEVEL 2

DIRECTIONS (Qs. 1-3) : *In the following questions, four items (figures, letter clusters or numbers) are given. Three of them are alike in a certain way. Find the one which is different from others.*

1. 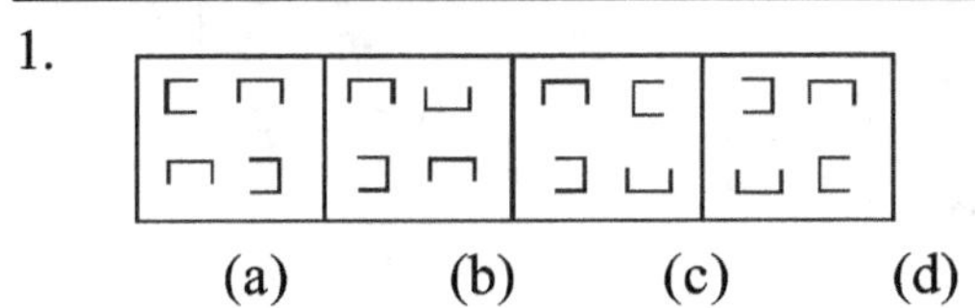

(a) (b) (c) (d)

2.

(a) (b) (c) (d)

3. 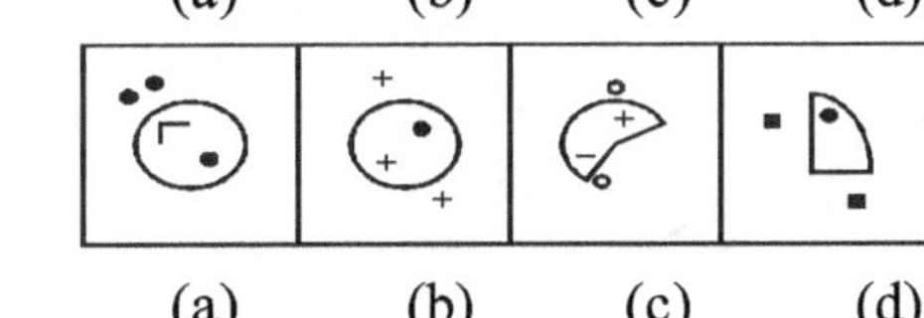

(a) (b) (c) (d)

4. Choose the figure which is different from the rest.

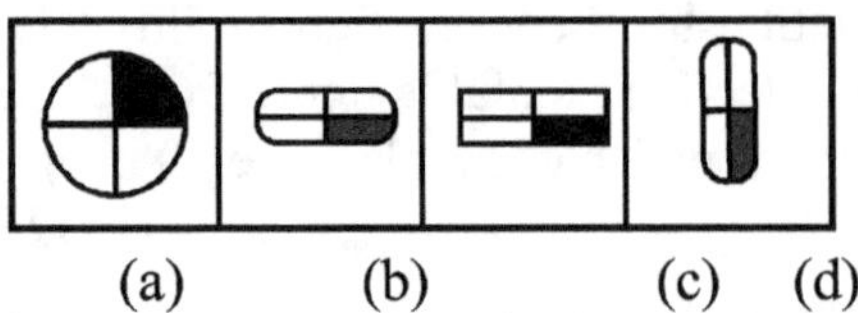

(a) (b) (c) (d)

DIRECTIONS (Qs. 5 & 6) : *In the following questions, find the one that does not fit in the sequence established by the six figures given.*

5.

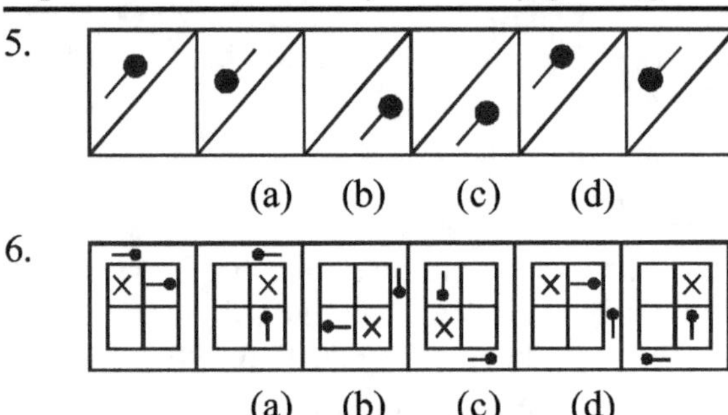

(a) (b) (c) (d)

6.

(a) (b) (c) (d)

7. Choose the figure which is different from the rest.

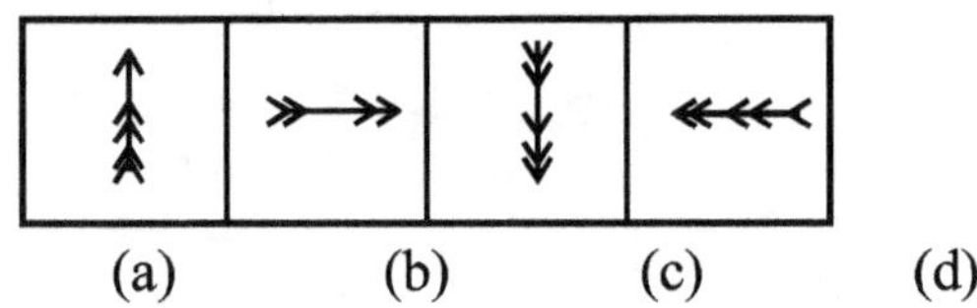

(a) (b) (c) (d)

8. Choose the figure which is different from the rest.

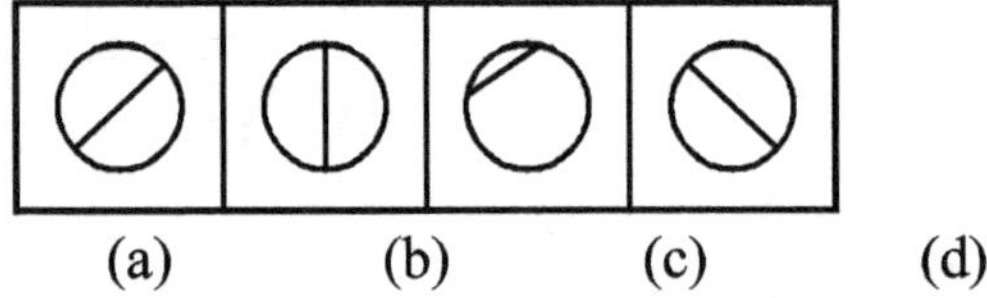

(a) (b) (c) (d)

DIRECTIONS (Qs. 9 – 11) : Find the odd figure out.

9. (a)

(b)

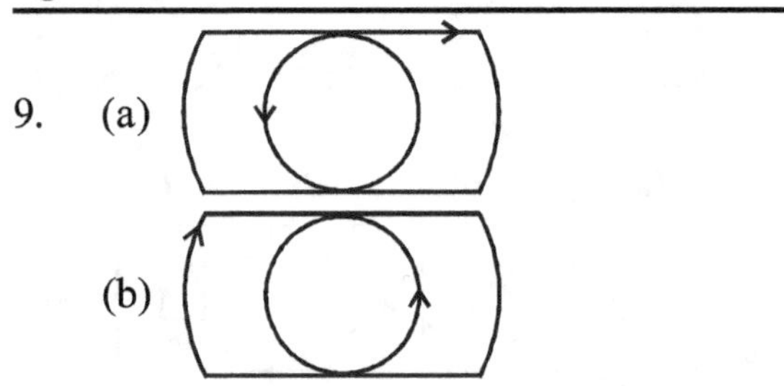

(c)

(d)

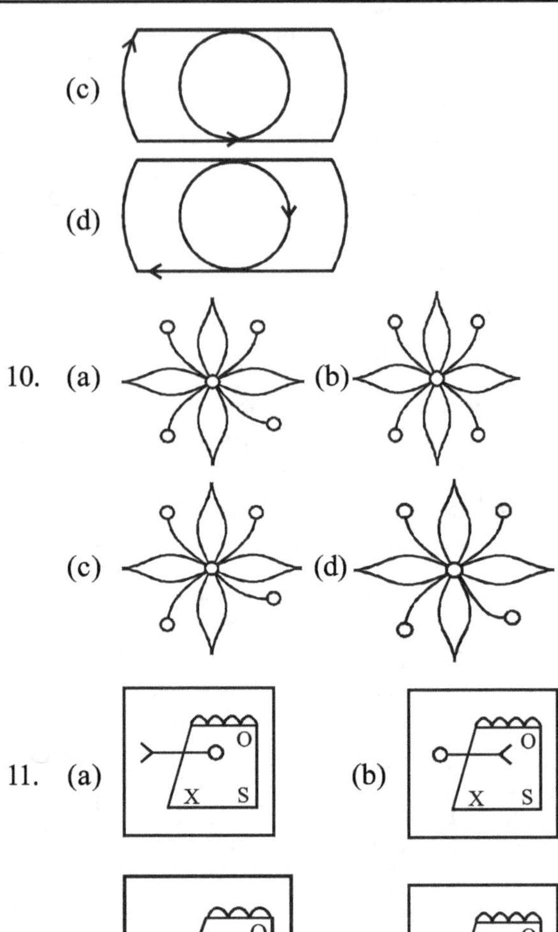

10. (a) (b)

(c) (d)

11. (a) (b)

(c) (d)

12. If 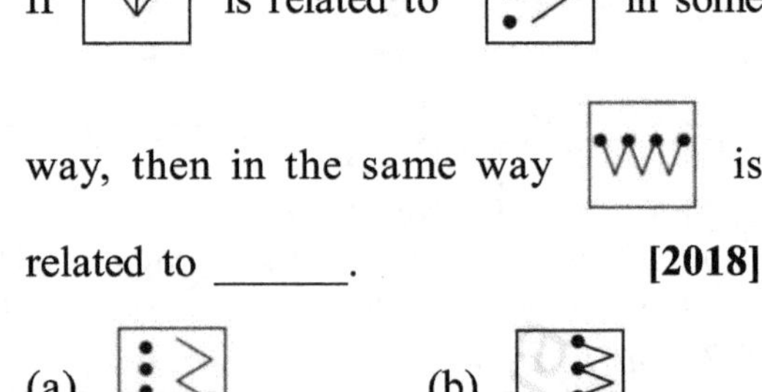 is related to in some way, then in the same way is related to ______. **[2018]**

(a) (b)

(c) (d)

13. There is a certain relationship between figures (i) and (ii). Establish the similar relationship between figures (iii) and (iv) by selecting a suitable figure from the given options which will replace the (?) in Fig. (iv).

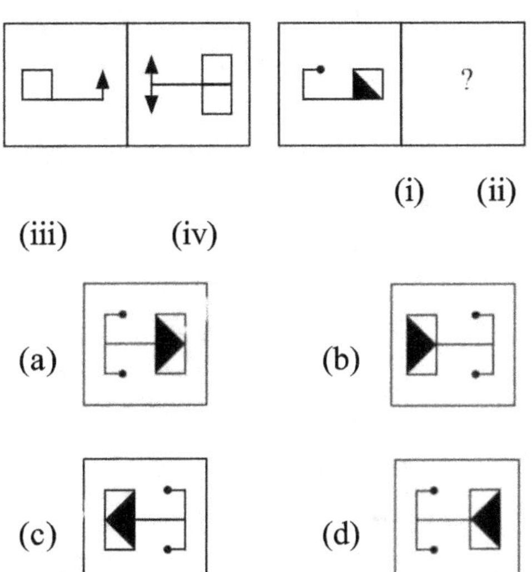

14. There is a certain relationship between figures (i) and (ii). Establish the similar relationship between figures (iii) and (iv) by selecting a suitable figure from the options which will replace the (?) in figure (iv).

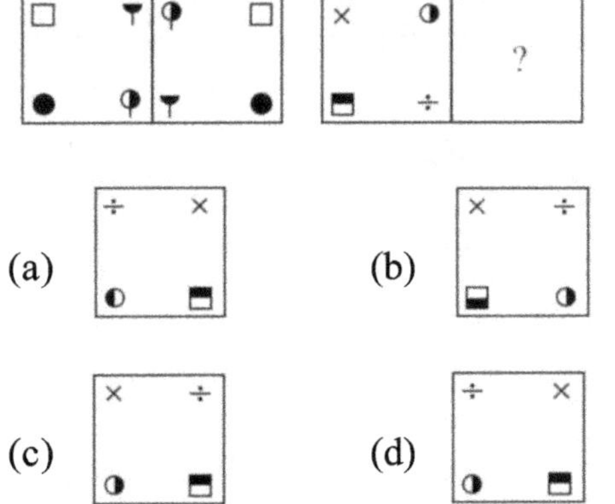

15. There is a certain relationship between figures (1) and (2). Establish the same relationship between the figures (3) and (4) by selecting a suitable figure from the options that would replace the (?) in figure (4). **[2018]**

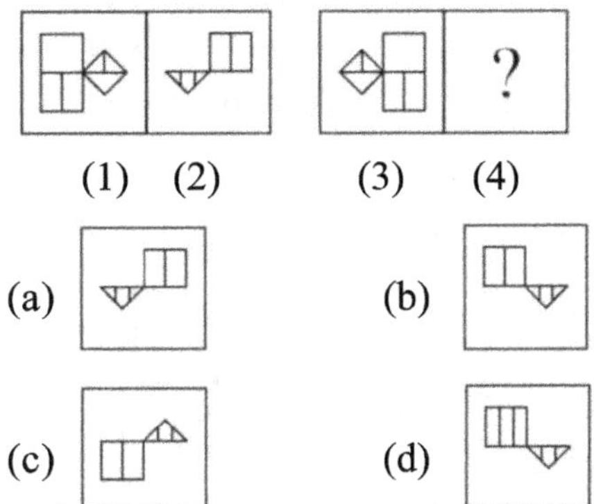

16. There is a certain relationship between figures (1) and (2). Establish the similar relationship between figures (3) and (4) by selecting a suitable figure from the options which will replace the (?) in Fig. (4). **[2019]**

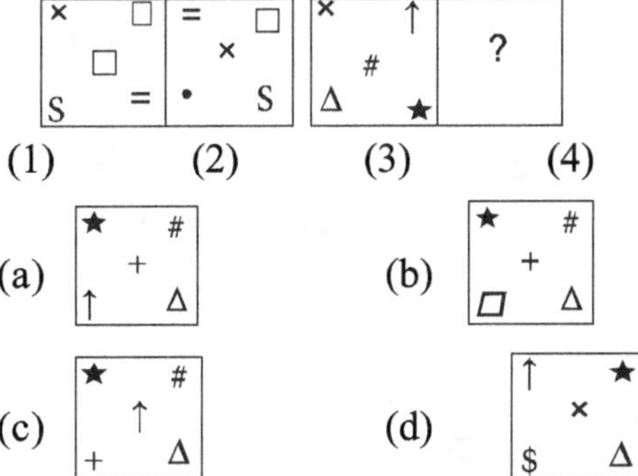

17. There is a certain relationship between figures (i) and (ii). Establish the similar relationship between figures (iii) and (iv) by selecting a suitable figure from the options which will replace the (?) in Fig. (iv). **[2019]**

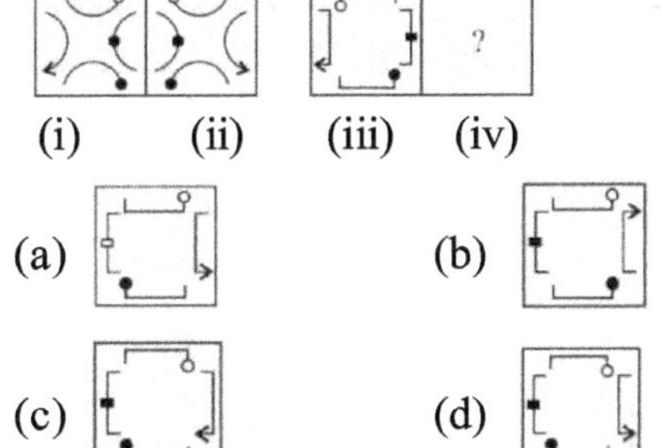

18. There is a certain relationship between figures (i) and (ii). Establish a similar relationship between figures (iii) and (iv) by selecting a suitable figure from the given options that would replace the (?) in fig. (iv). **[2021]**

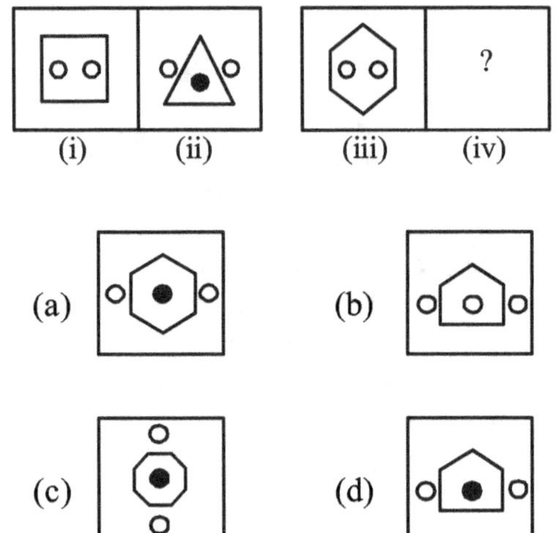

19. There is a certain relationship between the pair of figures on either side of ::. Identify the relationship between the given pair and find the missing figure. **[2021]**

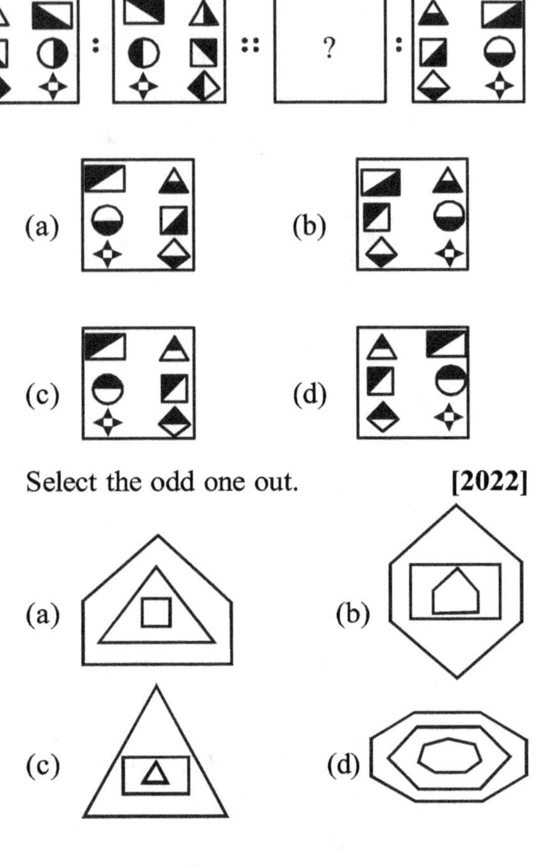

20. Select the odd one out. **[2022]**

(a) (b) (c) (d)

ANSWER KEY																			
LEVEL-1																			
1	(a)	**2**	(a)	**3**	(d)	**4**	(a)	**5**	(d)	**6**	(d)	**7**	(a)	**8**	(d)	**9**	(c)	**10**	(c)
11	(d)	**12**	(b)																
LEVEL-2																			
1	(b)	**2**	(a)	**3**	(c)	**4**	(a)	**5**	(c)	**6**	(d)	**7**	(b)	**8**	(c)	**9**	(d)	**10**	(b)
11	(c)	**12**	(c)	**13**	(a)	**14**	(d)	**15**	(b)	**16**	(b)	**17**	(d)	**18**	(d)	**19**	(c)	**20**	(c)

HINTS & EXPLANATIONS

CHAPTER-1

LEVEL 1

1. **(a)** Except (a) all are natural disaster. Seismograph is an instrument used to measure earthquakes by scientists.
2. **(a)** Except (a) rest of all are divisible by 3.
3. **(c)** **4. (c)**
5. **(c)** The logic is $x : \frac{x^2}{2}$.
6. **(b)** Sum of the digits of the first number is 2 more than the sum of the digits of the second number.
7. **(d)** The logic is $x^3 : (x + 1)^3 + 1$
8. **(c)** 'Oxygen' helps in burning while 'carbon dioxide' extinguishes fire.
9. **(b)** As Major heads a battalion, the Colonel commands a regiment.
10. **(c)** Whisper is of lesser intense than shouting, so is walking to running.
11. **(d)** Each letter of JKLM stands for each corresponding letter of XYZA, 14 places before.
12. **(b)** $3 + 6 + 3 = 12$, sum of the digits $= 1 + 2 = 3$
    $4 + 8 + 9 = 21$, sum of the digits $= 2 + 1 = 3$
    $5 + 7 + 9 = 21$, sum of the digits $= 2 + 1 = 3$
    $\Rightarrow$ $471 = 4 + 7 + 1 = 12$, sum of the digits
    $= 1 + 2 = 3$.
13. **(a)** In all the numbers, the sum of the digits is 12, and the largest digit lies in the middle.
14. **(b)** First digit of the given numbers 1, 2, 3, 4.
    Second digit of the given numbers are 3, 4, 5, 6.
    The last digit of the given numbers are 4, 6, 8, 0.
15. **(c)** In each set, 2nd number = 1st number + 7 3rd number = 2nd number + 9.
16. **(b)** Sum of the digits = 36.
17. **(d)** **18. (c)** **19. (a)** **20. (b)** **21. (c)**
22. **(a)** A successful finish of 'Education' equips one with 'Diploma'. Similary, a successful finish in 'Sports' equips one with 'Trophy'.
23. **(c)** Jewellery consists of Necklace ie 'Necklace' is a kind of 'Jewellery'. Similarly, 'Shirt' is a kind of 'Apparel'.
24. **(b)** Here, the first is the working place of the second.
25. **(b)** Uncle and Aunt are opposite words, similarly Cock is opposite to Hen.
26. **(d)** Table is made of wood, like that Coat is made of cloth.
27. **(b)** (Boy - Girl) are opposite pair word like that (Nephew - Neice) are opposite Pair word.
28. **(d)** Physicist deals with the subject Physics and biologist with subject anatomy.

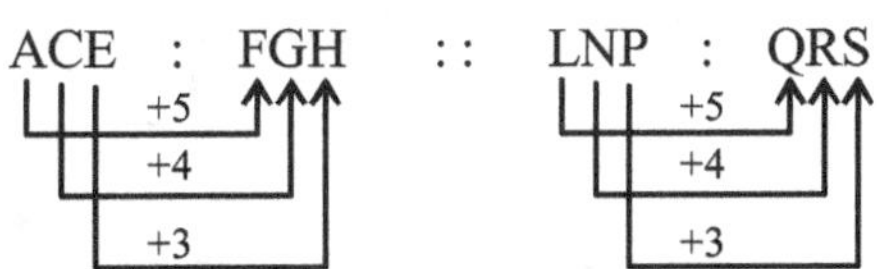

29. **(c)** The related words are near in meaning.
30. **(a)** The three letters are moved 5, 4 and 3 steps forward respectively.
31. **(d)** The word is divided into two sections and the letters are written backwards.

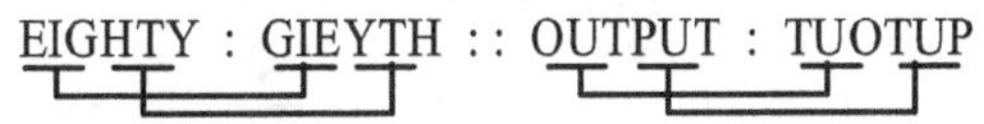

32. **(b)** The missing number is
    $(13)^2 = 169$
    $(17)^2 = 289$
33. **(c)**
34. **(c)** According to the question,
    12 : 168 :: 16 : ?
    As, $12 \times 14 = 168$
    So, $16 \times 14 = 224$

35. **(b)** **36.** **(c)** **37.** **(a)** **38.** **(a)** **39.** **(d)**

40. **(d)** Except option (d), all other options are divisible by 5

41. **(c)** 14 : 72
14 × 5 + 2 = 72
? : 82
? × 5 + 2 = 82
? = 80/5
? = 16

42. **(c)**

R (18)	+2	T (20)	+3	W (23)
K (11)	+2	M (13)	+3	P (16)
A (1)	+2	C (3)	+2	E (5)
Q (17)	+2	S (19)	+3	V

43. **(c)** $\frac{3\times4\times6}{9}=\frac{72}{9}=8$

Similarly

$\frac{5\times9\times2}{9}=\frac{90}{9}=10$

44. **(c)**

−1
+1
L N Q : M O P
+1

Similarly

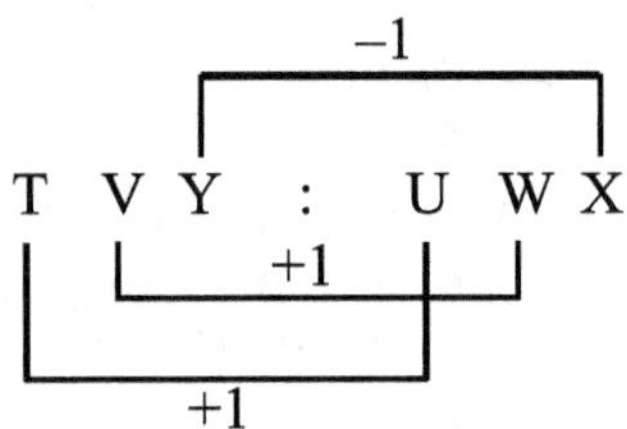

45. **(d)**

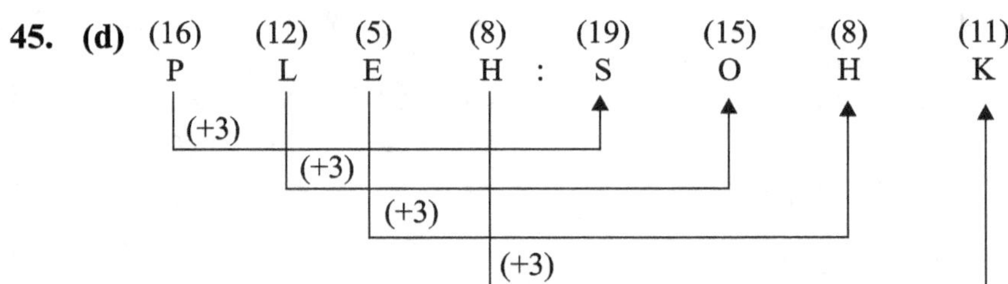

Similarly

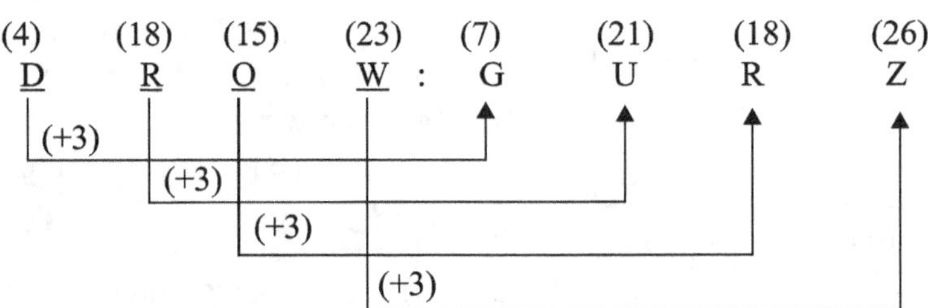

46. **(d)**

LEVEL 2

1. **(c)** All except Astrology are concerned with biology.
2. **(c)** Name of colours are writer in reverse order except (d).
3. **(d)** Ally is Antonym of Remaining three.
4. **(d)** Only FQMV is without any Vowel

5. **(d)** Difference between 36 – 48, 56 – 44 and 78 – 64 is 12 where as 33 – 64 is different.

6. **(d)** Except (d), all others belong to the period of before sunset.

7. **(b)** Except (b), all others are principles of society.

8. **(a)** Option (b): E V H S (– 3, + 3)

Option (c): H S K P

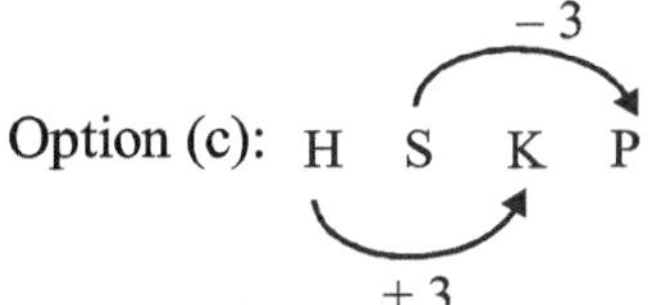

Option (d): K Q N N

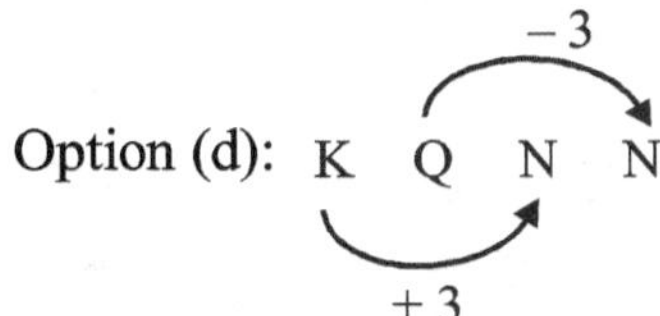

Option (a): D W F U (– 2, + 2)

Hence, option (a) is the group of odd letters.

9. **(d)** Option (a):

$C \xrightarrow{-1} B \xrightarrow{+3} E \xrightarrow{+1} F$

Option (b):

$E \xrightarrow{-1} D \xrightarrow{+3} G \xrightarrow{+1} H$

Option (c):

$I \xrightarrow{-1} H \xrightarrow{+3} K \xrightarrow{+1} L$

Option (d):

$G \xrightarrow{-1} F \xrightarrow{+1} H \xrightarrow{+1} J$

Hence, option (d) is the odd group of letters.

10. **(d)** $4+0+2+5=11$
$6+0+2+3=11$
$7+2+0+2=11$
$5+0+6+1=12$
Hence, (d) is the odd one out.

11. **(a)** 64 : 48
$\downarrow$ $\downarrow$
(8×8) (8×6)

80 : 60
$\downarrow$ $\downarrow$
(10×8) (10×6)

104 : 78
$\downarrow$ $\downarrow$
(13×8) (13×6)

Hence, option (a) is odd one out

12. **(c)** Except Deimos (It is a satellite), All others are Star systems.

13. **(c)** except (c) left side is the study of the right side.

14. (c) Except, XYZ, All others are opposite alphabetical sequence.

15. (b) 1919 Þ $1+9+1+9=20$
5656 Þ $5+6+5+6=22$
6761 Þ $6+7+6+1=20$
7760 Þ $7+7+6+0=20$
Except 5656, Sum of all digit of number is equal to 20.

16. (a) Except 2890, All are cube of a number. $(15)^3 = 3375$, $(12)^3 = 1728$, $(11)^3 = 1331$.

17. **(c)** The sequence of alphabets in each group is in reverse order (–1). Only option (3) has sequence in disturbed order, i.e.,

T S R; L K J P Q O; H G F
–1 –1   –1 –1   +1, –1   –1 –1

18. **(d)** In other groups, only the alphabet in the centre is in lower case. In option (d) letter 'L' on the left is in lower case.

but, G H
$\downarrow$ $\downarrow$
$7 + 8 = 15 \times 2 = 30 \neq 24$

19. (d) $25 = 5 \times 5$; $51 = 3 \times 17$; $96 = 6 \times 16$

$\boxed{75} \neq 5 \times 25$

125

20. (b) As,

E F

↓ ↓

(positonal value)

$5 + 6 = 11 \times 2 = 22$

J K

↓ ↓

$10 + 11 = 21 \times 2 = 42$

V W

↓ ↓

$22 + 23 = 45 \times 2 = 90$ and

I J

↓ ↓

$9 + 10 = 19 \times 2 = 38$

21. (c) (a)

–1

M G D L F C

13 7 4 12 6 3

–1 –1

(b)

–1

J Q V I P U

10 17 22 9 16 21

–1 –1

(c)

–1

Z U B X T A

26 21 2 24 20 1

–2 –1

(d)

–1

D Y S C X R

4 25 19 3 24 18

–1 –1

22. (d) All the groups contain 5 continuous letters arranged in a different way. Only (d) is different as there is a gap of 'U' between 'T' and 'V'.

23. (b) pQr follows Mno in sequence.

24. (c) 3rd and 4th terms are sums of digits of Ist and 2nd terms.

25. (c) Similarly placed letters on either side of : : show the same pattern such as (WX, YZ) and (JK, LM).

26. (a) The first and third letters are moved two and three step backwards respectively and the second letter three steps forward.

27. (c) In each set of letters, the 1st and 3rd letters are consecutive.

CJDL : FMGR :: IKJR : LSMT

28. (a) If A corresponds to X (the third from the end) then B should correspond to the fourth letter W.

29. (b) Because KLM are assigned No. 11, 12 & 13 from A onwards, this corresponds to PON, which are also numbered 11, 12 and 13 from Z to A in reverse order. Hence NOP will correspond to MLK.

30. (b)

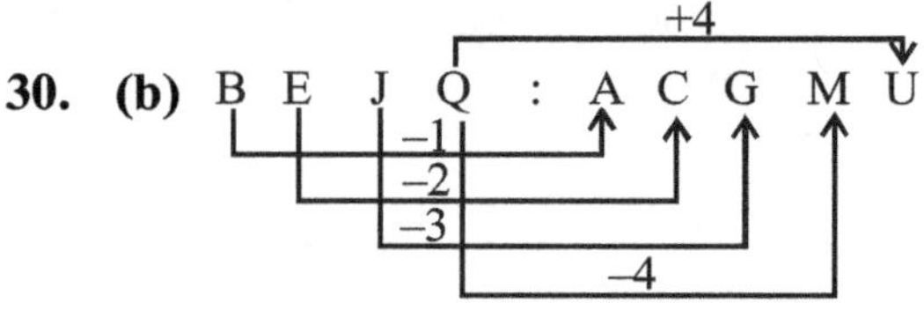

Similarly,

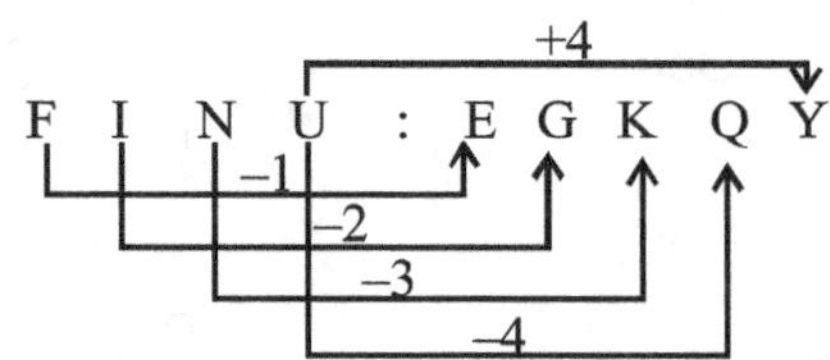

31. (c) B D G K : O K H F

+2 +3 +4 −4 −3 −2

Similarly,

K M P T : X T Q O

+2 +3 +4 −4 −3 −2

32. (d) As, guitar is for music. Similarly, book is for knowledge.

So in option (3) both are synonyms

33. (d) 34. (b) 35. (a) 36. (c) 37. (b)

38. (c) India, Pakistan & Bangladesh are countries of Indian sub-continent and Iran, Iraq and Kuwait are the countries of the Arabian sub-continent.

39. (c) Second follows the first and third follows the second.

40. (b)

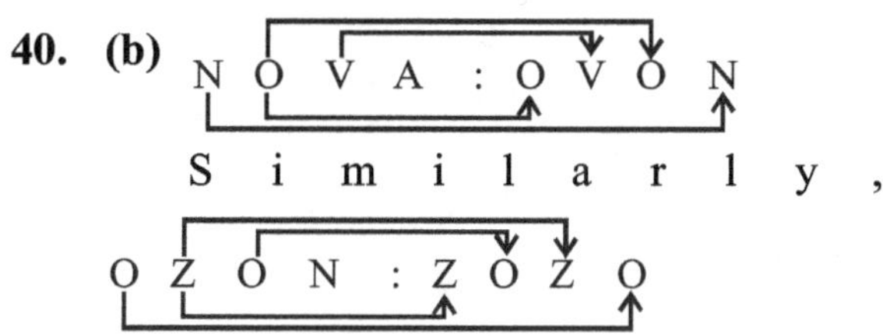

41. (a) B E K C

+3 −1 −4 +3

E D B F

Similarly, V Y Z W

+3 −1 −4 +3

Y X V Z

42. (c) Both the words are based on the fact. Like Famini means extreme hunger while war means destruction.

43. (c) Both are synonyms

44. (a) As,

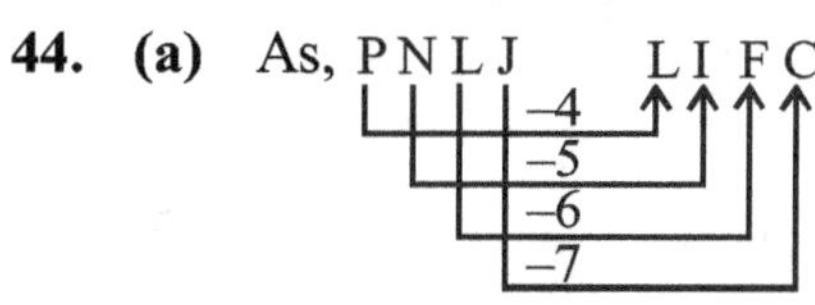

Similarly,

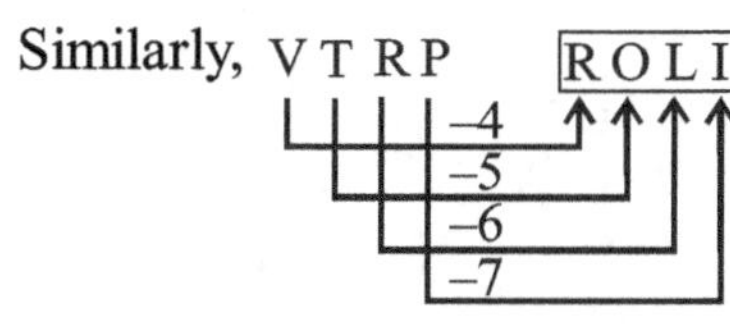

45. (a)

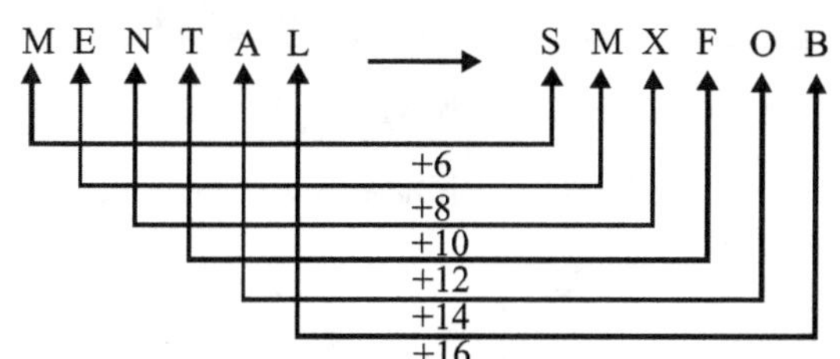

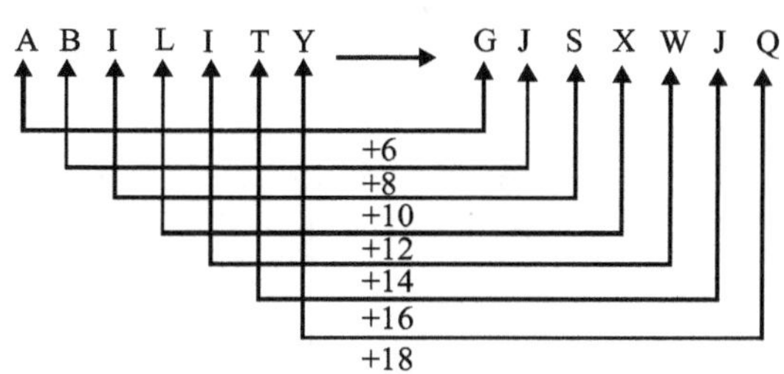

Option 1 is correct.

46. (a)

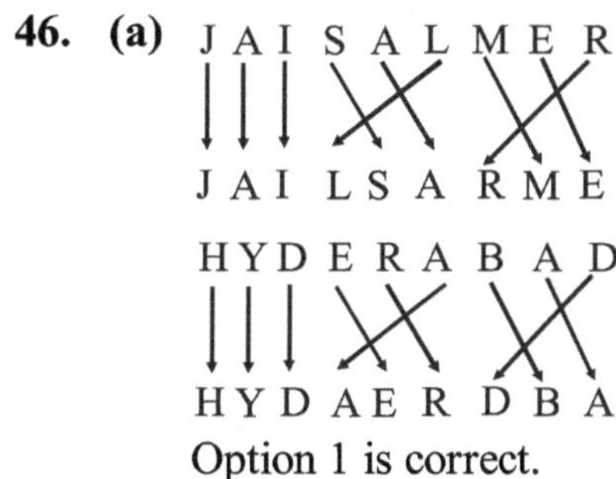

Option 1 is correct.

47. (c) .

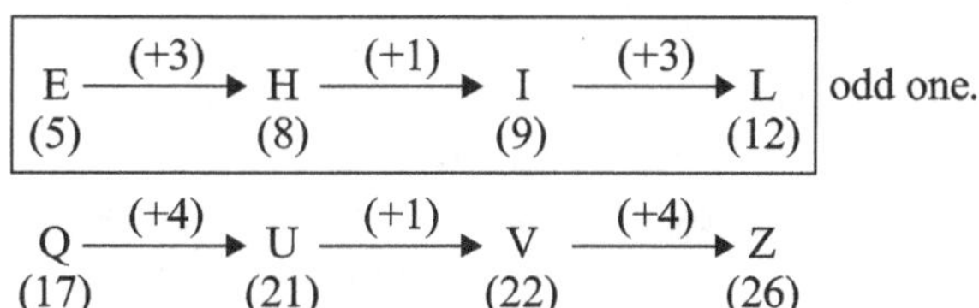

48. (c) $8:56::9:\boxed{72}$

$8\times(8-1)=56$

Similarly

$9\times(9-1)=72$

49. (c) 50. (d)

CHAPTER-2

LEVEL 1

1. **(c)** Type – Alphanumeric coding.

Word ⟶	V	I	S	H	A	L
Value in ⟶ alphabet series	22	9	19	8	1	12
		+1	+2	+3	+4	+5
Code	22	10	21	11	5	17

similarly, for the word	S	A	C	H	I	N
	19	1	3	8	9	14
		+1	+2	+3	+4	+5
Final code	19	2	5	11	13	19

Thus code is 1925111319, option (c).

2. **(b)** Direct Substitution.
3. **(c)** Direct Substitution.
4. **(c)** Type – Alphanumeric coding.

Word ⟶	V	I	S	H	A	L
Value in ⟶ alphabet series	22	9	19	8	1	12
		+1	+2	+3	+4	+5
Code	22	10	21	11	5	17

similarly, for the word	S	A	C	H	I	N
	19	1	3	8	9	14
		+1	+2	+3	+4	+5
Final code	19	2	5	11	13	19

Thus code is 1925111319, option (c).

5. **(b)** Direct Substitution.
6. **(c)** Direct Substitution.
7. **(a)** The first, second, third, fourth & fifth letters in the word are respectively one, two, three, four and five steps ahead of the corresponding letter of the code. Hence, answer is MMXQG.

Sol. (8-11)

The code is that A is substituted by Z, B is substituted by Y, C is substituted by X and so on. (This is also known as mirror coding.)

A B C D E F -------- U V W X Y Z.

Z Y X W V U -------- F E D C B A.

8. **(a)** LIMIT.
9. **(b)** MAXIMUM.
10. **(a)** MINIMUM
11. **(d)** CHAPEL.
12. **(*)** how can you go → Jede ke ...(i)

you come here → ne ke se ...(ii)

come and go → re pe se ...(iii)

The code for the word here is "ne".

13. **(a)** The code for 62830 will be written as HATCB
14. **(a)** 'BHICK' will be coded as 06734.

From (ii) here → ne

15. **(a)** From given statements :–

Blue → 2

Sky → 1

Was → 3

People → 8

Like → 0

In→ 0

Bird → 9

'People like birds' → 809

16. **(d)**

P	A	P	E	R
(16)	(1)	(16)	(5)	(18)
–1	–1	–1	–1	–1
O	Z	O	D	Q
(15)	(26)	(15)	(4)	(17)

Similarly

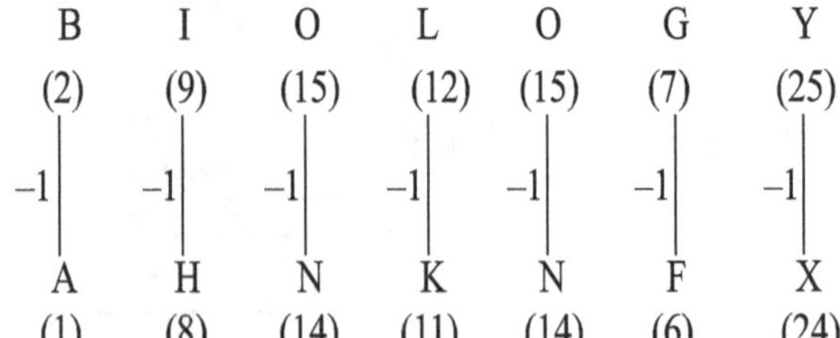

17. (a)

A	C	N	E
(1)	(3)	(14)	(5)
+2	+2	+2	+2
3	5	16	7

Similarly

P	A	I	R
(16)	(1)	(9)	(18)
+2	+2	+2	+2
18	3	11	20

18. (a) Men [are] very busy – 1 [2] 3 4

busy persons need (encouragement) – 4 (5) 6 7

(encouragement) is very important – 3 (5) 8 9

important persons [are] rare – [6] 8 0

'5' is the code for 'encouragement'.

19. (b)

LEVEL 2

1. (b) [Car is] Good → [1] 4 [5]

[Car is] Previous → [1 5] 9

From these statements, Good is coded as '4'.

2. (b) Amit's code = 8 Precious's Code = 9

Wants's code = 3 Scooter's code = 6

Amit Wants Precious Scooter = 8 3 9 6

3. (b) Extreme comes at middle while middle comes at the extreme. Hence, UMU is the correct answer.

4. (c) According to the given coding language:

(S) T [A] T → θ δ θ (γ) ...(i)

R [A] T → [δ] θ β ...(ii)

(S) [A] Y → ε (γ) [δ] ...(iii)

From the above coding language,

→ T is common in (i) and (ii), and the code for T is θ

→ A is common in (ii) and (iii), and the code for A is δ.

→ S is common in (i) and (iii), and the code for S is γ.

So, T → θ

R → β

A → δ

Y → ε

Therefore, from the given options, only option (3) is correct answer.

5. (d) A F R A I D

↓ ↓ ↓ ↓ ↓ ↓

O Y W O T I

6. (b) B U L L E T

↓ ↓ ↓ ↓ ↓ ↓

Z A M M X I

7. (c) Following the examples given, the code for SUGAR should be a combination of the following symbols <•, •], [•, _| and ∧ either in the same order or jumbled up.

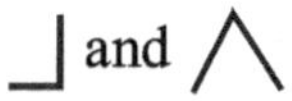

As S = <•, U = •], G = [•, A = _| and R = ∧.

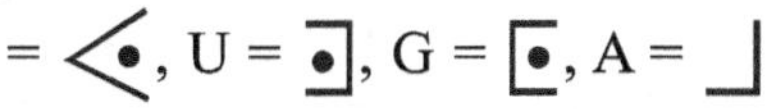

8. (a) Similarly, S P I C E is coded as <• •>⊓L⌉

9. (b) Similarly PATCH is coded as •>⌋□L<

10. (c)

S	T	U	D	E	N	T
–1	–1	–1	+1	–1	–1	
R	S	T	E	D	M	S

T	E	A	C	H	E	R
–1	–1	–1	+1	–1	–1	–1
S	D	Z	D	G	D	Q

11. (d)

12. (b) F A S T
6 1 19 20
Therefore, $6^2 + 1^2 + 19^2 + 20^2 = 798$
Also,
L A S T
12 1 19 20
Threrefore, $12^2 + 1^2 + 19^2 + 20^2 = 906$
So,
B U S Y
2 21 19 25
Therefore, $2^2 + 21^2 + 19^2 + 25^2 = 1431$

13. (c)

14. (b)

15. (d) @ # * # @ $ % & therefore, option (4) is correct.

16. (c)

17. (a) A s ,

I	M	P	H	A	L
+1 ↓	–1 ↓	+2 ↓	–2 ↓	+3 ↓	–3 ↓
J	L	R	F	D	I

Similarly,

M	Y	S	U	R	U
+1 ↓	–1 ↓	+2 ↓	–2 ↓	+3 ↓	–3 ↓
N	X	U	S	U	R

18. (d) S T A R = 50
19 20 1 18
Subtracting numbers from 27, we get (27 – 19), (27 – 1), (27 – 18) and now adding them, we get
$8 + 7 + 26 + 9 = 50$
Similary for CIRCUS we get = 65
∵ For P L A N E T
16 12 1 14 5 20
⇒ (27 –16) + (27 –12) + (27 – 1) + (27 – 14)
+ (27 – 5) + (27 – 20) = 94
Hence, option (d) is correct.

19. (b) Busy bees → Cpu (↑ Capital) Cff (↑ small)
Busy Crow → Cpu (↑ small) hup (↑ small)
Bright Crows → CSJ (↑ capital) HVP (↑ capital)

Busy crows are cleaves
From options → 3 & 4 → Eiminated becaused code for Busy' is either " CPu" or "Cff"
Similarly option → 1 → Eliminated becaused code for crows is either "CPu & HVp" option 2 is correct.

20. (b)

21. (b) TOME → @ $ * , ?
ARE → ! & ?
By direct comparision
REMOTE → & ? * $ @ ?

22. (b) As,

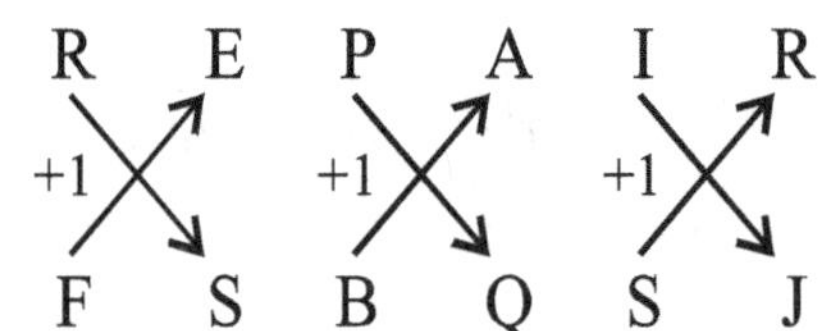

Similarly,

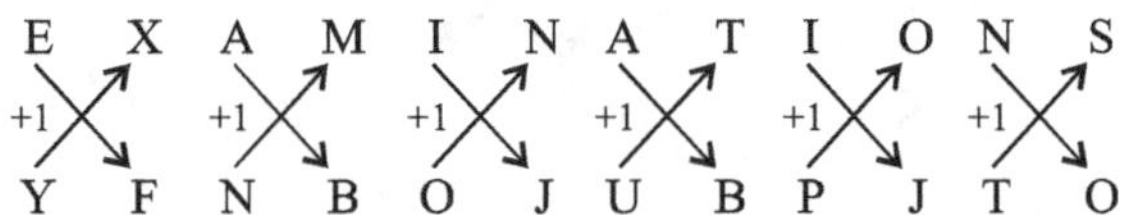

23. (b) 5 4 6 — you are best
5 3 8 — you can do
6 9 2 — all are good

'4' digit is written as 'best'.

24. (b) (cd + ef) × bc
⇒ (23 + 45) × 12
⇒ 68 × 12
⇒ 816

25. (c)

26. (b)

27. (c) 1 + 1 + 5 + 2 + 9 = 7 + 2 + 1 + 3 + 5
18 = 18
Similarly
1 + 5 + 2 + 9 + 4 + 3
= 2 + 1 + 3 + 5 + 4 + 9
24 = 24

28. (c) Whatelse can you do for me Mr. Ajay
1 2 3 4 5 6 7 8 9
you Mr what can Ajay else do me for
4 8 1 3 9 2 5 7 6
Similarly
anyone else who can do such favour to me
1 2 3 4 5 6 7 8 9

Can to anyone who me else do favour such
4 8 1 3 9 2 5 7 6

29. (d)

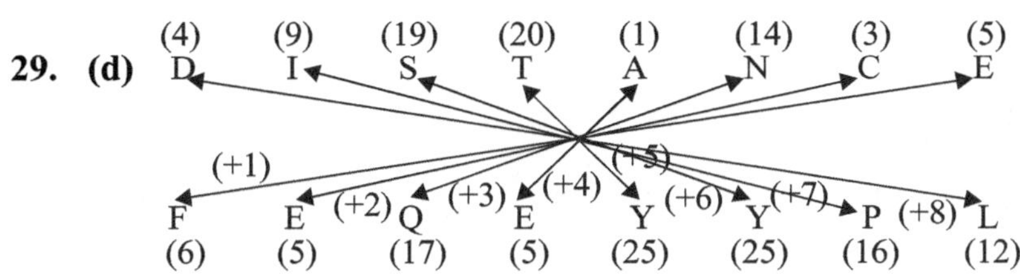

Similarly

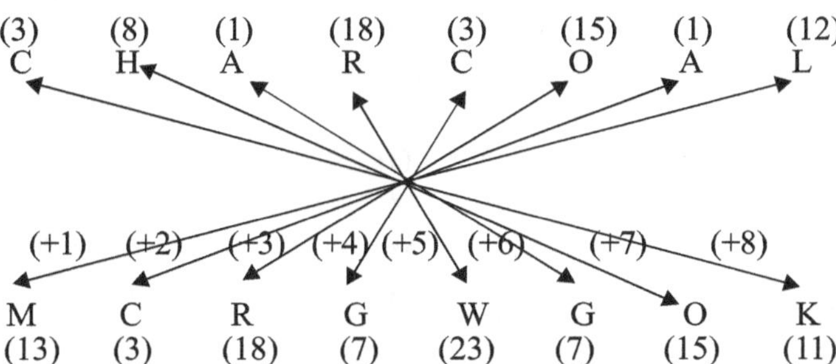

30. (c)

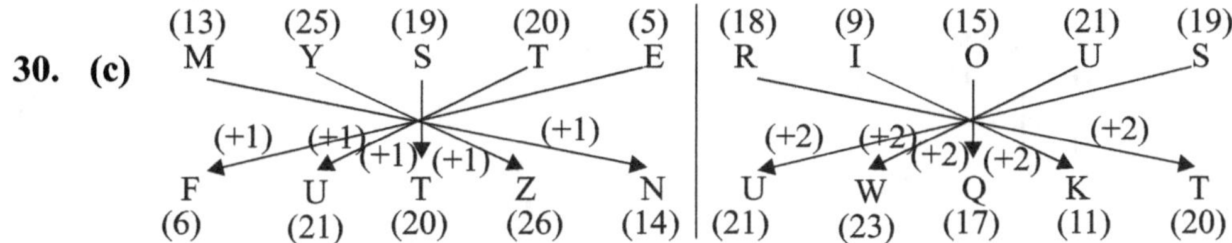

Similarly

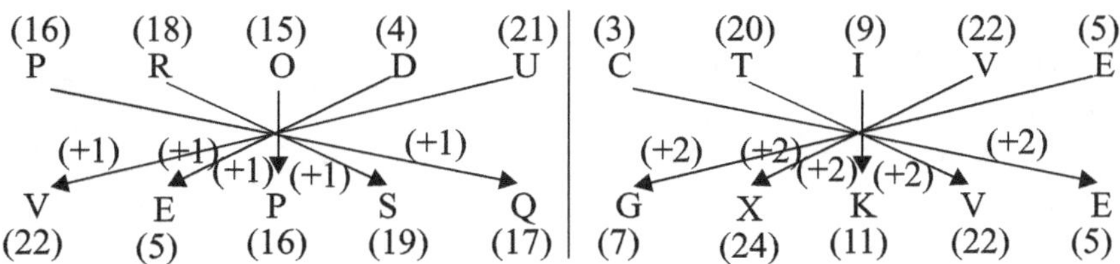

31. (d)

O	R	D	I	N	A	R	Y
(15)	(18)	(4)	(9)	(14)	(1)	(18)	(25)
+5	+5	+5	+5	–4	–4	–4	–4
T	W	I	N	J	W	N	U
(20)	(23)	(9)	(14)	(10)	(23)	(14)	(21)

Similarly

P	R	E	C	I	O	U	S
(16)	(18)	(5)	(3)	(9)	(15)	(21)	(19)
+5	+5	+5	+5	–4	–4	–4	–4
U	W	J	H	E	K	Q	O
(21)	(23)	(10)	(8)	(5)	(11)	(17)	(15)

32. (c)

(16)	(8)	(9)	(12)	(15)	(19)	(15)	(16)	(8)	(25)
P	H	I	L	O	S	O	P	H	Y
(+3)	(–2)	(+3)	(–2)	(+3)	(–2)	(+3)	(–2)	(+3)	(-2)
S	F	L	J	R	Q	R	N	K	W
(19)	(6)	(12)	(10)	(18)	(17)	(18)	(14)	(11)	(23)

Similarly,

(16)	(19)	(25)	(3)	(8)	(15)	(12)	(5)	(7)	(25)
P	S	Y	C	H	O	L	O	G	Y
(+3)	(–2)	(+3)	(–2)	(+3)	(–2)	(+3)	(–2)	(+3)	(-2)
S	Q	B	A	K	M	O	M	J	W
(19)	(17)	(2)	(1)	(11)	(13)	(15)	(13)	(10)	(23)

33. (c)

(4)	(5)	(6)	(5)	(14)	(19)	(9)	(22)	(5)
D	E	F	E	N	S	I	V	E
(+2)	(–2)	(+2)	(–2)	(+2)	(–2)	(+2)	(–2)	(+2)
F	C	H	C	F	Q	K	T	G
(6)	(3)	(8)	(3)	(16)	(17)	(11)	(20)	(7)

Similarly,

(16)	(18)	(15)	(20)	(5)	(3)	(20)	(5)	(4)
P	R	O	T	E	C	T	E	D
(+2)	(–2)	(+2)	(–2)	(+2)	(–2)	(+2)	(–2)	(+2)
R	P	Q	R	G	A	V	C	F
(18)	(16)	(17)	(18)	(7)	(1)	(22)	(3)	(6)

34. (c)

CHAPTER-3

LEVEL 1

1. **(b)** There is a gap of four letters between first and second, second and third letter of each term. Also there is a gap of 4 letters between the last letter of a term and the first letter of the next term.

2. **(d)** The first letters in odd numbered terms from the series J, I, H and in even numbered terms from the series K, L, M.

   The sequence followed by the numbers is +2, +3, +4, +5, +6. The third letter of each term is moved two steps backward to obtain the third letter of the next term.

3. **(d)** $3 = 2^2 - 1,$ $8 = 3^2 - 1:$

   $35 = 6^2 - 1,$ $48 = 7^2 - 1:$

   $? = 10^2 - 1,$ $120 = 11^2 - 1.$

4. **(a)** The sequence is $\times 2 - 1, \times 2 + 3, \times 2 - 5, \times 2 + 7, \times 2 - 9$ etc.

   The next number is $81 \times 2 - 9 = 153$.

5. **(b)**

   240 [240] 120 40 10 2

   ×1 ×2 ×3 ×4 ×5

6. **(d)** AABBCC/AABBCC/AABBCC

   Therefore the required missing letters are 'ACBA'

7. **(a)** CDBC/CDBC/CDBC/CDBC/CDBC

   Therefore the required missing letters are 'DBCD'

8. **(c)** Multiply each number in the series by 2, and then add '1' to get the next number, like $(16 \times 2 + 1) = 33$, $(33 \times 2 + 1) = 67$, and so on.

9. **(d)**

10. **(d)** The given sequence comprises of three sequences

    1, 4, 9, 16 (Square on 1, 2, 3, 4)
    2, 3, 5, 7 (Prime number series)
    10, 14, 18, 22 (Common difference 4)

    The missing number belongs to series number three, so it is 18.

11. **(a)** A careful look will show that there are two series of group of letters namely

    (i) ZYYZR, (?), XWABT
    (ii) ABVUM, BCUTL, CDTSK

    In the first series, Let us see the relations of letters in different positions.

Positions	Rule	(?)
I. Z ? X	1 letter backward	Y
II. Y ? W	1 letter backward	X
III. Y ? A	1 letter forward	Z
IV. Z ? B	– do –	A
V. R ? T	– do –	S

Hence the missing letter group is YXZAS i.e it is the answer.

12. **(a)** The sequence is consisting of two series. Z, W, T, Q,.......and S, O, K, G. The logic is three steps backward and four step backward respectively.

13. **(c)** There are three alternate series.

    A L W B M X C N Y

    Series I : ABC
    Series II : LMN
    Series III : WXY

14. **(a)** The sequence is $0^3 + 1, 1^3 + 1, 2^3 + 1, 3^3 + 1, 4^3 + 1, 5^3 + 1$ etc.

15. **(c)** This is a series of prime number

16. **(d)** Let x = 8

    then $15 = 2x - 1 = y$
    $28 = 2y - 2 = z$
    $53 = 2z - 3 = m$
    Next term in the pattern should be $2m - 4 = 2 \times 53 - 4 = 102$

17. (c) Note that $0 = 1^3 - 1$
$6 = 2^3 - 2$
$24 = 3^3 - 3$

18. (d) The terms exhibit the pattern $n^3 + 1$, n taking values 1, 2, 3.......

19. (b) Consider pairs of numbers:
24 : 6, 6 is one-fourth of 24 :
18 : 9, 9 is half of 18;
36 : 9, 9 is one fourth of 36

20. (b) The series is $\times 0.5 + 0.5, \times 1 + 1, \times 1.5 + 1.5$ .... Hence, 12 is wrong. It should be 14.

21. (b) The series is $+ 1^3, + 2^3, + 3^3, + 4^3$ ..... Hence, 229 is wrong. It should be 227.

22. (a) The series is $\times 2.5, \times 2$ alternately.

23. (c) $3^2 - 1 : 3^3 + 1 :: 4^2 - 1 : 4^3 + 1$
i.e. missing term is 15.

24. (a) The pattern of the series is as follows:

16 19 28 43 64 [91]
+3 +9 +15 +21 +27
+6 +6 +6 +6

25. (a) Explanation I : the sequence in the series is $\times 6, \div 3$ which is repeated .

8 48 16 96 32 192
×6 ÷3 ×6 ÷3 ×6

Explanation II : there are two alternate series and the numbers are multiplied by 2.

×2 ×2
8 48 16 96 32 192
×2 ×2

26. (b)

3 14 26 [44] 68 98
(+6) (+12) (+18) (+24) (+30)

27. (c)

3 8 15 24 35 48 [63]
+5 +7 +9 +11 +13 +15

28. (d)

21 25 33 49 81 [145]
+4 +8 +16 +32 +64

29. (c)

30. (c) Pattern of the series -

J $\xrightarrow{+2}$ L $\xrightarrow{+2}$ N $\xrightarrow{+2}$ P $\xrightarrow{+2}$ R
12 $\xrightarrow{+3}$ 15 $\xrightarrow{+3}$ 18 $\xrightarrow{+3}$ 21 $\xrightarrow{+3}$ 24
M $\xrightarrow{-2}$ K $\xrightarrow{-2}$ I $\xrightarrow{-2}$ G $\xrightarrow{-2}$ E

31. (c)

B	E	H
+1	+2	+3
C	G	K
+1	+2	+3
D	I	N
+1	+2	+3
E	K	Q
+1	+2	+3
F	M	T

32. (b)

33. (d)

34. (a)

5	6	8
6	9	10
121	?	324

Applying rule column wise
i.e in column 1
$5 + 6 = (11)^2 = 121$
In column 3
$8 + 10 = (18)^2 = 324$
Similarly
In column 2
$6 + 9 = (15)^2 = 225$
So ? = 225

35. (b) $(15 + 4) \times 3 = 57$
$(7 + 18) \times 5 = 125$
Similarly
$(12 + 20) \times 2 = 64$

LEVEL 2

1. (c) The pattern is :

   1 1 2 4 7 11 16 (22)

   +2, +7, +11 (alternate terms: 1 → 4 → 11 → 22)

   +1, +5, +9 (alternate terms: 1 → 2 → 7 → 16)

2. (c) abc – c–c– ba – – bca
   Option (c) i.e, baabc gives the pattern abc/bca/cab /abc/ bca (abc rotate in cyclic order)

3. (d) ab – – a – dcacb – acd –
   Option (d) i.e, cdbdb provides the pattern abcd/ abdc/ acbd/acdb

4. (c) Multiply each term by $\frac{3}{2}$ to get the next term.

5. (b) In each term, the first letter is moved two steps forward and the last letter is moved one step backward. The number series run as follows : Previous no × n + n, where, n = 1, 2,

6. (d) Consider pair of numbers
   $(1, 1) = (1, 1^3)$
   $(2, 4) = (2, 2^2)$
   $(3, 27) = (3, 3^3)$
   $(4, 16) = (4, 4^2)$
   Next number will be 5.

7. (c) The numbers in series are in the order of $3^2 - 1, 4^2 - 1, 5^2 - 1$, etc.

8. (c) It is the combination of two series, 1, 2, 3, 4, 5,......... and $1^2, 2^2, 3^2, 4^2$, ... etc., the numbers of the two series are placed alternatively.

9. (a)

   F N H L J: +2, +2 (F→H→J); –2 (N→L)

   W O U Q S: –2, –2 (W→U→S); +2 (O→Q)

   B N E K H: +3, +3 (B→E→H); –3 (N→K)

   N B K E H: –3, –3 (N→K→H); +3 (B→E)

   D T H P L: +4, +4 (D→H→L); –4 (T→P)

10. (a) Sequence is cabbac
    cabbaccabbaccabbac
    acbcb

11. (c) The pattern the series is as follows :

    D —+3→ G —+3→ J —+3→ M —+3→ P

    3 —$(3)^2$→ 9 —$(3)^3$→ 27 —$(3)^4$→ 81 —$(3)^5$→ 243

    Y —–4→ U —+3→ Q —+3→ M —+3→ I

    104 —–13→ 91 —–13→ 78 —–13→ 65 —–13→ 52

    So, the next term will be P243I52.

12. (c) The pattern of the series is as follows :

    9, 23, 51, [106] 107, 219, [643] 443

    14, 28, 55, 113, 424

    So, option (3) is correct answer.

13. (c) The pattern of the series is as follows :

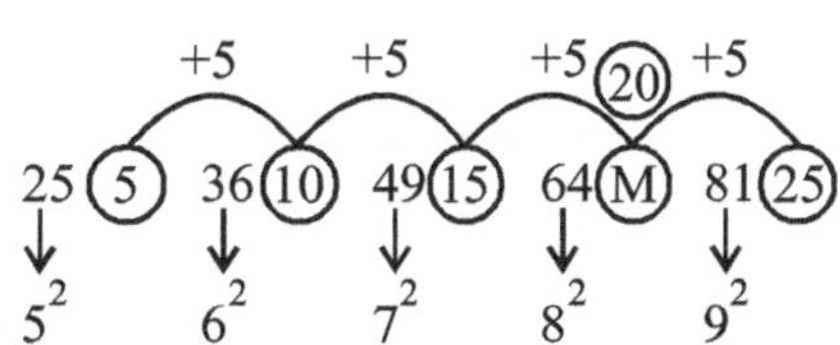

    So 6420 will fit in place of M.

14. (c) 6, 15, 35, ?, 143, 221
    (2×3),(3×5),(5×7), ?, (11×13),(13×17)
    This is a series of multiplication of consecutive prime number.
    ⇒ Missing number = 7 × 11 = 77

15. (c) 108, 135, 144, 171 (9); 132, 192, 156, 168 (12); 323, 357, 272, ? (17)

    ⇒ (108 + 135 + 144 + 171) ÷ 9 = 558 ÷ 9 = 62

    ⇒ (132 + 192 + 156 + 168) ÷ 12 = 648 ÷ 12 = 54

    Similarly (323 + 357 + 272 + [374]) ÷ 17
    = 1326 ÷ 17 = 78
    So, ? = 374.

16. (b) $\frac{6+4}{2}=\frac{10}{2}=5$ ——— E

$\frac{11+3}{2}=\frac{14}{2}=7$ ——— G

Similarly

$\frac{9+13}{2}=\frac{22}{2}=$ ——— K

17. (d)

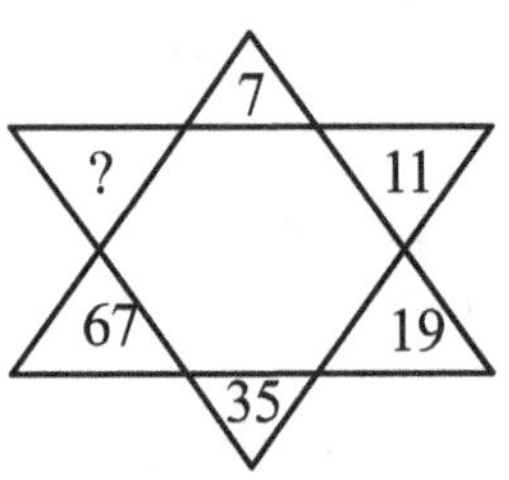

Starting from 7 ; 7 + 4 → 11

7 + 8 → 19

19 + 16 → 35

35 + 32 → 67

67 + 64 → 131

∴ ? = 131.

18. (a)

B	G	N
D	J	R
H	P	Z

→

2	7	14
4	10	18
8	16	26

In column 1.

2 + 2 ⟶ 4 + 4 ⟶ 8 (×2)

7 + 3 ⟶ 10 + 6 ⟶ 16 (×2)

14 + 4 ⟶ 18 + 8 ⟶ 26 (×2)

∴ ? = 26 and 26 represent Z in alphabetical series.

19. (c)

42	28	38
28	35	23
39	14	37

Difference between Column 1 and Column 3 will be equal to the Quotients when column 2 is divided by 7.

i.e 42 – 38 = 4 ; 28 % 7 = 4

28 – 23 = 5 ; 35 % 7 = 5

Similarly

39 – 37 = 2 ; ☐ % 7 = 2 i.e 14.

20. (a)

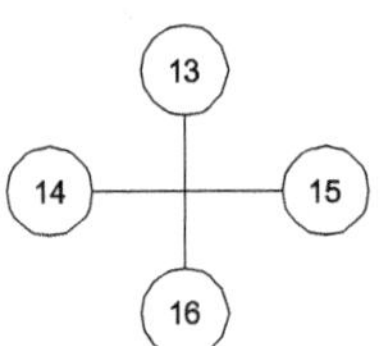

13 + 16 = 14 + 15

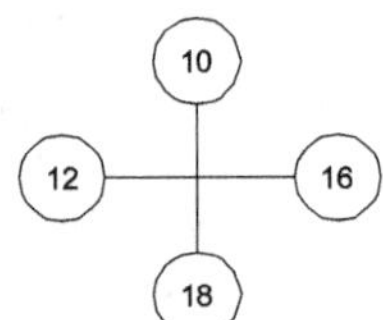

10 + 18 = 12 + 16

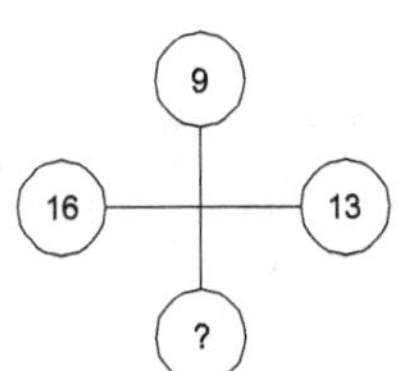

9 + ? = 16+13

? = 29 – 9

29 = 29

28 = 28 ? = 20

21. (a)

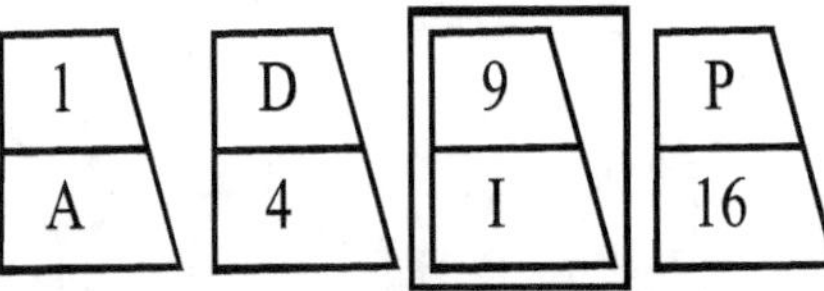

⇒ $(1)^2, (2)^2, (3)^2, (40)^2$

⇒ 1, 4, 9, 16, in english alphabets.

⇒ A, D, I, P

22. (a)

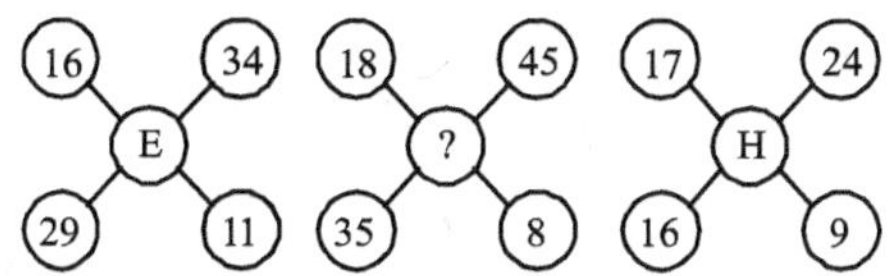

In middle circle, the alphabets which is at the place value of the difference between two diagonal no. is inserted.

Eg- $\left.\begin{array}{r}16-15=5\\34-29=4\end{array}\right\}\rightarrow$ is at place value of 5.

Similarly $\left.\begin{array}{r}17-9=8\\24-16=8\end{array}\right\}\rightarrow$ H is the place value of 8.

$\left.\begin{array}{r}18-8=10\\45-35=10\end{array}\right\}\rightarrow$ J is the place value of 10.

So ? = J

23. (b) $(3 \times 5) \times 2 = 30$
$(4 \times 6) \times 2 = 48$
$(5 \times 7) \times 2 = 70$

24. (b) 25. (c) 26. (c) 27. (a) 28. (c)

29. (c)

A (1) —50 $(1^2 + 7^2)$— G (7)
+8 | | +8
I (9) —306 $(9^2 + 15^2)$— O (15)
+8 | | +8
Q (17) —818 $(17^2 + 23^2)$— W (23)
+8 | | +8
Y (25) —650 $(25^2 + 5^2)$— E (5)
+8 | | +8
G (7) —218 $(7^2 + 13^2)$— M (13)

30. (b)

31. (d) $(6 \times 3 + 3) \times 2 = 42$
$(7 \times 7 + 2) \times 2 = 102$
Similarly
$(3 \times ? + 4) \times 2 = 50$
$3 \times ? = 21$
$\boxed{? = 7}$

32. (a) $(6 \times 3 + 2 \times 4) \times 2 = 52$
$(1 \times 3 + 4 \times 2) \times 2 = 22$
Similarly
$(15 \times 9 + 20 \times 3) \times 2 = 390$

33. (a) $15^2 + 20^2 = 25^2$
$18^2 + 24^2 = 30^2$
Similarly
$21^2 + 28^2 = 35^2$

34. (b)

A (1) $\xrightarrow{(+1)}$ B (2) $\xrightarrow{(+2)}$ D (4) $\xrightarrow{(+3)}$ **G (7)** $\xrightarrow{(+4)}$ K (11)
Y (25) $\xrightarrow{(-3)}$ V (22) $\xrightarrow{(-4)}$ R (18) $\xrightarrow{(-5)}$ **M (13)** $\xrightarrow{(-6)}$ G (7)
D (4) $\xrightarrow{(+2)}$ F (6) $\xrightarrow{(+2)}$ H (8) $\xrightarrow{(+2)}$ **J (10)** $\xrightarrow{(+2)}$ L (12)

So, GMJ is the missing term.

35. (a)

3	?	5
5	9	7
4	4	6
30	72	105

In column 1, $3 \times 5 \times 4 = 60 \div 2 = 30$
In column 2, $5 \times 7 \times 6 = 210 \div 2 = 105$
Similarly
In column 3, $\boxed{4} \times 9 \times 4 = 144 \div 2 = 72$
So ? = 4.

36. (d)

5	6	7
3	4	5
9	10	11
289	?	529

Applying operation column wise:
In column $1 \rightarrow 5 + 3 + 9 \rightarrow (17)^2 = 289$

In column 3 → 7 + 5 + 11 → $(23)^2$ = 529
Similarly in column 2,
6 + 4 + 10 = $(20)^2$ = 400
So, ? = 400.

37. (c) $\frac{3+7+9+5}{2}=\frac{24}{2}=12$

$\frac{13+9+16+18}{2}=\frac{56}{2}=28$

Similarly

$\frac{11+?+17+19}{2}=31$

? = 62 – 47

? = 15

38. (d) $\left.\begin{matrix}16\div4=4\\27\div3=9\end{matrix}\right\}\longrightarrow 9+4=13$

$\left.\begin{matrix}65\div13=5\\42\div7=6\end{matrix}\right\}\longrightarrow 5+6=11$

Similarly

$\left.\begin{matrix}72\div8=9\\27\div9=3\end{matrix}\right\}\longrightarrow 9+3=12$

39. (d) 18 + 17 = 12 + 23
35 = 35
21 + 23 = 24 + 20
44 = 44
Similarly
16 + 14 = ? + 9
30 = ? + 9

$\boxed{? = 21}$

40. (a) 4 + 0 + 3 = $(7)^3$ → 343
5 + 1 + 4 = $(10)^3$ → 1000
Similarly,
3 + 2 + 6 = $(11)^3$ → 1331

41. (a) **42. (d)** **43. (c)**
44. (c) **45. (d)**

CHAPTER-4

LEVEL 1

1. **(a)** D is the brother of E and E is the daughter of B. This means that D is the son of B. Also, A is the mother of B. So, A is the grandmother of D.

2. **(b)** Father's Wife — Mother; Mother's daughter — Sister Deepak's sister's younger brother— Deepak's brother.

3. **(c)** P @ Q $ M # T means P is the husband of Q who is the mother of M who is the father of T i.e, P is the father of T's father i.e, P is T's paternal grandfather.

4. **(b)** R is the sister of H means R is the daughter of the father of H i.e., R is the daughter of the husband (say D) of the mother (say F) of H i.e, R % D @ F $ H.

5. **(a)** F @ D % K # H means F is the husband of D who is the daughter of K who is the father of H i.e, F is the husband of D who is the sister of H i.e, F is H's brother in-law.

6. **(b)** H is the brother of N means N is the daughter of H's father and H is a male i.e, N is the daughter of the husband (say F) i.e, N% F @ D $ H # R or N% F @ D $ H @ R. husband of some other person (say, F) or the father (say, D) of H and H is the father or husband of some other person (say, R) i.e, N% F @ D $ H # R or N% F @ D$ H @ R.

7. **(a)** G $ M @ K means G is the mother of M who is the husband of K i.e, K is the wife of G's son i.e, K is G's daughter-in-law

8. (a)

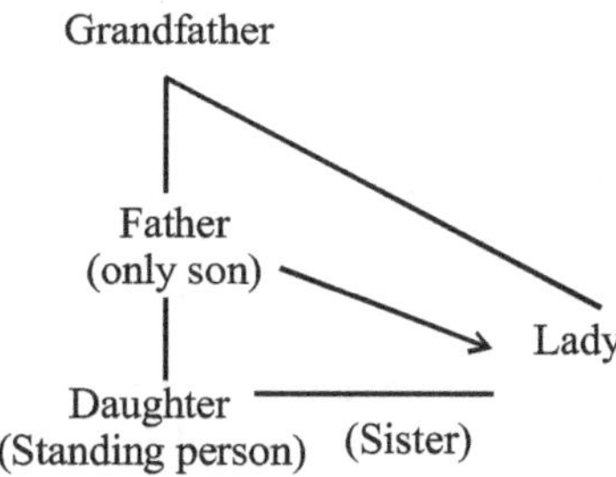

Lady's grandfather's son is lady's father and father's daughter will only be lady's sister.

9. (b) Girl's Father's only son— Girl's brother Grandmother of Girl's brother – Girl's Grandmother; Daughter-in-law of girl's grandmother — Girls' mother.

10. (a) Father's wife means mother ; mother's only son means himself and thus the girls is the daughter of the man.

11. (c) Clearly, the lady is the grandmother of man's sister's son i.e, the mother of the mother of man's sister's son i.e, the mother of man's sister.

12. (b) Father of shilpa's son— Shilpa's husband.
So, kapil is the son of sister of shilpa's husband. Thus, Kapil is shilpa's nephew.

13. (c) R × S ? T means R is the daughter of S whose mother is T i.e, R is the granddaughter of T.
P = Q. ? R means R is the mother of Q who is the father of P i.e, R is the grandmother of P.
L$M * O means L is the brother of M who is the sister of O i.e, L is the brother of O i.e, O is the brother or sister of L.
M * O ς P = Q means Q is the father of the son (P) i.e, Q is the father and O is the mother of P i.e Q and O are husband and wife.

14. (d) The gender of Q is not given hence the exact relation ship between N & Q cannot be established.

15. (d) The father of his brother means " his father" is the only son of my mother means " my brother" It means lady's is the father's sister of the man's father.

16. (a) Preeti's mother Shyama is youngest sister of Dubey & Sister of Prabhat. Therefore Prabhat is Preeti's uncle.

17. (d)

H ⟺ F
↓ H → I, F → G
J — I

○ means female member
□ means male member
⟺ means couple
— means brother/sister
↓ means son/daughter

18. (a) Rajesh is the husband of woman's father's sister.

19. (a) The relation is as follows :
Father wife→ Mother
Mother's only→ Uncle
brother
Uncle's son→ Cousin
So, Mahipal is cousin to sailesh

20. (d)

Hemant(+)
Rani(+) Reena(–) ——— Raju(+)

Ram is the son-in-law of Hemant.

21. (a)

Rohit's father's mother in law
Rohit's father == Anaya Daughter/mother
Rohit

∵ " ==" represents husband/wife relation
∵ " | " represents daughter/son relation
So, Aanya is mother of Rohit.

LEVEL 2

1. **(d)** V × T * P means V is the daughter of T who is the sister of P i.e, P is the brother/ sister of the mother of V i.e, P is either maternal uncle or maternal aunt of V.
   D ? V × T means V is the mother of D and daughter of T i.e, D is the son/ daughter of T's daughter i.e, D is the grandson or grand daughter of T.
   L ς M $ R means M is the son of L and the brother of R i.e, R is the son of L.
   M $ R * D? V means M is the brother of R who is the sister of D whose mother is V i.e, M is the brother of R who is the daughter of V i.e, M is the son of V.
2. **(d)** M × A = N = B means B is the father of N who is the father of A i.e., B is the grandfather of A.
   B $ L × Q × A means B is the brother of L who is daughter of Q. Q is daughter of A. i.e., A is grandfather or grandmother of B.
   B × L × A means B is daughter of L who is daughter of A. So, A is grandfather or grandmother of B.
   L * B = S $ Q = A means L is sister of B whose father is S. S is brother of Q whose father is A. So, A is grandfather of B.
3. **(a)** Nidhi is the daughter of Anurag and Aman is the son of Anurag's sister. So, Aman and Nidhi are cousins.
4. **(b)** Deepti is Anurag's wife and Komal is Anurag's sister. So, Komal is Deepti's sister in law
5. **(c)** Tarun is the father of Anurag and Deepti is Anurag's wife. So, Tarun is Deepti father-in-law.
   Aman is the son of Komal and Harshit. Garima is Anurag's and hence Komal's mother while harshit is komal's husband So, Garima is Harshit's mother-in-law.
   Nidhi is Anurag's daughter and Komal is Anurag's sister. So, Nidhi is Komal's niece.
6. **(a)** A × B – C + D

   [A] = (B) ↔ [C]
   ↓
   D

   Here, A is brother of B, B is wife of C and C is father of D.
   Hence, A is the brother of D's mother.
   ∴ A is the maternal uncle of D.
7. **(c)** Given, T – S × B – M

   (–)B ←Wife— M(+)
   ↓ Son
   (–)T ←Wife— S(+)

   S is son of B, not daughter.
   So, option (c) is correct answer.
8. **(c)**

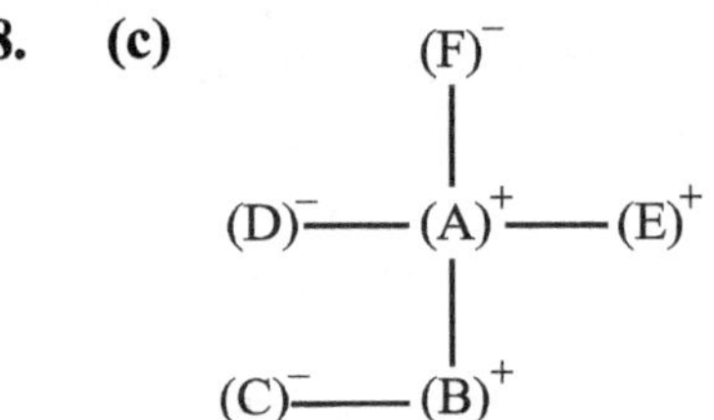

C is the daughter of E.

9. **(b)** (B)⁺ —— (C)⁻ —— (A)
   |
   (D)⁺

   D is the nephew of A.
10. **(d)**

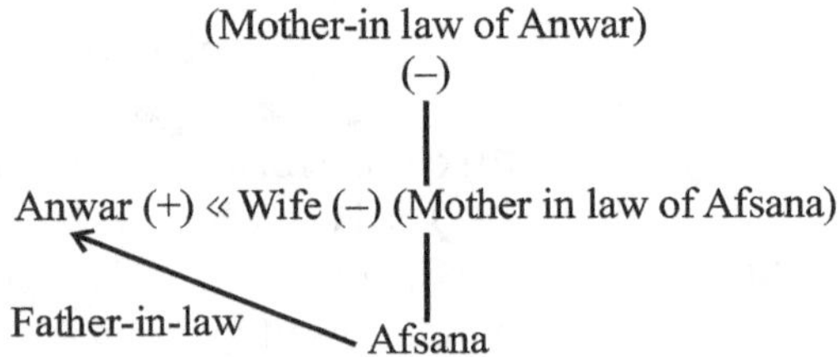

11. (b) A, C and D

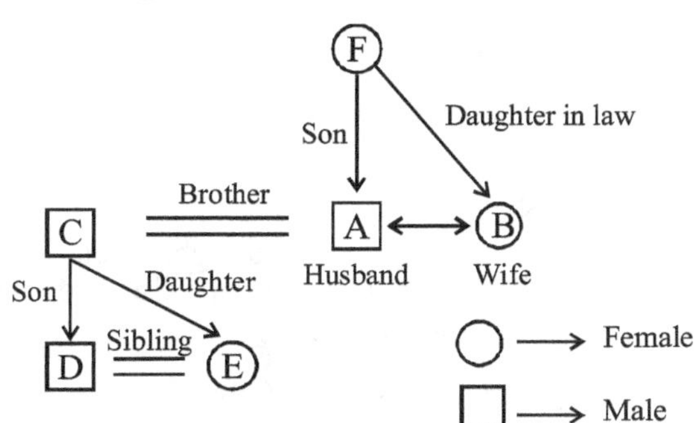

12. (b)

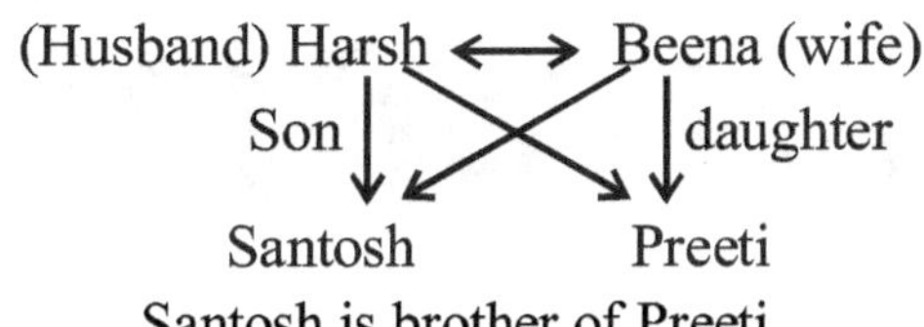

Santosh is brother of Preeti.

13. (b)

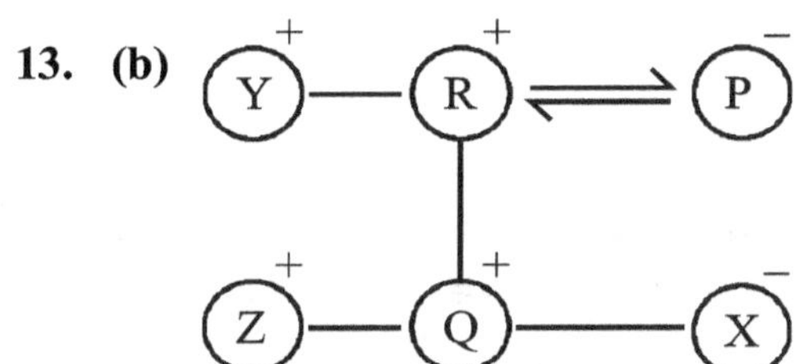

Q, X, Z represents all the children of P. Hence, option (b) is correct.

14. (c)

15. (c)

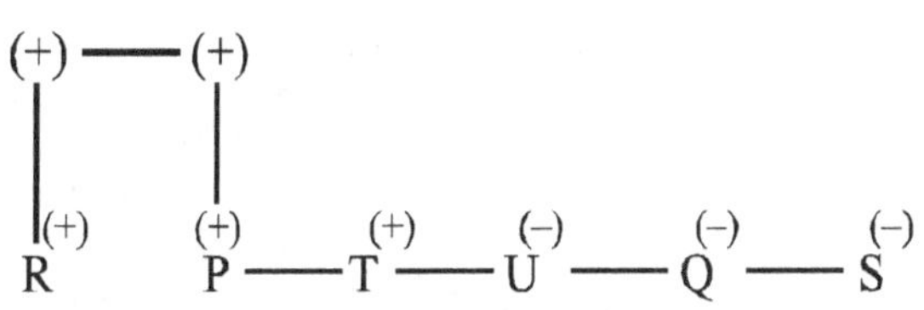

'3' female players are there.

16. (c)

17. (b)

18. (d)

19. (c)

$N^{(+)}$ — J

$I^{(-)}$ — $C^{(-)}$

So, I is the niece of J.

20. (c)

S

$(Q)^{-}$ — $(R)^{-}$

$(P)^{+}$

'P' is the grandson of 'S'.

21. (c) O^{+} → Represent male

"|" → represents son/daughter relation

"–" → represents brother/sister relation

"=" represents husband/wife relation.

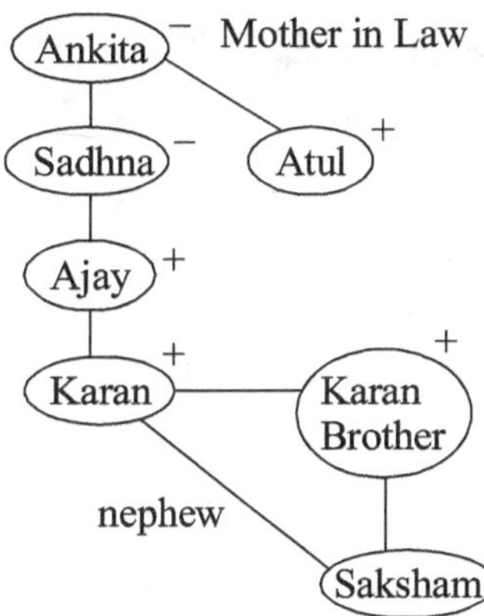

Karan is grandson of Atul.

22. (b)

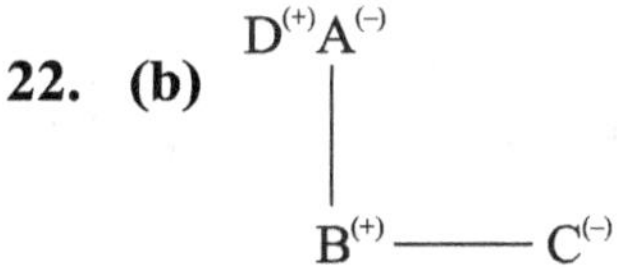

'D' is the father of 'B'.

23. (c)

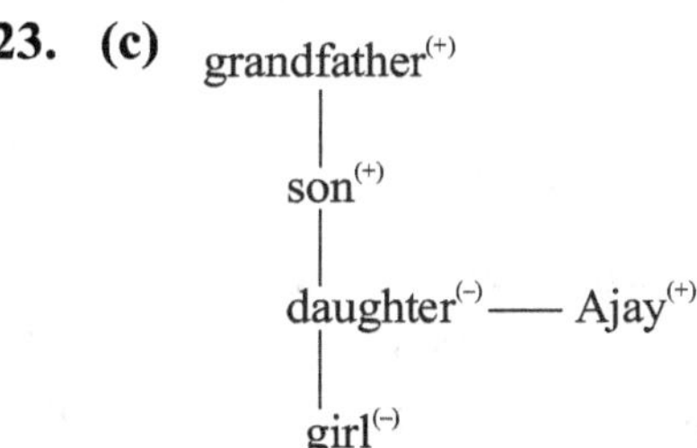

Girl is the niece of Ajay

24. (c) T @ U % S # R © Q

Diagramatically,

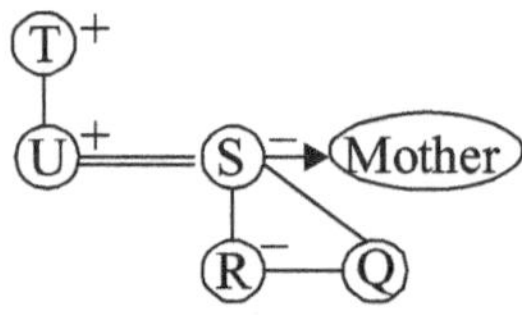

"==" represents husband/wife relation

"|" represents son/daughter relation

"_" represents brother/sister relation

O^+ → represents male

O^- → represents female.

25. (b) $P \div Q + R - T \times K$

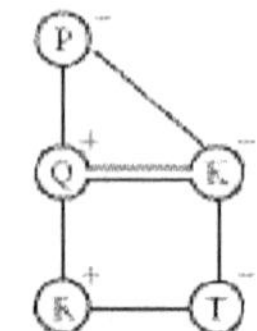

" | " → represents son/daughter relation

" — " → represents brother/sister relation

" O^+ " → represents male

" O^- " → represents female

" == " → represents husband/wife relations

P is K's mother in law

26. **(b)** **27.** **(b)**

CHAPTER-5

LEVEL 1

1. **(b)** The movements of the child from A to E are as shown in fig

Clearly, the child meets his father at E.

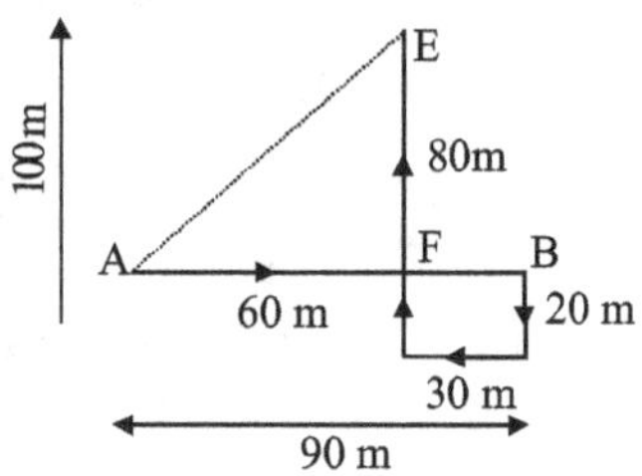

Now AF = (AB – FB) = (AB – DC)

= (90 – 30) m = 60 m.

EF = (DE – DF) = (DE – BC)

= (100 – 20) m = 80 m.

∴ Required distance

$= AE = \sqrt{AF^2 + EF^2} = \sqrt{(60)^2 + (80)^2}$

$= \sqrt{3600 + 6400} = \sqrt{10000} = 100$ m.

2. **(b)** As per the data, D faces North. A faces towards west. So, its partner B will face towards A and hence towards East. So, C who will face D will face towards south.

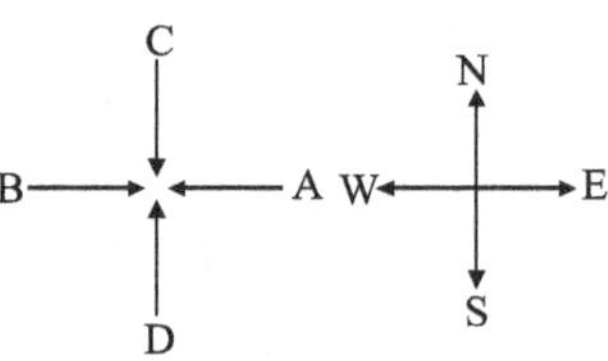

3. **(d)** The movements of Deepak are as shown in fig.

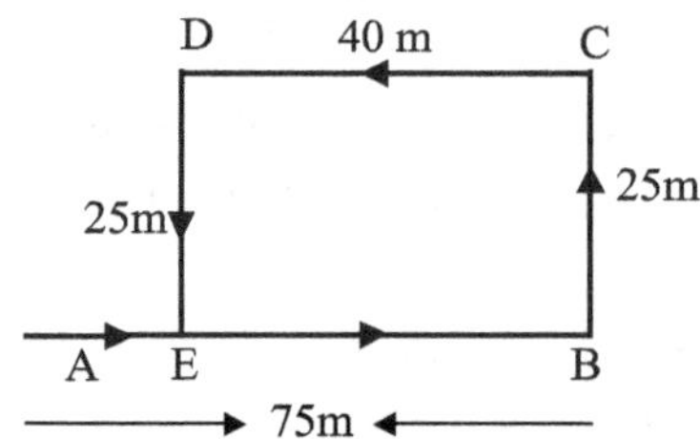

Clearly, FB = DC = 40 m .

∴ Deepak's distance from the starting point A

= (AB – EB) = (75 – 40) m = 35m.

4. **(a)** The Sun rises in the east. So, in morning, the shadow falls towards the west. Now, shadow of pole falls to the right of Gopal.Therefore, Gopal's right side is the west. So, he is facing South.

5. **(b)** The movements of the man from A to F are as shown in fig Clearly DC = AB + EF.

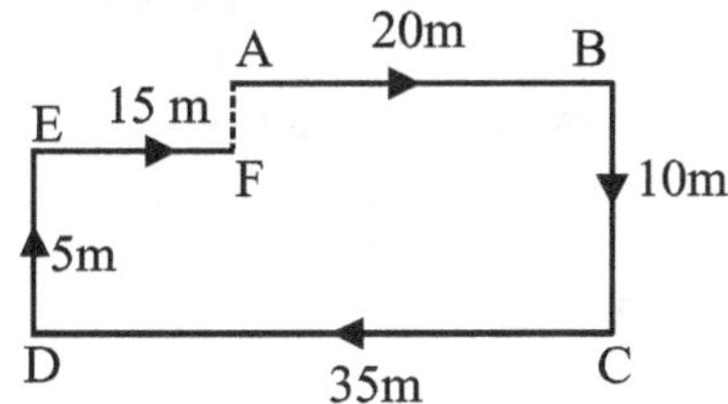

∴ F is in line with A.
Also, AF = (BC – DE) = 5 m.

6. **(d)** Aman has taken a rectangular path as is clear from the diagram below.

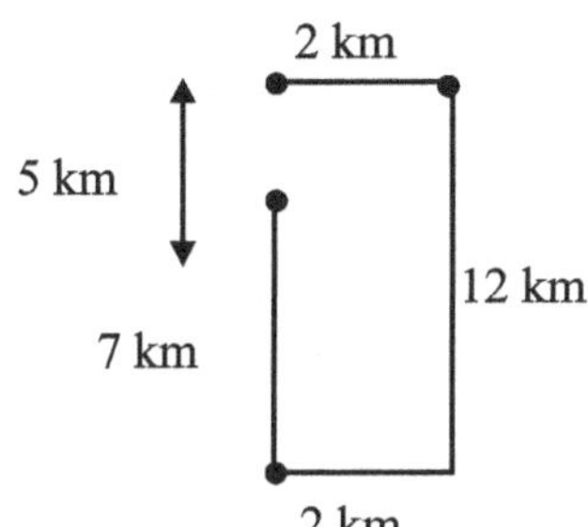

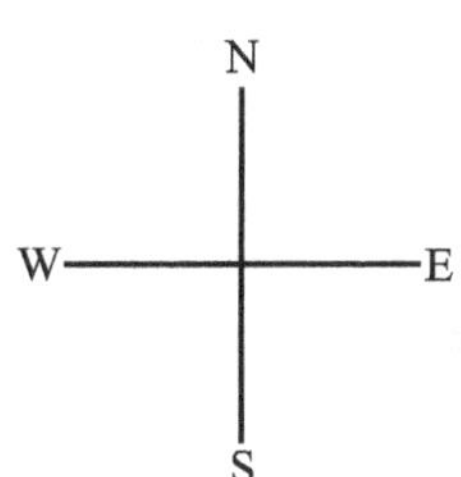

7. **(b)** **8.** **(c)**
9. **(b)**

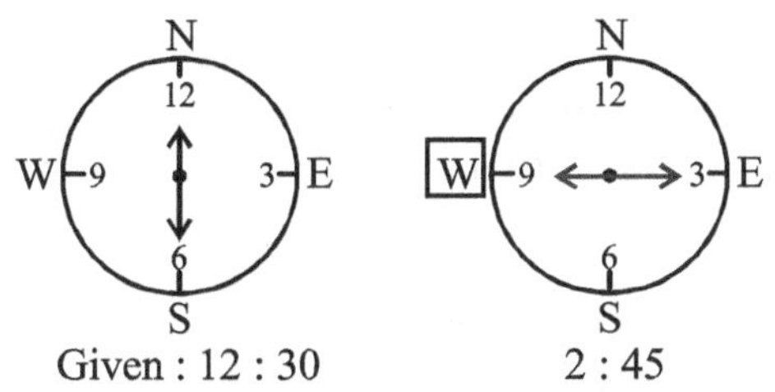

It is clearly shown that the minutes hand will be in west direction.

10. **(b)** The movements of the man from A to F are as shown in fig Clearly DC = AB + EF.

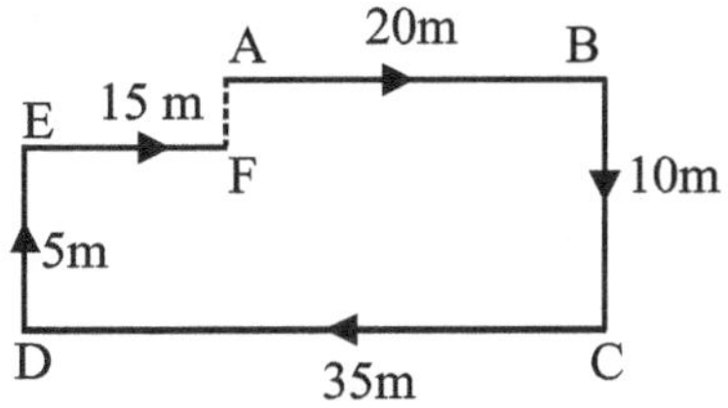

∴ F is in line with A.
Also, AF = (BC – DE) = 5 m.

11. **(b)**

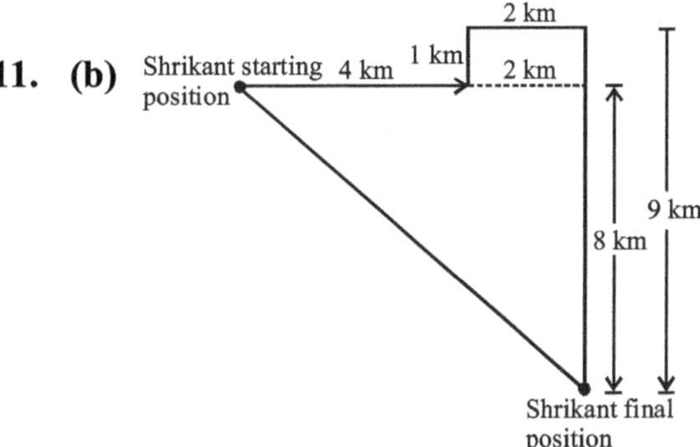

∴ Distance from original position

$= \sqrt{(6)^2 + (8)^2}$

$= \sqrt{36+64} = \sqrt{100} = 10$ km.

12. **(b)** Short cut method-
Take clockwise as '+' and anticlockwise as '–'

Person N
W E
S

∴ $+90° - 135° = -45°$
As person is facing North west. Now, rotate that person 45° anticlockwise. Now, he is facing west direction.

13. **(c)**

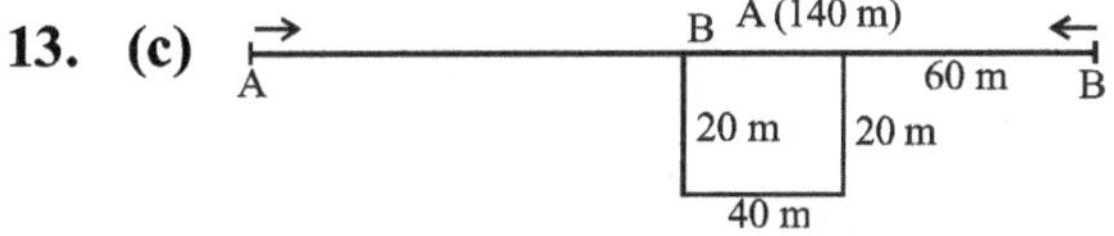

Distance travelled by A on road
= 60 + 20 + 40 + 20 = 140 m
Disance travelled by B on road
= 60 + 40 = 100 m
Required difference = 140 – 100
= 40 m

14. **(d)** Aman has taken a rectangular path as is clear from the diagram below.

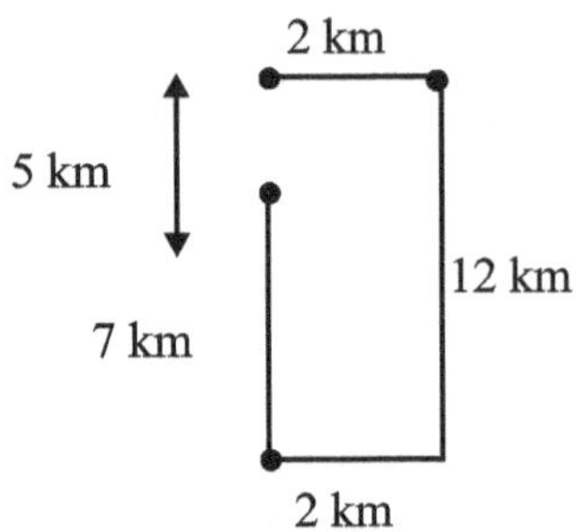

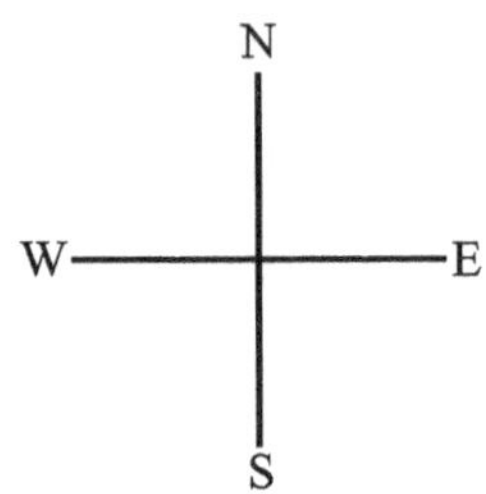

15. **(b)**

16. **(b)**

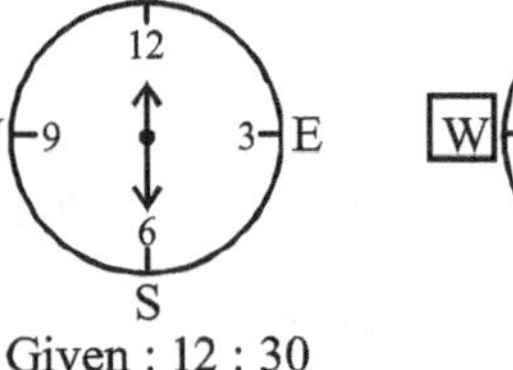

Given : 12 : 30 2 : 45

It is clearly shown that the minutes hand will be in west direction.

17. **(c)**

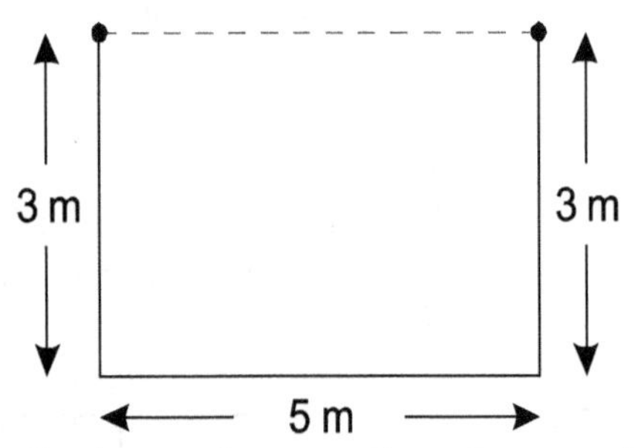

She is 5m for now from her starting point

18. **(b)**

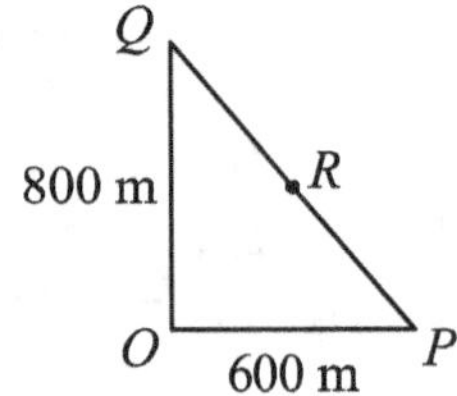

By Pythoagoras theorem -

$(QP)^2 = (OQ)^2 + (OP)^2$

$= 640000 + 360000$

$\Rightarrow QP = \sqrt{1000000} = 1000$ m

Hence,

$QR = \frac{1000}{2} = 500$ m ($\because QR = RP$)

19. **(b)**

20. **(c)**

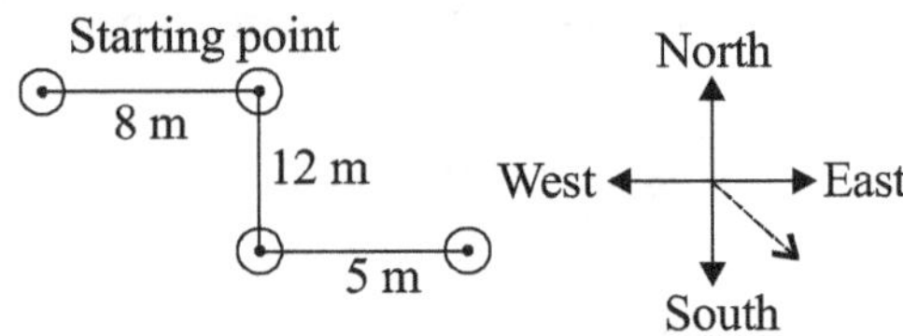

Sonal is in south east direction with respect to her starting point.

21. **(b)**

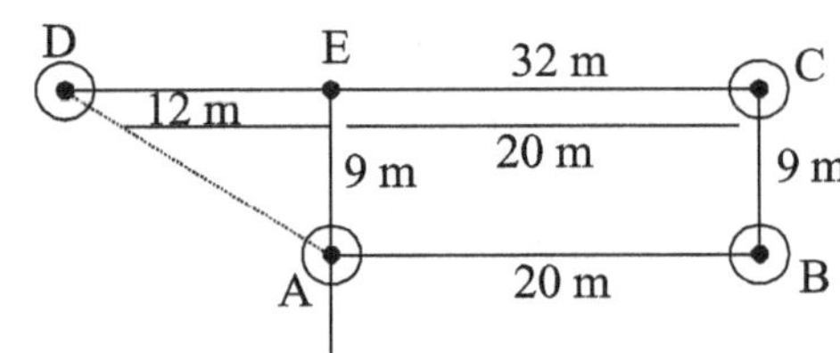

In ΔAED

By pythagoras theorem.

$(AD)^2 = (AE)^2 + (DE)^2$

$AD = \sqrt{(9)^2 + (144)}$

$= \sqrt{81 + 144}$

$AD = \sqrt{225} = 15$ m.

15 m north-west from starting point.

22. **(d)**

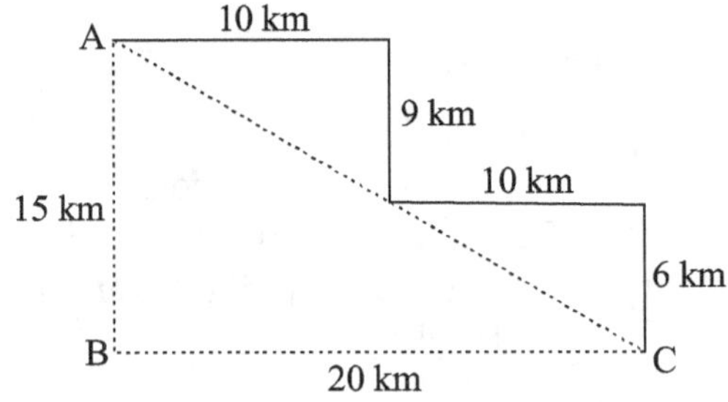

In ΔABC

$AB = 15, BC = 20$

By pythogoras theorem

$AC^2 = AB^2 + BC^2$

$AC = \sqrt{(15)^2 + (20)^2}$

$= \sqrt{225 + 400}$

$AC = \sqrt{625}$

$AC = 25$ km.

23. (c)

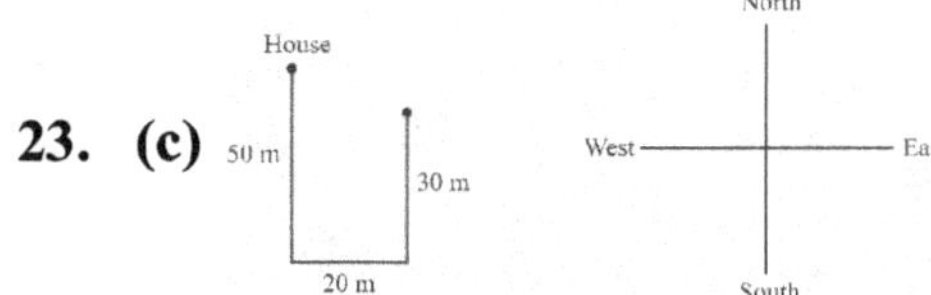

This home is in north west with respect to final point

LEVEL 2

1. (b) Rohit originally is facing east but he turns to his left from O.

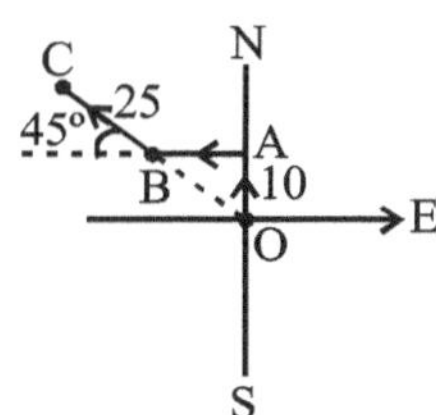

Here onwards his travel plans are shown in the diagram. He is finally at C which is North-west with respect to his starting point O.

2. (d) The movements of Rasik from A to F are as shown in figure.

Since CD = AB + EF, so F lies in line with A.

Rasik's distance from original position A = AF

= (AG + GF) = (BC + DE) = (30 + 15) m = 45m.

Also, F lies to the east of A.

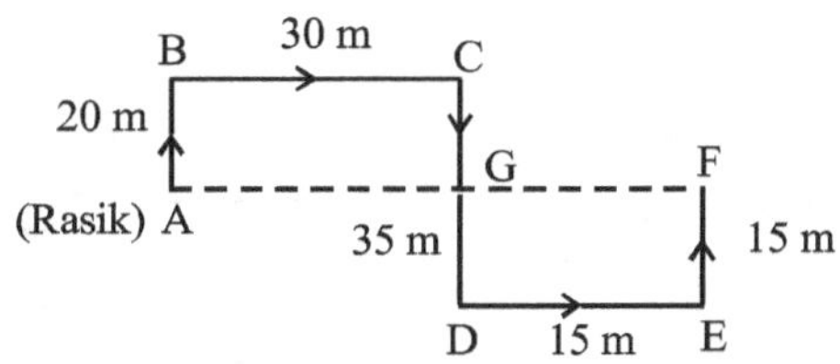

3 to 5 :

Peanuts		
	Rice	
		Vegetable

3. (d) Since Wheat and Barley should be continuous, therefore, Barley will be planted in the square immediately north east of the rice field.

4. (c) The square immediately west of the rice field cannot be planted with wheat.

5. (d) The square immediately north east of the rice square cannot be planted with soyabeans.

6 to 10.

6. (c)

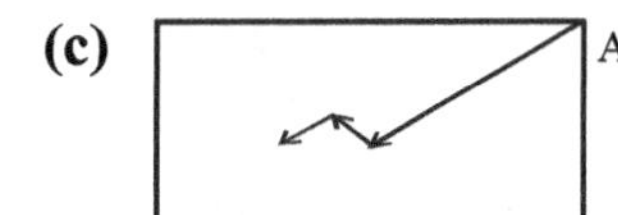

7. (a)

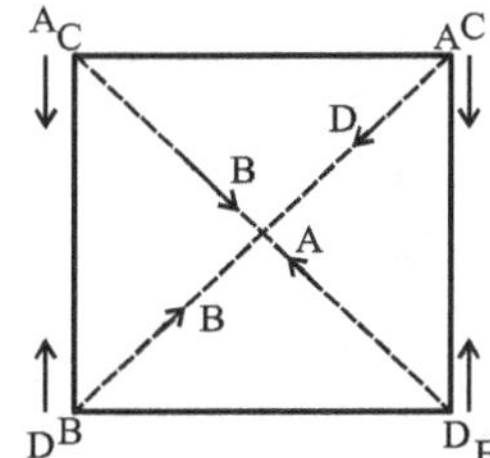

8. (a)

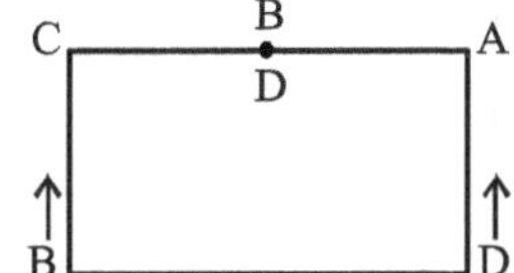

9. (d) As per directions given in the questions, the new figure formed is as follows :

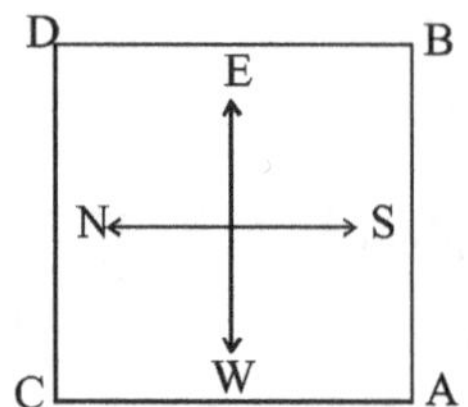

10. (b) It is clear from above diagram

11. (c)

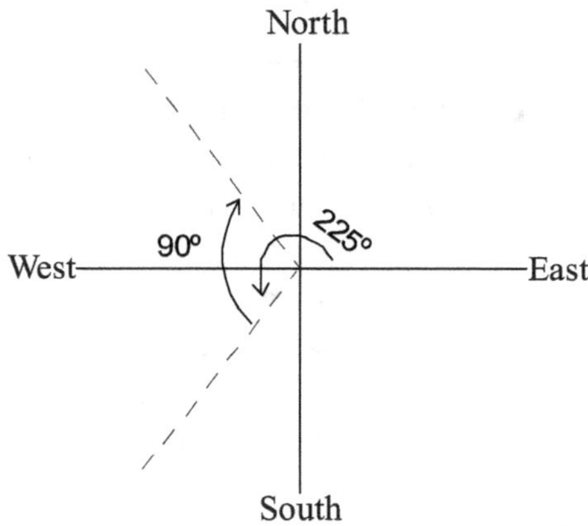

12. (c)

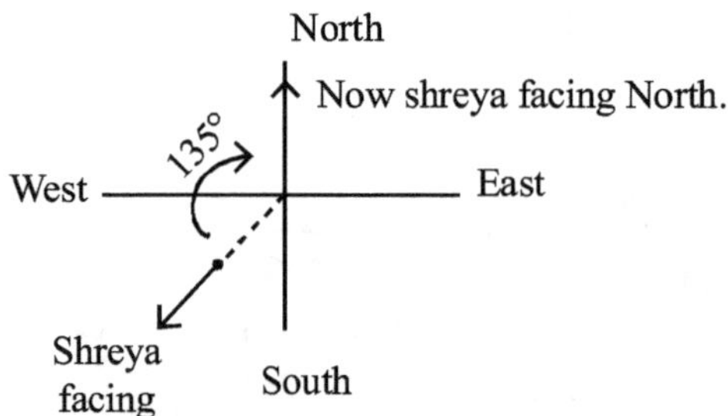

After turning 135° clockwise, now Shreya is facing North direction.

13. (a)

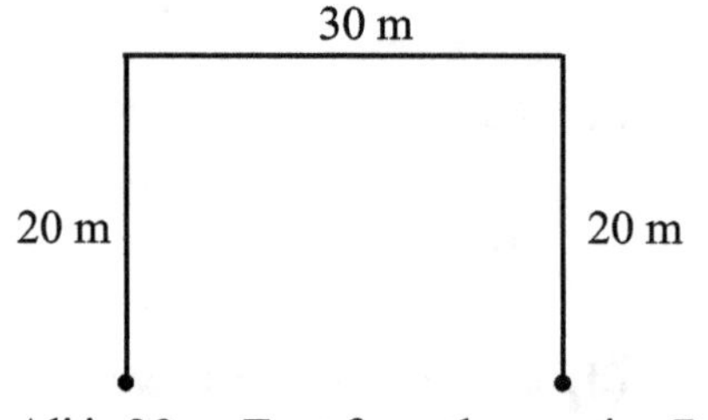

Ali is 30 m, East from the starting Point.

14. (b) 15. (d)

16. (d)

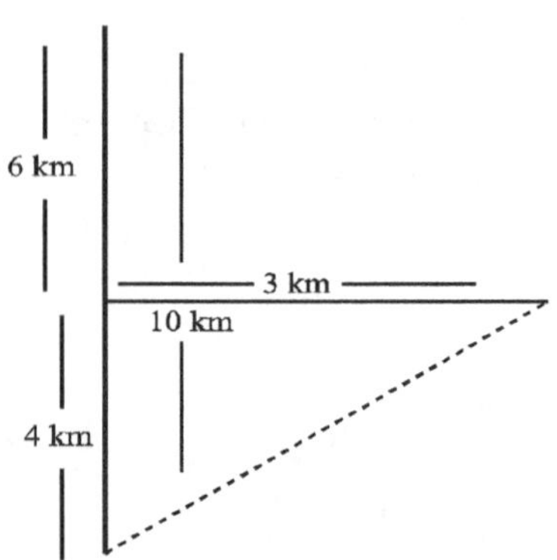

She is 5km North-East with respect to the starting point.

17. (b)

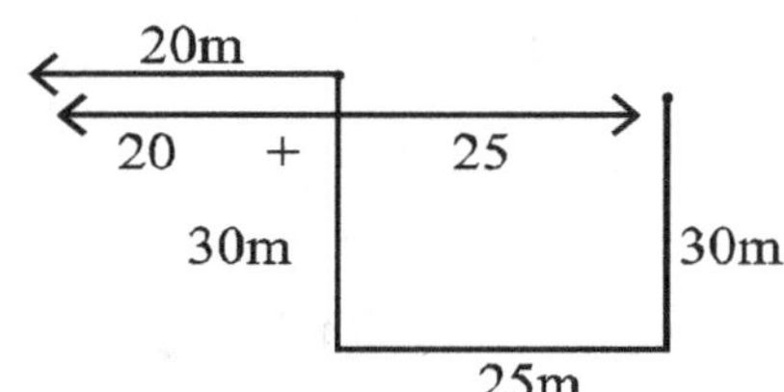

Hence, she is 45m in west from her starting point.

18. (c)

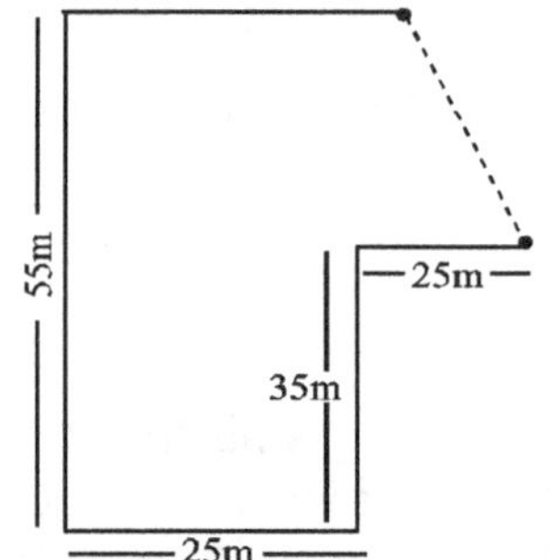

She is North-West from her starting point.

19. (c)

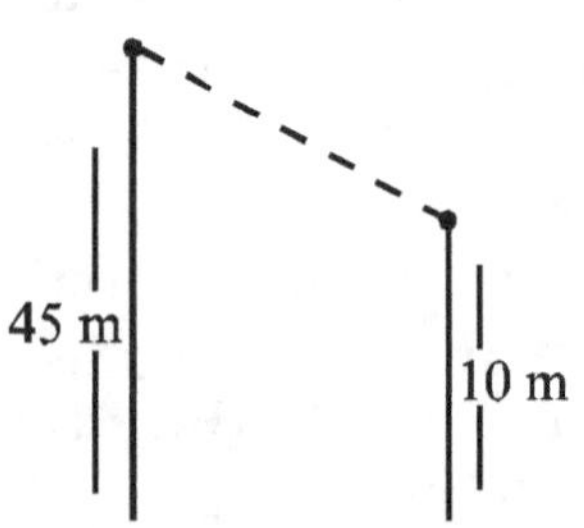

He is in North-West from his starting point.

20. (b) 21. (c) 22. (c)

23. (b) The movement of the person are as shown in fig.

Clearly, AB = 3 km,

BC = 3AB = (3 × 3) km = 9 km

CD = 5AB = (5 × 3) km = 15 km.

Draw AE ⊥ CD.

Then CE = AB = 3 km and

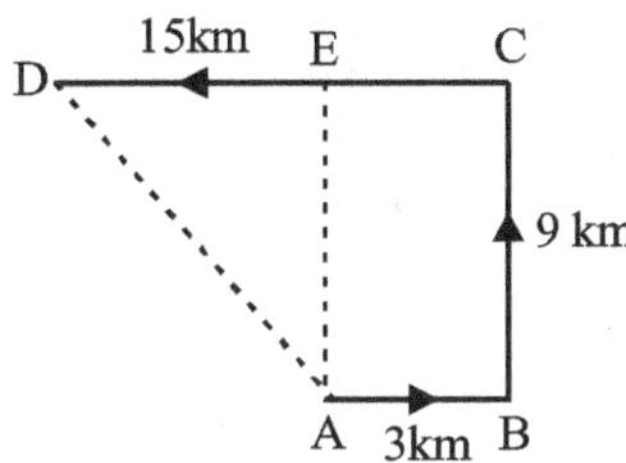

AE = BC = 9 km

DE = (CD – CE) = (15 – 3) km = 12 km.

In Δ AED, $AD^2 = AE^2 + DE^2$

$\Rightarrow$ $AD = (\sqrt{9^2 + (12)^2})\,km = \sqrt{225}\,km = 15$ km.

∴ Required distance = AD = 15 km.

24. (d)

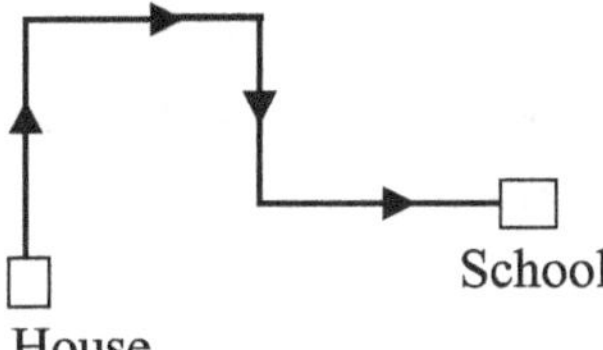

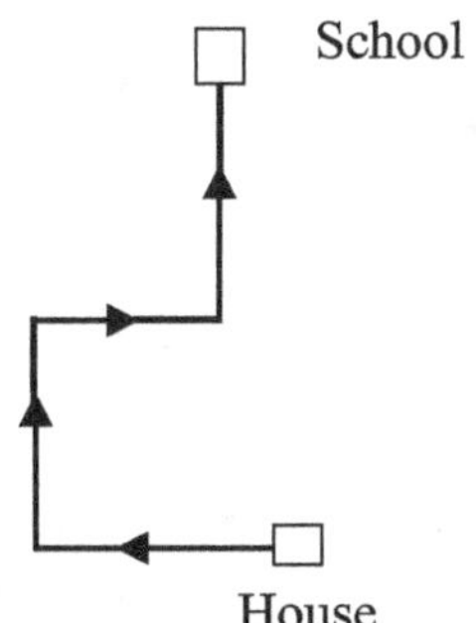

In fig 1, the route of the bus from Lokesh's house to the school is shown. It is given that the bus faces North on reaching the school. Now turning fig. 1 90° anti-clockwise. We obtain fig. 2 which satisfies the specified conditions. It is evident from fig. 2 that the bus faces west in front of Lokesh's house.

25. (d)

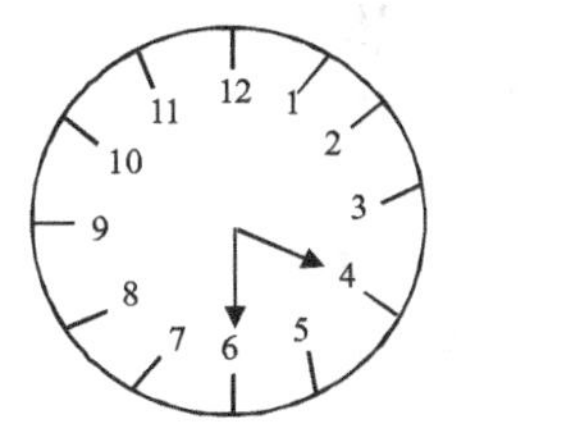

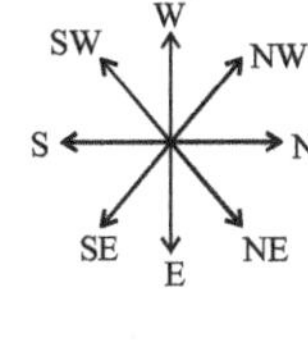

26. (c)

27. (c) The angle covered will be

$= \frac{12}{60} \times 360 = 72°$ from North.

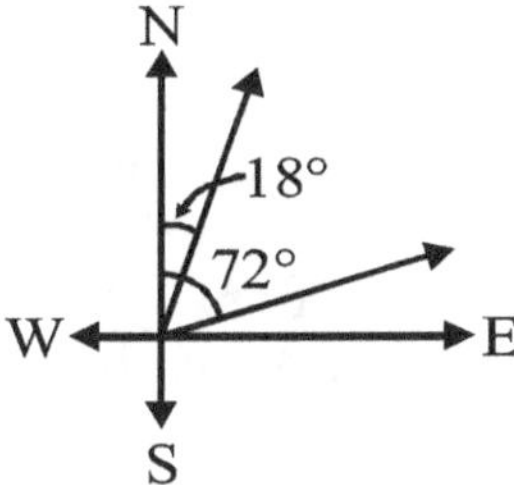

So it can be said to beat 18° North of East of 72° East of North.

28. (a) According to the given information, the direction movements of Amita is as follows:

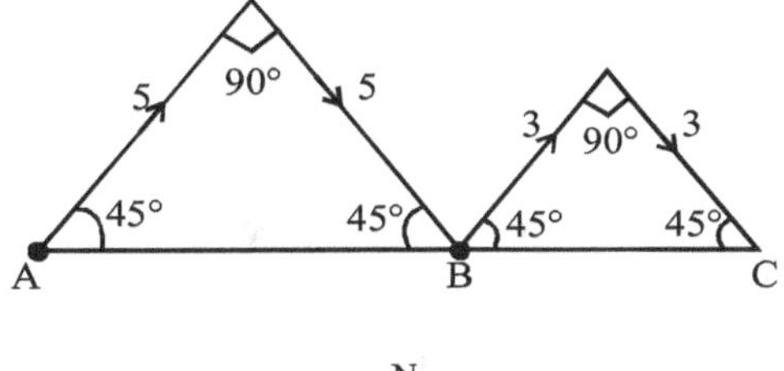

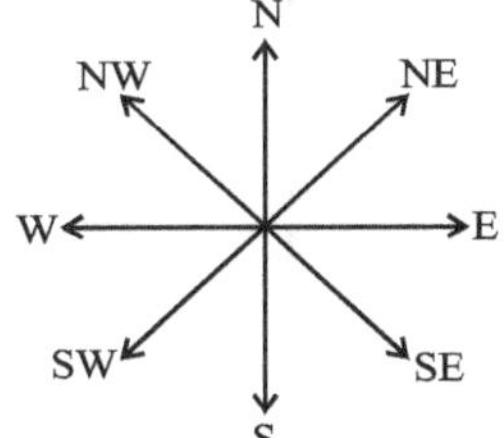

Here, A is the starting point and C is the final point. It is clearly shown from the above direction diagram that the direction of point B and C is east direction with respect to point A. Hence option (1) is correct answer.

29. (a) The direction diagram is as follows :

North

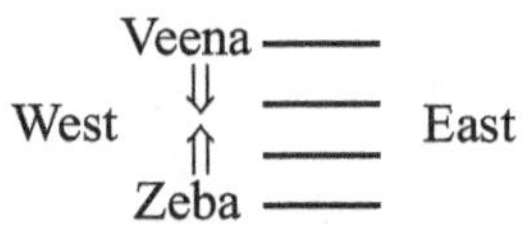

South

Clearly, from the diagram, veena was facing south direction.

30. (b) Starting point

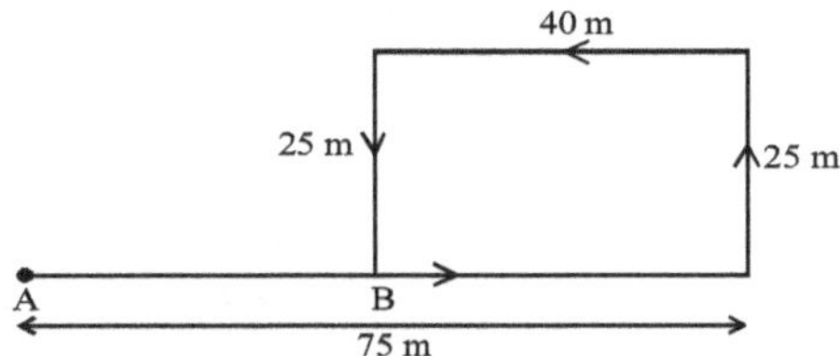

Distance from A to B = 75 – 40 = 35.
options (b) is correct.

31. (d)

32. (d)

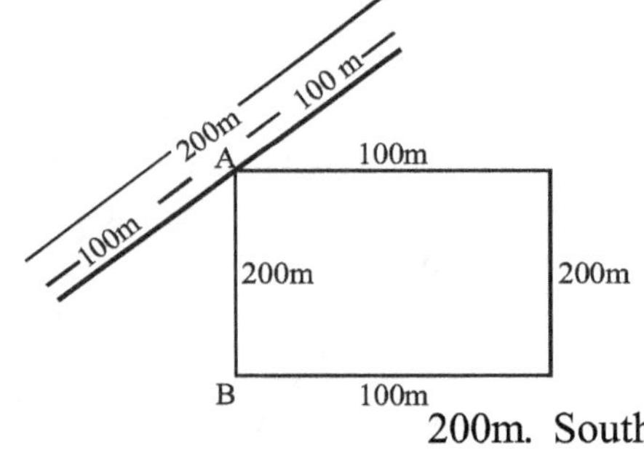

Option (d) is correct.

33. (d)

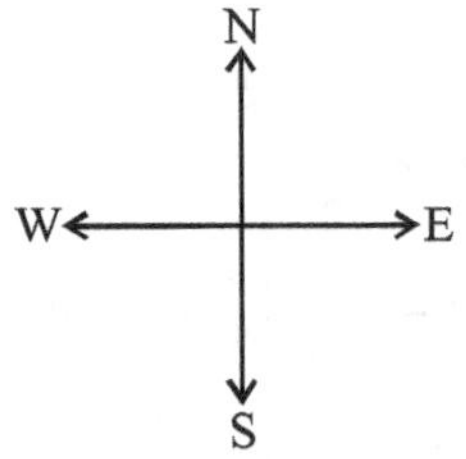

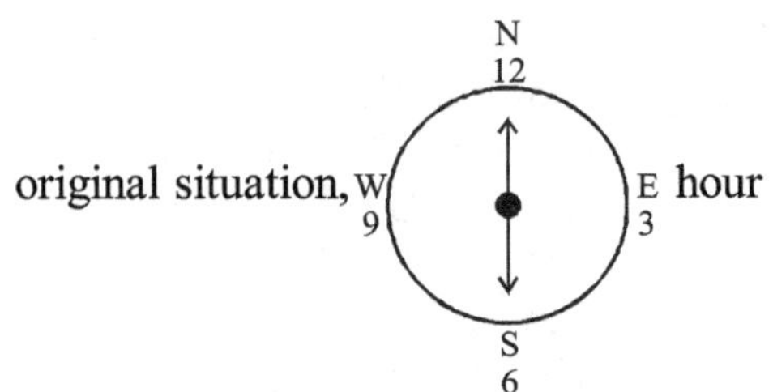

hand denotes south.

ATQ,

At 6:00 PM

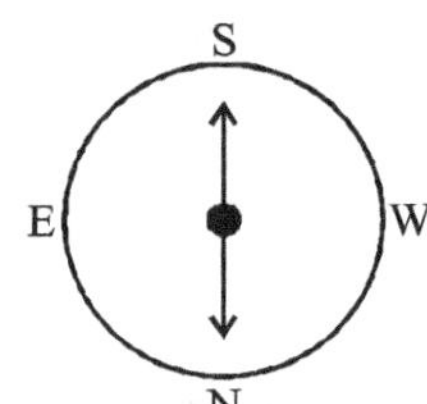

Now,

At 9 : 15 PM

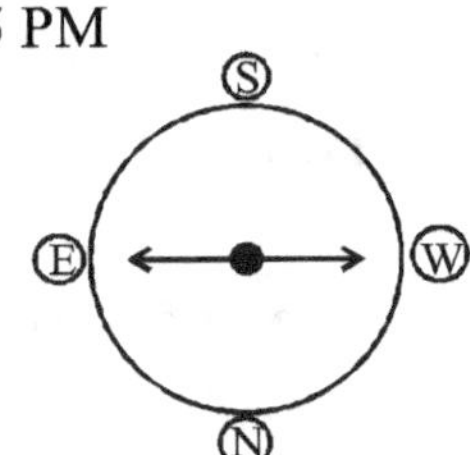

Minute hand denotes **West** option (d) is correct.

34. (c) Sunset

Sunset

N
Opposite to Sun
Rajni
W
E
Sanjeev
(right)
Shadows
S

Hence, Rajni was facing towards south.

35. (c)

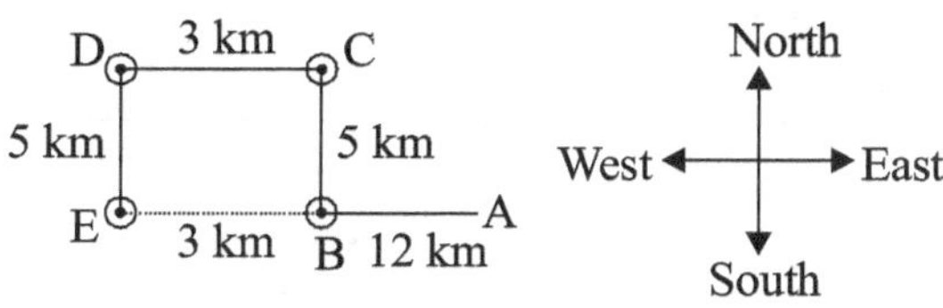

AE = AB + BE

12 + 3 = 15 km.

Samay is 15 km west from his starting position.

36. (c)

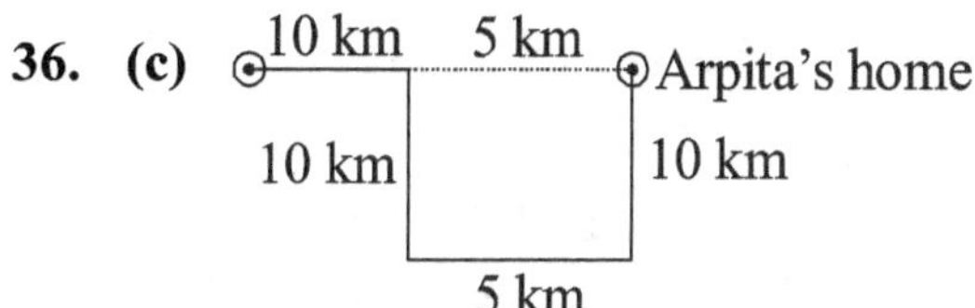

Arpita is 15 km away from her house.

37. (d)

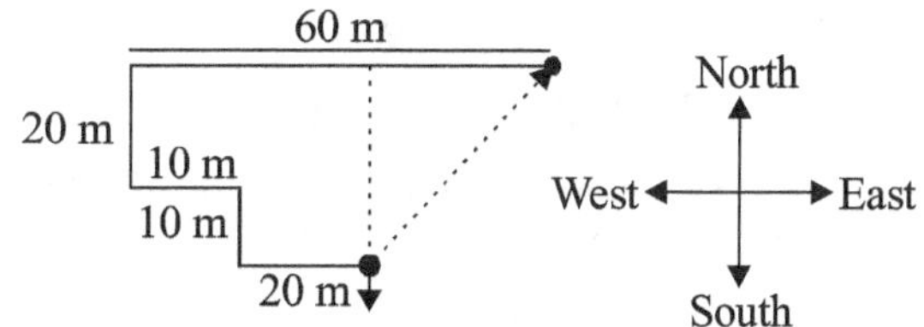

Sudhir is in north east direction with respect to the starting point.

38. (a)

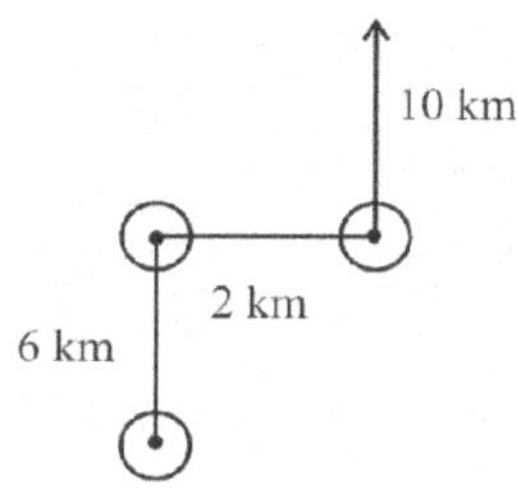

Mohit started his Journey in North Direction.

39. (a)

CHAPTER-6

LEVEL 1

1. **(d)** Clearly, we have :
   COMPREHENSION → (COM) (PREHENS) (ION)
   → MOCIONSNEHERP
   The middle letter is the seventh letter, which is S.
2. **(d)** The new letter sequence is EDRPSEISNO.

   The seventh letter from the right is P.

   D E P R E S S I O N

   1 2 3 4 5 6 7 8 9 10
3. **(d)** Clearly, the given letters, when arranged in the order 5, 1, 2, 3, 4 form the word 'TRACE'.
4. **(b)**
5. **(a)**
6. **(b)**
7. **(c)**
8. **(c)**
9. **(c)** TUB when interchanged will term a meaningful word BUT.
10. **(a)** The order of words in dictionary will be BUT, CAR, HID, LAP, SON
11. **(c)** LAP and CAR both have 'A' at the same position.
12. **(d)** All 5 will have no vowels – LBP, BVT, CBR, SPN, HJD.
13. **(d)** 486 441 634 932 873

    –2 –2 –2 –2 –2

484 439 632 930 871

highest no. → 930

2nd highest no. → 871

Required sum of 2nd digit of both these two no.→ 3 + 7 = 10.

14. (d) Five consonants are there in the series which is immediately procceded by a vowel

ET, ES, AW, IP, OT

15. (b)

16. (b) $40 + 1 - 11 = 30^{th}$

17. (b)

d_1, d_2 — In front of three ducks

d_3

d_4, d_5 — Behind three ducks

18. (a)

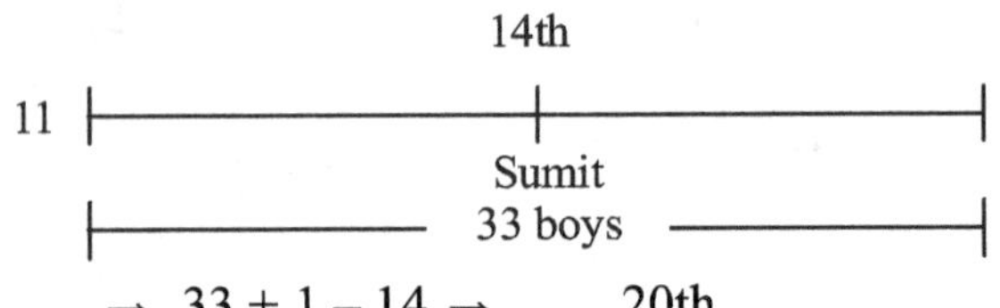

⇒ 33 + 1 – 14 ⇒ 20th

19. (c) Total girls in the row

⇒ 12 + 5 – 1 = 16

To make 30 girls in the row

⇒ 30 – 16 = 14

(girls should join the row)

20. (c) **21. (b)** **22. (d)**

23. (c) There are '3'8's which are immediately preceded by a number which does not divide it but followed by a number which divides it.

588 384 382

24. (d)

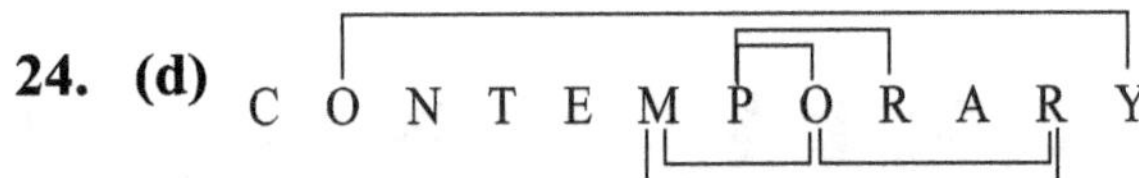

There are 5 pairs of letters which have as many letters between them in the word as in the English alphabets.

25. (d)

(4)	(5)	(16)	(1)	(18)	(20)	(13)	(5)	(14)	(20)
D	E	P	A	R	T	M	E	N	T

D, E; D,– A–,A; P – R ; A– – – E ; R– – –N;

More than four.

26. (c) 876 786 756 797 61677 6886 976 87

768 ; 768

These are two combinations which are following the given condition in the question.

27. (a) When the first and second digits are interchanged and "1" is subtracted from 3rd digit.

734 642 656 277 368

When No. are arranged in increasing order, then

277, 368, 642, 656, 734

Sum of the digit of third highest numbers = 6 + 4 + 2 = 12

28. (d) 8 6 7; 6, 8, 9; 2, 2, 3; 2, 8, 1

29. (c) 2 – District

1 – Town

3 – Street

5 – Home

4 – Room

30. (b) 864 549 968 742 963 721

Second highest number ⇒ 963

Third digit of the number ⇒ 3

LEVEL 2

1. (c) C O R P O R A T E

Three pairs — (P, R), (R, T) and (P, O) have as many letters between them in the word as in the English alphabet. But since the letters must be in the same sequence in the word as in English alphabet, so that desire pairs are (P, R) and (R, T) only.

2. (d) A M B Z A N A A B Z A B A Z B A P Z A B A Z A B

3. (a) Since the letters of the alphabet are reversed, take the left and right as right and left. Thus fourteenth letter from the right of the alphabet is M and the fifth letter from M to the right is R.

4. (b) Position of BLUE → 1st

Position of UBLE → 20th

UBLE's position is 20 according to dictionary.

∴ Option (b) is correct answer.

5. (d) 22nd letter from the left is V and 21st letter from the right is F. The letter midway F and V is N.

6. (b) The new alphabet series is

M L K J I H G F E D C B A

N O P Q R S T U V W X Y Z

The 9th letter from right is R and the ninth letter to the left of R is E.

7. (c) The name of the vegetable is PUMPKIN. The last letter is N.

8. (b) The name of the game is BADMINTON.

9. (c) Counting from the right end i.e. from Z, the 16th letter is K. Counting from K towards the left, the 8th letter is C.

10. (a) There are ten letters between H and S and as such there is no letter which lies in the middle.

11. (d) J is the tenth letter in the first half. The tenth letter in the later half is W.

12. (d) 22nd letter from the left is V and 21st letter from the right is F. The letter midway F and V is N.

13. (b) The new alphabet series is

M L K J I H G F E D C B A

N O P Q R S T U V W X Y Z

The 9th letter from right is R and the ninth letter to the left of R is E.

14. (c) The new alphabet series is B A D C F E H G J I L K N

M P O R Q T S V U X W Z Y

The seventeenth letter from the right is I.

15. (a) The sixth letter from the right is F. E comes immediately before F.

16. (d) The new series is

A 3 C 5 E 7 G 9 I 11 K 13 M 15 O 17 Q 19 S 21 U 23 W 25 Y 27

Counting from the right, the tenth character is Q, and the third character to the right of Q is 21.

17. (d)

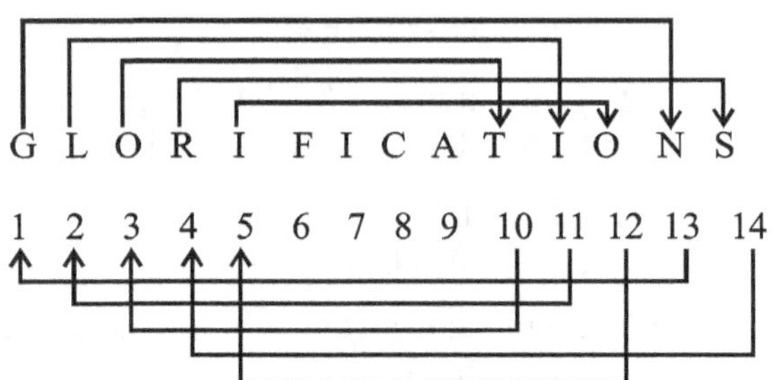

The new letter sequence is NITSOFICAOLIGR.

The twelfth letter from the right is T.

18. (a) Garv > Raj > Mohit > Avinash > Sumit

Hence, Raj finished the race at second position.

19. (a) B A D C F E H G J I L K N M P O R Q T [S] V U X W Z Y

'S' will be the seventh letter from the right end.

20. (b) 547, 747, 345

Hence, there are 3 such sequence of numbers.

21. (a) Second, fifth, seventh and tenth letters = N, U, I and T

Meaningful work → UNIT

Hence, second letter of word formed is 'N'.

22. (b) Kewa's position from left end = 26 – 10 = 16th

∴ Satish's position from left end = 16 + 3 + 1 = 20th

Hence, Rohan's position from left end = 20 – 10 = 10th

23. (c) After adding three

$$\begin{array}{r} 8\ 7\ 8 \\ -\ 2\ 6\ 7 \\ \hline 6\ \textcircled{1}\ 1 \end{array}$$

24. (c)

25. (d)

26. (c)

27. (b)

28. (b)

29. (c)

30. (c) Z Y X W V T S R Q P N M L [K] J H G F D C B

'K' will be the 8th letter from the right end.

31. (c)

Dilip → 10th; Jagdish 20th ← ; 23rd ← Jagdish

⇒ 10 + 23 – 1

⇒ 32 students are there in the row.

32. (b) 475 ; 875

There are only two sequence which follow condition.

33. (a) A E C B % 7 D $ E B 5 C ? 3 D ε 9 @ 2 #

After arrangement, series will be

C B % 9 D $ B 7 C ? 5 D 3 @ 2 #

12th element from right = D

5th to right of D = ?

34. (c) Triangle represents students who like cricket = 8, 12, 3, 11

Rectangle represents students who like football = 12, 11, 10, 14

circle represents students who like swimming = 3, 12, 4, 5.

No. of students who like swimming and football but not circket = 4.

35. (b) 9 6 2 6 9 4 7 6 2 5 6 4 6 7 8 3 2 6 9 2 2 6 5 6 2

Two such arrangements are there in the series, i.e. 2 6 9 ; 2 6 9

36. (d)

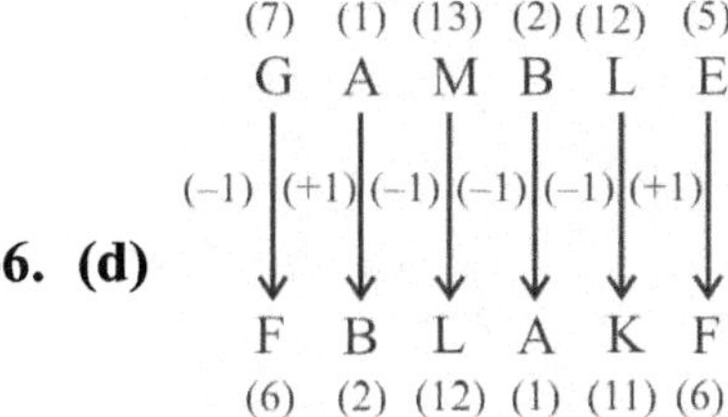

When letters are arranged in alphabetical order i.e.

(1)	(2)	(6)	(6)	(11)	(12)
A	B	F	F	K	L

"F" will be the fourth letter from right.

37. (c) There are 5 symbols which satisfies the condition given in the question which are as follows:

$A \times 2$; P \$ 7 ; Q 9 ; $P + 6$; $F \div 8$

38. (c)

(T)	(E)	C	H	(N)	O	L	(O)	G	Y
(20)	(5)	(3)	(8)	(14)	(15)	(12)	(15)	(7)	(25)
↓	↓	↓	↓	↓	↓	↓	↓	↓	↓
1	2	3	4	5	6	7	8	9	10

Words are : NOTE, TONE

39. (d)

|——————||15th|——————|27th|——|——|

Akhil Vivek

$15 + 12 + 3 = 30$

30 students are sitting in the given figure.

40. (b) 8 # B ; 4 * M : 7 * H.

3 such symbols are there which satisfies

41. (b) Raw 1

16 14 2

By rule (iii) i.e

$\rightarrow 16 + 14 \quad 2$

$\rightarrow 30 \quad 2$

By rule (iv) i.e

$\rightarrow 30 \div 2 = 15$

Resultant of Rawl = 15

According to question,

$15 \div 3 = 5$

Raw 2

8 7 12

By rule (ii) i.e

$8 + 7 \quad 12$

15 12

By rule (i) i.e,

$15 - 12 = 3$

Resultant of Raw 2 = 3

42. (c) 5, 3, 7 ; 1, 3, 5

43. (c)

CHAPTER-7

LEVEL 1

1. **(a)** From the relationship given in the question, we observe that each of the objects carries something in common to one another. A Tennis fan can be a cricket player as well as student. Hence Diagram (1) represents this relationship.

2. **(a)**

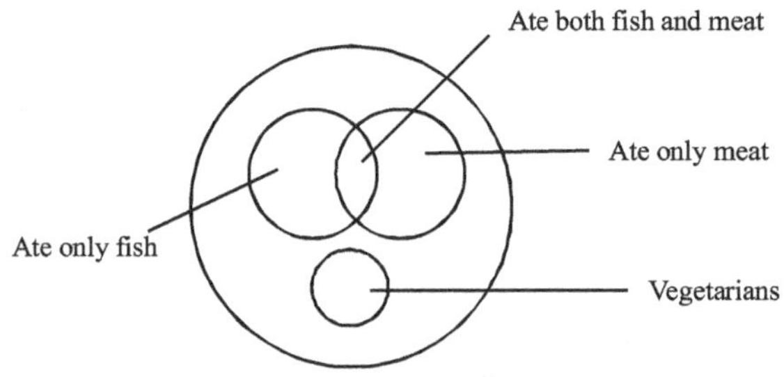

3. **(a)** The required set of students is denoted by region common to any three circle only

   ∴ Required number

   = (13 + 13 + 18 + 18) = 62.

4. **(a)** The required set of students is denoted by regions lying inside the circles representing History, Mathematics and Science. ∴ Required number = (9 + 14 + 18 + 15 + 16 + 13 + 13 + 20 + 18 + 13 + 16 + 19) = 183.

5. **(b)** The required set of students is denoted by the regions common to the circles representing History and Geography.

   ∴ Required number

   = (20 + 13 + 12 + 18) = 63.

6. **(b)** Number of students who took History

   = (16 + 12 + 18 + 20 + 18 + 14 + 13) = 111.

   Number of students who took Geography

   = (9 + 16 + 13 + 20 + 13 + 12 + 18) = 101.

   Number of students who took science

   = (19 + 15 + 18 + 20 + 18 + 16 + 13) = 119.

   Number of students who took mathematics

   = (9 + 14 + 13 + 20 + 13 + 15 + 18) = 102.

7. **(c)**

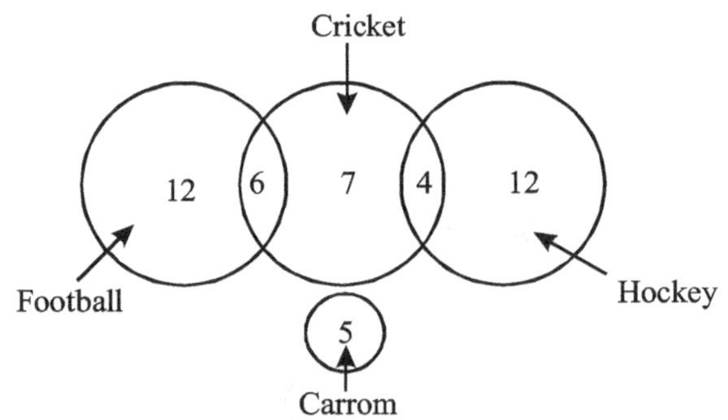

8. **(c)** 9. **(b)** 10. **(a)**

11. **(c)** The correct venn diagram represents female, mother and doctor is as shown below.

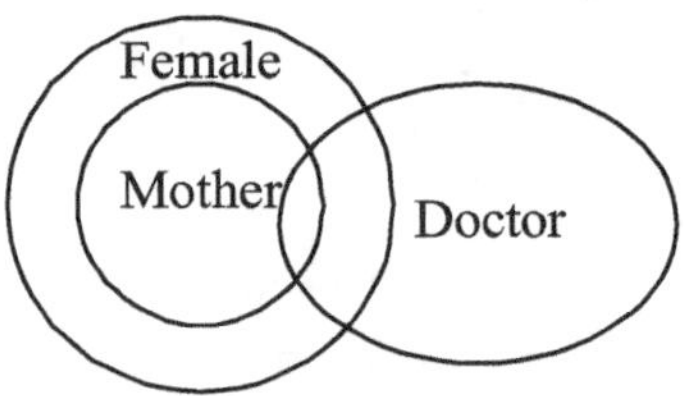

12. **(a)** English and Hindi both are the the languages.

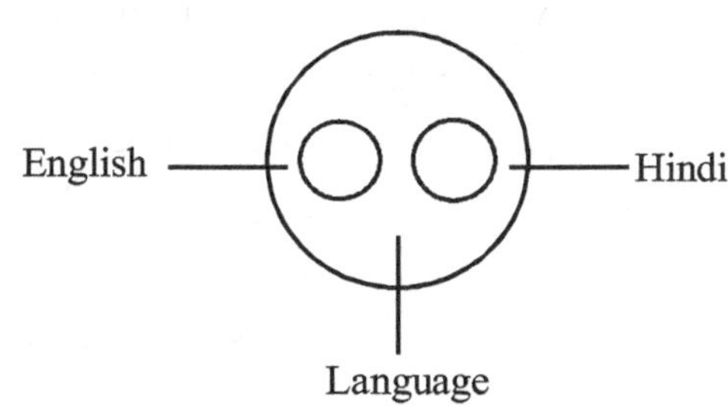

13. (b)

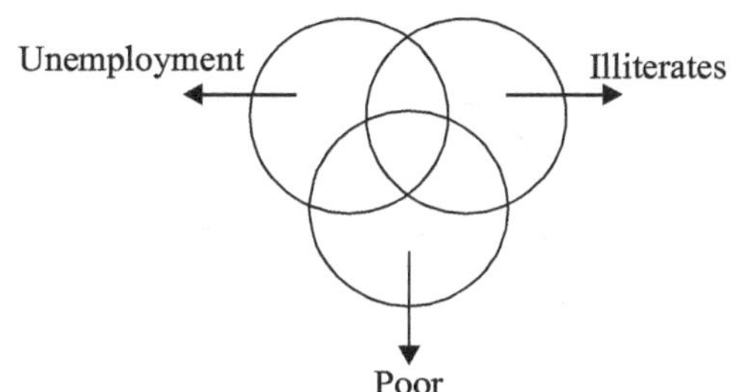

14. (a)

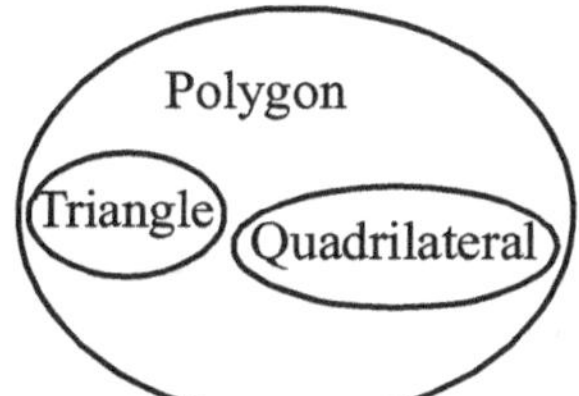

15. (c)

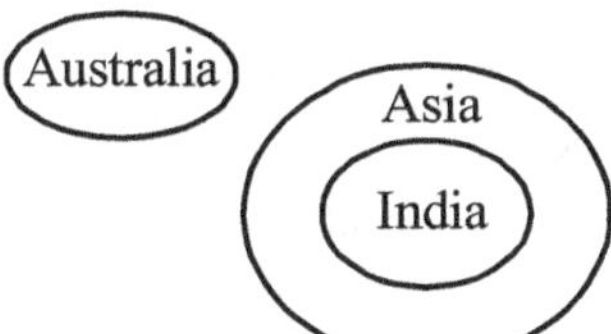

16. (d)

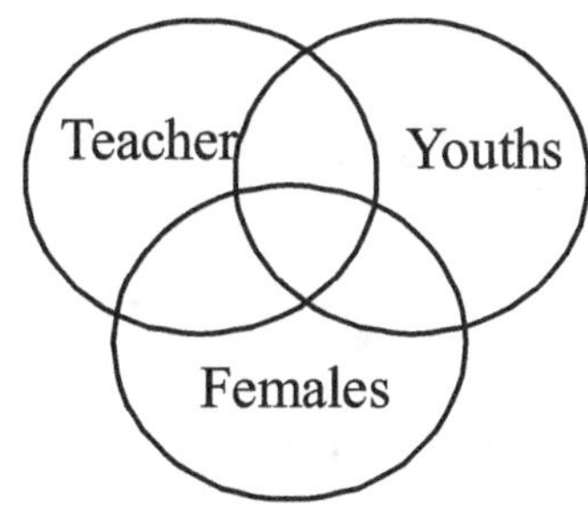

17. (d)

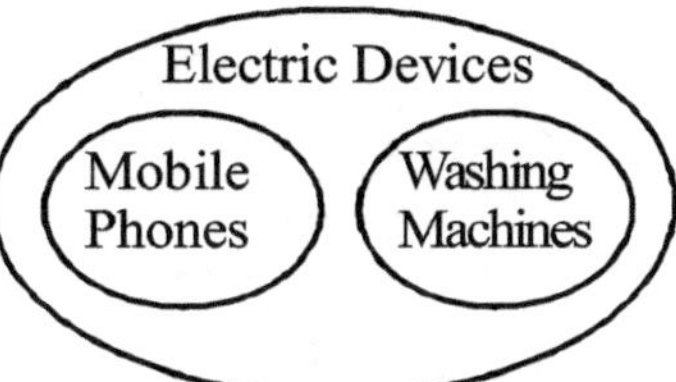

18. (a)

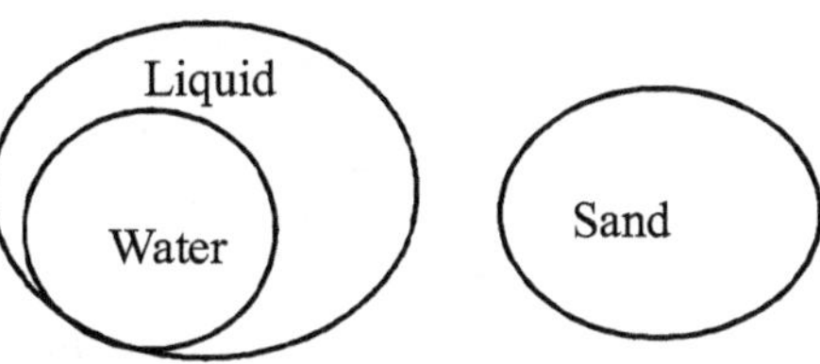

19. (b)

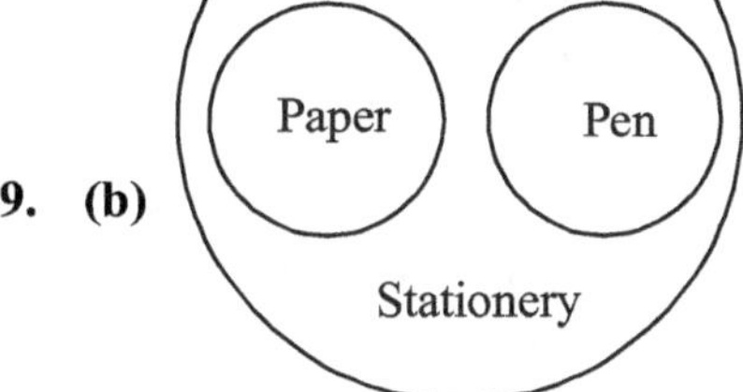

20. (d)

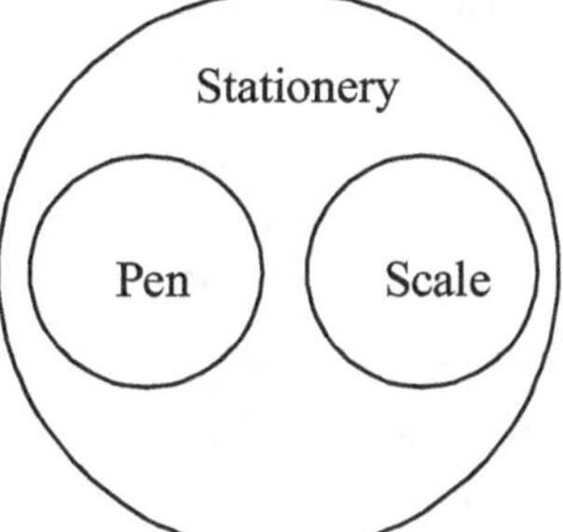

21. (b)

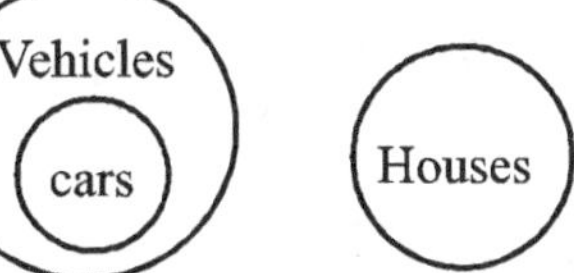

22. (c)

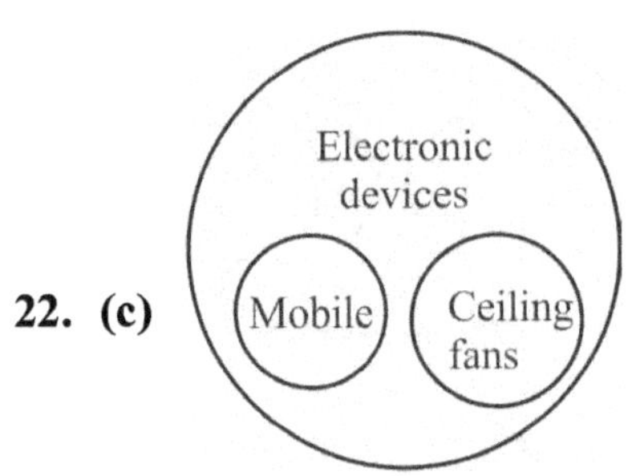

23. (c)

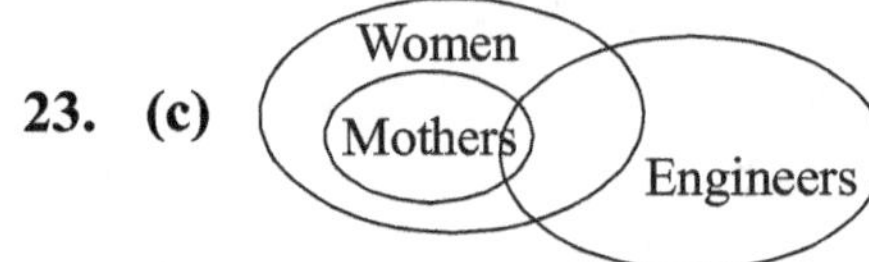

LEVEL 2

1. (a) The required region is the one common to the rectangle, square, circle and the triangle i.e., 7.

2. (d) The required region is the one which is common to only the rectangle and the circle and is not a part of either the triangle or the square i.e., 4.

3. (b) The required region is the one which lies inside the triangle and outside the rectangle. Square and circle i.e., 1.

4. (c) The required region is the one which lies inside the circle but outside the rectangle square and triangle i.e., 3.

5. (c) The required region is the one which is common to only the triangle and the circle i.e., 2.

6. (a) Clearly athletes among youths are represented by 'f + g'.

The ones, among them, who are not footballers are g.

7. (c)

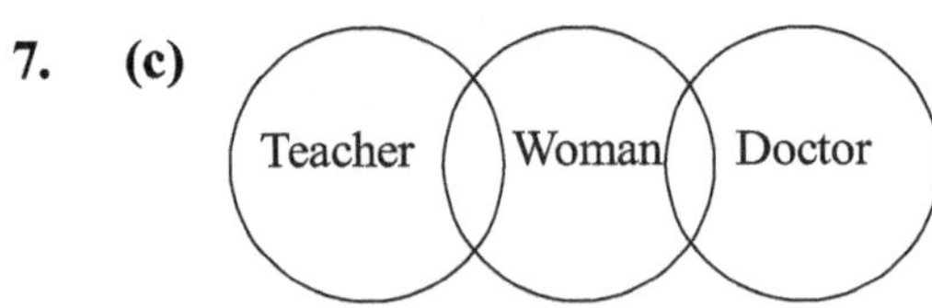

8. (b) The best relation among men, fathers and teachers is as shown below :

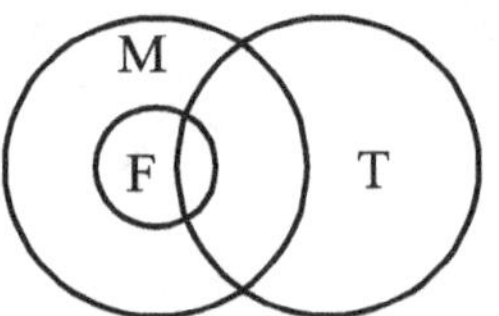

Here, all fathers are men and some fathers can be teachers. So, option (b) is correct answer.

9. (c)

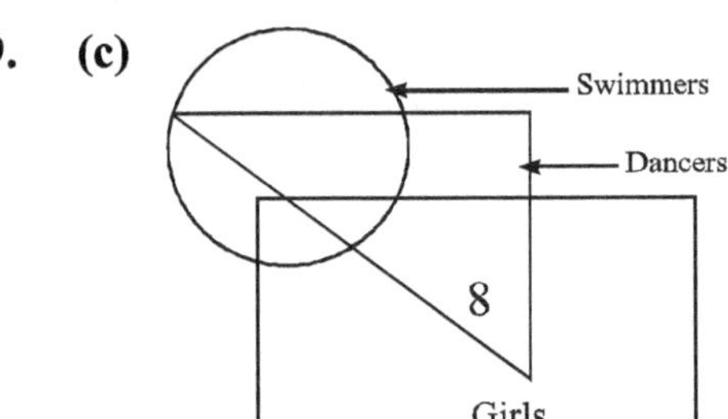

10. (d)

11. (c)

12. (a)

13. (c)

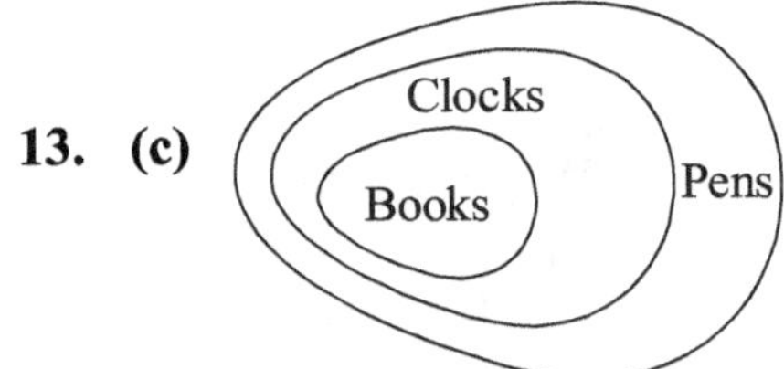

Both 1 and II follow.

14. (a) Number '4' is representing youth who are employed but not educated.

15. (d)

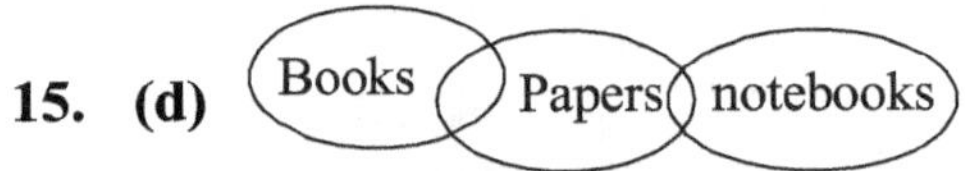

Both I and II follow.

16. (b) Circle represents boy child → 8, 9

Triangle represents girl child → 7, 4

Square represents twin child born → 4, 5.

in a day in particular hospital

4 represents twin girl child bron in a day in hospital.

17. (c) Persons who like banana and strawberry but not apple:

$5 + 4 = 9$

CHAPTER-8

LEVEL 1

1. (a) On interchanging + and ÷, and 2 and 3, we get the equations as $(2 + 4) \div 3$

$= 2$ or $6 \div 3 = 2$ or $2 = 2$, which is true.

2. (c) Given expression

$= (10 \times 4) + (4 \times 4) - 6 = 50$

3. (c) The rule is Difference of the digits of the number

$84 \oplus 72 = (8 - 4)(7 - 2) = 45$ etc.

$\therefore \quad 94 \oplus 82 = (9 - 4)(8 - 2) = 56$

4. (a) The rule is $a \times b = (b + a)(b - a)$

$\therefore \quad 2 \times 5 = (2 + 5)(5 - 2) = 73$

5. (b) Using the proper notations in (b), we get the statement as $5 \times 2 \div 2 < 10 - 4 + 2$ or $5 < 8$, which is true.

6. (c) Using the proper notations in (c), we get the statement as $5 \times 2 \div 2 < 10 - 4 + 8$ or $5 \times 1 < 18 - 4$ or $5 < 14$, which is true.

7. (d) Interchanging (+ and ÷) and (2 and 4), we get :

(a) $4 \div 2 + 3 = 3$ or $5 = 3$, which is false

(b) $2 \div 4 + 6 = 1.5$ or $6.5 = 1.5$, which is false.

(c) $2 + 4 \div 3 = 4$ or $\frac{10}{3} = 4$, which is false.

(d) $4 \div 2 + 6 = 8$ or $8 = 8$, which is true.

8. (c) Using the usual notations, we have

(a) The statement is $a > b < c \Rightarrow a = c < b$, which is false $[\because c > b]$

(b) The statement is $a > b < c \Rightarrow b \nless a > c$, which is false. $[\because b < a]$

(c) The statement is $a > b < c \Rightarrow a \nless b \ngtr c$, which is true

(d) The statement is $a > b < c \Rightarrow b \nless a = c$, which is false. $[\because b < a]$

9. (d) Given $A + B = C + D$

$\Rightarrow A - D = C - B$ ....(a)

and $A + D > B + C$ ....(b)

Subtracting (a) from (b) we get $2D > B$ or $D > B$.

hence $B > D$ is a wrong statement,

10. (c) The rule is $a + b = \left(\frac{a+b}{2}\right)^2$

$3 + 5 = \left(\frac{3+5}{2}\right)^2 = 16$ etc. \ $11 + 3 = \left(\frac{11+3}{2}\right)^2 = 49$

11. (a) $\frac{(36 \times 4) - 8 \times 4}{4 + 8 \times 2 + 16 \div 1}$

Replacing sign according to question. We get,

$\frac{(36 - 4) \div 8 - 4}{4 \times 8 \div 2 \times 16 + 1}$

$\Rightarrow \frac{32 \div 8 - 4}{4 \times 4 \times 16 + 1} = \frac{4 - 4}{256 + 1} = 0$

12. **(a)** $p \times q \times r$ means q is greater than or equal to r.

13. **(d)** $p + q \times r$ means p is not equal to q which is not possible.

14. **(c)** $p \Delta q O r$ means q is greater than r.

15. **(c)**

16. **(a)** By option (a),

$\Rightarrow 6 \div 20 \times 12 + 7 - 1 = 70$

By putting signs,

$\Rightarrow 6 - 20 + 12 \times 7 \div 1 = 70$

$\Rightarrow 6 - 20 + 12 \times 7 = 70$

$\Rightarrow 6 - 20 + 84 = 70$

$\Rightarrow 70 = 70$

17. **(d)** As, $(5 - 4) + (4 - 3) \Rightarrow 1 + 1 \Rightarrow 2$

and $(6 - 0) + (5 - 1) \Rightarrow 6 + 4 \Rightarrow 10$

Similarly, $(6 - 2) + (7 - 2)$

$\Rightarrow 4 + 5 \Rightarrow \boxed{9}$

18. **(b)** 25 M 5 L 10 P 2 J 15

$25 \div 5 - 10 \times 2 + 15$

$5 - 20 + 15$

$= 0$

19. **(c)** $34 \times 2 + 14 \div 7 - 8$

$= 34 \times 2 - 8$

$= 68 + 2 - 8 = 62$

20. **(c)** $14 \times 10 + 42 \div 2 - 8$

$= 140 + 21 - 8 = 153.$

21. **(b)** $40 \div 8 - 6 + 3 \times 4$

$= 5 - 6 + 12 = 11.$

22. **(a)** 52 © 4 @ 5 £ 8 $ 2

After changing the sign,

$52 - 4 \times 5 + 8 \div 2$

$= 52 - 20 + 4 = 36.$

23. **(d)** $2 + 14 - 4 \div 11 \times 5$

$\Rightarrow 2 \times 14 \div 4 - 11 + 5$

$\Rightarrow 2 \times - 11 + 5$

$\Rightarrow 1$

24. **(c)**

25. **(a)** $16 - 8 \div 4 + 5 \times 2 = 8$

Taking L.H.S.

$\rightarrow 16 \div 8 - 4 + 5 \times 2$

$\rightarrow 2 - 4 + 5 \times 2$

$\rightarrow 2 - 4 + 10$

$= 8.$

26. **(d)** $9 \times 6 - 2$

$= 54 - 2$

$= 52$

27. **(d)** Equation $\rightarrow 1 \div 14 \times 30 + 20 - 10 = 12.$

Taking L.H.S.

$1 + 14 \times 30 \div 20 - 10$

$1 + \cancel{14} \times \frac{3\cancel{0}}{\cancel{20}} - 10$

$\rightarrow 1 + 21 - 10$

$\rightarrow 22 - 10 = 12$ R.H.S.

LEVEL 2

1. **(d)** Using the proper notations in (4), we get

$8 \times 8 + 8 \div 8 - 8 = 8 \times 8 + 1 - 8$

$= 64 + 1 - 8 = 57$

2. **(d)** Using the proper notations in (d), we get

$8 \times 8 + 8 \div 8 - 8 = 8 \times 8 + 1 - 8 = 64 + 1 - 8 = 57$

3. **(b)** Using the proper signs, we get

Expression in (a) $= 15 - 5 \div 5 \times 20 + 10$

$= 15 \times 5 + 5 - 2 = 75 + 5 - 2 = 78$

Expression in (b)

$= 8 + 10 \times 3 \div 5 - 6 = 8 + 10 \times \frac{3}{5} - 6$

$= 8 + 6 - 6 = 8.$

Expression in (c)

$= 6 - 2 \div 3 + 12 \times 3 = 6 - \frac{2}{3} + 36$

$= 42 - \frac{2}{3} = \frac{124}{3}$

Expression in (d)

$= 3 + 7 \times 5 - 10 \div 3 = 3 + 7 \times 5 - \frac{10}{3} =$

$\frac{104}{3}$

$\therefore$ Expression (b) is true

4. **(c)** By making the interchanges given in (a), we get the equations as 2 – 5 + 3 = 4 or 0 = 4, which is false.

By making the interchanges given in (b), we gets the equations as 3 – 2 + 5 = 4 or 6 = 4, which is false.

By making the interchanges given in (c), we get the equations as 5 – 3 + 2 = 4, which is true.

So, the answer is (c)

5. **(d)** Given : $36 \div 12 \times 6 + 9 - 6 = 38$

Let us consider option (a) : – and ×

After putting it in given equation we get $36 \div 12 - 6 + 9 \times 6 = 36$

$36 \neq 38$. So it is wrong option.

Option (b) : ÷ and ×

After putting in given equation we get $36 \times 12 \div 6 + 9 - 6 = 75$

$75 \neq 38$. So it is wrong option.

Option (c) : – and +

After putting it in given equation we get $36 \div 12 \times 6 - 9 + 6 = 15$

$15 \neq 38$. So it is wrong option.

Option (d) : ÷ and +

After putting it in given equation we get $36 + 12 \times 6 \div 9 - 6 = 38$

38 is required answer. So, it is correct option.

6. **(a)** Given : $= \to >, - \to +, + \to -$ and a = b = c

Taking option (a) : b = a + c

By Changing the signs we get,

$b > a - c$

$b > a - a$ $(\because a = c)$

$b < 0$

$\therefore$ This is the correct option.

7. **(c)** Given, $100 - 81 \div 27 @ 3 < 6 = 115$

After replacing the symbols,

$\Rightarrow 100 - 81 \div 27 + 3 \times 6$

$\Rightarrow 100 - 3 + 18$

$\Rightarrow 100 + 18 - 3$

$\Rightarrow 118 - 3 \Rightarrow 115$

8. **(c)** Given, $56\delta(6\sigma 8)\sum 4 \propto 1$

After putting the signs,

$56 \div (6 + 8) \times 4 - 1$

$56 \div 14 \times 4 - 1$

$4 \times 4 - 1$

$16 - 1 = 15$

9. **(a)** + and +, 64 and 96

$\Rightarrow (64 + 128) + 96 \Rightarrow 192 \div 96 = 2.$

10. **(b)** $23 + 26 = 49 - 7 = 42$

$11 + 15 = 26 - 7 = 19$

$32 + 16 = 48 - 7 = 41$

11. **(a)**

12. **(b)** $3 + 2 - 4 > 6 \div 3 - 2$

$1 > 0$

13. **(c)** $5 \times 15 + 7 - 20 \div 4 = 77$

$75 + 7 - 5 = 77$

$\boxed{77 = 77}$

14. **(d)** $a - b - c = a < b < c$

As

$a - b + c = a < b > c$

$b + a - c = b > a < c$

$c \times b + a = c \leq b > a$

None of these implies.

15. **(b)** $13 \div 13 - 13 + 13 \times 13$

$\Rightarrow 1 - 13 + 169$

$\Rightarrow 157$

16. **(b)** $(7 \times 6) + (16 \div 8) + (4 + 3)$

$\Rightarrow 42 + 2 + 7$

$\Rightarrow 51$

17. **(b)** $- \longleftrightarrow +$

$\times \longleftrightarrow \div$

$10 + 8 \times 4 \div 8 - 9$

$= 10 + 8 \times \frac{1}{2} - 9$

$= 5$

18. **(c)**

CHAPTER-9

LEVEL 1

1. **(c)** To be together between 9 and 10, the minute hand has to gain 45 minute spaces.

Now, 55 min. spaces are gained in 60 minutes.

$\therefore$ 45 min. spaces are gained in $\left(\frac{60}{55} \times 45\right)$ min. or $49\frac{1}{11}$ min.

So, the hands are together at $49\frac{1}{11}$ min. past 9.

2. **(a)** Between 2 and 4 O'clock, 8 and 10 O'clock, the hands are at right thrice in each case. Between 4 and 8'O clock, the hands are at right angles.

So total number of times the hands are at right angles

$= 3 + 3 + (2 \times 4) = 14.$

3. **(c)** Starting with 1988, we go on counting the number of odd days till the sum is divisible by 7.

Years $\rightarrow$ 1988 1989 1990 1991 1992

Odd days $\rightarrow$ 2 1 1 1 2

= 7 i.e. odd days

$\therefore$ Calendar for 1993 the same as that of 1988.

4. **(c)** 1600 years have 0 odd day and 300 years have 1 odd day.

49 years contain 12 leap years and 37 ordinary years and therefore (24 + 37) odd days i.e., 5 odd days

i.e., 1949 years contain (0 + 1 + 5) or 6 odd days.

26 days of January contain 5 odd days.

Total odd days = (6 + 5) = 11 or 4 odd days.

So, the day was Thursday.

5. **(b)** The year 1979 being an ordinary year, it has 1 odd day.

So, the day on 12th January 1980 is one day beyond on the day on 12th January, 1979.

But, January 12, 1980 being Saturday.

$\therefore$ January 12, 1979 was Friday.

6. **(b)** A leap year has (52 weeks + 2 days). So, the number of odd days in a leap year is 2.

7. **(c)** Counting the number of days after 3rd November, 1987, we have :

Nov. Dec. Jan. Feb. March April

days 27 + 31 + 31 + 29 + 31 + 4

= 153 days containing 6 odd days.

8. **(c)** 1600 years contain 0 odd day, 300 years contain 1 odd day. Also, 83 years contain 20 leap years and 63 ordinary years and therefore (40 + 0) odd days i.e., 5 odd days.

∴ 1983 years contain (0 + 1 + 5) i.e., 6 odd days.

Number of days from Jan. 1984 to 31st Oct. 1984

$= (31 + 29 + 31 + 30 + 31 + 30 + 31 + 31 + 30 + 31)$

= 305 days = 4 odd days

∴ Total number of odd days

= 6 + 4 = 3 odd days

So, 31st Oct. 1984 was Wednesday.

9. **(c)** The hands coincide 11 times in every 12 hours (between 11 and 1 O'clock there is a common position at 12 O'clock). Hence, the hands coincide 22 times in a day.

10. **(d)** In 60 min. hour hand moves by 360/12

In 20 min. hour hand moves by

$$\frac{360}{12 \times 60} \times 20 = 10$$

11. **(d)**

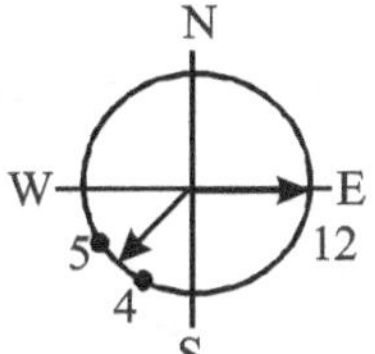

12. **(a)** At 2'O Clock, Minute Hand will be 10 × 6 = 60° behind the Hour Hand.

In 30 minutes, Minute Hand will gain $\left(5\frac{1}{2}\right)^{\circ} \times 30 = 150 + 15 = 165°$

∴ Angle between Hour Hand and Minute Hand

= 165 – 60 = 105°

13. **(a)** 2000 year have 0 odd day

Year 2001 2002 2003 2004 2005 2006 2007 2008 2009

Odd days 1 1 1 2 1 1 1 2 1

= 11 odd days = 4 odd days.

1st January, 2010 has 1 odd day. Total number of odd days = (4 + 1)

∴ 1st January, 2010 will be Friday.

14. **(c)** Count the number of days from 2005 onwards to get 0 odd day.

Year 2005 2006 2007 2008 2010 2011

Odd days 1 1 1 2 1 1

= 7 or 0 odd day.

∴ Calender for the year 2005 is the same as that for the year 2012.

15. (c) In a day the two hands of a clock coincide 22 times.

16. (a)

At 4 : 30, minute hand will be 15 × 6 = 90°

In twenty minutes, hour hand will gain

$20\times\frac{1}{2}=10°$

∴ Required angle = 90 + 10 = 100°

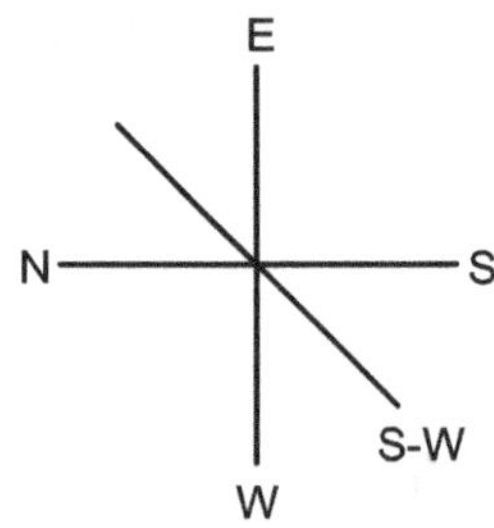

LEVEL 2

1. (a) At 4 O'clock, the minute hand will be 20 min. spaces behind the hour hand.

Now, when the two hands are at right angles, they are 15 min. spaces apart.

So, they are at right angles in following two cases.

Case I :

When minute hand is 15 min. spaces behind the hour hand :

In this case min. hand will have to gain (20 – 15) = 5 min. spaces.

55 min. spaces are gained by it in 60 min.

5 min. spaces will be gained by it in $\left(\frac{60}{55}\times 5\right)$ min. $= 5\frac{5}{11}$ min.

∴ They are at right angles at $5\frac{5}{11}$ min. past 4.

Case II :

When the minute hand is 15 min. spaces ahead of the hour hand :

To be in this position, the minute hand will have to gain (20 + 15) = 35 minute spaces.

55 min. spaces are gained in 60 min.

35 min. spaces are gained in $\left(\frac{60}{55}\times 35\right)$ min $= 38\frac{2}{11}$ min.

∴ They are at right angles at $38\frac{2}{11}$ min. past 4.

2. (d) Clearly, every day repeats itself on the seventh day. Now, 17th Dec. 2002 - 16th Dec.

2003 is a period of 365 days. Dividing by 7, we get 52 weeks and one day. Thus, the 365th day will be the same as the first day, i.e., 16th Dec. 2003 is also Saturday.

Now, 16th Dec. 2003 - 15th Dec. 2004 is a period of 366 days (because 2004, being a leap year, has 29 days in February). Thus, as shown above, 14th Dec. 2004 will be the same as 16th Dec. 2003, i.e., Saturday. So, 21st Dec. 2004 is also Saturday and thus, 22nd Dec. 2004 is a Sunday.

3. (a) 16th July, 1776 mean (1775 years + 6 months + 16 days)

Now, 1600 years have 0 odd days.

100 years have 5 odd days

75 years contain 18 leap years and 57 ordinary years and therefore (36 + 57) or 93 or 2 odd days.

∴ 1775 years given 0 + 5 + 2 = 7 and so 0 odd days.

Also number of days from 1st Jan. 1776 to 16th July, 1776

Jan. Feb. March April May June July

31 + 29 + 31 + 30 + 31 + 30 + 16

= 198 days = 28 weeks + 2 days = 2 odd days

∴ Total number of odd days = 0 + 2 = 2.

Hence the day on 16th July, 1776 was 'Tuesday'.

4. **(d)** They will be opposite to each other when there is a space of 30 minutes between them.

This will happen when the minute hand gains (30 + 20) minutes = 50 minutes.

The minute hand gains 50 minutes in

$\frac{50 \times 60}{55} = 54\frac{6}{11}$ minutes.

i.e., they will point in opposite directions at $54\frac{6}{11}$ minutes past 4.

5. **(a)** Time interval indicated by incorrect clock

= 6 p.m – 1 p.m = 5 hrs.

Time gained by incorrect clock in one hour

$= +1 \text{ min} = +\frac{1}{60} \text{hr.}$

Using the formula,

$$\frac{\text{True time interval}}{\text{Time interval in incorrect clock}}$$

$$= \frac{1}{1 + \text{hour gained in 1 hour by incorrect clock}}$$

$$\Rightarrow \frac{\text{True time interval}}{5} = \frac{1}{1+\frac{1}{60}}$$

$$\Rightarrow \text{True time interval} = \frac{5 \times 60}{61} = 4\frac{56}{61}$$

$$\therefore \text{True time} = 1 \text{ p.m.} + 4\frac{56}{61} \text{ hrs.}$$

$$= 5 \text{ p.m.} + \frac{56}{61} \text{ hrs.} = 5 \text{ p.m.} + \frac{56}{61} \times 60 \text{ min.}$$

$$= 55\frac{5}{61} \text{ minutes past 5.}$$

6. **(b)** Time from noon on Sunday to 3 pm on Wednesday = 75 hours.

24 hours 2 minutes of the first clock

= 24 hours of the correct one.

⇒ 1 hour of the first clock = 24 × (30/721) hours
of correct one.

⇒ 75 ours of the first clock

= 24 × 30 × (75/721) hours of correct one

= 54000/721 hours = 74 hours 53.7 min.

Hence the answer is 2:54 pm.

7. **(a)** At 9'O clock, the Minute Hand is ahead of Hour Hand by 45 minutes. The hands will be opposite to each other when there is a space of 30 minutes between them.

This will happen when the Minute Hand gains 15 minutes' space over Hour Hand.

Time taken by Minutes Hand to gain

15 minutes

$$=15\times\left(1+\frac{1}{11}\right)=15+\frac{15}{11}=15+1\frac{4}{11}=16\frac{4}{11} \text{ minutes.}$$

Hence the Hands are opposite to each other at $16\frac{4}{11}$ minutes past 9.

8. **(a)** The clock gains 15 min in 24 hours.

Therefore, in 16 hours, it will gain 10 minutes.

Hence, the time shown by the clock will be 4.10 am.

9. **(d)** Required angle

= 240 – 24 × (11/2)

= 240 –132 = 108°.

10. **(b)** In a watch than is running correct the minute hand should cross the hour hand once in every $65+\frac{5}{11}$ min. So they should ideally cross 3 times once in

$$3\times\left(\frac{720}{11}\right)\frac{-2060}{11}\text{min}=196.36 \text{ minutes.}$$

But in the watch under consideration, they meet after every 3hr, 18 min and 15 seconds,

i.e. $\left(3\times 60+18+\frac{15}{60}\right)=\frac{793}{4}$ min.

Thus, our watch is actually losing time (as it is slower than the normal watch). Hence when our watch elapsed

$$\left(1440\times\frac{196.36}{198.25}\right)=1426.27.$$

Hence the amount of time lost by our watch in one day $=(1440\sim 1426.27)=13.73$ i.e. 13 min and 50s (approx).

11. **(c)** 26th Jan., 1950 = (1949 years + Period from 1st Jan., 1950 to 26th Jan., 1950)

1600 years have 0 odd day. 300 years have 1 odd day.

49 years = (12 leap years + 37 ordinary years)

= [(12 × 2) + (37 × 1)] odd days = 61 odd days = 5 odd days.

Number of days from 1st Jan. to 26th Jan = 26 = 5 odd days

Total number of odd days

= (0 + 1 + 5 + 5) = 11 = 4 odd days

∴ The required days was 'Thursday'

12. **(c)** 2000 years have 2 odd days.

Year	2001	2002	2003	2004	2005	2006	2007	2008	2009
Odd days	1	1	1	2	1	1	1	2	1

= 11 odd days = 4 odd days.

1st January, 2010 has 1 odd day. Total number of odd days = (2 + 4 + 1) = 7 = 0.

∴ 1st January, 2010 will be Sunday.

13. **(c)** Count the number of days from 2005 onwards to get 0 odd day.

Year	2005	2006	2007	2008	2010	2011
Odd days	1	1	1	2	1	1

= 7 or 0 odd day. ∴ Calendar for the year 2005 is the same as that for the year 2012.

14. (d) 09/12/2001—— Sunday

No. of days between 9/ 12/ 71 & 9 / 12/ 2001

we know every year has 1 odd days

we know leap year has 2 odd days

Here, No. of normal years = 22

And no. of leap years = 8

So odd days = 22 + 16

= 38 i.e. 3odd days

(remainder when 38 is divided by 7, i.e. 3)

Hence it was a Thursday

15. (c) 15th August, 1947 = (1946 years + Period from 1st Jan., 1947 to 15th Aug., 1947)

Counting of odd days :

1600 years have 0 odd day. 300 years have 1 odd day.

47 years = (11 leap years + 36 ordinary years)

= [(11 × 2) + (36 × 1)] odd days = 58 odd days

⇒ 2 odd days.

Jan.	Feb.	March	April	May	June
31	28	31	30	31	30

July	Aug.
31	15

= 227 days = (32 weeks + 3 days)

= 3 odd days.

Total number of odd days

= (0 + 1 + 2 + 3) odd days

= 6 odd days.

Hence, the required day was 'Friday'.

16. (d) 100 years contain 5 odd days. So, last day of 1st century is 'Friday'

200 years contain (5 × 2) = 10 odd days = 3 odd days.

So, last day of 2nd century is 'Wednesday'.

300 years contain (5 × 3)

= 15 odd days = 1 odd day.

∴ Last day of 3rd century is 'Monday'.

400 years contain 0 odd day.

∴ Last day of 4th century is 'Sunday'

Since the order is continually kept in successive cycles, we see that the last day of a century cannot be Tuesday, Thursday or Saturday.

CHAPTER-10

LEVEL 1

Sol. (1-5)

Person	Vehicle	Profession	Sex
A	II	Teacher	Female
B	I	Engineer	Male
C	III	Doctor	Female
D	II	Doctor	Male
E	III	Teacher	Male
F	II	Engineer	Female
G	I	Teacher	Female

1. (c) C travels in vehicle III.

2. (b) There are four ladies in the group — A, C, F and G.

3. (b) F is an engineer by profession.

4. (d) Since F is an engineer, so F – Female - Teacher is the incorrect combination.

5. (a) A, E and G are the three teachers.

Sol. (6-7)

Arrangement from Richest to poorest

Bhanudas > Akhil > Amar > Chaitanya > Gopal (Farmer) (Lawyer) (Doctor) (Teacher) (Photographer)

6. (d) Chaitanya's occupation is Teacher.

7. (b) Bhanudas is a farmer.

8. (a) 1st Row ⇒ D

2nd Row ⇒ E

3rd Row ⇒ C

4th Row ⇒ A

5th Row ⇒ B

9. (d)

Persons	LANGUAGES			
	Tamil	Malayalam	English	Hindi
A	✓	✓	✓	×
B	✓	✓	×	✓
C	✓	×	✓	✓
D	×	✓	✓	✓

D can speak English, Hindi, and Malayalam.

10. (a) Left • M R P L O • Right

Hence, P coach is in the middle of the five coaches.

11. (b) A B (E) D C

12. (d) Standing arrangement : (facing south)

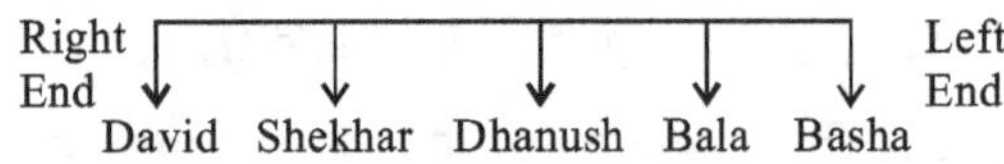

Hence, Dhanush is standing at the middle of the row.

13. (d) Standing Arrangement:

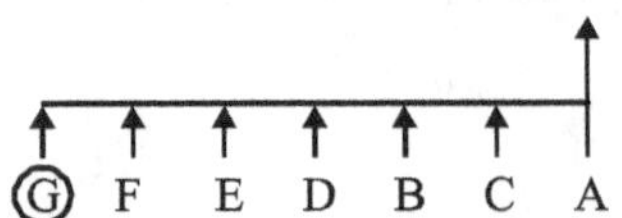

G is standing on the extreme left.

14. (a) C > D > A > E > B

So, A is in the middle.

15. (c) East

T B V M S H Y

So, vehicle B is second to the left of the M.

16. (a)

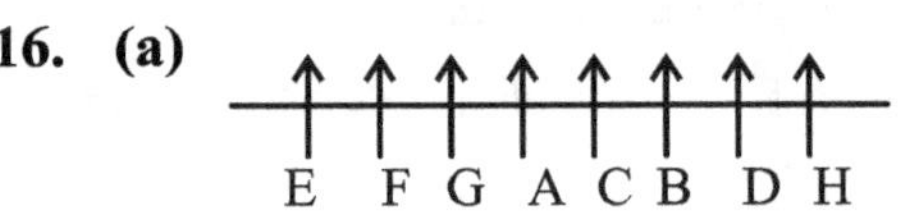

E is sitting at the other corner.

17. (d)

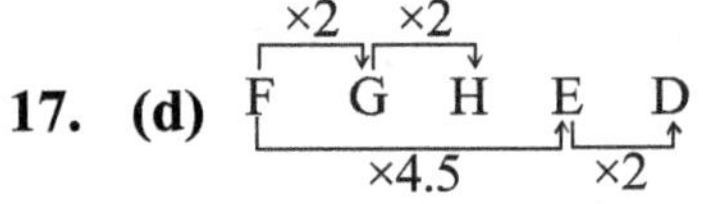

18. (d)

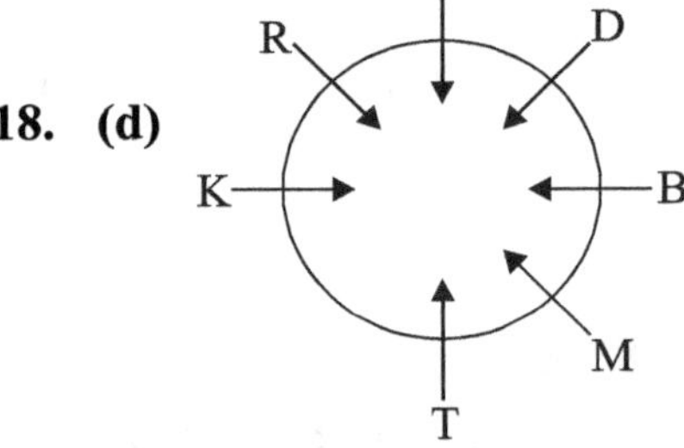

T is sitting second to the right of R.

LEVEL 2

Sol. (1-2)

C is the second reader. A is the second last reader.

E is not the first or last to read. So, E is the third reader. There were two readers between B and A.

So, the order of reading the newspaper is : B, C, E, A, D.

1. (b) B passed the newspaper to C.

2. (d) D read the newspaper last.

Sol. (3-4)

C is the second reader. A is the second last reader.

E is not the first or last to read. So, E is the third reader. There were two readers between B and A.

So, the order of reading the newspaper is : B, C, E, A, D.

3. **(b)** B passed the newspaper to C.
4. **(d)** D read the newspaper last.
5. **(b)** We may prepare a table as follows:

	Delhi	Bangalore	Tall	Short	Girls	Boys
A	✓			✓	✓	
B	✓			✓		✓
C		✓		✓	✓	
D		✓	✓		✓	
E		✓		✓		✓
F		✓	✓			✓

Clearly, D is the tall girl from Bangalore.

6. **(c)** The four vocal musicians and one actress in the group are given. Two dancers are Shailja and Tanuja. Two violinists are Girija and Vanaja. Since Jalaja and Shailja cannot be violinists, so remaining two violinists are Tanuja and Pooja. Clearly, Tanuja is both a violinist and a dancer.
7. **(c)** Clearly moving left from β, third person will be ϕ at positioin 2.
8. **(b)** $1 \rightarrow \delta$ is to the left of ψ

   $2 \rightarrow \beta$ is to the right of $\in$

   $3 \rightarrow \eta$ & β are not neighbours

   $4 \rightarrow \psi$ is to the left of η
9. **(a)** Clearly ϕ is third towards right of ψ.
10. **(c)** Only $\in$ is between α & β.
11. **(d)** There are 3 persons between γ and β both clockwise and anti-clockwise.

Sol. (12-14)

According to the given information, the arrangement of six boys is as following :

BOYS	GAMES					
	Foot-ball	Cri-cket	Tennis	(Tallest) Kabaddi	Squash	(Shortest) Vollyball
Tarun	✓	×	×	×	×	×
Umesh	×	×	×	✓	×	×
Prem	×			×		×
Kamal	×			×		×
Ramesh	×	×	×	×	×	✓
Shyam	×			×		×

According to their heights : U > K > T > P > S > R

12. **(d)** Umesh plays Kabaddi among them
13. **(a)** According to the descending order of their heights, Prem will be at fourth place.
14. **(a)** We can't determine that who plays tennis.

Sol. (15-18)

15. **(c)** Talyang is sitting opposite to Ribiya.
16. **(d)** Silva is sitting between Ribiya and Ninong.
17. **(a)** Nazeli is sitting Talyang Yaangba. Option 1 is correct.
18. **(d)** Silva is sitting on the left of Hinong. Hence, option (d) is correct.

19. (a)

R →		S →
→		Q →
P →	Or	P →
Q →		→
S →		R →

S cannot be seat at 2nd place in either case because it is given in question that R and S cannot be together.

20. (d)

21. (d)

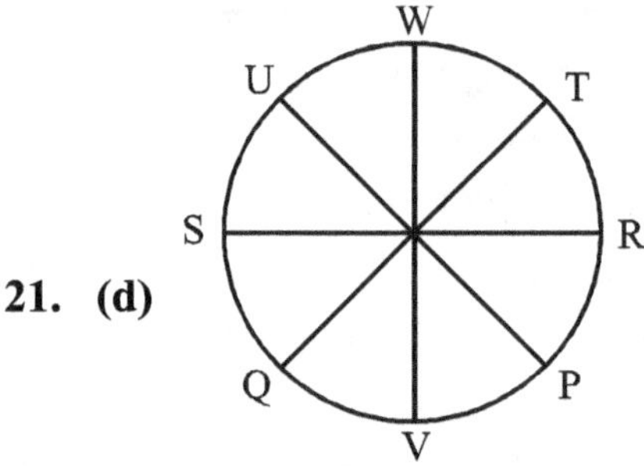

'U' is sitting between W and S.

22. (c) Monday → L

Tuesday → K

Wednesday → N

Thursday → J

Friday → M

L is unloaded on Monday.

23. (d)

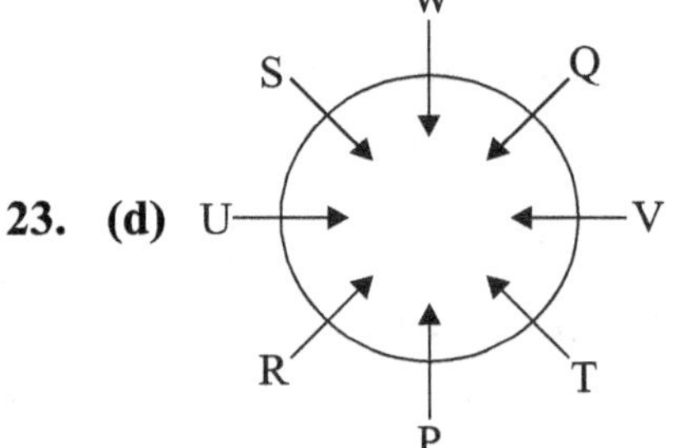

R is the immediate right of U.

24. (c)

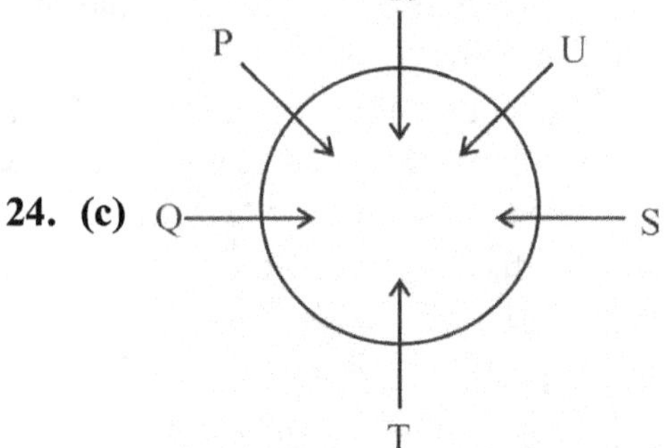

U is sitting third to the left of Q

25. (b)

P	Men	Vegetarian	Non swimmer
Q	Women	Vegetarian	Swimmer
R	Women	Vegetarian	Non swimmer
S	Men	Non vegetarian	Non swimmer
T	Women	Vegetarian	Swimmer
U	Men	Non vegetarian	Swimmer

'Q' is the vegetarian female who knows swimming.

26. (a)

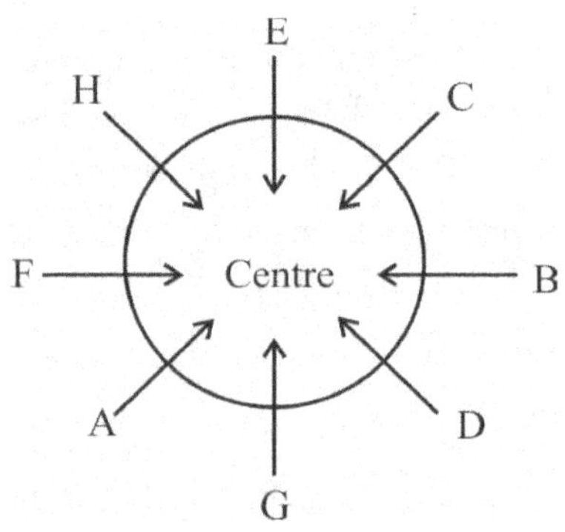

B sits in between D and C

27. **(a)** **28.** **(c)**

CHAPTER-11

LEVEL 1

1. **(d)** We have three squares with vertical and horizontal sides. Each such square has $1^2 + 2^2 = 5$ squares in it. Thus there are 15 such squares.

   In addition, we have two obliquely placed squares.

   Hence total no. of squares = 17

2. **(c)** Name the squares as square 1, 2, 3, 4 5 beginning with the largest.

   The space between square 1 and 2 is subdivided into 4 triangles.

   The space between square 2 and 3 has 12 triangles as below.

   From each vertex of square no. 2, there are two small triangles and one large triangle consisting of these two triangles.

   Thus from four vertices, there are 12 triangles.

   Each diagonal of square no. 2 divides it into two triangles, making 4 triangles in this manner, each half the size of the square.

   The two diagonals together sub- divide the square into four triangles, each 1/ 4th the size of the square .

   Thus there are 20 triangles in square no.

   2 Pattern of square no. 1 and 2 is repeated in no. 3 and 4 respectively.

   There are no triangles in square no.

   Hence, total no. of triangles

   $= 4 + 20 + 4 + 20 = 48$

3. **(b)** In figure (X), one of the dots lies in the region common to the circle and the triangle only and the other dot lies in the region common to the circle and the square only. In figures (a), (c) and (d), the region common to the circle and the triangle lies within the square. Only figure (b) contains a region common to the circle and the triangle only and also a region common to the circle and the square.

4. **(d)** One point in all three figures and the second point only in one figure.

5. **(a)** One point lies in all three figures. Two points lie in between two figures.

6. **(c)** In fig. (X), the dot is placed in the region common to the circle and the triangle. Amongst the four alternatives only in figure (c), we have a region common to circle and triangle only. Hence figure, (c) is the answer.

7. **(b)** Total number of Parallelograms are 17.

8. **(a)** **9.** **(d)** **10.** **(d)**

11. **(c)** The figure may be labelled as shown.

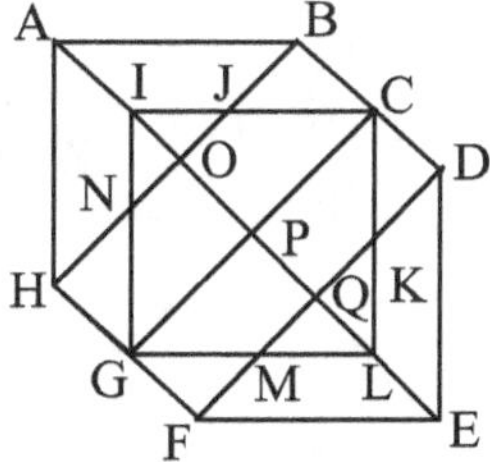

The simplest triangles are IJO, BCJ, CDK, KQL, MLQ, GFM, GHN and NIO i.e. 8 in number.

The triangles composed of two components each are ABO, AHO, NIJ, IGP, ICP, DEQ, FEQ, KLM, LCP and LGP i.e. 10 in number

The triangles composed of four components each are HAB, DEF, LGI, GIC,

ICL and GLC i.e. 6 in number.

Total number of triangles in the figure = 8 + 10 + 6 = 24.

12. (d) There are 60 triangles in the given figure.

13. (d) There are 30 triangles in the given figure.

14. (d) There are 31 triangles in the given figure.

15. (d) There are 30 triangles in the given figure.

16. (d) More than 15 or 22 exactly.

LEVEL 2

1. (d) The figure may be labelled as shown :

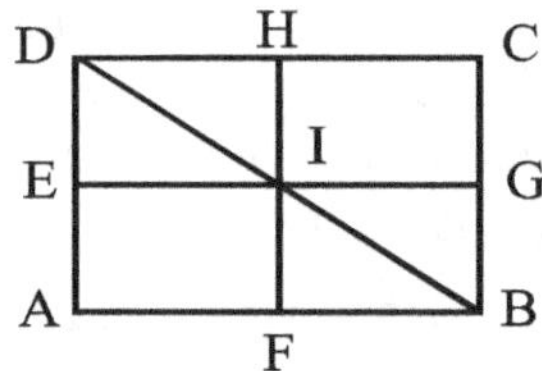

The simplest triangles are – DHI, DEI, IFB, IGB, i.e. 4 in number.

The triangles composed of three components each are – DAB, DCB i.e. 2 in number.

So, total triangles are = (4 + 2) = 6

The simple quadrilaterals are – DEHI, HIGC, EIFA, FIGB i.e. 4 in number.

The quadrilaterals composed of two components each are – DHFA, HFBC, DECG, EABG, i.e. 4 in number.

The quadrilateral composed of your components is – ABCD. So quadrilaterals are = (4 + 4 + 1) = 9

2. (c) The figure may be labelled as shown :

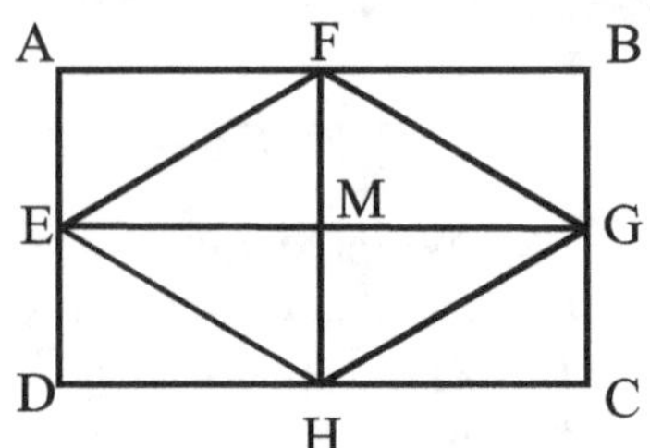

The quadrilaterals composed of two components each are –

AFME, FMGB, EMHD, MGCH i.e. 4 in number.

The quadrilaterals composed of four components each are –

AEGB, AFHD, FBCH, EDCG, EFGH i.e. 5 in number

The quadrilateral composed of eight components is –

ABCD i.e. in number

So, quadrilaterals are = (4 + 5 + 1) = 10

3. (a)

4. (a) The figure may be labelled as shown.

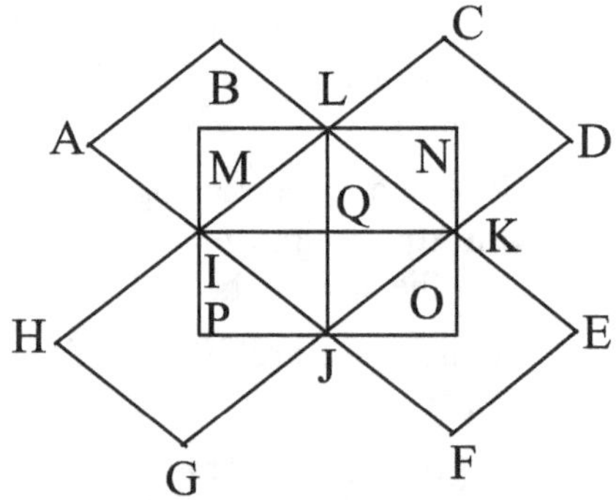

The simplest squares/rectangles are - ABCI, LCDK, HIJG, JKEF, MLQI, LNK, QKOJ and QJPIQ i.e 8.

The squares/rectangles composed of two components each are ABKJ, ILEF,

HLKG, IJCD, MLQJP, LNOJ, MNKI and IKOP i.e 8

The squares/rectangles composed of three/four components each are - ABEF, HGDC, ILKJ and MNOPL i.e 4.

Total no. of squares/rectangles in the figure = 8 + 8 + 4 = 20.

5. **(c)** Largest size square formed in this diagram is of size 3 × 3.

No. of 3 × 3 squares = 2 = 1 × 2 (from points 1, 5)

No . of 2 × 2 squares = 6 = 2 × 3 (from points 1, 2, 5, 6, 9, 10)

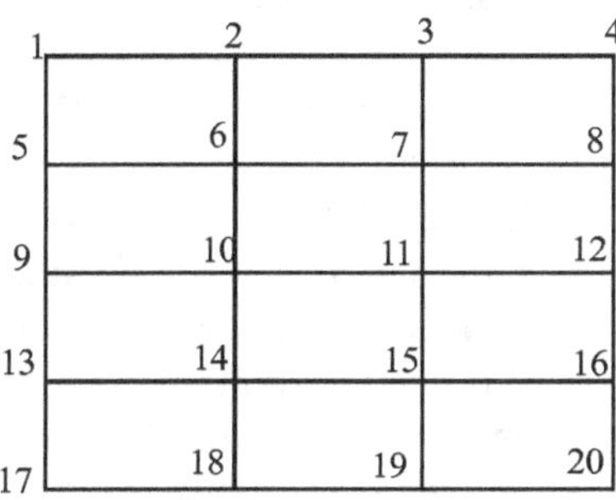

No. of 1 × 1 squares = 12 = 3 × 4

Hence , total = 1 × 2 + 2 × 3 + 3 × 4

= 3 × 4 + 2 × 3 + 1 × 2 = 20

6. **(d)** There are 3 trips parallel to AB and 3 strips parallel to AC. There are 6 horizontal parallelograms in the first. 3 in the second and 1 in the third strip parallel to AB. Kite shaped parallelograms in these strips are 6 + 3 + 1 = 10.

The pattern is repeated for strips parallel to AC except that top-most kite is common to both type of strips.

There are 3 parallelograms each made up of 4 small parallelograms (horizontal and kite shaped.)

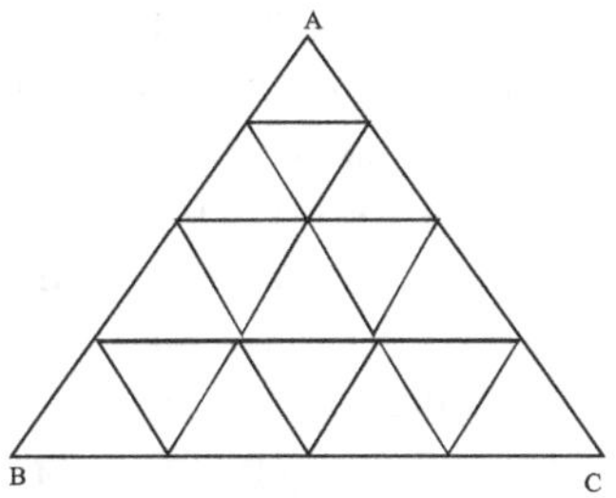

Hence total no. of parallelograms

= [2 (10 + 10) – 1] + 3 = 42

7. **(d)** Within the triangle with vertices 1, 2, 6, there are

4 + 3 + 2 + 1 = 10 triangles. In the triangle with vertices

1, 2, 14 there are 6 triangles.

In the triangle with vertices 1, 14, 15 there are 8 triangles.

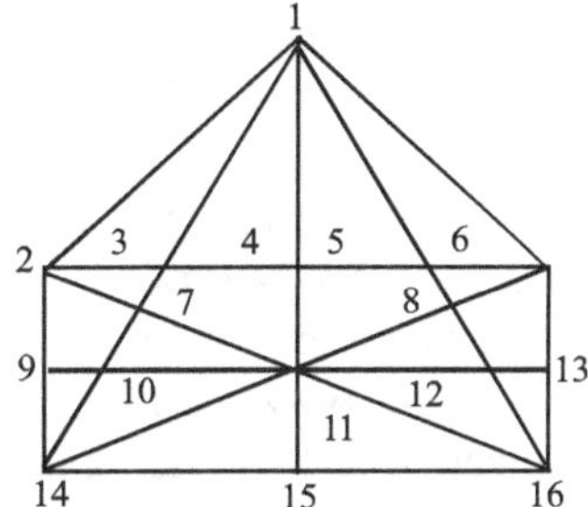

This pattern is repeated for triangle 1, 6, 16 and for triangle 1, 15, 16.

In the triangle with vertices 1, 6, 14 there are 3 triangles and the pattern is repeated for the triangle with vertices 1, 2, 16.

In the parallelogram, there are 4 triangles each half the size, 4 triangles of quarter size and 6 triangles each made up of two small triangles.

Finally, there two triangles with vertices 1, 10, 12 and 1, 14, 16 respectively

Hence total no. of triangles.

= 10 + 2 (6 + 8) + 2 × 3 + (4 + 4 + 6) + 2 = 60

8. **(b)** In fig. (X), one of the dots lies in the region common to the circle and the square only, another dot lies in the region common to all the three figures– the circle, the square and the triangle and the third dot lies in the region common to the circle and the triangle only. In each of the alternatives (a), (c) and (d), there is no region common to the circle and the triangle only. Only fig. (b) consists of all the three types of regions.

9. **(a)** In fig. (X), one of the dots lies in the region common to the circle and the square only, another dot lies in the region common to all the three figures—the circle, the square and the triangle and the third dot lies in the circle alone. In fig. (b) there is no region common to the circle and the square only and in each of the figures (c) and (d) there are regions which lie in the circle alone. Only fig. (a) consists of all the three types of regions.

10. **(c)** In fig. (X), one of the dots lies in the region common to the circle and the triangle only, another dot lies in the circle alone and the third dot lies in the region common to the circle and the square only. In fig. (a) there is no region common to the circle and the triangle only, in fig. (b), there is no region common to the circle and the square and in fig. (d), there is no region which lies in the circle alone. Only, fig. (c) consists of all the three types of regions.

11. **(a)** In fig. (X), one of the dots lies in the region common to the square and the rectangle only, another dot lies in the region common to all the four elements—the circle, the square, the triangle and the rectangle and the third dot lies in the region common to the triangle and the rectangle only. In fig. (b) there is no region common to the triangle and the rectangle only. In fig. (c) there is no region common to the square and the rectangle only. In fig. (d) there is no region common to all the four elements—the circle, the square, the triangle and the rectangle. Only fig. (a) consists of all the three types of regions.

12. **(d)** In fig. (X), one of the dots lies in the region common to the circle and the square only, another dot lies in the region common to the square, the triangle and the rectangle only and the third dot lies in the region common to the triangle and the rectangle only. In each of the figures (a), (b) and (c) there is no region common to the square, the triangle and the rectangle only. Only fig. (d) consists of all the three types of regions.

13. **(d)** In fig. (X), one of the dots lies in the region common to the circle and the square only, another dot lies in the region common to the circle and the rectangle only and the third dot lies in the region common to the triangle and the rectangle only. In fig. (a) there is no region common to the circle and the square only. In figures (b) and (c) there are no regions common to the triangle and the rectangle only. Only fig. (d) consists of all the three types of regions.

14. **(d)** There are 52 triangles in the figure.

15. **(d)** There are 19 squares in the given figure.

16. **(d)** There are 30 triangles in the given figure.

17. **(b)** **18. (c)** **19. (c)**

20. **(d)** There are 44 triangles in the given figure.

21. **(d)** There are 40 triangles in the given figure.

22. **(d)** More than 27 triangles are present.

23. **(d)** There are 48 triangles in the given figure.

24. **(a)** More than 12 triangles are there i.e, 14.

25. **(a)**

CHAPTER-12

LEVEL 1

1. **(c)** Mirror image for the letters 'D' is 'ɑ', 'R' is 'Я', 'E' is 'Ǝ', 'A' is 'A' and 'M' is 'M' . Since the word ends with M, i.e., where the mirror is placed, therefore the mirror image will start from the mirror image of M, i.e., M. Thus the mirror image for water is MAƎЯɑ.
2. **(a)** Mirror image for the letters 'N' is 'И', 'E' is 'Ǝ', 'W' is 'W' and 'S' is 'Ƨ'.
3. **(d)** Mirror image for the letters 'j' is ᒑ, 'e' is 'ɘ', 'a' is 'ɒ', 'I' is I, 'O' is 'O', 'u' is 'u' and 'S' is 'Ƨ'
4. **(d)** Mirror image of numbers — '3' is 'Ɛ', '1' is '1', '2' is 'S', '5' is 'ट', '6' is 'ə' and '8' is '8'.
5. **(b)** If we rotate the mirror image, i.e., '8' 90° clockwise, then it will be 'm'.
6. **(c)** If we rotate the mirror image, i.e., 'ƧƖ' to 90° anticlockwise, then it will be 'ᔕ'.
7. **(c)** Assume that the mirror is placed on the right hand side of the given object, unless mentioned or drawn near the object.

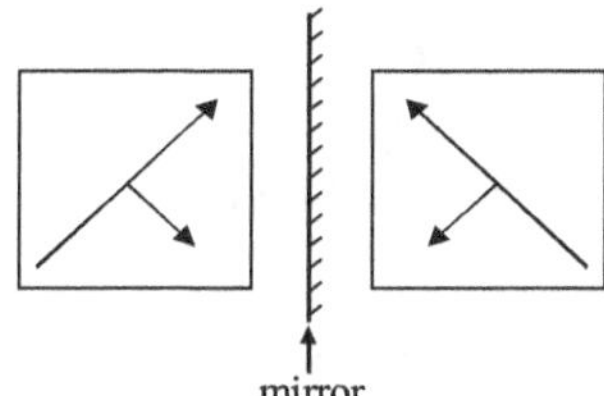

8. **(c)**
9. **(c)**
10. **(d)**

11. **(a)**
12. **(d)** This object has mirror placed under the object.

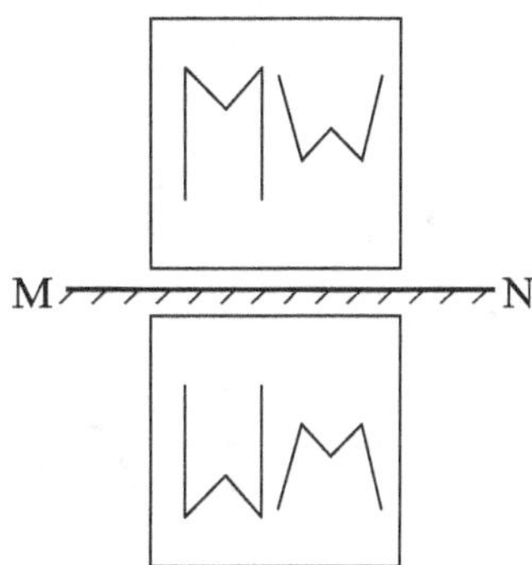

13. **(a)**
14. **(a)**

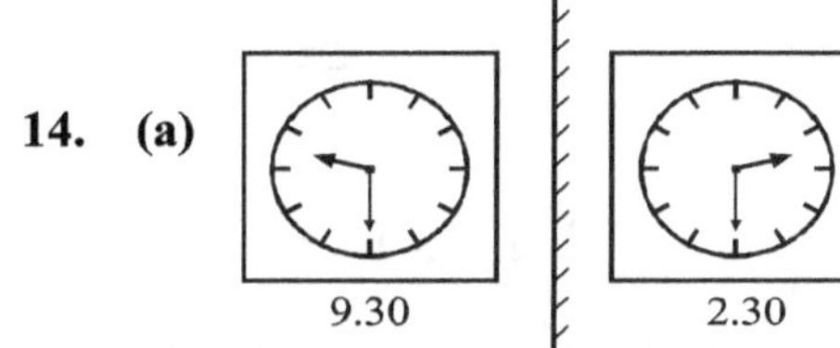

15. **(d)**

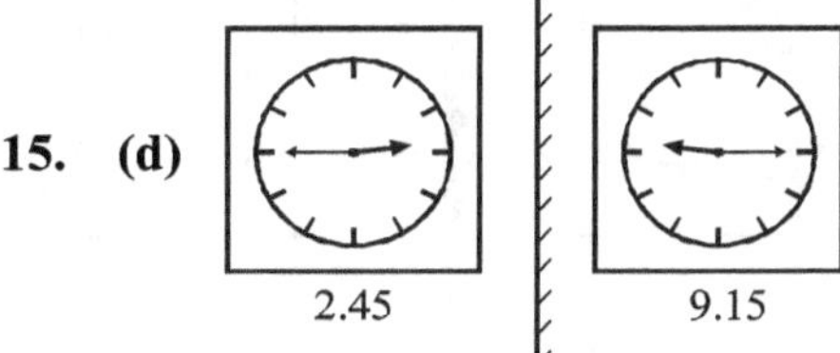

16. **(c)**
17. **(c)**
18. **(b)**
19. **(a)**
20. **(d)**
21. **(b)**
22. **(b)**
23. **(c)**

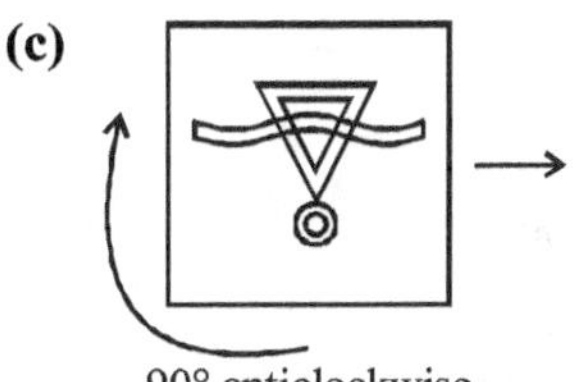

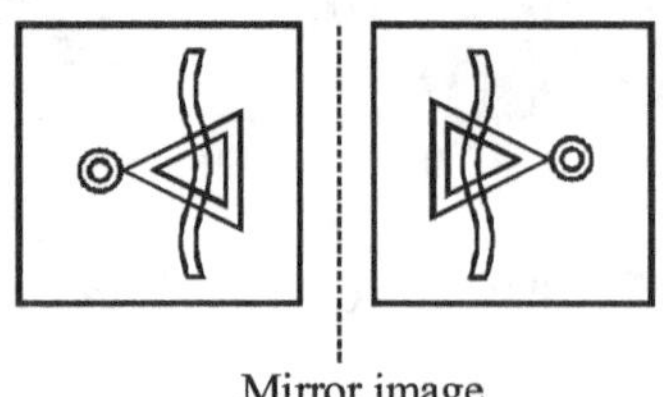

24. (a)

25. (c)

26. (b) SWIMMING

27. (d)

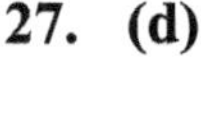

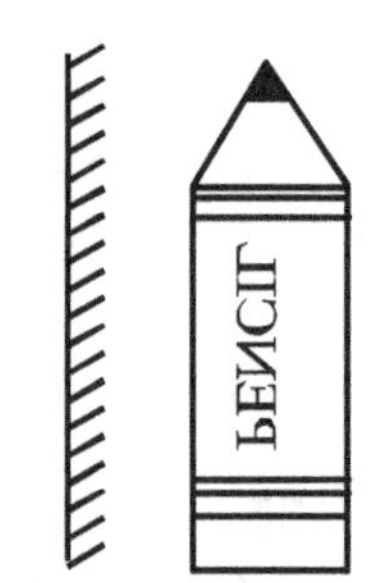

28. (a) INDIANAIRFORCE

29. (b)

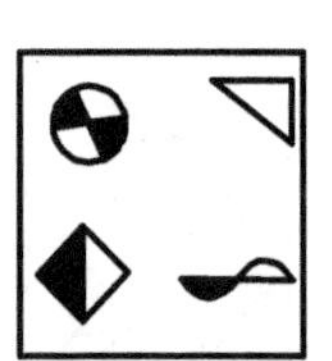

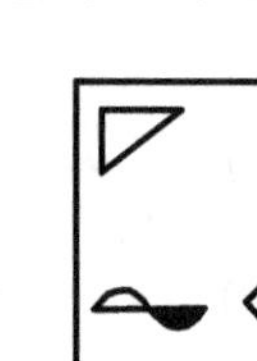

30. (a)

31. (a)

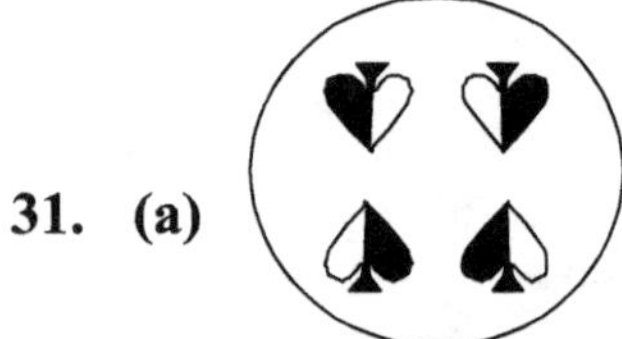

32. (a) PLAY

33. (b) HINDI

34. (a)

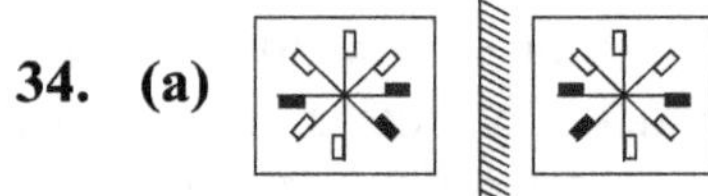

35. (b) US91Q4M5W3

36. (a)

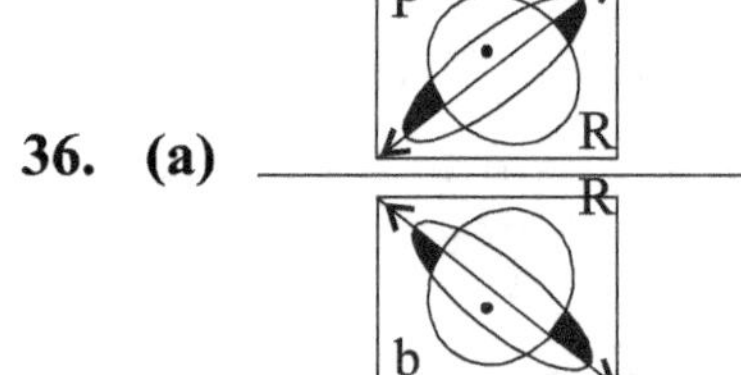

37. (a) HR26DA$2O?@90

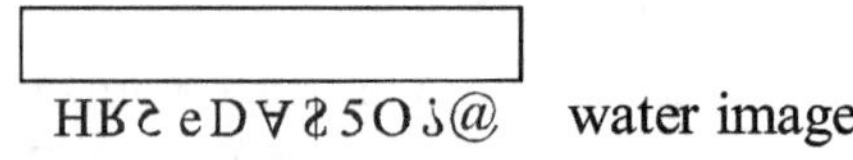

water image.

38. (a)

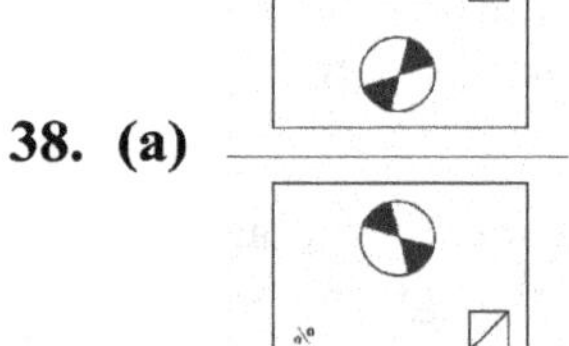

39. (a)

40. (b)

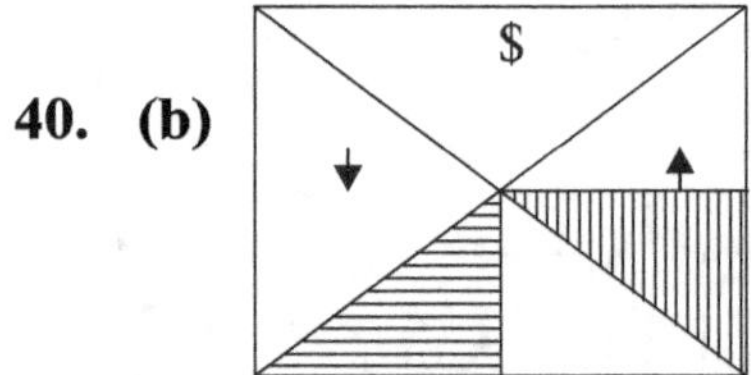

LEVEL 2

1. **(d)** 2. **(d)**

3. **(c)** 4. **(d)**

5. **(d)** The water image of number — '9' is 'ə', '1' is 'ɿ', '8' is '8', '4' is 'ᔭ', '2' is 'ᘔ' and '3' is '3'

6. **(b)** The water image of '?' is '¿'.

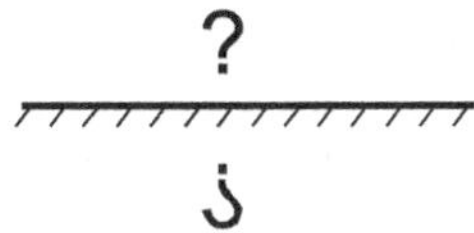

7. **(c)** The water image of 'g' is 'ə', 'L' is 'Γ', 'a' is 'ɘ' and 'd' is 'q'.

8. **(a)** The water image of 'S' is 'Ƨ', 'N' is 'И', 'O' is 'O' and 'W' is 'M'

9. **(b)** The water image of 'd' is 'q', 'r' is 'ɭ', 'a' is 'ɘ', 'i' is 'ṛ' and 'n' is 'u'

10. **(c)** The water image of 'Z' is 'Z', 'E' is 'E', 'B' is B, 'R' is 'ᴚ' and 'A' is '∀'

11. **(b)** The water image of '6' is 'ɘ', '7' is 'ㄥ' and '1' is ɿ.

12. **(c)** The water image of '9' is 'ə', '2' is 'ᘔ', '8' is '8' and '3' is '3'.

13. **(a)** Since, in case of water images, usually the image drawn is just under the actual object. So the shaded and dotted portion will come up on their respective sides, because the portion of the object near water surface will remain near the water surface in case of the image as well.

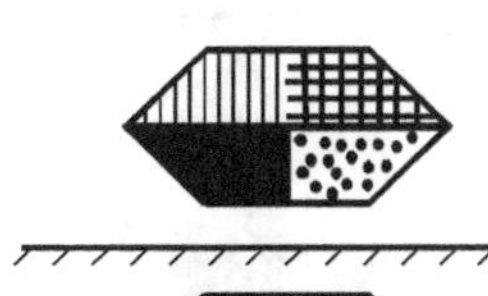

← Water surface

14. **(d)**

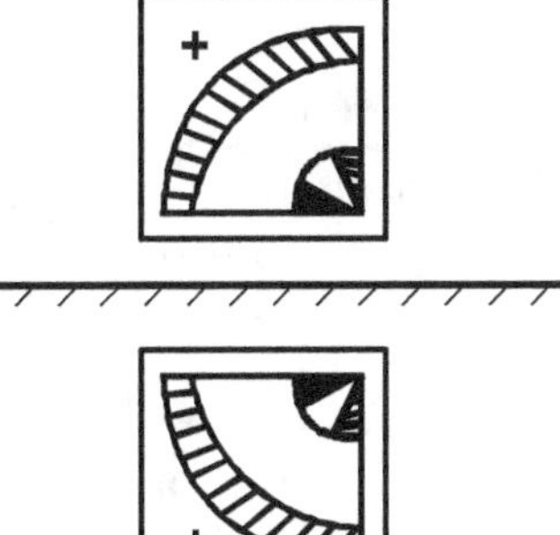

15. **(d)**

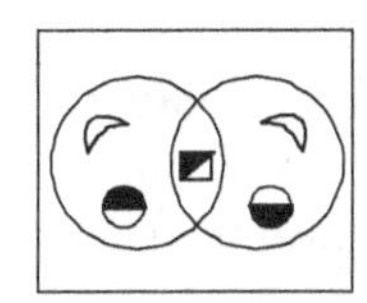

16. **(b)**

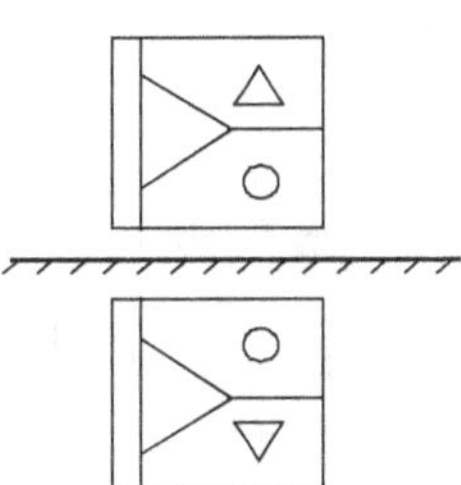

17. **(c)**

18. **(a)**

19. **(d)**

20. **(b)**

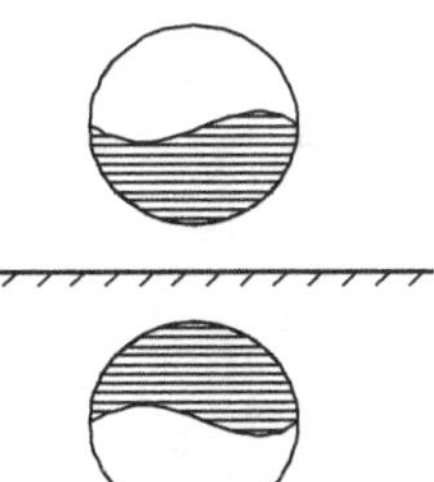

21. (b)

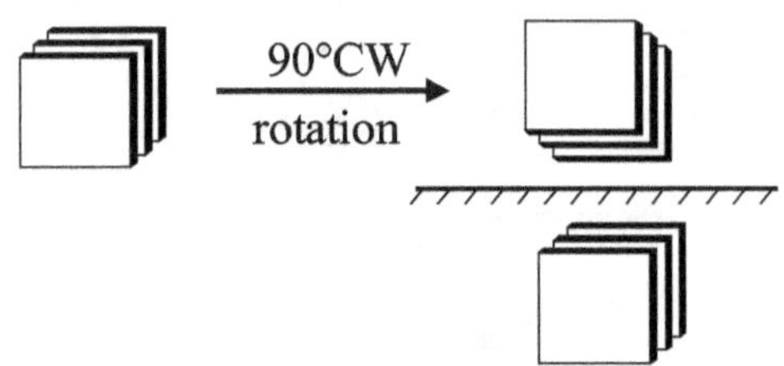

This is the final image

Thus option (b) is the correct answer.

22. (b)

23. (d) In all others head of "T" faces the vertex of the triangle.

24. (d) Figure in options (a), (b) and (c) have shaded fraction equal to $\frac{1}{2}$.

25. (a) Options (b) and (c), (d) have line of symmetry.

26. (d) Options (a), (b) and (c) have same outer most and inner most element.

27. (b)

28. (b)

29. (d)

30. (a)

31. (c)

32. (a)

33. (b)

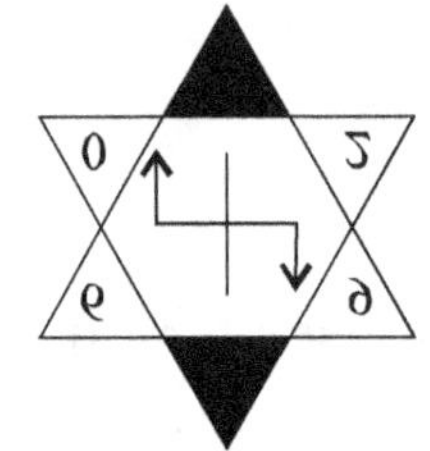

34. (d)

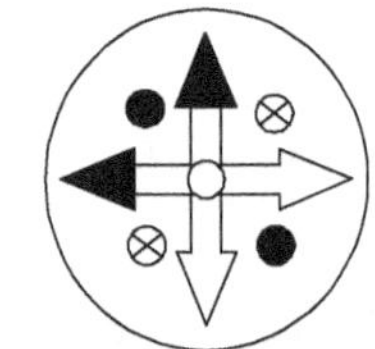

35. (d) @ > W Ƨ #∇ꓘ?

36. (b) ЯƧƧƆƆƐ٢OƧ | S O 7 3 C C 2 2 R

CHAPTER-13

LEVEL 1

1. (d)

2. (a) 3. (b) 4. (a) 5. (d)

6. (d)

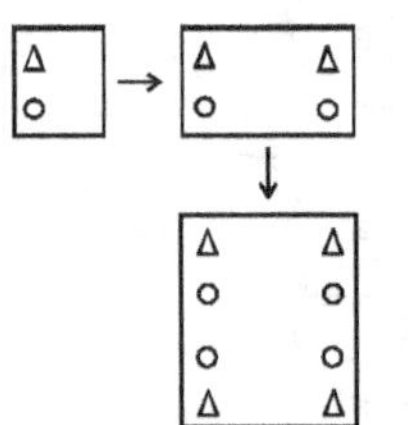

7. (b)

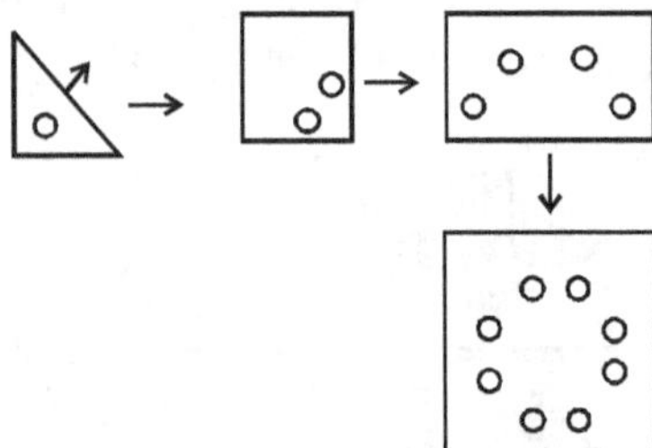

8. (c) **9.** (d) **10.** (a)
11. (b)
12. (a)
13. (b)
14. (a)

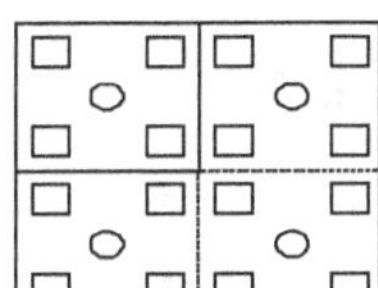

15. (c)

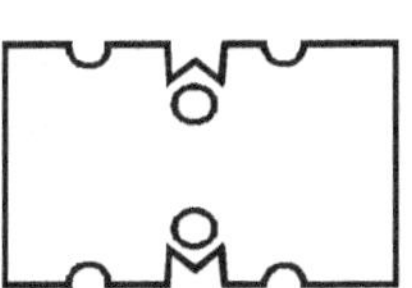

LEVEL 2

1. (c) **2.** (d) **3.** (d) **4.** (c) **5.** (a)
6. (d) **7.** (a) **8.** (d) **9.** (b) **10.** (b)
11. (c) **12.** (d) **13.** (d) **14.** (c) **15.** (a)
16. (d) **17.** (a)
18. (a)

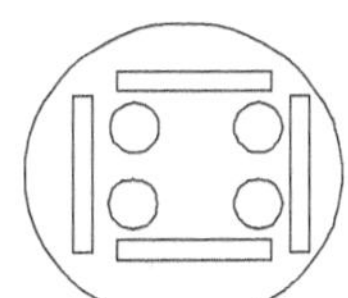

19. (c)

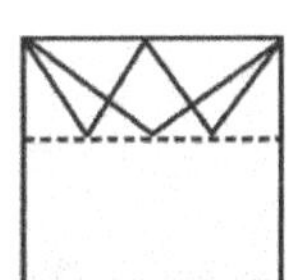

20. (a)

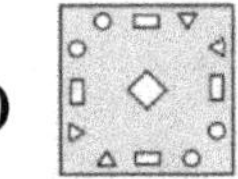

21. (a)

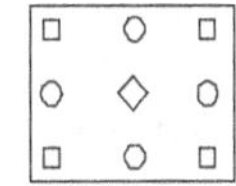

22. (b)

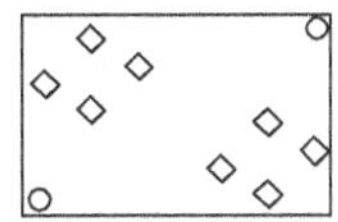

23. (b)

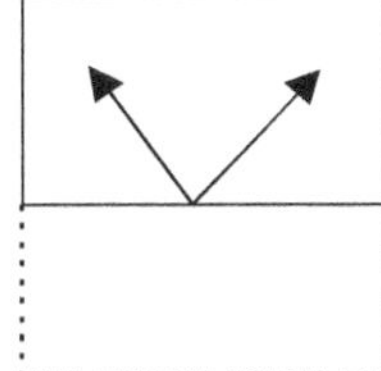

24. (b)

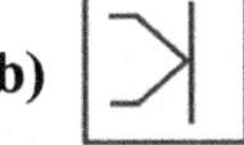

25. (c)

26. (a)

CHAPTER-14

LEVEL 1

1. (c)

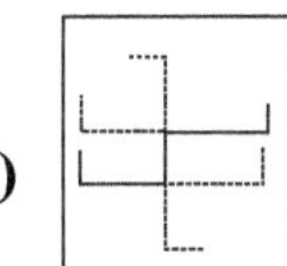

2. (d)

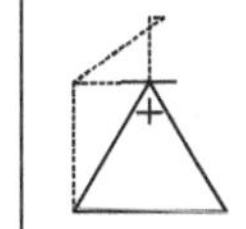

3. (b)

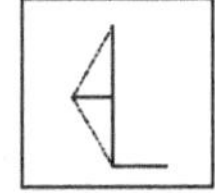

4. (c)

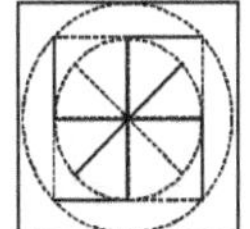

5. (b)
6. (b)

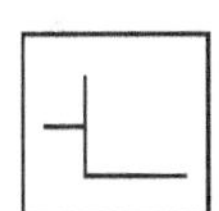

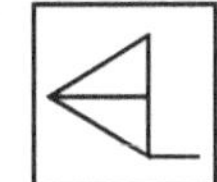

7. (d) 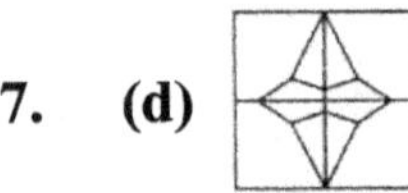

8. (d) 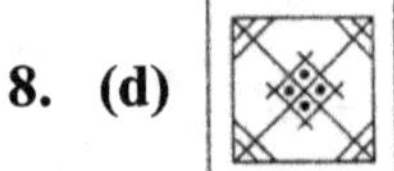

9. (c) 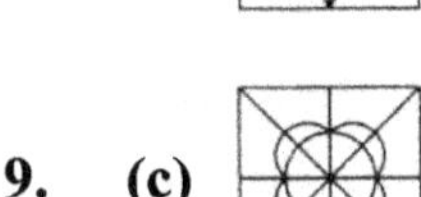

10. (d) 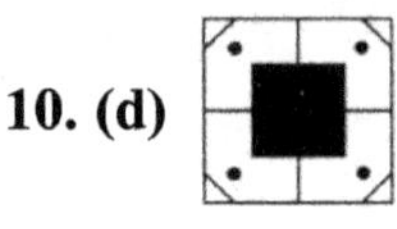

11. (b) 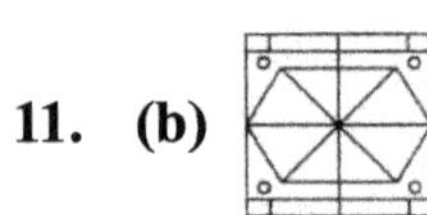 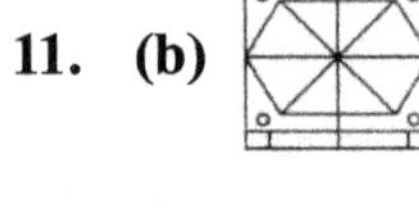

12. (c) 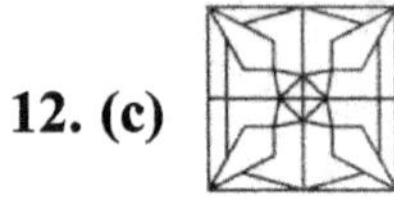

13. (d)

14. (c)

15. (a)

16. (d)

17. (b) 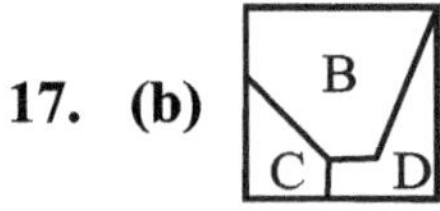

18. (c) 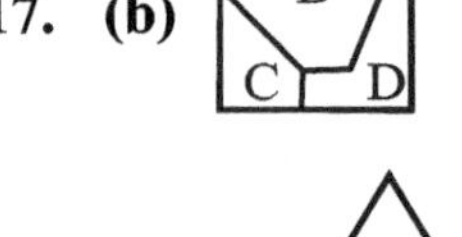

19. (a) 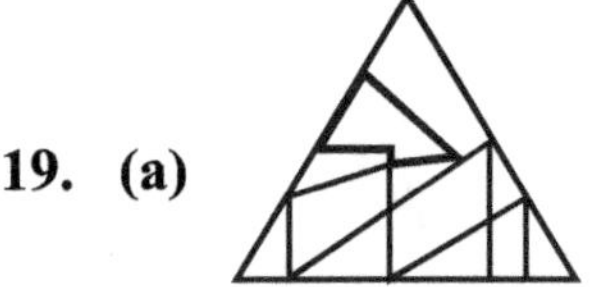

20. (b) 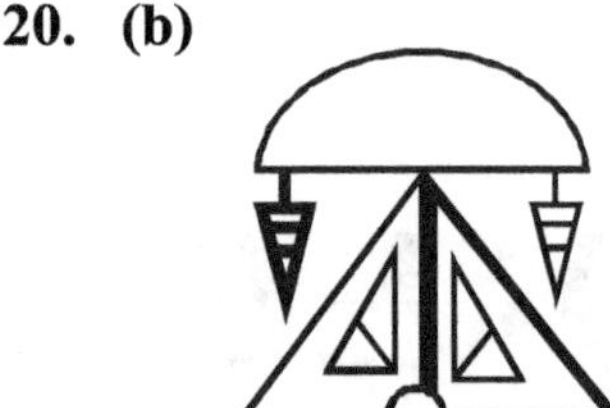

21. (d)

22. (b) 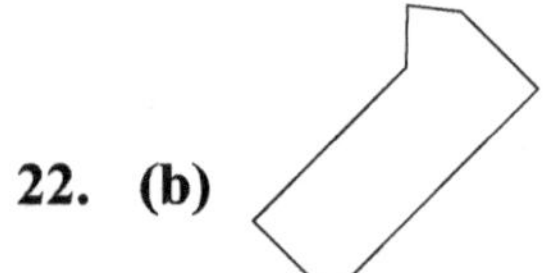

The given figure is exactly embedded in option (b) as one of its parts.

23. (c) 

24. (b) 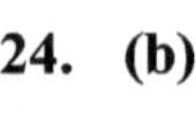 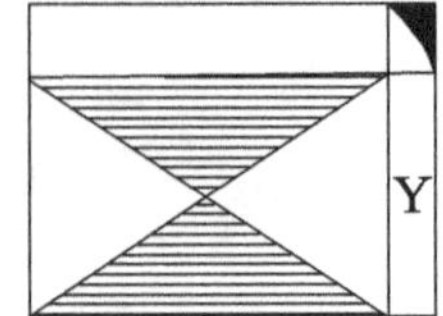

25. (c) 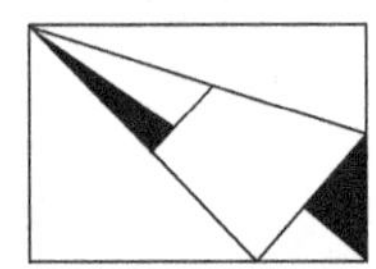

26. (a) 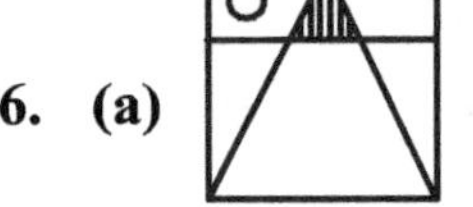

Option (a) would complete the pattern

27. (d)  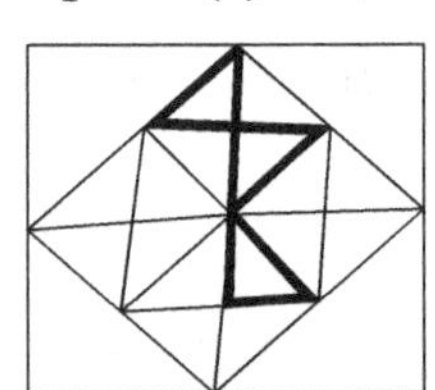

LEVEL 2

1. (d) 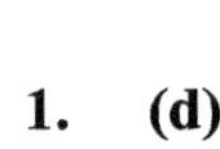 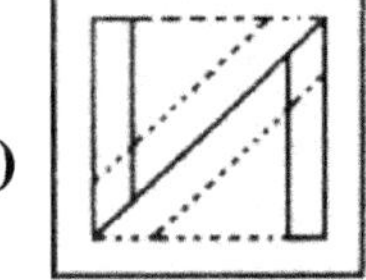

2. (a) 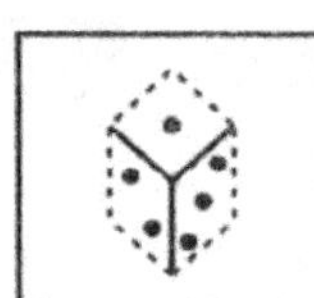

3. (d) 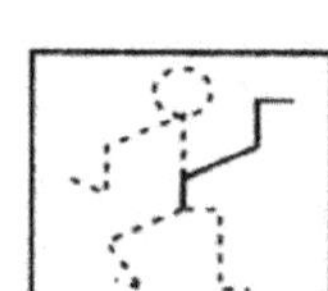

4. (c) 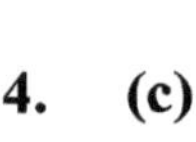 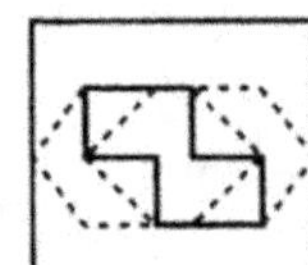

5. (d)

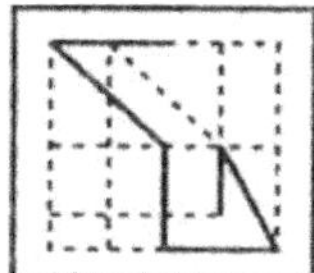

6. (a)

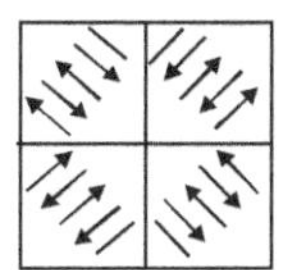

7. (a)

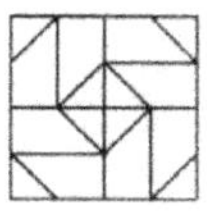

8. (d)

9. (d)

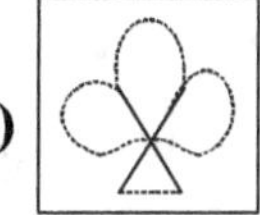

10. (b)

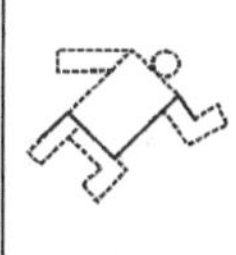

11. (d) Fig. (X) is embedded in figure (d) as shown below :

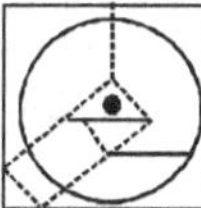

12. (c)

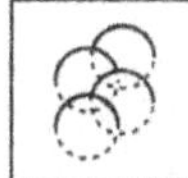

13. (c)

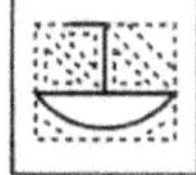

14. (a)

15. (b)

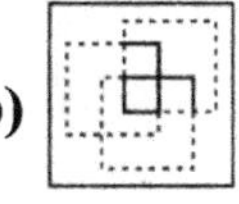

16. (d)

[**Note :** Figure is rotated.]

17. (a)

18. (c)

19. (c)

20. (d) all except (d) dots are on either side of the line.

21. (c) Except (c) rest elements of figures are diagonally opposite direction.

22. (a) all other figure can be rotated into each other. The middle element is obtained by rotating the outer element through 90 degree clock wise and the inner element is obtained by rotating the middle element through 90 degree clock wise.

23. (a) only in figure (a) two of the four elements are oriented in the same direction.

24. (a) Elements in option (b), (c) and (d) have diagonals.

25. (d) Letters in options (a), (b) and (c) are vowels.

26. (d) Except option (d), all the figures can be obtained by rotating each other.

27. (d) In option (d), the two elements drawn inside the circle are different from other figures.

28. (b) **29. (b)** **30. (c)** **31. (d)**

32. (d)

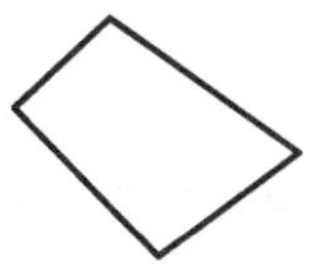

33. (b)

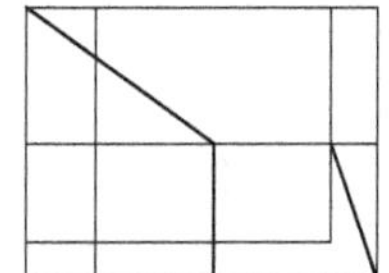

34. (a)
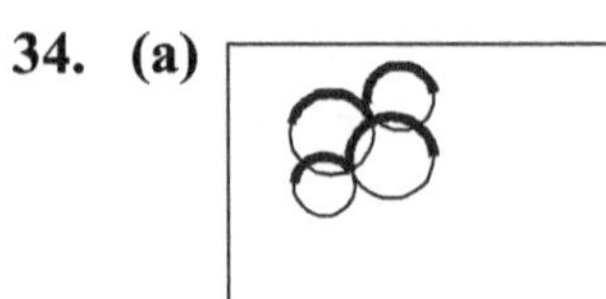

35. (a)
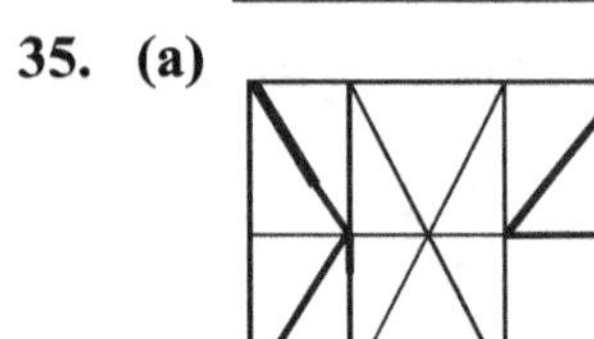

36. (d)
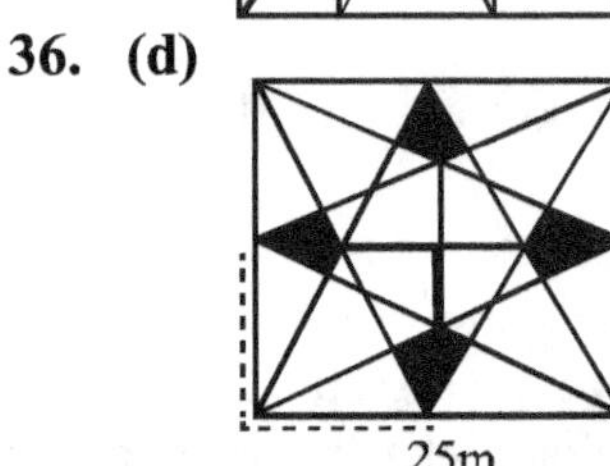

37. (a)
38. (d)
39. (c)
40. (c)
41. (c) Option (c) will complete the given figure.
42. (d)
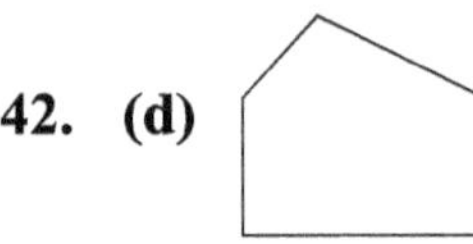

43. (b)
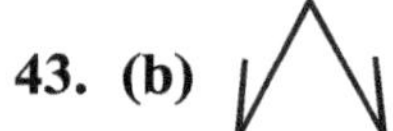

CHAPTER-15

LEVEL 1

1. (a) In each row, the central part of the first figure rotates either 90o CW or 90o ACW to form the central part of the second figure and the central part of the first figure rotates through 180 degrees to form the central part of the third figure. Also, in each row, there are 3 types of side elements - rectangles, circles, and triangles.
2. (d) One line is increasing in each subsequent figure.
3. (c) There are 3 types of shadings in the triangles, 3 types of legs, 3 positions of circles, each of which is used only once in a single row. The circle is shaded in alternate figures.
4. (d) In each row, the third figure is a combination of the first and second figures.
5. (b) There are types of arrows - a single-headed arrow, a double-headed arrow, and a triple-headed arrow. There are three positions of arrows-Upwards, downwards, and towards the right. The arrows have 3 types of base-plane, rectangular and circular. Each of these features is used once in each row.
6. (a) The contents of the third figure in each row (and column) are determined by the contents of the first two figures. Lines are carried forward from the first two figures to the third one, except where two lines appear in the same position, in which they are cancelled out.
7. (a) In each row (and column), the superimposition of all the three figures results in a darkened circle.
8. (d) The third figure in each row comprises parts that are not common to the first two figures.
9. (c) The third figure in each row comprises of parts which are not common to the first two figures.
10. (a) In each row, the third figure comprises of a black circle and only those line segments which are not common to the first and the second figures.

11. **(a)**

12. **(b)** Group (1, 5, 6) '! Same figure inside the figure.
Group (2, 4, 8) '! Two same figure one small and one bigger.
Group (3, 7, 9) '! Figure divided in 4 equal parts.

13. **(b)** Group (1, 5, 7) divides the figure in four equal parts.
Group (2, 4, 9) divides the figure in two equal parts.
Group (3, 6, 8) has different small figure inside the big figure.

14. **(b)** 1, 6, 8 (Both the figures touches externally)
2, 4, 7 (figure is contained in another figure)
3, 5, 7 (exact figure is contained in same figure)

15. **(b)** 1, 6, 7 → Fig. inside fig. is there with two lines intesecting both the figures.
2, 4, 9 → Groups of two same figures.
3, 5, 8 → all are 3d figures.

LEVEL 2

1. **(c)** In each column, the second figure (middle figure) is obtained by removing the upper part of the first figure (uppermost figure) and the third figure (lowermost figure) is obtained by vertically inverting the upper part of the first figure.

2. **(b)** There are 3 types of faces, 3 types of bodies, 3 types of hands and 3 types of legs, each of which is used only once in a single row. So, the features which have not been used in the first two figures of the third row would combine to produce the missing figure.

3. **(b)** In each row, the figures are getting laterally inverted in each step. The number of components or the quantities are either increasing or decreasing from left to right sequentially.

4. **(a)** The number of components in each row either increases or decreases from left to right . In the third row, it increases.

5. **(a)** In each row, the second figure is obtained from the first figure by adding two mutually perpendicular line segments at the centre and the third figure is obtained from the first figure by adding four circles outside the main figure.

6. **(d)**

7. **(d)**

8. **(d)**

9. **(c)**

10. **(c)**

11. **(c)**

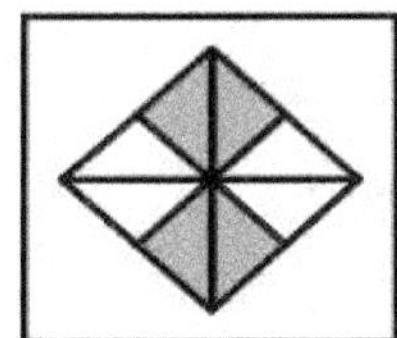

Column 1 and Column 2 is added to get column 3.

12. **(b)** Group (1, 3, 8) has different Small figures in the big figures.
Group (2, 4, 6) has two figures inter connected.
Group (5, 7, 9) has the figures divided in four equal parts.

13. **(c)** Rotate the figure 135° anticlockwise.

Option (c) will complete the figure.

14. **(d)** Group (1, 5, 9) has one big and one small same figures.
Group (2, 6, 7) has different small figure inside the big figure.

Group (3, 4, 8) has five sides figure.

Option (d) is the correct Answer.

15. (c)

A (1)	C (3)	D (4)
F (6)	I (9)	O (15)
H (8)	Q (17)	Y (25)

Addition of place value of alphabets in alphabetical series of first two column results in 3rd column.

i.e., $1 + 3 \rightarrow 4$

$8 + 17 \rightarrow 17$

Similarly

$6 + \square \rightarrow 15$

$\square \rightarrow 15 - 6$

$\square \rightarrow$ a i.e. I

16. (d) Property used in grouping is number of figures which are shaded and manner in which shaded,

So, 1, 5, 9 (3 figure are shaded continuously)

2, 4, 6, (2 figures are shaded, which are opposite to each other)

3, 7, 8 (1 figure is shaded)

17. (b) In first row – sum of all the (×) is 18.
In second row – sum of all the (○) is 18.
In third row – sum of all the (□) is 18

So, $5 + 9 + ? = 18$

$? = 4$

$\boxed{? = 4}$

18. (d) Group (1, 3, 6) '! Figure divided in two equal parts.
Group (2, 4, 8) '! Different small figure inside the big figure.
Group (5, 7, 9) '! Same small figure inside the big figure.

19. (a)

20. (c) In row 1, column 2 and 3 figure is rotatate 135° in clockwise direction in subsequent figure in comparison with column 1.
Similarly in Row 2.
∴ In row 3, column 2. fig. will be

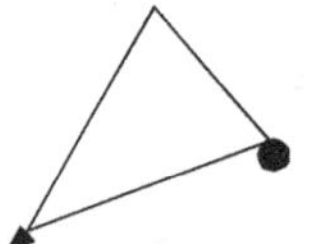

21. (c) 1, 4, 9 → all these are polygon.
2, 5, 8 → all are 3d figures.
3, 6, 7 → figure contains figure.

22. (a) 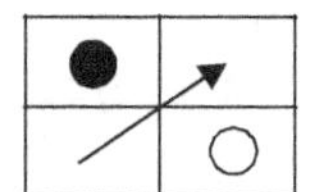

23. (c) 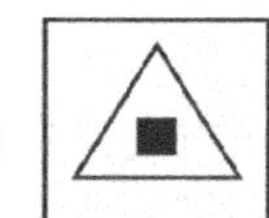

CHAPTER-16

LEVEL 1

1. (c) In the figure, there are 9 columns containing 5 cubes each, 7 columns containing 4 cubes each, 5 columns containing 3 cubes each and 1 columns containing 1 cube.

∴ Total number of cubes
$= (9 \times 5) + (7 \times 4) + (5 \times 3) + (1 \times 1)$
$= 89.$

2. (a) When the sheet in fig. (X) is folded, then one of the faces of the cube formed will be of the from [|] . Thus, a cube of the type as shown in fig. (a) will be formed.

3. **(d)** When the sheet in fig.(X) is folded to form a cube, then the face bearing a dot appears opposite to a blank face, the face bearing a '+' sign appears opposite to another blank face and the face bearing a circle appears opposite to the third blank face. Clearly, all the four cubes shown in figures (a), (b),(c) and (d) can be formed.

4. **(c)** From figure (i) (ii) and (iv), we conclude that 6, 4, 1 and 2 dots appear adjacent to 3 dots. Clearly, there will be 5 dots on the face opposite the face with 3 dots.

5. **(c)** When this figure is folded to form a cube then the face bearing three dots will lie opposite the face bearing five dots.

6. **(d)** From figures (i) and (iv) we conclude that 6, 5, 2 and 3 lie adjacent to 4. It follows that 1 lies opposite 4.

7. **(b)** From the three given figures, it is clear that the 1,2,5 and 4 appear adjacent to 3, so none of these can appear opposite 3. Therefore, 6 appears opposite 3.

8. **(d)**

	4	
5	2	3
	1	
	6	

Hence, the numbers that are adjacent to 1 are 5, 2, 6 and 3.

9. **(d)** The opposite pairs are – (2, 4), (1, 6) and (3, 5)

Therefore, option (d) is correct choice.

10. **(b)** The opposite pairs are – (F, B), (A, D) and (E, C). Hence option (b) is the correct choice.

11. **(d)** When the sheet in fig.(X) is folded to form a cube, then the face bearing a dot appears opposite to a blank face, the face bearing a '+' sign appears opposite to another blank face and the face bearing a circle appears opposite to the third blank face. Clearly, all the four cubes shown in figures (a), (b),(c) and (d) can be formed.

Sol. (12-15)

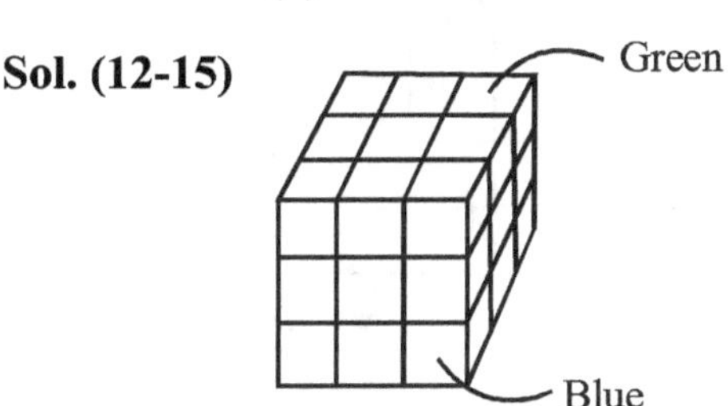

12. **(d)** There are four cubes in the middle layer which have one face painted only in blue.

13. **(b)** There is one (central) cube in top layer and one (central) cube in the bottom layer which have one face painted in green only.

14. **(a)** Four (corner) cubes in the top layer and four (corner) cubes in the bottom layer have three sides painted. There are no such cubes in the middle layer. Hence, there are 8 such cubes.

15. **(a)** Only one central cube in the middle layer has no face painted at all.

16. **(d)** The opposite pairs are – (2, 4), (1, 6) and (3, 5)

Therefore, option (d) is correct choice.

17. (b)

	4	
6	3	5
	2	
	1	

So, if 1 is at the bottom then 3 will be on the top.

Sol. (18 – 19)

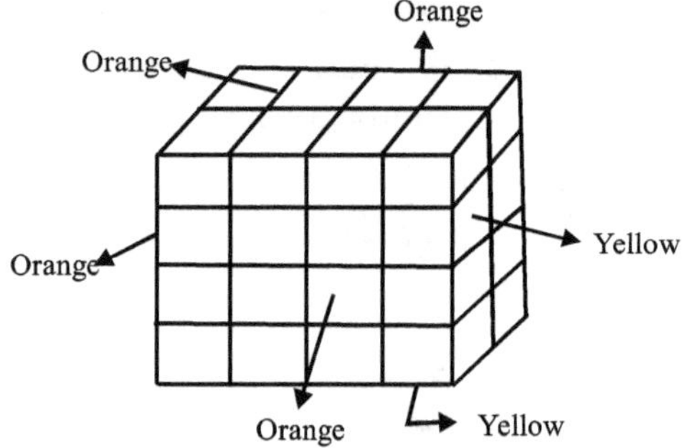

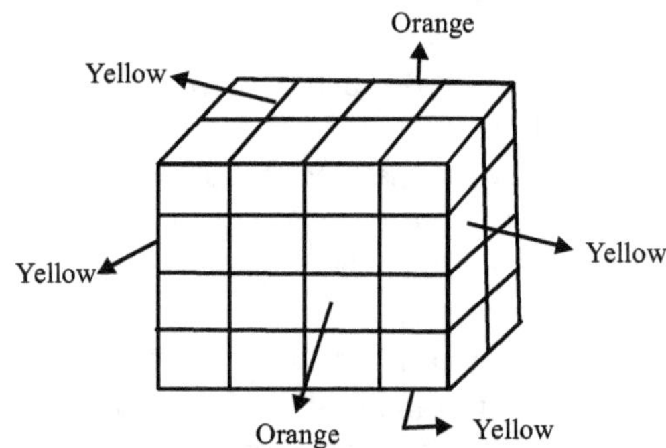

18. (a) All the smaller cubes have colour on their faces.

19. (b) The larger faces will have one face coloured cube which is four on each face.
So, in total there are four larger faces.
$4 \times 4 = 16$
16 cubes will have only one face colour.

20. (c) Number '3' is common on both the dice. Write from '3' clockwise.

3	6	4
3	1	5

Number '4' will be on the face opposite to the face having number 5.

21. (b) In dice (1) and dice (3) numbers 5 and 3 are common. So, 4 will be at the bottom of 6.

22. (b) % $\xleftrightarrow{\text{opposite}}$ \$

\# $\xleftrightarrow{\text{opposite}}$ @

© $\longleftrightarrow$ ★

Symbol opposite to ★ is ©

LEVEL 2

1. (b) There are 4 blocks in the lower layer close to the ground. Also, there are 3 blocks standing over the lower layer of blocks.

2. (c) In the figure there are 34 columns containing 2 cubes each.
∴ Total number of cubes = $(34 \times 2) = 68$

3. (b) In the figure, there are 4 columns containing 5 cubes each and 38 columns containing 1 cube each.
∴ Total number of cubes = $(4 \times 5) + (38 \times 1) = 20 + 38 = 58$.

4. (a) When the sheet shown in fig.(X) is folded to from a box (cuboid), then the two rectangular-shaded faces lie opposite to each other, the two rectangular white faces lie opposite to each other and the two square shaped faces (one shaded and one white) lie opposite to each other. Clearly, the cuboids shown in fig. (b) and (d) cannot be formed as in each of the two cuboids the two shaded rectangular faces appear adjacent to each other. So, only the cuboids in figures (a) and (c) can be formed.

5. (a) Since the total number of dots on opposite faces is always 7, therefore 1 dot must lie opposite 6 dots, 2 dots must lie opposite 5 dots and 3 dots must lie

opposite 4 dots. In the figures (b) and (d), 2 dots appear adjacent to 5 dots, and in fig. (c), 3 dots appear adjacent to 4 dots. Hence, figures are incorrect. Therefore, only fig. (a) is correct.

6. (b) From these two figures, it has been seen that dots 1, 2, 5 and 6 are adjacent to 4. So, 3 is opposite to 4.

7. (c) From figure I, II and IV, ◇, ○, ◆ and △ are adjacent to ◎.

So, '=' is opposite to ◎ and vice versa.

8. (c) In the figure there are 34 columns containing 2 cubes each.

∴ Total number of cubes = (34 × 2) = 68

9. (c) In the figure, there are 4 columns containing 3 cubes each, 12 columns containing 2 cubes each and 4 columns containing 1 cube each.

∴ Total numbers of cubes

= (4 × 3) + (12 × 2) + (4 × 1)

= 12 + 24 + 4 = 40

10. (b) In the figure, there are 11 columns containing 4 cubes each, 7 columns containing 3 cubes each and 2 columns containing 2 cubes each.

∴ Total number of cubes

= (11 × 4) + (7 ×3) + (2 × 2)

= 44 + 21 + 4 = 69.

11. (d) The number 3 occurs most often in the given three figures. From these three figures it is clear that 1, 2, 5 and 4 lie adjacent to 3. Clearly, 6 lies opposite the face showing 3.

= 12 + 24 + 4 = 40

12. (a) When the sheet shown in fig.(X) is folded to from a box (cuboid), then the two rectangular-shaded faces lie opposite to each other, the two rectangular white faces lie opposite to each other and the two square shaped faces (one shaded and one white) lie opposite to each other. Clearly, the cuboids shown in fig. (b) and (d) cannot be formed as in each of the two cuboids the two shaded rectangular faces appear adjacent to each other. So, only the cuboids in figures (a) and (c) can be formed.

13. (a) Since the total number of dots on opposite faces is always 7, therefore 1 dot must lie opposite 6 dots, 2 dots must lie opposite 5 dots and 3 dots must lie opposite 4 dots. In the figures (b) and (d), 2 dots appear adjacent to 5 dots, and in fig. (c), 3 dots appear adjacent to 4 dots. Hence, figures are incorrect. Therefore, only fig. (a) is correct.

Sol. (14 – 18)

After the first cut and painting green, we have

	Coloured faces	**No. of cubes**
I	3 faces red and 3 green	1
II	2 faces red and 4 green	3
III	1 face red and 5 green	3
IV	No face red and 6 green	1
	Total	8

After the second cut, the following types of cubes will be there:

			Type			
		Colour on Faces	**I**	**II**	**III**	**IV**
A	:	3 red, none green	1	–	–	–
B	:	2 red, 1 green	3	6	–	–
C	:	1 red, 2 green	3	12	12	–
D	:	3 green only	1	6	12	8

14. (a) **15. (d)** **16. (d)** **17. (d)**

18. (d)

19. (b) From these two figures, it has been seen that dots 1, 2, 5 and 6 are adjacent to 4. So, 3 is opposite to 4.

20. (c) From figure I, II and IV, ◇, ○,

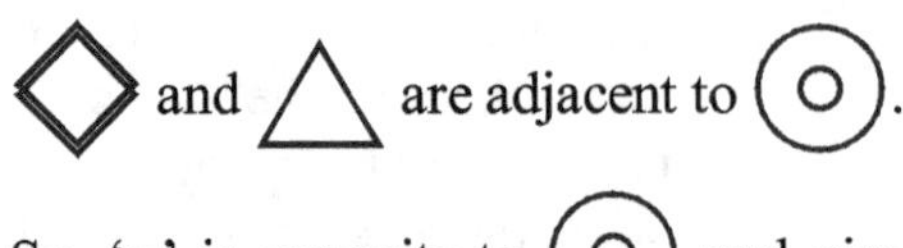

So, '=' is opposite to ◎ and vice versa.

21. (d) The cube formed will be

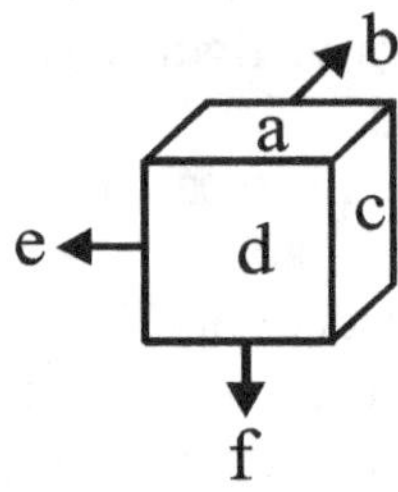

(a) is wrong as with c on top f and a are opposite to each other.
(b) is wrong as with a on top c and e
(c) is wrong as with b is opposite to d
(d) is correct

22. (d) 1. With club in front; chess board is at bottom

2. Chess board & Brick pattern are opposite. So wrong.

3. Lines are opposite to star. So Wrong.

4. This is the correct dice

23. (b) There are 6 cubes in the second layer from the top do not have any coloured faces.

24. (b)

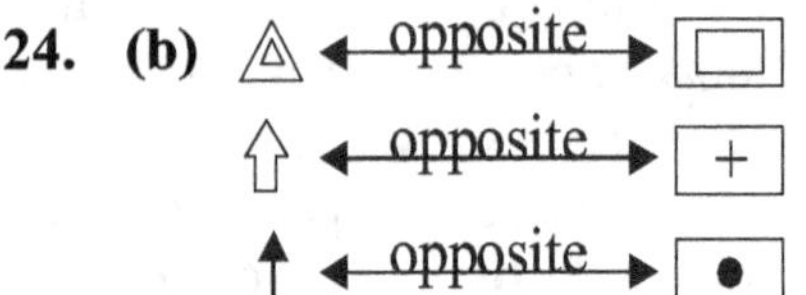

Only 2 is possible.

25. (c) Rotating dice from 4 in clockwise direction i.e

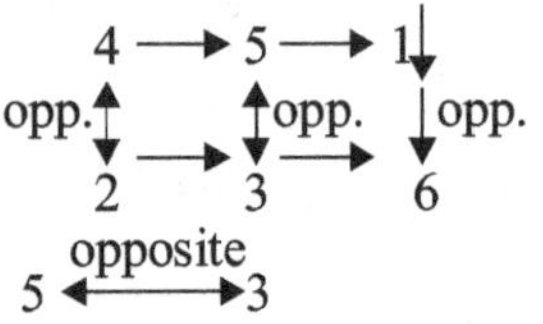

26. (b)

· ← opposite → ∷

⋱ ← opposite → ⋮⋮

⋱ ← opposite → ⁙

∴ dots is opposite to 3 dots.

27. (c) Symbol '+' is opposite to 'O'.

Symbol 'Δ' is opposite to '□'.

and

Empty face is opposite to empty face.
So, dice (3) and (4) can not be formed.
Only (1) and (2) dices can be formed.

28. (a) 25 cubes are there.

29. (c)

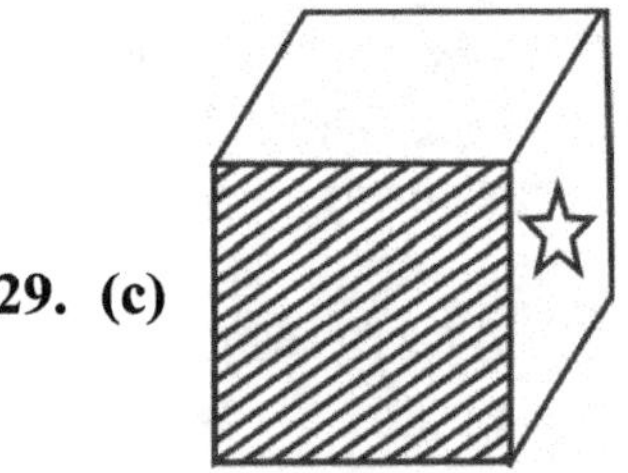

CHAPTER-17

LEVEL 1

1. (b) In figure (X), one of the dots lies in the region common to the circle and the triangle only and the other dot lies in the region common to the circle and the square only. In figures (a), (c) and (d), the region common to the circle and the triangle lies within the square. Only figure (b) contains a region common to the circle and the triangle only and also a region common to the circle and the square.

2. **(c)** In figure (X) the dot lies in the region common to the circle and the triangle only.
Such a region is present in fig. (c).

3. **(a)** One point lies in all three figures. Two points lie in between two figures.

4. **(c)** In fig. (X), the dot is placed in the region common to the circle and the triangle. Amongst the four alternatives only in figure (c), we have a region common to circle and triangle only. Hence figure, (c) is the answer.

5. **(d)**

6. **(b)**

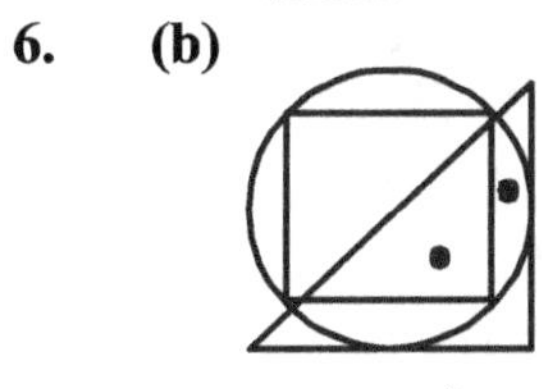

7. **(b)**

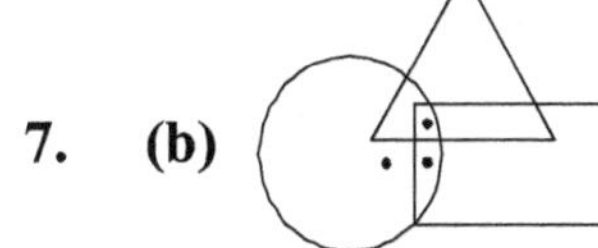

8. **(b)**

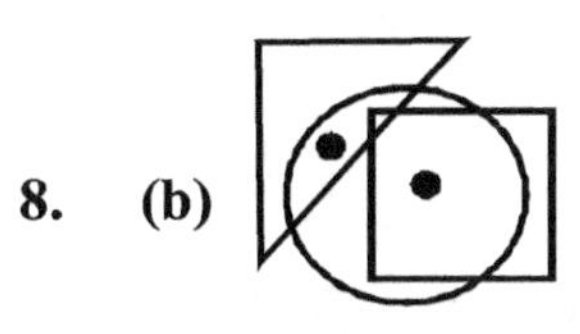

9. **(b)**

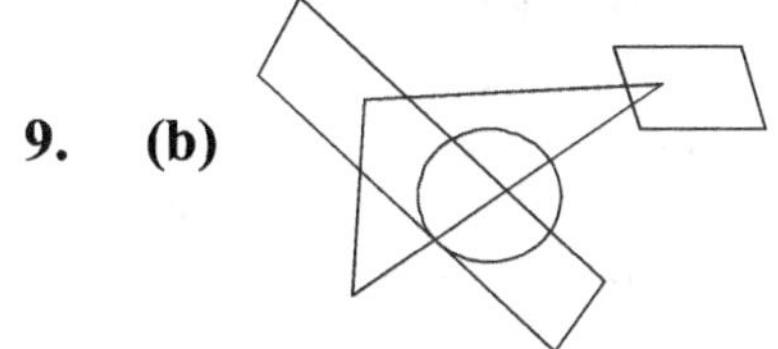

10. **(d)** Copy paste Fig. from question paper

11. **(d)** We can not make the dot made by the circle and square only.
So, option (d) is correct

12. **(b)**

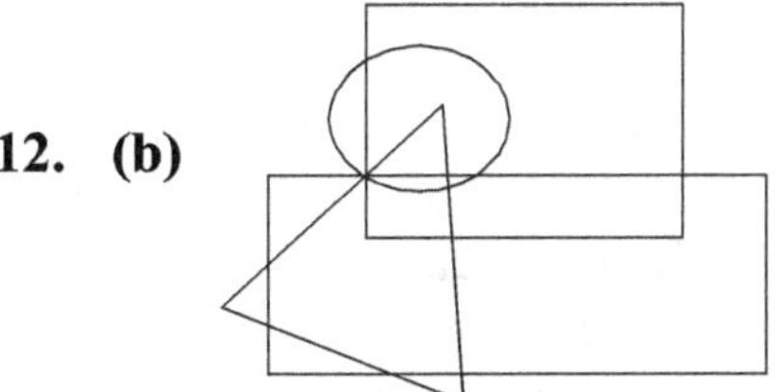

LEVEL 2

1. **(d)** In fig. (X), one of the dots lies in the region common to the square and the triangle only and the other dot lies in the region common to all the three figures—the circle, the square and the triangle. In each of the alternatives (a) and (b), there is no region common to the square and the triangle only. In alternative (c), there is no region common to all the three figures. Only, alternative (d) consists of both the types of regions.

2. **(a)** In fig. (X), one of the dots lies in the region common to the square and the triangle only, another dot lies in the region common to the circle and the triangle only and the third dot lies in the region common to the triangle and the rectangle only. In fig. (b), there is no region common to the square and the triangle only. In fig. (c), there is no region common to the circle and the triangle only. In fig. (d) there is no region common to the triangle and the rectangle only. Only fig. (a) consists of all the three types of regions.

3. **(b)** In fig. (X), one of the dots lies in the region common to the circle and the triangle only and the other dot lies in the region common to the circle and the square only. In each of the figures

(a), (c) and (d), there is no region common to the circle and the triangle only. Only fig. (b) consists of both the types of regions.

4. **(d)** In fig. (X), one of the dots lies in the region common to the circle and the triangle only, another dot lies in the region common to all the three figures– the circle, the square and the triangle and the third dot lies in the region common to the circle and the square only. In each of the figures (a) and (c), there is no region common to the circle and the square only and in fig. (b), there is no region common to the circle and the triangle only. Only fig. (d) consists of all the three types of regions.

5. **(d)** In fig. (X), one of the dots lies in the region common to the circle and the rectangle only, another dot lies in the region common to the circle, the square and the rectangle only and the third dot lies in the region common to the circle, the square and the triangle only. In each of the figures (a) and (c) there is no region common to the circle, the square and the rectangle only and in fig. (b), there is no region common to the circle, the square and the triangle only. Only fig. (d) consists of all the three types of regions.

6. **(b)** In fig. (X), one of the dots lies in the region common to the circle and the triangle only, another dot lies in the region common to the circle, the square and the triangle only and the third dot lies in the region common to the circle, the square and the rectangle only. In each of the figures (a) and (c) there is no region common to the circle and the triangle only. In fig. (d) there is no region common to the circle, the square and the rectangle only. Only fig. (b) consists of all the three types of regions.

7. **(c)**

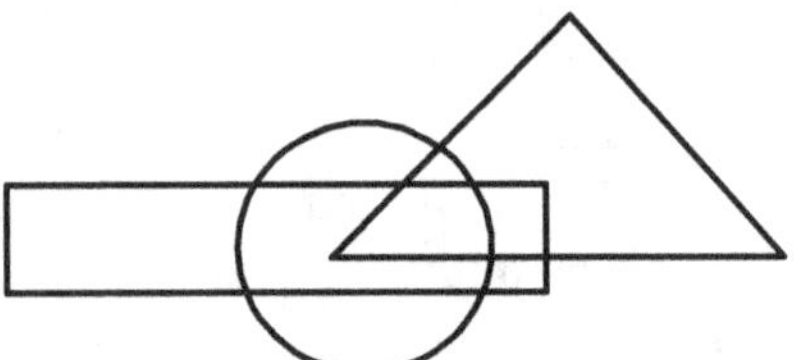

8. **(c)**

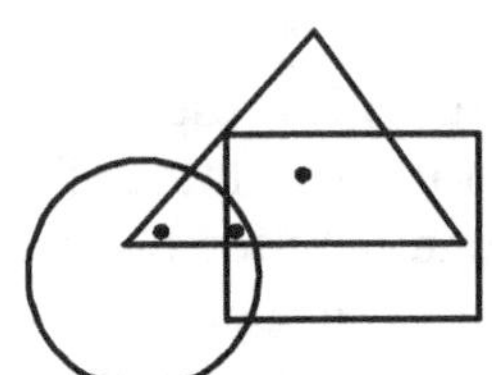

9. **(b)**

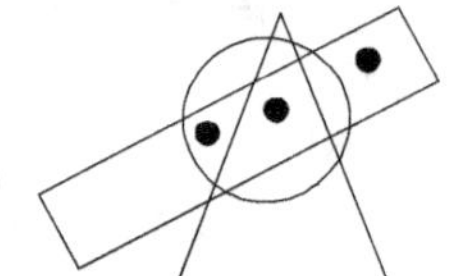

10. **(a)**

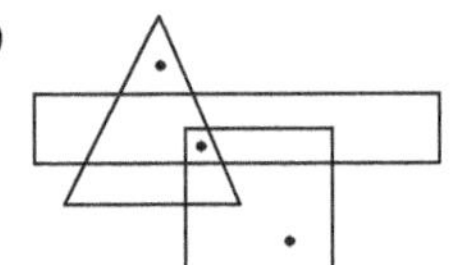

11. **(c)**

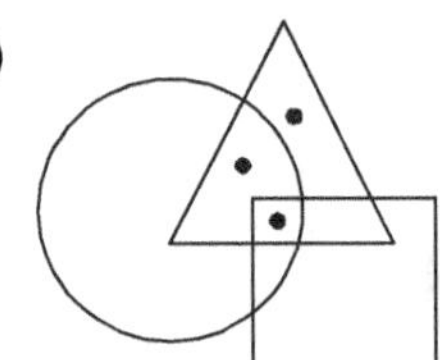

12. **(d)**

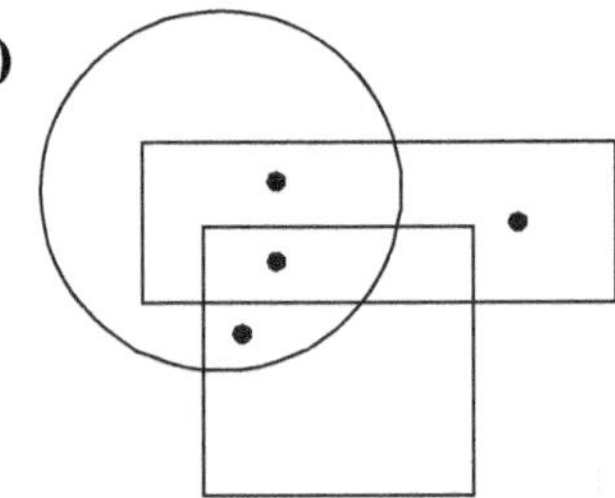

13. **(a)** One dot is only in triangle.
One dot is common for rectangle and triangle.
One dot is common for all.
But in option (a), there is no dot which is common for rectangle and triangle.

14. (b)

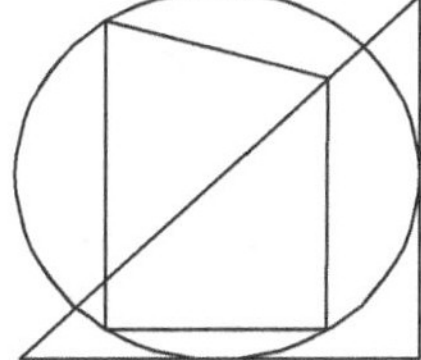

There is no common place of triangle and square only.

15. (c)

16. (a)

17. (d)

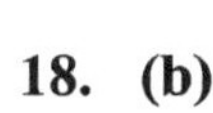

18. (b)

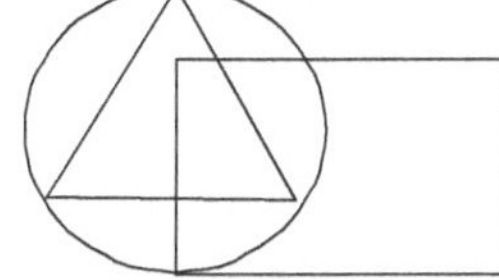

option (b) does not satisfy as a dot which is in only triangle cannot be made in option (b).

19. (c)

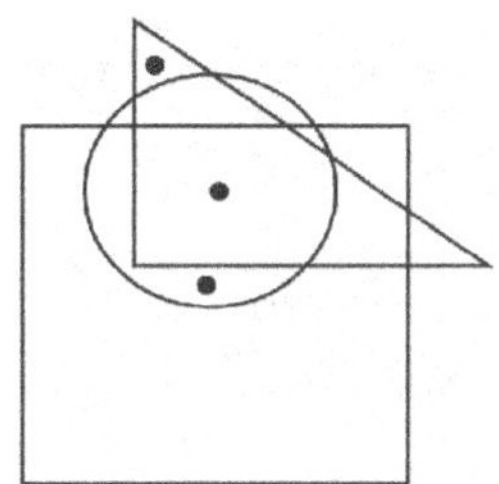

20. (c)

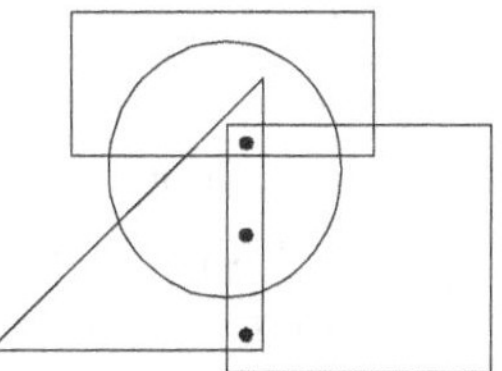

21. (c)

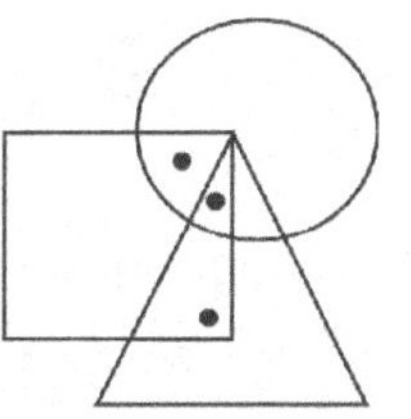

CHAPTER-18

LEVEL 1

Sol. (1 to 7):

For simplicity, let us replace all the Ps with 4 as P = 4 (given).

$$\begin{array}{cccc} M & N & O & 4 \\ +A & Q & R & 4 \\ \hline Z & Z & Z & Z \\ \hline \end{array}$$

As 4 + 4 = Z that means Z = 4 + 4 = 8. Now, replacing all Zs by 8.

$$\begin{array}{cccc} M & N & O & 4 \\ +A & Q & R & 4 \\ \hline 8 & 8 & 8 & 8 \\ \hline \end{array}$$

1. **(c)** $Z = 8$
2. **(d)** If $N > 5$, then N can either be 6 or 7 or 8, but $Z = 8$. So, N = 6 or 7. Hence option (d).
3. **(d)** When $N = 6$ and $M > N$, then $M = 7$. But since the value of R has no relation with the values of either M or N, therefore, the value of R cannot be determined with the given information. Thus option (d) is the answer.
4. **(b)** As $N = 6$, $M = 7$. Therefore, $A = Z - M = 8 - 7 = 1$. Therefore, option (b).
5. **(b)** $M = 7$, A = 1 and $N = 6$. Therefore, the numbers that stand for $M\ A\ N$ have to be a combination of 7, 1 and 6. Therefore, option (b) 716 is the answer.
6. **(a)** P O A R should be a combination of the numbers 4, 5, 1 & 3. Thus option (a) 4513 is the answer. As it is given that O = 5.

7. (b) P = 4 and Q = 2. So, when P ÷ Q = 4 ÷ 2, remainder is 0. Thus option (b) is the answer.

Sol. (8 to 14):

For simplicity, let us replace all the *C*s with 9, as $C = 9$ (given)

	A	B	9	D
+	S	R	O	P
	9	9	9	9

8. (c) Since A is a prime number smaller than 3. As 1 is neither a prime number nor a composite number and 0 is just a non negative number. Thus A = 2, option (c).

9. (a) As $A + S = C$, i.e., $A + S = 9$ and $A = 2$. Therefore, $S = 7$.

10. (d) $C = 9, A = 2$ but value for R is unknown. Thus the number for *C A R* cannot be determined.

As $A = 2, R < 5$ where *R* is a prime number, the only option available is $R = 3$.

11. (b) *S, C, A & R* are denoted by 7, 9, 2 and 3 respectively, the representation for the word *S C A R* should be a combination of 7, 9, 2, & 3. Thus option (b) 2973 is the answer.

12. (b) $SOAP \rightarrow 7021$. As 9 + O = 9,

so $O = 0$ and $P = C - D = 9 - 8 = 1$.

13. (d) $B \div O = 6 \div 0 = \infty$ because any integer divide by 0 is ∞.

14. (b) Row 1 means *A B C D*. Sum of all integers means $A + B + C + D = 25$.

Sol. (15 to 18):

	T	X	7
+	X	T	7
	A	7	T

As the first column is the sum of two 7s, *i.e.*, 7 + 7 = 14. So $T = 4$ and 1 is carried over. Therefore, now $1 + X + T = L = 7$ and since $T = 4$ $X = L - T - 1 = 7 - 4 - 1 = 2$.

Thus $A = T + X = 4 + 2 = 6$.

15. (a) $X = 2$.

16. (a) $A\ L\ T = 467$ (jumbled up)

17. (a) T A X = 426 (jumbled up)

18. (b) Sum of second row = $X + T + L = 13$.

Third multiple of 13 = 39.

19. (d)

LEVEL 2

Sol. (1to 5):

For simplicity, we substitute *O* with 2 and *B* with 4. Since L is neither prime nor composite, thus $L = 1$.

	4	2	T	H
−	2	N	1	Y
	2	2	2	2

$O - N = O$, *i.e.*, $2 - N = 2$, So $N = 0$.

As *T, H & Y* are prime numbers they will take values 3, 5, or 7.

1. (b) $BOON = 4220$

2. (c) As $T - 1 = 2 \Rightarrow T = 3$.

Thus $TOON = 3202$ (jumbled up)

3. (a) As $H > Y$ and both *H & Y* are prime numbers, so $H = 7$ & $Y = 5$ Thus the number for *T H Y* is 375.

4. (c) Product of *B, Y & T* $= 4 \times 5 \times 3 = 60$. Second multiple of 60 = 120.

5. (d) Product of *H, N, L & T* $= 7 \times 0 \times 1 \times 3 = 0$. Fifth multiple = 0

Sol. (6 to 9) :

As $A = 2$ and $N = 3$.

	B	2	3	2
+	3	2	3	2
	V	L	W	L

$2 + 2 = L = 4$ and $3 + 3 = W = 6$.

6. (b) If *V* is a prime number, it can hold the values 2, 3, 5 or 7. As $A = 2$, N = 3 and if $V = 5$, then *B* will be 2 which is not possible. Hence, $V = 7$ thus $B = 4$.

7. **(c)** $V = 7$.

8. **(b)** $B + A + N + A + N + A$

$= 4 + 2 + 3 + 2 + 3 + 2 = 16$

9. **(b)** $V \times L \times W \times L = 7 \times 4 \times 6 \times 4 = 672$.

Sol. (10- 14):

Here $A = 3$ and $Q = 8$.

$$\begin{array}{cccc} & B & 3 & N & 3 \\ + & N & 3 & N & 3 \\ \hline & 8 & B & P & B \end{array}$$

As, $3 + 3 = B = 6$, $N = 8 - B = 8 - 6 = 2$. So, $P = N + N = 4$.

10. **(a)** $2 \times 6 = 12$.

11. **(c)** $6 \times 4 = 24$.

12. **(b)** $N^2 = 2^2 = 4$.

13. **(d)** $P \times Q = 4 \times 8 = 32$

14. **(b)** $B \times A \times N \times A \times N \times A$

$= 6 \times 3 \times 2 \times 3 \times 2 \times 3 = 648$.

15. **(a)**

$$\begin{array}{ccccc} & & T & A & R \\ + & R & A & T & E \\ \hline & 4 & 4 & 4 & 4 \end{array}$$

As we see, at the Thousand's place $R = 4$. Therefore, at the unit's place

$R + E = 4 \Rightarrow E = 0$.

Now, at Ten's and Hundred's place $A + T = 4$, so if $A = 1$ then $T = 3$ and if $A = 3$ then $T = 1$.

Thus the word $T\ E\ A$ has to be either 301 or 103. Thus option (a) 103 since that is one of the options.

16. **(c)**

CHAPTER-19

LEVEL 1

1. **(c)** In the every consecutive figure, a new design comes at the lower middle and then that is sliding as follows–

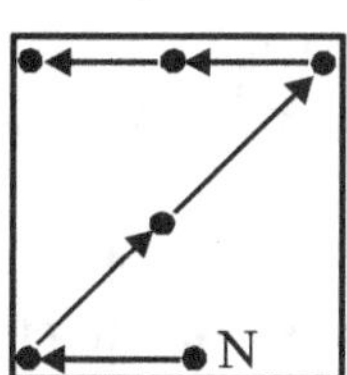

2. **(d)** In the every consecutive figure the designs their position as follows —

3. **(b)** In the every consecutive figure the left side design comes in next figure with changing and sliding half arm as follows –

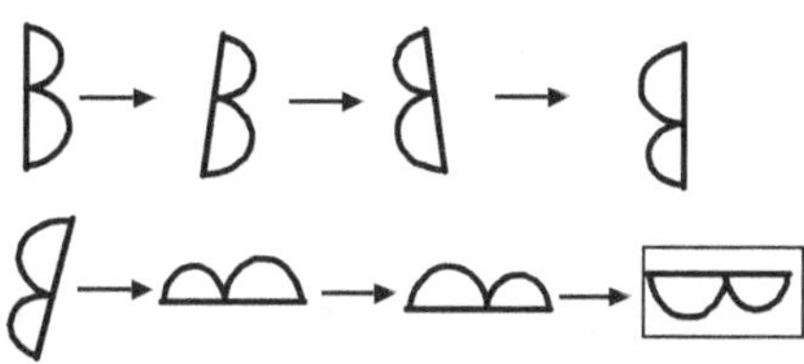

Similarly, In the every consecutive figure the right side design comes after sliding half arm and rotating 45° clockwise one time and second time slides half arm in the same direction after changing as follows–

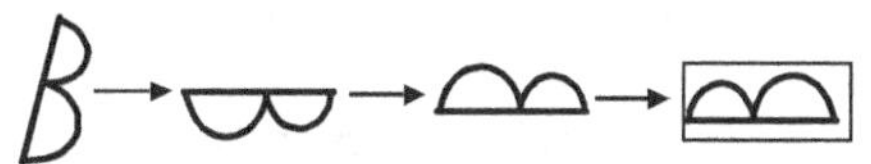

4. **(a)** In the every consecutive figure the designs are changing their places two types respectively as follows and a new design comes at the place of N–

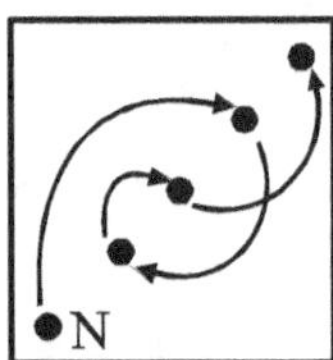

In B from A In C from B

In D from C In V from IV

5. (b) The pin moves diagonally (between upper-right and lower-left corners) in a sequence and gets inverted in each step. The square moves CW two spaces (each spaces is equal to half the side of the square boundary) and one space alternately. The triangle moves ACW one space and two spaces alternately.

6. (c) In each step, the outer larger element disappears; the inner smaller element enlarges to become the outer element and a new small element appears inside it.

7. (c) The 'S' shaped figure reverses its direction and gets rotated through 45°CW in each step.

8. (c) In every step, shaded region moves 90° clockwise.

9. (a) In each step, fish is rotating 90° clockwise.

10. (a) In each step, one line is added at every corner, in clockwise direction.

11. (c) One small circle is added on the outer side of the semicircle in every step.

12. (a) All the elements moves clockwise to the adjacent corner in each step.

13. (b) and moves 90° clockwise in each step.

14. (b) Shaded circle moves half step clockwise.

15. (a) One line and one circle is added in each step.

16. (c) All symbols moves 1 step in anti-clockwise direction while the line segment changes to its mirror images.

17. (b) The slanting lines changes to the vertical lines in each alternate step and the region containing lines moves 1 step clockwise.

18. (b) In each next step number of leaves are increased by one on alternate side.

19. (d) Number of sides in each next figure is increased by 2.

20. (b) Number of petals in each next flower is decreased by 1.

21. (a) Each next figure is half of the previous figure.

22. (c) One circle is added in each next figure.

23. (d) One circle is added on each side of square in each step. So, answer (d) is correct.

24. (d)

25. (b) Triangle at the corner moves one step anti-clockwise and elements comes inside and outside the triangles alternately.

26. (a) Vertical line becomes horizontal and a new line is inserted in upper most part alternately.

27. (d) Figure is rotating 90° anti-clockwise in each step.

28. (b) Original figure is rotated by 90° in clockwise direction in every next step.

29. (a) In every next figure, a part of flower pattern added in clockwise direction.

30. (c)

31. (d) Original figure is rotated by 90° in anti-clockwise direction in every next figure.

32. (b) Here we get the pattern the arrow rotate ahead first anticlockwise and then anticlockwise direction again and so on.

33. (b) Here all the shapes with in the figure rotate one step ahead in clockwise direction as we can start from arrow.

34. (b) The figure is rotating 90° anti-clockwise in every next step.

35. (b)

36. (b)

37. (c) The figure is rotating 90° anti-clockwise in every next step.

38. (a)

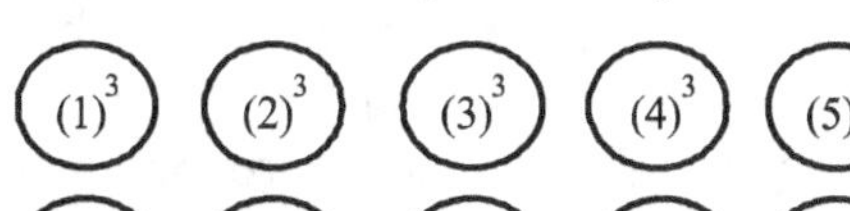

Numbers in circle are cubes of consecutive natural numbers.
So in place of ? = $(6)^3 = 216$.

39. (b)

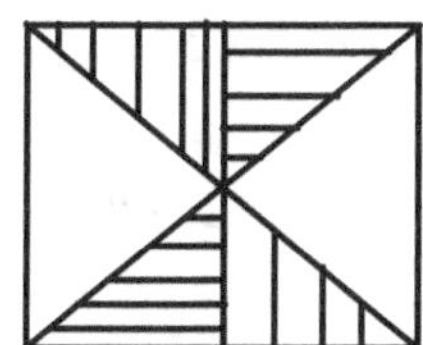

Rotation of figure at 90° in anticlockwise direction is followed in alternate figure.

40. (d) Symbol Δ, + and A (which is changed to C and E) are rotating clockwise. Symbol \$ and ÷ are changing their position in every next figure.

LEVEL 2

1. (d) The arrow moves one, two, three, four,..........spaces CW sequentially.

2. (d) In each step, the figure gets laterally inverted and a new line segment is added to the figure at the end opposite to the one having a dot.

3. (b) In each step, all the existing arrow get laterally inverted; the line segment is replaced by a new arrow pointing toward the left and a new line segment appears at the lowermost position.

4. (b) Similar figure repeats in every second step. Each time a particular figure reappears, it gets vertically inverted.

5. (c) In one step, the figure gets laterally inverted and a new circle is introduced inside the existing figure on the RHS and in the next step, the figure gets laterally inverted.

6. (b) Option (b) will be the next figure.

7. (d) Option (d) will be the next figure.

8. (d) option (d) is mathematical symbol.

9. (c) all outer elements having the replica of its present inside of that, except option (c)

10. (d) all inner figures are enclosed one except (d)

11. (c) the shaded region is present on the left bottom region, where as rest all has on top right region.

12. (a)

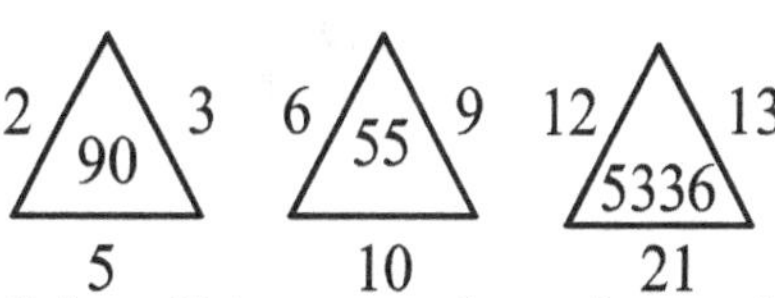

Cube of bigger number – [sum of cube of other two no]

i.e. $(5)^3 - [(2)^3 + (3)^3]$

$= 125 - [8 + 27]$

$= 90$

Similarly

$(10)^3 - [(6)^3 + (9)^3]$

$= 1000 - [216 + 729]$

$= 1000 - 945$

$= 55$

So, $(21)^3 - [(12)^3 + (13)^3]$

$\Rightarrow 9261 - [1728 + 2197]$

$\Rightarrow 5,336$

13. (b) In each subsequent figure no. of lines are increased by "4",

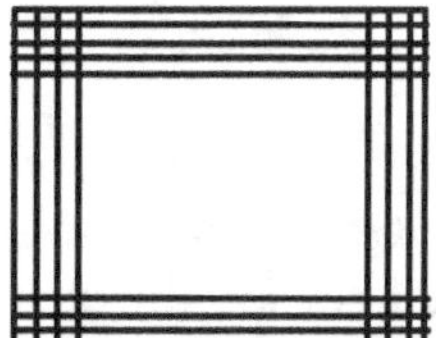

14. (d)

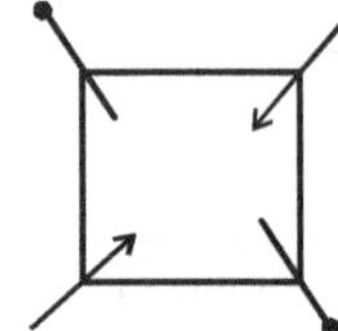

Repetition of figures after the 4th figure in sequence.

15. (d) Symbols C,N, + and ↑are moving one step clockwise than shifts diagonally and so on.
Option (d) will continue the series.

16. (b) In the series alternatively ↑ and ⫯ added one in each step. Also ↑ and ⫯ flip alternatively in each step.

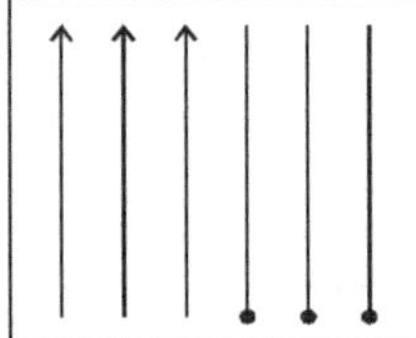

17. (a)

18. (b)

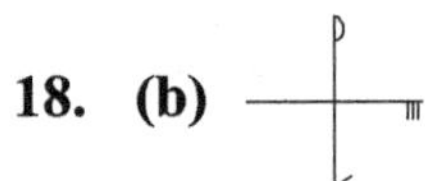

Option (b) will continue the same series as established by the problem figures.

19. (b) A small line is added to the line '|' at the right side then at the left side and so on. Arrow '↑' is moving up and down continuously. A part of circle 'O' is removed clock-wise. Symbol '–O' is moving 90° clock-wise.

20. (a) There is a series of letters and their opposite of english alphabets.
'=' is moving anti-clock wise.

21. (a) All the symbols are moving three steps forward to the next figure and then one step forward to the next figure anti-clockwise.
Symbol 'C' is changed to 'S'
Symbol 'O' is changed to '★'
Symbol '=' is changed to '□'
and
Symbol 'X' is changed to '∆'

22. (d)

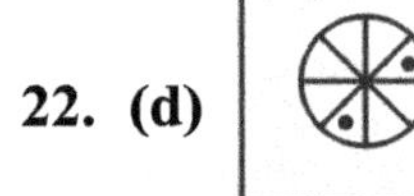

Both the dots are shifted to one place in their reverse direction

23. (b)

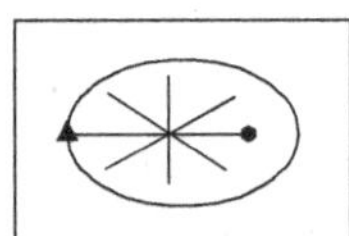

CHAPTER-20

LEVEL 1

1. (a) Except (a) in all others, the outer and inner figures are the same.
2. (a) Except (a) in all others, the first two outer figures are same.
3. (d)

4. (a) The element at the bottom is moved to the diagonal corner, the element in the top is enlarged and moved to the centre and element in the middle is reduced and moved to the bottom right corner.
5. (d) Second image is the mirror image of (vertically placed mirror along y-axis) first image.
6. (d) Except option (d) all other figures have base.

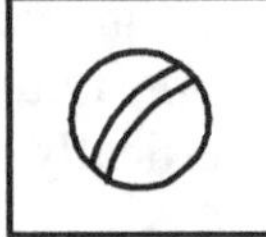

7. **(a)** Sign X, – and + are moving diagonally

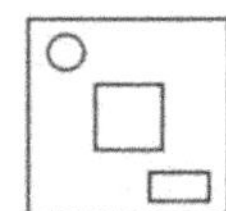

So, option (a) will be the correct figure.

8. **(d)** No. of sides in Outer figures is one more than the no. of sides in inside figure.
But in option "D" outer figure consistes of no. of sides less than the no. of sides than inside figure.

9. **(c)** Except option (c), in rest figures between ↑ and ↑ have three parts.

10. **(c)**

11. **(d)** Option (d) shows the same relation as between (i) and (ii) have.

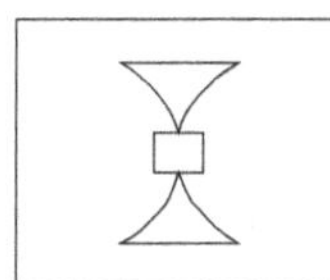

12. **(b)**

1		2	5		3
	3			1	
4		5	6		4

Similarly

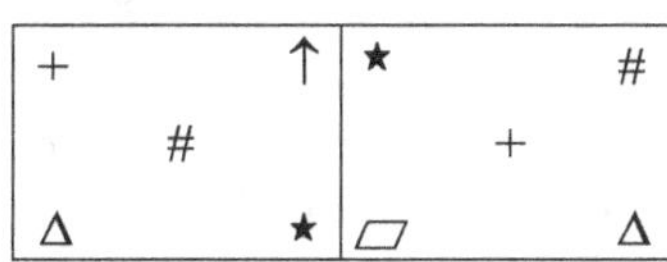

LEVEL 2

1. **(b)**

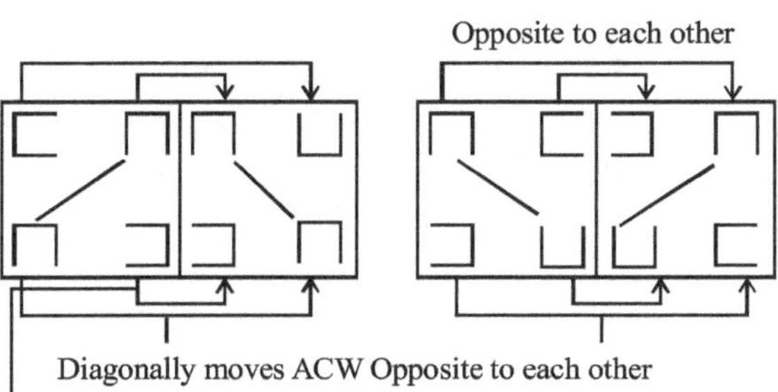

2. **(a)**

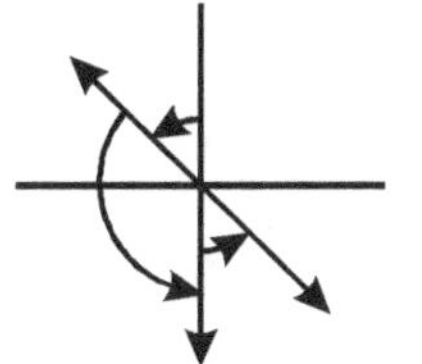

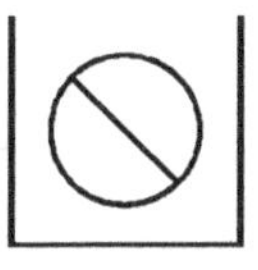

1st figure → 45° → 135° → 45° anti-clockwise movement. But first figure is not correct. It should be like

3. **(c)** In figure, third outmost two diagrams (two small circles) must be at one place or nearby to each other like figure first, outmost two small darken circles.

4. **(a)** In all other figures, the lower-right quarter portion is shaded.

5. **(c)** In figure (c), darken circle is not changing their place and same as in figure (b).

6. **(d)**

7. **(b)** Each one of the figures except fig. (b), consists of five arrow heads.

8. **(c)** Only in fig. (c), the line segment is not a diameter of the circle.

9. **(d)** In all the figures except (d) inside circle is rotating in anticlockwise direction while outer curve rotating in clockwise direction. Hence option (d) is odd figure.

10. **(b)** By visualizing the figure, we figure out that option (b) is odd one out.

11. **(c)** In all the figures except (c) outer curve elements count is 4 but in figure (c), it's having 3 elements. Hence, it's odd one out.

12. **(c)**

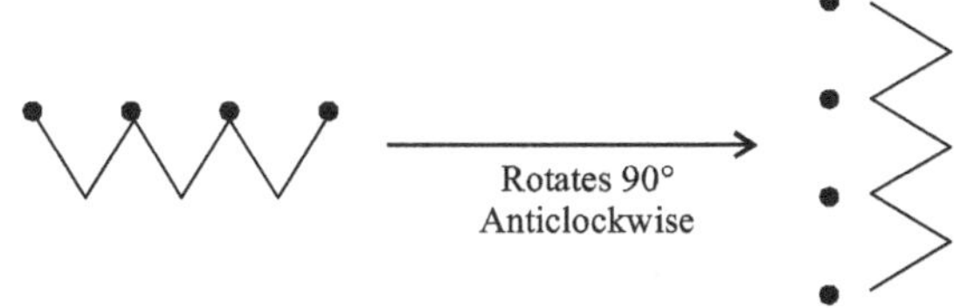

13. (a) Pattern is -

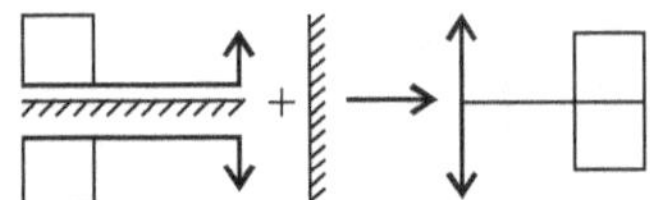

Similarly,

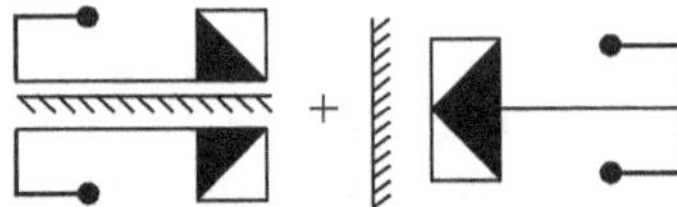

14. (d) Symbols '÷' and '◑' are moving diagonaly.
Symbols '×' and '▬' are moving left to right in the figure.

15. (b)

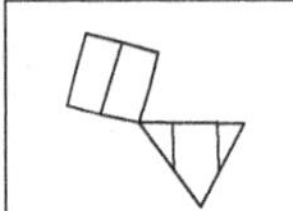

Option (b) shows the same relation as between (1) and (2).

16. (b) Replace symbols with digits to clearly understand and the relationship.

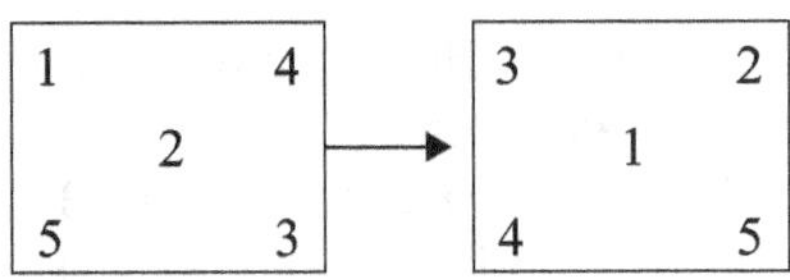

Representation
∵ 1 → x
2 → □
3 → =
4 → ©
5 → S
No. 4 is replaced with π in fig. 2. Similar pattern is to be followed in fig. 3 and 4

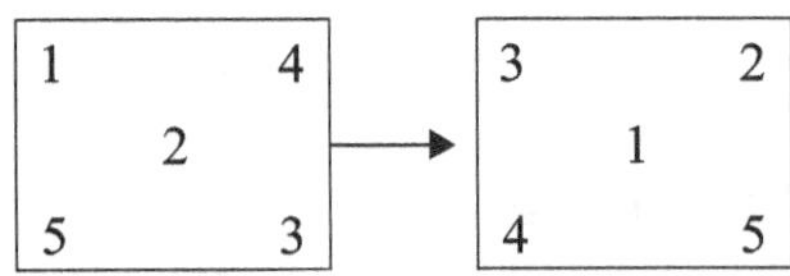

So,

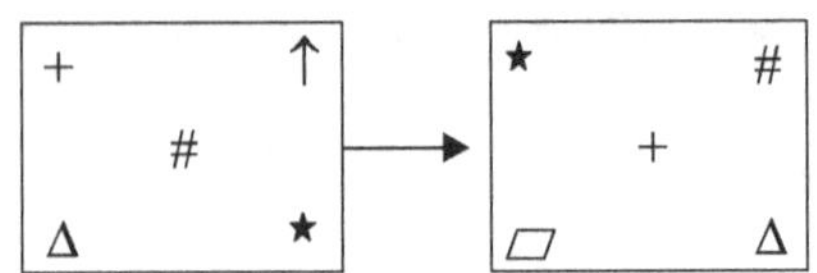

Representation
∵ 1 → +
2 → #
3 → ★
4 → ↑
5 →

17. (d) Fig. (iii) is mirror image of fig. (i) when mirror is kept on right hand side of fig. (i) Similarly:

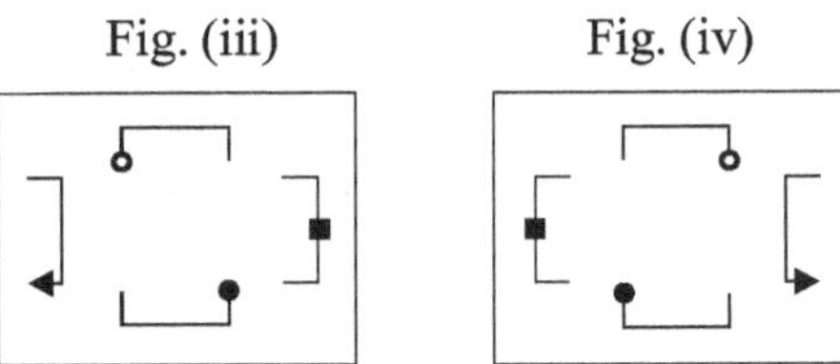

18. (d) Fig. (ii) contains "one side less than fig. (i)" and Q one shaded dot more than Fig. (i) inside the figure and same no. of dots outside the fig. So,

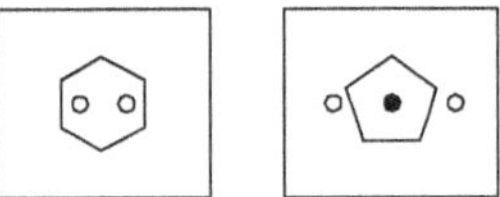

19. (c) Interchange the position of (first and second figure), (third and fourth figure) and (fifth and six figure). Dark the other side of the figure.

20. (c)

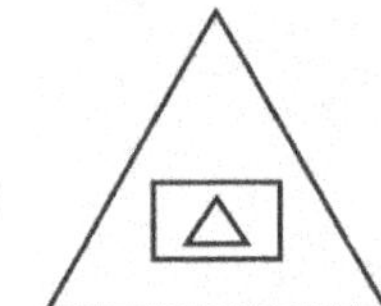

Other than "C", in all options the 1st inner figure contains sides less than the outer figure.

www.ingramcontent.com/pod-product-compliance
Lightning Source LLC
LaVergne TN
LVHW080850170826
845678LV00006B/1760

* 9 7 8 9 3 5 5 6 4 3 9 9 5 *